NOT SPARKING JOY

ALSO BY JERRY SCOTT AND JIM BORGMAN

Zits: Sketchbook 1
Growth Spurt: Zits Sketchbook 2
Don't Roll Your Eyes at Me, Young Man!: Zits Sketchbook 3
Are We an "Us"?: Zits Sketchbook 4
Zits Unzipped: Zits Sketchbook 5
Busted!: Zits Sketchbook 6
Road Trip: Zits Sketchbook 7
Teenage Tales: Zits Sketchbook No. 8
Thrashed: Zits Sketchbook No. 9
Pimp My Lunch: Zits Sketchbook No. 10
Are We Out of the Driveway Yet?: Zits Sketchbook No. 11
Rude, Crude, and Tattooed: Zits Sketchbook No. 12
Jeremy and Mom
Pierced
Lust and Other Uses for Spare Hormones
Jeremy & Dad
You're Making That Face Again
Drive!
Triple Shot, Double Pump, No Whip Zits
Zits en Concert
Peace, Love, and Wi-Fi
Zits Apocalypse
Extra Cheesy Zits
Dance Like Everybody's Watching!

TREASURIES

Humongous Zits
Big Honkin' Zits
Zits: Supersized
Random Zits
Crack of Noon
Alternative Zits
My Bad
Sunday Brunch
What Was That All About?: 20 Years of Strips and Stories

GIFT BOOK

A Zits Guide to Living with Your Teenager

NOT SPARKING JOY

A ZITS® Treasury by Jerry Scott and Jim Borgman

Andrews McMeel
PUBLISHING®

For Andrew Rubin
—JS

For Gail Loos, who rocked first grade.
—JB

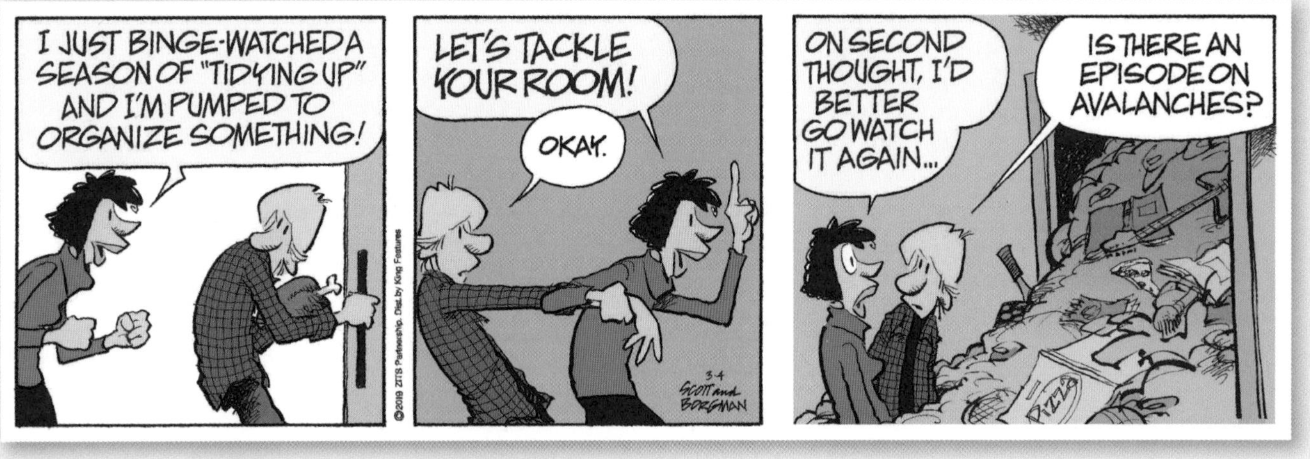
I JUST BINGE-WATCHED A SEASON OF "TIDYING UP" AND I'M PUMPED TO ORGANIZE SOMETHING!
LET'S TACKLE YOUR ROOM!
OKAY.
©2019 ZITS Partnership. Dist. by King Features
3-4
SCOTT and BORGMAN
ON SECOND THOUGHT, I'D BETTER GO WATCH IT AGAIN...
IS THERE AN EPISODE ON AVALANCHES?
PIZZA

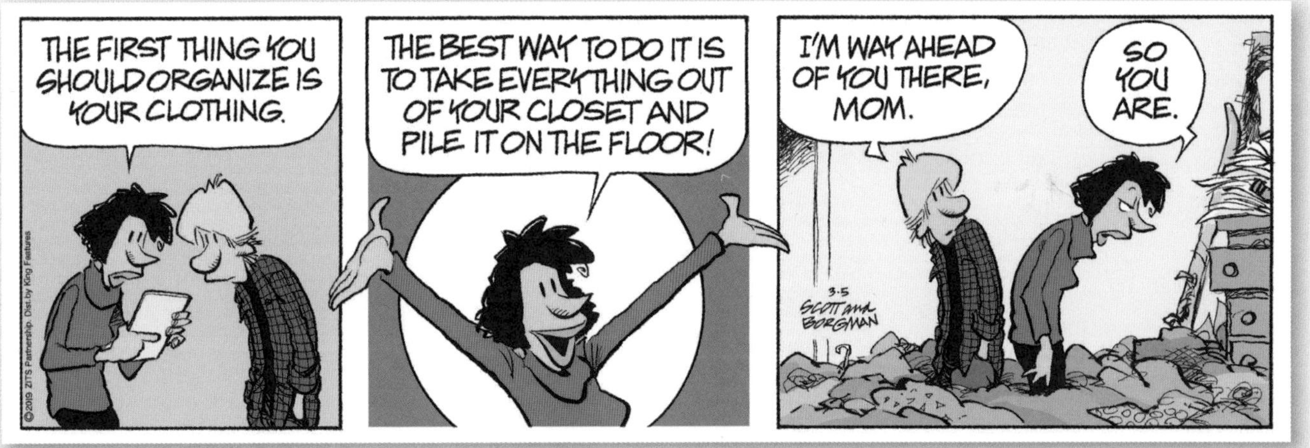
THE FIRST THING YOU SHOULD ORGANIZE IS YOUR CLOTHING.
©2019 ZITS Partnership. Dist. by King Features
THE BEST WAY TO DO IT IS TO TAKE EVERYTHING OUT OF YOUR CLOSET AND PILE IT ON THE FLOOR!
I'M WAY AHEAD OF YOU THERE, MOM.
SO YOU ARE.
3-5
SCOTT and BORGMAN

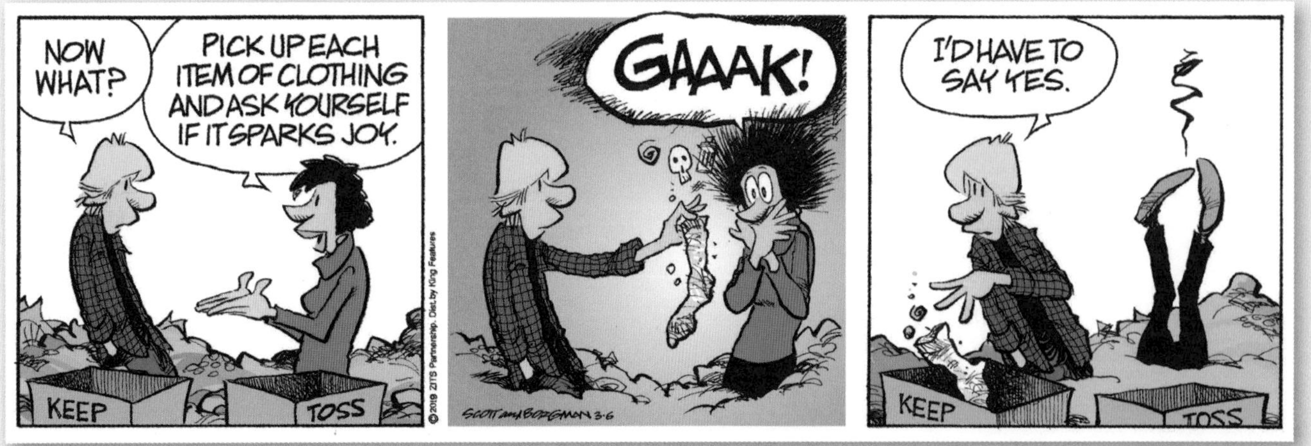
NOW WHAT?
PICK UP EACH ITEM OF CLOTHING AND ASK YOURSELF IF IT SPARKS JOY.
KEEP
TOSS
©2019 ZITS Partnership. Dist. by King Features
GAAAK!
SCOTT and BORGMAN 3-6
I'D HAVE TO SAY YES.
KEEP
TOSS

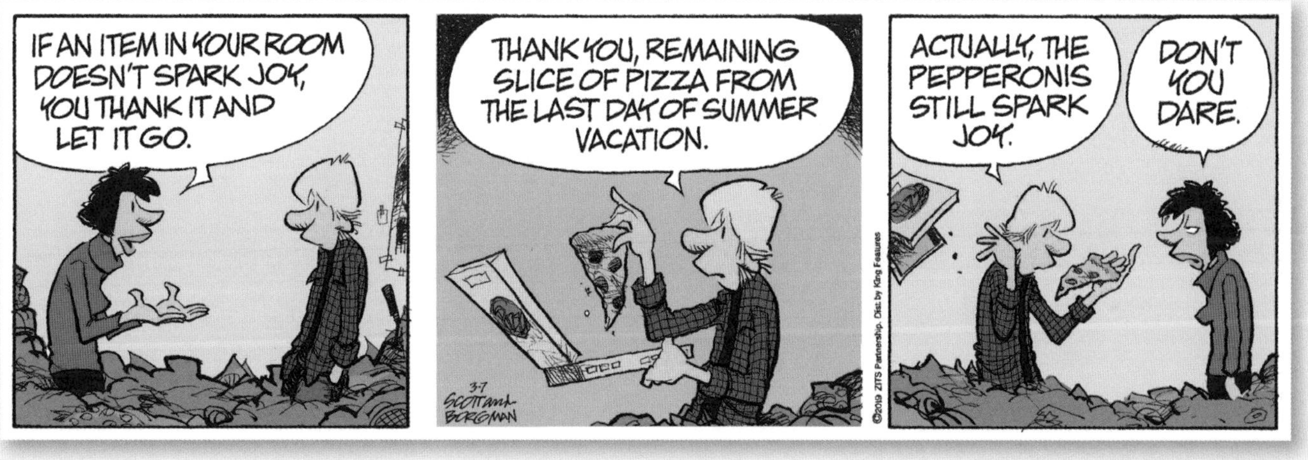
IF AN ITEM IN YOUR ROOM DOESN'T SPARK JOY, YOU THANK IT AND LET IT GO.
THANK YOU, REMAINING SLICE OF PIZZA FROM THE LAST DAY OF SUMMER VACATION.
3-7 SCOTT and BORGMAN
ACTUALLY, THE PEPPERONIS STILL SPARK JOY.
DON'T YOU DARE.
©2019 ZITS Partnership. Dist. by King Features

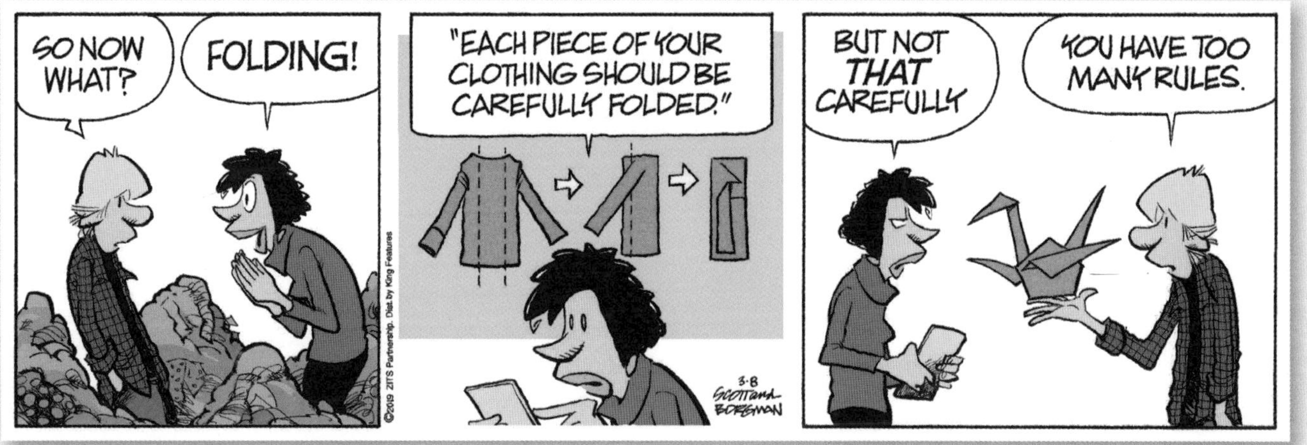
SO NOW WHAT?
FOLDING!
©2019 ZITS Partnership. Dist. by King Features
"EACH PIECE OF YOUR CLOTHING SHOULD BE CAREFULLY FOLDED."
3-8 SCOTT and BORGMAN
BUT NOT THAT CAREFULLY
YOU HAVE TOO MANY RULES.

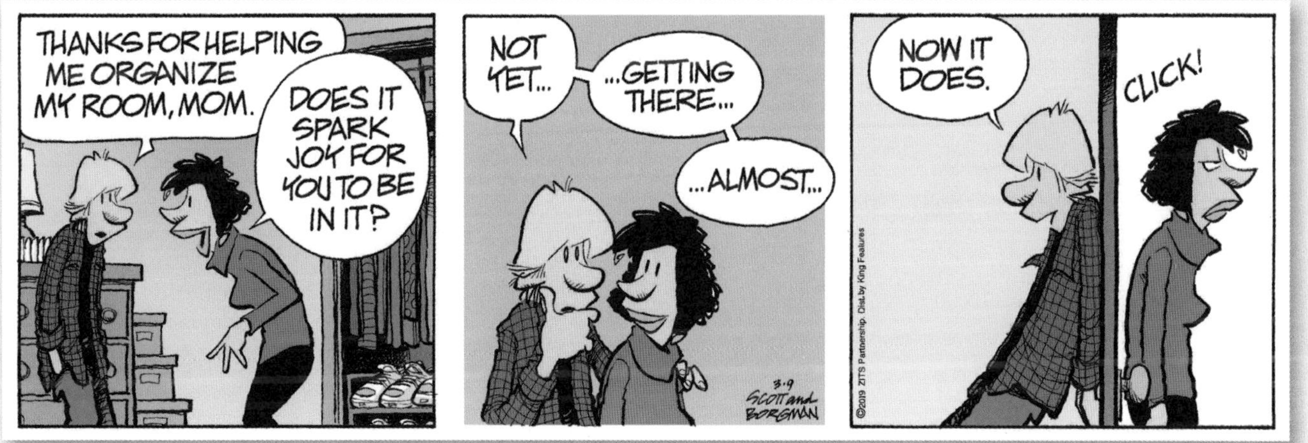
THANKS FOR HELPING ME ORGANIZE MY ROOM, MOM.
DOES IT SPARK JOY FOR YOU TO BE IN IT?
NOT YET...
...GETTING THERE...
...ALMOST...
3-9 SCOTT and BORGMAN
NOW IT DOES.
CLICK!
©2019 ZITS Partnership. Dist. by King Features

ZITS

by JERRY SCOTT and JIM BORGMAN

THIS- THIS IS UNBELIEVABLE!
I KNOW, AL...
...BUT THERE IT IS! A GIANT DUCK MADE OF FLOWERS!
LOTS OF 'EM!
WHAT?? AND A MARCHING BAND!
WHAT WILL THEY THINK OF NEXT?
AND LOOK! BEHIND THE BAND IS SOME OLD GUY WHO MAYBE USED TO BE A MINOR CELEBRITY!
(SWOON!)
WATCHING THE PARADE WAS MORE FUN WHEN HE WAS LITTLE.
AND NOT SUCH A SMARTASS!
CAN I GO LIVE IN THE PRESENT CENTURY NOW?
©2017 ZITS Partnership. Dist. by King Features
SCOTT AND BORGMAN

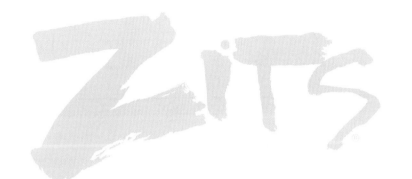

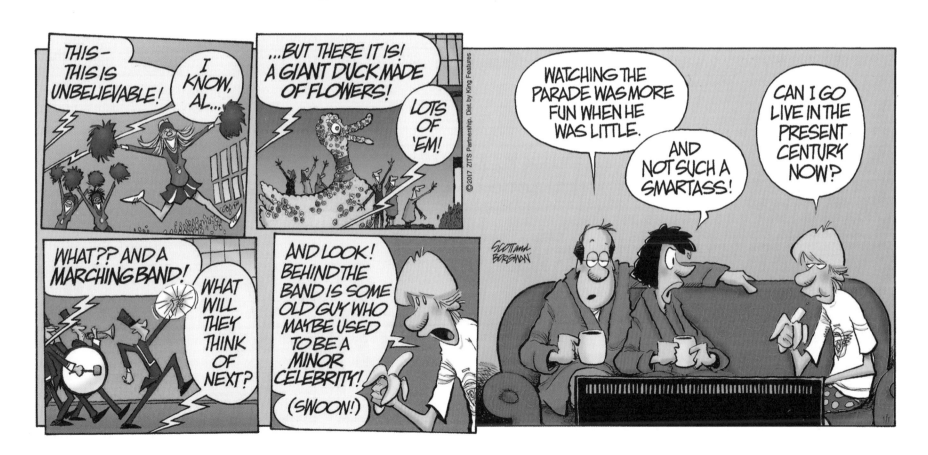

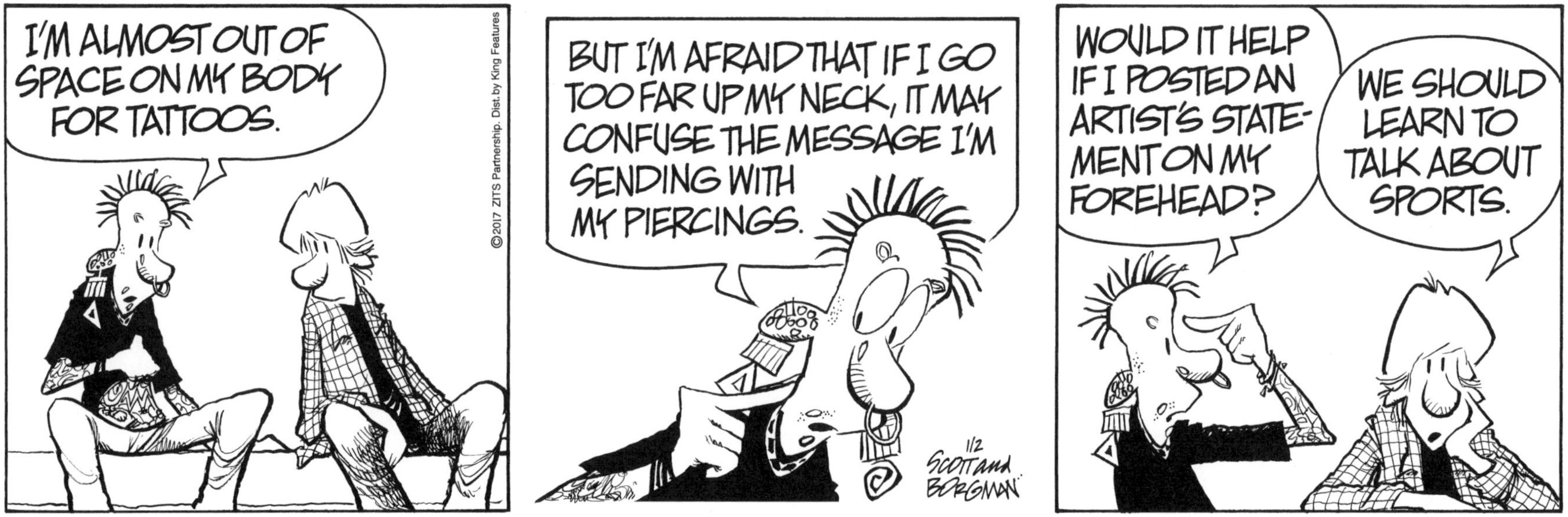
I'M ALMOST OUT OF SPACE ON MY BODY FOR TATTOOS.
©2017 ZITS Partnership. Dist. by King Features
BUT I'M AFRAID THAT IF I GO TOO FAR UP MY NECK, IT MAY CONFUSE THE MESSAGE I'M SENDING WITH MY PIERCINGS.
1/2 SCOTT and BORGMAN
WOULD IT HELP IF I POSTED AN ARTIST'S STATE-MENT ON MY FOREHEAD?
WE SHOULD LEARN TO TALK ABOUT SPORTS.

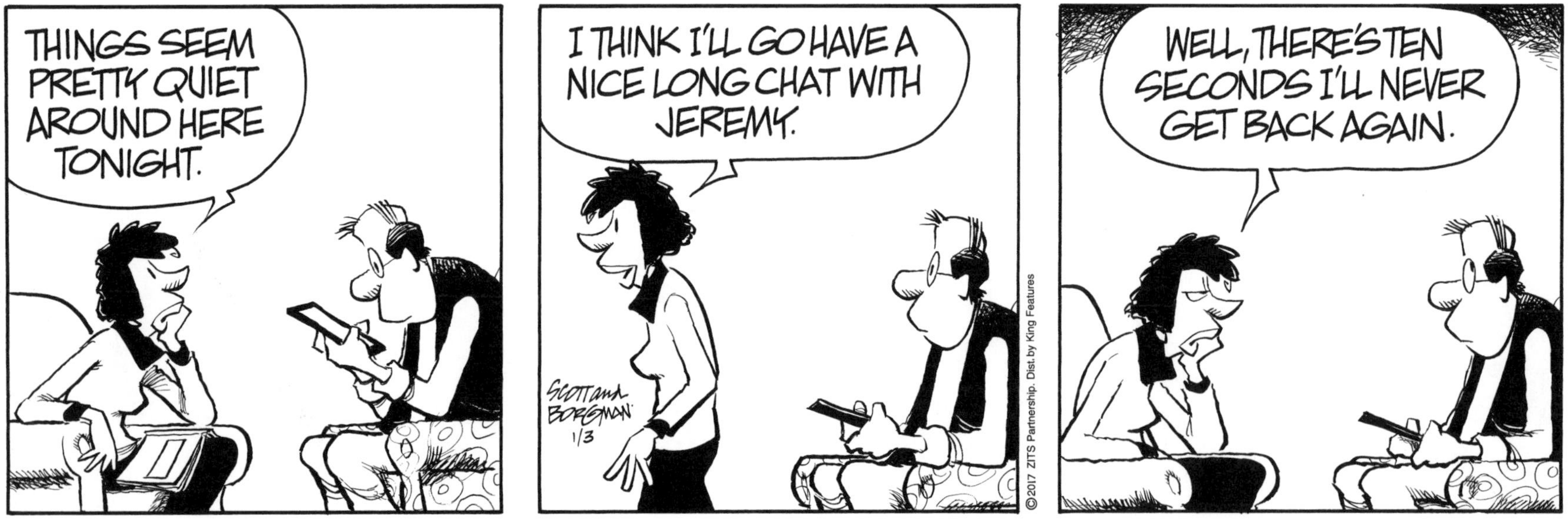
THINGS SEEM PRETTY QUIET AROUND HERE TONIGHT.
I THINK I'LL GO HAVE A NICE LONG CHAT WITH JEREMY.
SCOTT and BORGMAN 1/3
©2017 ZITS Partnership. Dist. by King Features
WELL, THERE'S TEN SECONDS I'LL NEVER GET BACK AGAIN.

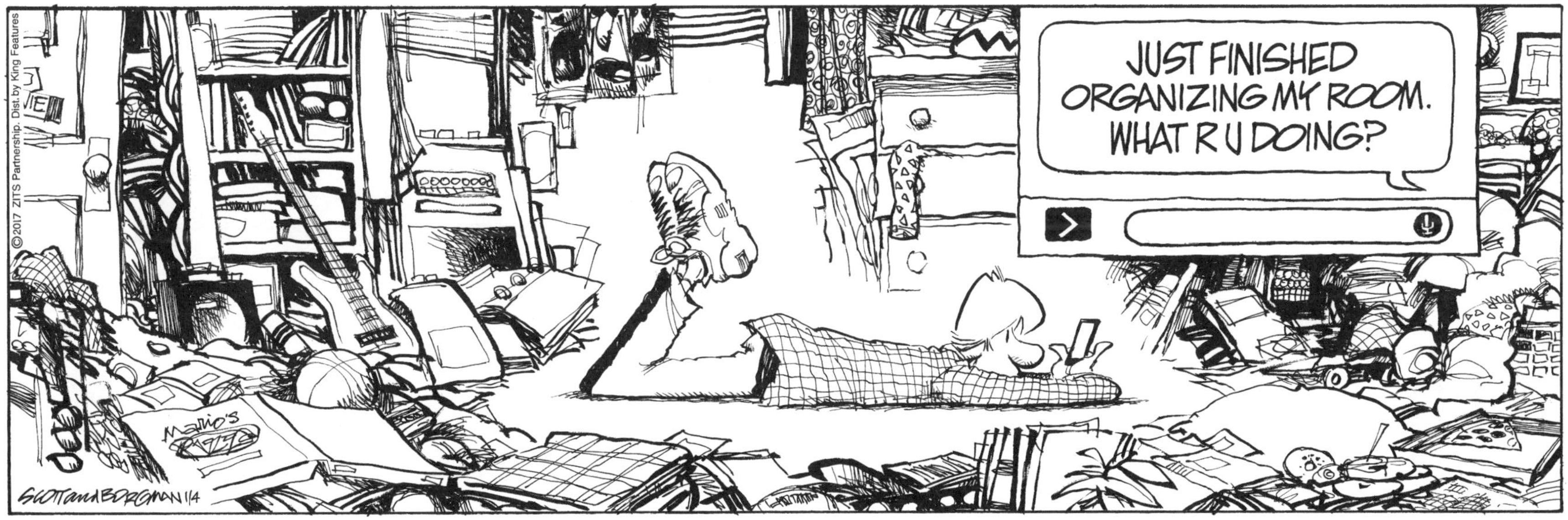
©2017 ZITS Partnership. Dist. by King Features
JUST FINISHED ORGANIZING MY ROOM. WHAT R U DOING?
SCOTT and BORGMAN 1/4

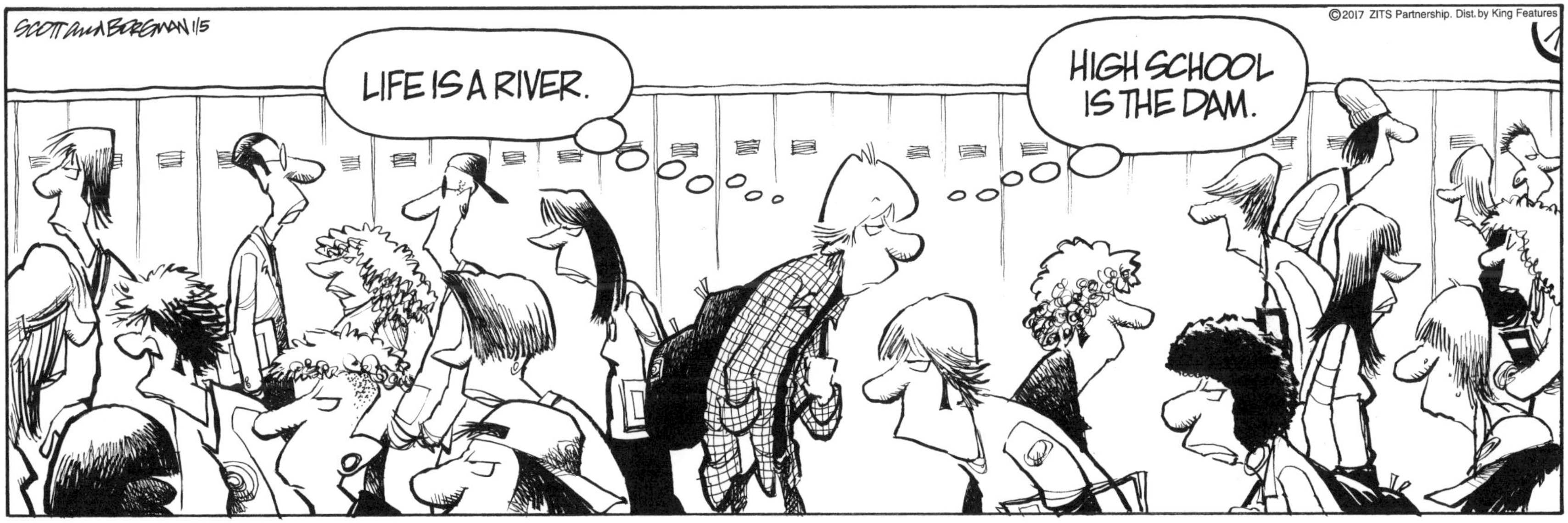
SCOTT and BORGMAN 1/5
©2017 ZITS Partnership. Dist. by King Features
LIFE IS A RIVER.
HIGH SCHOOL IS THE DAM.

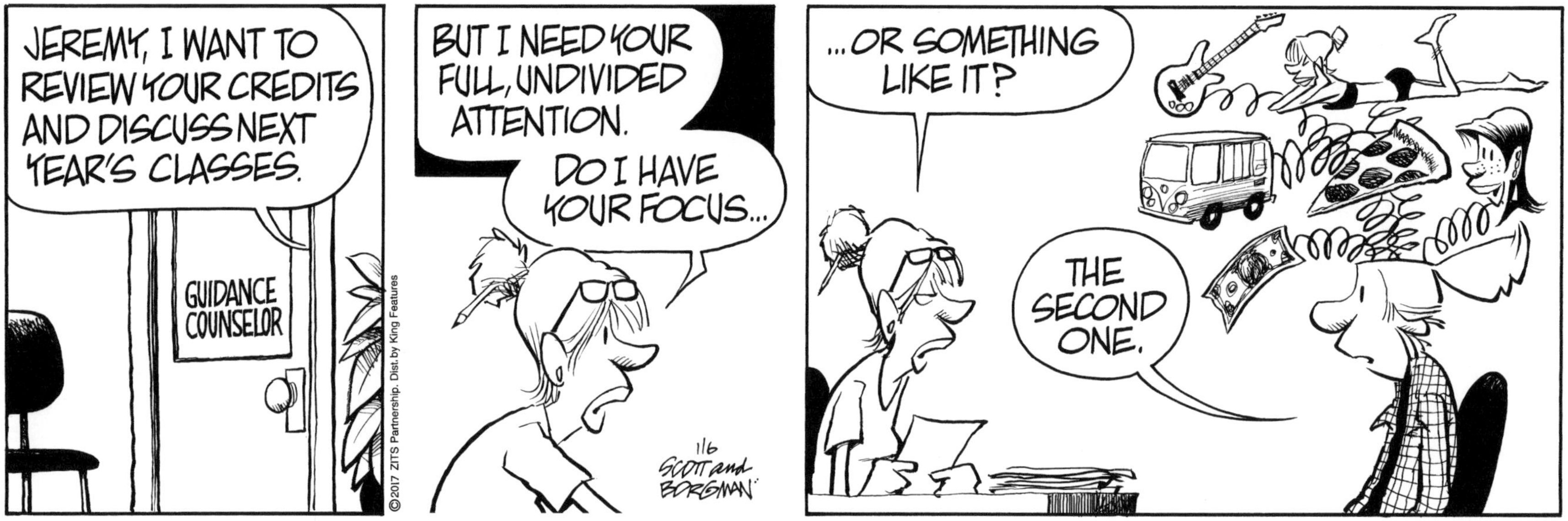
JEREMY, I WANT TO REVIEW YOUR CREDITS AND DISCUSS NEXT YEAR'S CLASSES.
GUIDANCE COUNSELOR
©2017 ZITS Partnership. Dist. by King Features
BUT I NEED YOUR FULL, UNDIVIDED ATTENTION.
DO I HAVE YOUR FOCUS...
1/6
SCOTT and BORGMAN
...OR SOMETHING LIKE IT?
THE SECOND ONE.

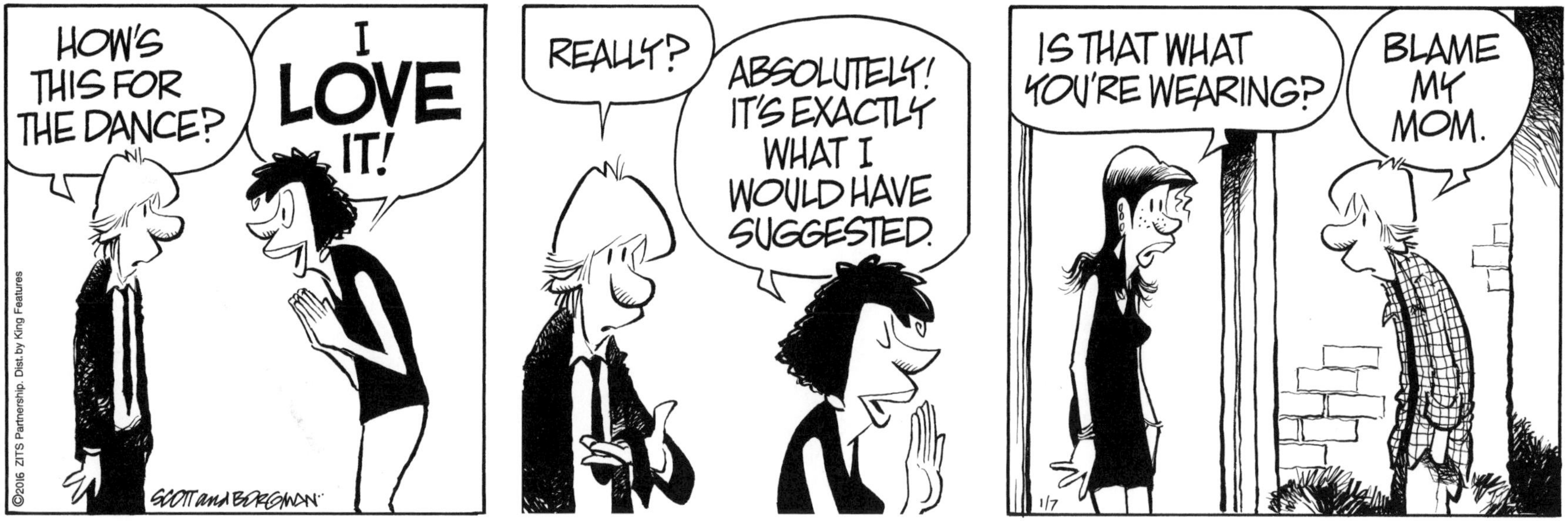
HOW'S THIS FOR THE DANCE?
I LOVE IT!
©2016 ZITS Partnership. Dist. by King Features
SCOTT and BORGMAN
REALLY?
ABSOLUTELY! IT'S EXACTLY WHAT I WOULD HAVE SUGGESTED.
IS THAT WHAT YOU'RE WEARING?
BLAME MY MOM.
1/7

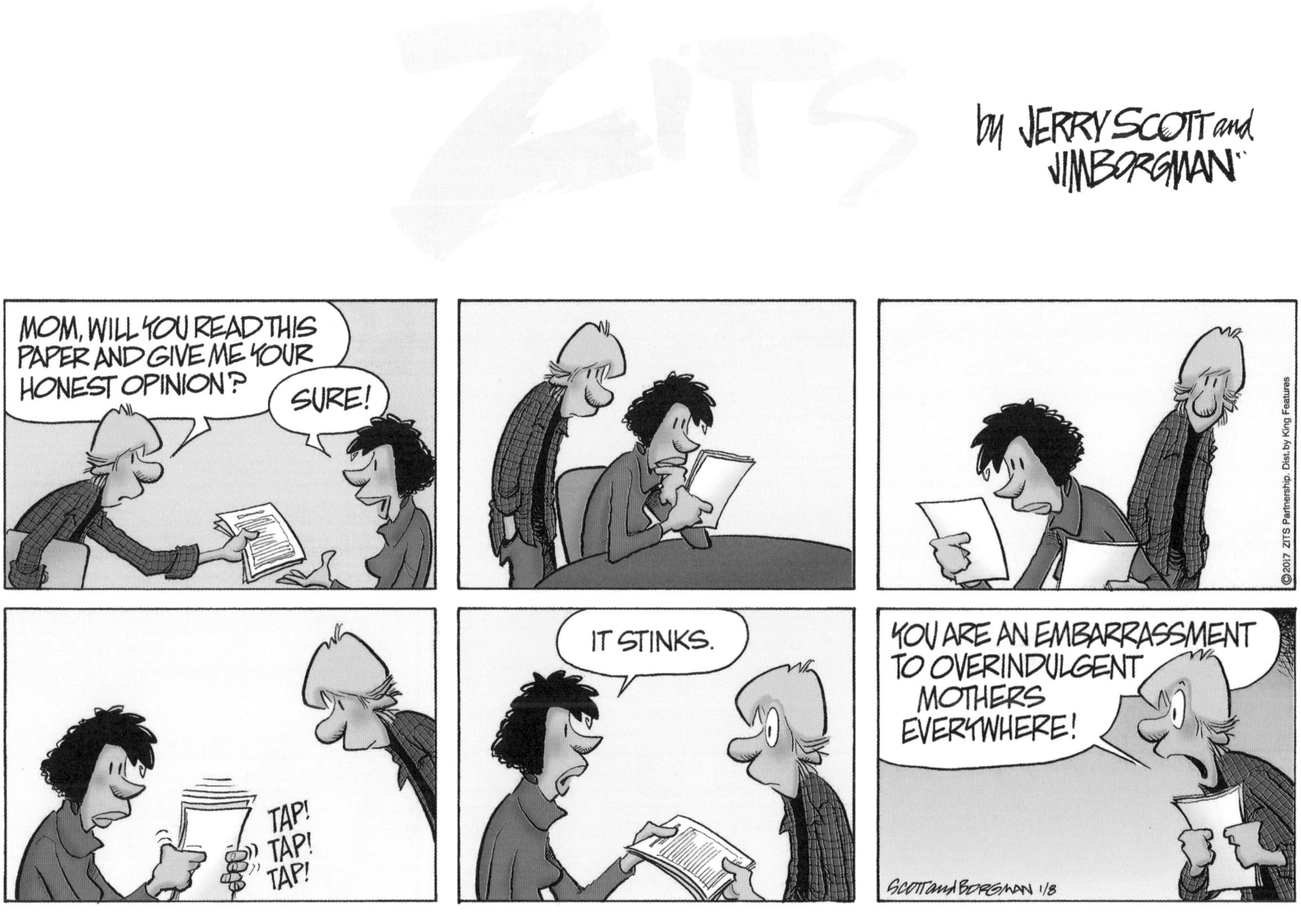
ZITS
by JERRY SCOTT and JIM BORGMAN
MOM, WILL YOU READ THIS PAPER AND GIVE ME YOUR HONEST OPINION?
SURE!
©2017 ZITS Partnership. Dist. by King Features
TAP! TAP! TAP!
IT STINKS.
YOU ARE AN EMBARRASSMENT TO OVERINDULGENT MOTHERS EVERYWHERE!
SCOTT and BORGMAN 1/8

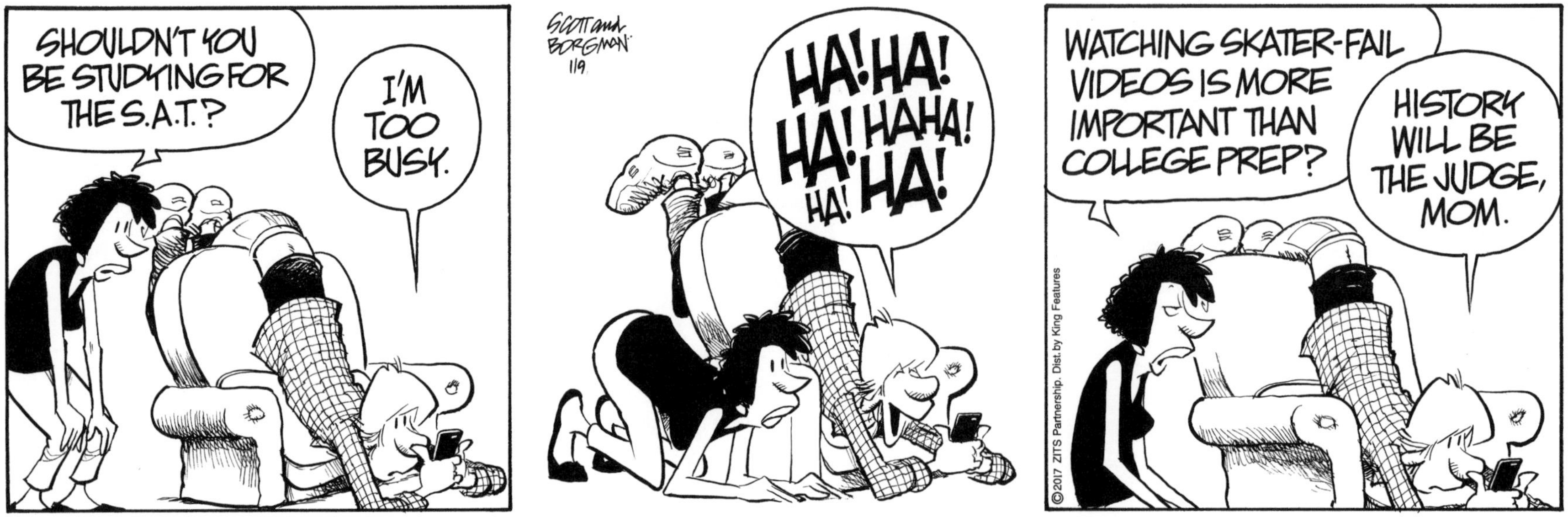
SHOULDN'T YOU BE STUDYING FOR THE S.A.T.?
I'M TOO BUSY.
HA! HA! HA! HAHA! HA! HA!
WATCHING SKATER-FAIL VIDEOS IS MORE IMPORTANT THAN COLLEGE PREP?
HISTORY WILL BE THE JUDGE, MOM.
©2017 ZITS Partnership. Dist. by King Features

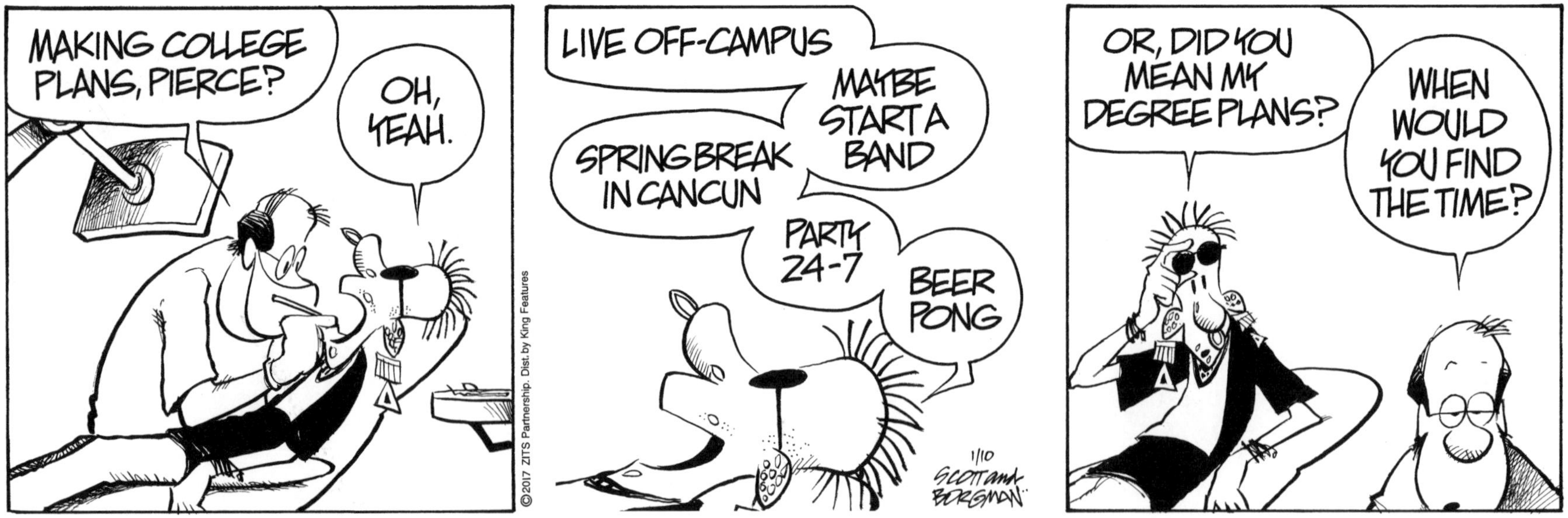
MAKING COLLEGE PLANS, PIERCE?
OH, YEAH.
©2017 ZITS Partnership. Dist. by King Features
LIVE OFF-CAMPUS
MAYBE START A BAND
SPRING BREAK IN CANCUN
PARTY 24-7
BEER PONG
OR, DID YOU MEAN MY DEGREE PLANS?
WHEN WOULD YOU FIND THE TIME?

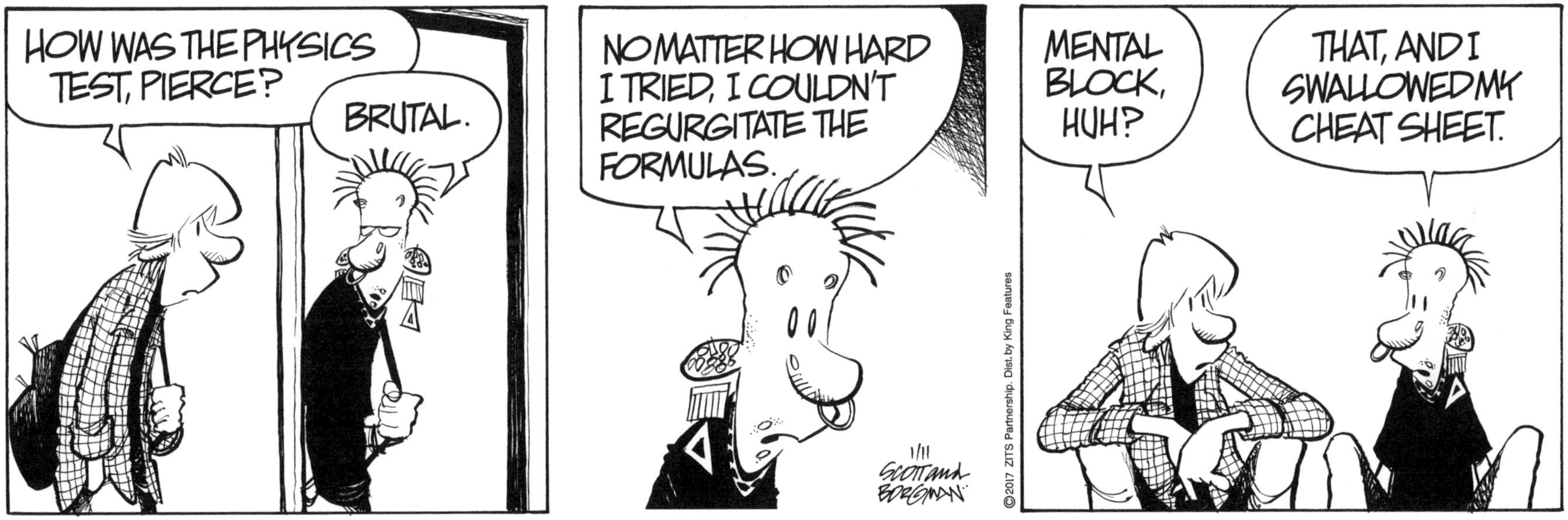
HOW WAS THE PHYSICS TEST, PIERCE?
BRUTAL.
NO MATTER HOW HARD I TRIED, I COULDN'T REGURGITATE THE FORMULAS.
1/11
SCOTT AND BORGMAN
©2017 ZITS Partnership. Dist. by King Features
MENTAL BLOCK, HUH?
THAT, AND I SWALLOWED MY CHEAT SHEET.

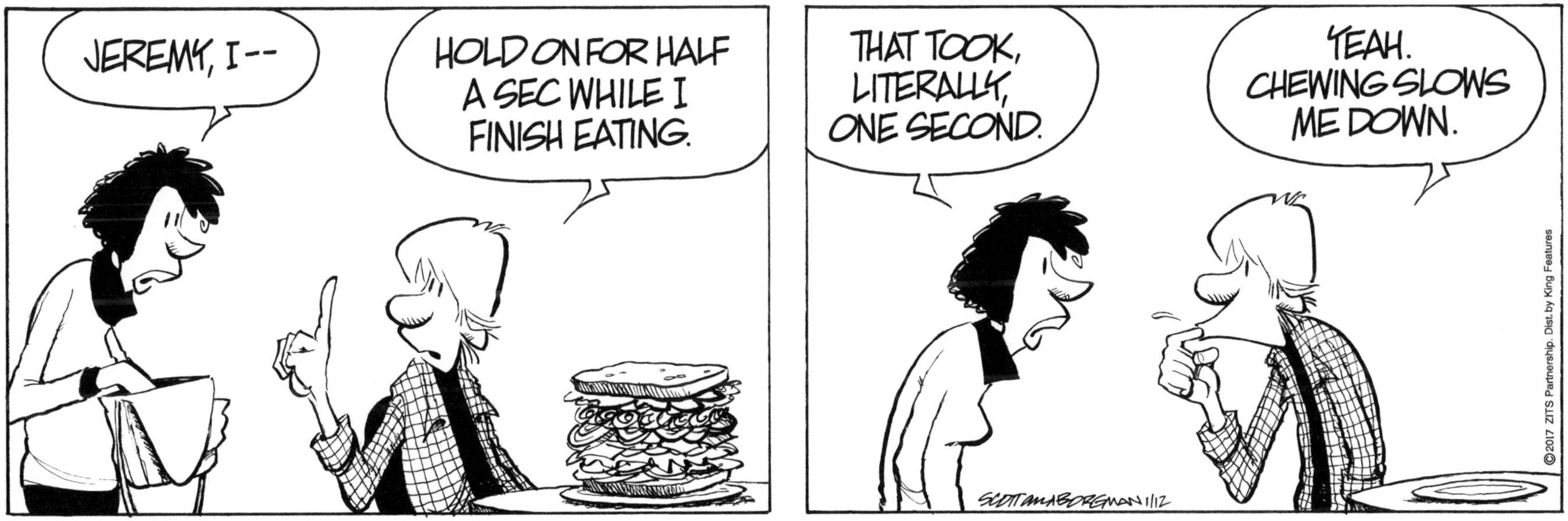
JEREMY, I--
HOLD ON FOR HALF A SEC WHILE I FINISH EATING.
THAT TOOK, LITERALLY, ONE SECOND.
YEAH. CHEWING SLOWS ME DOWN.
SCOTT AND BORGMAN 1/12
©2017 ZITS Partnership. Dist. by King Features

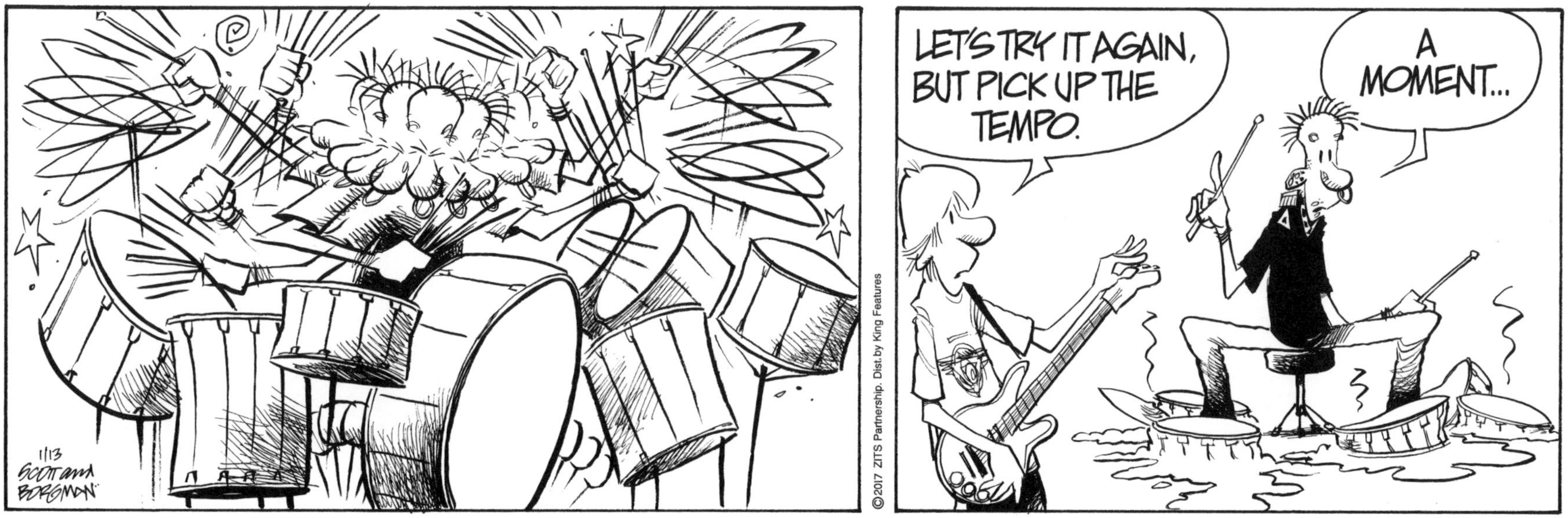
LET'S TRY IT AGAIN, BUT PICK UP THE TEMPO.
A MOMENT...
1/13 SCOTT and BORGMAN
©2017 ZITS Partnership. Dist. by King Features

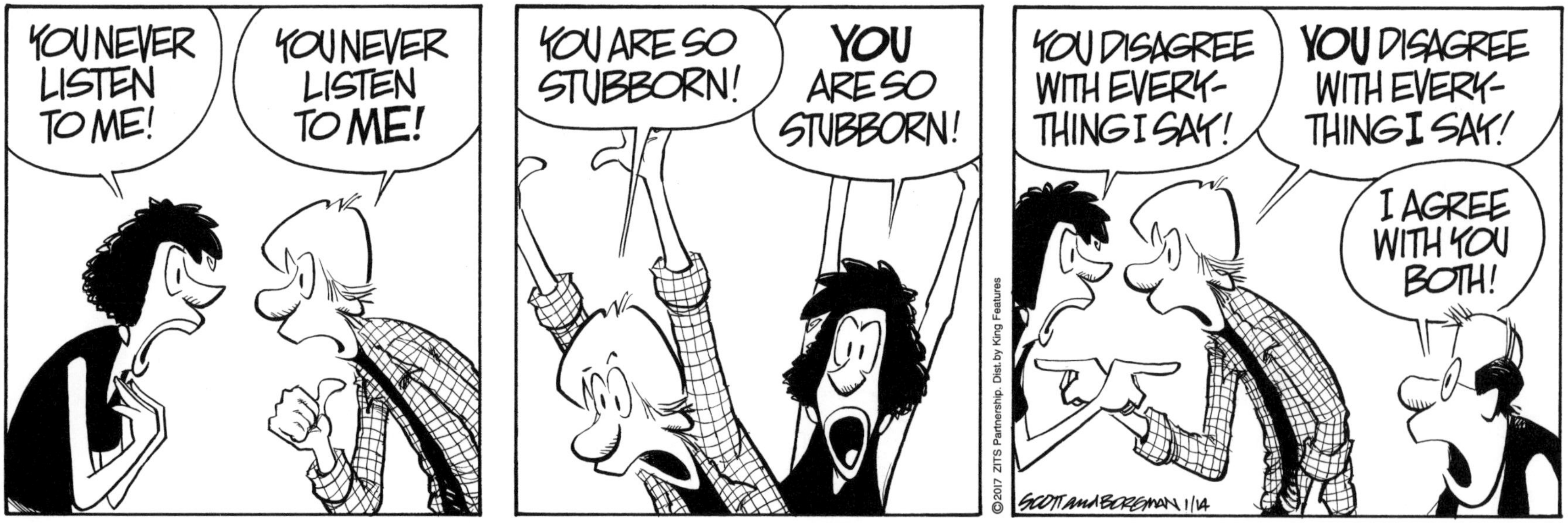
YOU NEVER LISTEN TO ME!
YOU NEVER LISTEN TO **ME**!
YOU ARE SO STUBBORN!
YOU ARE SO STUBBORN!
YOU DISAGREE WITH EVERY-THING I SAY!
YOU DISAGREE WITH EVERY-THING **I** SAY!
I AGREE WITH YOU BOTH!
SCOTT and BORGMAN 1/14
©2017 ZITS Partnership. Dist. by King Features

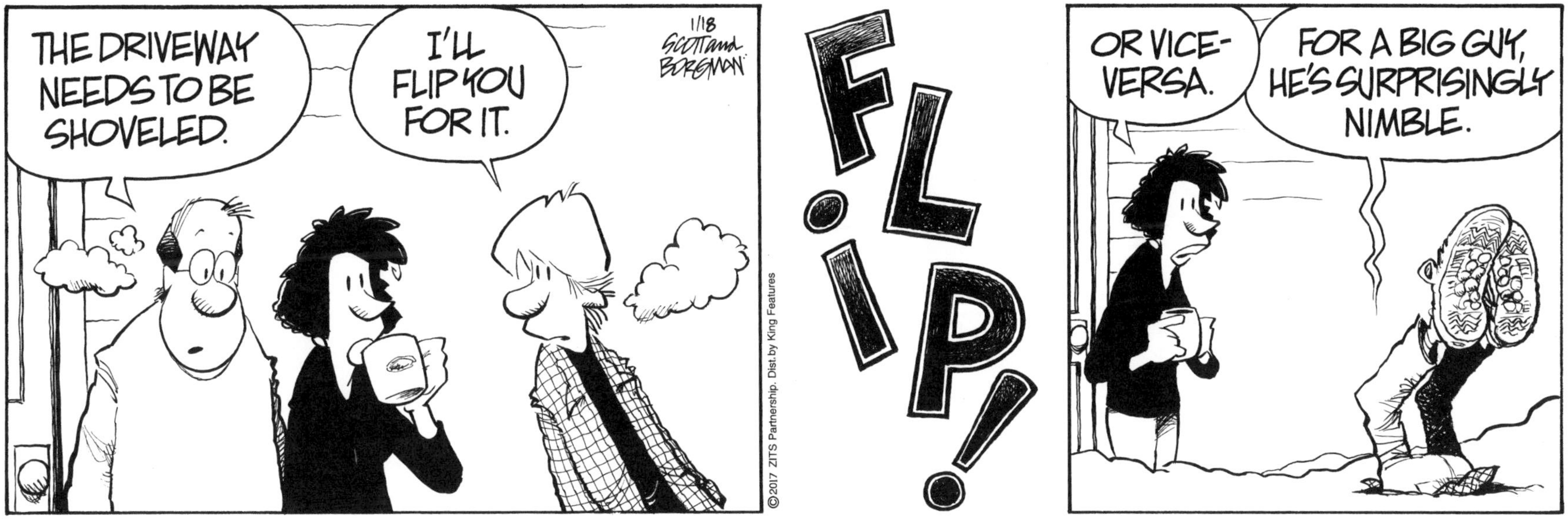
THE DRIVEWAY NEEDS TO BE SHOVELED.
I'LL FLIP YOU FOR IT.
1/18 SCOTT and BORGMAN
©2017 ZITS Partnership. Dist. by King Features
FLIP!
OR VICE-VERSA.
FOR A BIG GUY, HE'S SURPRISINGLY NIMBLE.

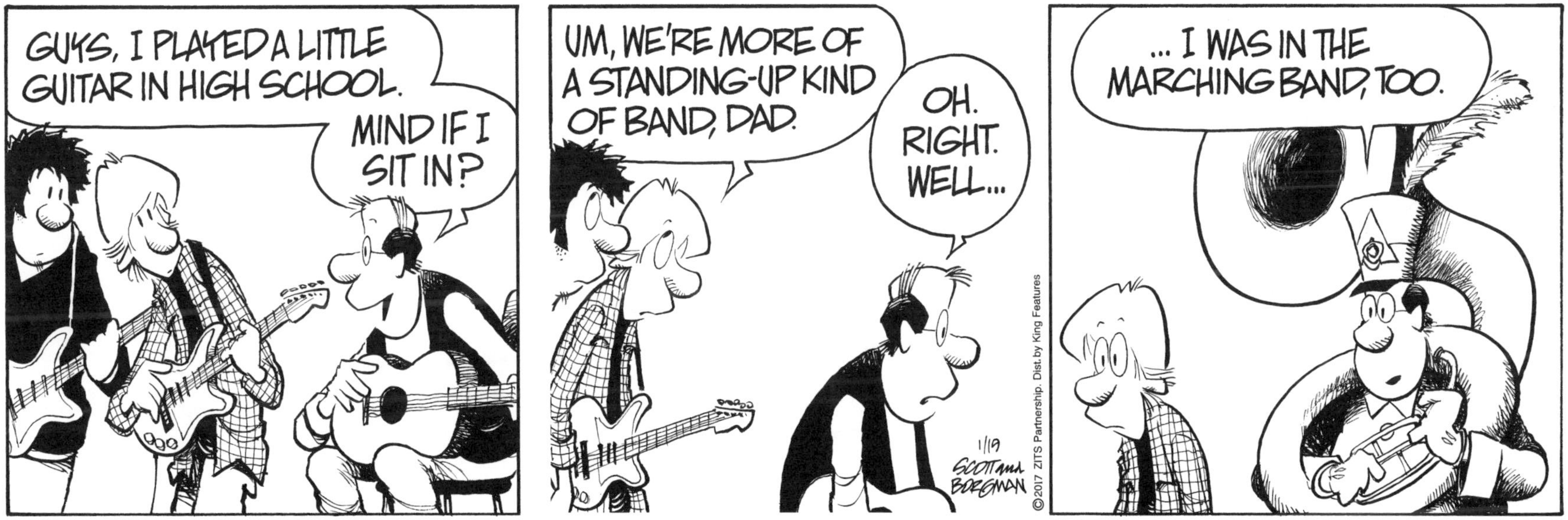
GUYS, I PLAYED A LITTLE GUITAR IN HIGH SCHOOL.
MIND IF I SIT IN?
UM, WE'RE MORE OF A STANDING-UP KIND OF BAND, DAD.
OH. RIGHT. WELL...
1/19 SCOTT and BORGMAN
©2017 ZITS Partnership. Dist. by King Features
... I WAS IN THE MARCHING BAND, TOO.

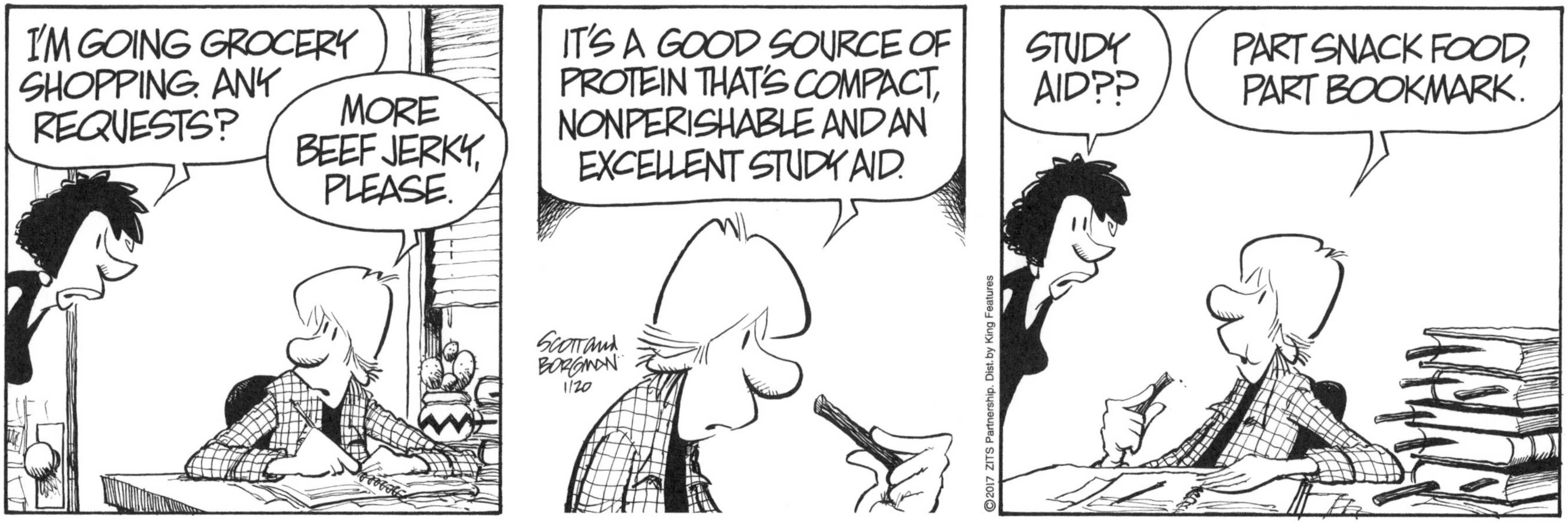
I'M GOING GROCERY SHOPPING. ANY REQUESTS?
MORE BEEF JERKY, PLEASE.
IT'S A GOOD SOURCE OF PROTEIN THAT'S COMPACT, NONPERISHABLE AND AN EXCELLENT STUDY AID.
SCOTT and BORGMAN 1/20
STUDY AID??
PART SNACK FOOD, PART BOOKMARK.
©2017 ZITS Partnership. Dist. by King Features

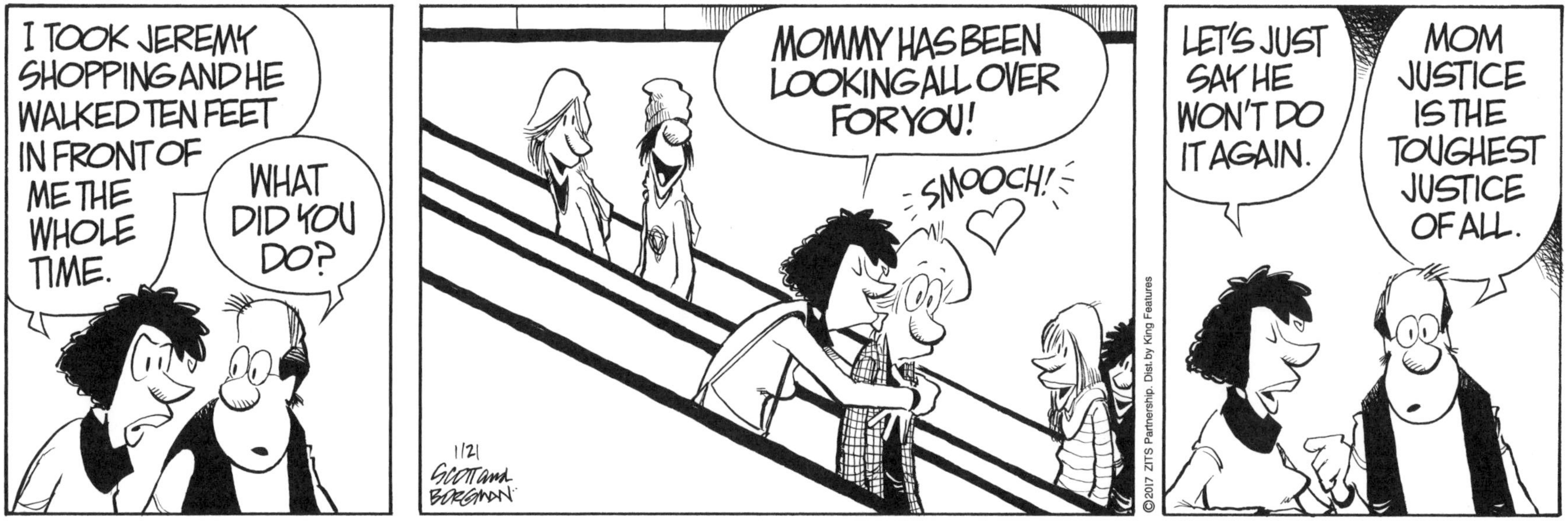
I TOOK JEREMY SHOPPING AND HE WALKED TEN FEET IN FRONT OF ME THE WHOLE TIME.
WHAT DID YOU DO?
MOMMY HAS BEEN LOOKING ALL OVER FOR YOU!
SMOOCH!
1/21 SCOTT and BORGMAN
©2017 ZITS Partnership. Dist. by King Features
LET'S JUST SAY HE WON'T DO IT AGAIN.
MOM JUSTICE IS THE TOUGHEST JUSTICE OF ALL.

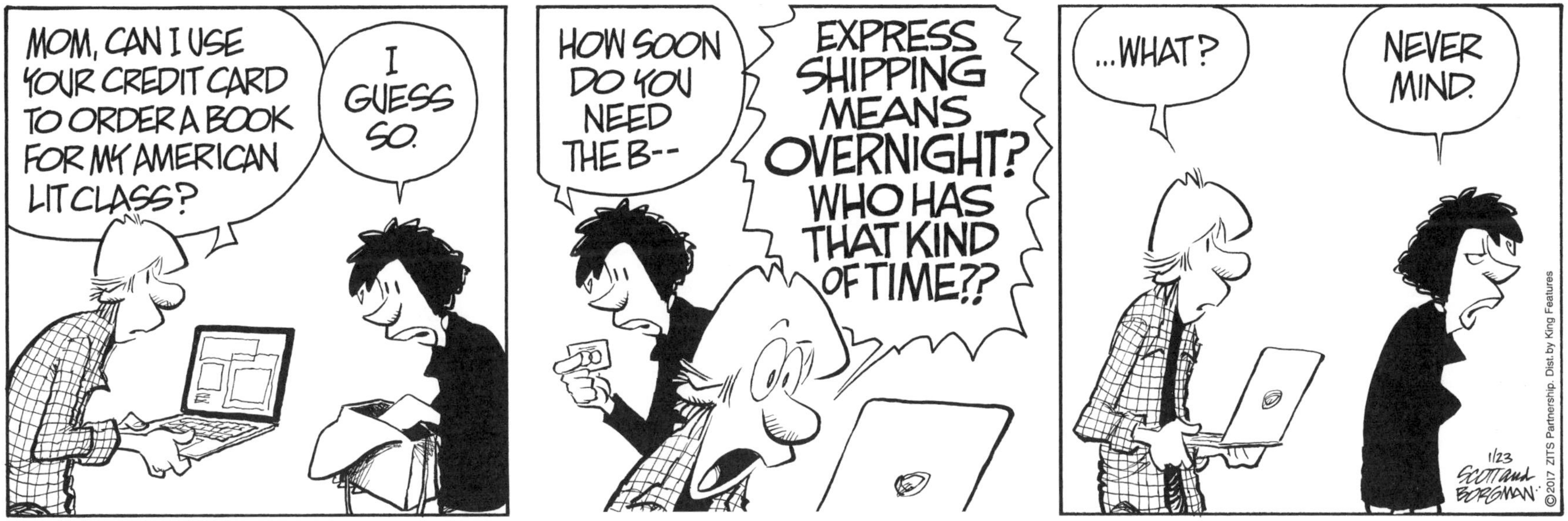
MOM, CAN I USE YOUR CREDIT CARD TO ORDER A BOOK FOR MY AMERICAN LIT CLASS?
I GUESS SO.
HOW SOON DO YOU NEED THE B--
EXPRESS SHIPPING MEANS OVERNIGHT? WHO HAS THAT KIND OF TIME??
...WHAT?
NEVER MIND.
1/23
SCOTT and BORGMAN
©2017 ZITS Partnership. Dist. by King Features

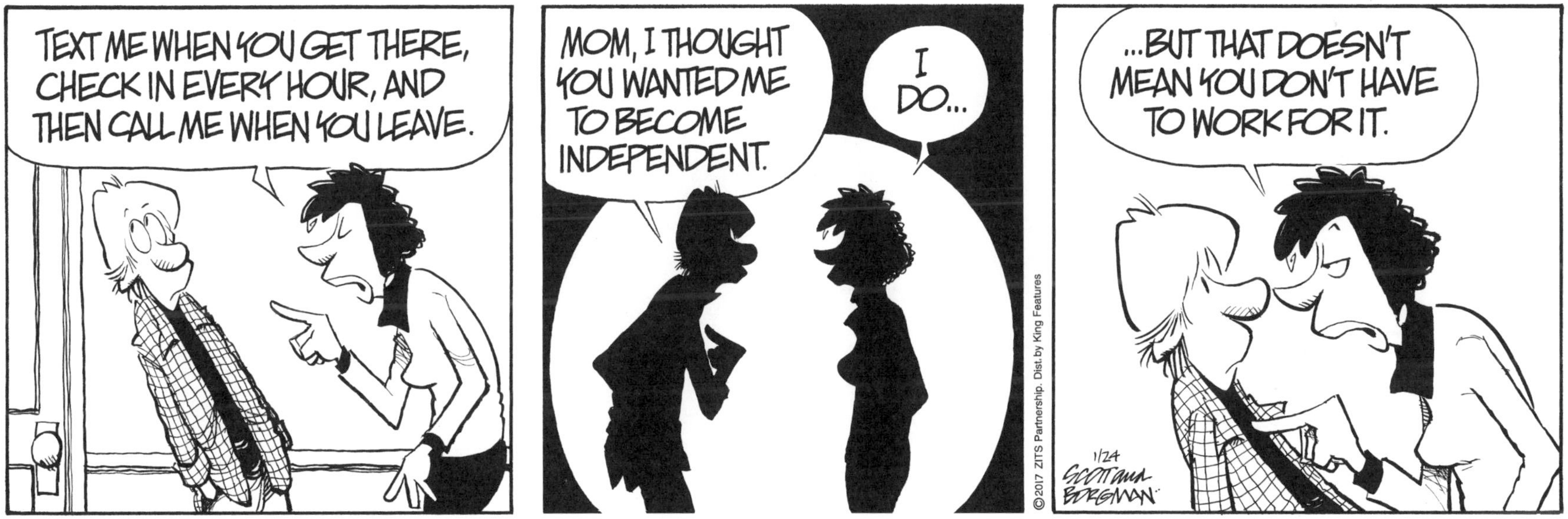
TEXT ME WHEN YOU GET THERE, CHECK IN EVERY HOUR, AND THEN CALL ME WHEN YOU LEAVE.
MOM, I THOUGHT YOU WANTED ME TO BECOME INDEPENDENT.
I DO...
...BUT THAT DOESN'T MEAN YOU DON'T HAVE TO WORK FOR IT.
©2017 ZITS Partnership. Dist. by King Features
1/24
SCOTT and BORGMAN

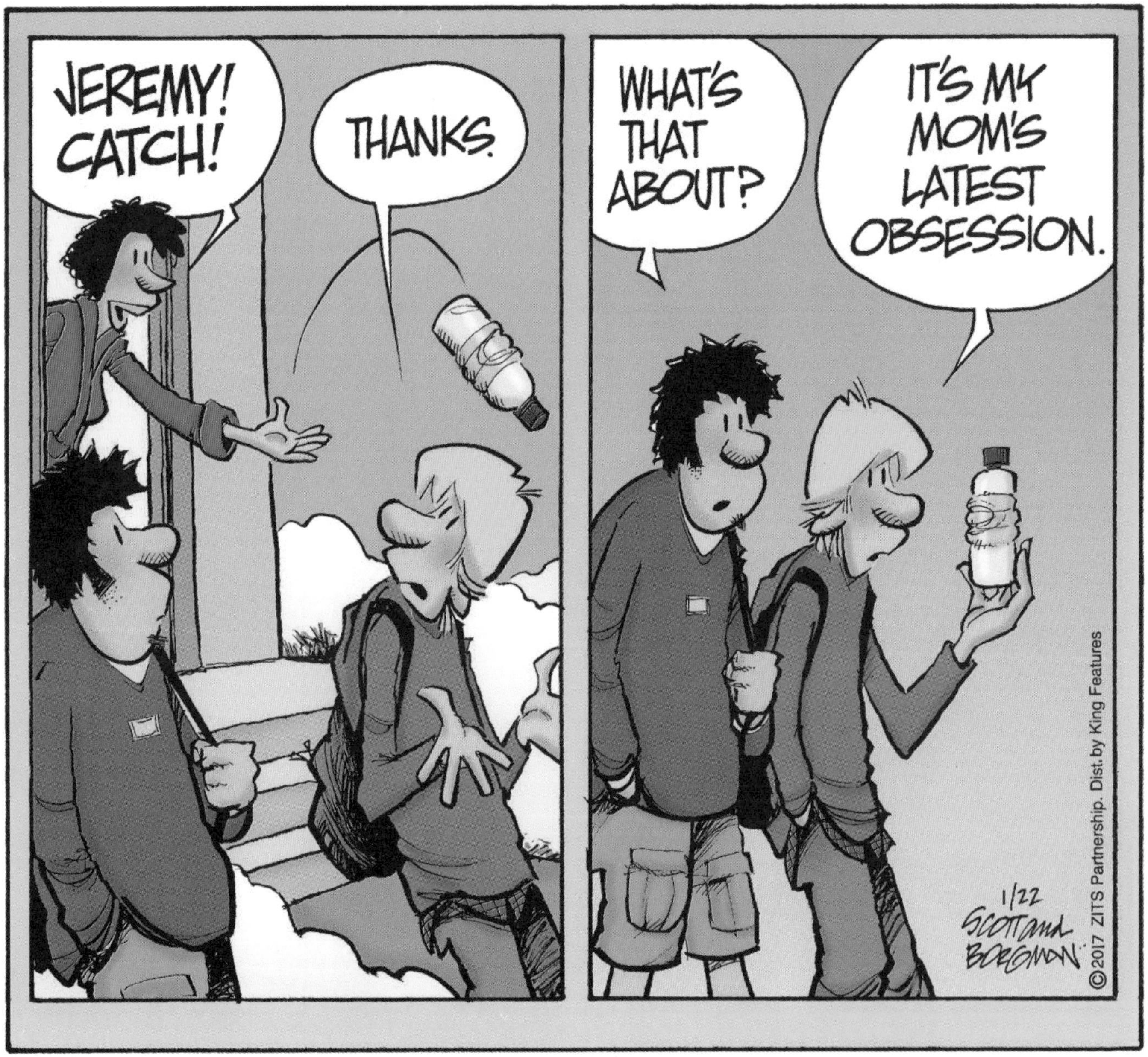
JEREMY! CATCH!
THANKS.
WHAT'S THAT ABOUT?
IT'S MY MOM'S LATEST OBSESSION.
1/22
SCOTT and BORGMAN
©2017 ZITS Partnership. Dist. by King Features

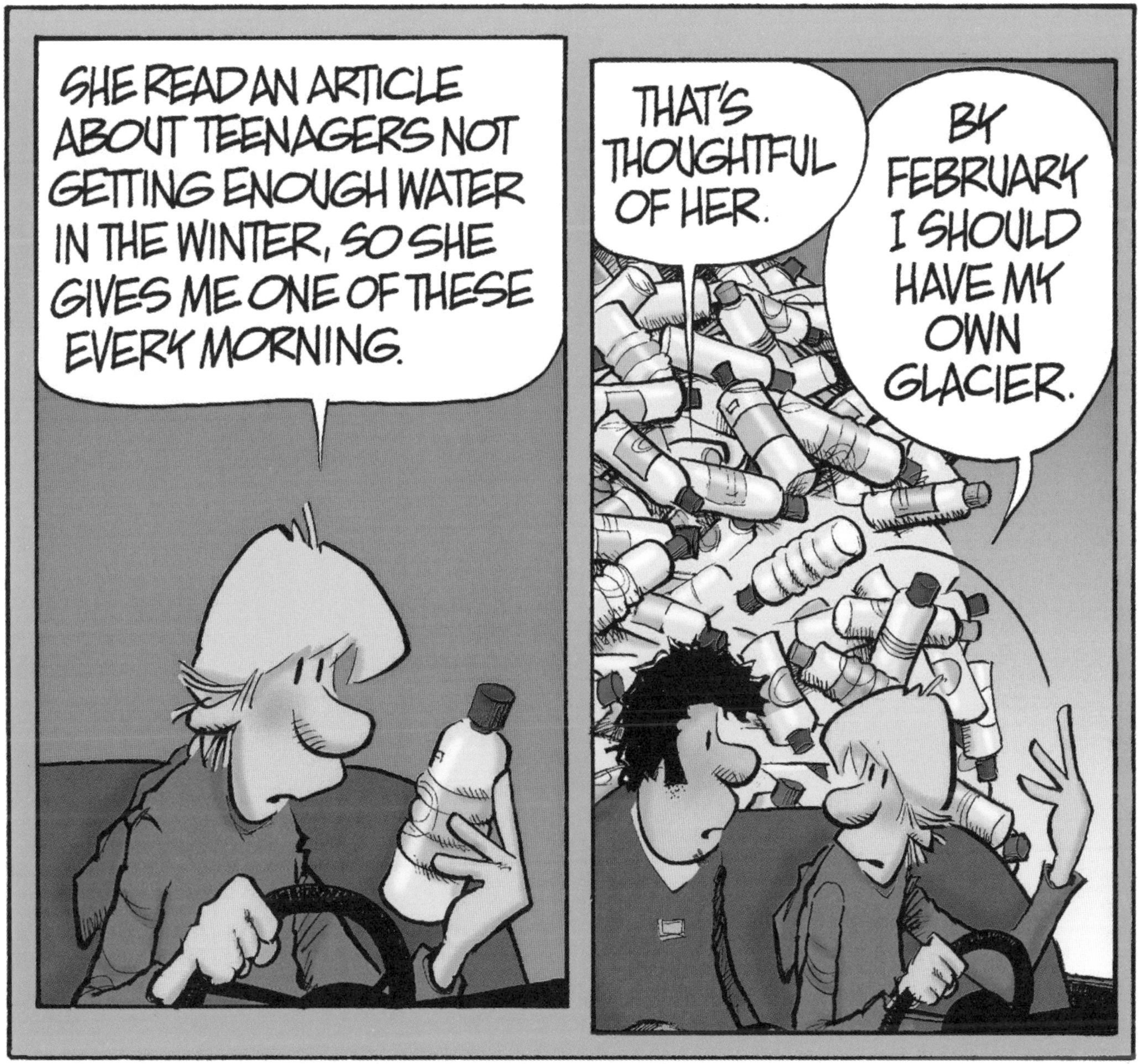
SHE READ AN ARTICLE ABOUT TEENAGERS NOT GETTING ENOUGH WATER IN THE WINTER, SO SHE GIVES ME ONE OF THESE EVERY MORNING.
THAT'S THOUGHTFUL OF HER.
BY FEBRUARY I SHOULD HAVE MY OWN GLACIER.

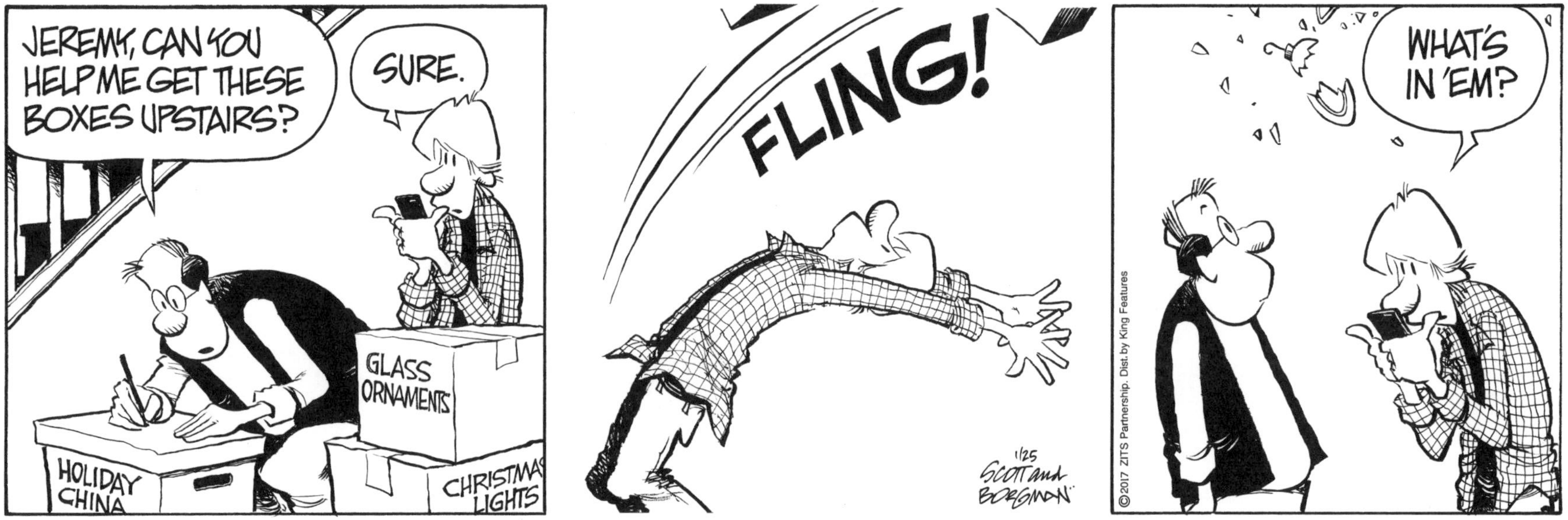
JEREMY, CAN YOU HELP ME GET THESE BOXES UPSTAIRS?
SURE.
GLASS ORNAMENTS
HOLIDAY CHINA
CHRISTMAS LIGHTS
FLING!
1/25 SCOTT and BORGMAN
WHAT'S IN 'EM?
©2017 ZITS Partnership. Dist. by King Features

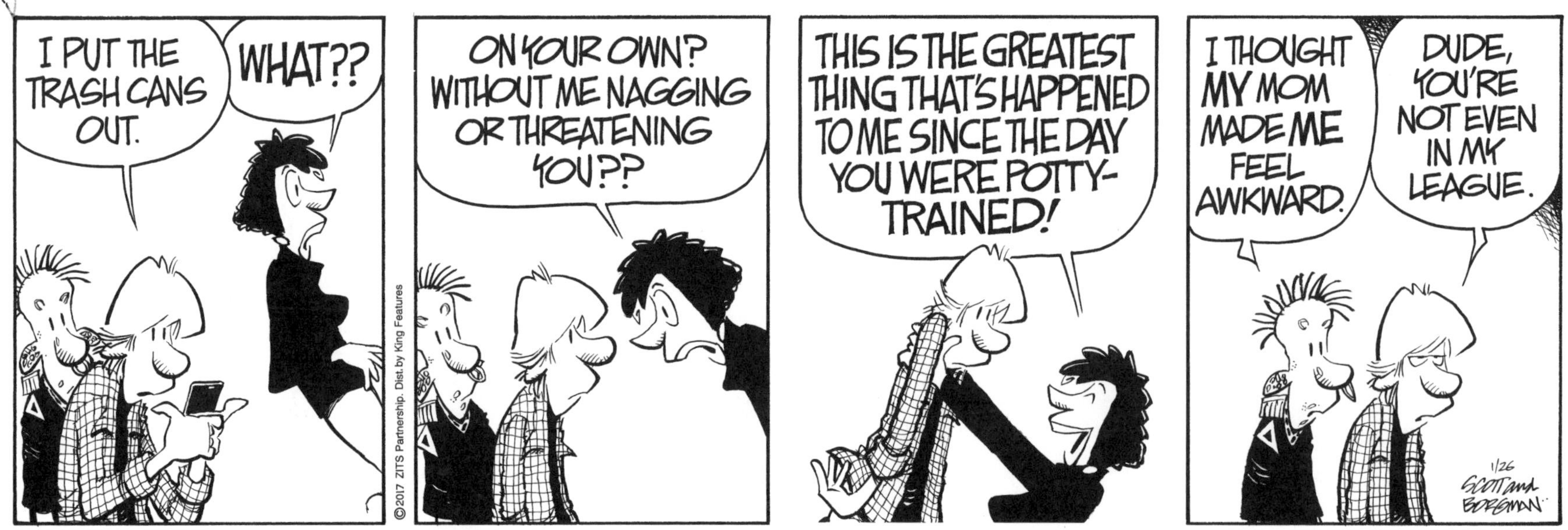
I PUT THE TRASH CANS OUT.
WHAT??
©2017 ZITS Partnership. Dist. by King Features
ON YOUR OWN? WITHOUT ME NAGGING OR THREATENING YOU??
THIS IS THE GREATEST THING THAT'S HAPPENED TO ME SINCE THE DAY YOU WERE POTTY-TRAINED!
I THOUGHT MY MOM MADE ME FEEL AWKWARD.
DUDE, YOU'RE NOT EVEN IN MY LEAGUE.
1/26 SCOTT and BORGMAN

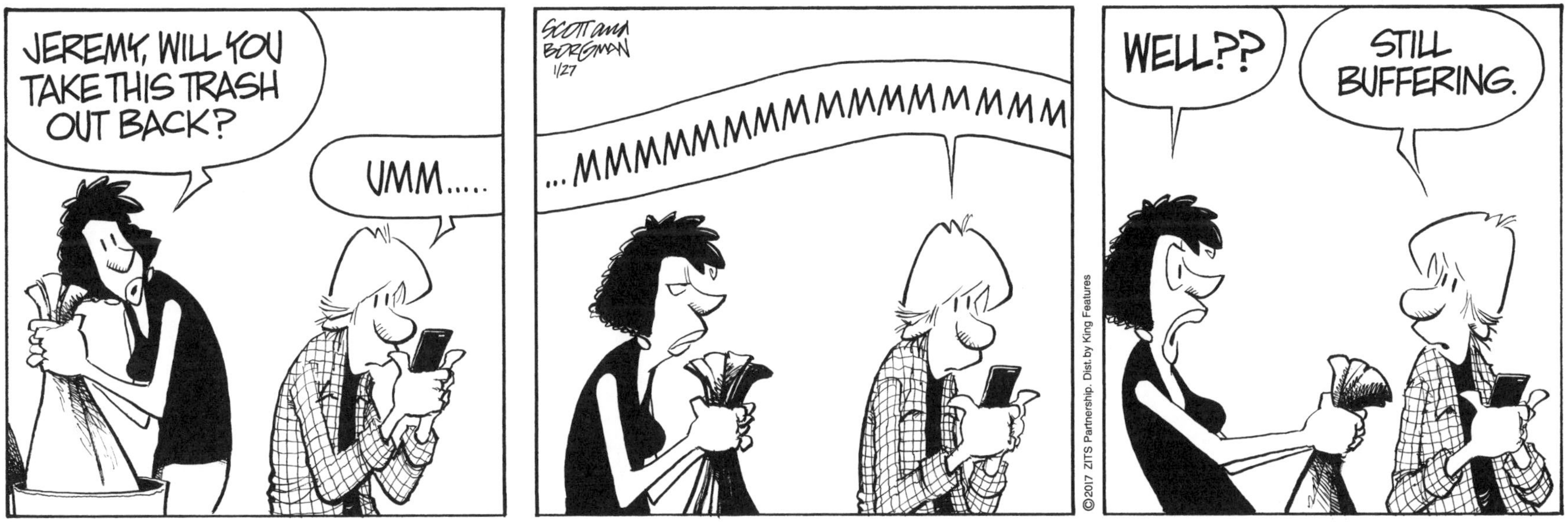
JEREMY, WILL YOU TAKE THIS TRASH OUT BACK?
UMM.....
SCOTT and BORGMAN 1/27
...MMMMMMMMMMMMMMMMMMMMM
©2017 ZITS Partnership. Dist. by King Features
WELL??
STILL BUFFERING.

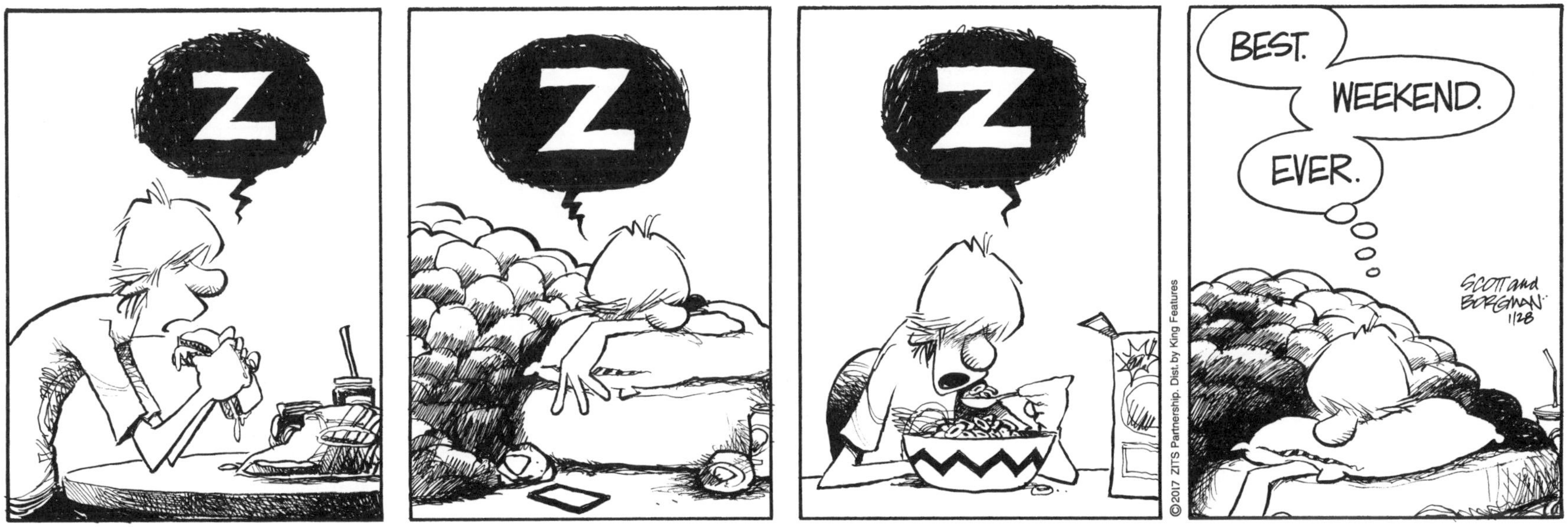
Z
Z
Z
©2017 ZITS Partnership. Dist. by King Features
BEST.
WEEKEND.
EVER.
SCOTT and BORGMAN 1/28

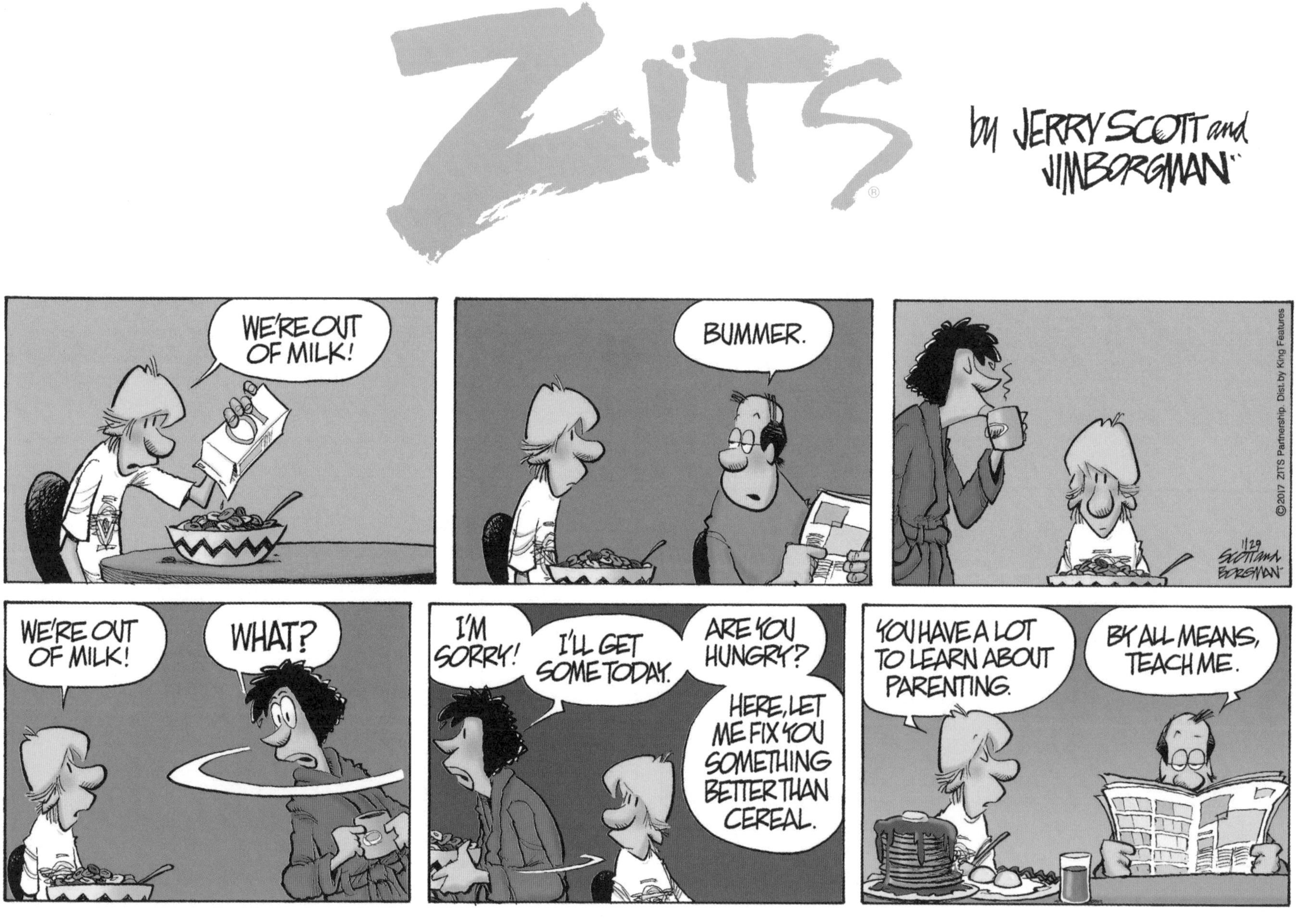
ZITS
by JERRY SCOTT and JIM BORGMAN
WE'RE OUT OF MILK!
BUMMER.
©2017 ZITS Partnership. Dist. by King Features
1/29 SCOTT and BORGMAN
WE'RE OUT OF MILK!
WHAT?
I'M SORRY!
I'LL GET SOME TODAY.
ARE YOU HUNGRY?
HERE, LET ME FIX YOU SOMETHING BETTER THAN CEREAL.
YOU HAVE A LOT TO LEARN ABOUT PARENTING.
BY ALL MEANS, TEACH ME.

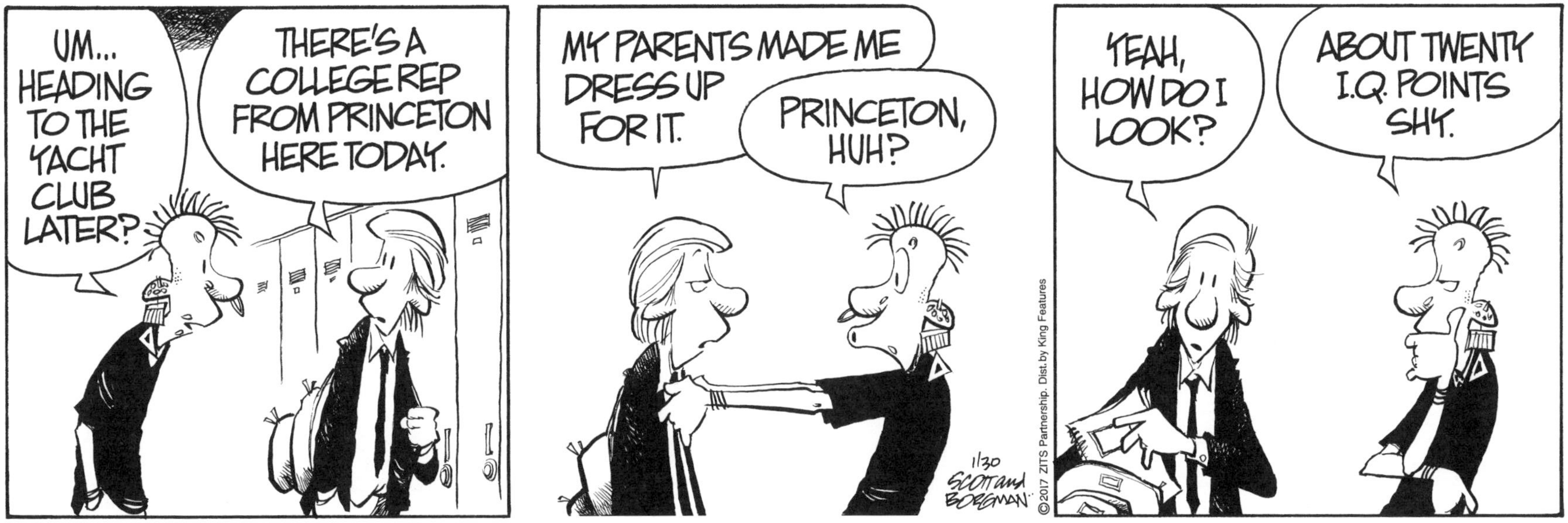
UM... HEADING TO THE YACHT CLUB LATER?
THERE'S A COLLEGE REP FROM PRINCETON HERE TODAY.
MY PARENTS MADE ME DRESS UP FOR IT.
PRINCETON, HUH?
1/30 SCOTT and BORGMAN
©2017 ZITS Partnership. Dist. by King Features
YEAH, HOW DO I LOOK?
ABOUT TWENTY I.Q. POINTS SHY.

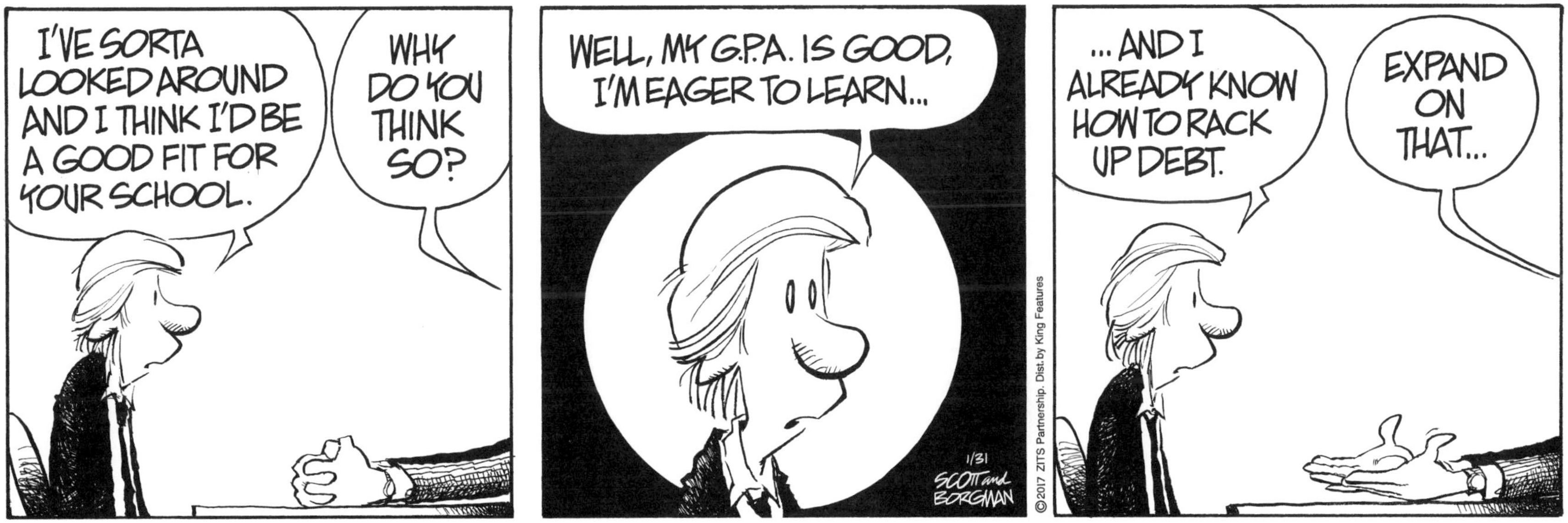
I'VE SORTA LOOKED AROUND AND I THINK I'D BE A GOOD FIT FOR YOUR SCHOOL.
WHY DO YOU THINK SO?
WELL, MY G.P.A. IS GOOD, I'M EAGER TO LEARN...
1/31 SCOTT and BORGMAN
©2017 ZITS Partnership. Dist. by King Features
...AND I ALREADY KNOW HOW TO RACK UP DEBT.
EXPAND ON THAT...

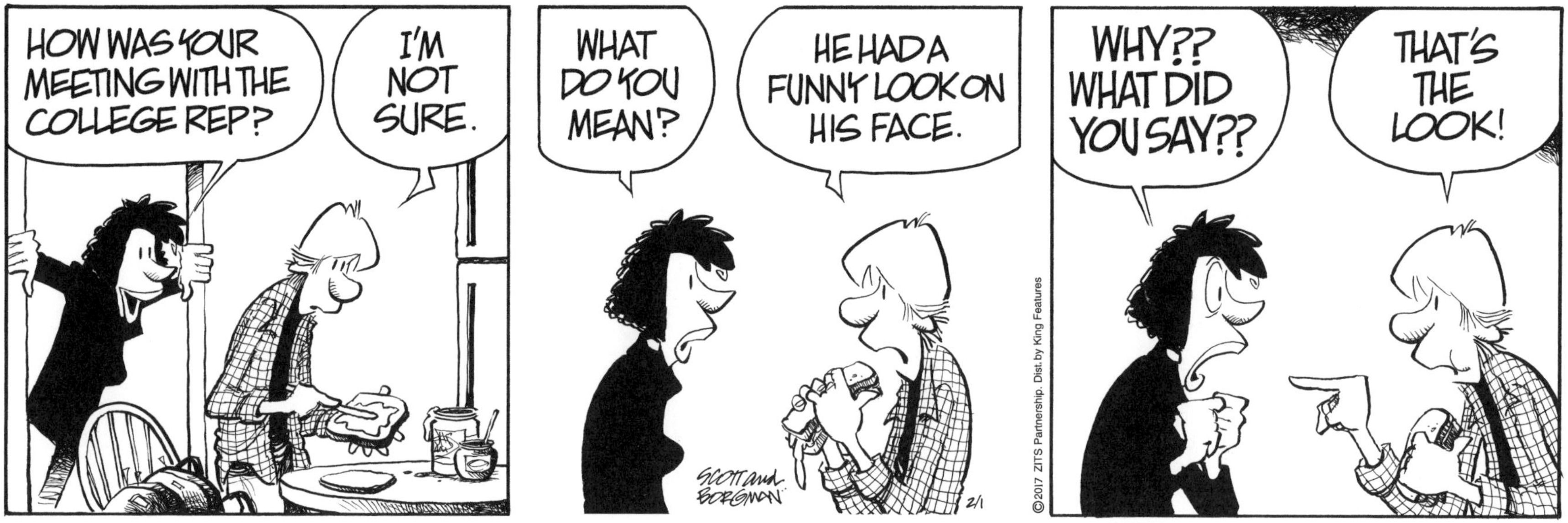
HOW WAS YOUR MEETING WITH THE COLLEGE REP?
I'M NOT SURE.
WHAT DO YOU MEAN?
HE HAD A FUNNY LOOK ON HIS FACE.
SCOTT and BORGMAN 2/1
©2017 ZITS Partnership. Dist. by King Features
WHY?? WHAT DID YOU SAY??
THAT'S THE LOOK!

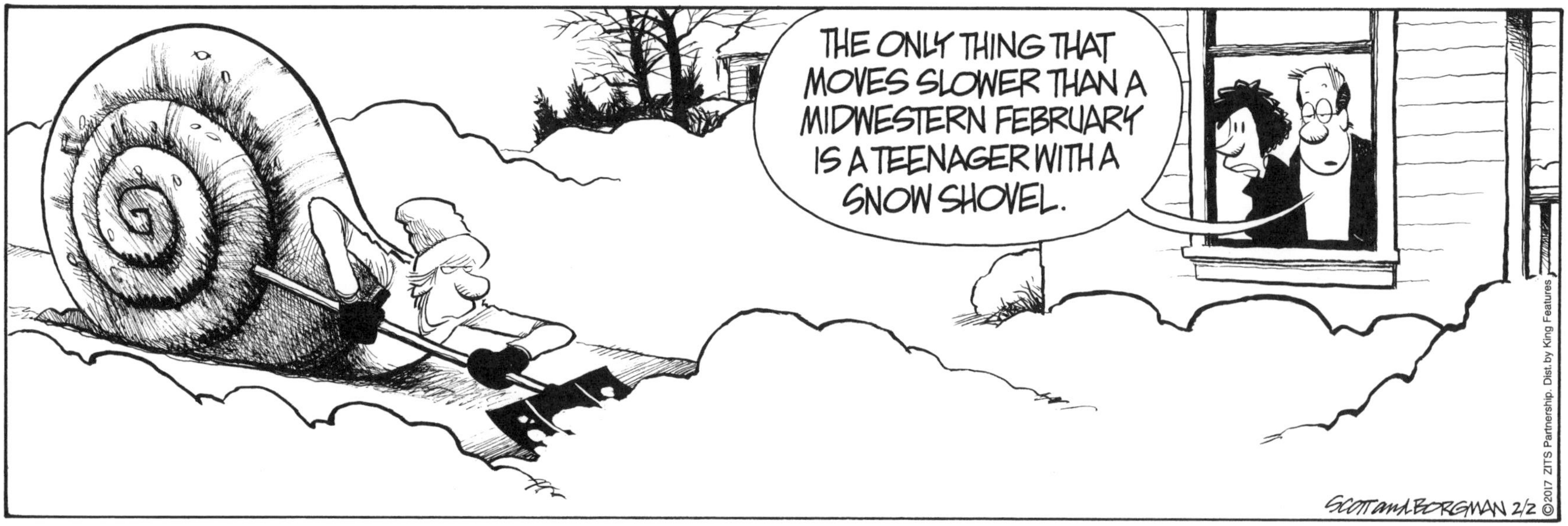
THE ONLY THING THAT MOVES SLOWER THAN A MIDWESTERN FEBRUARY IS A TEENAGER WITH A SNOW SHOVEL.
SCOTT and BORGMAN 2/2
©2017 ZITS Partnership. Dist. by King Features

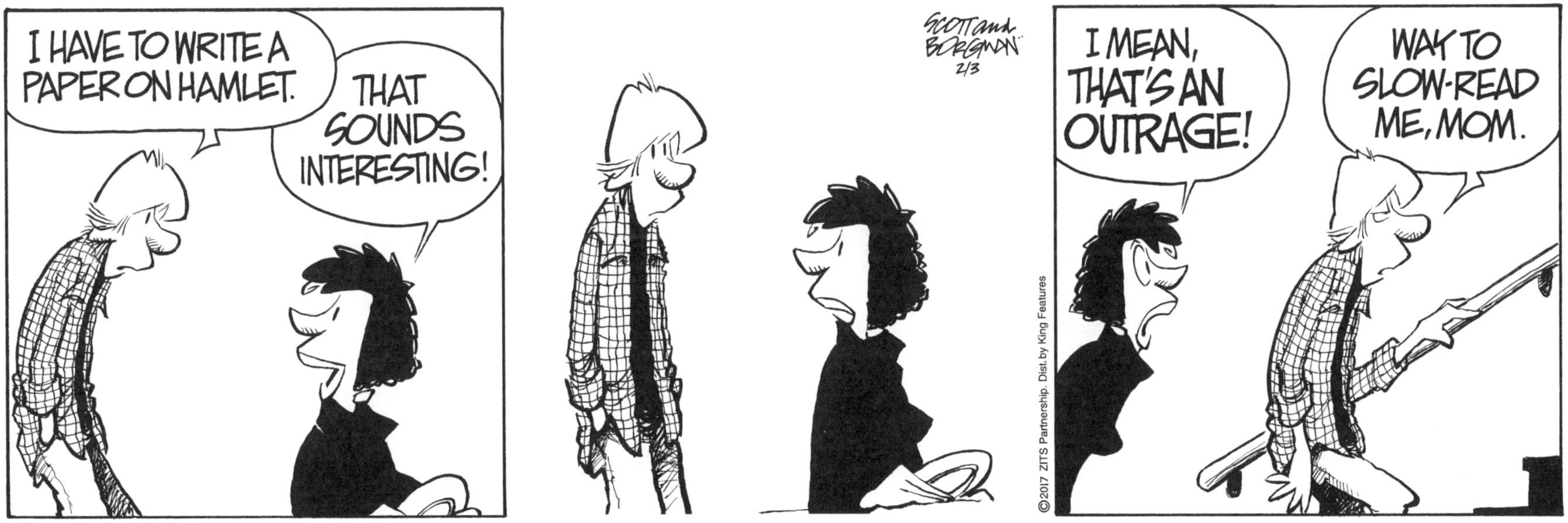
I HAVE TO WRITE A PAPER ON HAMLET.
THAT SOUNDS INTERESTING!
SCOTT and BORGMAN 2/3
I MEAN, THAT'S AN OUTRAGE!
WAY TO SLOW-READ ME, MOM.
©2017 ZITS Partnership. Dist. by King Features

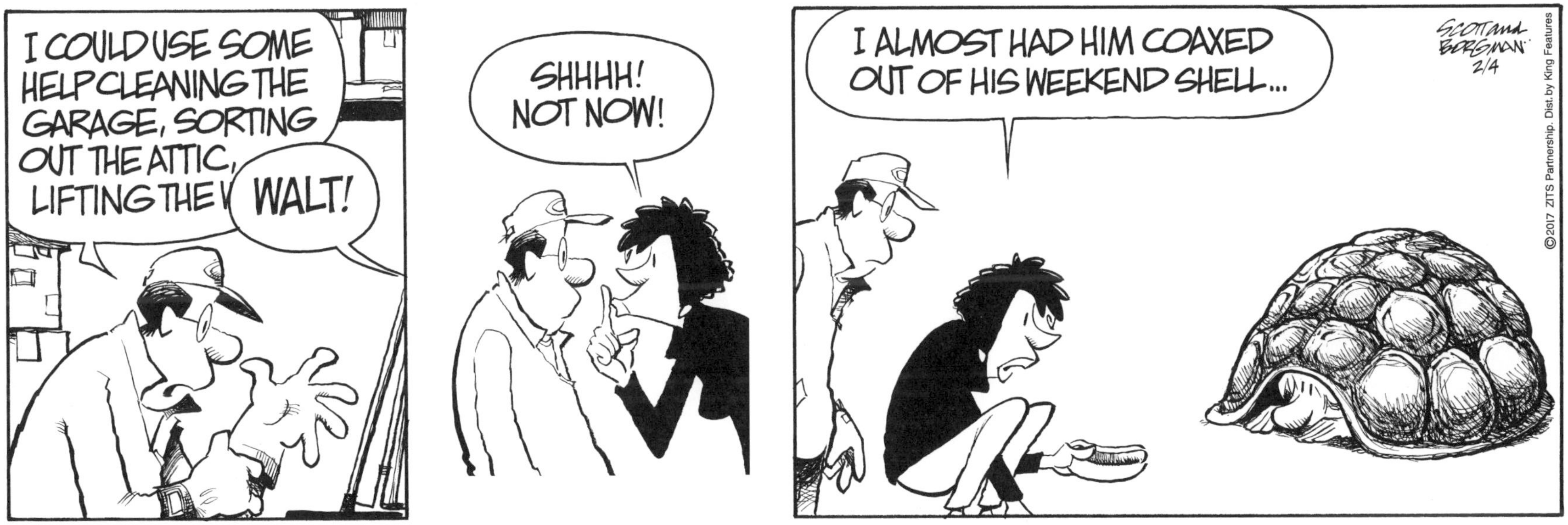
I COULD USE SOME HELP CLEANING THE GARAGE, SORTING OUT THE ATTIC, LIFTING THE
WALT!
SHHHH! NOT NOW!
I ALMOST HAD HIM COAXED OUT OF HIS WEEKEND SHELL...
SCOTT and BORGMAN 2/4
©2017 ZITS Partnership. Dist. by King Features

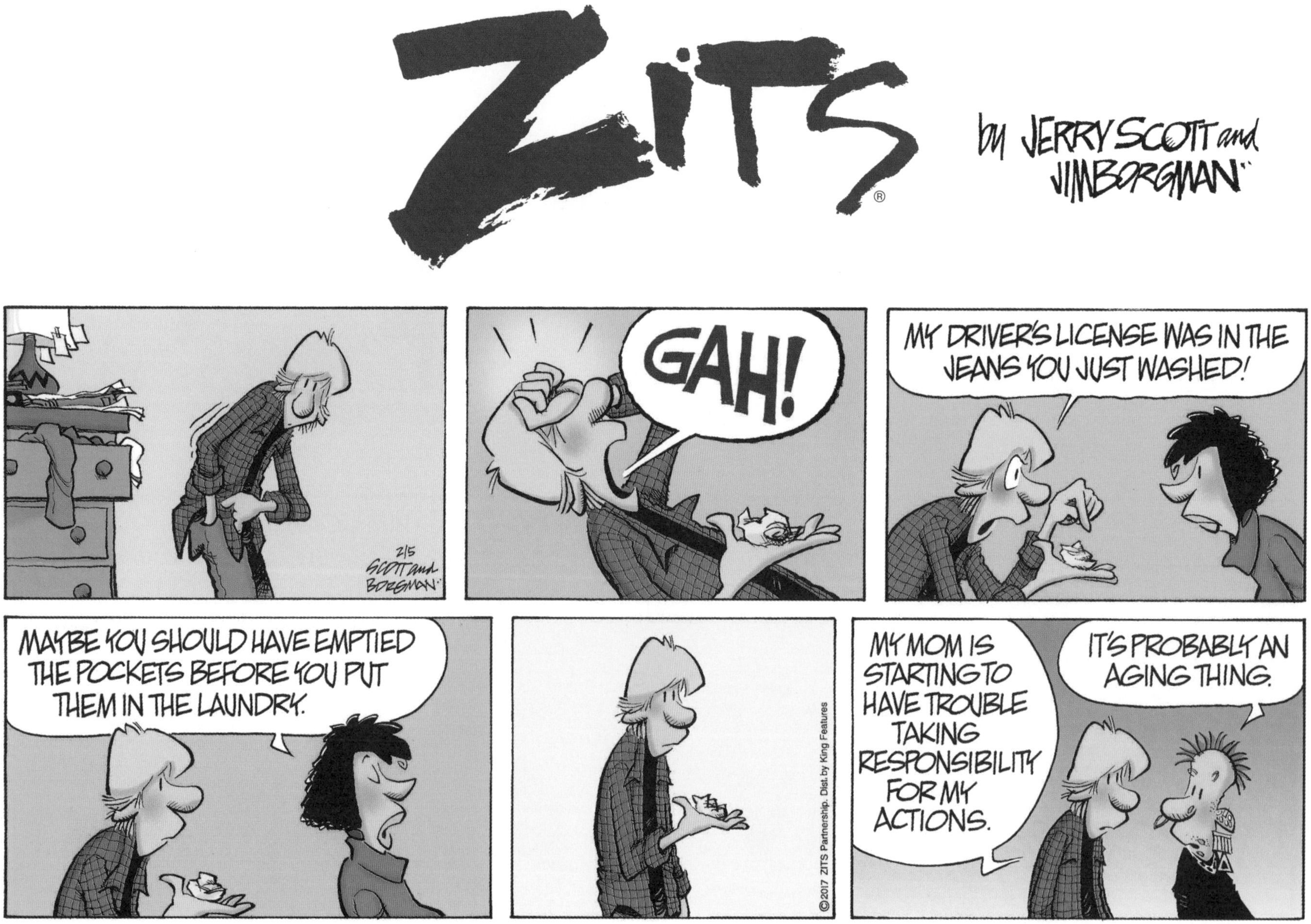
ZITS®
by JERRY SCOTT and JIM BORGMAN
2/5 SCOTT and BORGMAN
GAH!
MY DRIVER'S LICENSE WAS IN THE JEANS YOU JUST WASHED!
MAYBE YOU SHOULD HAVE EMPTIED THE POCKETS BEFORE YOU PUT THEM IN THE LAUNDRY.
©2017 ZITS Partnership. Dist. by King Features
MY MOM IS STARTING TO HAVE TROUBLE TAKING RESPONSIBILITY FOR MY ACTIONS.
IT'S PROBABLY AN AGING THING.

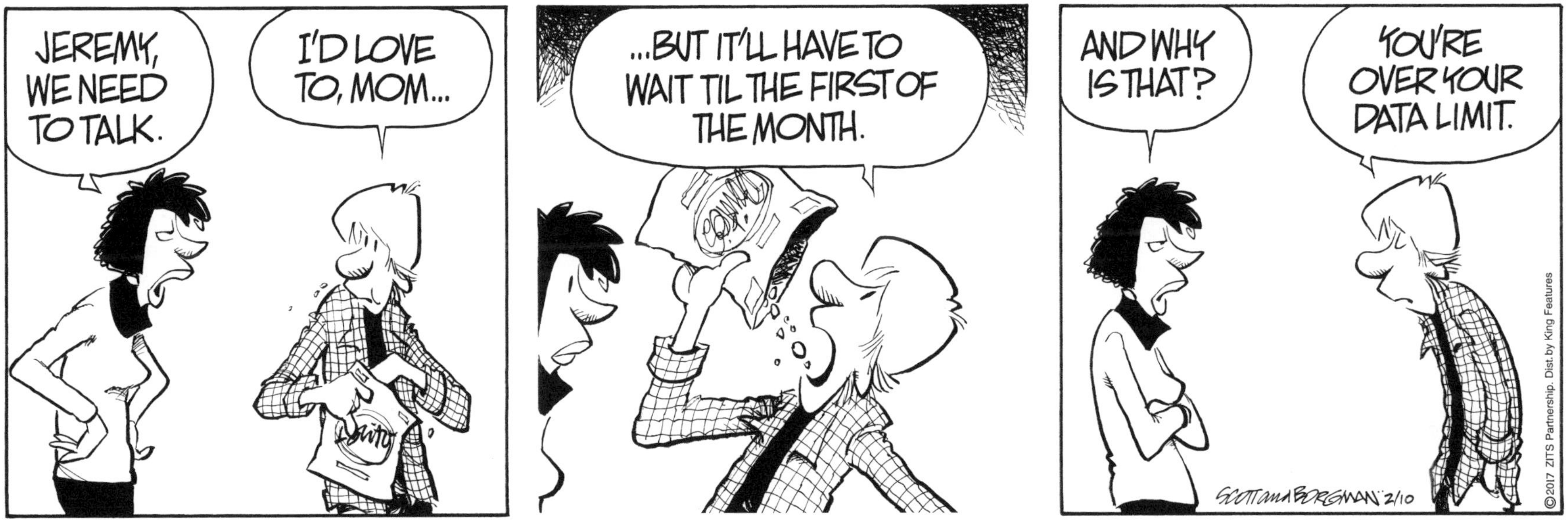

JEREMY, WE NEED TO TALK.
I'D LOVE TO, MOM...
...BUT IT'LL HAVE TO WAIT TIL THE FIRST OF THE MONTH.
AND WHY IS THAT?
YOU'RE OVER YOUR DATA LIMIT.
SCOTT and BORGMAN 2/10
©2017 ZITS Partnership. Dist. by King Features

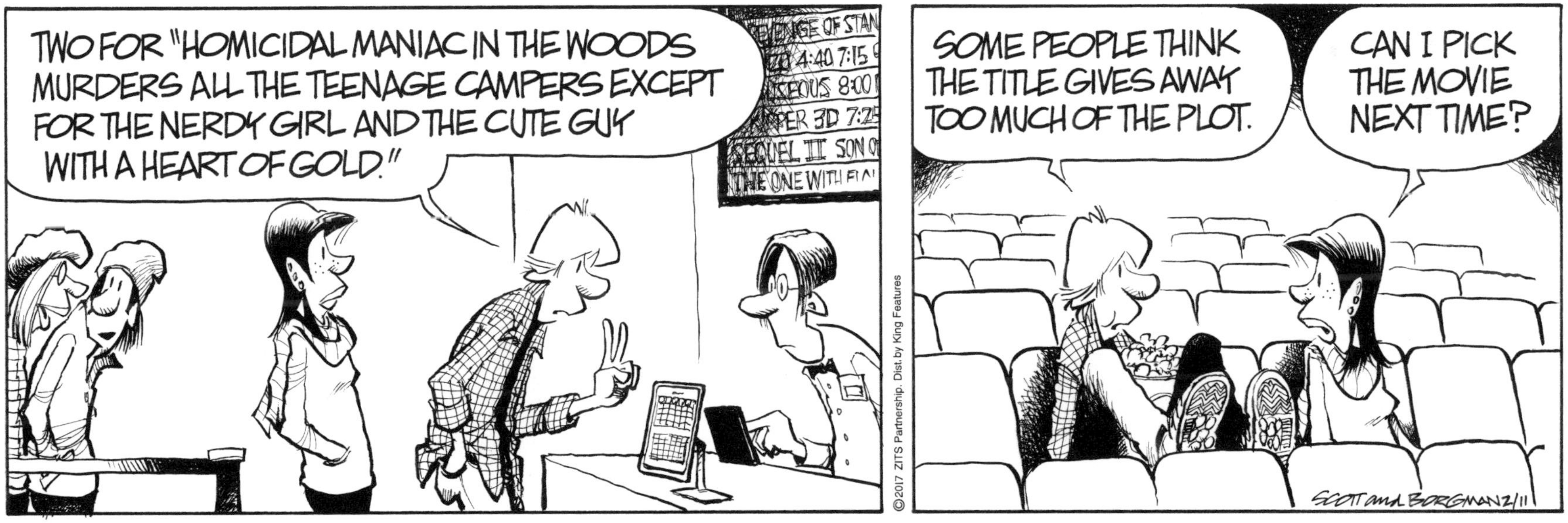

TWO FOR "HOMICIDAL MANIAC IN THE WOODS MURDERS ALL THE TEENAGE CAMPERS EXCEPT FOR THE NERDY GIRL AND THE CUTE GUY WITH A HEART OF GOLD."
©2017 ZITS Partnership. Dist. by King Features
SOME PEOPLE THINK THE TITLE GIVES AWAY TOO MUCH OF THE PLOT.
CAN I PICK THE MOVIE NEXT TIME?
SCOTT and BORGMAN 2/11

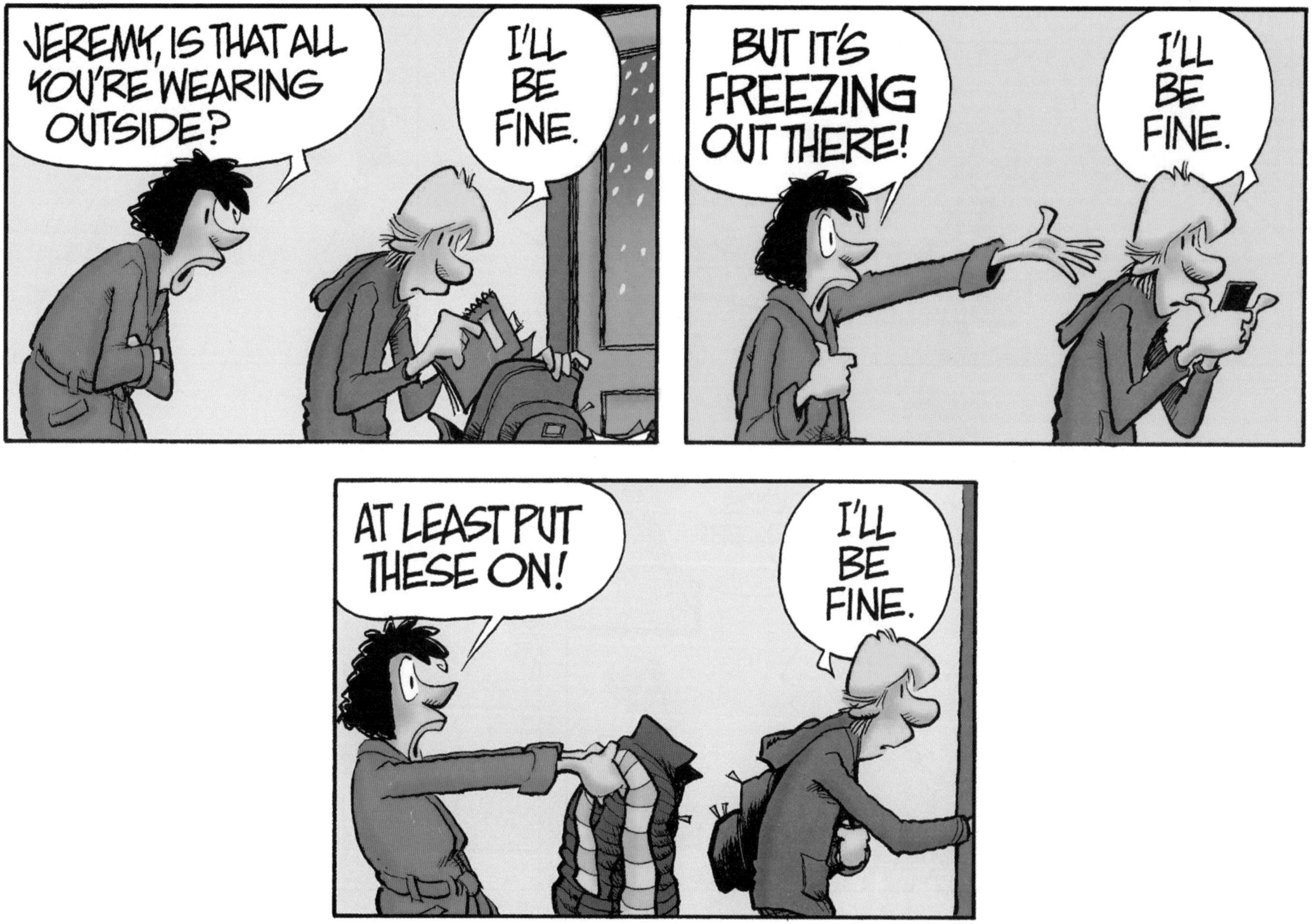
JEREMY, IS THAT ALL YOU'RE WEARING OUTSIDE?
I'LL BE FINE.
BUT IT'S FREEZING OUT THERE!
I'LL BE FINE.
AT LEAST PUT THESE ON!
I'LL BE FINE.

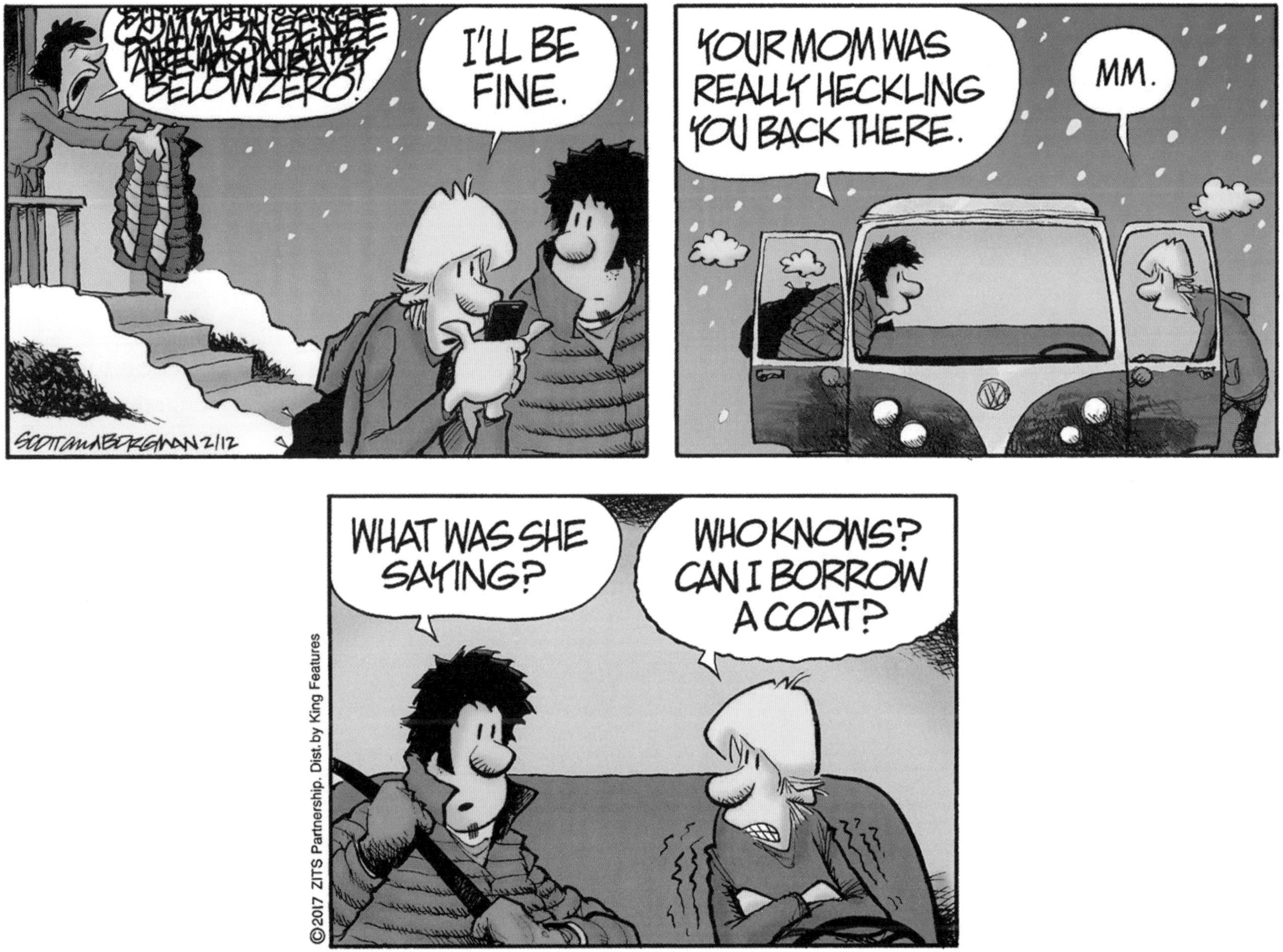
BELOW ZERO!
I'LL BE FINE.
YOUR MOM WAS REALLY HECKLING YOU BACK THERE.
MM.
WHAT WAS SHE SAYING?
WHO KNOWS? CAN I BORROW A COAT?

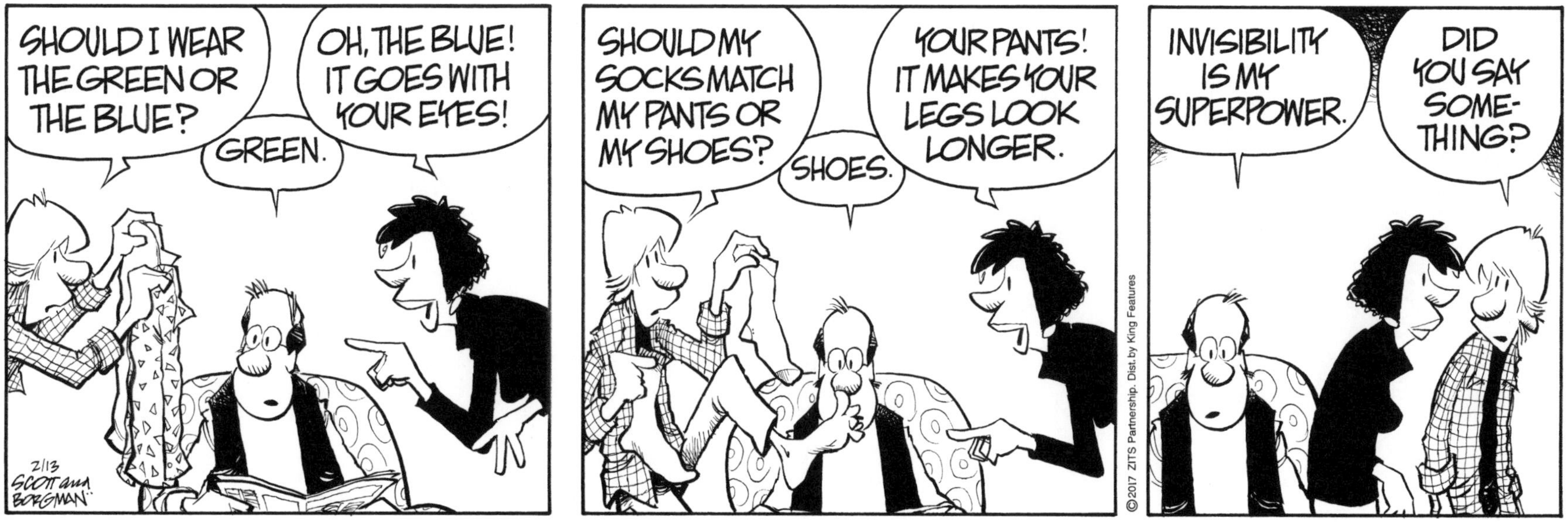
SHOULD I WEAR THE GREEN OR THE BLUE?
GREEN.
OH, THE BLUE! IT GOES WITH YOUR EYES!
SHOULD MY SOCKS MATCH MY PANTS OR MY SHOES?
SHOES.
YOUR PANTS! IT MAKES YOUR LEGS LOOK LONGER.
INVISIBILITY IS MY SUPERPOWER.
DID YOU SAY SOME-THING?
© 2017 ZITS Partnership. Dist. by King Features

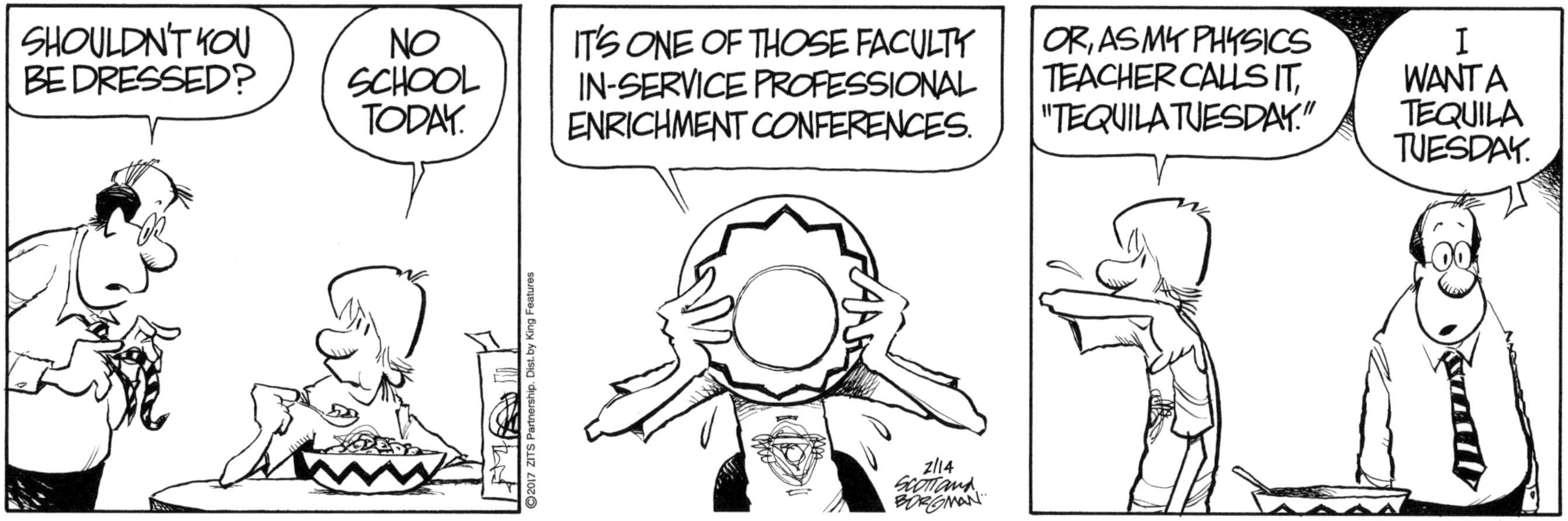
SHOULDN'T YOU BE DRESSED?
NO SCHOOL TODAY.
IT'S ONE OF THOSE FACULTY IN-SERVICE PROFESSIONAL ENRICHMENT CONFERENCES.
OR, AS MY PHYSICS TEACHER CALLS IT, "TEQUILA TUESDAY."
I WANT A TEQUILA TUESDAY.
© 2017 ZITS Partnership. Dist. by King Features

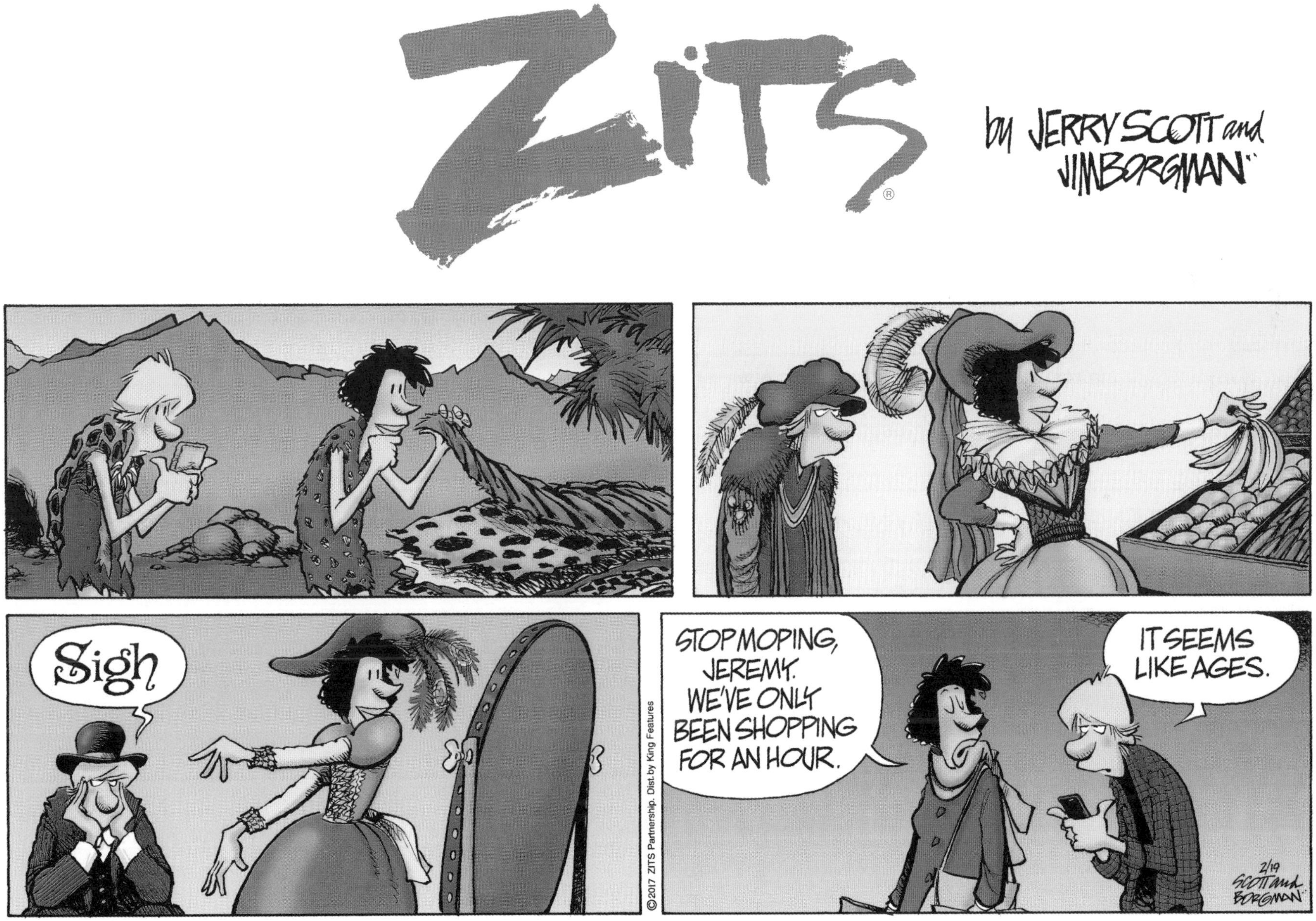
ZITS
by JERRY SCOTT and JIM BORGMAN
Sigh
©2017 ZITS Partnership. Dist. by King Features
STOP MOPING, JEREMY. WE'VE ONLY BEEN SHOPPING FOR AN HOUR.
IT SEEMS LIKE AGES.
2/19
SCOTT and BORGMAN

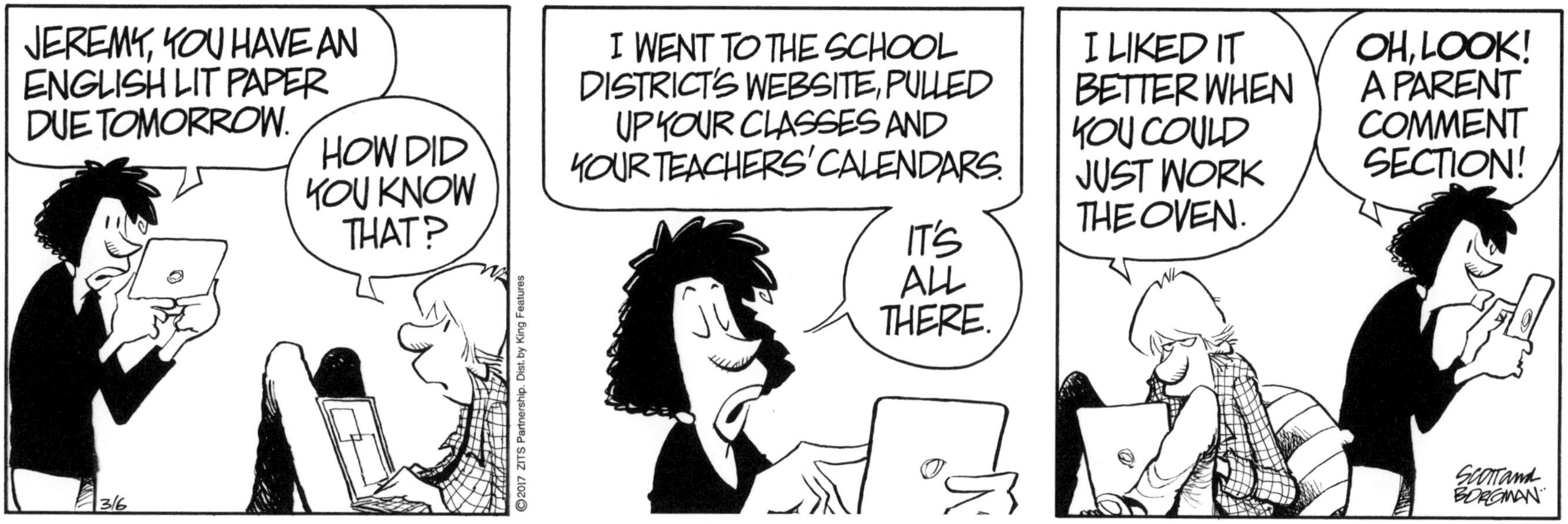
JEREMY, YOU HAVE AN ENGLISH LIT PAPER DUE TOMORROW.
HOW DID YOU KNOW THAT?
I WENT TO THE SCHOOL DISTRICT'S WEBSITE, PULLED UP YOUR CLASSES AND YOUR TEACHERS' CALENDARS.
IT'S ALL THERE.
I LIKED IT BETTER WHEN YOU COULD JUST WORK THE OVEN.
OH, LOOK! A PARENT COMMENT SECTION!
3/6
©2017 ZITS Partnership. Dist. by King Features
SCOTT and BORGMAN

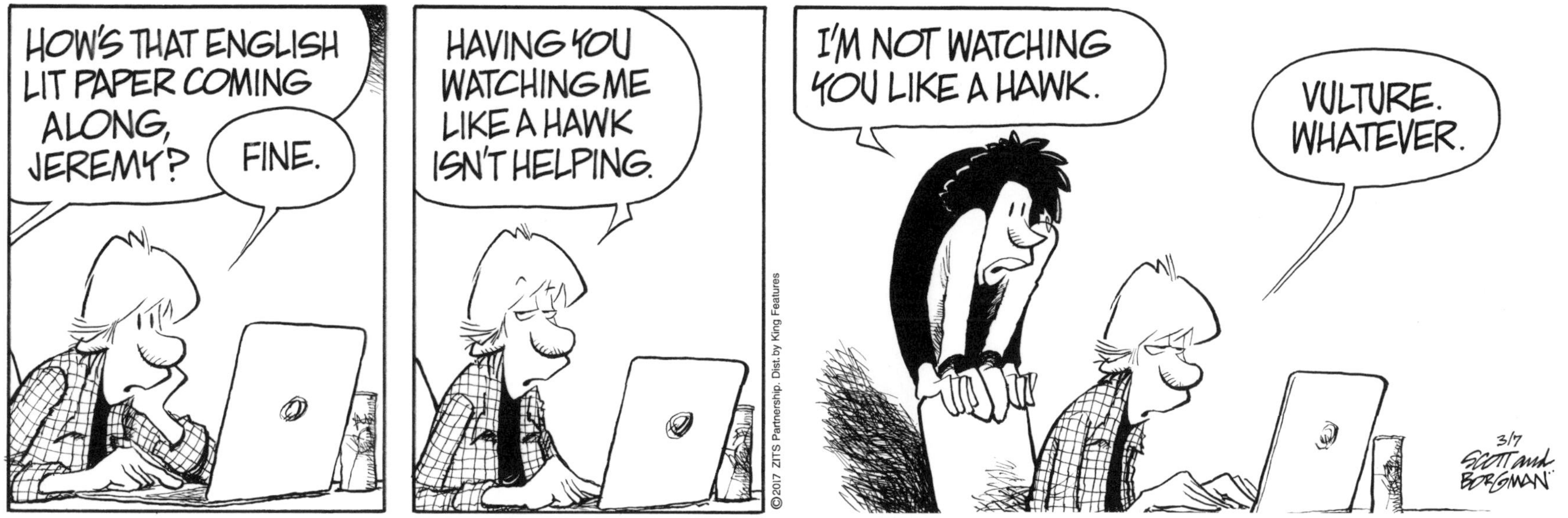
HOW'S THAT ENGLISH LIT PAPER COMING ALONG, JEREMY?
FINE.
HAVING YOU WATCHING ME LIKE A HAWK ISN'T HELPING.
I'M NOT WATCHING YOU LIKE A HAWK.
VULTURE. WHATEVER.
©2017 ZITS Partnership. Dist. by King Features
3/7
SCOTT and BORGMAN

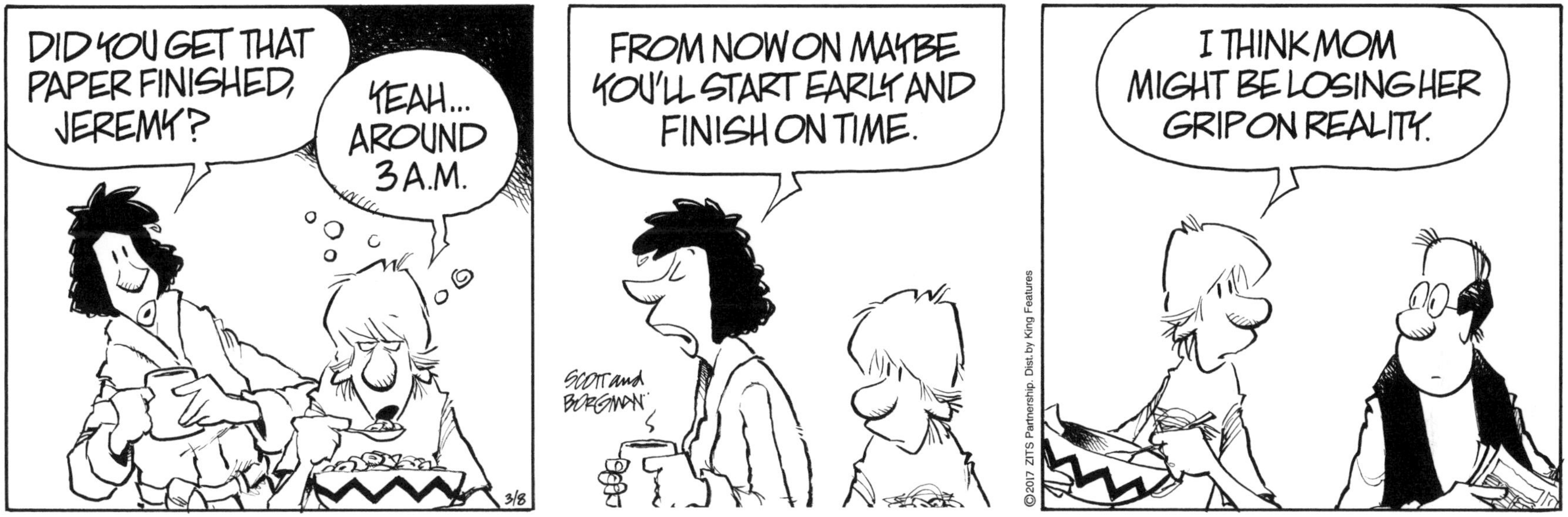
DID YOU GET THAT PAPER FINISHED, JEREMY?
YEAH... AROUND 3 A.M.
3/8
FROM NOW ON MAYBE YOU'LL START EARLY AND FINISH ON TIME.
SCOTT and BORGMAN
©2017 ZITS Partnership. Dist. by King Features
I THINK MOM MIGHT BE LOSING HER GRIP ON REALITY.

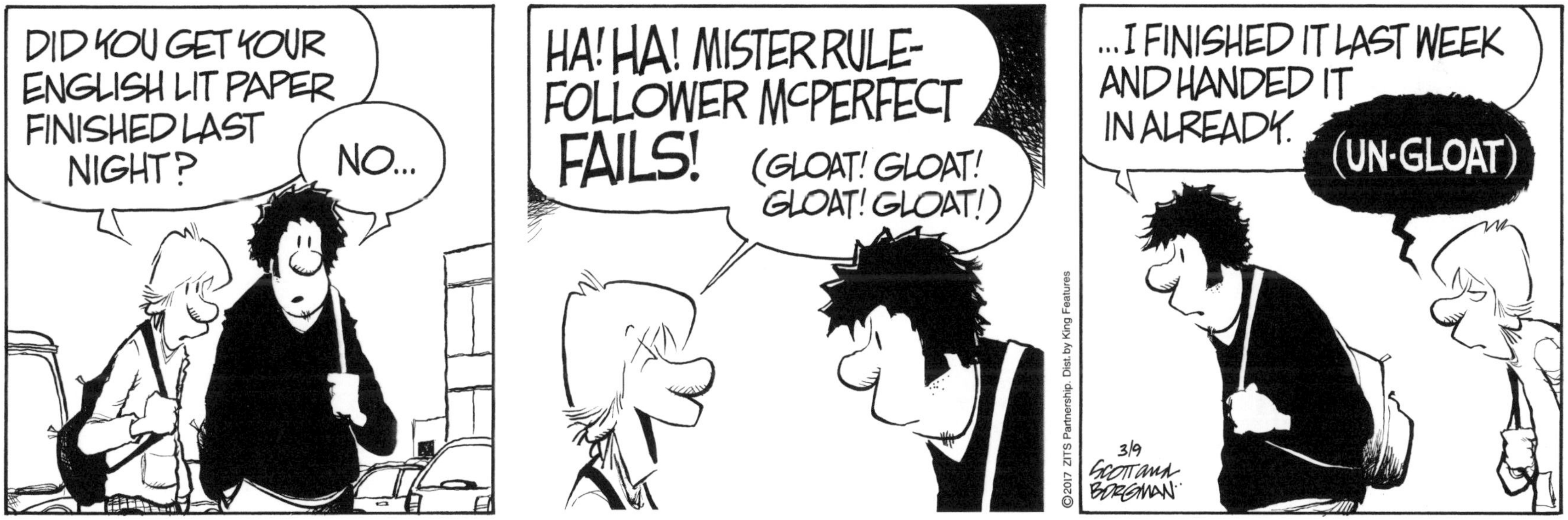
DID YOU GET YOUR ENGLISH LIT PAPER FINISHED LAST NIGHT?
NO...
HA! HA! MISTER RULE-FOLLOWER McPERFECT FAILS!
(GLOAT! GLOAT! GLOAT! GLOAT!)
©2017 ZITS Partnership. Dist. by King Features
...I FINISHED IT LAST WEEK AND HANDED IT IN ALREADY.
(UN-GLOAT)
3/9
SCOTT and BORGMAN

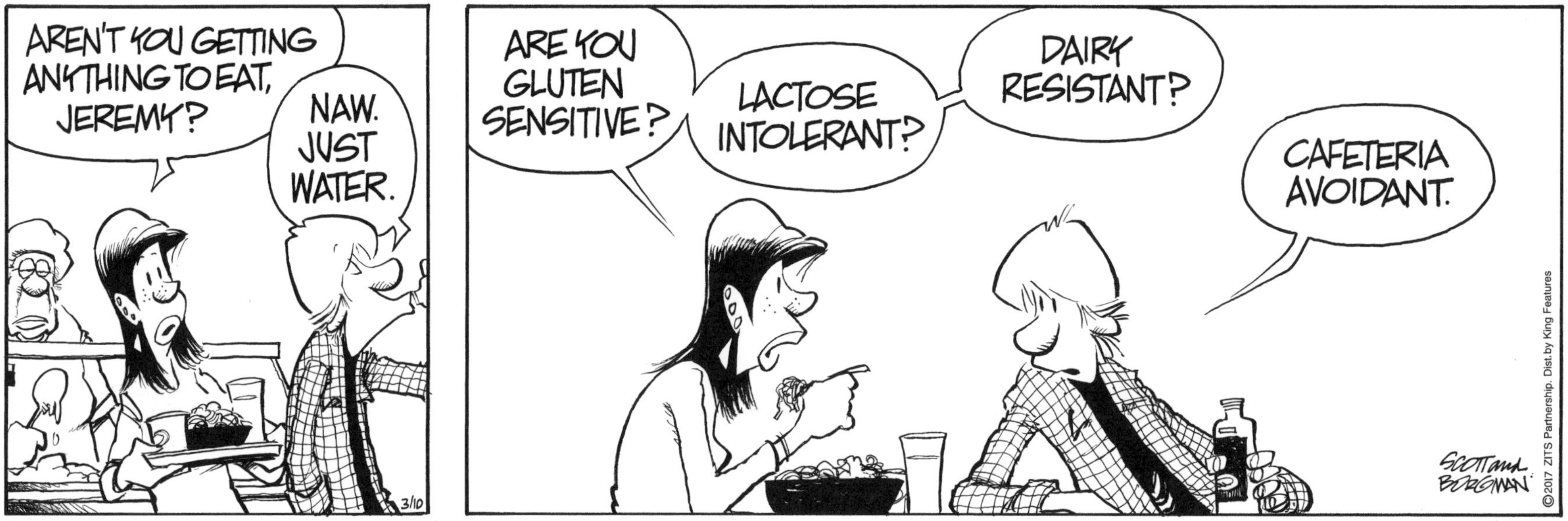
AREN'T YOU GETTING ANYTHING TO EAT, JEREMY?
NAW. JUST WATER.
3/10
ARE YOU GLUTEN SENSITIVE?
LACTOSE INTOLERANT?
DAIRY RESISTANT?
CAFETERIA AVOIDANT.
SCOTT and BORGMAN
©2017 ZITS Partnership. Dist. by King Features

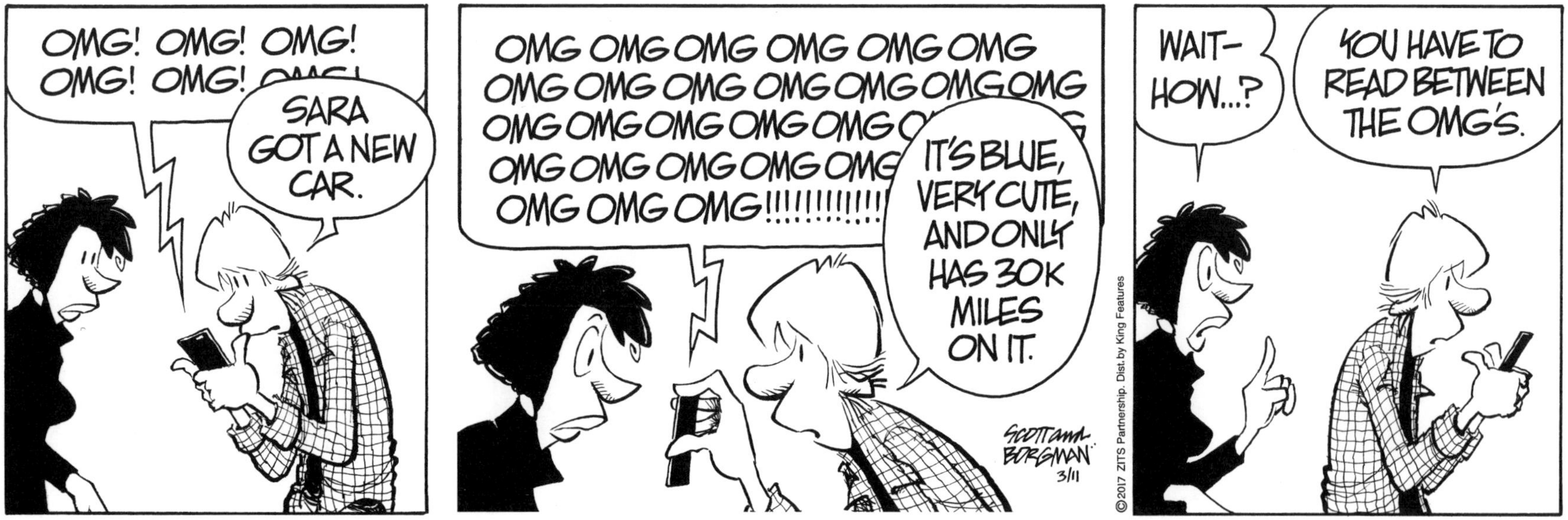
OMG! OMG! OMG! OMG! OMG!
SARA GOT A NEW CAR.
OMG OMG OMG OMG OMG OMG OMG OMG OMG OMG OMG OMG OMG OMG OMG OMG OMG OMG OMG OMG OMG OMG OMG OMG OMG OMG OMG!!!!!!!!!!!!
IT'S BLUE, VERY CUTE, AND ONLY HAS 30K MILES ON IT.
SCOTT and BORGMAN
3/11
©2017 ZITS Partnership. Dist. by King Features
WAIT- HOW...?
YOU HAVE TO READ BETWEEN THE OMG'S.

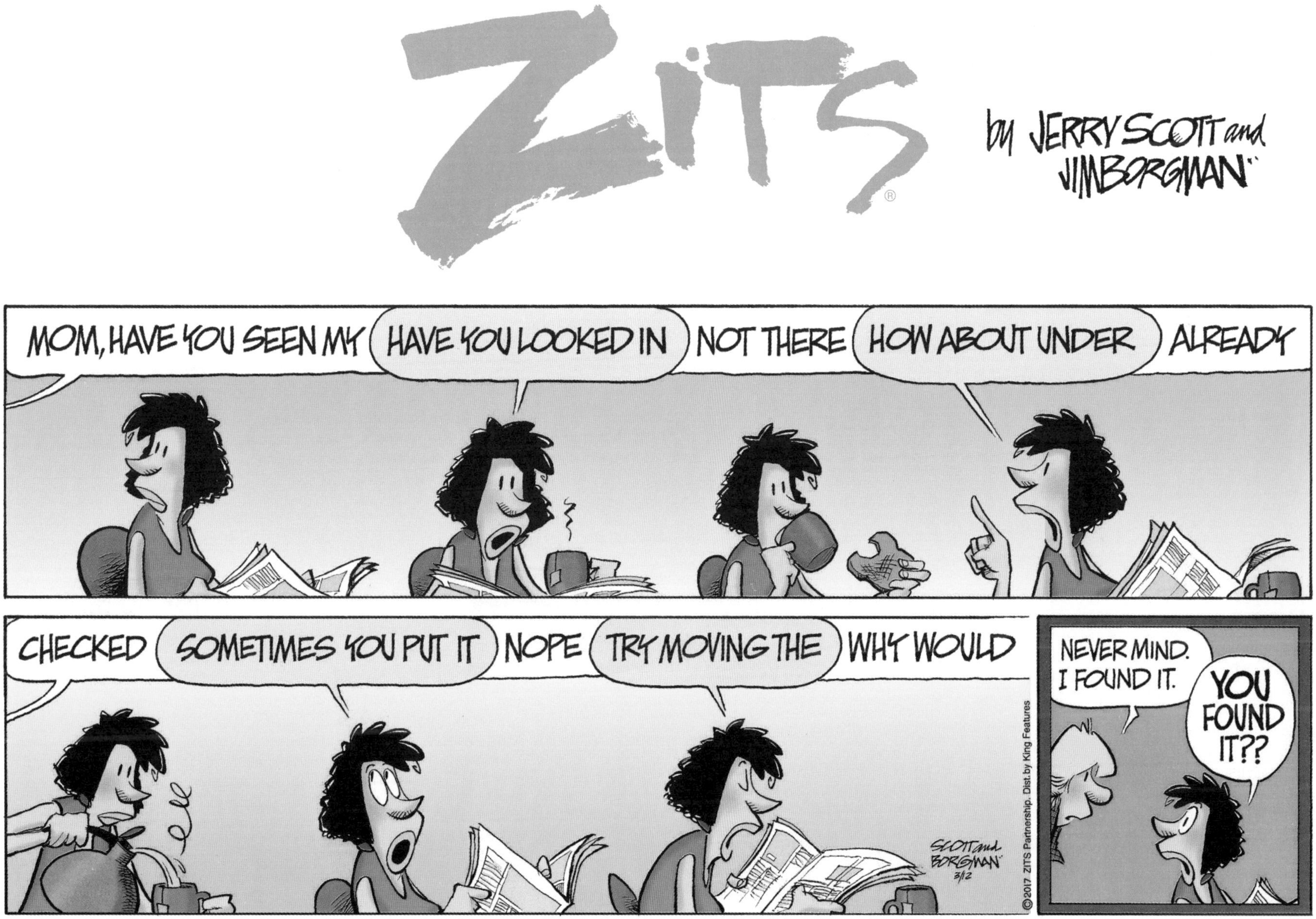
ZITS
by JERRY SCOTT and JIM BORGMAN
MOM, HAVE YOU SEEN MY
HAVE YOU LOOKED IN
NOT THERE
HOW ABOUT UNDER
ALREADY
CHECKED
SOMETIMES YOU PUT IT
NOPE
TRY MOVING THE
WHY WOULD
SCOTT and BORGMAN 3/12
© 2017 ZITS Partnership. Dist. by King Features
NEVER MIND. I FOUND IT.
YOU FOUND IT??

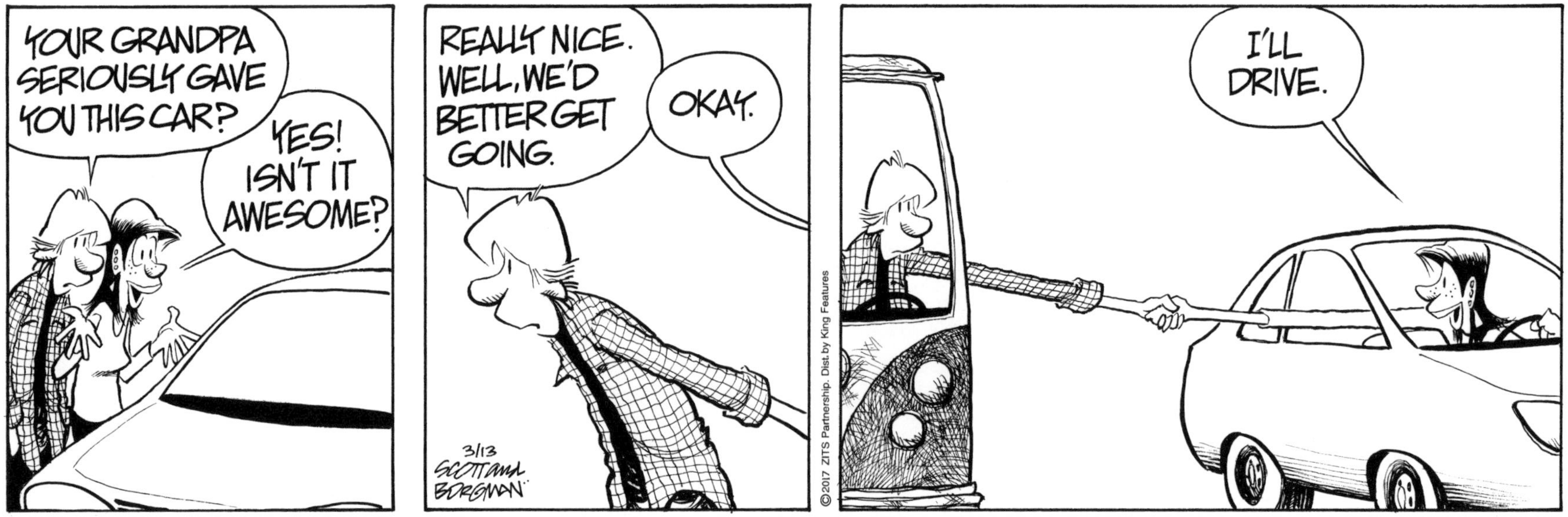
YOUR GRANDPA SERIOUSLY GAVE YOU THIS CAR?
YES! ISN'T IT AWESOME?
REALLY NICE. WELL, WE'D BETTER GET GOING.
OKAY.
3/13 SCOTT and BORGMAN
©2017 ZITS Partnership. Dist. by King Features
I'LL DRIVE.

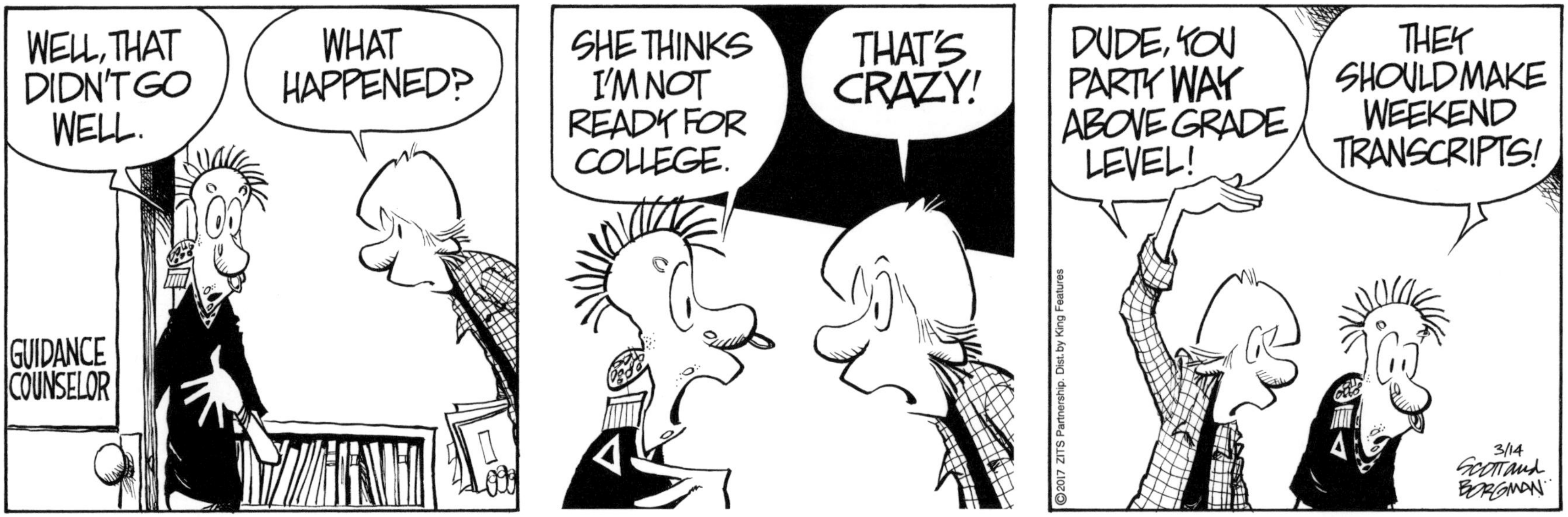
WELL, THAT DIDN'T GO WELL.
WHAT HAPPENED?
GUIDANCE COUNSELOR
SHE THINKS I'M NOT READY FOR COLLEGE.
THAT'S CRAZY!
©2017 ZITS Partnership. Dist. by King Features
DUDE, YOU PARTY WAY ABOVE GRADE LEVEL!
THEY SHOULD MAKE WEEKEND TRANSCRIPTS!
3/14 SCOTT and BORGMAN

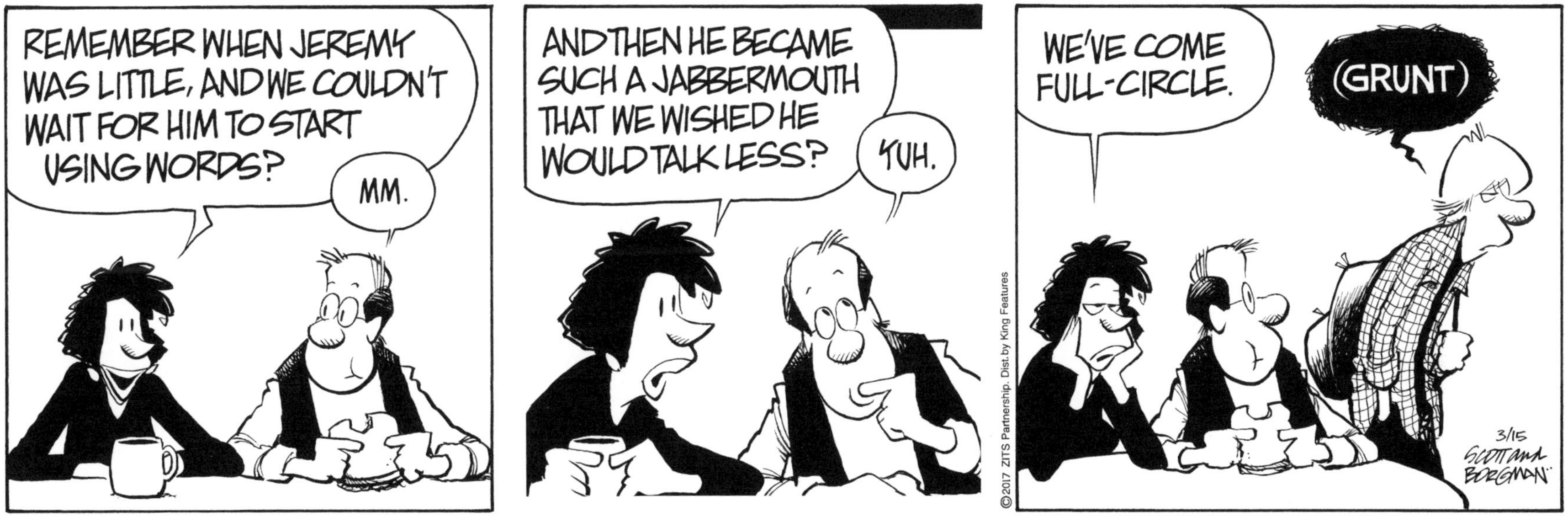
REMEMBER WHEN JEREMY WAS LITTLE, AND WE COULDN'T WAIT FOR HIM TO START USING WORDS?
MM.
AND THEN HE BECAME SUCH A JABBERMOUTH THAT WE WISHED HE WOULD TALK LESS?
YUH.
WE'VE COME FULL-CIRCLE.
(GRUNT)
3/15
SCOTT and BORGMAN
©2017 ZITS Partnership. Dist. by King Features

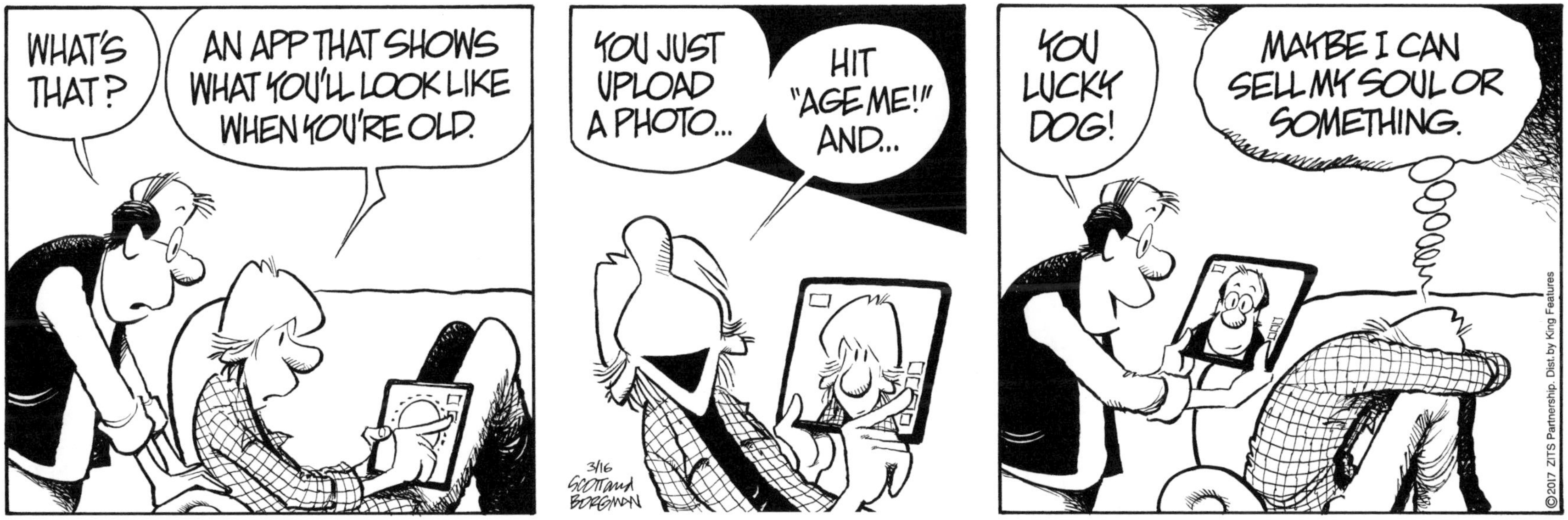
WHAT'S THAT?
AN APP THAT SHOWS WHAT YOU'LL LOOK LIKE WHEN YOU'RE OLD.
YOU JUST UPLOAD A PHOTO...
HIT "AGE ME!" AND...
3/16
SCOTT and BORGMAN
YOU LUCKY DOG!
MAYBE I CAN SELL MY SOUL OR SOMETHING.
©2017 ZITS Partnership. Dist. by King Features

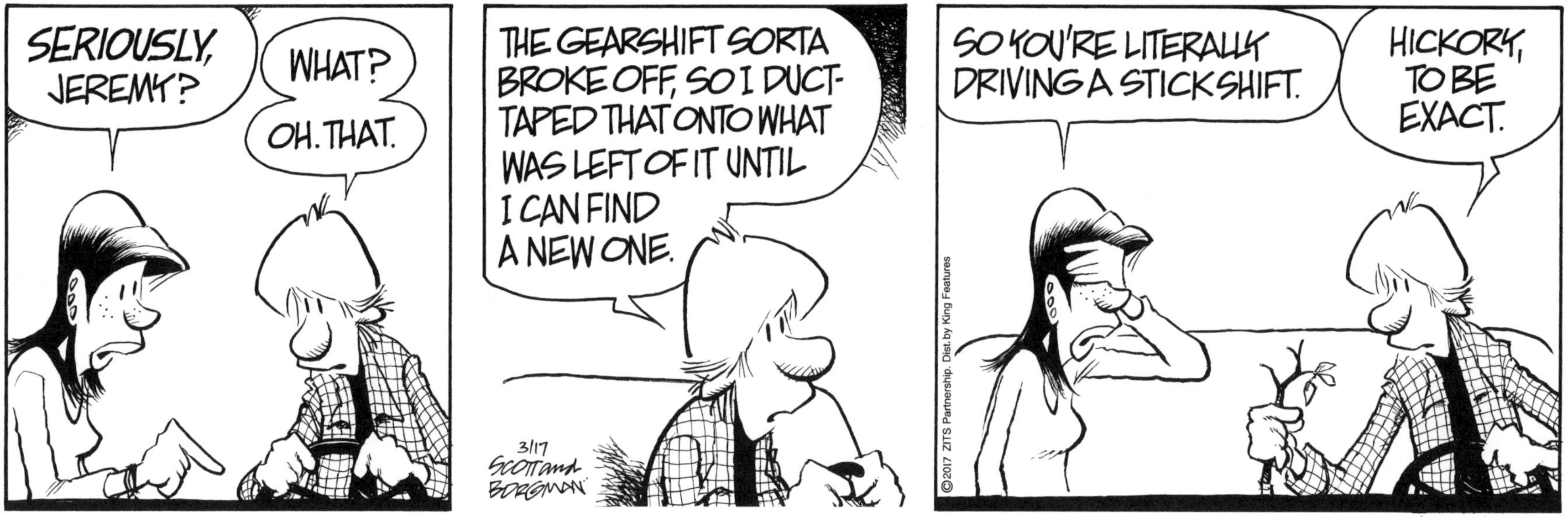
SERIOUSLY, JEREMY?
WHAT?
OH. THAT.
THE GEARSHIFT SORTA BROKE OFF, SO I DUCT-TAPED THAT ONTO WHAT WAS LEFT OF IT UNTIL I CAN FIND A NEW ONE.
3/17 SCOTT and BORGMAN
SO YOU'RE LITERALLY DRIVING A STICK SHIFT.
HICKORY, TO BE EXACT.
©2017 ZITS Partnership. Dist. by King Features

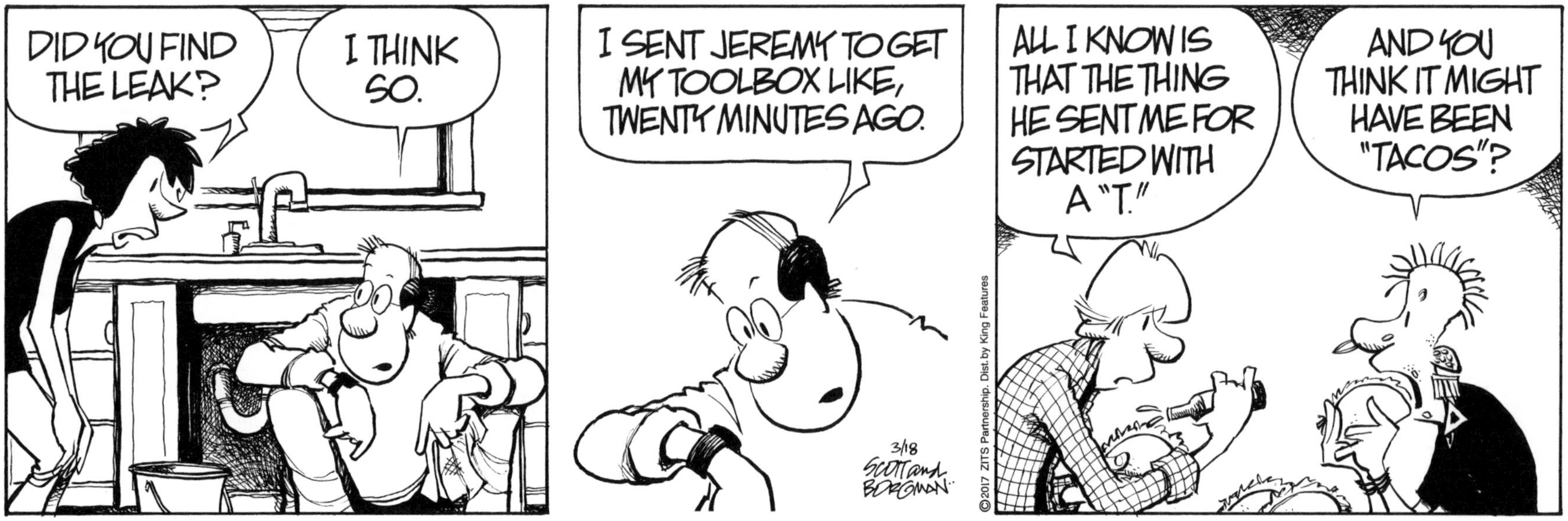
DID YOU FIND THE LEAK?
I THINK SO.
I SENT JEREMY TO GET MY TOOLBOX LIKE, TWENTY MINUTES AGO.
3/18 SCOTT and BORGMAN
ALL I KNOW IS THAT THE THING HE SENT ME FOR STARTED WITH A "T."
AND YOU THINK IT MIGHT HAVE BEEN "TACOS"?
©2017 ZITS Partnership. Dist. by King Features

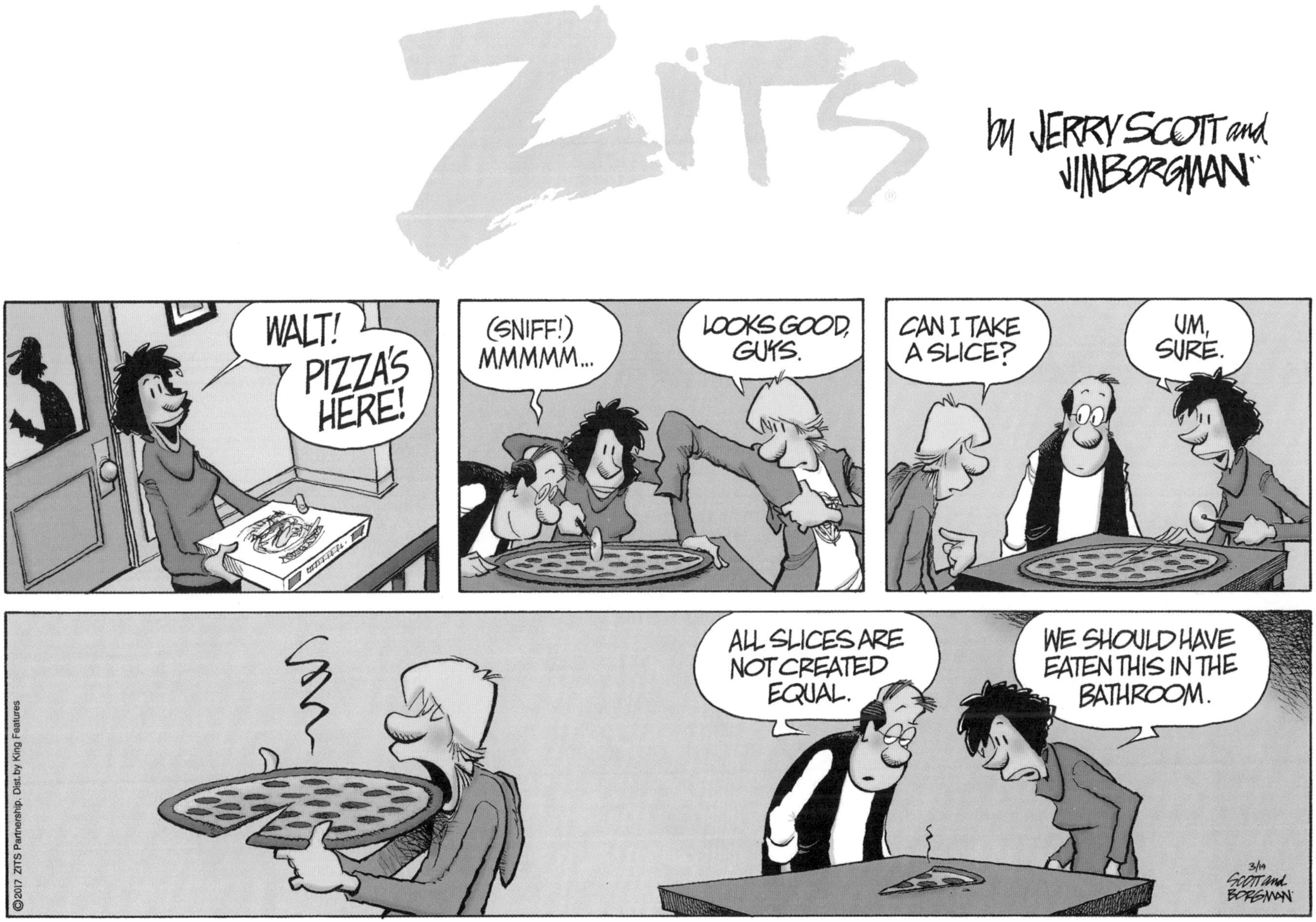
ZITS
by JERRY SCOTT and JIM BORGMAN
WALT! PIZZA'S HERE!
(SNIFF!) MMMMM...
LOOKS GOOD, GUYS.
CAN I TAKE A SLICE?
UM, SURE.
ALL SLICES ARE NOT CREATED EQUAL.
WE SHOULD HAVE EATEN THIS IN THE BATHROOM.
3/19 SCOTT and BORGMAN
©2017 ZITS Partnership. Dist. by King Features

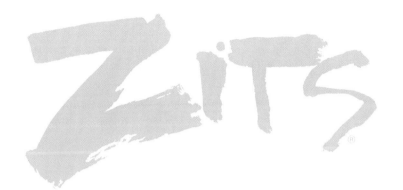

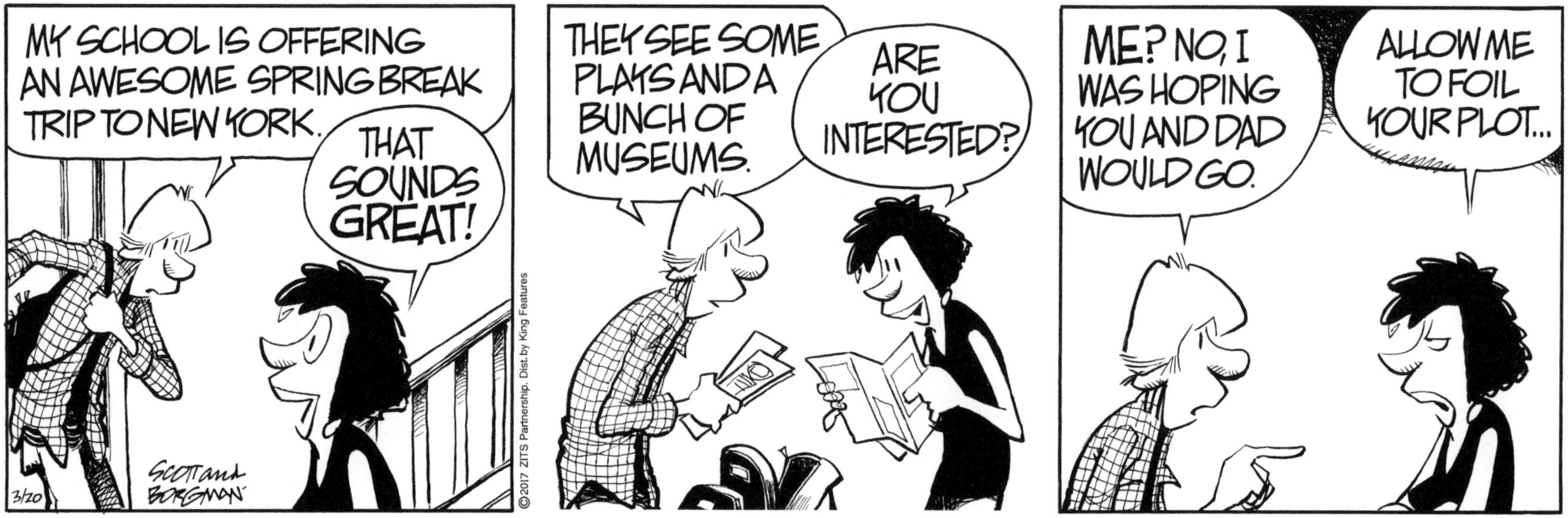
MY SCHOOL IS OFFERING AN AWESOME SPRING BREAK TRIP TO NEW YORK.
THAT SOUNDS GREAT!
THEY SEE SOME PLAYS AND A BUNCH OF MUSEUMS.
ARE YOU INTERESTED?
ME? NO, I WAS HOPING YOU AND DAD WOULD GO.
ALLOW ME TO FOIL YOUR PLOT...
SCOTT and BORGMAN
3/20
© 2017 ZITS Partnership. Dist. by King Features

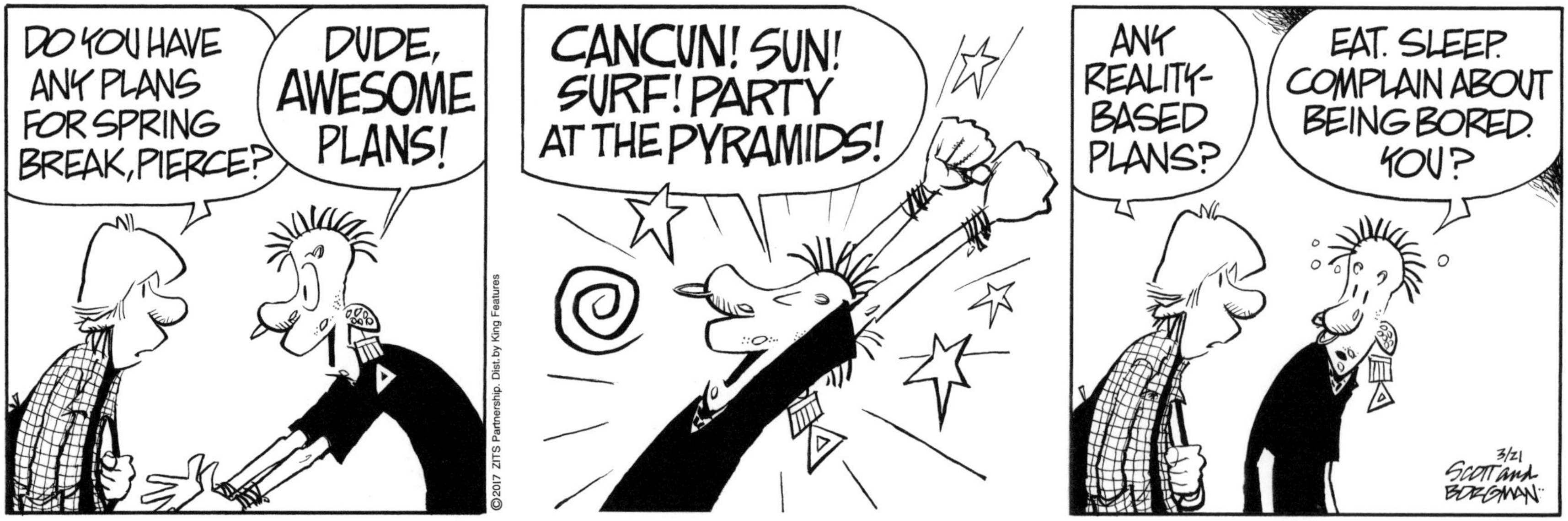
DO YOU HAVE ANY PLANS FOR SPRING BREAK, PIERCE?
DUDE, AWESOME PLANS!
CANCUN! SUN! SURF! PARTY AT THE PYRAMIDS!
ANY REALITY-BASED PLANS?
EAT. SLEEP. COMPLAIN ABOUT BEING BORED. YOU?
3/21
SCOTT and BORGMAN
© 2017 ZITS Partnership. Dist. by King Features

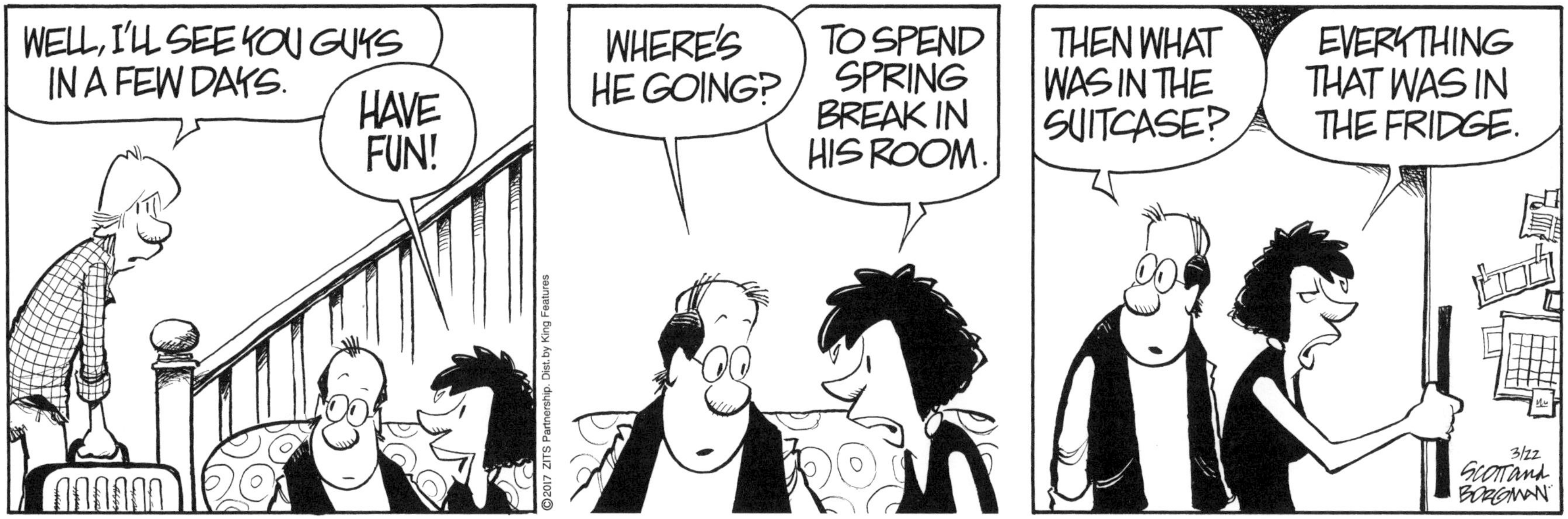
WELL, I'LL SEE YOU GUYS IN A FEW DAYS.
HAVE FUN!
©2017 ZITS Partnership. Dist. by King Features
WHERE'S HE GOING?
TO SPEND SPRING BREAK IN HIS ROOM.
THEN WHAT WAS IN THE SUITCASE?
EVERYTHING THAT WAS IN THE FRIDGE.
3/22
SCOTT and BORGMAN

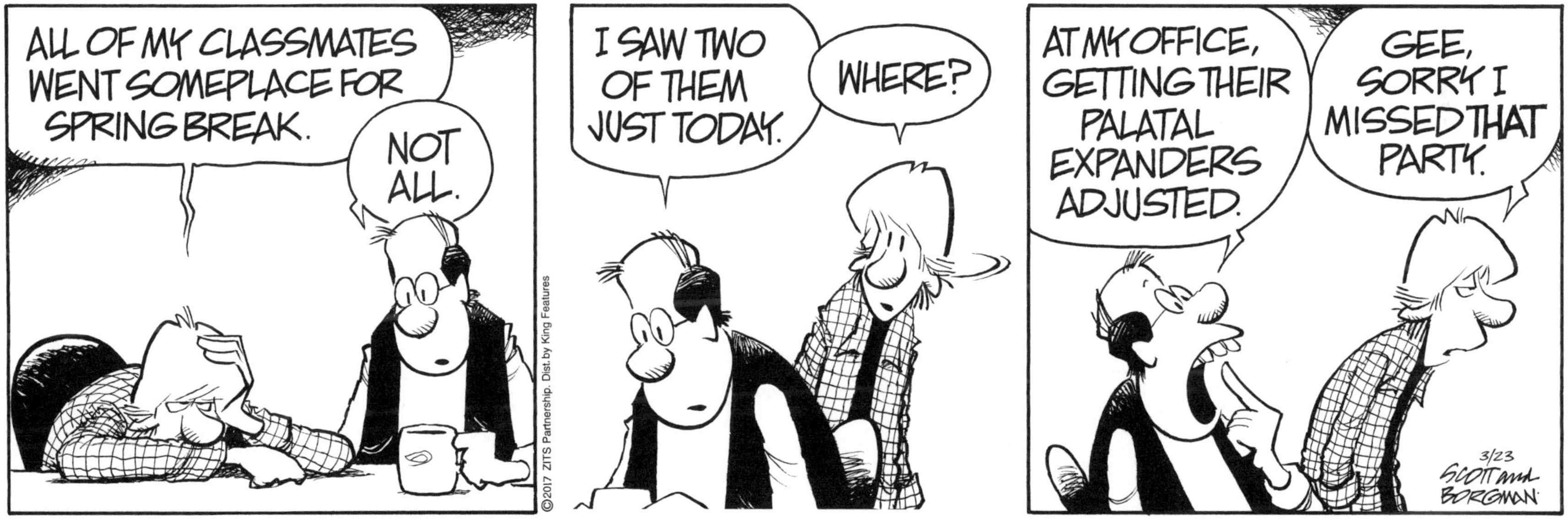
ALL OF MY CLASSMATES WENT SOMEPLACE FOR SPRING BREAK.
NOT ALL.
©2017 ZITS Partnership. Dist. by King Features
I SAW TWO OF THEM JUST TODAY.
WHERE?
AT MY OFFICE, GETTING THEIR PALATAL EXPANDERS ADJUSTED.
GEE, SORRY I MISSED THAT PARTY.
3/23
SCOTT and BORGMAN

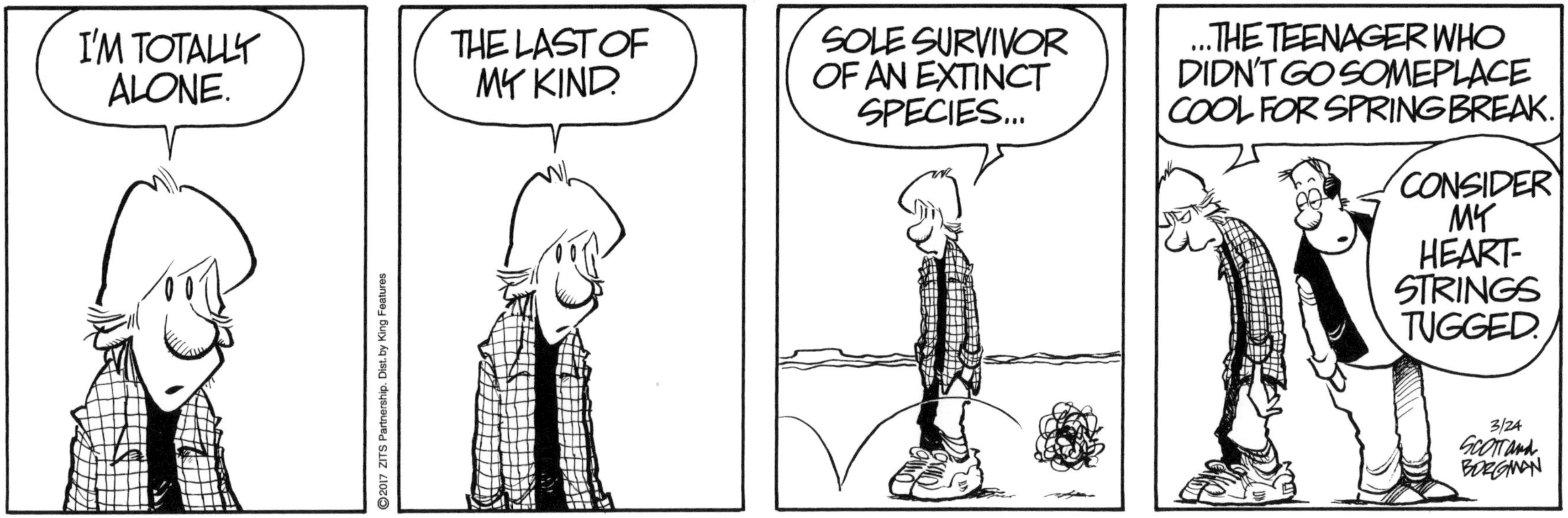

I'M TOTALLY ALONE.
THE LAST OF MY KIND.
SOLE SURVIVOR OF AN EXTINCT SPECIES...
...THE TEENAGER WHO DIDN'T GO SOMEPLACE COOL FOR SPRING BREAK.
CONSIDER MY HEART-STRINGS TUGGED.
©2017 ZITS Partnership. Dist. by King Features
3/24 SCOTT and BORGMAN

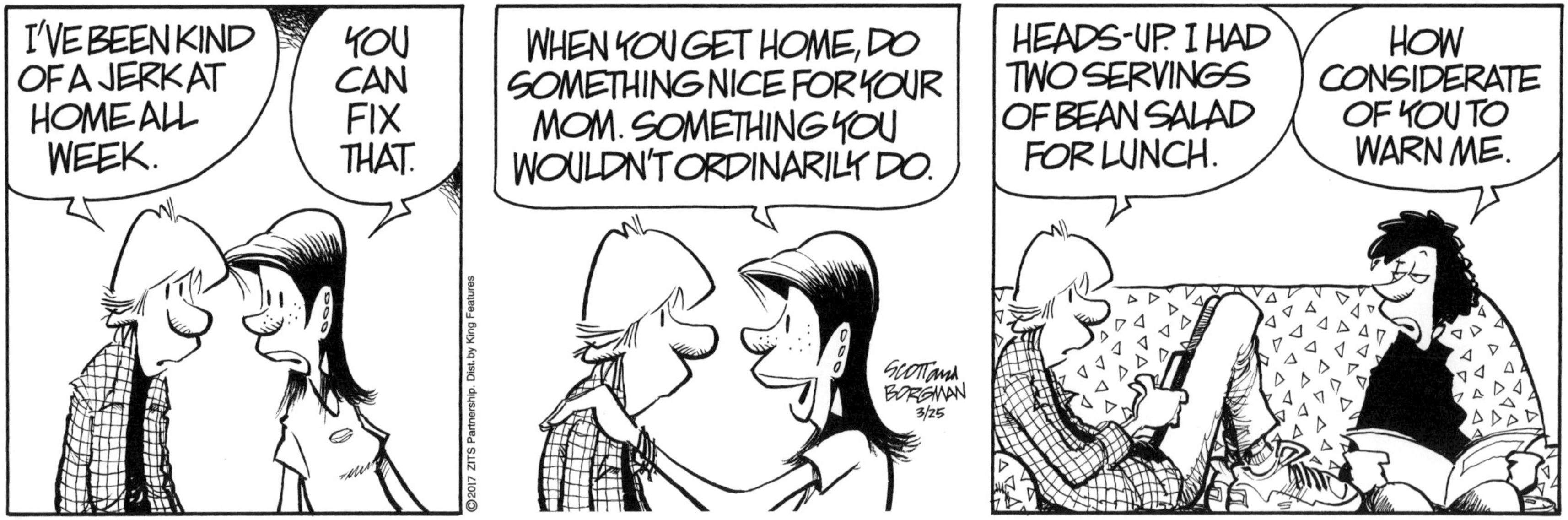

I'VE BEEN KIND OF A JERK AT HOME ALL WEEK.
YOU CAN FIX THAT.
WHEN YOU GET HOME, DO SOMETHING NICE FOR YOUR MOM. SOMETHING YOU WOULDN'T ORDINARILY DO.
HEADS-UP. I HAD TWO SERVINGS OF BEAN SALAD FOR LUNCH.
HOW CONSIDERATE OF YOU TO WARN ME.
©2017 ZITS Partnership. Dist. by King Features
SCOTT and BORGMAN 3/25

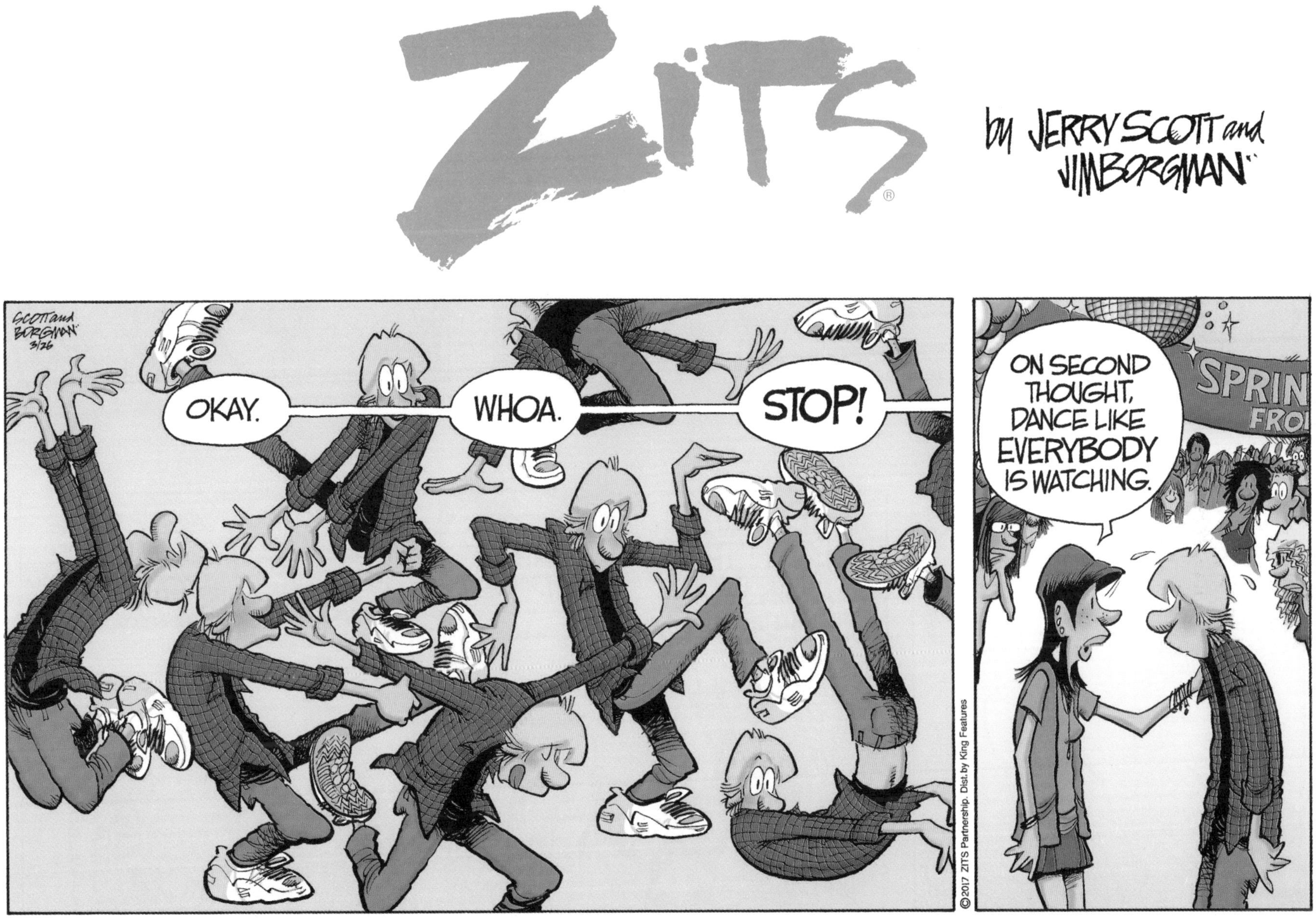
ZITS
by JERRY SCOTT and JIM BORGMAN
SCOTT and BORGMAN 3/26
OKAY.
WHOA.
STOP!
ON SECOND THOUGHT, DANCE LIKE EVERYBODY IS WATCHING.
©2017 ZITS Partnership. Dist. by King Features

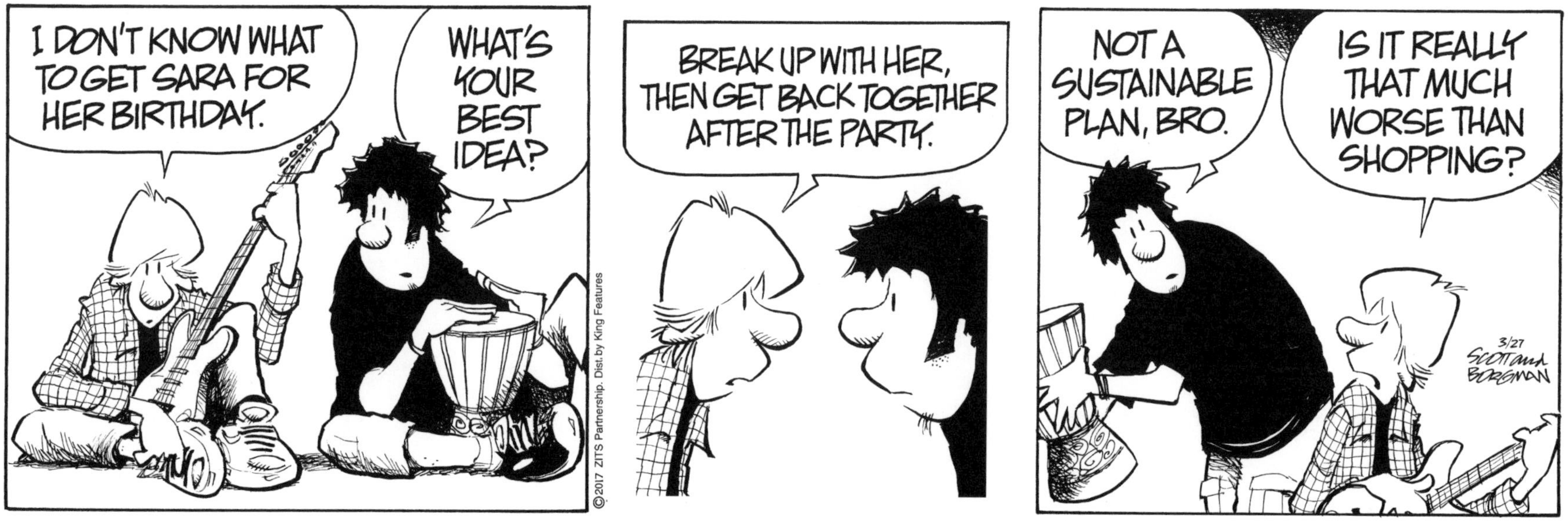
I DON'T KNOW WHAT TO GET SARA FOR HER BIRTHDAY.
WHAT'S YOUR BEST IDEA?
BREAK UP WITH HER, THEN GET BACK TOGETHER AFTER THE PARTY.
NOT A SUSTAINABLE PLAN, BRO.
IS IT REALLY THAT MUCH WORSE THAN SHOPPING?
3/27
SCOTT and BORGMAN

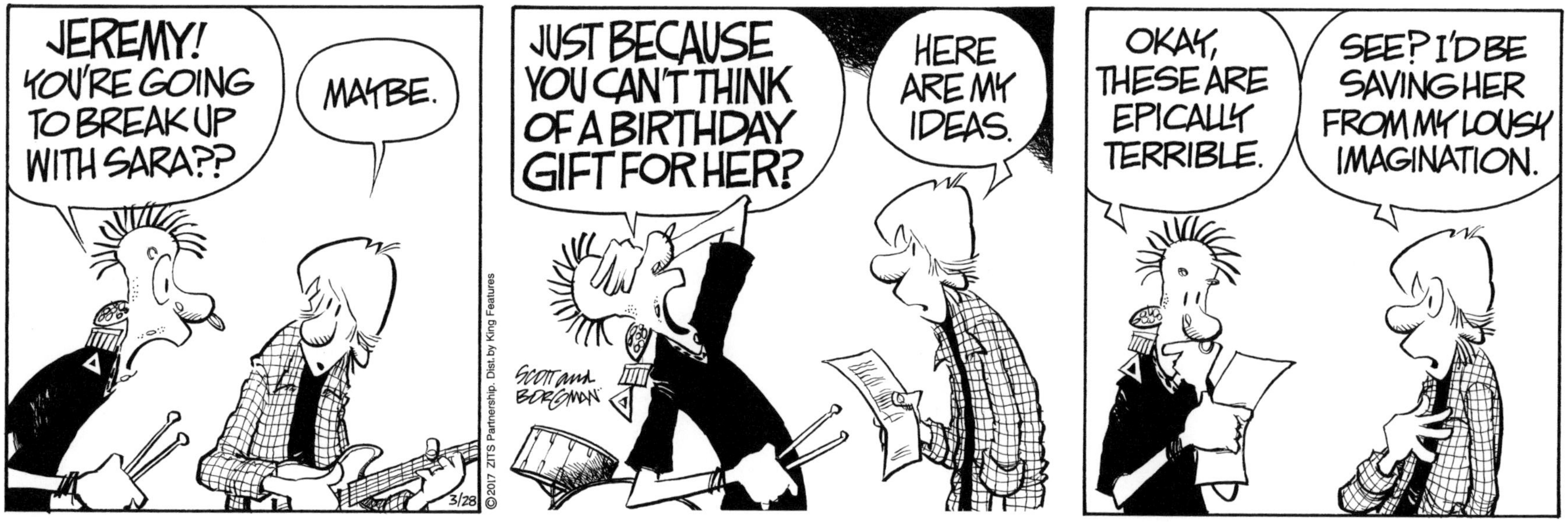
JEREMY! YOU'RE GOING TO BREAK UP WITH SARA??
MAYBE.
3/28
SCOTT and BORGMAN
JUST BECAUSE YOU CAN'T THINK OF A BIRTHDAY GIFT FOR HER?
HERE ARE MY IDEAS.
OKAY, THESE ARE EPICALLY TERRIBLE.
SEE? I'D BE SAVING HER FROM MY LOUSY IMAGINATION.

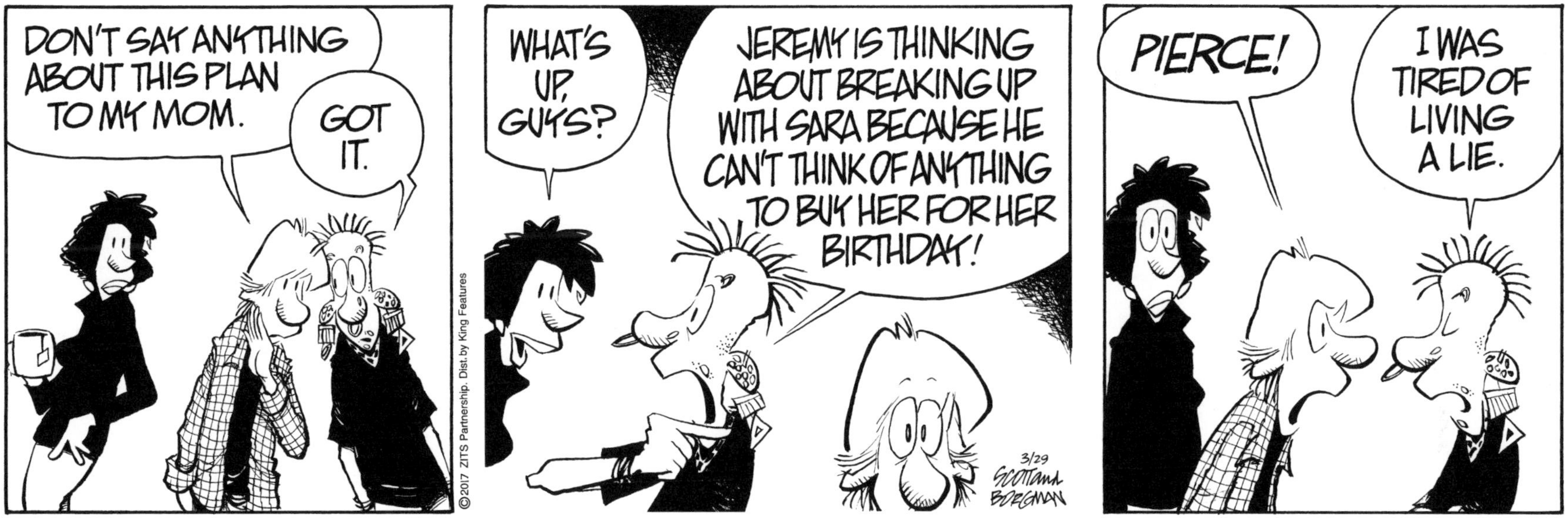
DON'T SAY ANYTHING ABOUT THIS PLAN TO MY MOM.
GOT IT.
© 2017 ZITS Partnership. Dist. by King Features
WHAT'S UP, GUYS?
JEREMY IS THINKING ABOUT BREAKING UP WITH SARA BECAUSE HE CAN'T THINK OF ANYTHING TO BUY HER FOR HER BIRTHDAY!
3/29 SCOTTMAN BORGMAN
PIERCE!
I WAS TIRED OF LIVING A LIE.

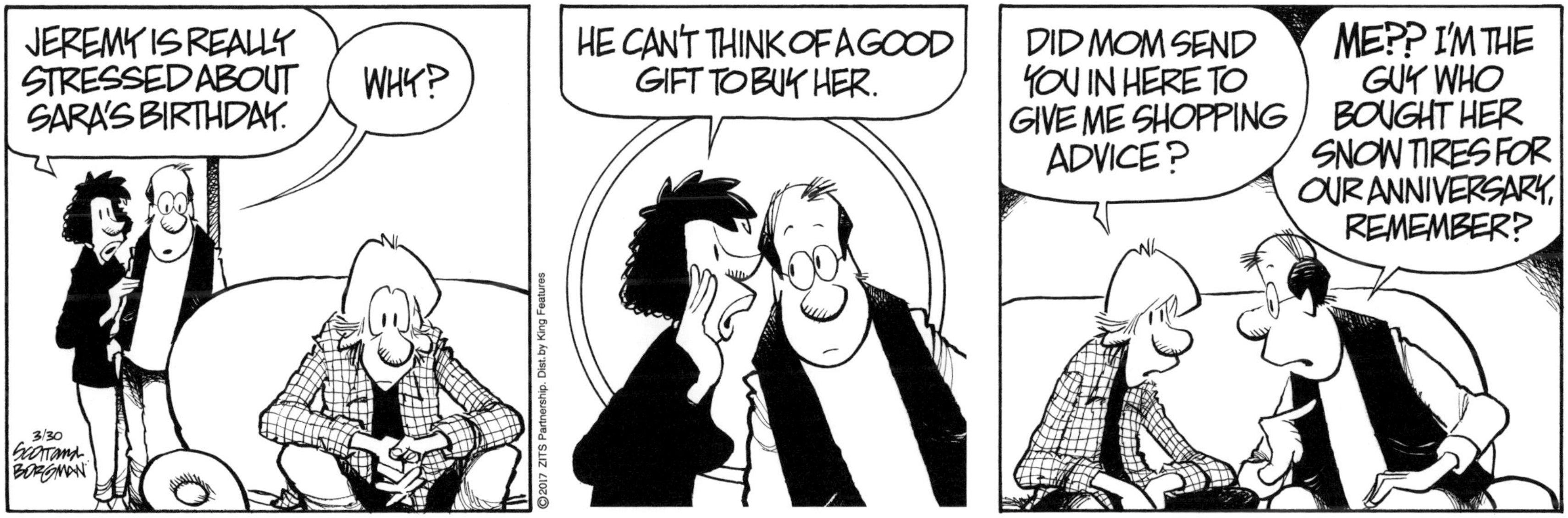
JEREMY IS REALLY STRESSED ABOUT SARA'S BIRTHDAY.
WHY?
3/30 SCOTTMAN BORGMAN
© 2017 ZITS Partnership. Dist. by King Features
HE CAN'T THINK OF A GOOD GIFT TO BUY HER.
DID MOM SEND YOU IN HERE TO GIVE ME SHOPPING ADVICE?
ME?? I'M THE GUY WHO BOUGHT HER SNOW TIRES FOR OUR ANNIVERSARY, REMEMBER?

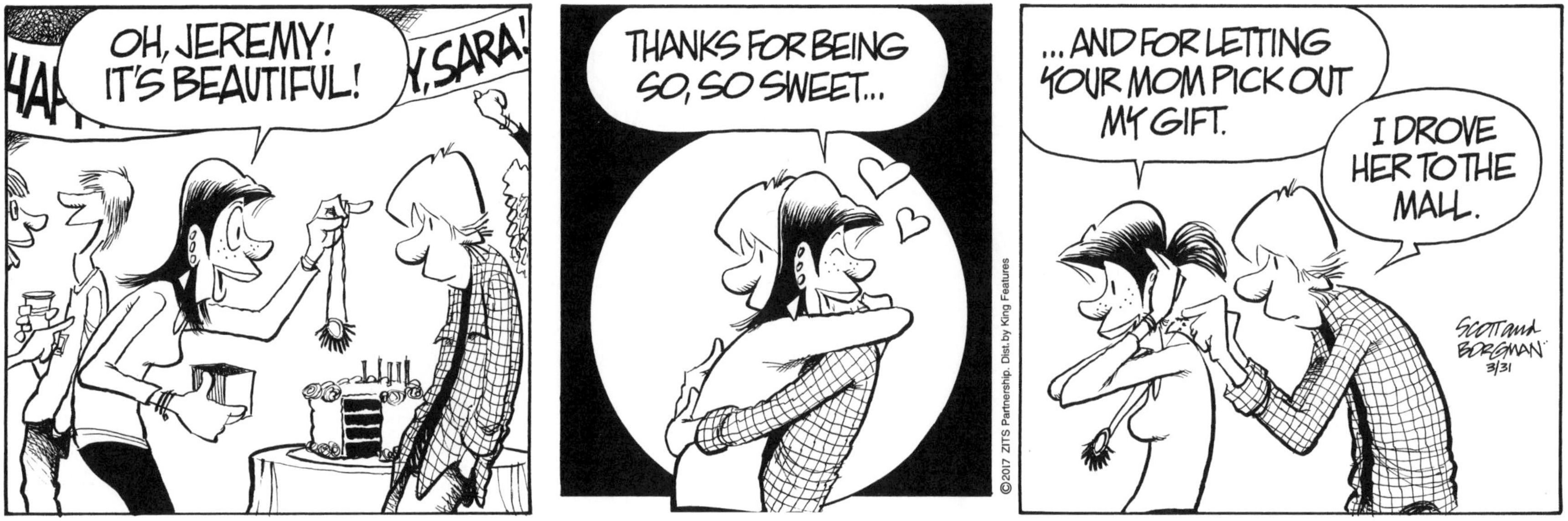
Y, SARA!
OH, JEREMY! IT'S BEAUTIFUL!
THANKS FOR BEING SO, SO SWEET...
...AND FOR LETTING YOUR MOM PICK OUT MY GIFT.
I DROVE HER TO THE MALL.
SCOTT and BORGMAN 3/31
©2017 ZITS Partnership. Dist. by King Features

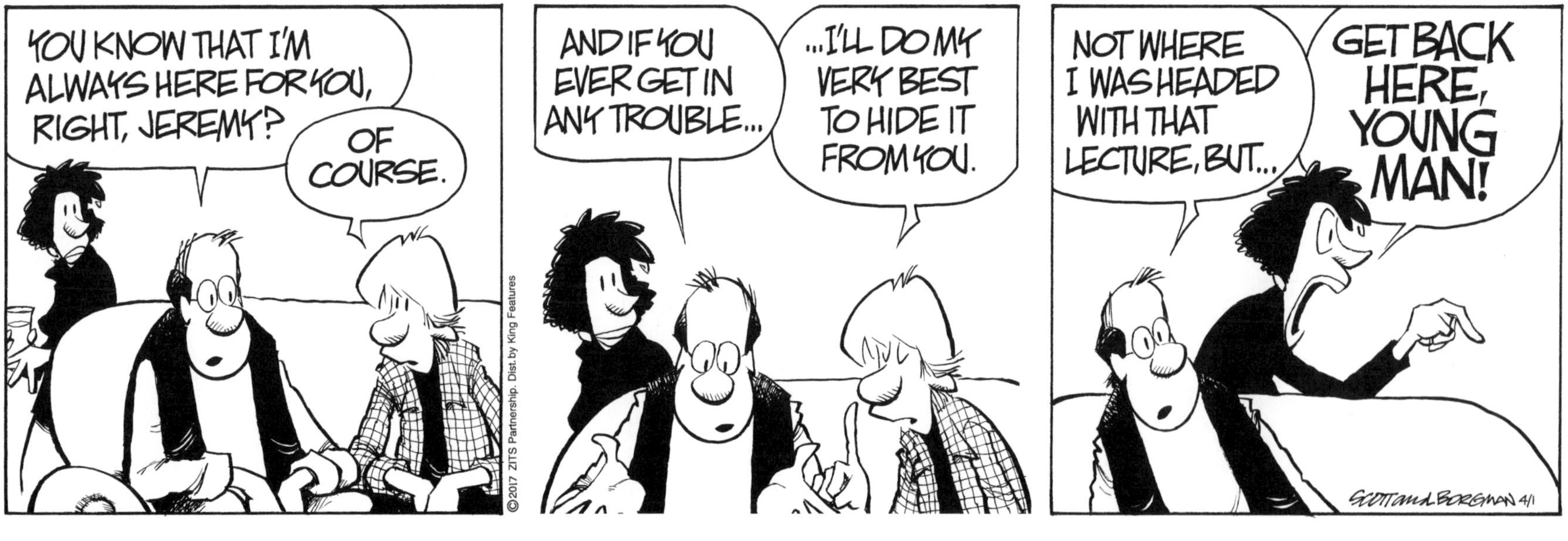
YOU KNOW THAT I'M ALWAYS HERE FOR YOU, RIGHT, JEREMY?
OF COURSE.
AND IF YOU EVER GET IN ANY TROUBLE...
...I'LL DO MY VERY BEST TO HIDE IT FROM YOU.
NOT WHERE I WAS HEADED WITH THAT LECTURE, BUT...
GET BACK HERE, YOUNG MAN!
SCOTT and BORGMAN 4/1
©2017 ZITS Partnership. Dist. by King Features

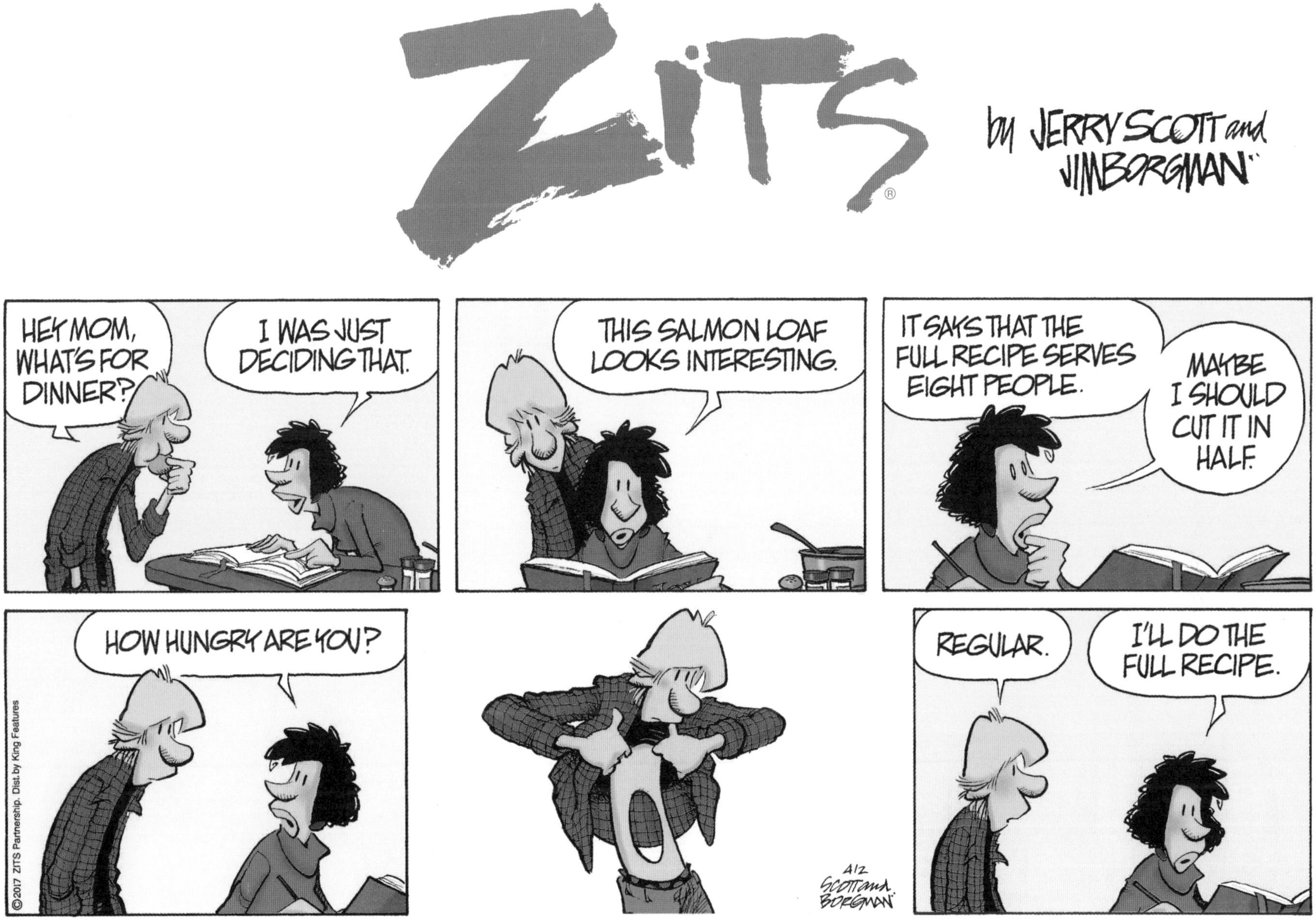
ZITS
by JERRY SCOTT and JIM BORGMAN
HEY MOM, WHAT'S FOR DINNER?
I WAS JUST DECIDING THAT.
THIS SALMON LOAF LOOKS INTERESTING.
IT SAYS THAT THE FULL RECIPE SERVES EIGHT PEOPLE.
MAYBE I SHOULD CUT IT IN HALF.
HOW HUNGRY ARE YOU?
REGULAR.
I'LL DO THE FULL RECIPE.
©2017 ZITS Partnership. Dist. by King Features
4/2
SCOTT and BORGMAN

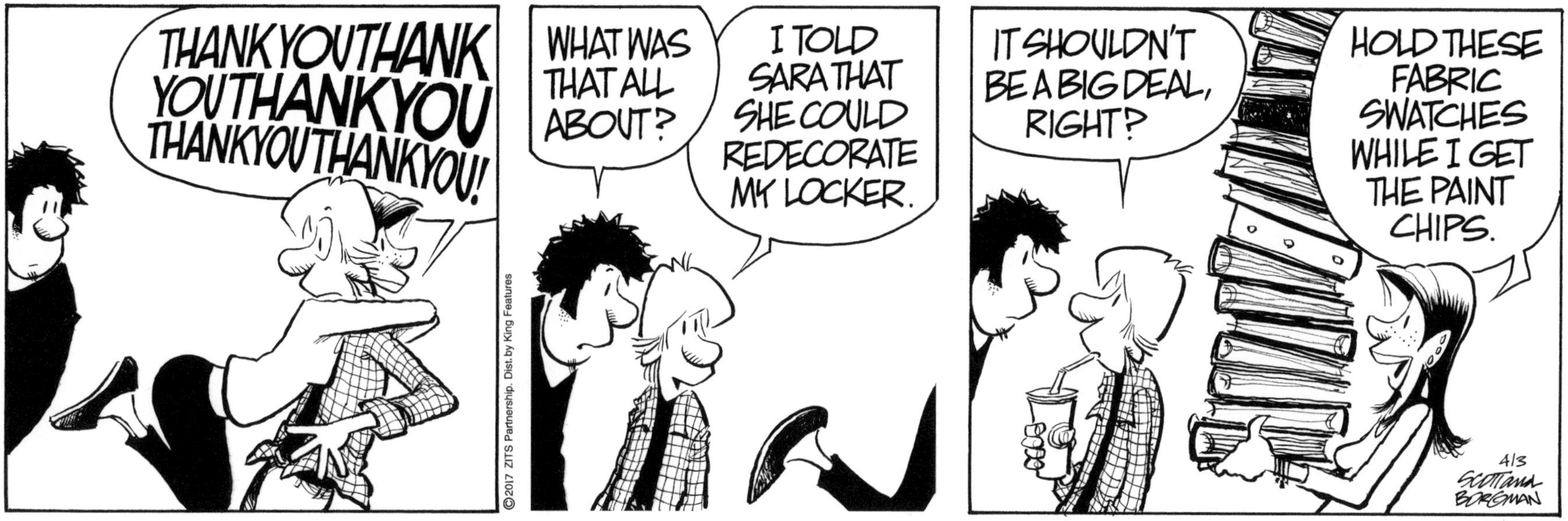
THANKYOUTHANK YOUTHANKYOU THANKYOUTHANKYOU!
WHAT WAS THAT ALL ABOUT?
I TOLD SARA THAT SHE COULD REDECORATE MY LOCKER.
IT SHOULDN'T BE A BIG DEAL, RIGHT?
HOLD THESE FABRIC SWATCHES WHILE I GET THE PAINT CHIPS.
©2017 ZITS Partnership. Dist. by King Features
4/3
SCOTT and BORGMAN

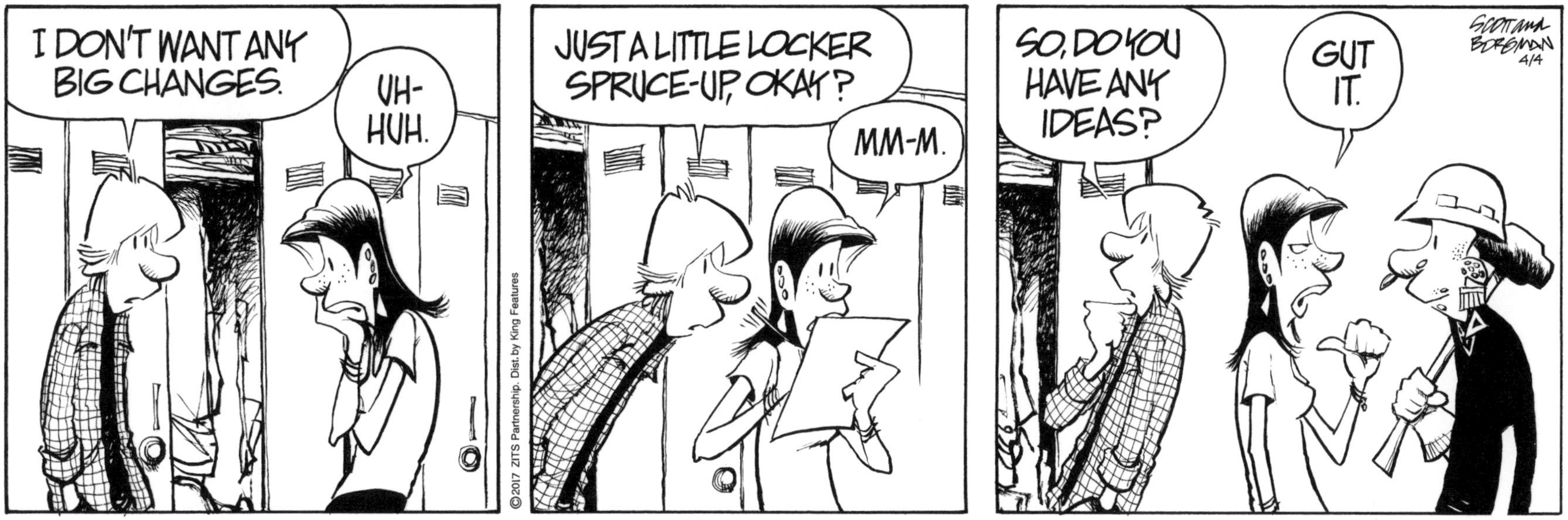
I DON'T WANT ANY BIG CHANGES.
UH-HUH.
JUST A LITTLE LOCKER SPRUCE-UP, OKAY?
MM-M.
SO, DO YOU HAVE ANY IDEAS?
GUT IT.
©2017 ZITS Partnership. Dist. by King Features
SCOTT and BORGMAN 4/4

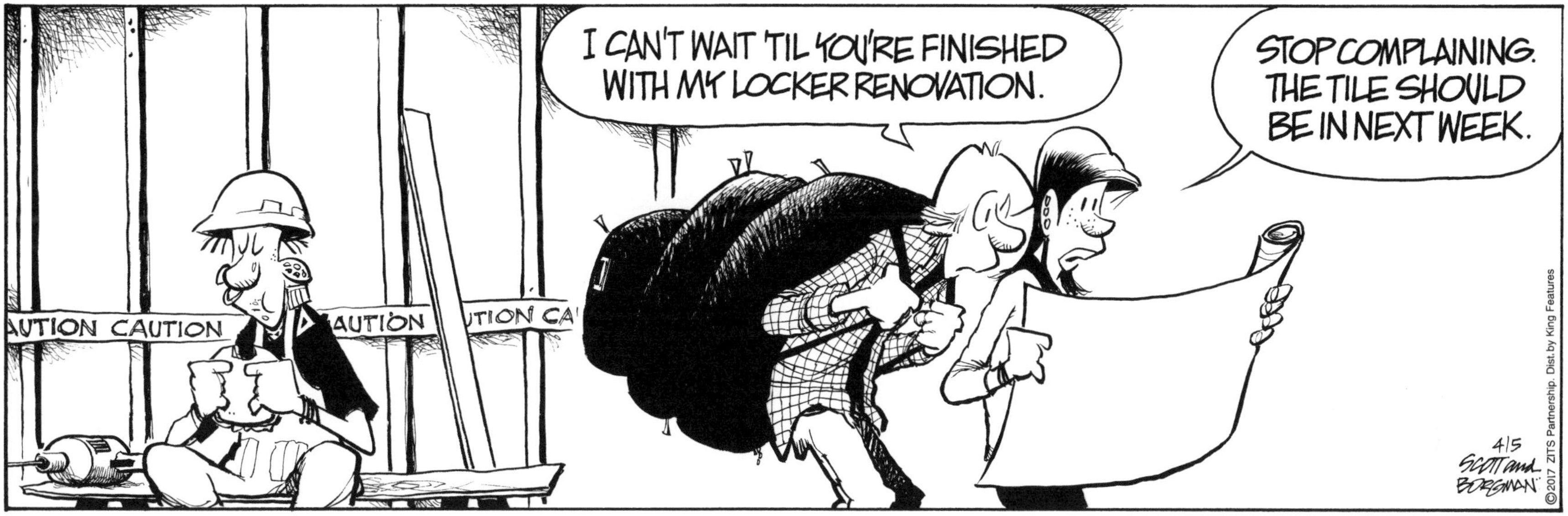
AUTION CAUTION
AUTION
UTION CA
I CAN'T WAIT 'TIL YOU'RE FINISHED WITH MY LOCKER RENOVATION.
STOP COMPLAINING. THE TILE SHOULD BE IN NEXT WEEK.
4/5
SCOTT and BORGMAN
©2017 ZITS Partnership. Dist. by King Features

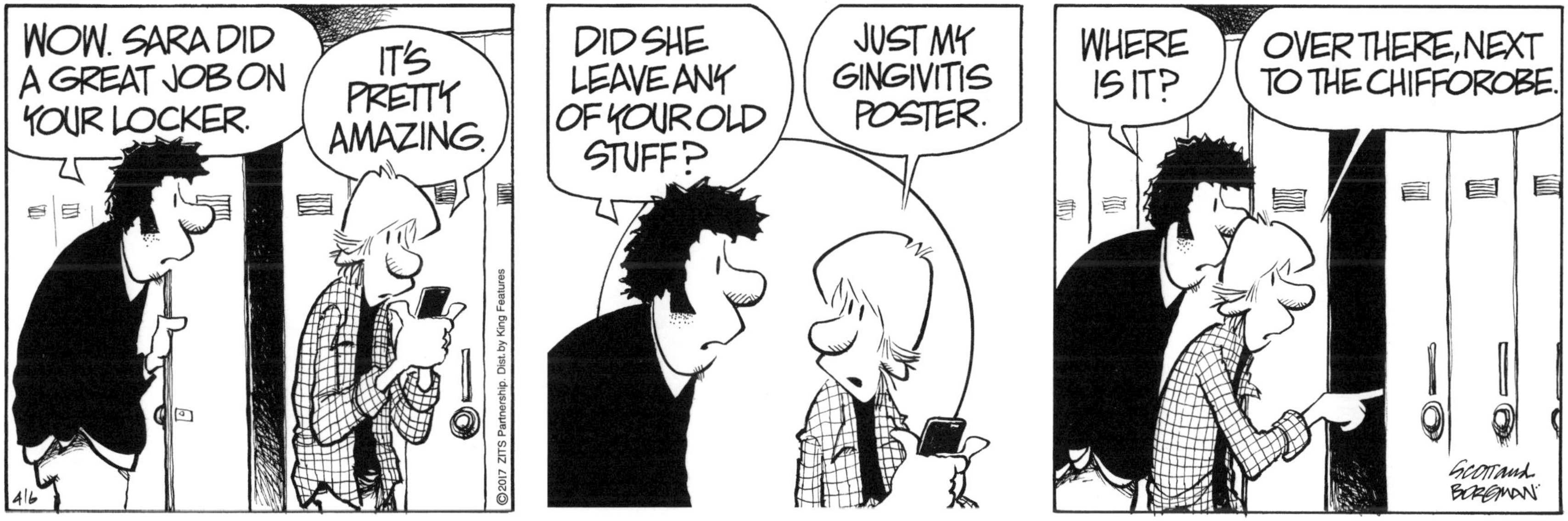
WOW. SARA DID A GREAT JOB ON YOUR LOCKER.
IT'S PRETTY AMAZING.
4/6
©2017 ZITS Partnership. Dist. by King Features
DID SHE LEAVE ANY OF YOUR OLD STUFF?
JUST MY GINGIVITIS POSTER.
WHERE IS IT?
OVER THERE, NEXT TO THE CHIFFOROBE.
SCOTT and BORGMAN

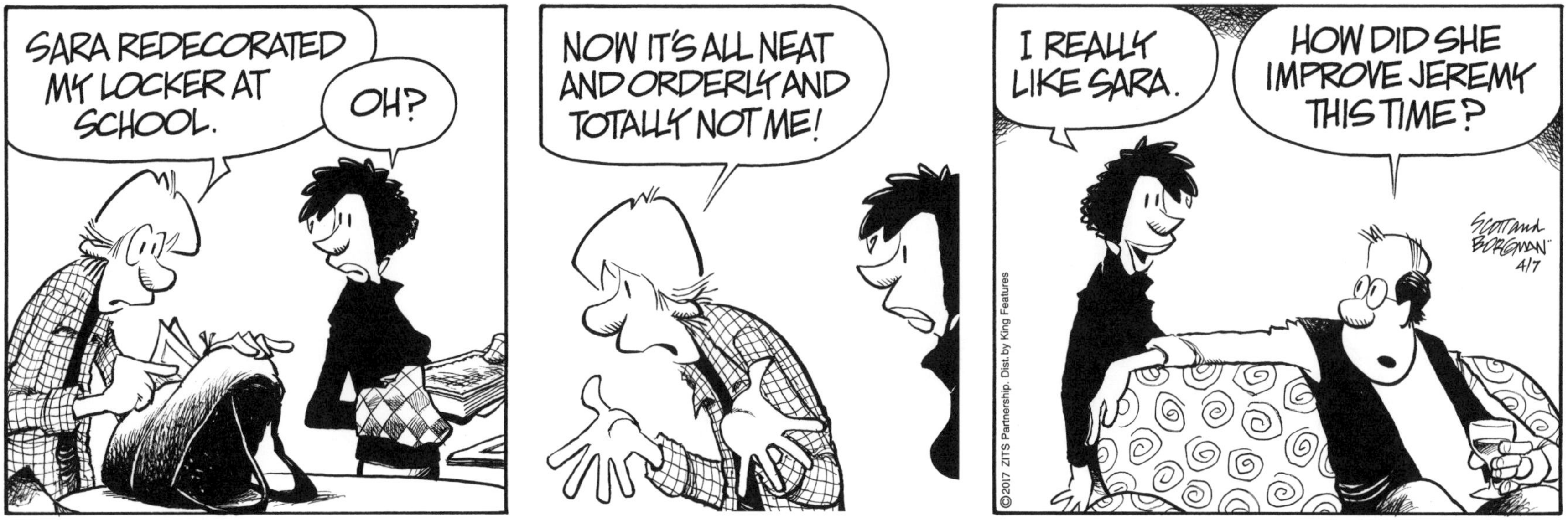
SARA REDECORATED MY LOCKER AT SCHOOL.
OH?
NOW IT'S ALL NEAT AND ORDERLY AND TOTALLY NOT ME!
I REALLY LIKE SARA.
HOW DID SHE IMPROVE JEREMY THIS TIME?
©2017 ZITS Partnership. Dist. by King Features

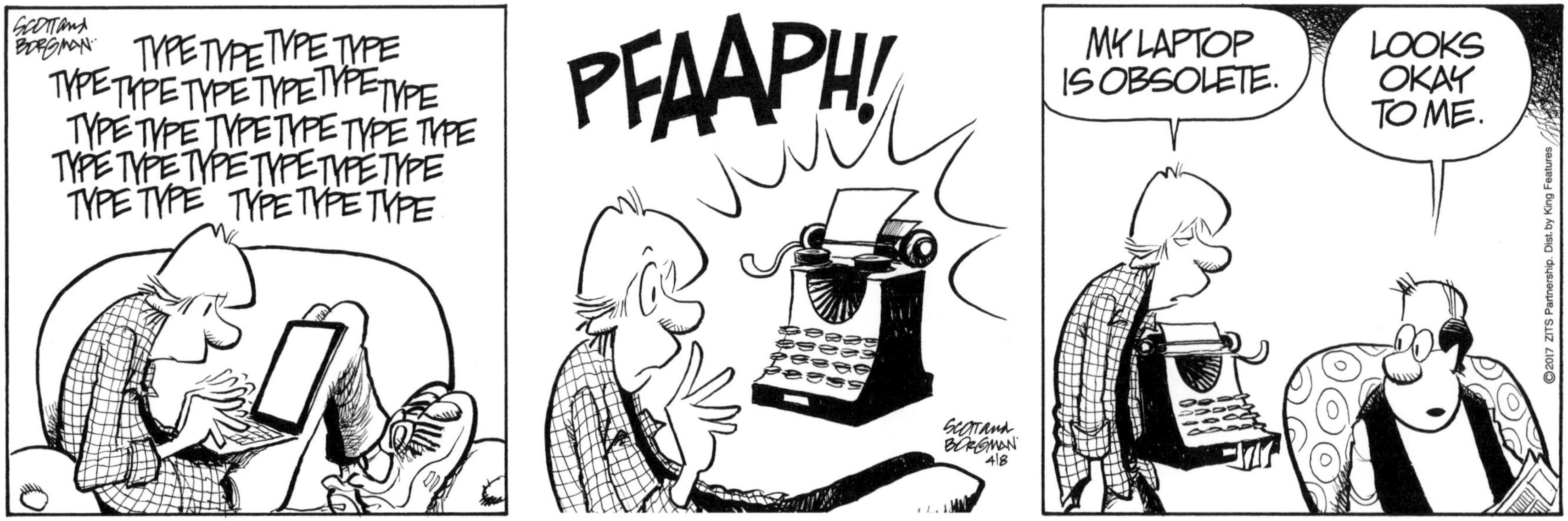
TYPE TYPE TYPE TYPE TYPE TYPE TYPE TYPE TYPE TYPE TYPE TYPE TYPE TYPE TYPE TYPE TYPE TYPE TYPE TYPE TYPE TYPE TYPE TYPE TYPE TYPE TYPE TYPE TYPE
PFAAPH!
MY LAPTOP IS OBSOLETE.
LOOKS OKAY TO ME.
©2017 ZITS Partnership. Dist. by King Features

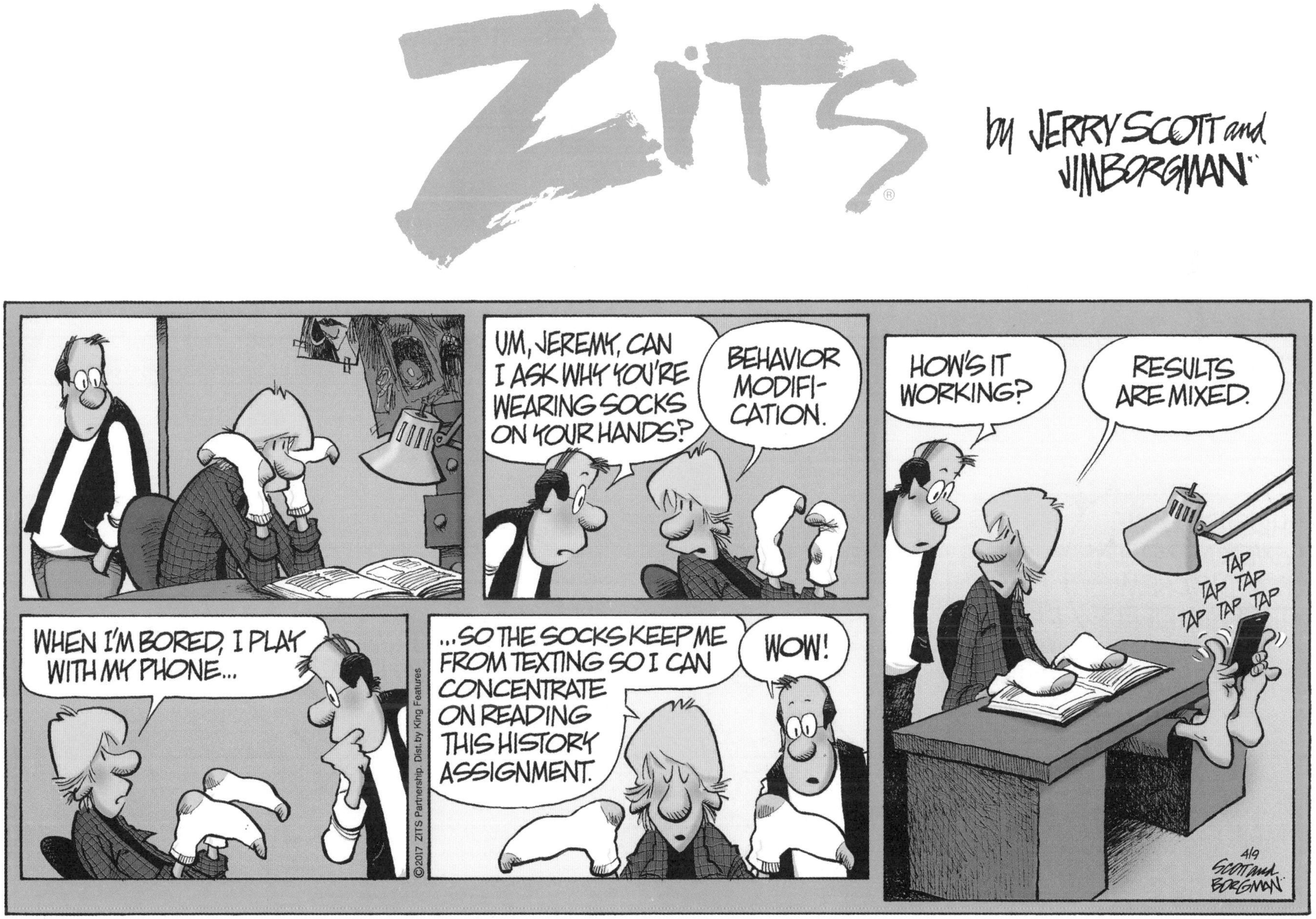
ZITS®
by JERRY SCOTT and JIM BORGMAN
UM, JEREMY, CAN I ASK WHY YOU'RE WEARING SOCKS ON YOUR HANDS?
BEHAVIOR MODIFI-CATION.
HOW'S IT WORKING?
RESULTS ARE MIXED.
WHEN I'M BORED, I PLAY WITH MY PHONE...
...SO THE SOCKS KEEP ME FROM TEXTING SO I CAN CONCENTRATE ON READING THIS HISTORY ASSIGNMENT.
WOW!
TAP TAP TAP TAP TAP TAP
©2017 ZITS Partnership. Dist. by King Features
4/9 SCOTT and BORGMAN

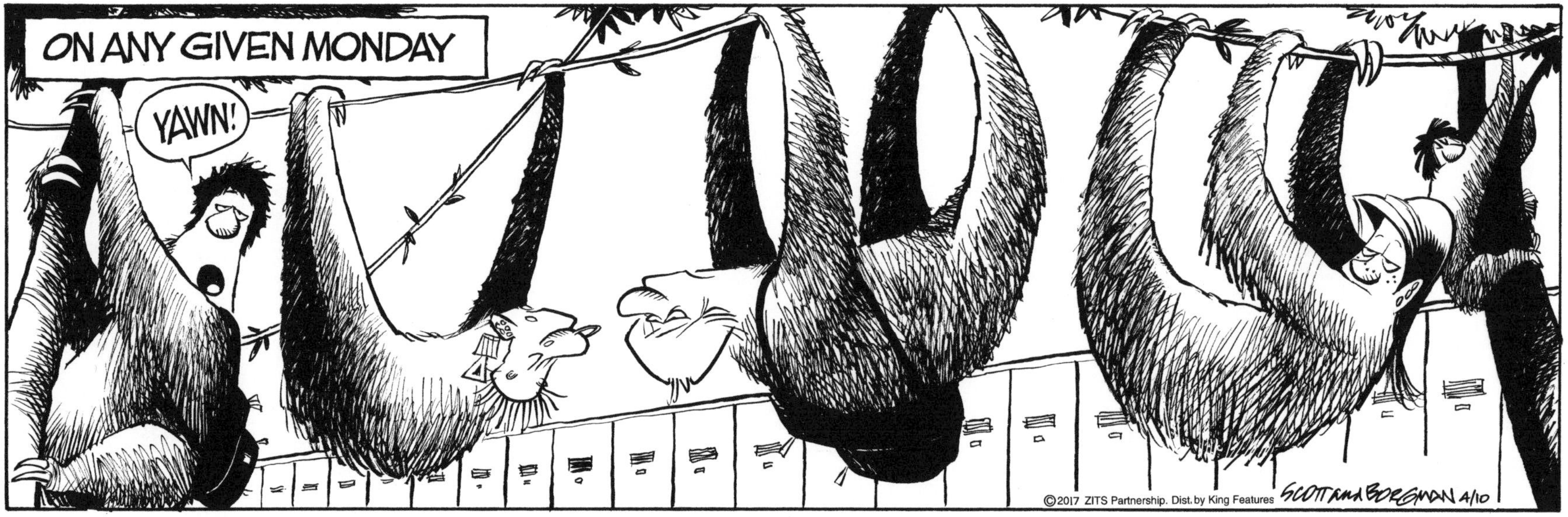
ON ANY GIVEN MONDAY
YAWN!
©2017 ZITS Partnership. Dist. by King Features
SCOTT AND BORGMAN 4/10

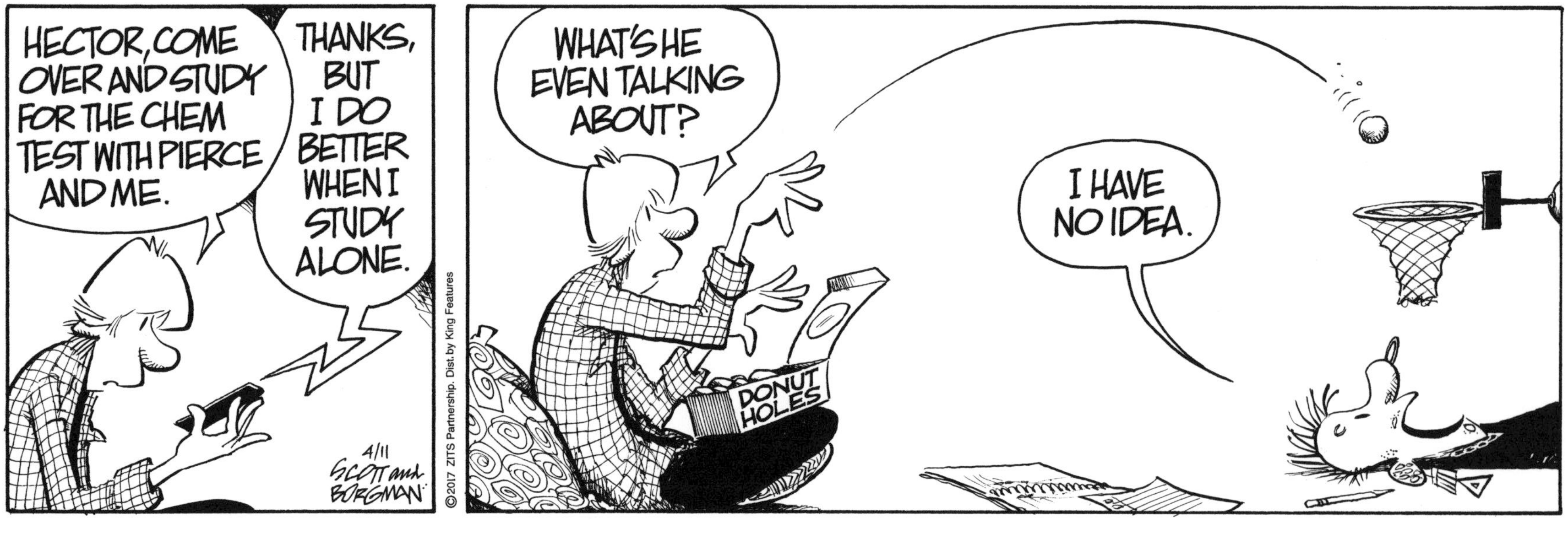
HECTOR, COME OVER AND STUDY FOR THE CHEM TEST WITH PIERCE AND ME.
THANKS, BUT I DO BETTER WHEN I STUDY ALONE.
4/11 SCOTT AND BORGMAN
©2017 ZITS Partnership. Dist. by King Features
WHAT'S HE EVEN TALKING ABOUT?
DONUT HOLES
I HAVE NO IDEA.

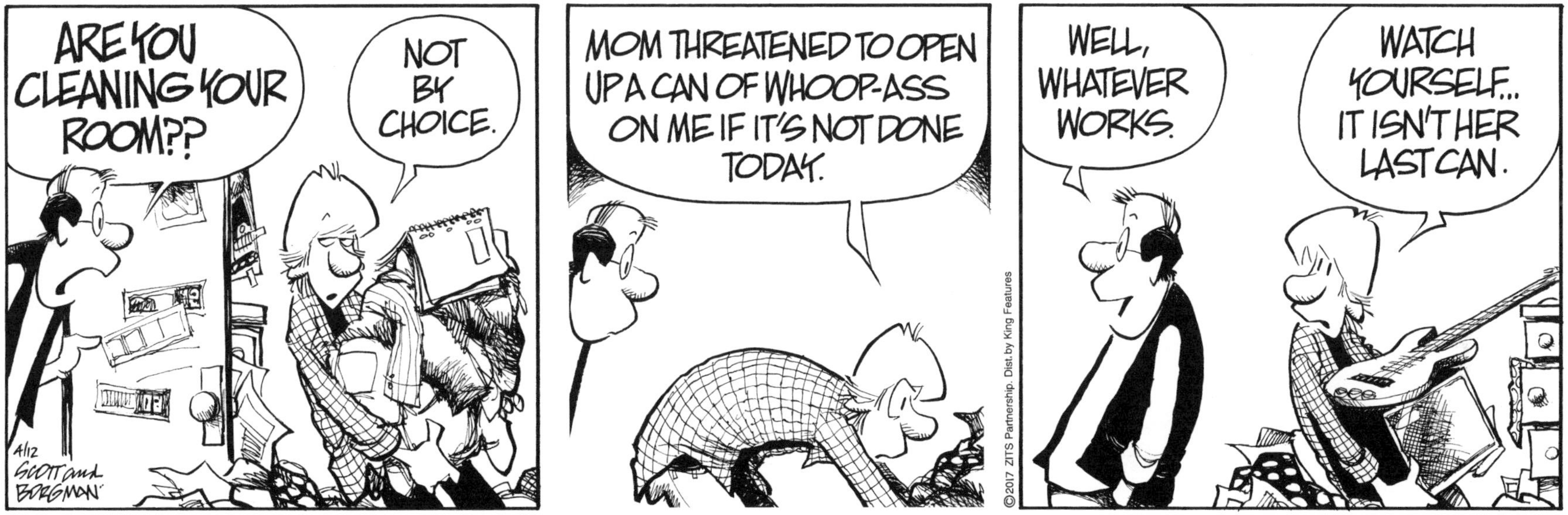
ARE YOU CLEANING YOUR ROOM??
NOT BY CHOICE.
4/12 SCOTT and BORGMAN
MOM THREATENED TO OPEN UP A CAN OF WHOOP-ASS ON ME IF IT'S NOT DONE TODAY.
©2017 ZITS Partnership. Dist. by King Features
WELL, WHATEVER WORKS.
WATCH YOURSELF... IT ISN'T HER LAST CAN.

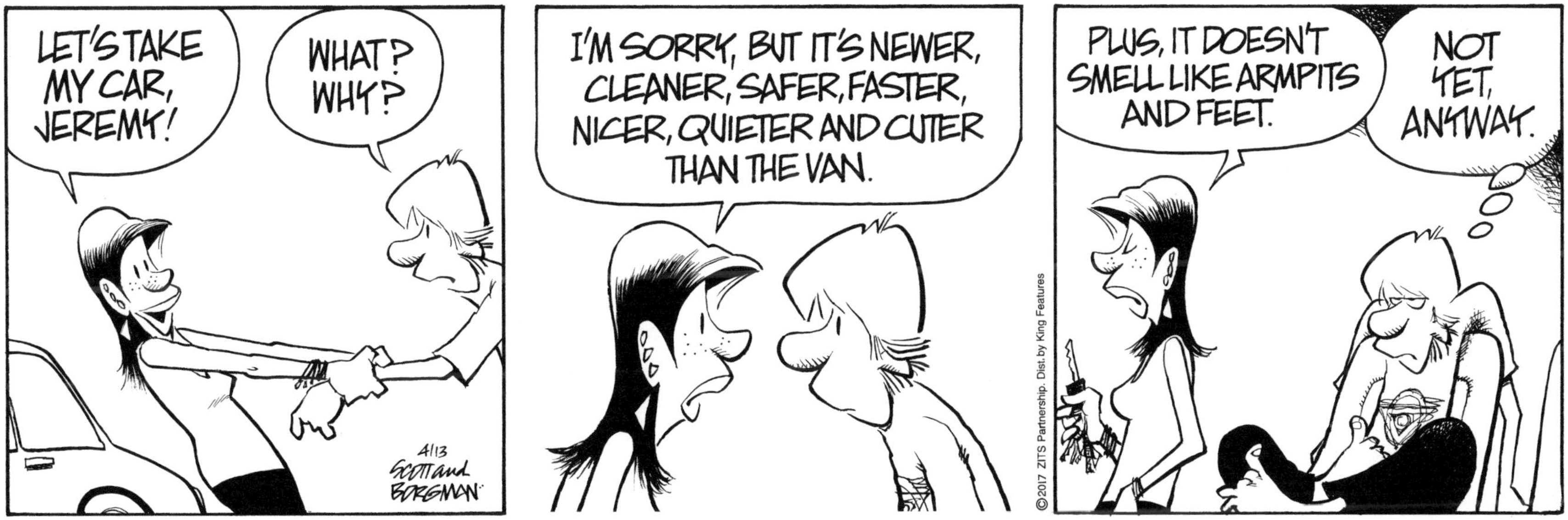
LET'S TAKE MY CAR, JEREMY!
WHAT? WHY?
4/13 SCOTT and BORGMAN
I'M SORRY, BUT IT'S NEWER, CLEANER, SAFER, FASTER, NICER, QUIETER AND CUTER THAN THE VAN.
©2017 ZITS Partnership. Dist. by King Features
PLUS, IT DOESN'T SMELL LIKE ARMPITS AND FEET.
NOT YET, ANYWAY.

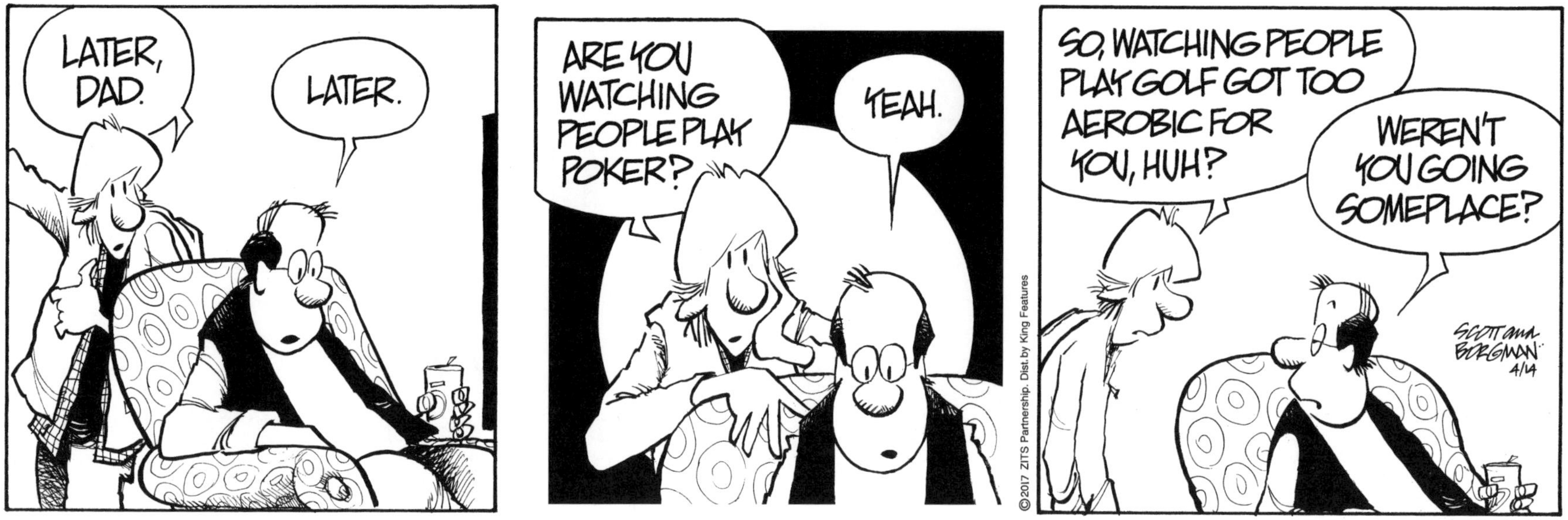
LATER, DAD.
LATER.
ARE YOU WATCHING PEOPLE PLAY POKER?
YEAH.
©2017 ZITS Partnership. Dist. by King Features
SO, WATCHING PEOPLE PLAY GOLF GOT TOO AEROBIC FOR YOU, HUH?
WEREN'T YOU GOING SOMEPLACE?
SCOTT and BORGMAN
4/14

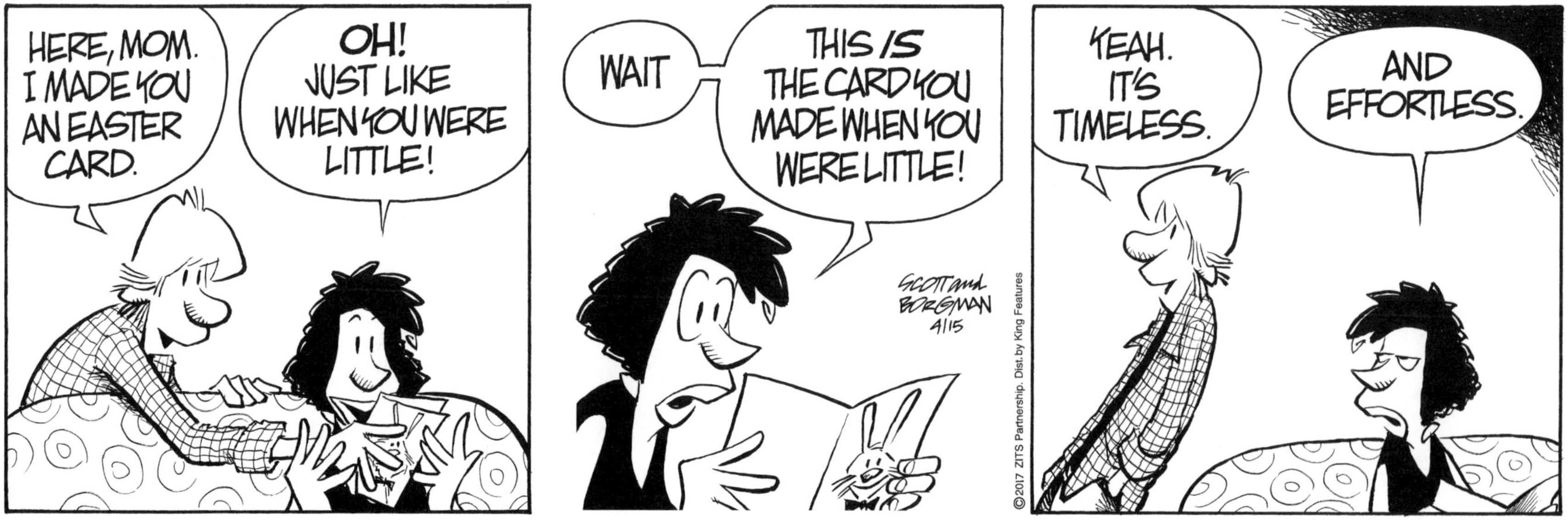
HERE, MOM. I MADE YOU AN EASTER CARD.
OH! JUST LIKE WHEN YOU WERE LITTLE!
WAIT
THIS *IS* THE CARD YOU MADE WHEN YOU WERE LITTLE!
SCOTT and BORGMAN
4/15
©2017 ZITS Partnership. Dist. by King Features
YEAH. IT'S TIMELESS.
AND EFFORTLESS.

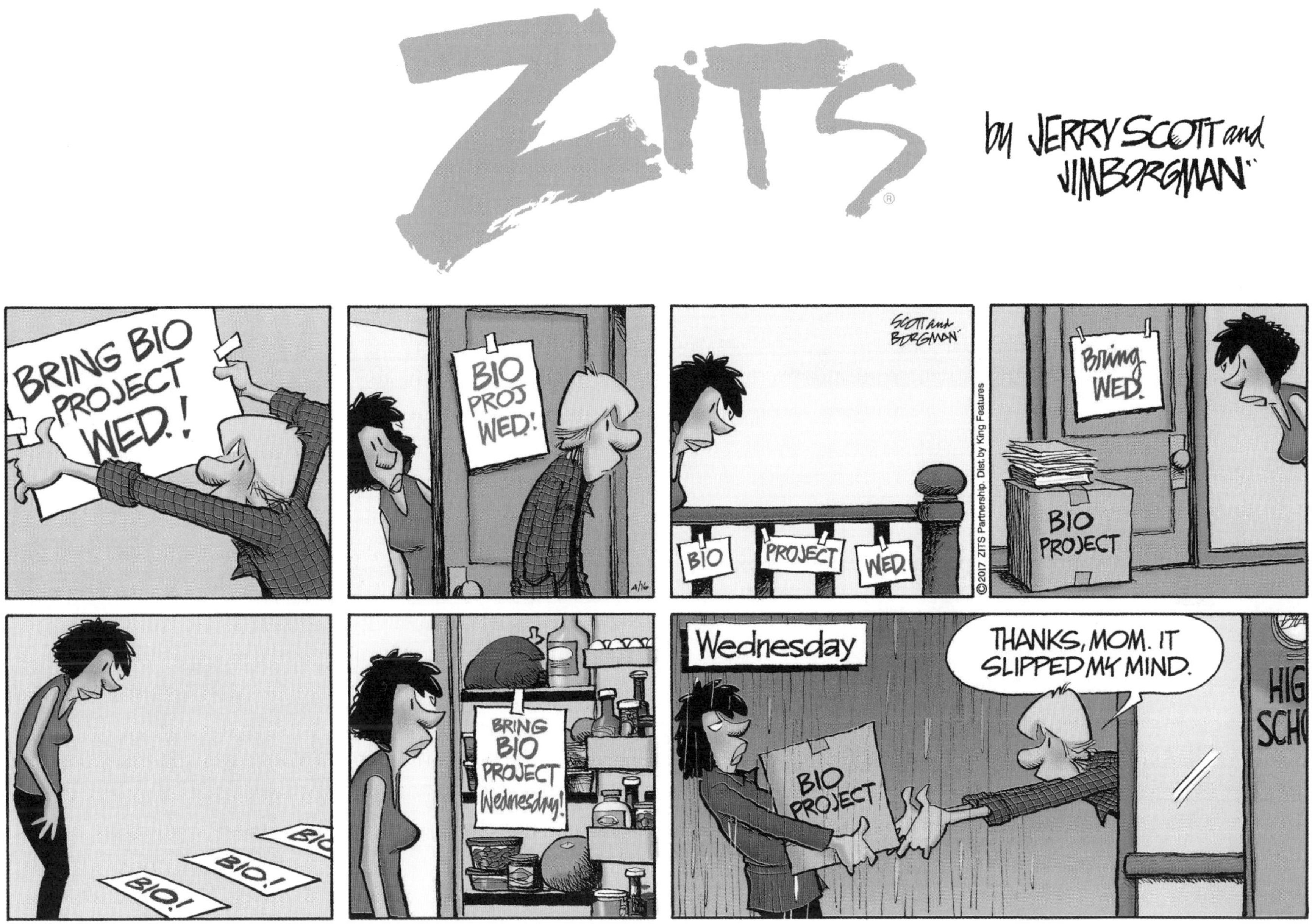
ZITS
by JERRY SCOTT and JIM BORGMAN
BRING BIO PROJECT WED.!
BIO PROJ WED!
SCOTT AND BORGMAN
BIO
PROJECT
WED.
©2017 ZITS Partnership. Dist. by King Features
Bring WED.
BIO PROJECT
BIO!
BIO!
BIO
BRING BIO PROJECT Wednesday!
Wednesday
THANKS, MOM. IT SLIPPED MY MIND.
BIO PROJECT

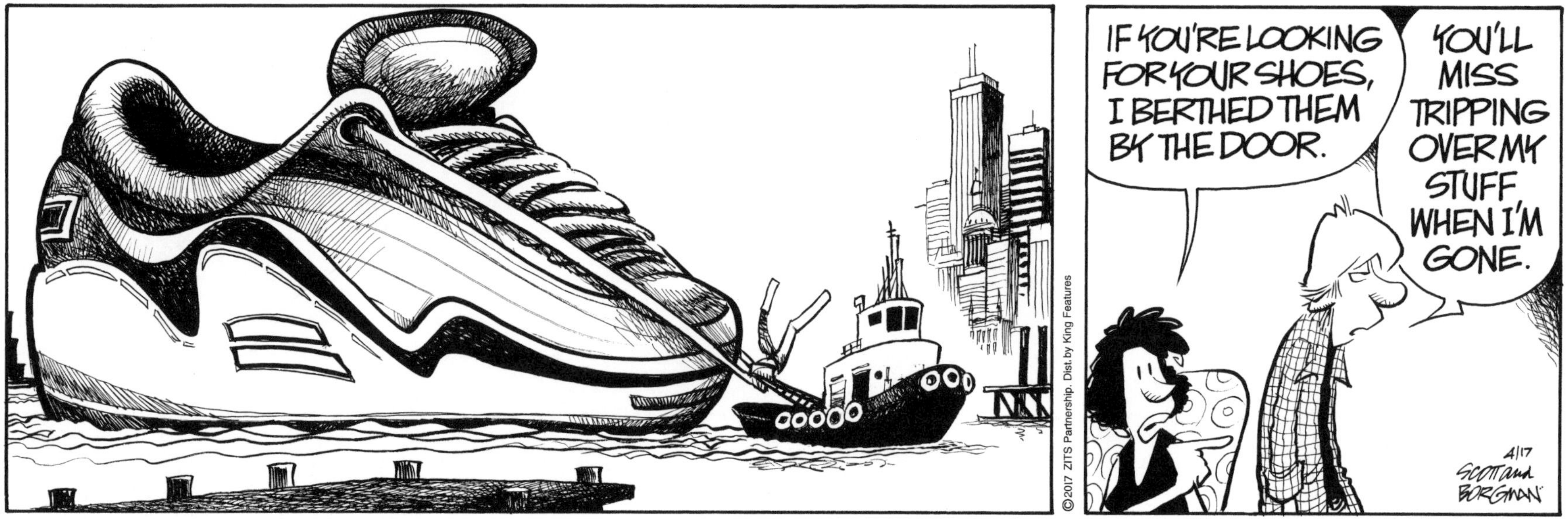
©2017 ZITS Partnership. Dist. by King Features
IF YOU'RE LOOKING FOR YOUR SHOES, I BERTHED THEM BY THE DOOR.
YOU'LL MISS TRIPPING OVER MY STUFF WHEN I'M GONE.
4/17
SCOTT and BORGMAN

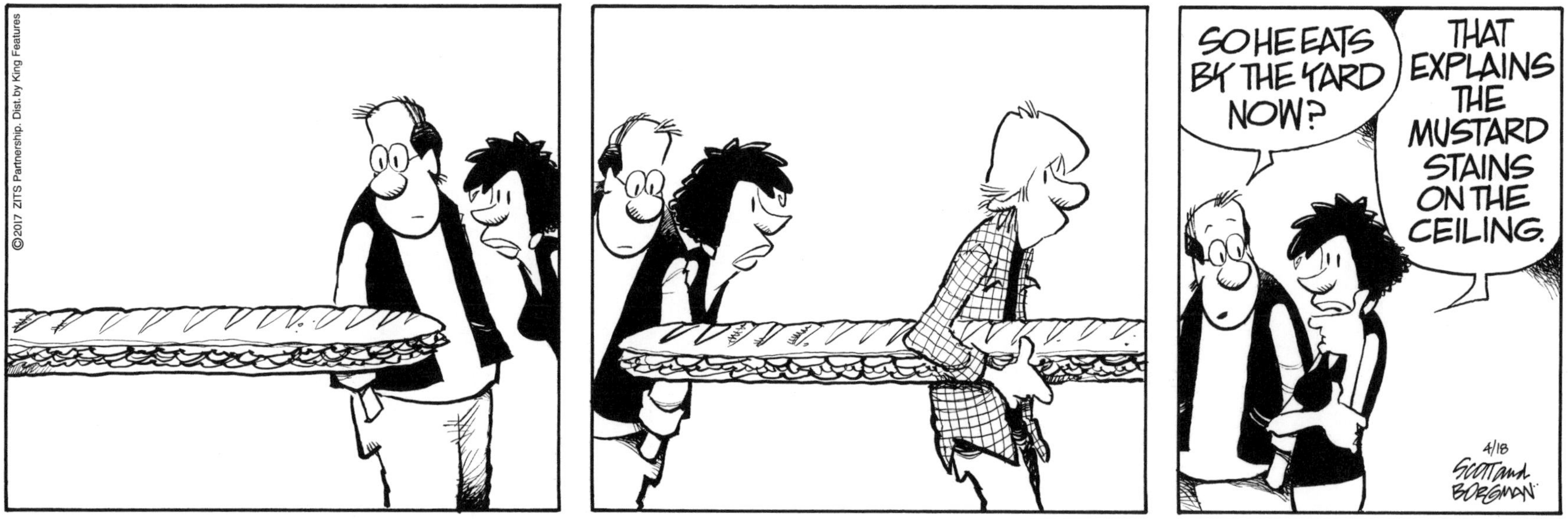
©2017 ZITS Partnership. Dist. by King Features
SO HE EATS BY THE YARD NOW?
THAT EXPLAINS THE MUSTARD STAINS ON THE CEILING.
4/18
SCOTT and BORGMAN

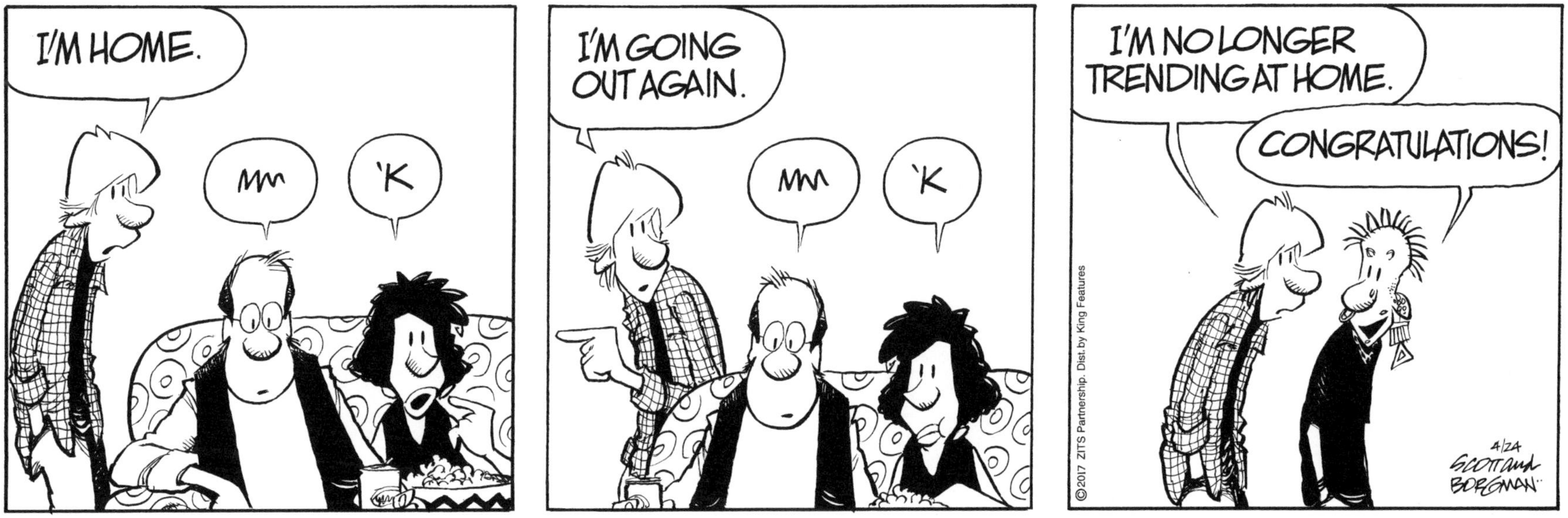
I'M HOME.
MM
'K
I'M GOING OUT AGAIN.
MM
'K
I'M NO LONGER TRENDING AT HOME.
CONGRATULATIONS!
©2017 ZITS Partnership. Dist. by King Features
4/24 SCOTT and BORGMAN

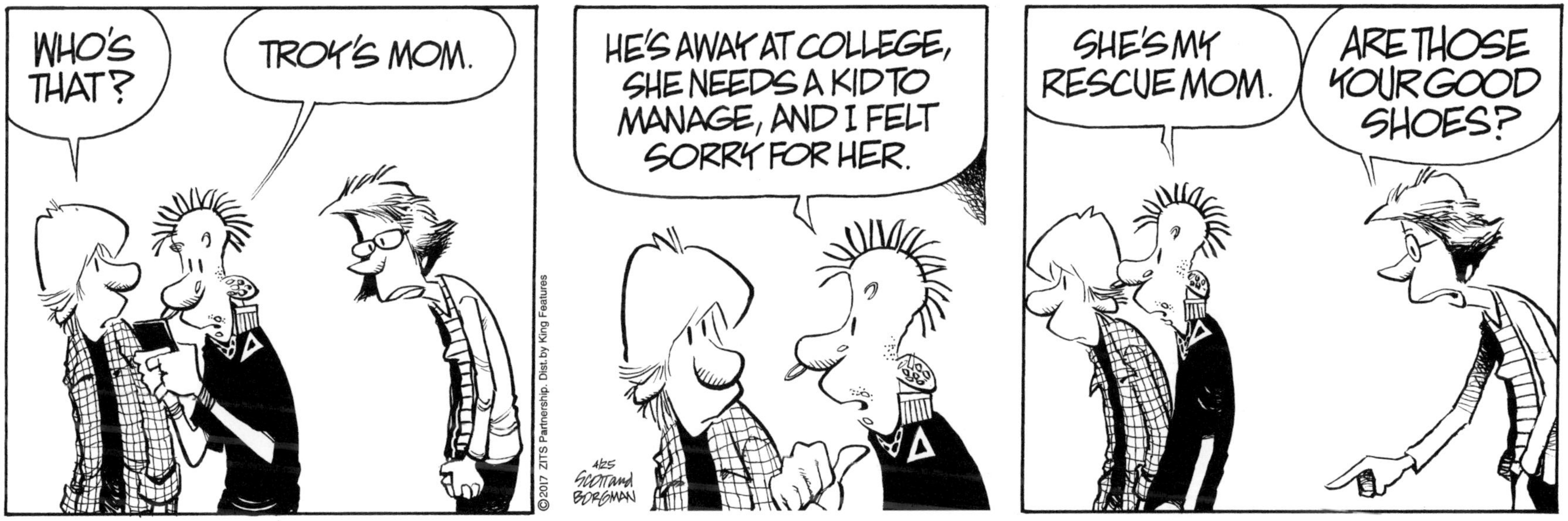
WHO'S THAT?
TROY'S MOM.
©2017 ZITS Partnership. Dist. by King Features
4/25 SCOTT and BORGMAN
HE'S AWAY AT COLLEGE, SHE NEEDS A KID TO MANAGE, AND I FELT SORRY FOR HER.
SHE'S MY RESCUE MOM.
ARE THOSE YOUR GOOD SHOES?

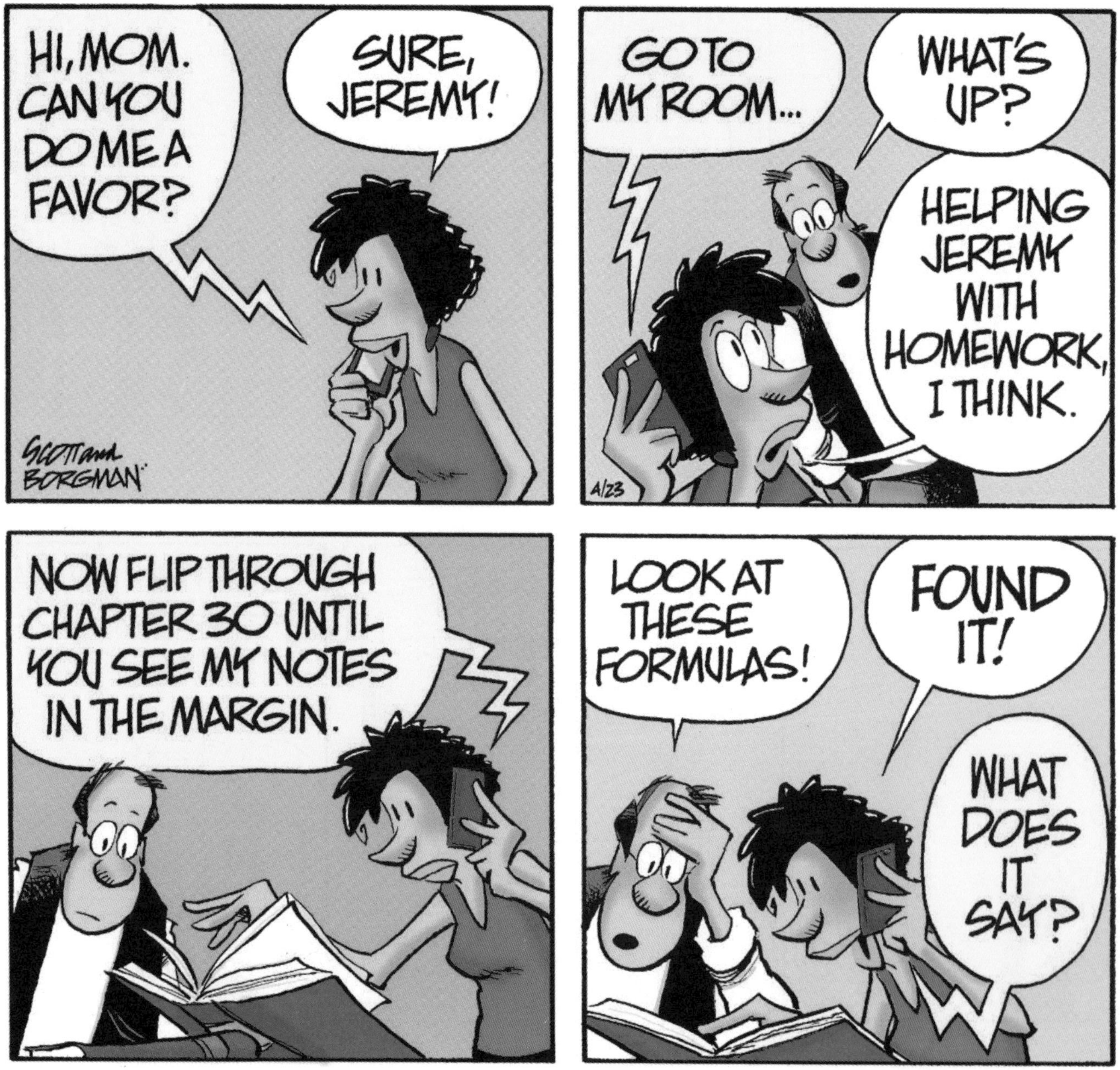
HI, MOM. CAN YOU DO ME A FAVOR?
SURE, JEREMY!
SCOTT and BORGMAN
GO TO MY ROOM...
WHAT'S UP?
HELPING JEREMY WITH HOMEWORK, I THINK.
4/23
NOW FLIP THROUGH CHAPTER 30 UNTIL YOU SEE MY NOTES IN THE MARGIN.
LOOK AT THESE FORMULAS!
FOUND IT!
WHAT DOES IT SAY?

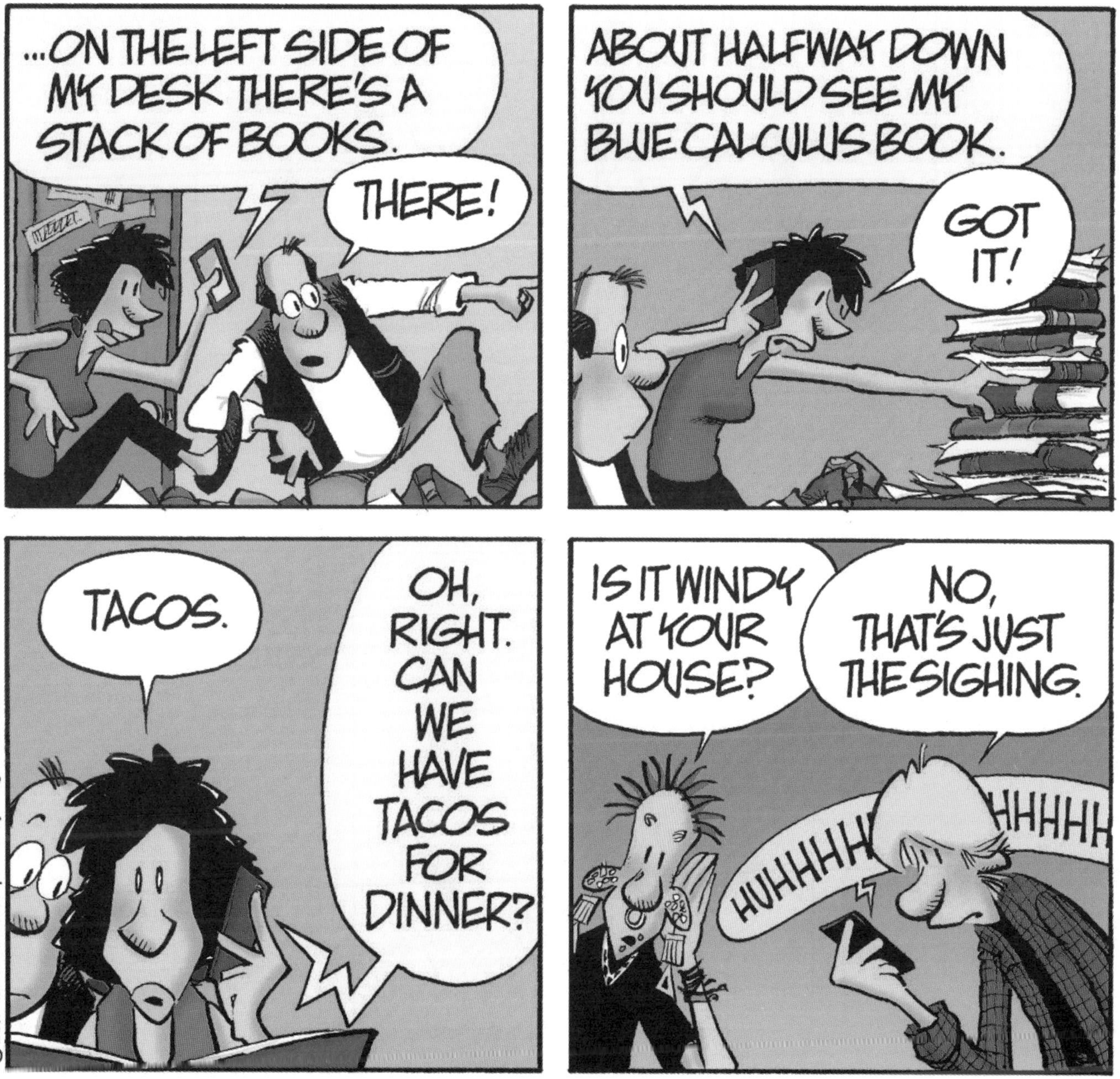
...ON THE LEFT SIDE OF MY DESK THERE'S A STACK OF BOOKS.
THERE!
ABOUT HALFWAY DOWN YOU SHOULD SEE MY BLUE CALCULUS BOOK.
GOT IT!
TACOS.
OH, RIGHT. CAN WE HAVE TACOS FOR DINNER?
IS IT WINDY AT YOUR HOUSE?
NO, THAT'S JUST THE SIGHING.
HUHHHH
HHHHH

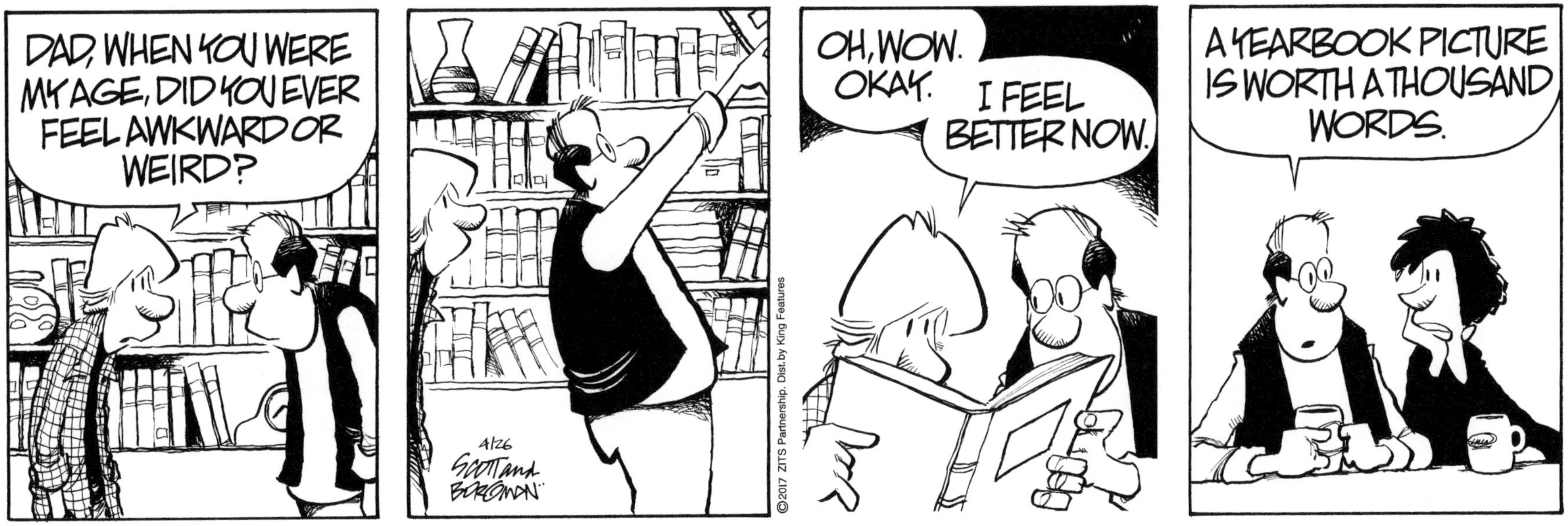
DAD, WHEN YOU WERE MY AGE, DID YOU EVER FEEL AWKWARD OR WEIRD?
4/26
SCOTT AND BORGMAN
© 2017 ZITS Partnership. Dist. by King Features
OH, WOW. OKAY.
I FEEL BETTER NOW.
A YEARBOOK PICTURE IS WORTH A THOUSAND WORDS.

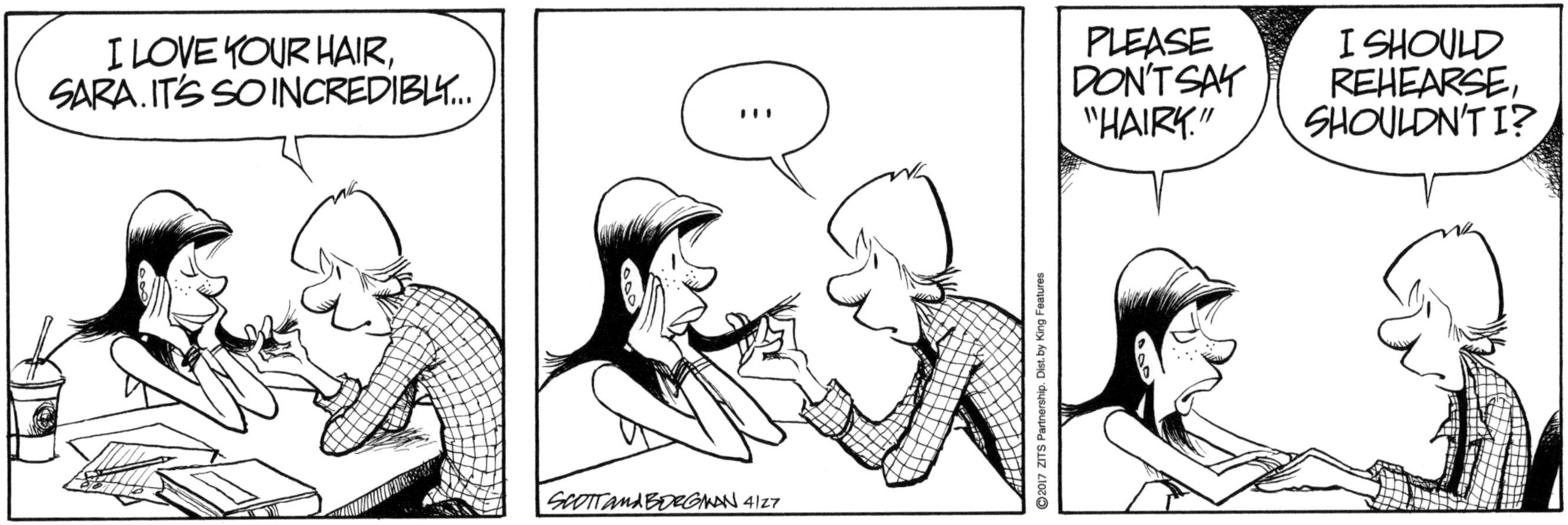
I LOVE YOUR HAIR, SARA. IT'S SO INCREDIBLY...
...
SCOTT AND BORGMAN 4/27
© 2017 ZITS Partnership. Dist. by King Features
PLEASE DON'T SAY "HAIRY."
I SHOULD REHEARSE, SHOULDN'T I?

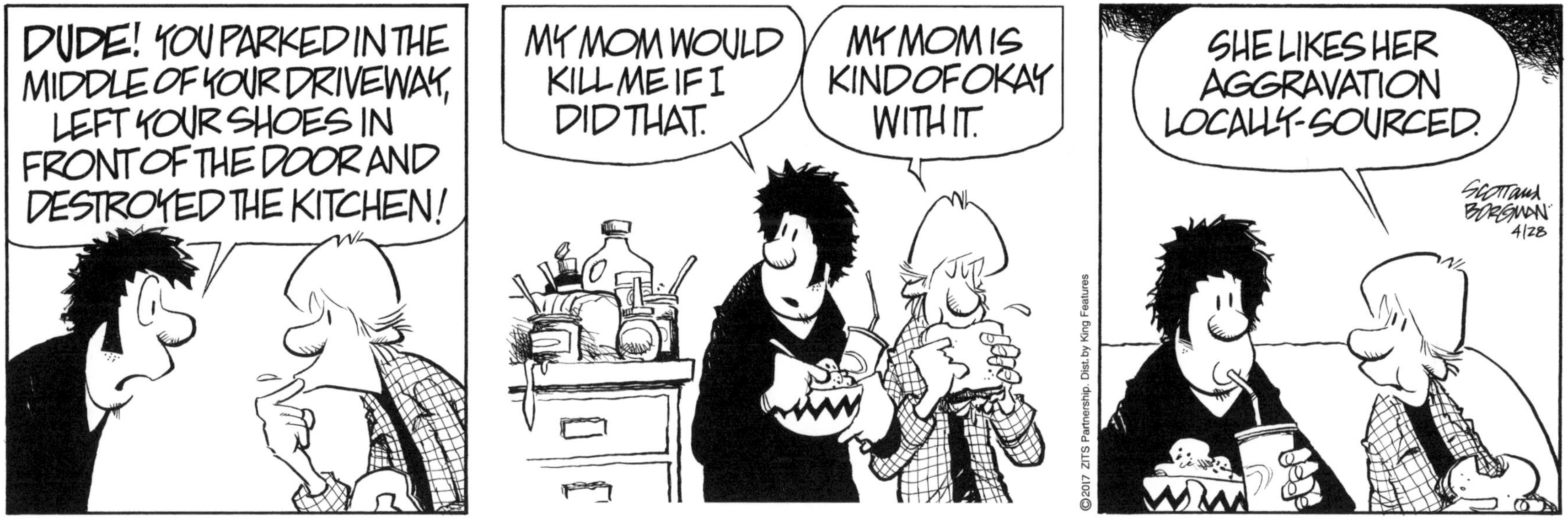
DUDE! YOU PARKED IN THE MIDDLE OF YOUR DRIVEWAY, LEFT YOUR SHOES IN FRONT OF THE DOOR AND DESTROYED THE KITCHEN!
MY MOM WOULD KILL ME IF I DID THAT.
MY MOM IS KIND OF OKAY WITH IT.
SHE LIKES HER AGGRAVATION LOCALLY-SOURCED.
SCOTT and BORGMAN 4/28
©2017 ZITS Partnership. Dist. by King Features

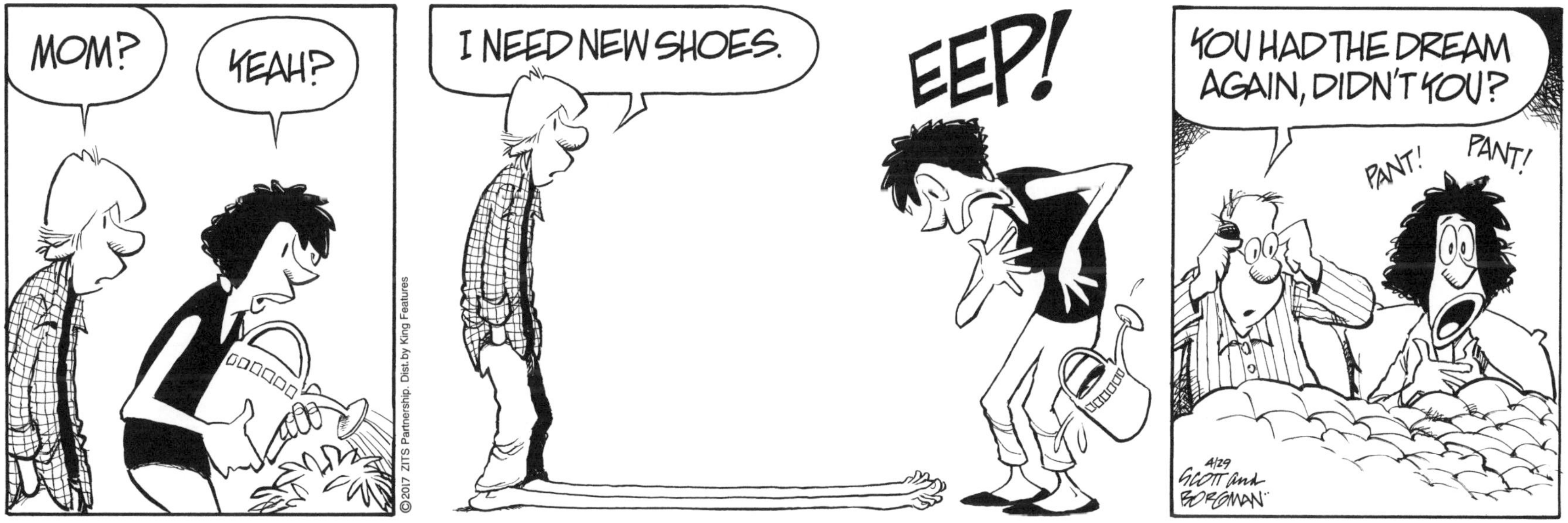
MOM?
YEAH?
I NEED NEW SHOES.
EEP!
YOU HAD THE DREAM AGAIN, DIDN'T YOU?
PANT!
PANT!
4/29 SCOTT and BORGMAN
©2017 ZITS Partnership. Dist. by King Features

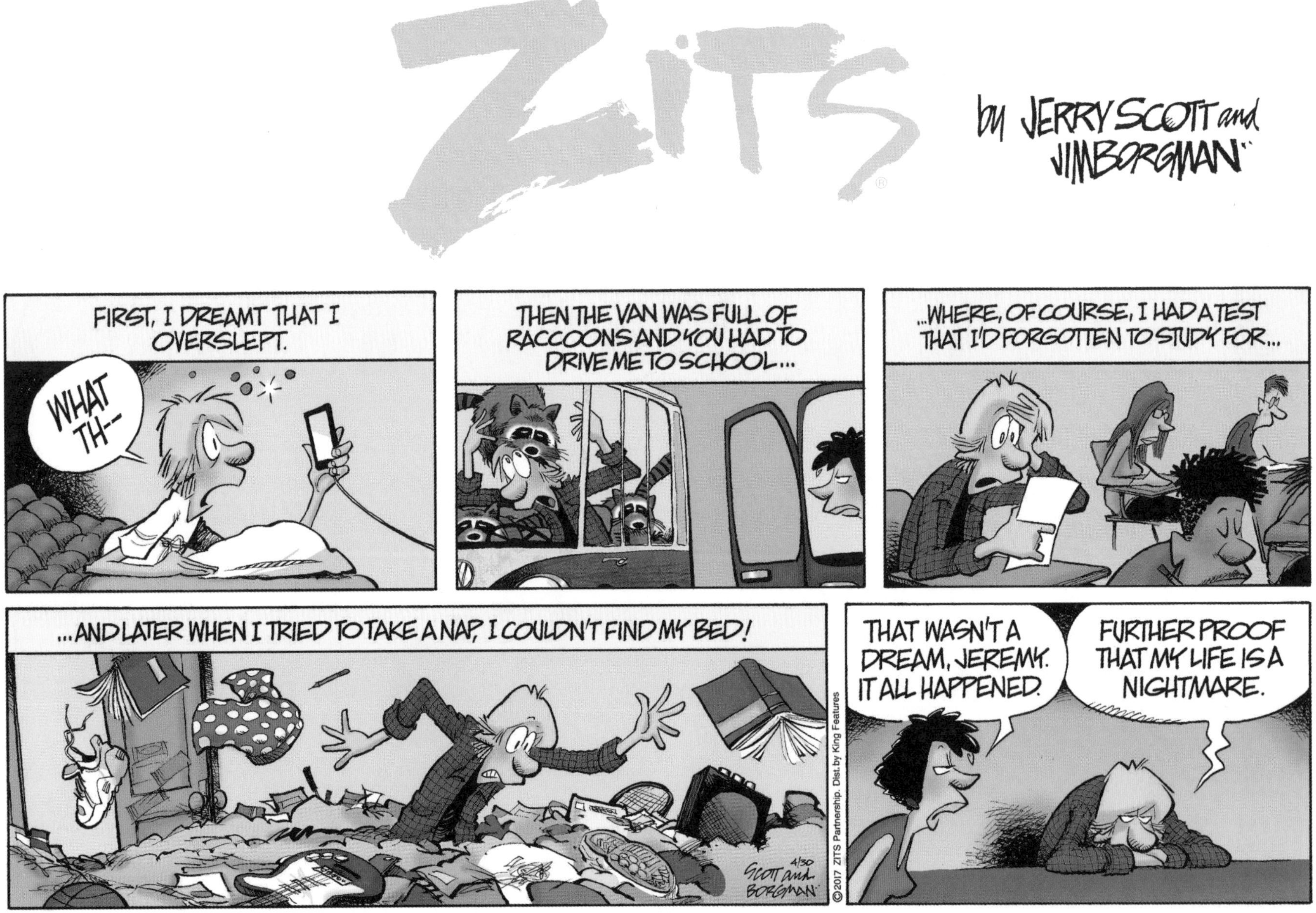
ZITS
by JERRY SCOTT and JIM BORGMAN
FIRST, I DREAMT THAT I OVERSLEPT.
WHAT TH--
THEN THE VAN WAS FULL OF RACCOONS AND YOU HAD TO DRIVE ME TO SCHOOL...
...WHERE, OF COURSE, I HAD A TEST THAT I'D FORGOTTEN TO STUDY FOR...
...AND LATER WHEN I TRIED TO TAKE A NAP, I COULDN'T FIND MY BED!
4/30 SCOTT and BORGMAN
©2017 ZITS Partnership. Dist. by King Features
THAT WASN'T A DREAM, JEREMY. IT ALL HAPPENED.
FURTHER PROOF THAT MY LIFE IS A NIGHTMARE.

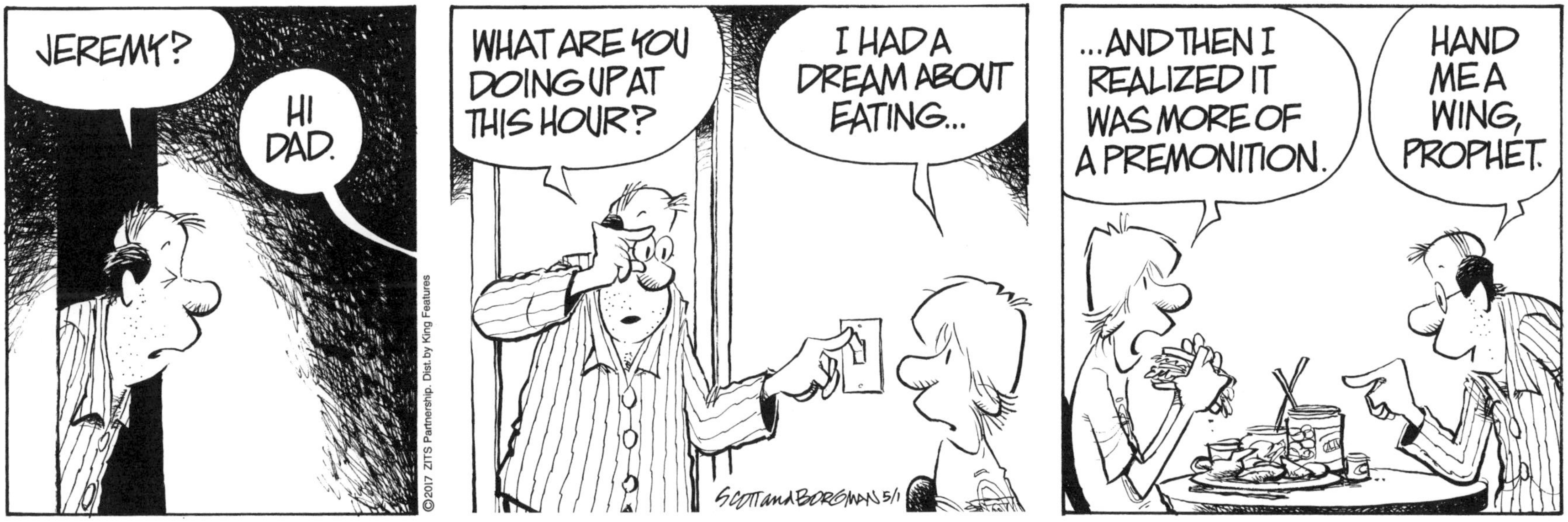
JEREMY?
HI DAD.
©2017 ZITS Partnership. Dist. by King Features
WHAT ARE YOU DOING UP AT THIS HOUR?
I HAD A DREAM ABOUT EATING...
SCOTT and BORGMAN 5/1
...AND THEN I REALIZED IT WAS MORE OF A PREMONITION.
HAND ME A WING, PROPHET.

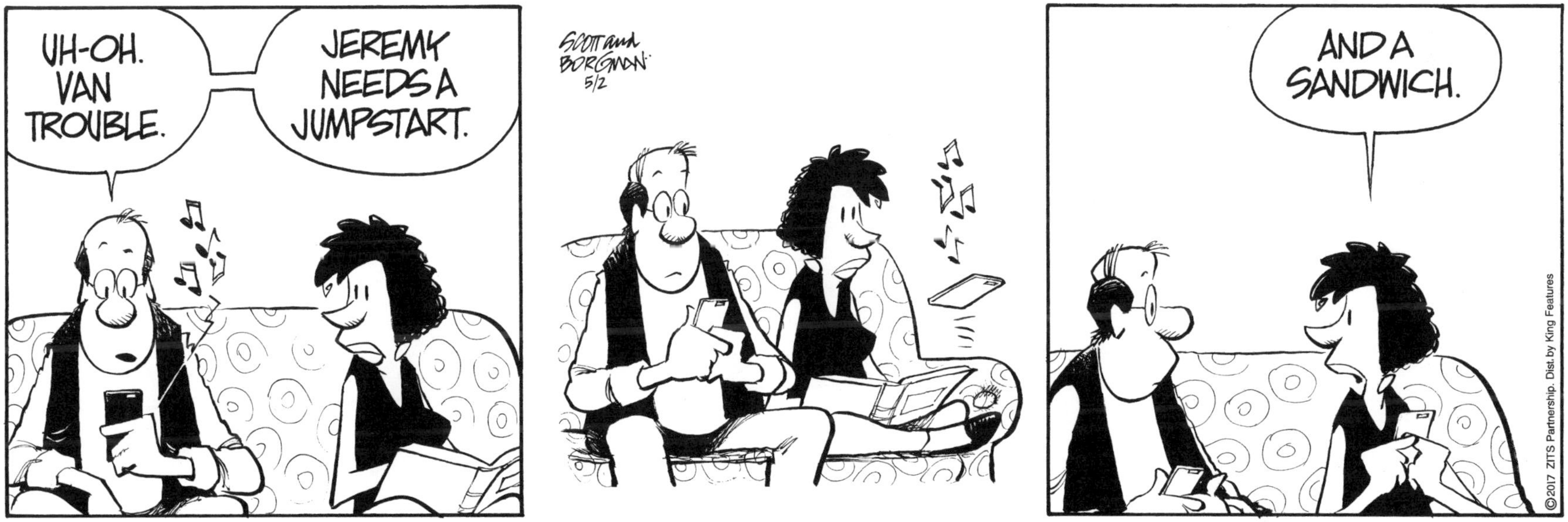
UH-OH. VAN TROUBLE.
JEREMY NEEDS A JUMPSTART.
SCOTT and BORGMAN 5/2
AND A SANDWICH.
©2017 ZITS Partnership. Dist. by King Features

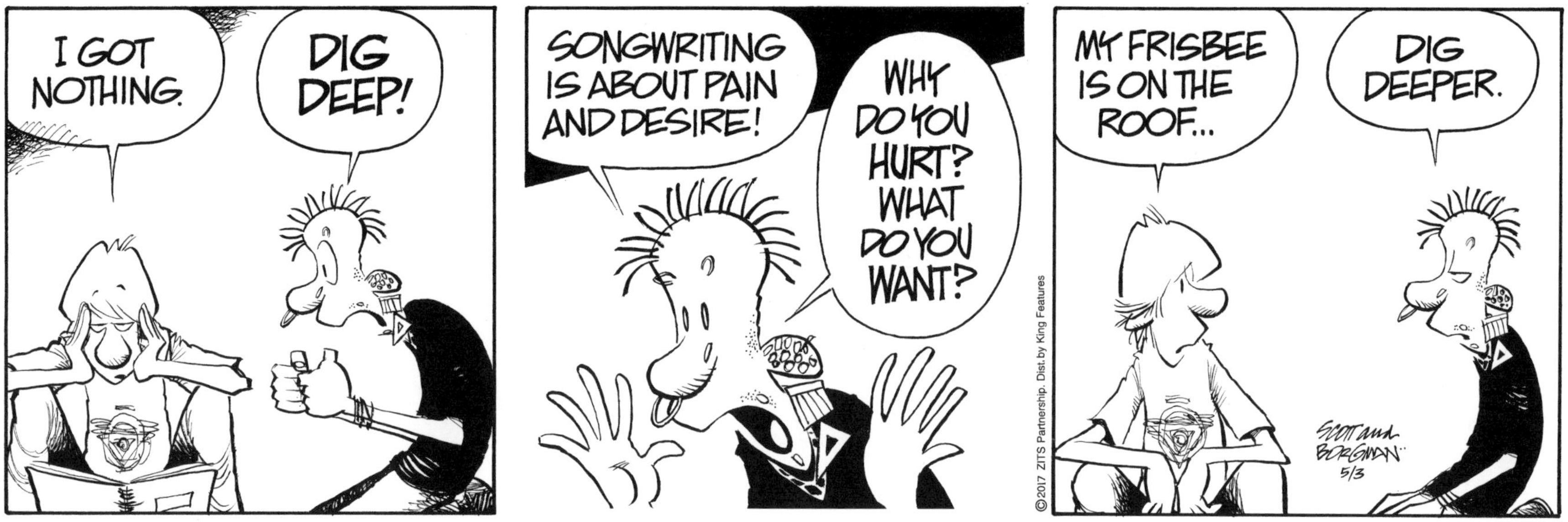
I GOT NOTHING.
DIG DEEP!
SONGWRITING IS ABOUT PAIN AND DESIRE!
WHY DO YOU HURT? WHAT DO YOU WANT?
©2017 ZITS Partnership. Dist. by King Features
MY FRISBEE IS ON THE ROOF...
DIG DEEPER.
SCOTT and BORGMAN 5/3

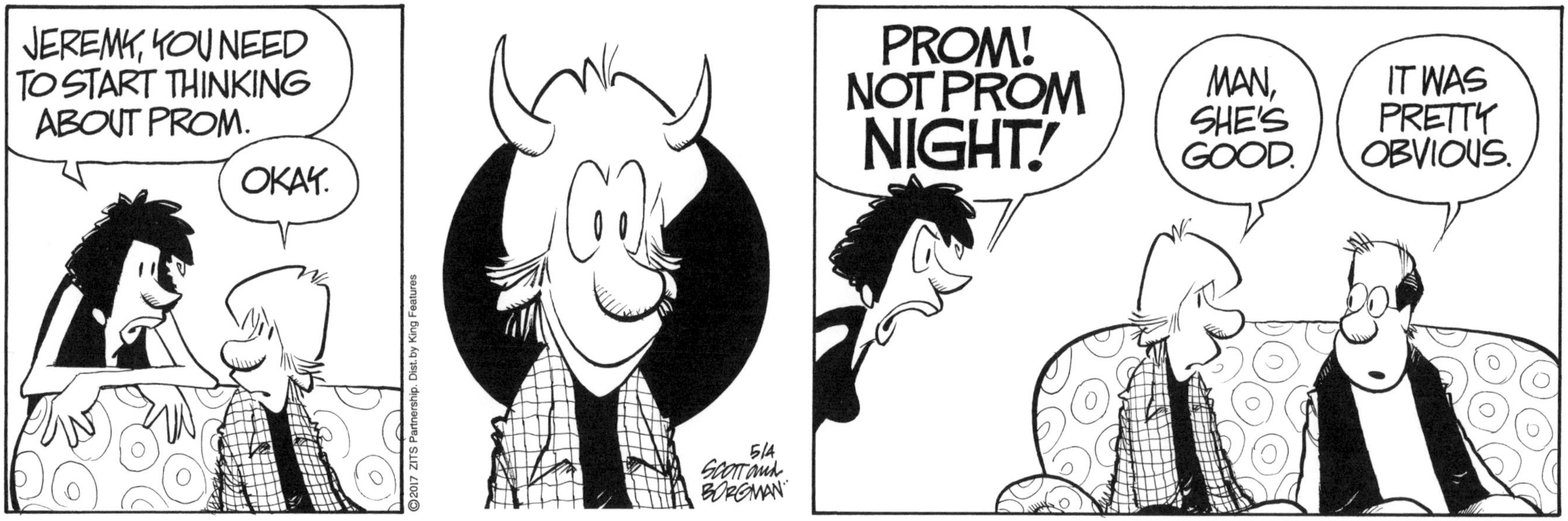
JEREMY, YOU NEED TO START THINKING ABOUT PROM.
OKAY.
©2017 ZITS Partnership. Dist. by King Features
5/4 SCOTT and BORGMAN
PROM! NOT PROM NIGHT!
MAN, SHE'S GOOD.
IT WAS PRETTY OBVIOUS.

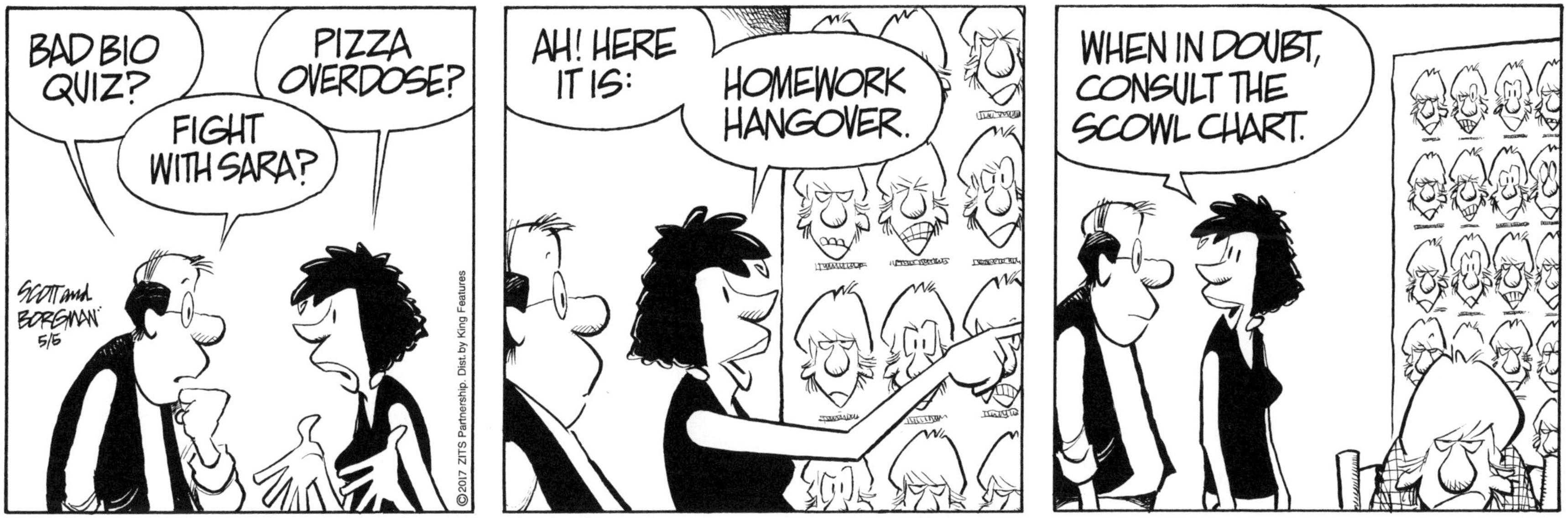
BAD BIO QUIZ?
FIGHT WITH SARA?
PIZZA OVERDOSE?
SCOTT and BORGMAN 5/5
©2017 ZITS Partnership. Dist. by King Features
AH! HERE IT IS:
HOMEWORK HANGOVER.
WHEN IN DOUBT, CONSULT THE SCOWL CHART.

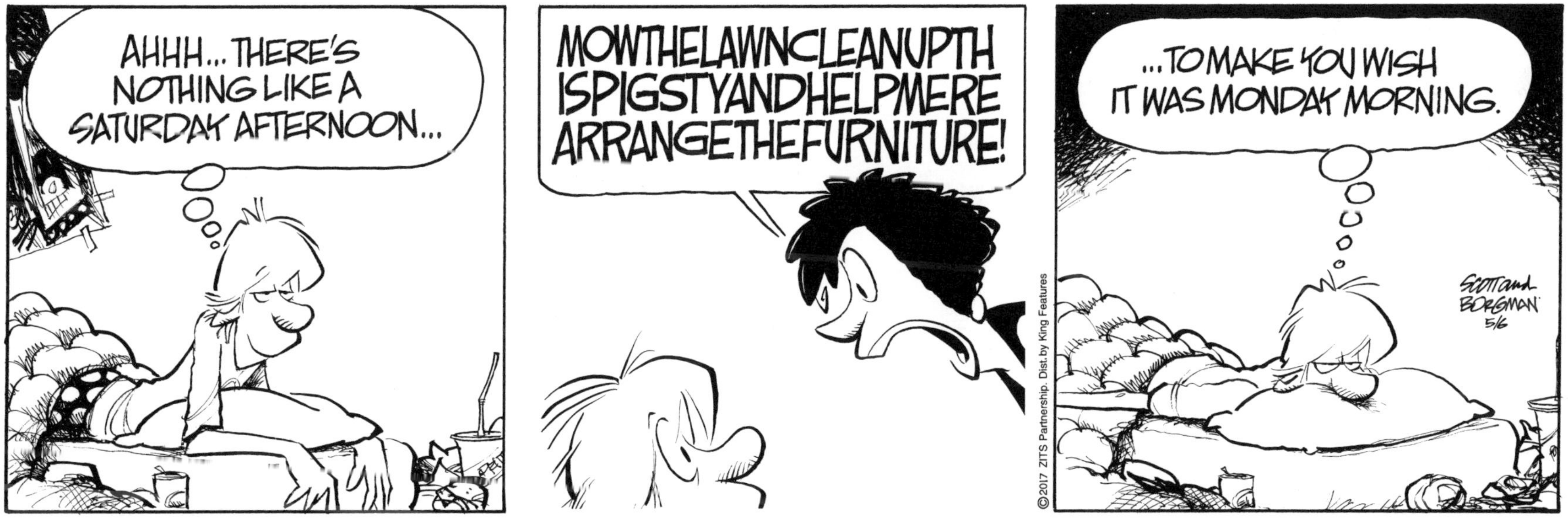
AHHH... THERE'S NOTHING LIKE A SATURDAY AFTERNOON...
MOWTHELAWNCLEANUPTH ISPIGSTYANDHELPMERE ARRANGETHEFURNITURE!
©2017 ZITS Partnership. Dist. by King Features
...TO MAKE YOU WISH IT WAS MONDAY MORNING.
SCOTT and BORGMAN 5/6

ZITS®

by JERRY SCOTT and JIM BORGMAN

CHOMP!
AWESOME, ISN'T IT?
I FEEL LIKE I SHOULD BE WEARING A HARD HAT.
WOULD YOU PLEASE GAWK SOMEWHERE ELSE?
©2017 ZITS Partnership. Dist. by King Features
SCOTT and BORGMAN 5/7

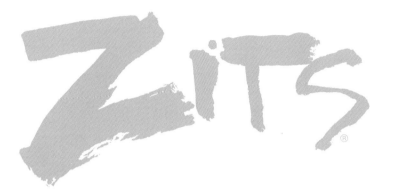

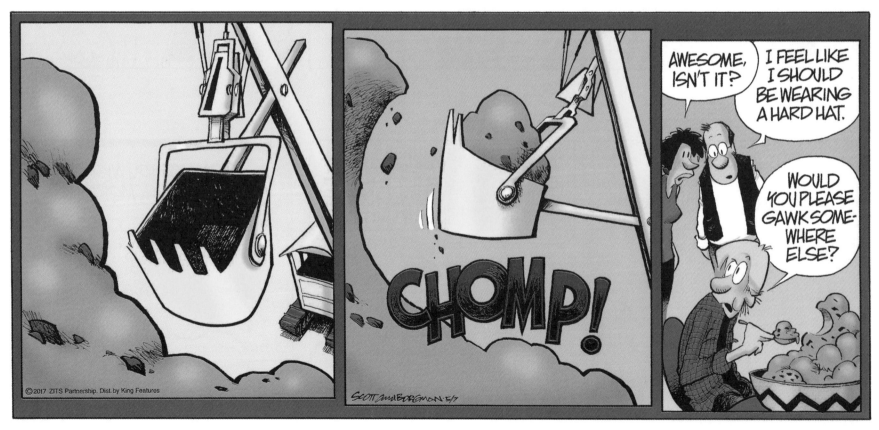

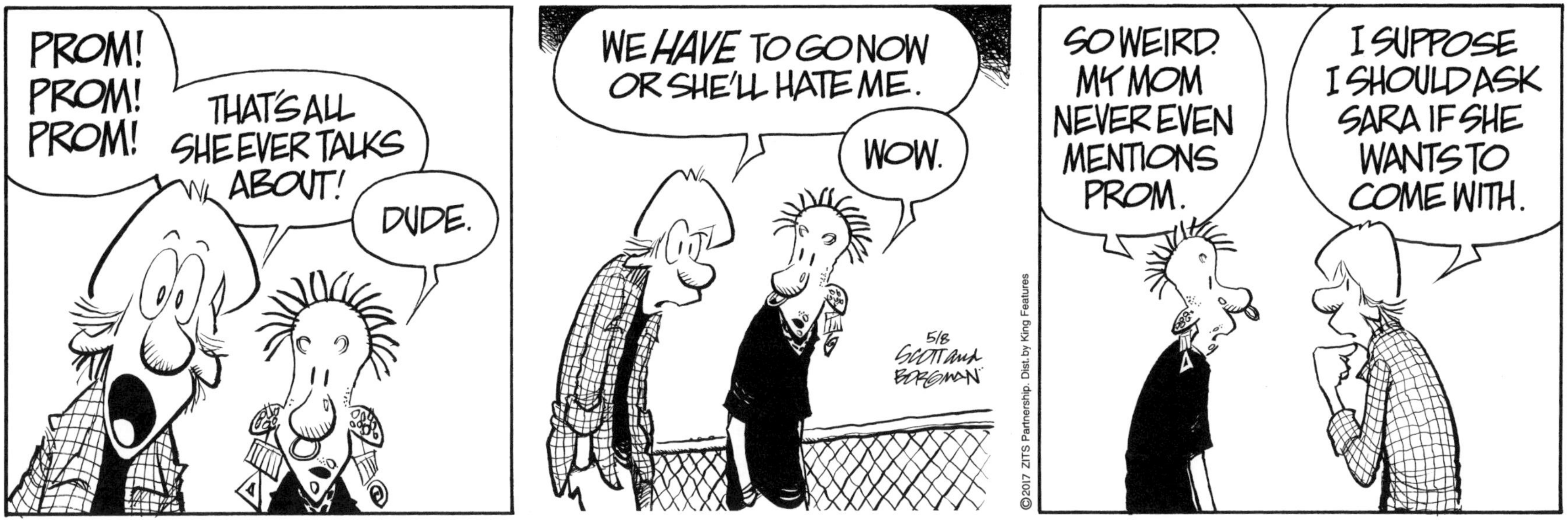
PROM! PROM! PROM!
THAT'S ALL SHE EVER TALKS ABOUT!
DUDE.
WE *HAVE* TO GO NOW OR SHE'LL HATE ME.
WOW.
5/8 SCOTT and BORGMAN
© 2017 ZITS Partnership. Dist. by King Features
SO WEIRD. MY MOM NEVER EVEN MENTIONS PROM.
I SUPPOSE I SHOULD ASK SARA IF SHE WANTS TO COME WITH.

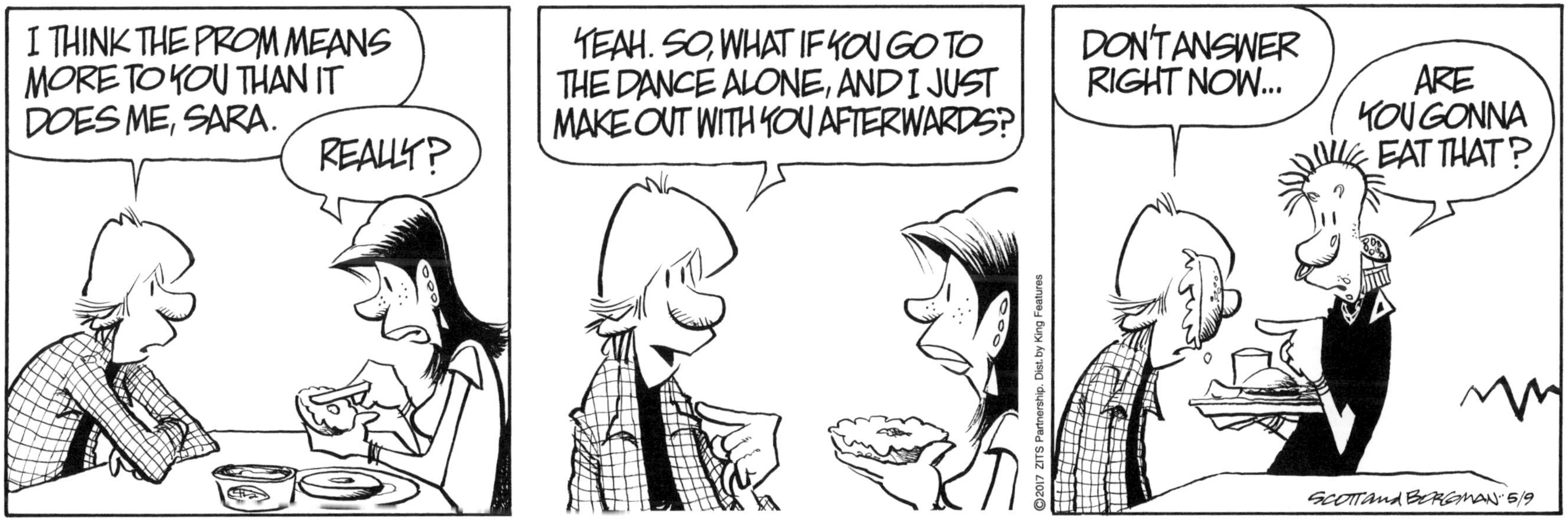
I THINK THE PROM MEANS MORE TO YOU THAN IT DOES ME, SARA.
REALLY?
YEAH. SO, WHAT IF YOU GO TO THE DANCE ALONE, AND I JUST MAKE OUT WITH YOU AFTERWARDS?
© 2017 ZITS Partnership. Dist. by King Features
DON'T ANSWER RIGHT NOW...
ARE YOU GONNA EAT THAT?
SCOTT and BORGMAN 5/9

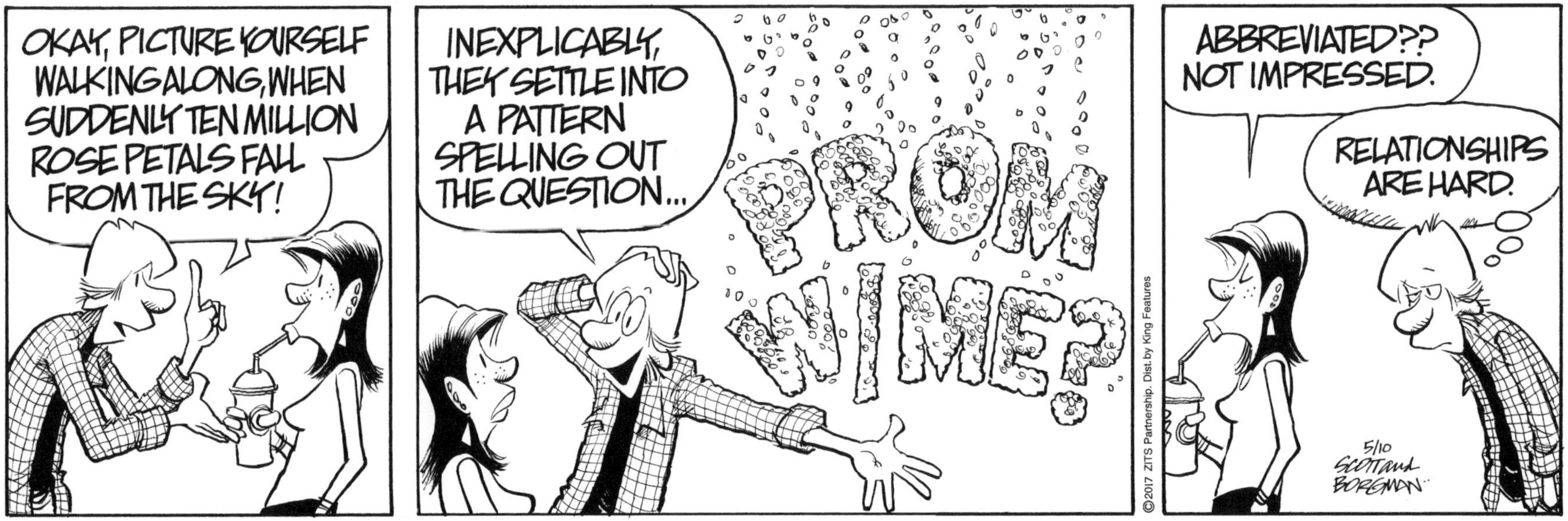
OKAY, PICTURE YOURSELF WALKING ALONG, WHEN SUDDENLY TEN MILLION ROSE PETALS FALL FROM THE SKY!
INEXPLICABLY, THEY SETTLE INTO A PATTERN SPELLING OUT THE QUESTION...
PROM W/ME?
ABBREVIATED?? NOT IMPRESSED.
RELATIONSHIPS ARE HARD.
5/10 SCOTT and BORGMAN
©2017 ZITS Partnership. Dist.by King Features

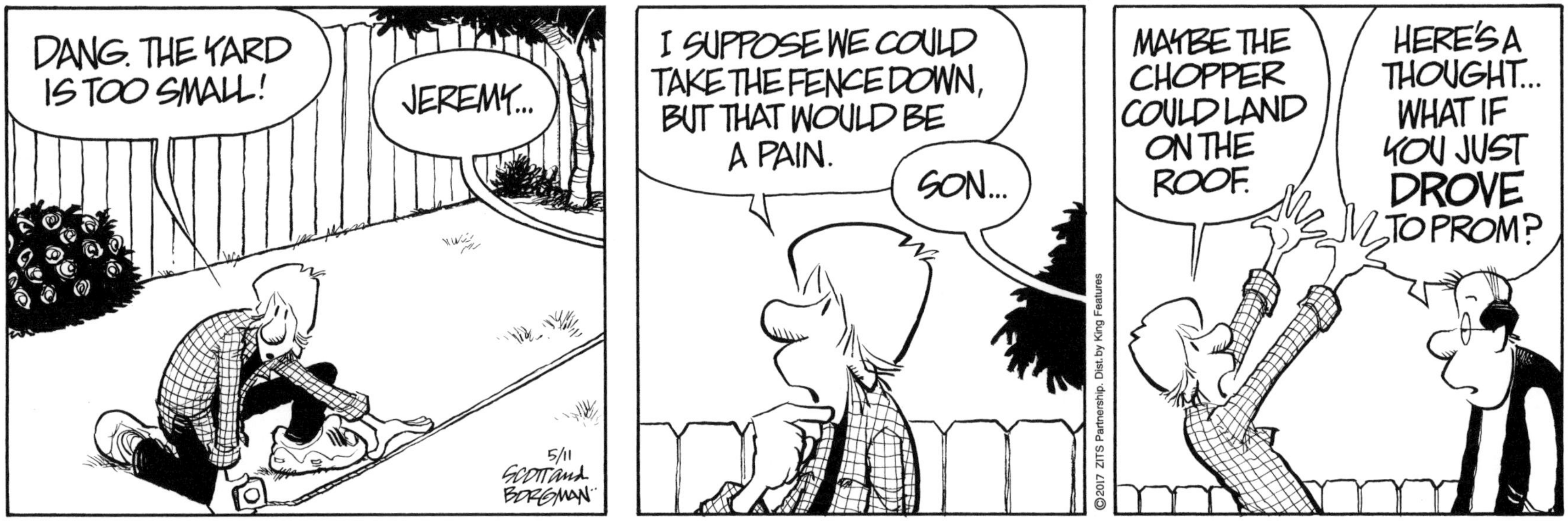
DANG. THE YARD IS TOO SMALL!
JEREMY...
5/11 SCOTT and BORGMAN
I SUPPOSE WE COULD TAKE THE FENCE DOWN, BUT THAT WOULD BE A PAIN.
SON...
MAYBE THE CHOPPER COULD LAND ON THE ROOF.
HERE'S A THOUGHT... WHAT IF YOU JUST **DROVE** TO PROM?
©2017 ZITS Partnership. Dist.by King Features

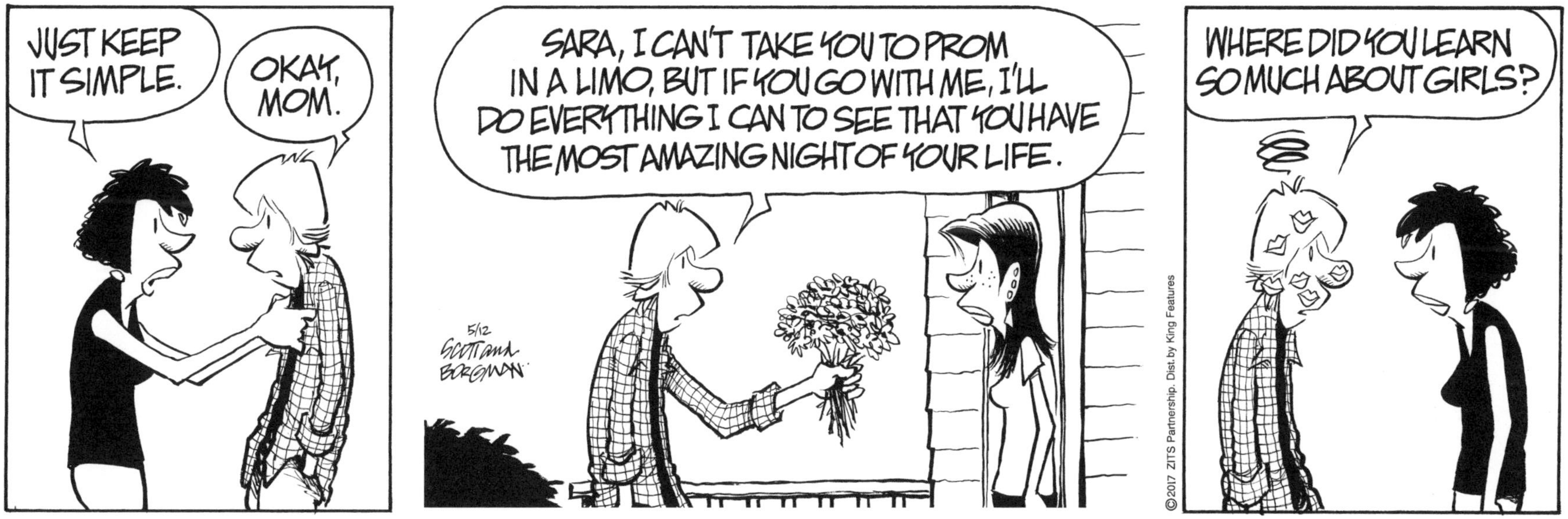
JUST KEEP IT SIMPLE.
OKAY, MOM.
SARA, I CAN'T TAKE YOU TO PROM IN A LIMO, BUT IF YOU GO WITH ME, I'LL DO EVERYTHING I CAN TO SEE THAT YOU HAVE THE MOST AMAZING NIGHT OF YOUR LIFE.
5/12
SCOTT and BORGMAN
WHERE DID YOU LEARN SO MUCH ABOUT GIRLS?
©2017 ZITS Partnership. Dist. by King Features

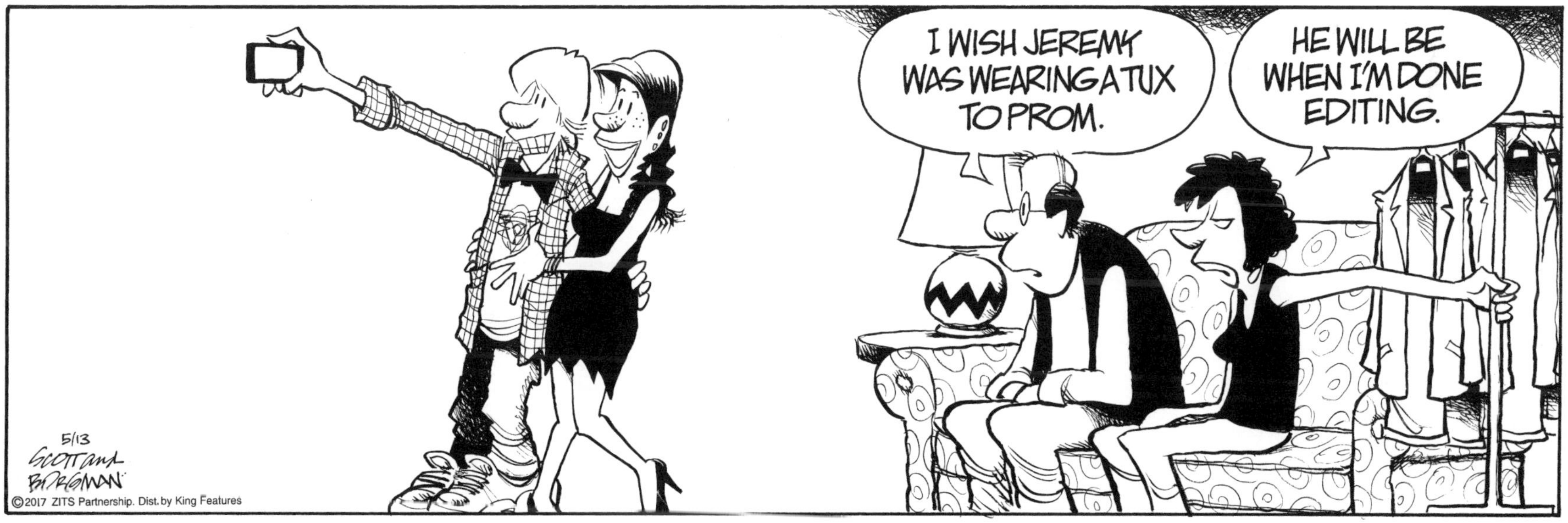
I WISH JEREMY WAS WEARING A TUX TO PROM.
HE WILL BE WHEN I'M DONE EDITING.
5/13
SCOTT and BORGMAN
©2017 ZITS Partnership. Dist. by King Features

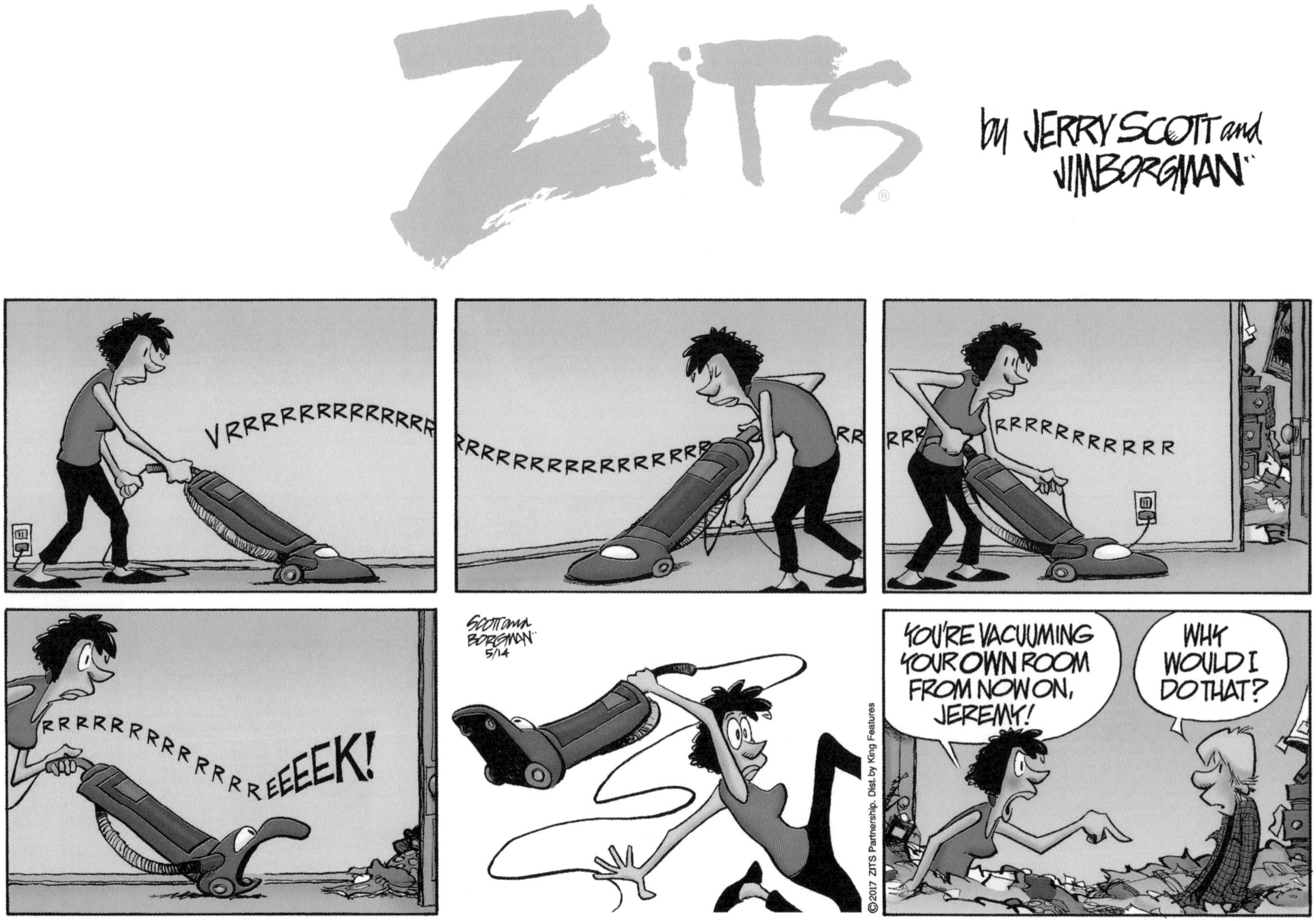
ZITS
by JERRY SCOTT and JIM BORGMAN
VRRRRRRRRRRRRR
RRRRRRRRRRRRRRRR
RR
RRR
RRRRRRRRRRR
RRRRRRRRRRRRRRRREEEEK!
SCOTT and BORGMAN 5/14
©2017 ZITS Partnership. Dist. by King Features
YOU'RE VACUUMING YOUR OWN ROOM FROM NOW ON, JEREMY!
WHY WOULD I DO THAT?

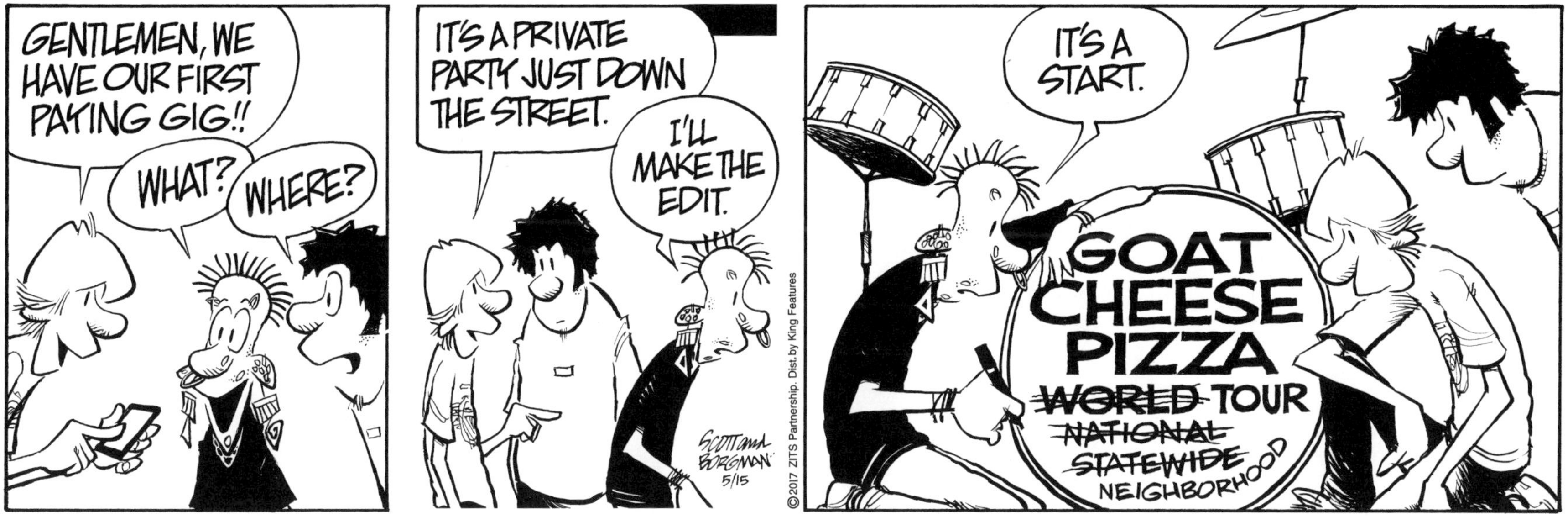
GENTLEMEN, WE HAVE OUR FIRST PAYING GIG!!
WHAT?
WHERE?
IT'S A PRIVATE PARTY JUST DOWN THE STREET.
I'LL MAKE THE EDIT.
SCOTT and BORGMAN 5/15
©2017 ZITS Partnership. Dist. by King Features
IT'S A START.
GOAT CHEESE PIZZA
~~WORLD~~ TOUR
~~NATIONAL~~
~~STATEWIDE~~
NEIGHBORHOOD

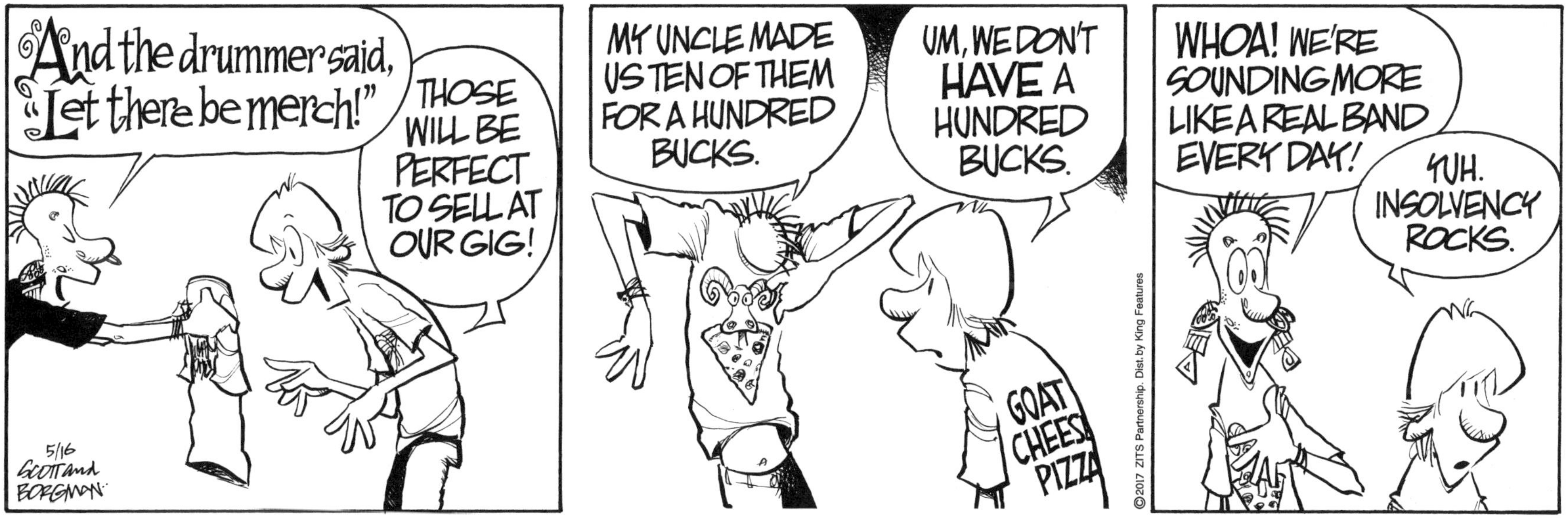
And the drummer said, "Let there be merch!"
THOSE WILL BE PERFECT TO SELL AT OUR GIG!
5/16 SCOTT and BORGMAN
MY UNCLE MADE US TEN OF THEM FOR A HUNDRED BUCKS.
UM, WE DON'T **HAVE** A HUNDRED BUCKS.
GOAT CHEESE PIZZA
©2017 ZITS Partnership. Dist. by King Features
WHOA! WE'RE SOUNDING MORE LIKE A REAL BAND EVERY DAY!
YUH. INSOLVENCY ROCKS.

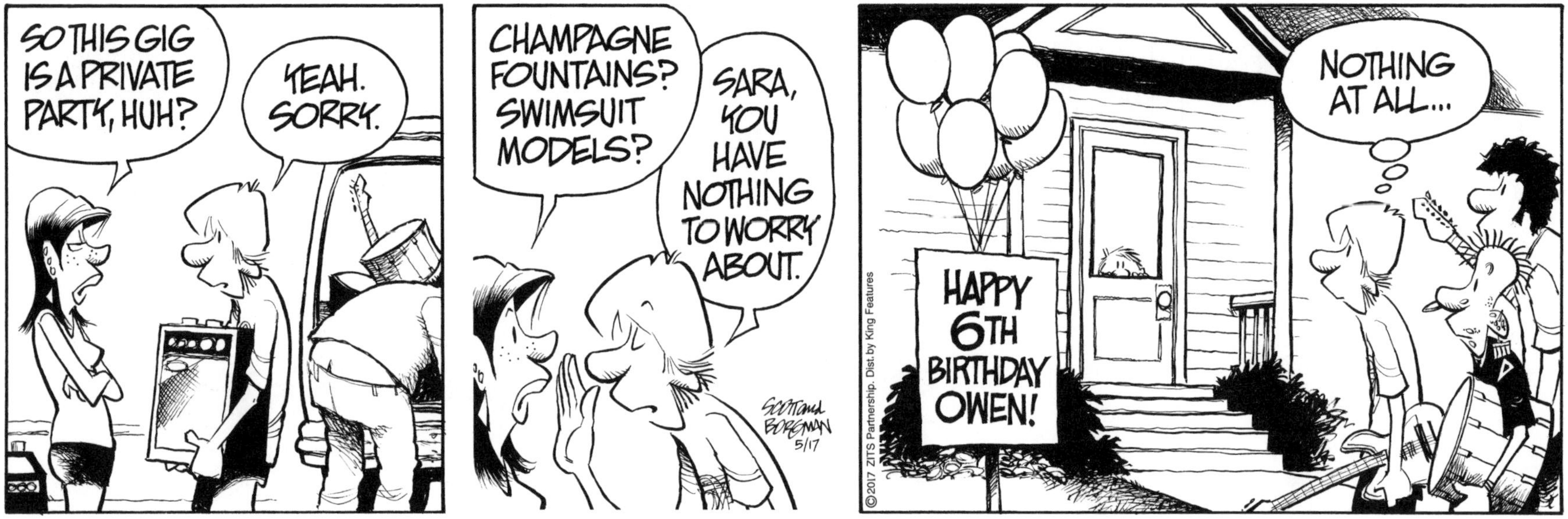
SO THIS GIG IS A PRIVATE PARTY, HUH?
YEAH. SORRY.
CHAMPAGNE FOUNTAINS? SWIMSUIT MODELS?
SARA, YOU HAVE NOTHING TO WORRY ABOUT.
SCOTT and BORGMAN 5/17
HAPPY 6TH BIRTHDAY OWEN!
NOTHING AT ALL...
©2017 ZITS Partnership. Dist. by King Features

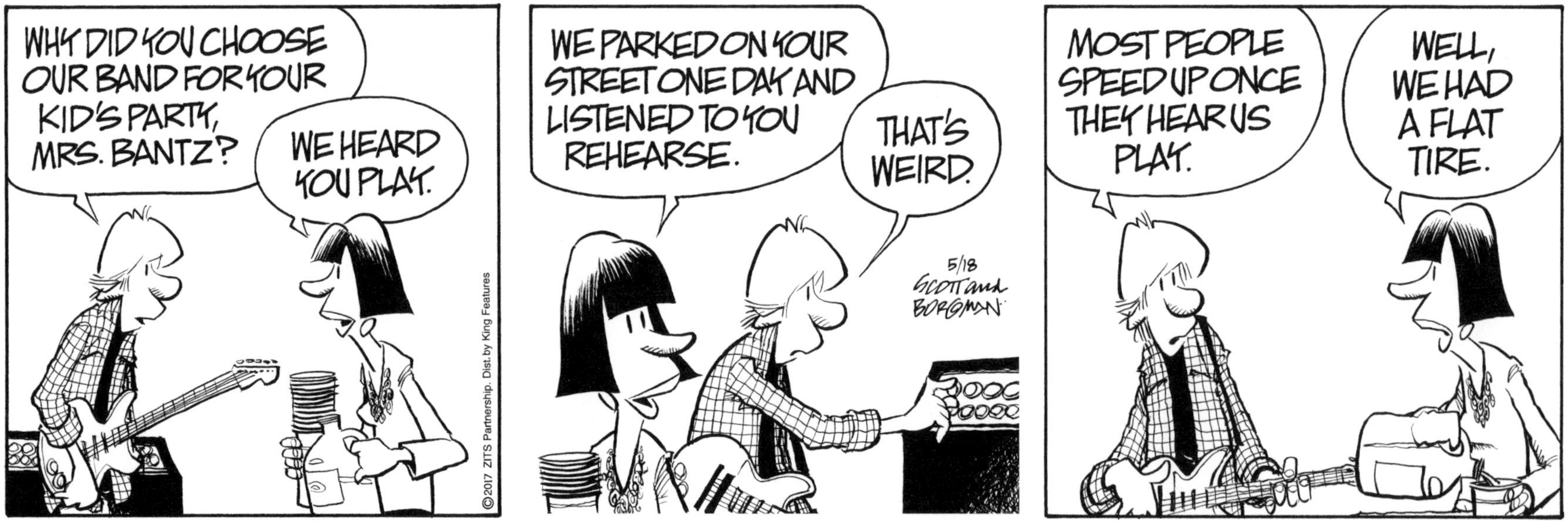
WHY DID YOU CHOOSE OUR BAND FOR YOUR KID'S PARTY, MRS. BANTZ?
WE HEARD YOU PLAY.
©2017 ZITS Partnership. Dist. by King Features
WE PARKED ON YOUR STREET ONE DAY AND LISTENED TO YOU REHEARSE.
THAT'S WEIRD.
5/18 SCOTT and BORGMAN
MOST PEOPLE SPEED UP ONCE THEY HEAR US PLAY.
WELL, WE HAD A FLAT TIRE.

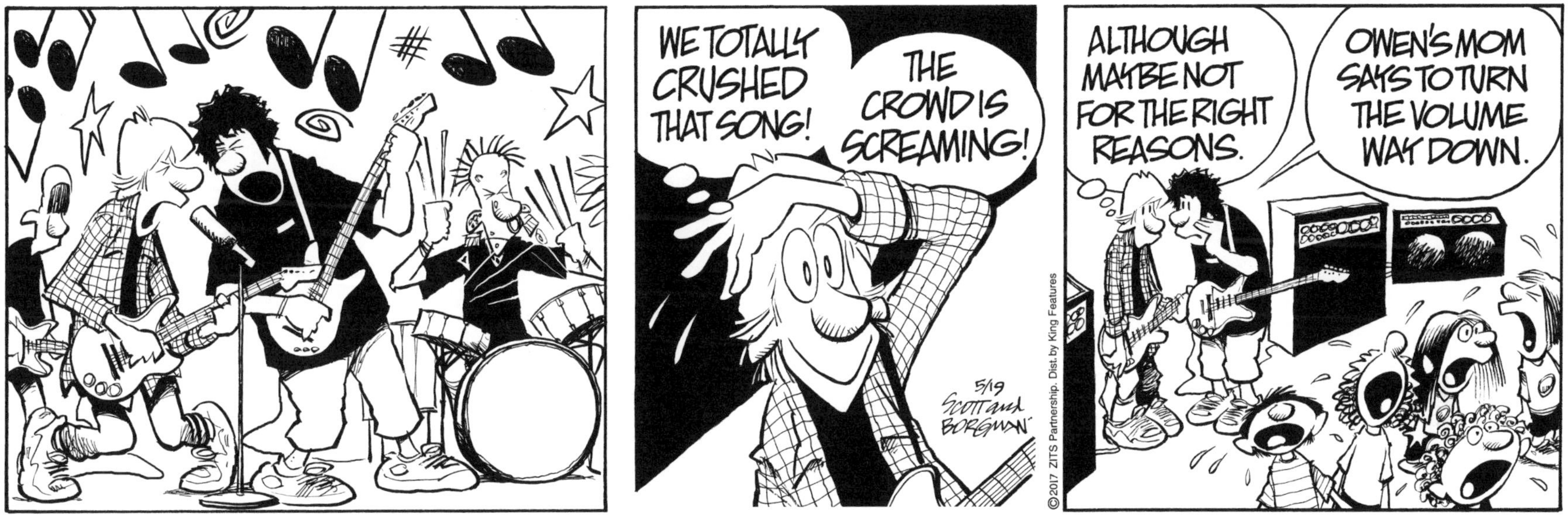
WE TOTALLY CRUSHED THAT SONG!
THE CROWD IS SCREAMING!
5/19 SCOTT and BORGMAN
© 2017 ZITS Partnership. Dist. by King Features
ALTHOUGH MAYBE NOT FOR THE RIGHT REASONS.
OWEN'S MOM SAYS TO TURN THE VOLUME WAY DOWN.

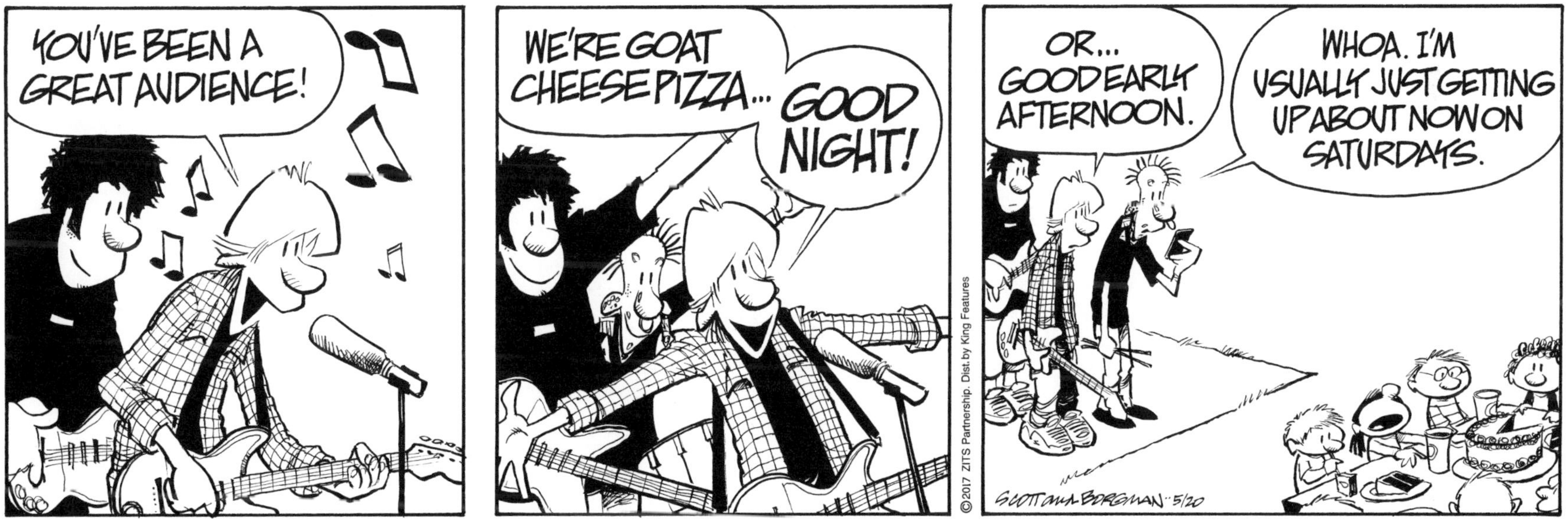
YOU'VE BEEN A GREAT AUDIENCE!
WE'RE GOAT CHEESE PIZZA...
GOOD NIGHT!
© 2017 ZITS Partnership. Dist. by King Features
OR... GOOD EARLY AFTERNOON.
WHOA. I'M USUALLY JUST GETTING UP ABOUT NOW ON SATURDAYS.
SCOTT and BORGMAN 5/20

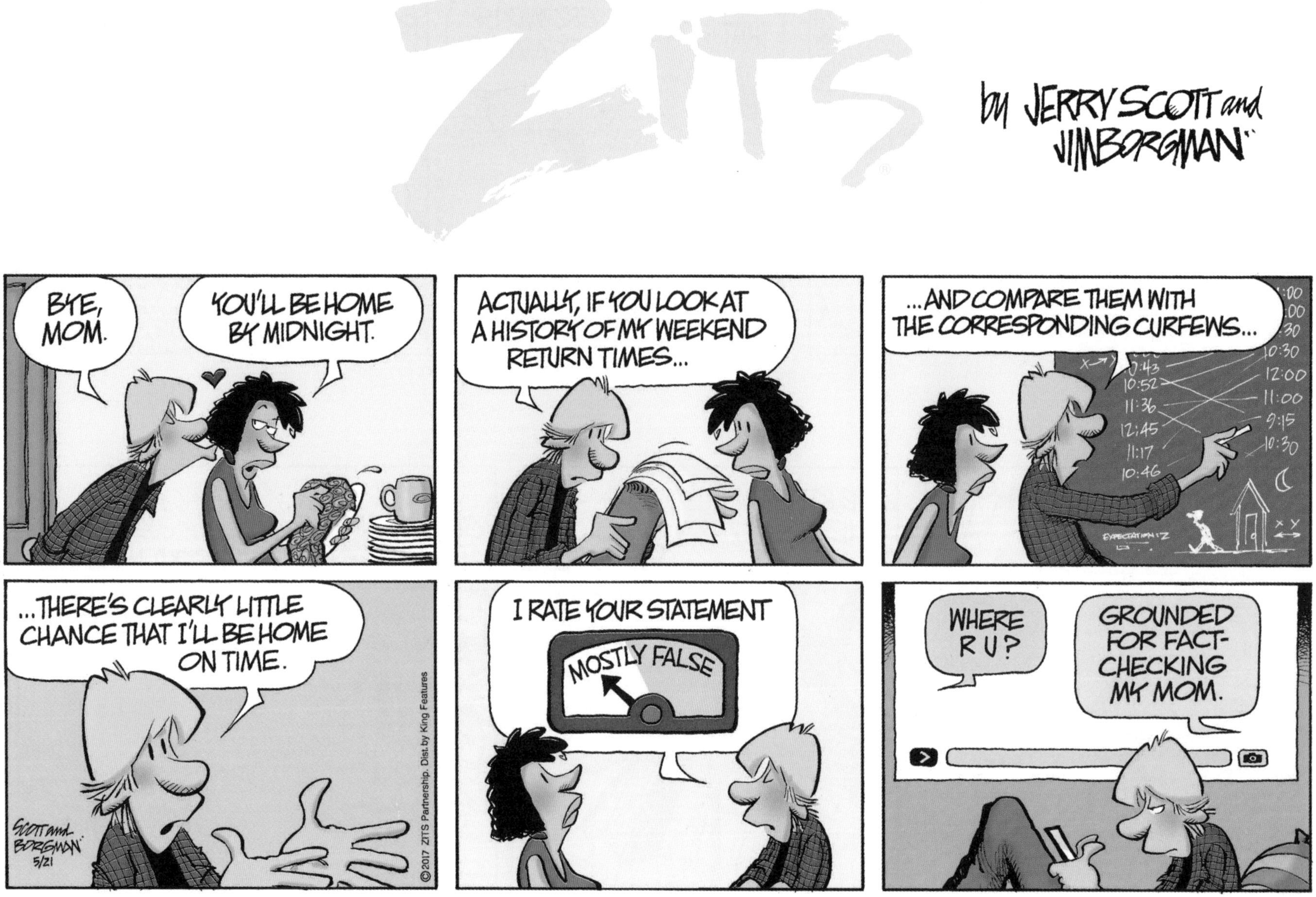
ZITS
by JERRY SCOTT and JIM BORGMAN
BYE, MOM.
YOU'LL BE HOME BY MIDNIGHT.
ACTUALLY, IF YOU LOOK AT A HISTORY OF MY WEEKEND RETURN TIMES...
...AND COMPARE THEM WITH THE CORRESPONDING CURFEWS...
...THERE'S CLEARLY LITTLE CHANCE THAT I'LL BE HOME ON TIME.
I RATE YOUR STATEMENT
MOSTLY FALSE
WHERE R U?
GROUNDED FOR FACT-CHECKING MY MOM.
SCOTT and BORGMAN 5/21
©2017 ZITS Partnership. Dist. by King Features

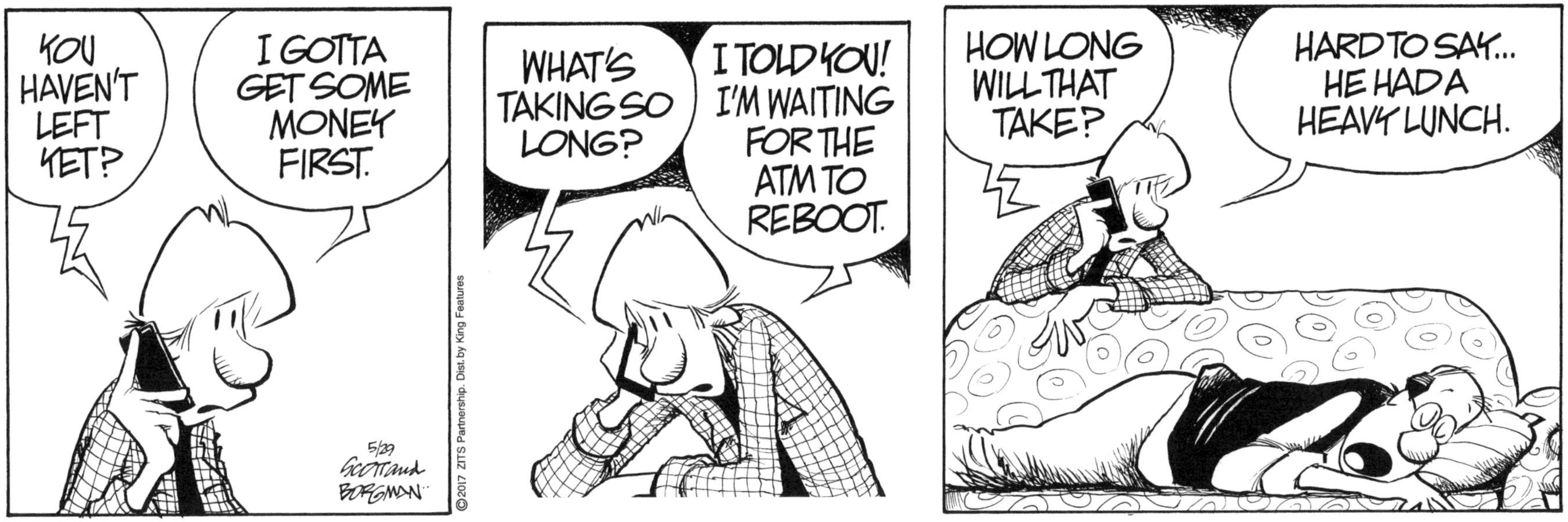
YOU HAVEN'T LEFT YET?
I GOTTA GET SOME MONEY FIRST.
5/29 SCOTT and BORGMAN
©2017 ZITS Partnership. Dist. by King Features
WHAT'S TAKING SO LONG?
I TOLD YOU! I'M WAITING FOR THE ATM TO REBOOT.
HOW LONG WILL THAT TAKE?
HARD TO SAY... HE HAD A HEAVY LUNCH.

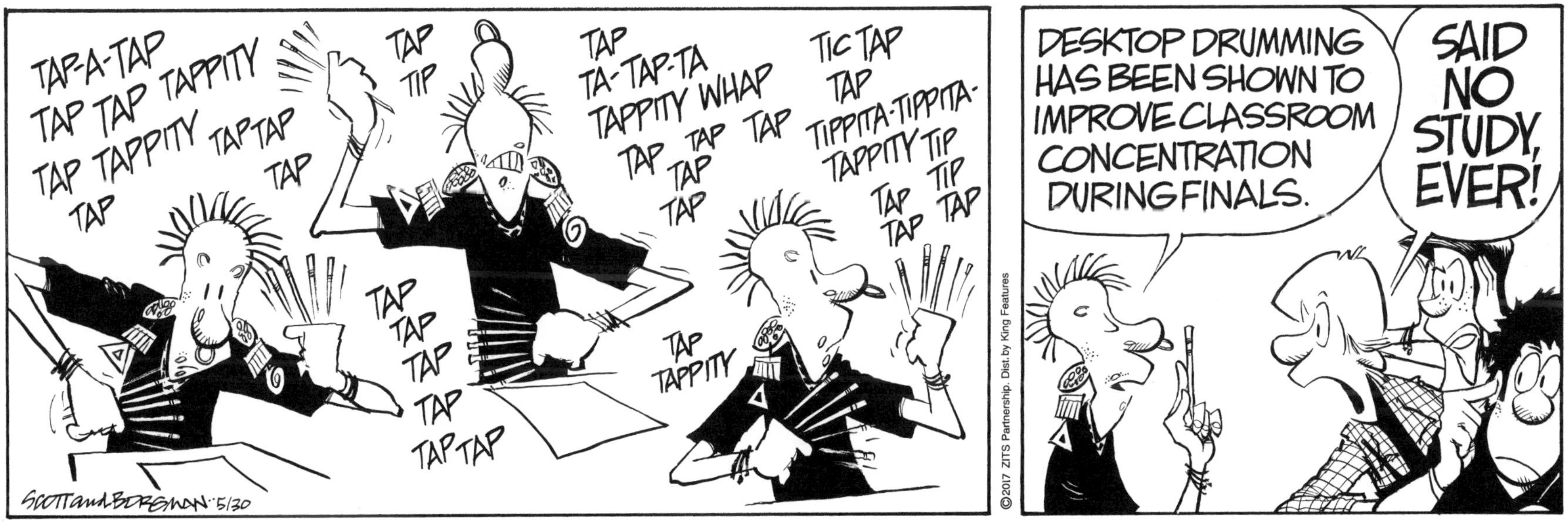
TAP-A-TAP TAP TAP TAPPITY TAP TAPPITY TAP TAP TAP TAP
TAP TIP
TAP TA-TAP-TA TAPPITY WHAP TAP TAP TAP TAP TAP
TIC TAP TAP TIPPITA-TIPPITA-TAPPITY TIP TAP TIP TAP TAP
TAP TAP TAP TAP TAP TAP
TAP TAPPITY
SCOTT and BORGMAN 5/30
©2017 ZITS Partnership. Dist. by King Features
DESKTOP DRUMMING HAS BEEN SHOWN TO IMPROVE CLASSROOM CONCENTRATION DURING FINALS.
SAID NO STUDY, EVER!

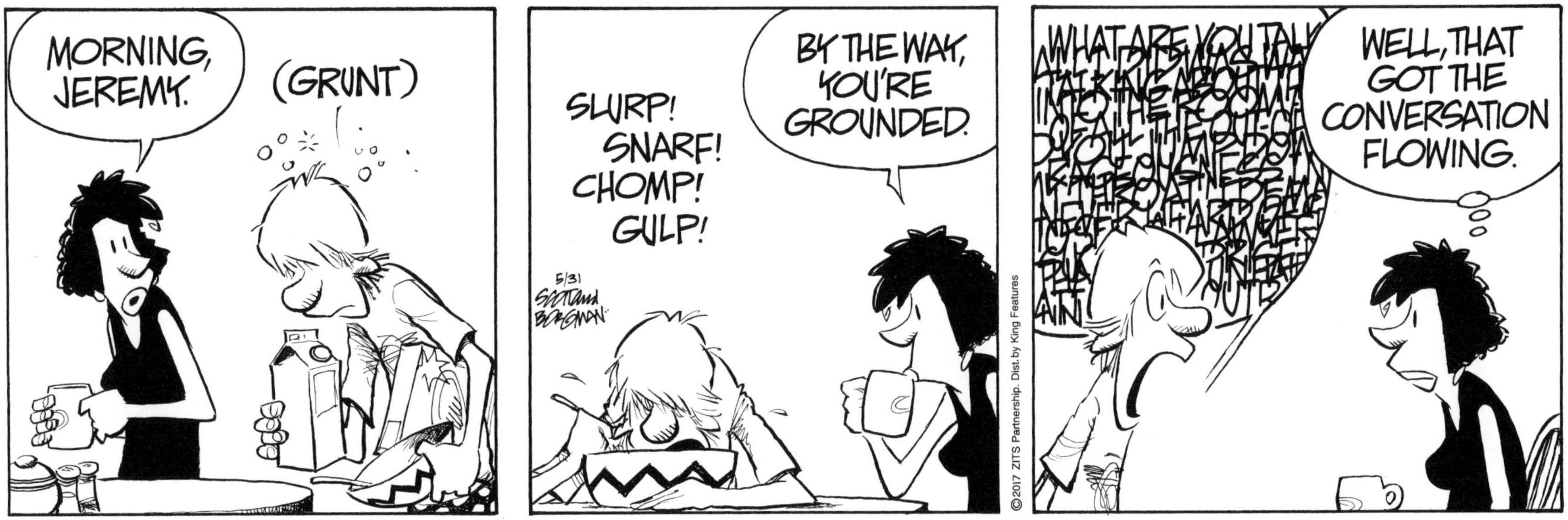
MORNING, JEREMY.
(GRUNT)
SLURP! SNARF! CHOMP! GULP!
BY THE WAY, YOU'RE GROUNDED.
5/31 SCOTT and BORGMAN
©2017 ZITS Partnership. Dist. by King Features
WELL, THAT GOT THE CONVERSATION FLOWING.

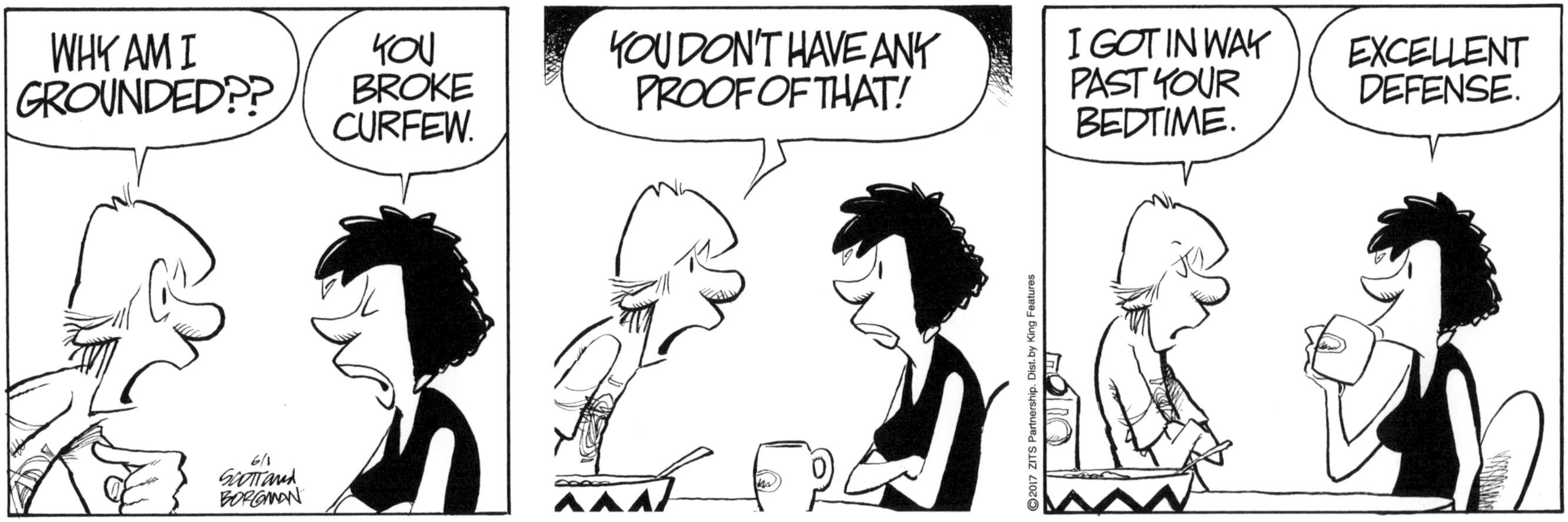
WHY AM I GROUNDED??
YOU BROKE CURFEW.
6/1 SCOTT and BORGMAN
YOU DON'T HAVE ANY PROOF OF THAT!
©2017 ZITS Partnership. Dist. by King Features
I GOT IN WAY PAST YOUR BEDTIME.
EXCELLENT DEFENSE.

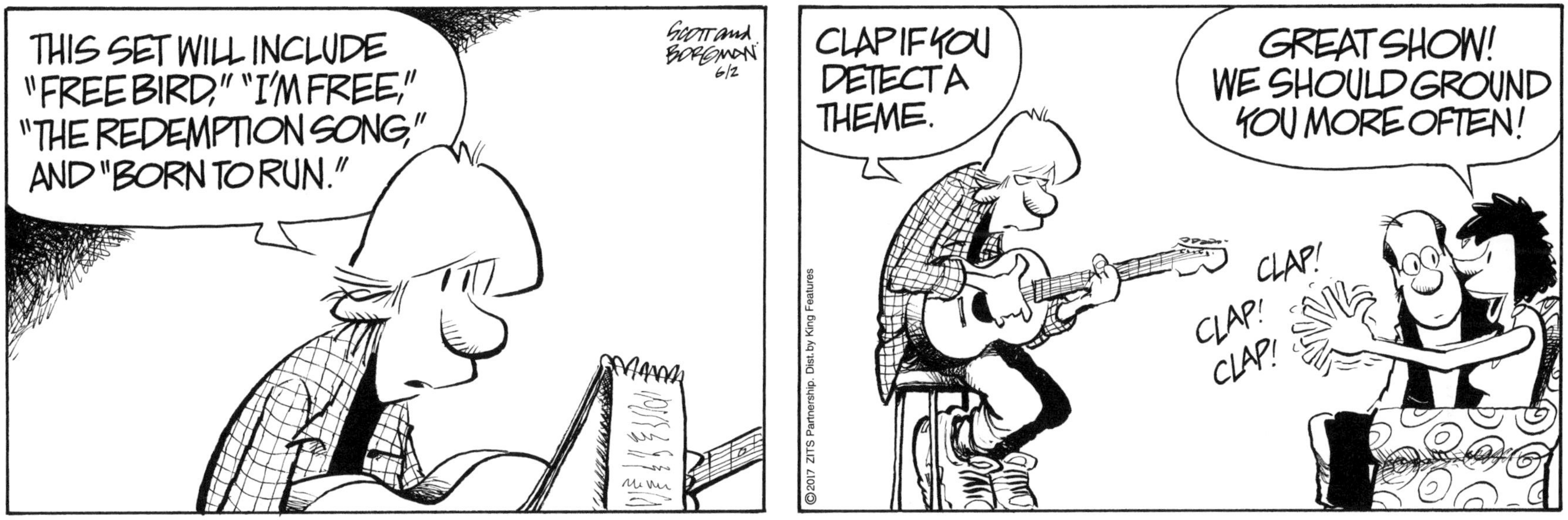
THIS SET WILL INCLUDE "FREE BIRD," "I'M FREE," "THE REDEMPTION SONG," AND "BORN TO RUN."
SCOTT AND BORGMAN 6/2
CLAP IF YOU DETECT A THEME.
GREAT SHOW! WE SHOULD GROUND YOU MORE OFTEN!
CLAP! CLAP! CLAP!
©2017 ZITS Partnership. Dist. by King Features

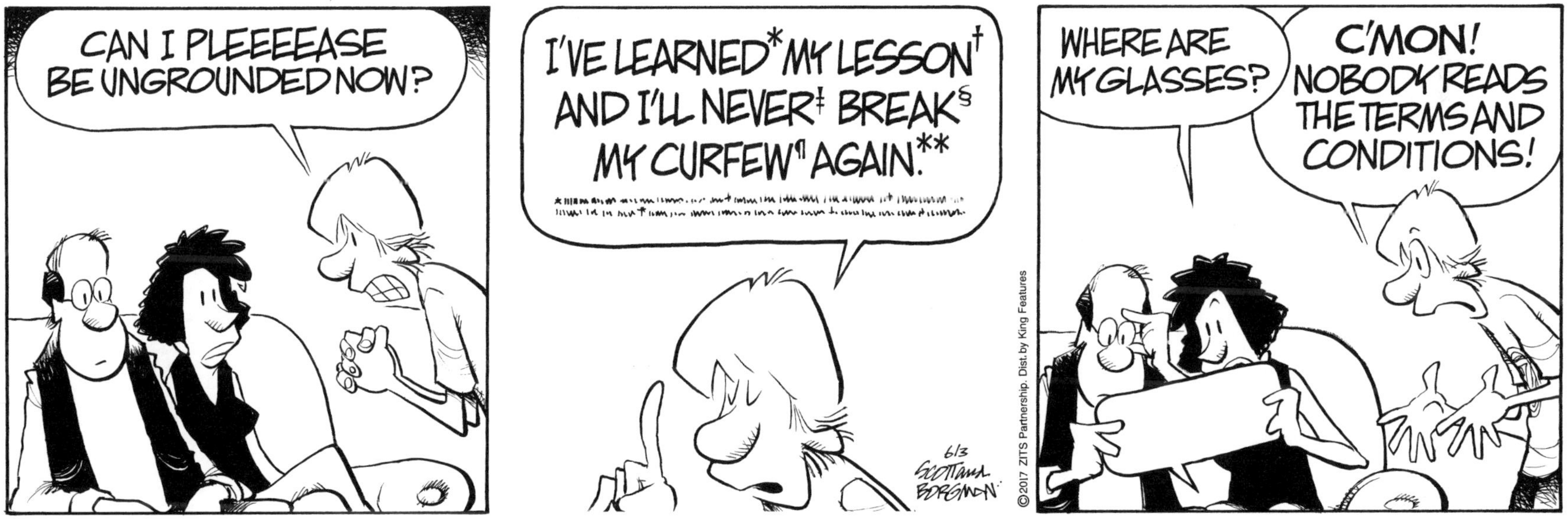
CAN I PLEEEEEASE BE UNGROUNDED NOW?
I'VE LEARNED* MY LESSON† AND I'LL NEVER‡ BREAK§ MY CURFEW¶ AGAIN.**
6/3 SCOTT AND BORGMAN
WHERE ARE MY GLASSES?
C'MON! NOBODY READS THE TERMS AND CONDITIONS!
©2017 ZITS Partnership. Dist. by King Features

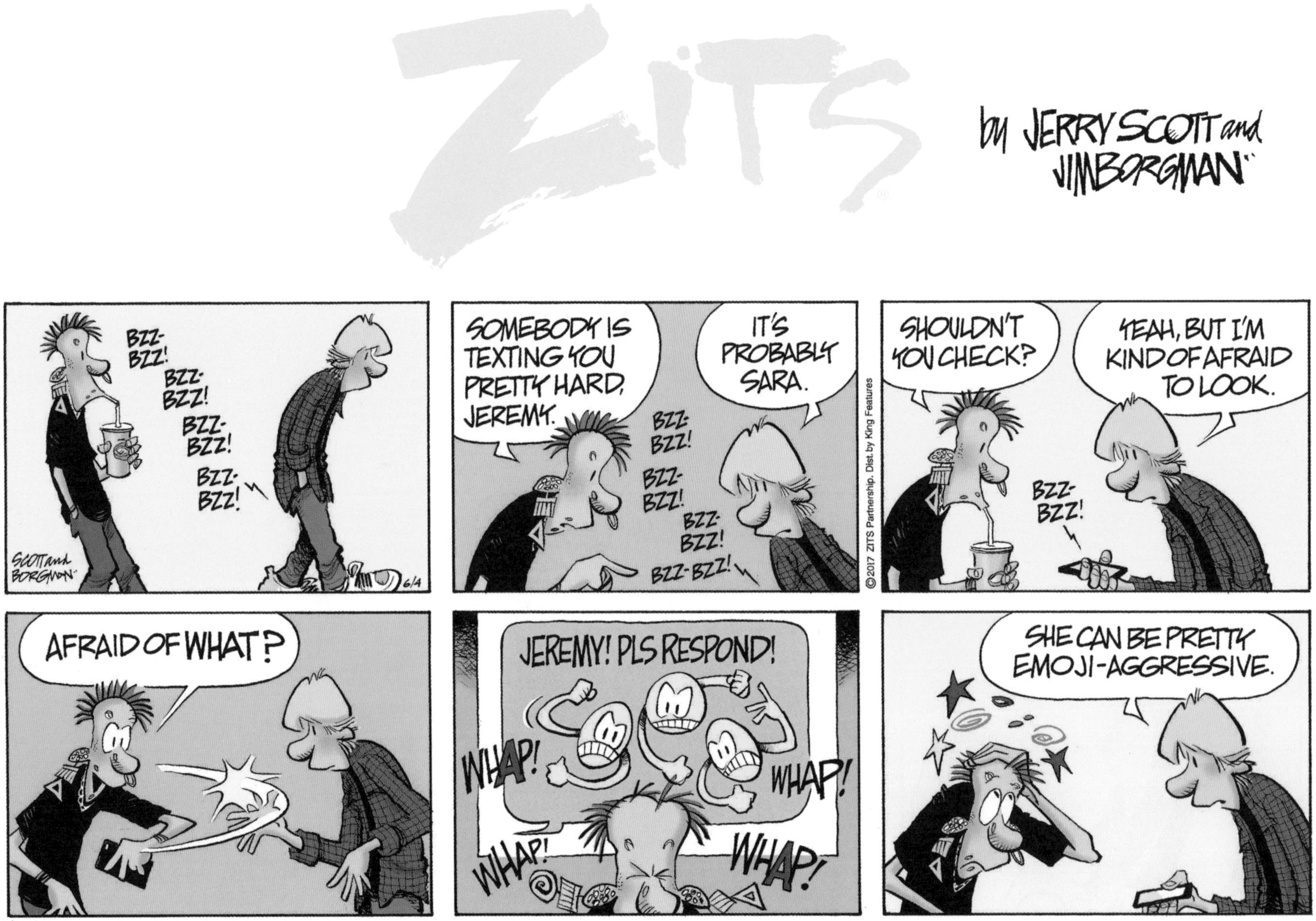
ZITS
by JERRY SCOTT and JIM BORGMAN
BZZ-BZZ! BZZ-BZZ! BZZ-BZZ! BZZ-BZZ!
SCOTT and BORGMAN
6/4
SOMEBODY IS TEXTING YOU PRETTY HARD, JEREMY.
BZZ-BZZ! BZZ-BZZ! BZZ-BZZ! BZZ-BZZ!
IT'S PROBABLY SARA.
©2017 ZITS Partnership. Dist. by King Features
SHOULDN'T YOU CHECK?
YEAH, BUT I'M KIND OF AFRAID TO LOOK.
BZZ-BZZ!
AFRAID OF WHAT?
JEREMY! PLS RESPOND!
WHAP! WHAP! WHAP! WHAP!
SHE CAN BE PRETTY EMOJI-AGGRESSIVE.

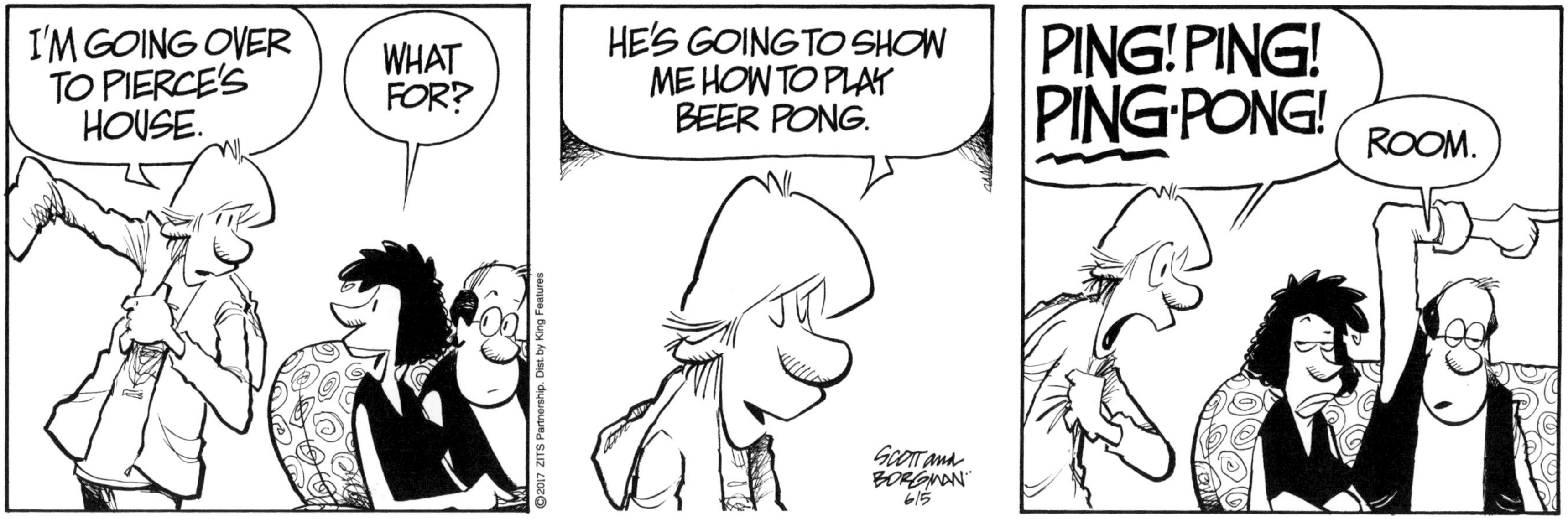
I'M GOING OVER TO PIERCE'S HOUSE.
WHAT FOR?
HE'S GOING TO SHOW ME HOW TO PLAY BEER PONG.
PING! PING! PING-PONG!
ROOM.
SCOTT and BORGMAN 6/5
©2017 ZITS Partnership. Dist. by King Features

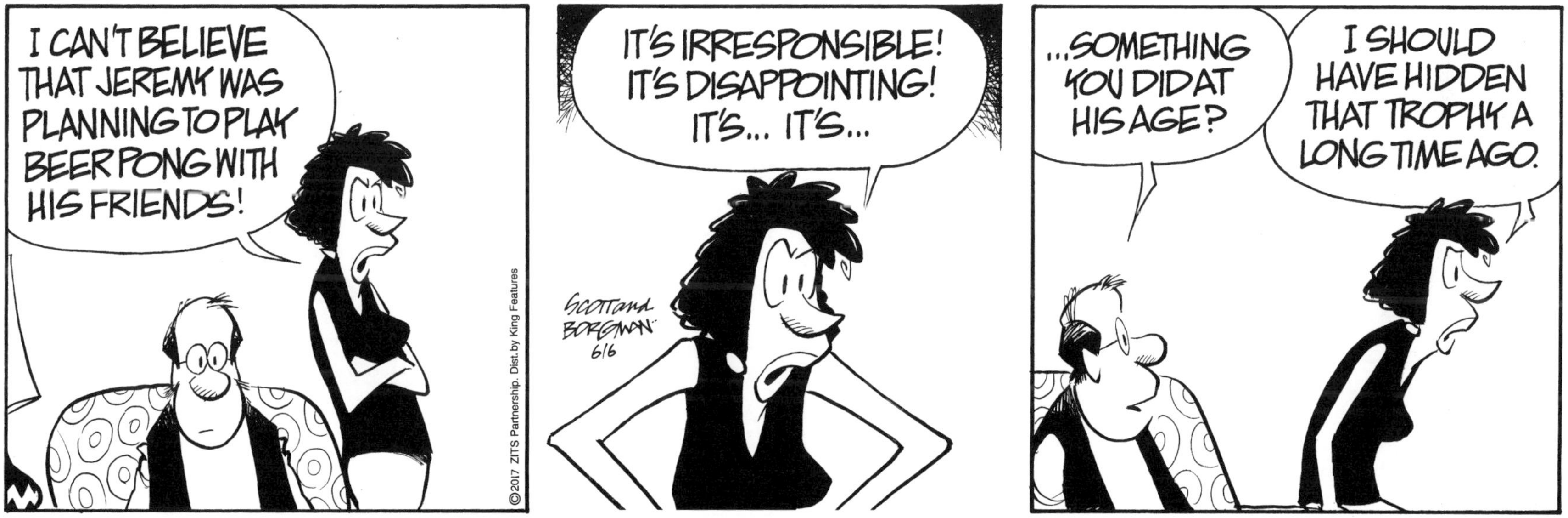
I CAN'T BELIEVE THAT JEREMY WAS PLANNING TO PLAY BEER PONG WITH HIS FRIENDS!
IT'S IRRESPONSIBLE! IT'S DISAPPOINTING! IT'S... IT'S...
...SOMETHING YOU DID AT HIS AGE?
I SHOULD HAVE HIDDEN THAT TROPHY A LONG TIME AGO.
SCOTT and BORGMAN 6/6
©2017 ZITS Partnership. Dist. by King Features

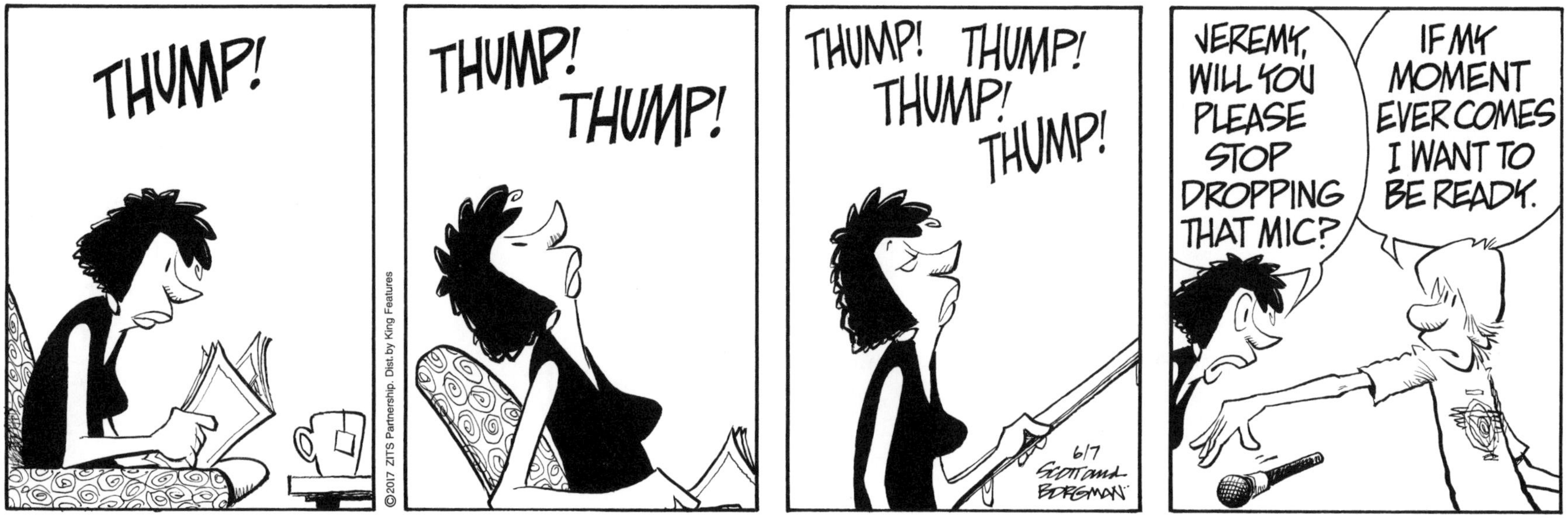
THUMP!
THUMP! THUMP!
THUMP! THUMP! THUMP! THUMP!
JEREMY, WILL YOU PLEASE STOP DROPPING THAT MIC?
IF MY MOMENT EVER COMES I WANT TO BE READY.
©2017 ZITS Partnership. Dist.by King Features
6/7 SCOTT and BORGMAN

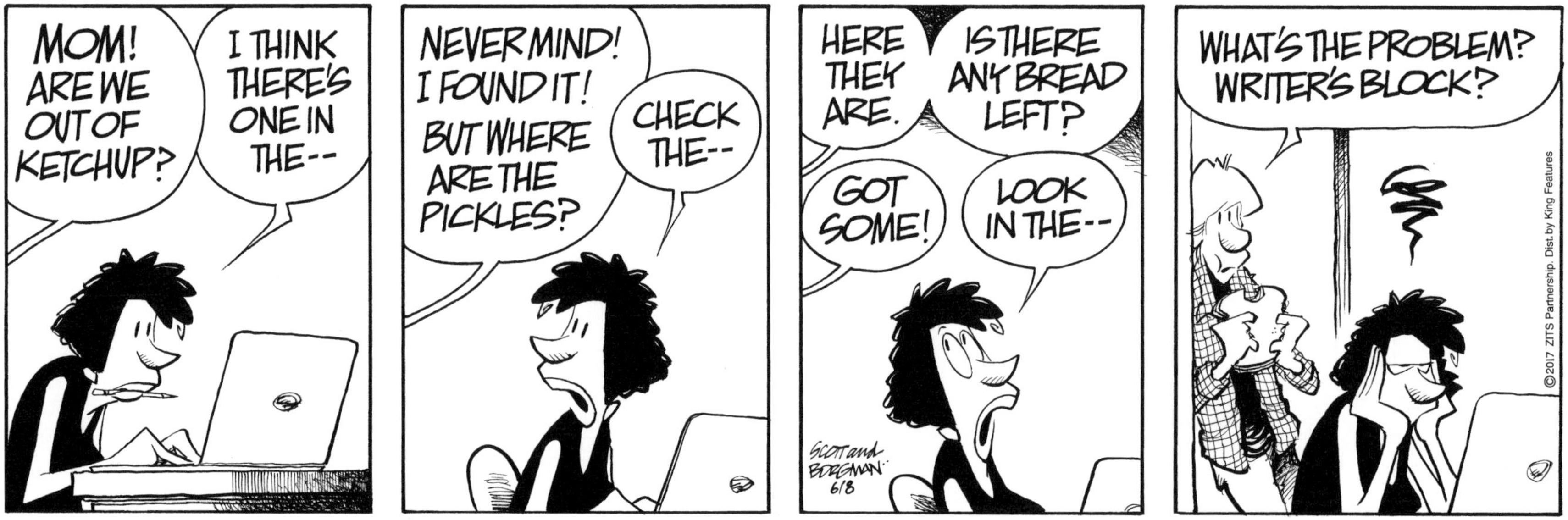
MOM! ARE WE OUT OF KETCHUP?
I THINK THERE'S ONE IN THE--
NEVER MIND! I FOUND IT! BUT WHERE ARE THE PICKLES?
CHECK THE--
HERE THEY ARE.
IS THERE ANY BREAD LEFT?
GOT SOME!
LOOK IN THE--
SCOTT and BORGMAN 6/8
WHAT'S THE PROBLEM? WRITER'S BLOCK?
©2017 ZITS Partnership. Dist.by King Features

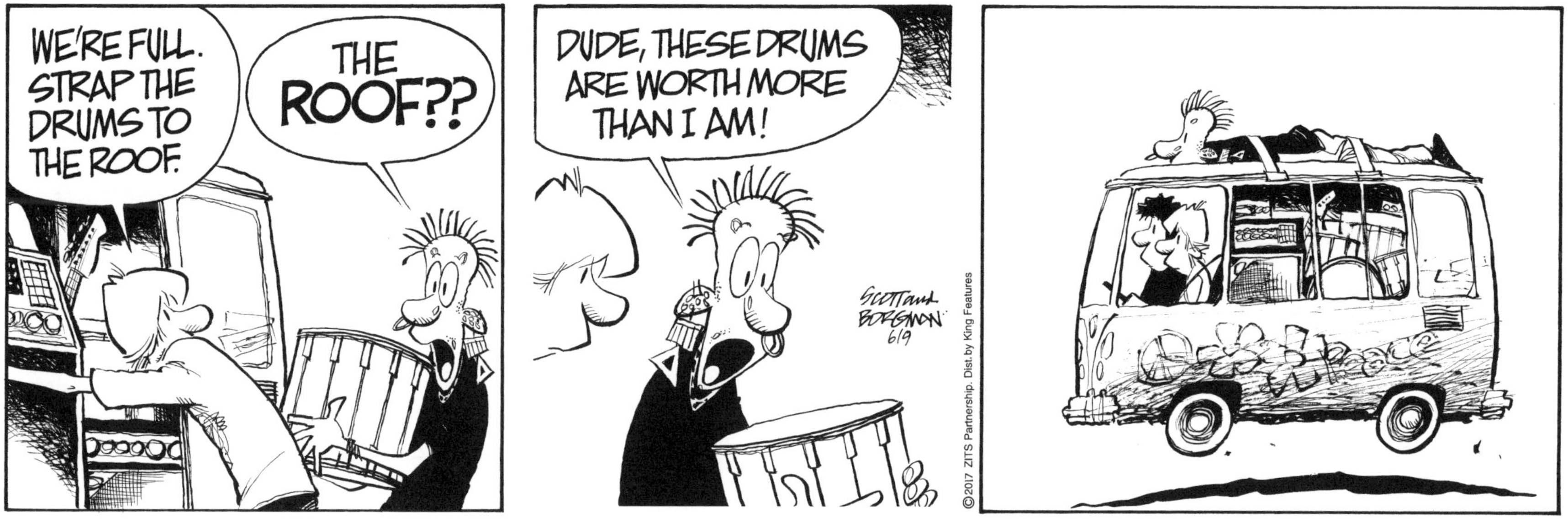
WE'RE FULL. STRAP THE DRUMS TO THE ROOF.
THE ROOF??
DUDE, THESE DRUMS ARE WORTH MORE THAN I AM!
SCOTT and BORGMAN 6/9
©2017 ZITS Partnership. Dist. by King Features

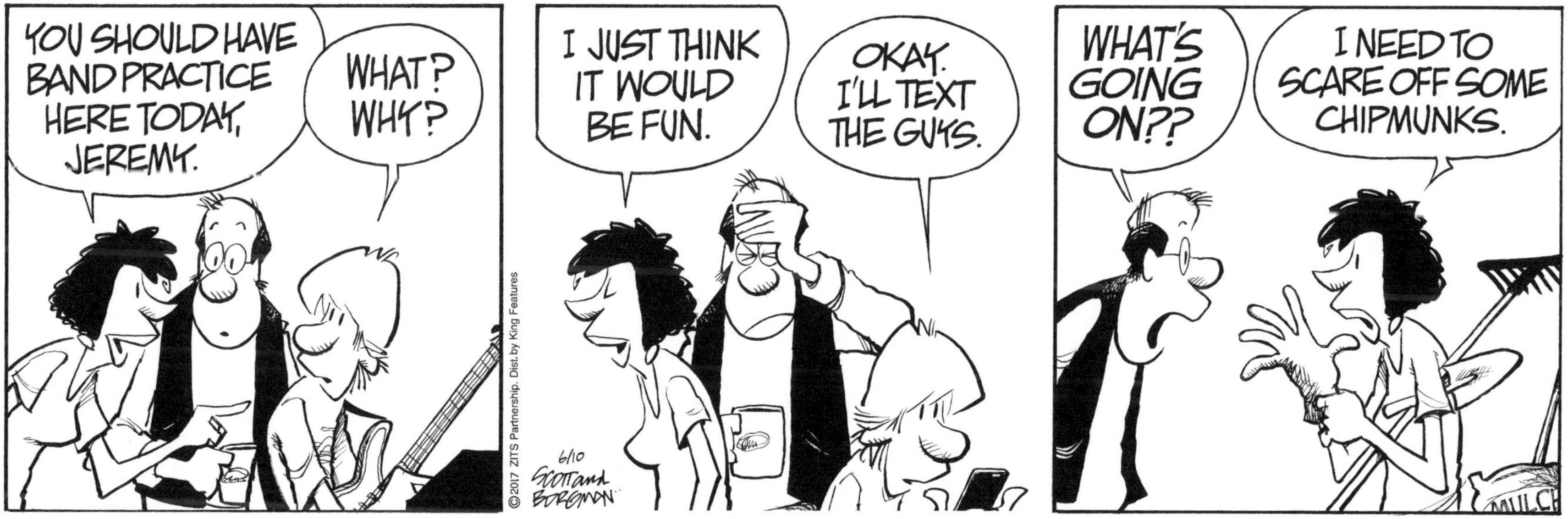
YOU SHOULD HAVE BAND PRACTICE HERE TODAY, JEREMY.
WHAT? WHY?
©2017 ZITS Partnership. Dist. by King Features
6/10 SCOTT and BORGMAN
I JUST THINK IT WOULD BE FUN.
OKAY. I'LL TEXT THE GUYS.
WHAT'S GOING ON??
I NEED TO SCARE OFF SOME CHIPMUNKS.
MULCH

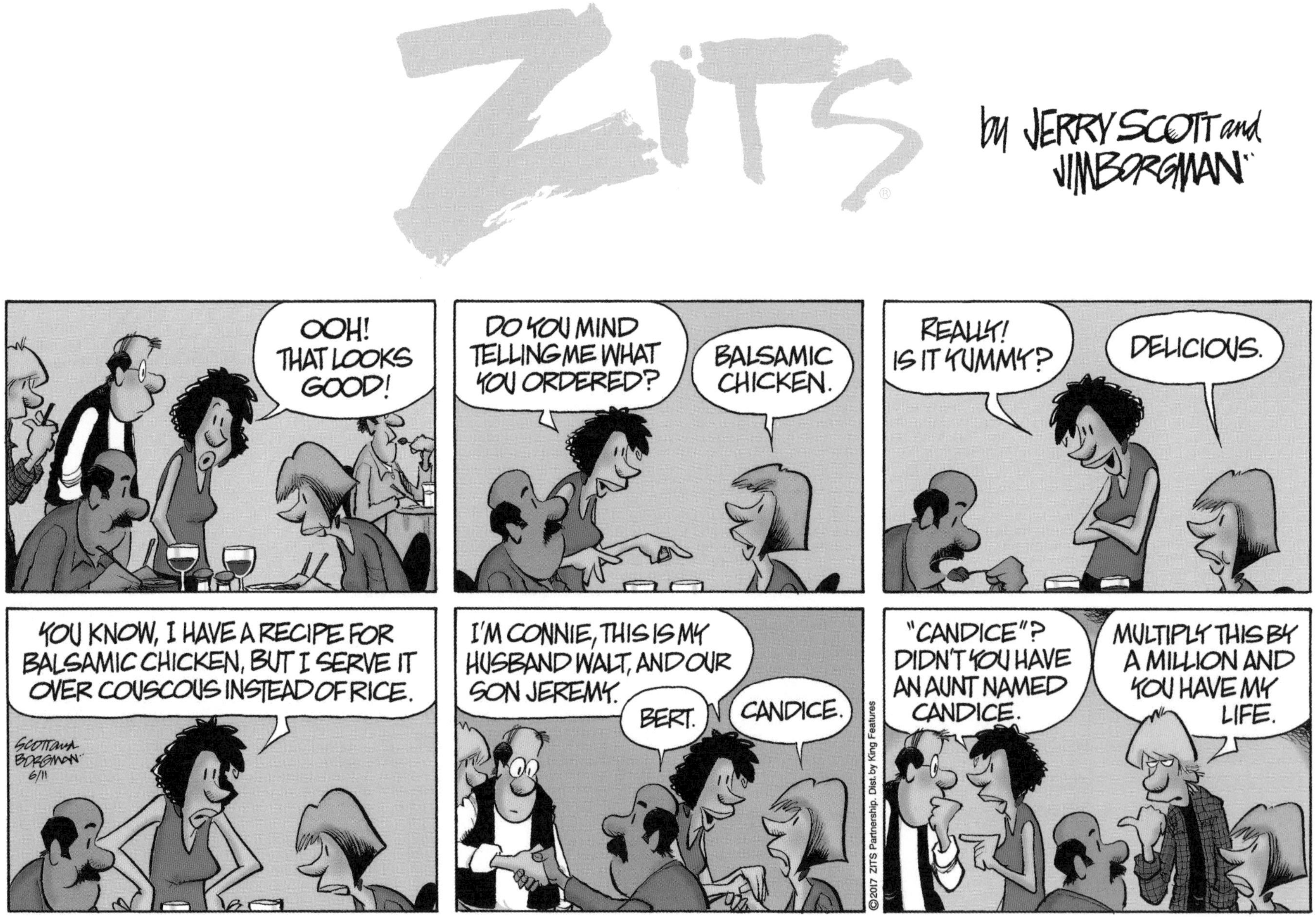
ZITS
by JERRY SCOTT and JIM BORGMAN
OOH! THAT LOOKS GOOD!
DO YOU MIND TELLING ME WHAT YOU ORDERED?
BALSAMIC CHICKEN.
REALLY! IS IT YUMMY?
DELICIOUS.
YOU KNOW, I HAVE A RECIPE FOR BALSAMIC CHICKEN, BUT I SERVE IT OVER COUSCOUS INSTEAD OF RICE.
I'M CONNIE, THIS IS MY HUSBAND WALT, AND OUR SON JEREMY.
BERT.
CANDICE.
©2017 ZITS Partnership. Dist. by King Features
"CANDICE"? DIDN'T YOU HAVE AN AUNT NAMED CANDICE.
MULTIPLY THIS BY A MILLION AND YOU HAVE MY LIFE.

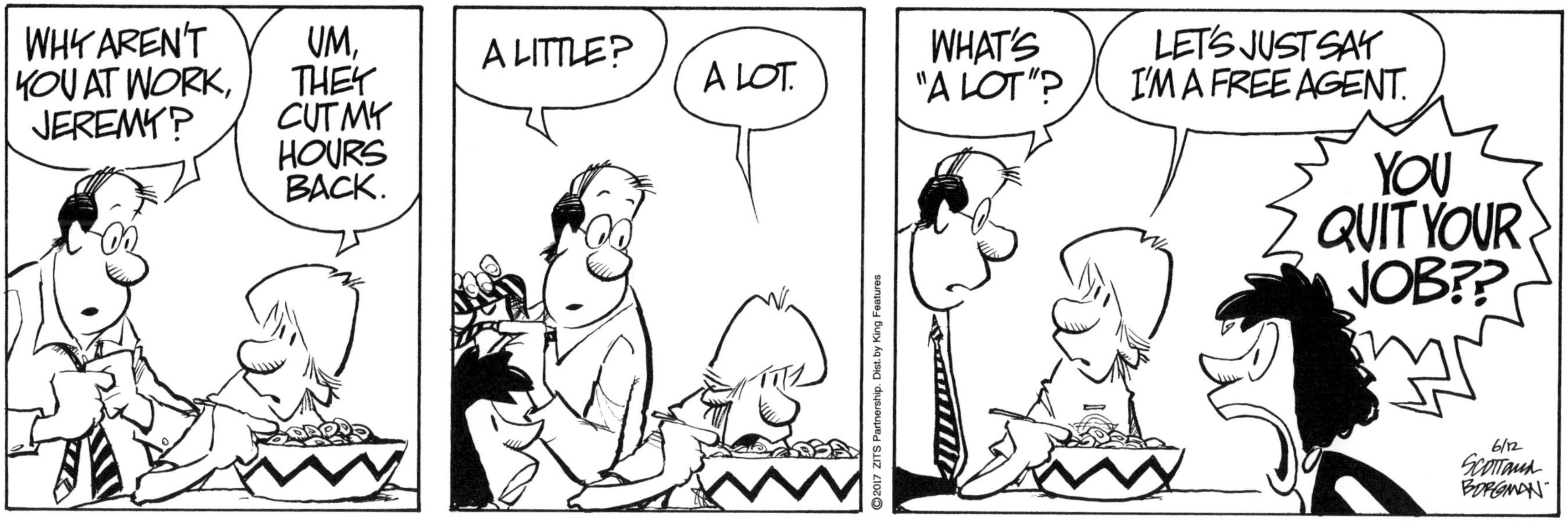
WHY AREN'T YOU AT WORK, JEREMY?
UM, THEY CUT MY HOURS BACK.
A LITTLE?
A LOT.
© 2017 ZITS Partnership. Dist. by King Features
WHAT'S "A LOT"?
LET'S JUST SAY I'M A FREE AGENT.
YOU QUIT YOUR JOB??
6/12
SCOTT and BORGMAN

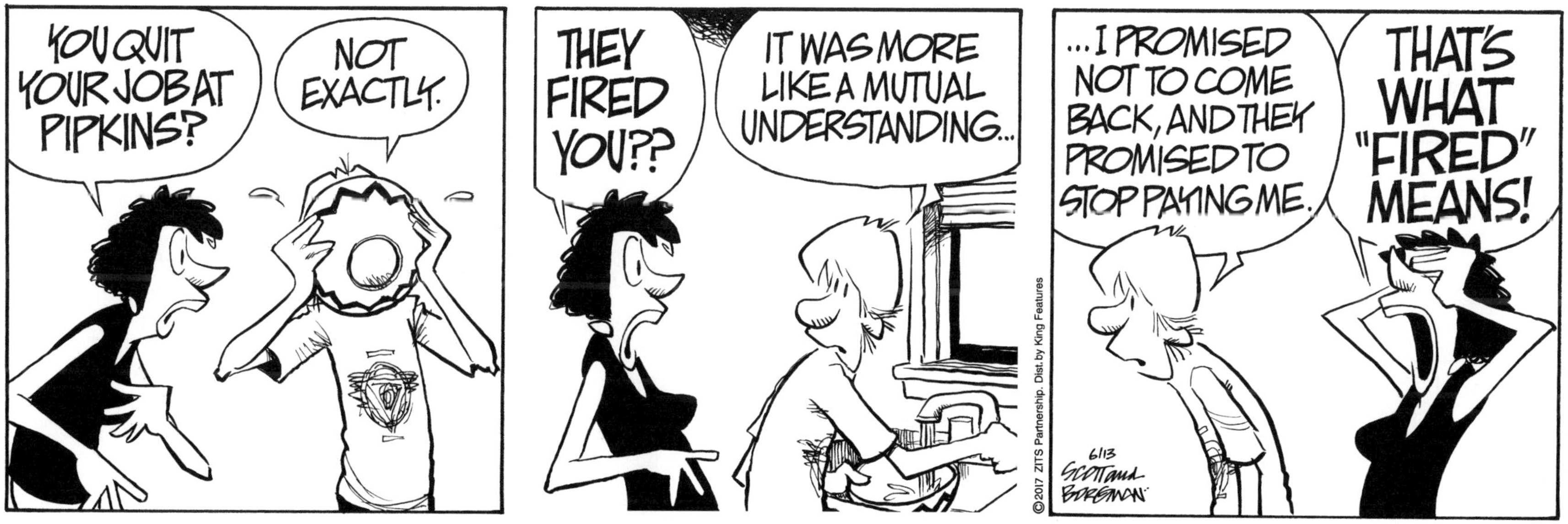
YOU QUIT YOUR JOB AT PIPKINS?
NOT EXACTLY.
THEY FIRED YOU??
IT WAS MORE LIKE A MUTUAL UNDERSTANDING...
© 2017 ZITS Partnership. Dist. by King Features
6/13
SCOTT and BORGMAN
...I PROMISED NOT TO COME BACK, AND THEY PROMISED TO STOP PAYING ME.
THAT'S WHAT "FIRED" MEANS!

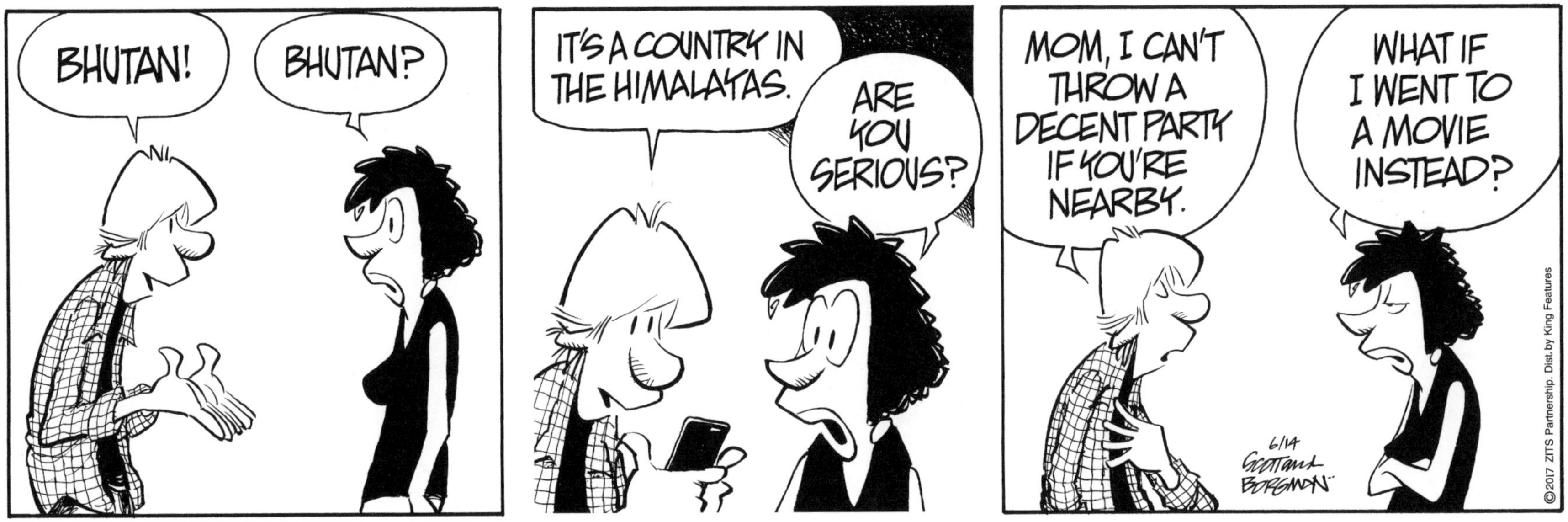
BHUTAN!
BHUTAN?
IT'S A COUNTRY IN THE HIMALAYAS.
ARE YOU SERIOUS?
MOM, I CAN'T THROW A DECENT PARTY IF YOU'RE NEARBY.
WHAT IF I WENT TO A MOVIE INSTEAD?
6/14 SCOTT AND BORGMAN
©2017 ZITS Partnership. Dist. by King Features

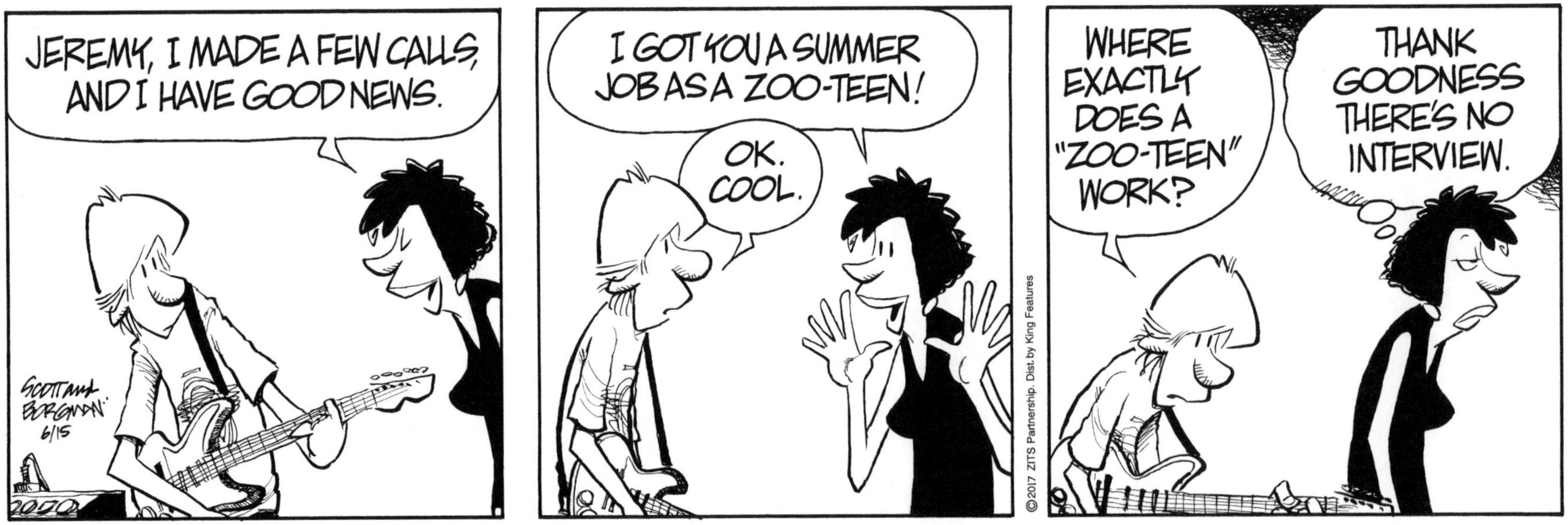
JEREMY, I MADE A FEW CALLS, AND I HAVE GOOD NEWS.
SCOTT AND BORGMAN 6/15
I GOT YOU A SUMMER JOB AS A ZOO-TEEN!
OK. COOL.
©2017 ZITS Partnership. Dist. by King Features
WHERE EXACTLY DOES A "ZOO-TEEN" WORK?
THANK GOODNESS THERE'S NO INTERVIEW.

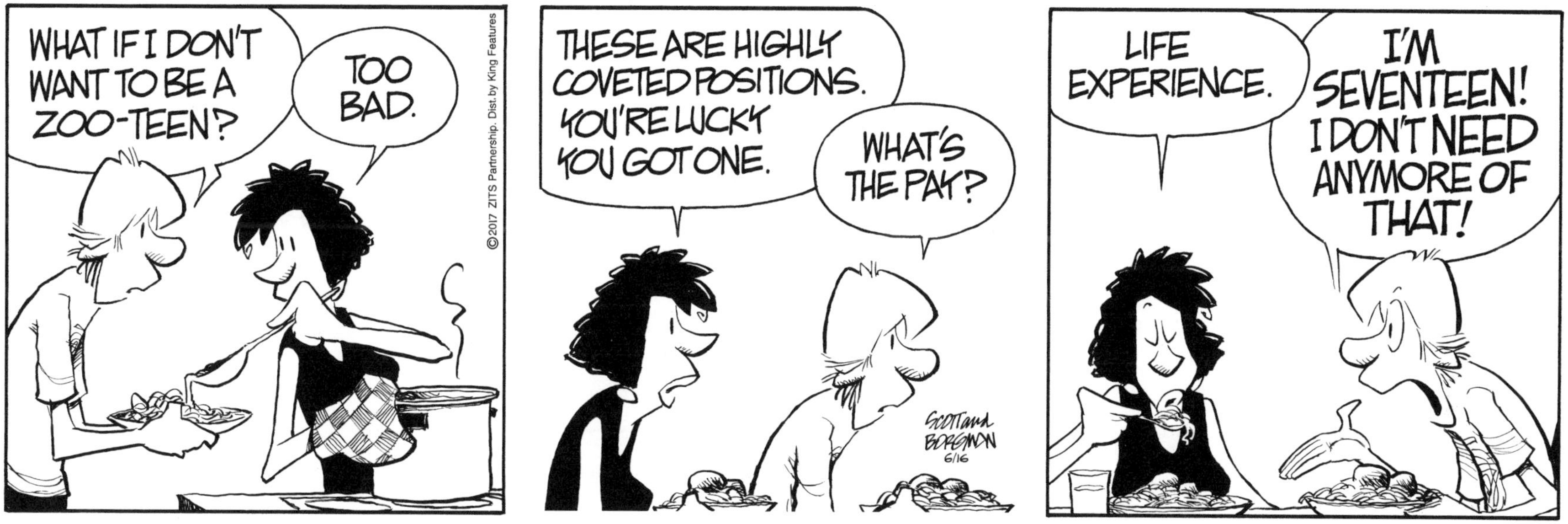
WHAT IF I DON'T WANT TO BE A ZOO-TEEN?
TOO BAD.
©2017 ZITS Partnership. Dist. by King Features
THESE ARE HIGHLY COVETED POSITIONS. YOU'RE LUCKY YOU GOT ONE.
WHAT'S THE PAY?
SCOTT and BORGMAN 6/16
LIFE EXPERIENCE.
I'M SEVENTEEN! I DON'T NEED ANYMORE OF THAT!

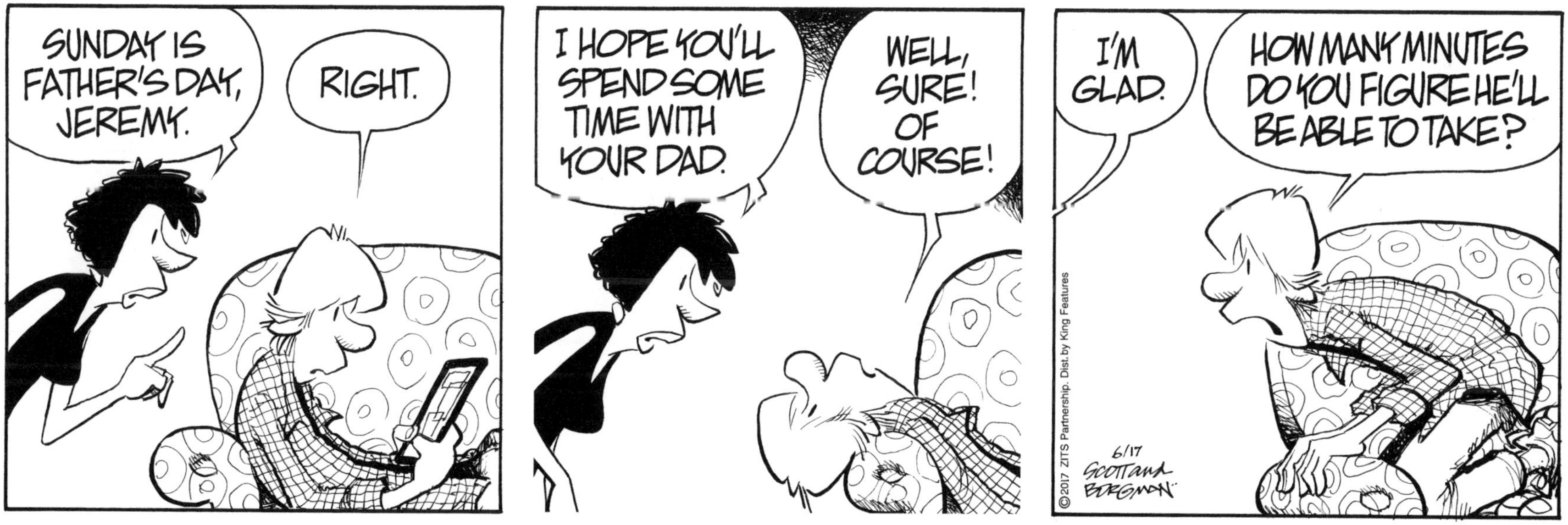
SUNDAY IS FATHER'S DAY, JEREMY.
RIGHT.
I HOPE YOU'LL SPEND SOME TIME WITH YOUR DAD.
WELL, SURE! OF COURSE!
I'M GLAD.
HOW MANY MINUTES DO YOU FIGURE HE'LL BE ABLE TO TAKE?
©2017 ZITS Partnership. Dist. by King Features
6/17 SCOTT and BORGMAN

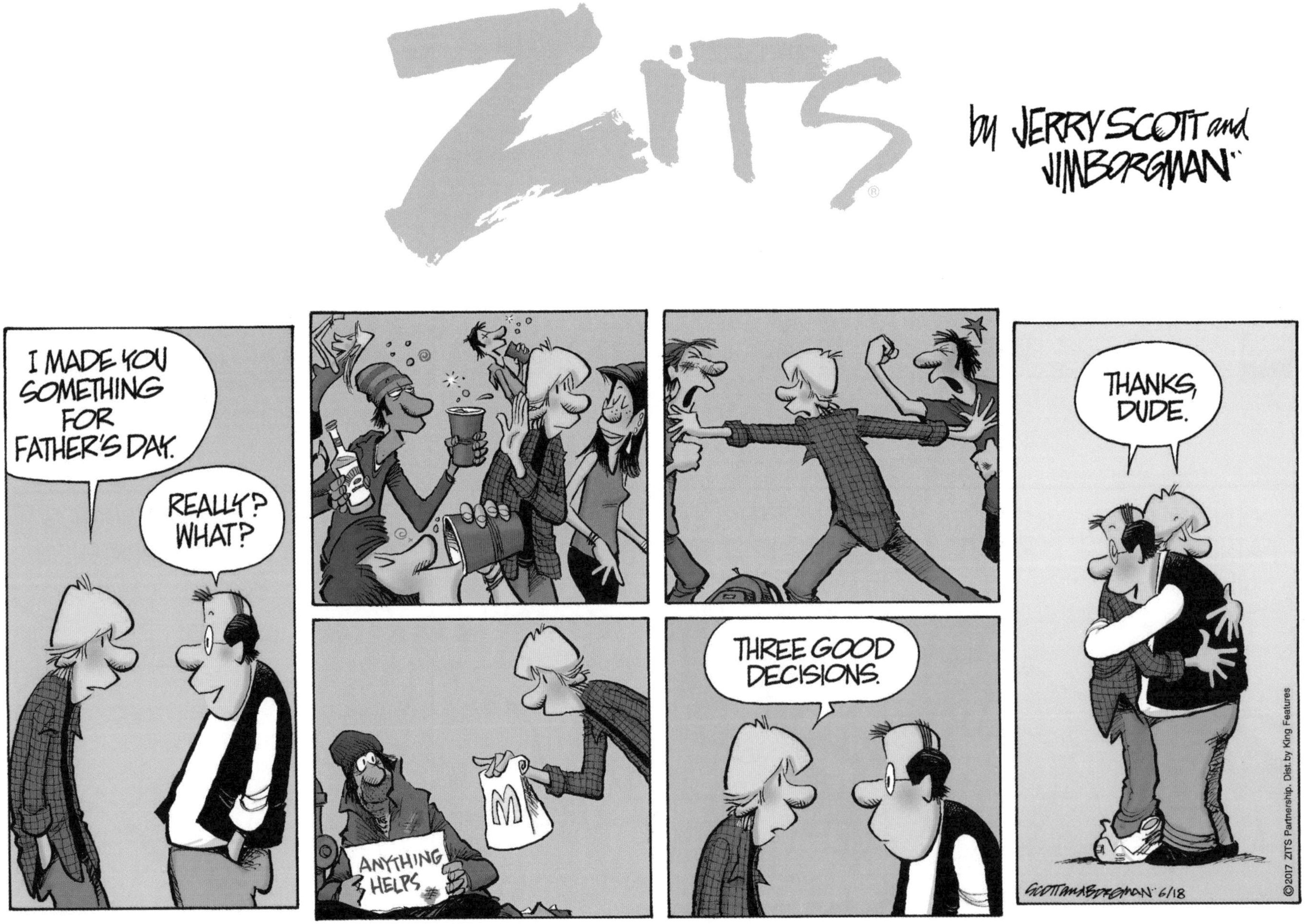
ZITS
by JERRY SCOTT and JIM BORGMAN
I MADE YOU SOMETHING FOR FATHER'S DAY.
REALLY? WHAT?
M
ANYTHING HELPS
THREE GOOD DECISIONS.
THANKS, DUDE.
SCOTT and BORGMAN 6/18
©2017 ZITS Partnership. Dist. by King Features

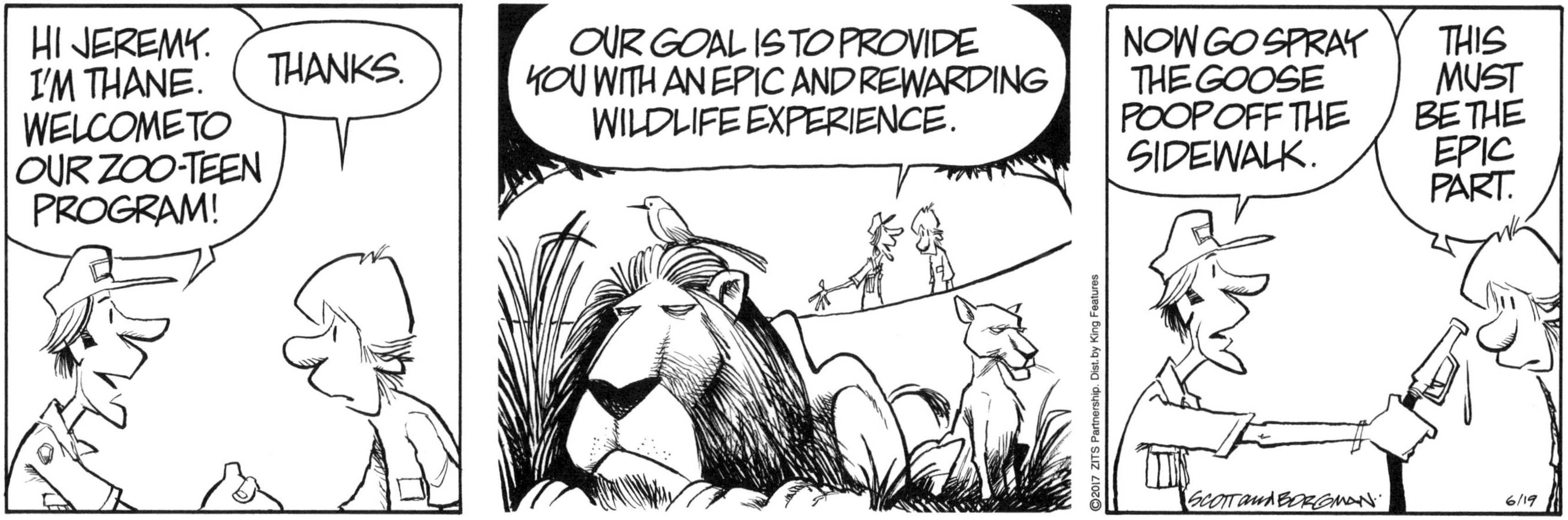
HI JEREMY. I'M THANE. WELCOME TO OUR ZOO-TEEN PROGRAM!
THANKS.
OUR GOAL IS TO PROVIDE YOU WITH AN EPIC AND REWARDING WILDLIFE EXPERIENCE.
NOW GO SPRAY THE GOOSE POOP OFF THE SIDEWALK.
THIS MUST BE THE EPIC PART.
©2017 ZITS Partnership. Dist. by King Features
SCOTT and BORGMAN 6/19

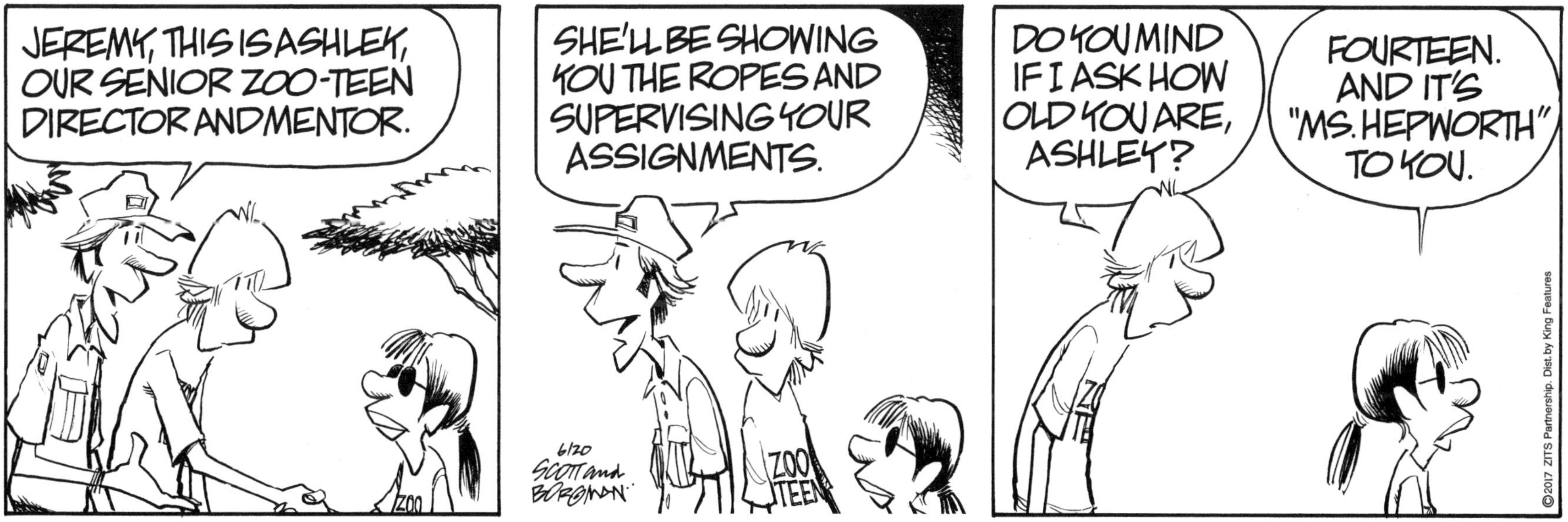
JEREMY, THIS IS ASHLEY, OUR SENIOR ZOO-TEEN DIRECTOR AND MENTOR.
ZOO
SHE'LL BE SHOWING YOU THE ROPES AND SUPERVISING YOUR ASSIGNMENTS.
6/20 SCOTT and BORGMAN
ZOO TEEN
DO YOU MIND IF I ASK HOW OLD YOU ARE, ASHLEY?
FOURTEEN. AND IT'S "MS. HEPWORTH" TO YOU.
©2017 ZITS Partnership. Dist. by King Features

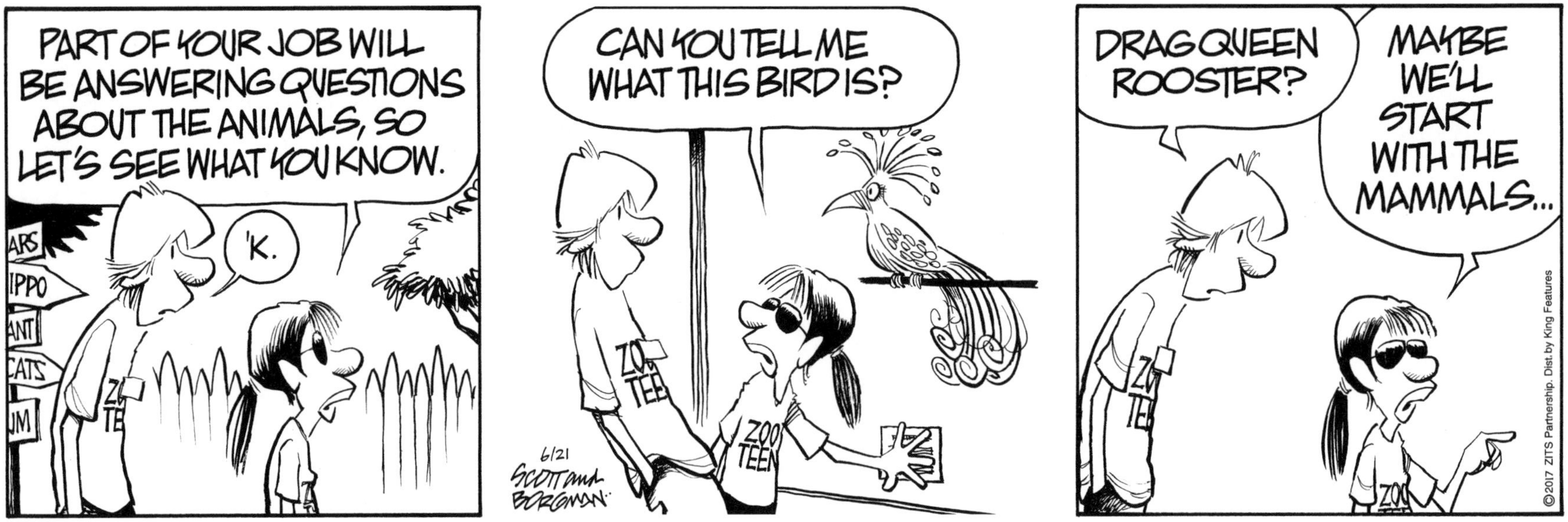
PART OF YOUR JOB WILL BE ANSWERING QUESTIONS ABOUT THE ANIMALS, SO LET'S SEE WHAT YOU KNOW.
'K.
CAN YOU TELL ME WHAT THIS BIRD IS?
6/21 SCOTT and BORGMAN
DRAG QUEEN ROOSTER?
MAYBE WE'LL START WITH THE MAMMALS...
©2017 ZITS Partnership. Dist. by King Features

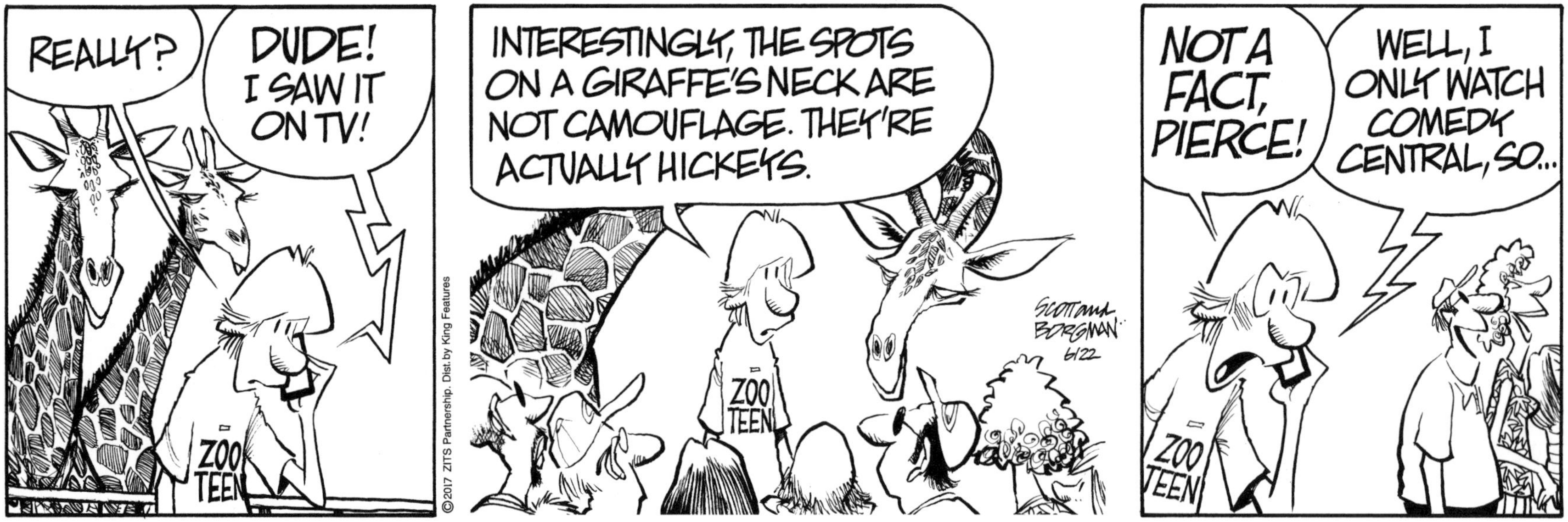
REALLY?
DUDE! I SAW IT ON TV!
©2017 ZITS Partnership. Dist. by King Features
INTERESTINGLY, THE SPOTS ON A GIRAFFE'S NECK ARE NOT CAMOUFLAGE. THEY'RE ACTUALLY HICKEYS.
SCOTT and BORGMAN 6/22
NOT A FACT, PIERCE!
WELL, I ONLY WATCH COMEDY CENTRAL, SO...

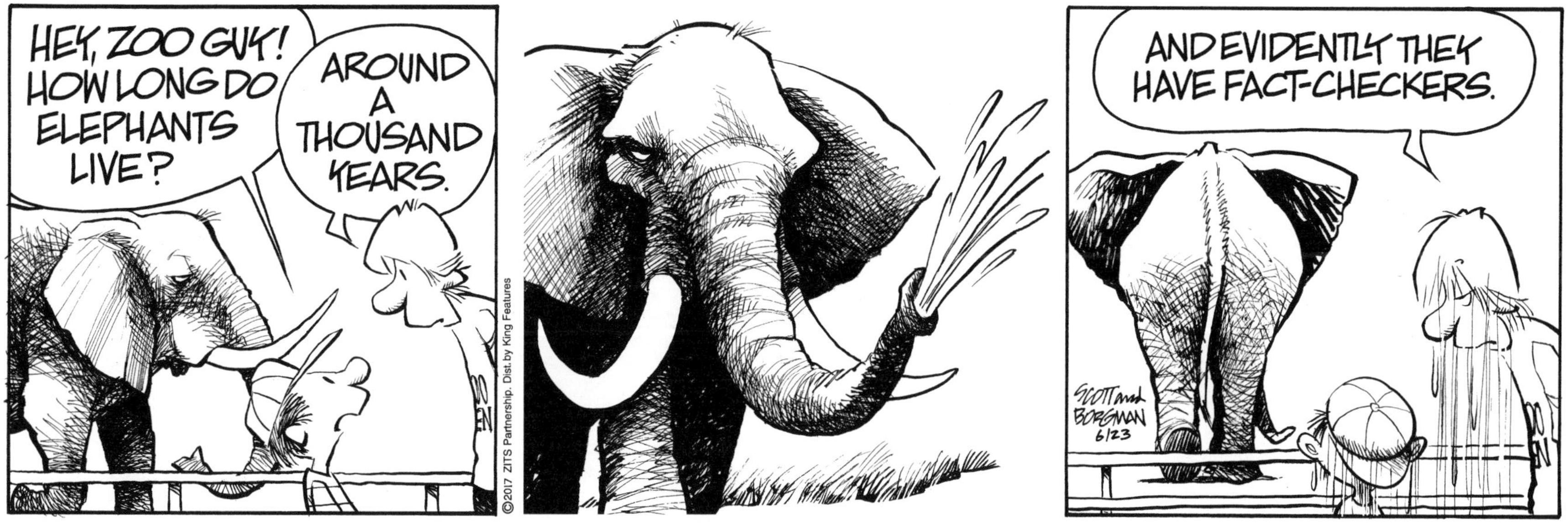
HEY, ZOO GUY! HOW LONG DO ELEPHANTS LIVE?
AROUND A THOUSAND YEARS.
AND EVIDENTLY THEY HAVE FACT-CHECKERS.
SCOTT and BORGMAN 6/23
© 2017 ZITS Partnership. Dist. by King Features

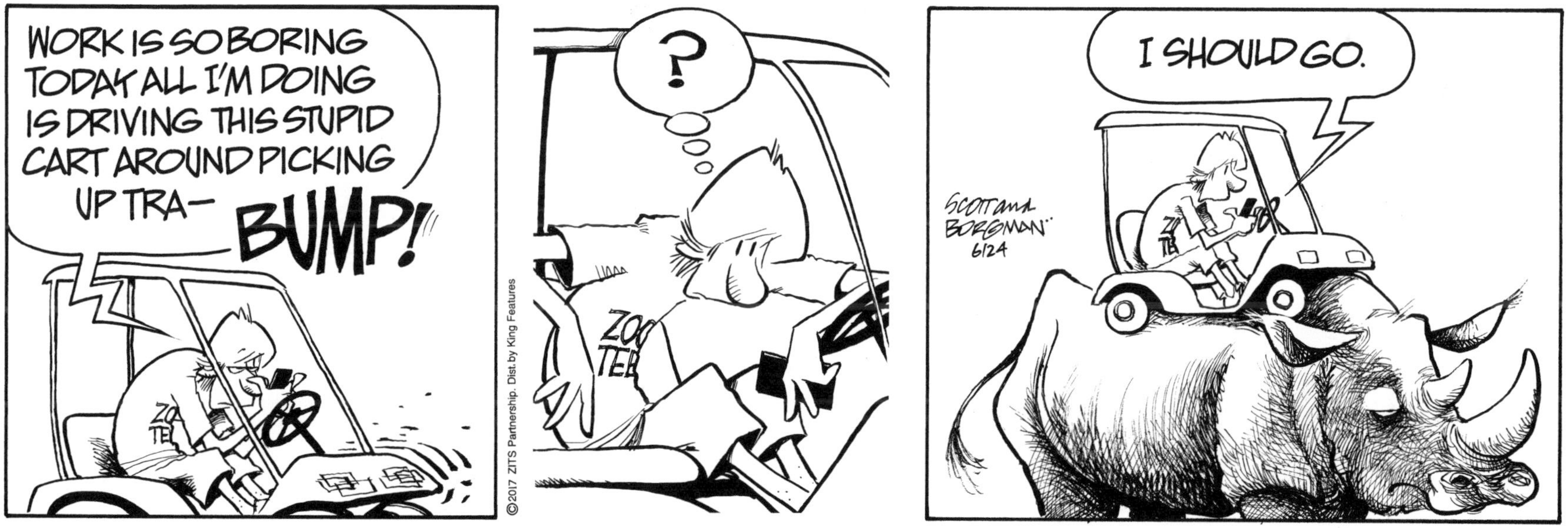
WORK IS SO BORING TODAY ALL I'M DOING IS DRIVING THIS STUPID CART AROUND PICKING UP TRA—
BUMP!
?
I SHOULD GO.
SCOTT and BORGMAN 6/24
© 2017 ZITS Partnership. Dist. by King Features

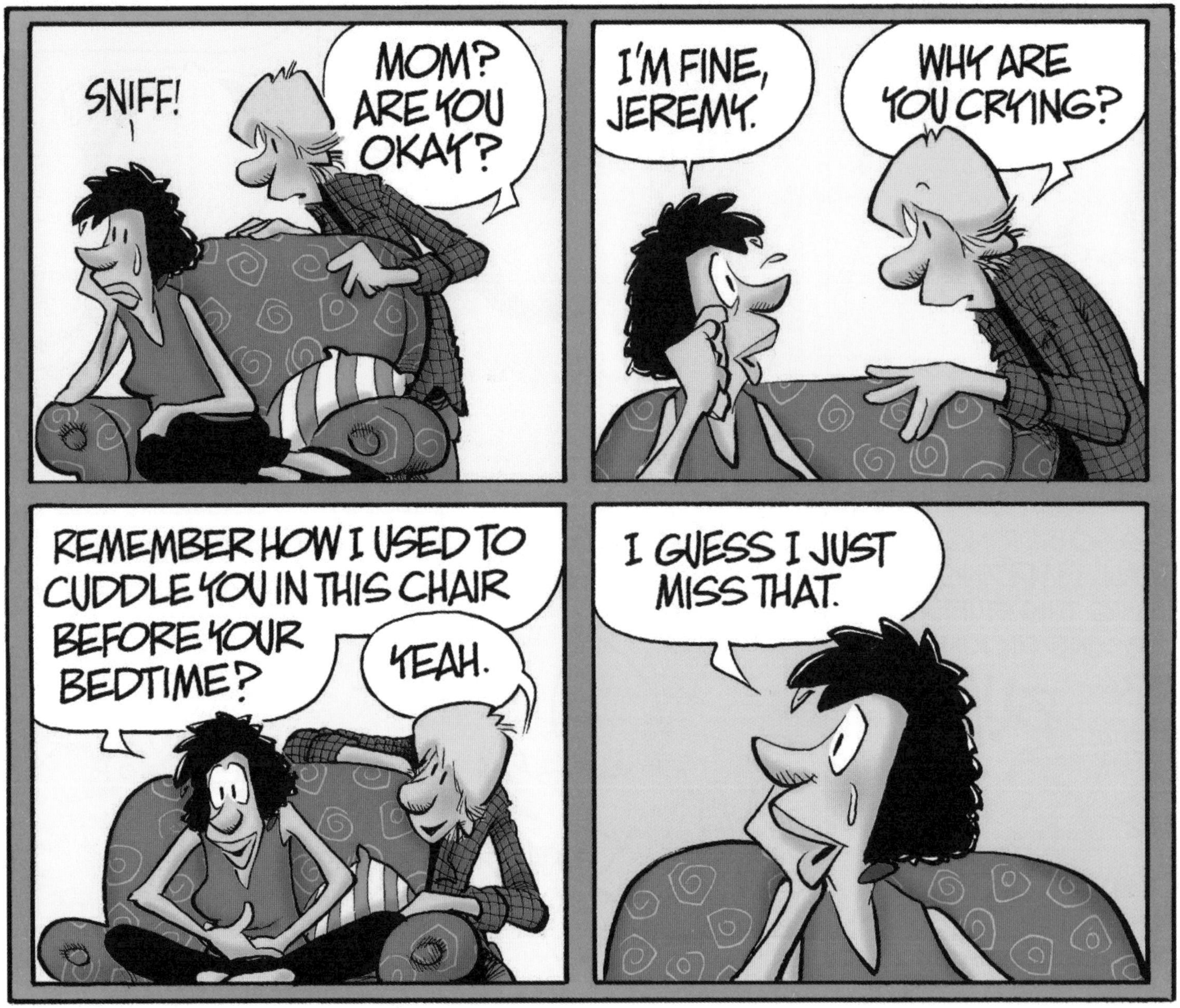
SNIFF!
MOM? ARE YOU OKAY?
I'M FINE, JEREMY.
WHY ARE YOU CRYING?
REMEMBER HOW I USED TO CUDDLE YOU IN THIS CHAIR BEFORE YOUR BEDTIME?
YEAH.
I GUESS I JUST MISS THAT.

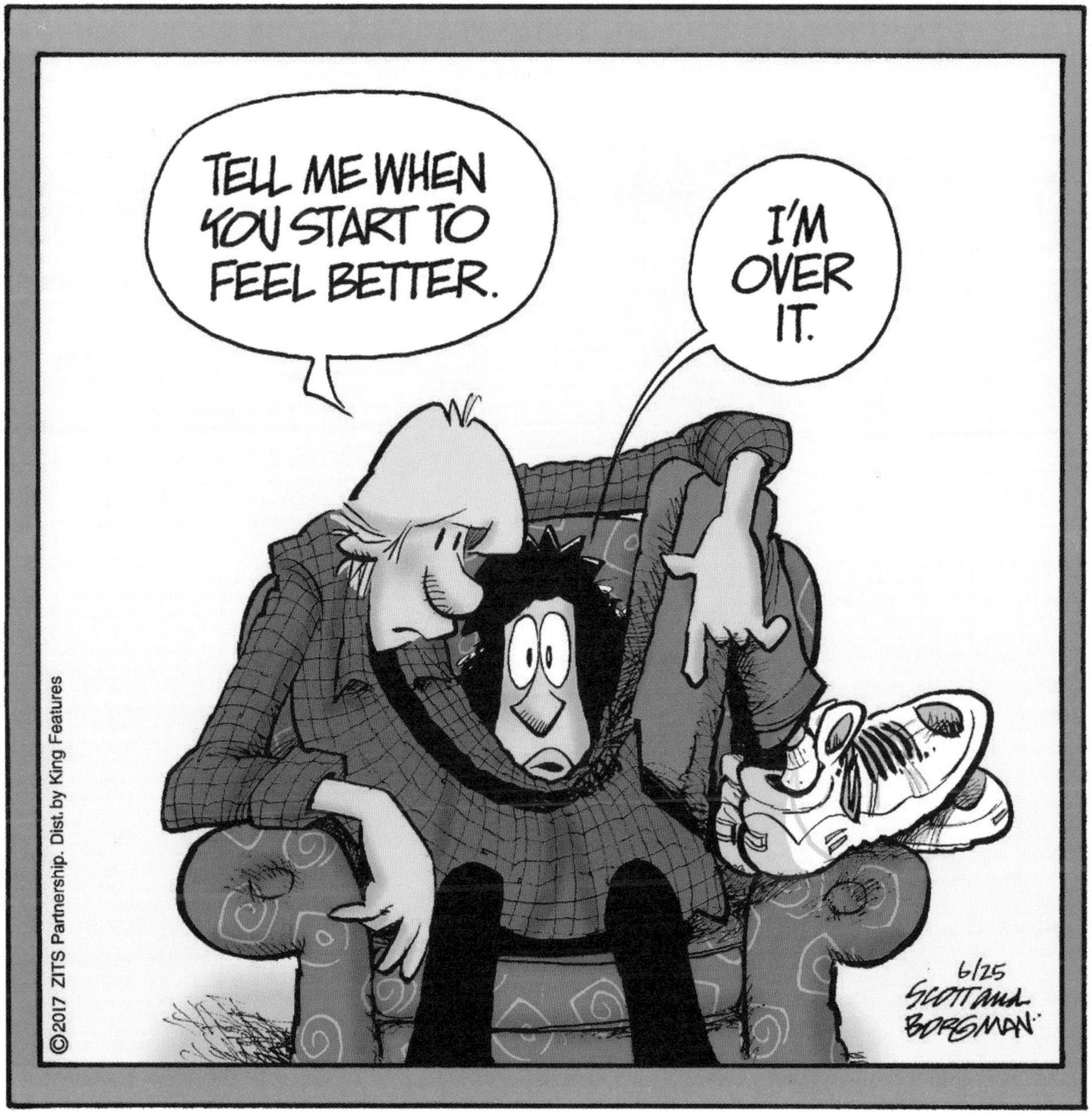
TELL ME WHEN YOU START TO FEEL BETTER.
I'M OVER IT.
6/25 SCOTT and BORGMAN
©2017 ZITS Partnership. Dist. by King Features

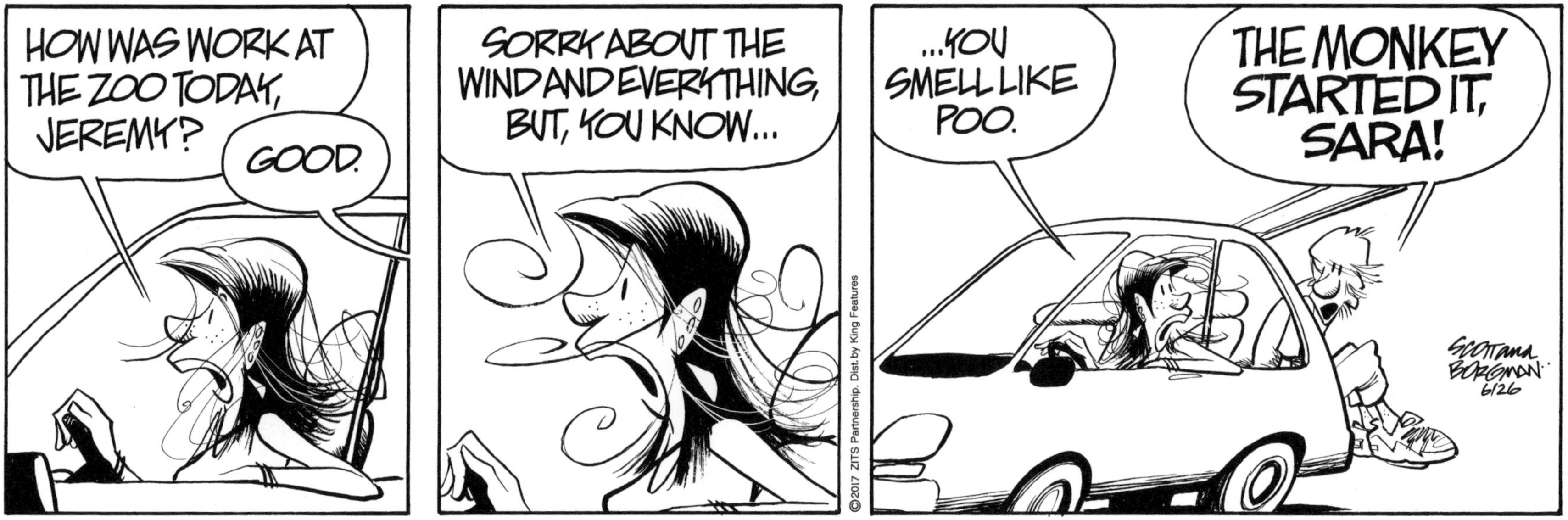
HOW WAS WORK AT THE ZOO TODAY, JEREMY?
GOOD.
SORRY ABOUT THE WIND AND EVERYTHING, BUT, YOU KNOW...
...YOU SMELL LIKE POO.
THE MONKEY STARTED IT, SARA!
SCOTT and BORGMAN 6/26
©2017 ZITS Partnership. Dist. by King Features

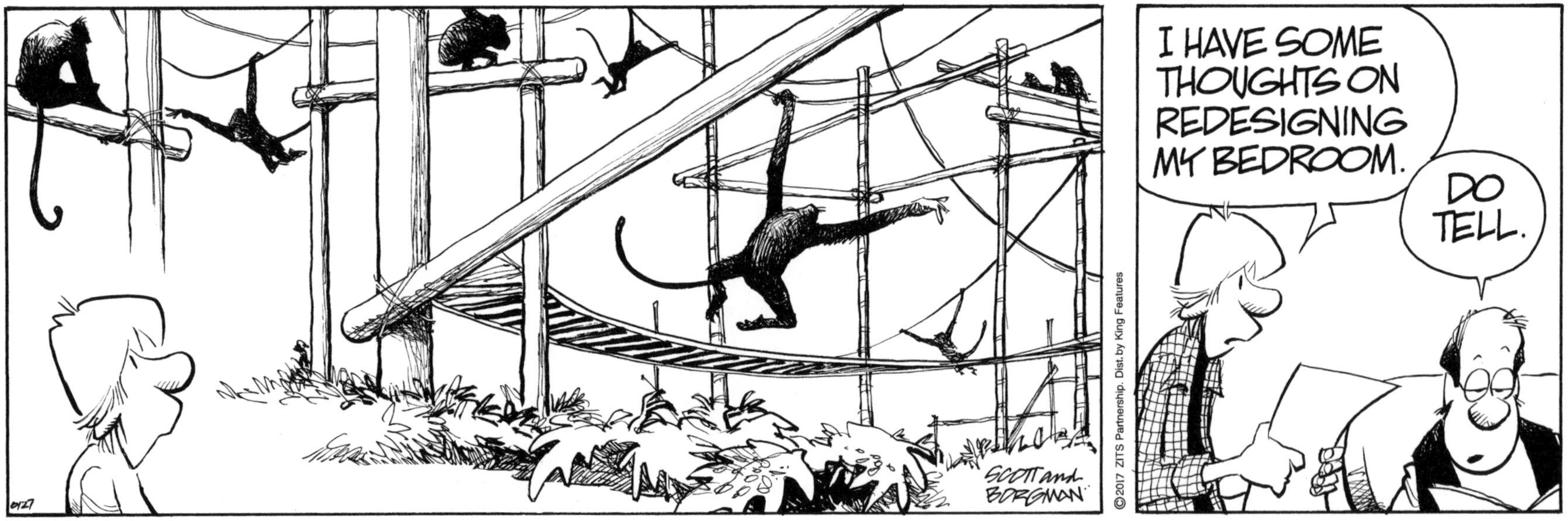
6/27
SCOTT and BORGMAN
©2017 ZITS Partnership. Dist. by King Features
I HAVE SOME THOUGHTS ON REDESIGNING MY BEDROOM.
DO TELL.

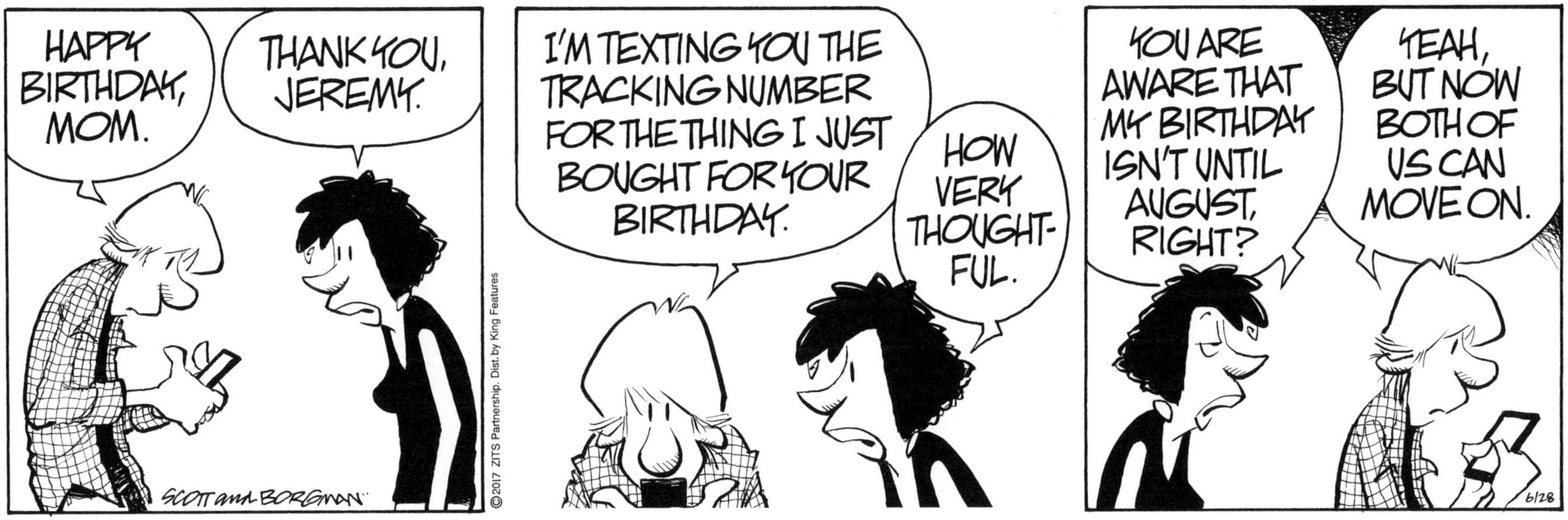
HAPPY BIRTHDAY, MOM.
THANK YOU, JEREMY.
I'M TEXTING YOU THE TRACKING NUMBER FOR THE THING I JUST BOUGHT FOR YOUR BIRTHDAY.
HOW VERY THOUGHT-FUL.
YOU ARE AWARE THAT MY BIRTHDAY ISN'T UNTIL AUGUST, RIGHT?
YEAH, BUT NOW BOTH OF US CAN MOVE ON.
SCOTT and BORGMAN
©2017 ZITS Partnership. Dist. by King Features
6/28

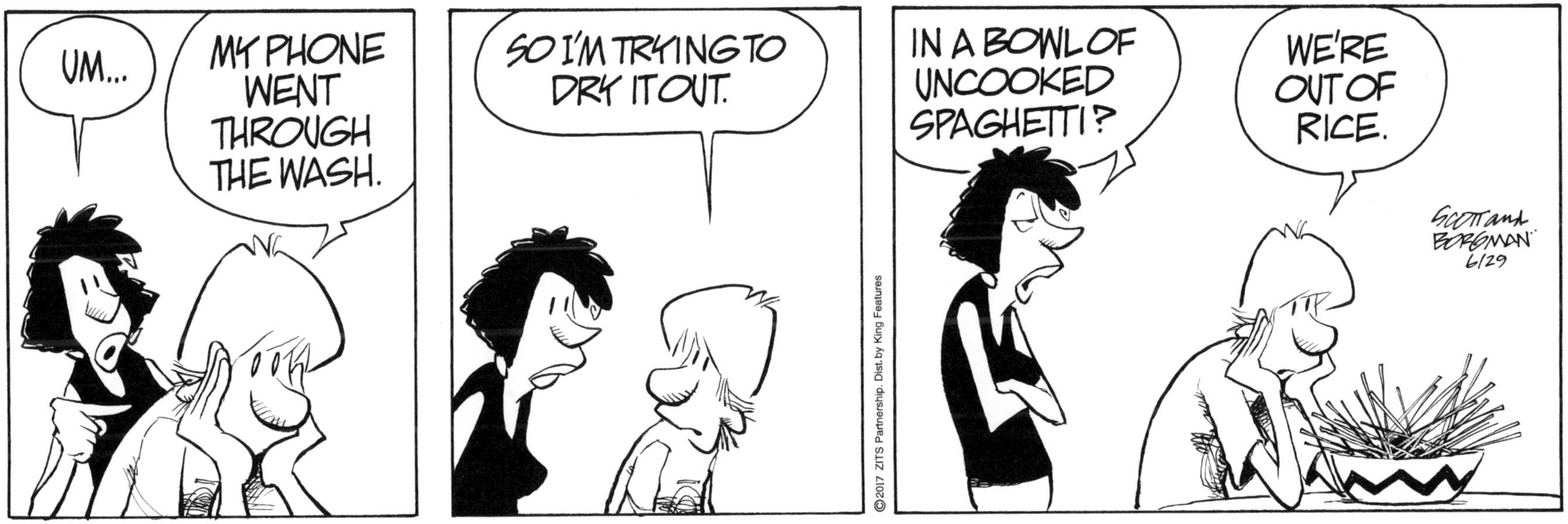
UM...
MY PHONE WENT THROUGH THE WASH.
SO I'M TRYING TO DRY IT OUT.
IN A BOWL OF UNCOOKED SPAGHETTI?
WE'RE OUT OF RICE.
SCOTT and BORGMAN
6/29
©2017 ZITS Partnership. Dist. by King Features

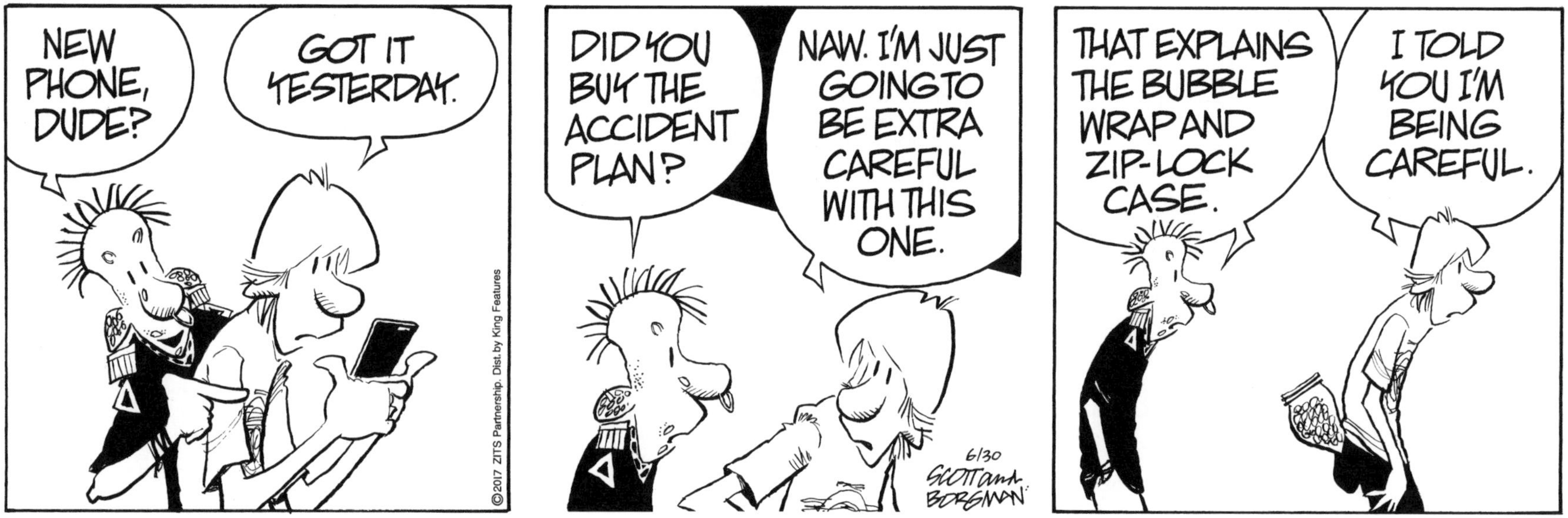
NEW PHONE, DUDE?
GOT IT YESTERDAY.
©2017 ZITS Partnership. Dist. by King Features
DID YOU BUY THE ACCIDENT PLAN?
NAW. I'M JUST GOING TO BE EXTRA CAREFUL WITH THIS ONE.
6/30
SCOTT and BORGMAN
THAT EXPLAINS THE BUBBLE WRAP AND ZIP-LOCK CASE.
I TOLD YOU I'M BEING CAREFUL.

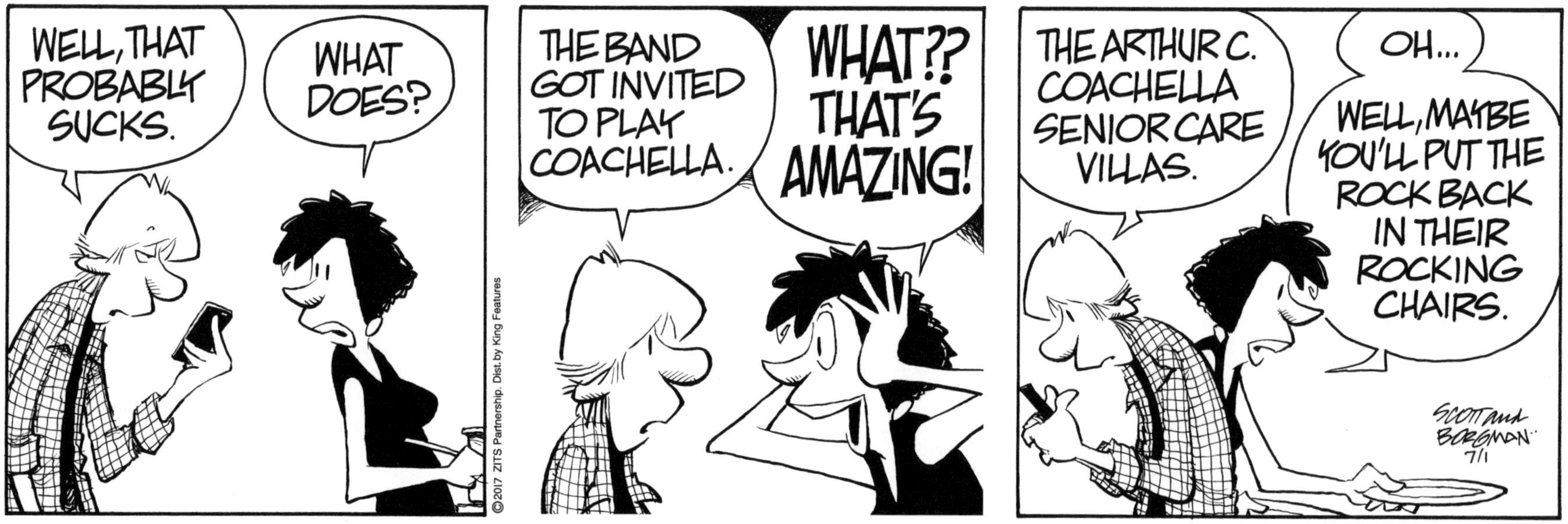
WELL, THAT PROBABLY SUCKS.
WHAT DOES?
©2017 ZITS Partnership. Dist. by King Features
THE BAND GOT INVITED TO PLAY COACHELLA.
WHAT?? THAT'S AMAZING!
THE ARTHUR C. COACHELLA SENIOR CARE VILLAS.
OH...
WELL, MAYBE YOU'LL PUT THE ROCK BACK IN THEIR ROCKING CHAIRS.
SCOTT and BORGMAN
7/1

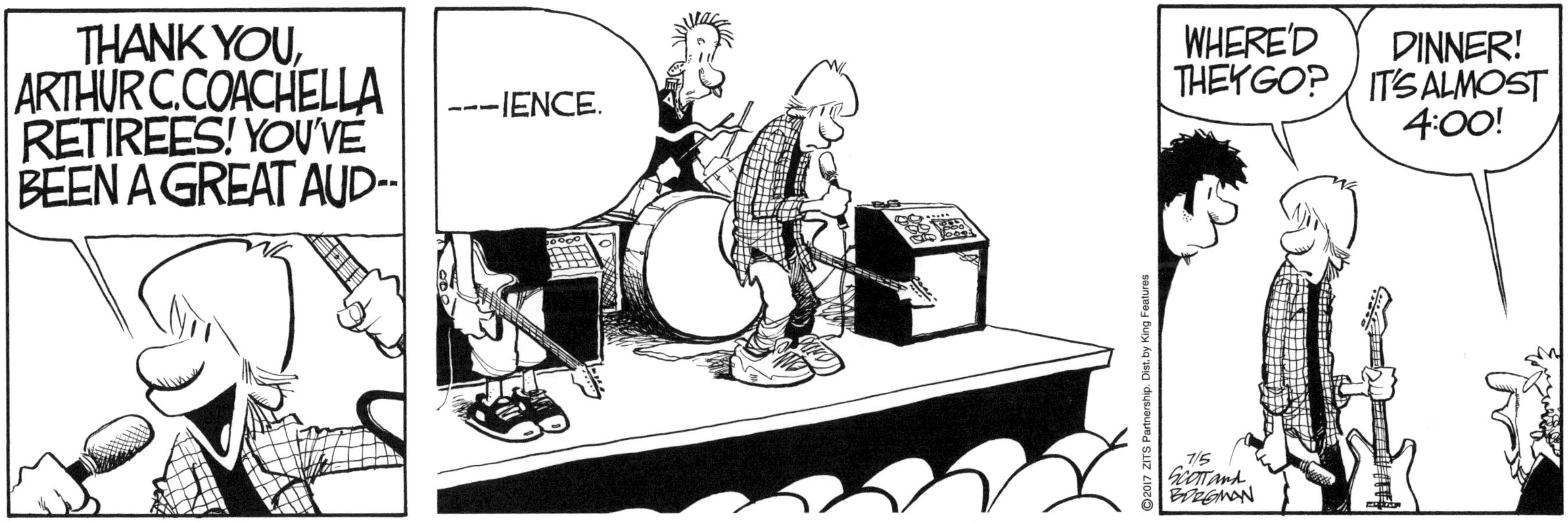
THANK YOU, ARTHUR C. COACHELLA RETIREES! YOU'VE BEEN A GREAT AUD--
---IENCE.
WHERE'D THEY GO?
DINNER! IT'S ALMOST 4:00!
7/5 SCOTT AND BORGMAN
© 2017 ZITS Partnership. Dist. by King Features

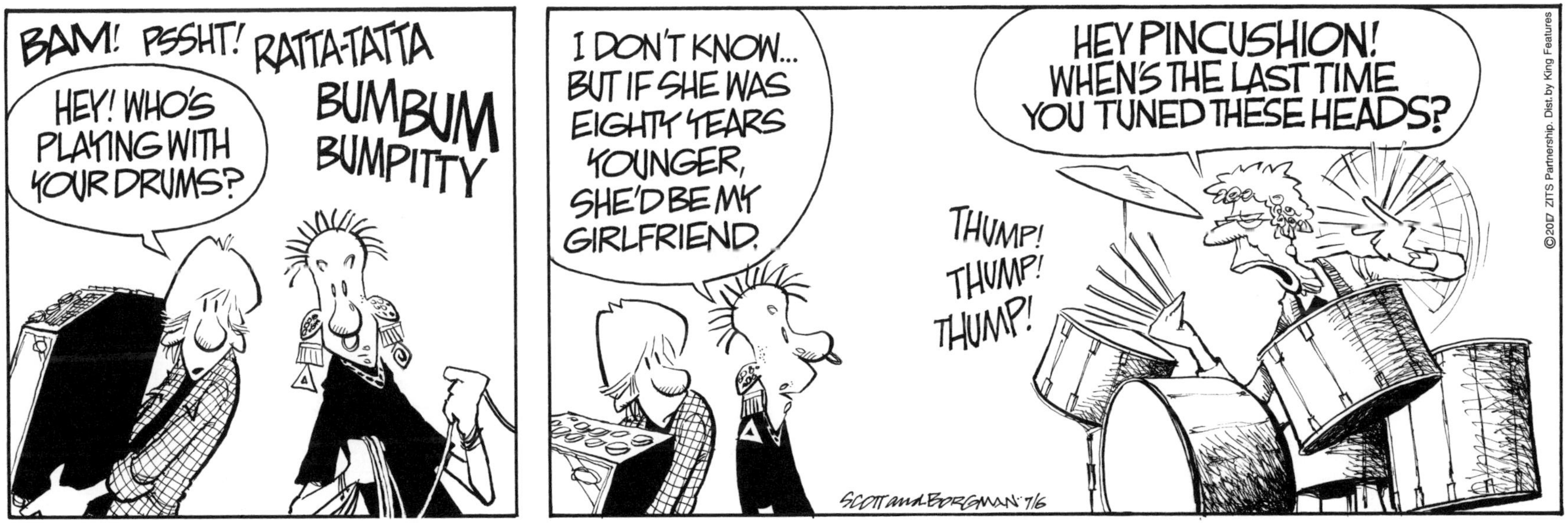
BAM! PSSHT! RATTA-TATTA
HEY! WHO'S PLAYING WITH YOUR DRUMS?
BUM BUM BUMPITTY
I DON'T KNOW... BUT IF SHE WAS EIGHTY YEARS YOUNGER, SHE'D BE MY GIRLFRIEND.
HEY PINCUSHION! WHEN'S THE LAST TIME YOU TUNED THESE HEADS?
THUMP! THUMP! THUMP!
SCOTT AND BORGMAN 7/6
© 2017 ZITS Partnership. Dist. by King Features

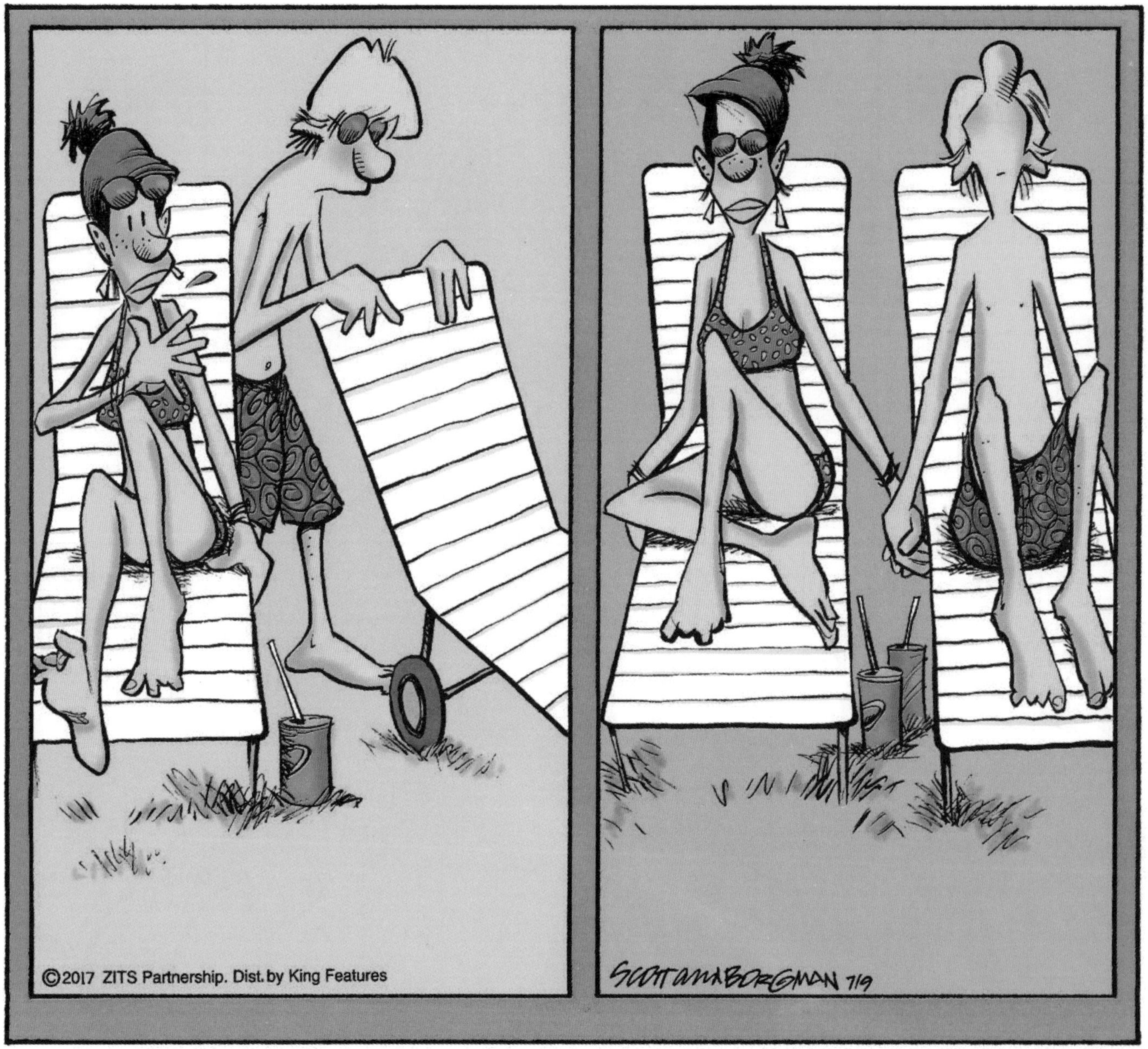
©2017 ZITS Partnership. Dist. by King Features
SCOTT AND BORGMAN 7/9

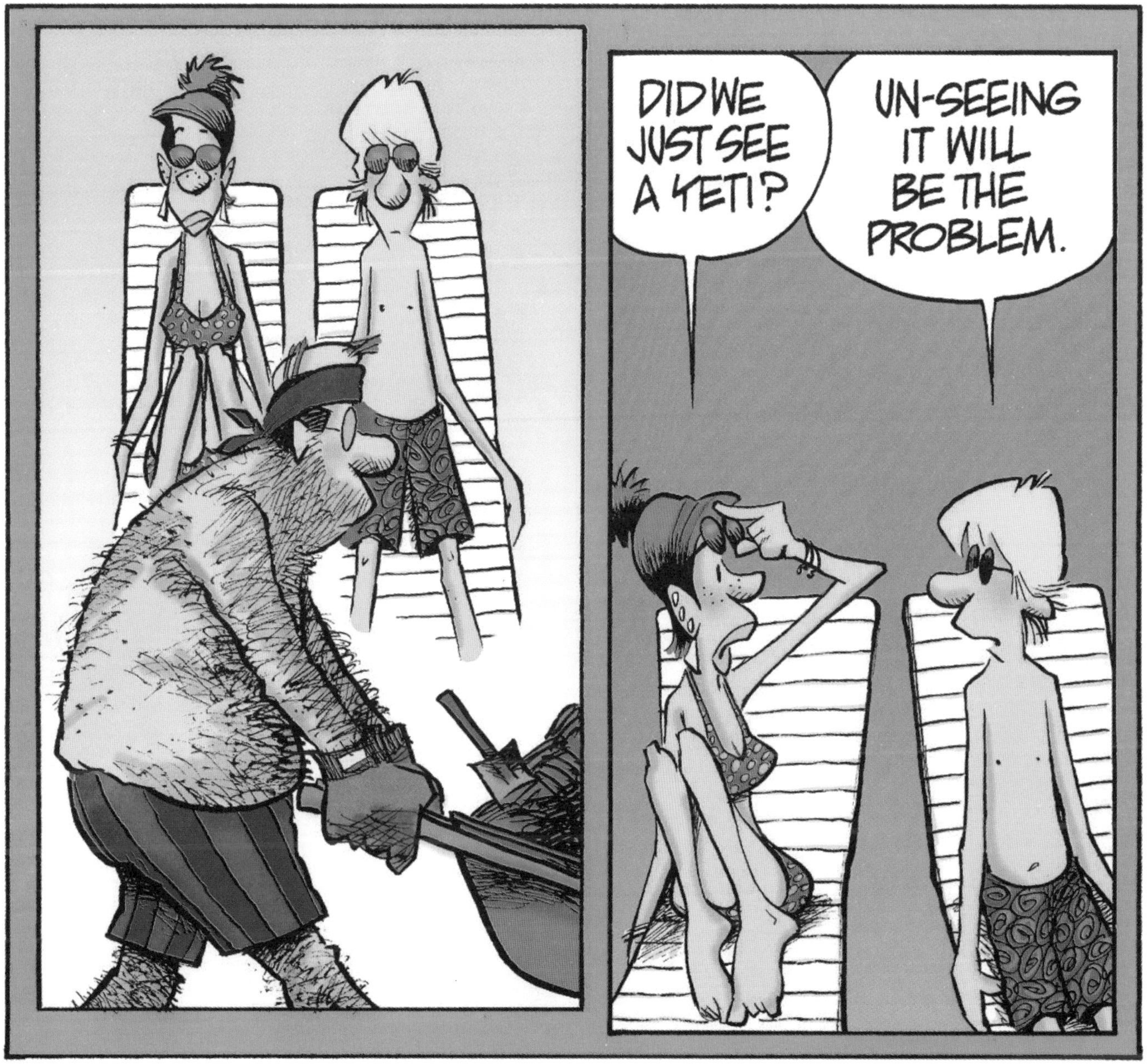
DID WE JUST SEE A YETI?
UN-SEEING IT WILL BE THE PROBLEM.

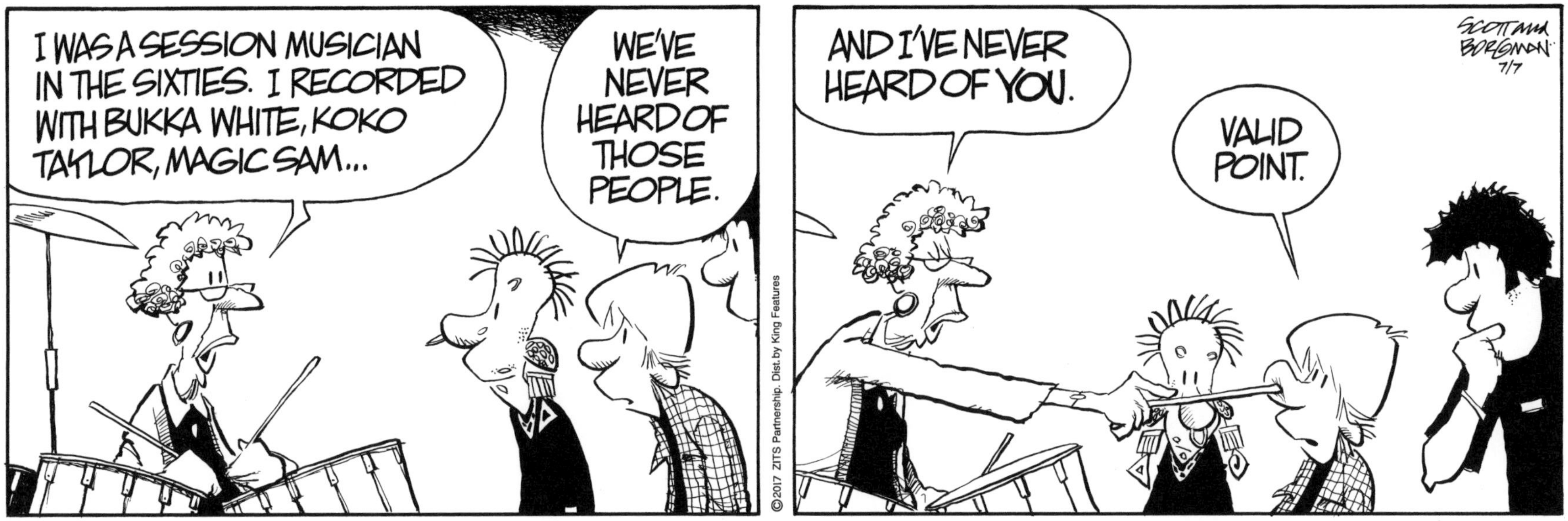

I WAS A SESSION MUSICIAN IN THE SIXTIES. I RECORDED WITH BUKKA WHITE, KOKO TAYLOR, MAGIC SAM...
WE'VE NEVER HEARD OF THOSE PEOPLE.
© 2017 ZITS Partnership. Dist. by King Features
AND I'VE NEVER HEARD OF YOU.
VALID POINT.
SCOTT AND BORGMAN 7/7

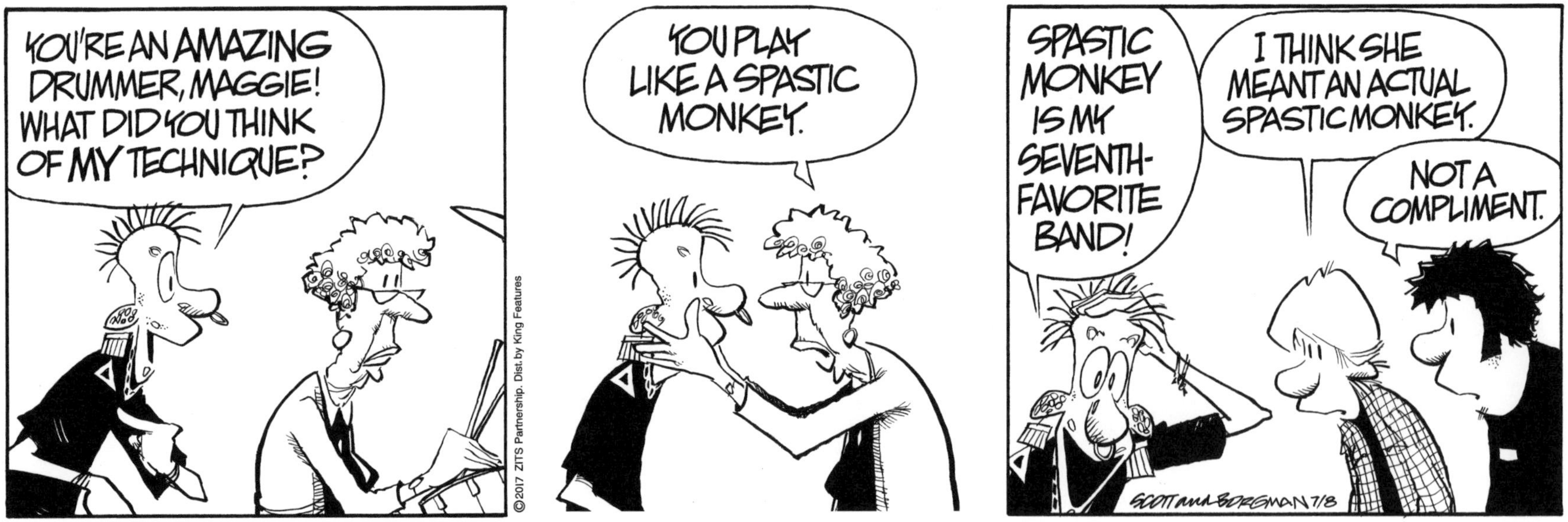

YOU'RE AN AMAZING DRUMMER, MAGGIE! WHAT DID YOU THINK OF MY TECHNIQUE?
© 2017 ZITS Partnership. Dist. by King Features
YOU PLAY LIKE A SPASTIC MONKEY.
SPASTIC MONKEY IS MY SEVENTH-FAVORITE BAND!
I THINK SHE MEANT AN ACTUAL SPASTIC MONKEY.
NOT A COMPLIMENT.
SCOTT AND BORGMAN 7/8

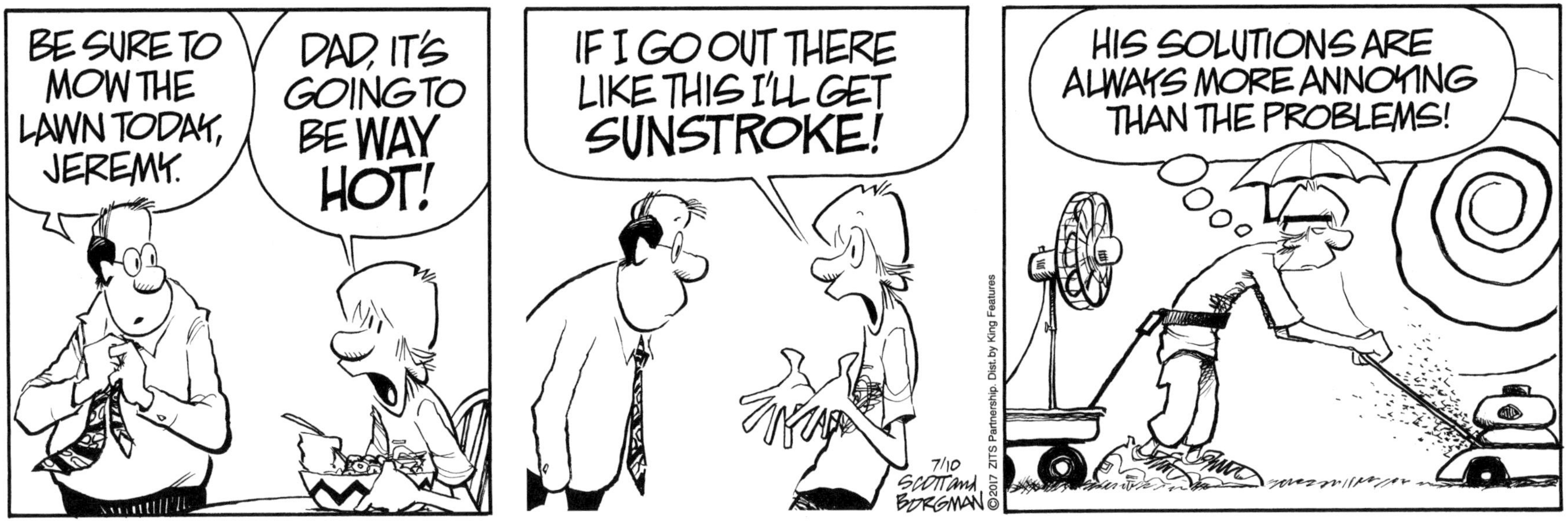
BE SURE TO MOW THE LAWN TODAY, JEREMY.
DAD, IT'S GOING TO BE WAY HOT!
IF I GO OUT THERE LIKE THIS I'LL GET SUNSTROKE!
7/10 SCOTT and BORGMAN
©2017 ZITS Partnership. Dist. by King Features
HIS SOLUTIONS ARE ALWAYS MORE ANNOYING THAN THE PROBLEMS!

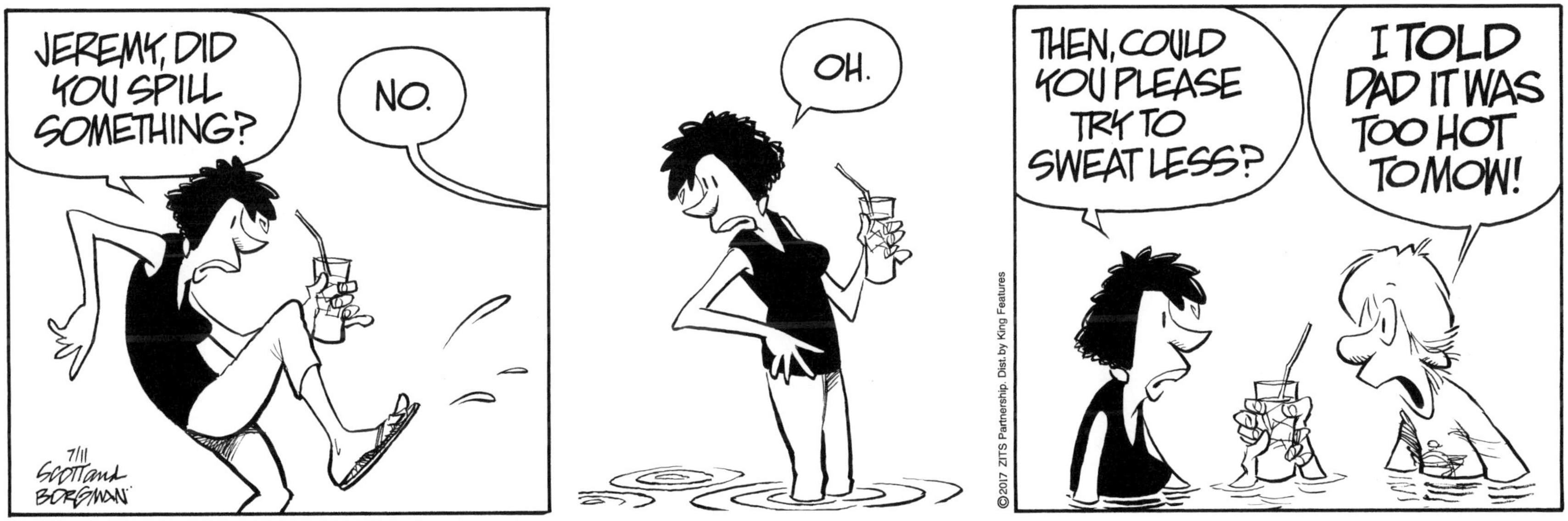
JEREMY, DID YOU SPILL SOMETHING?
NO.
7/11 SCOTT and BORGMAN
OH.
©2017 ZITS Partnership. Dist. by King Features
THEN, COULD YOU PLEASE TRY TO SWEAT LESS?
I TOLD DAD IT WAS TOO HOT TO MOW!

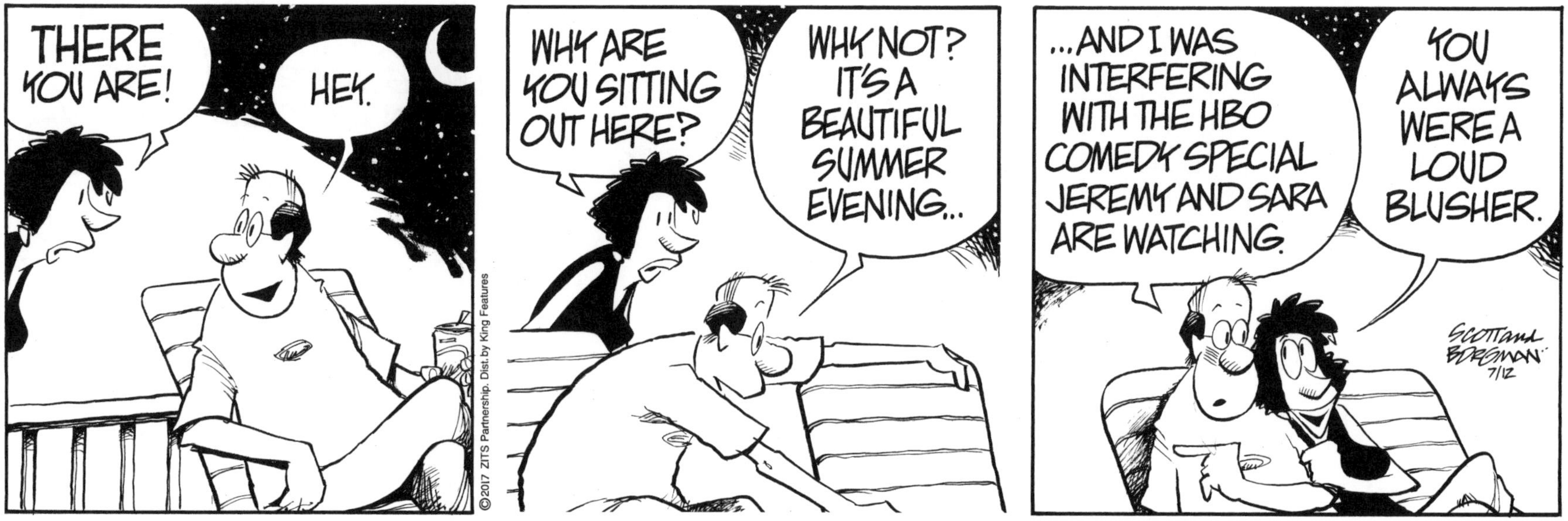
THERE YOU ARE!
HEY.
WHY ARE YOU SITTING OUT HERE?
WHY NOT? IT'S A BEAUTIFUL SUMMER EVENING...
...AND I WAS INTERFERING WITH THE HBO COMEDY SPECIAL JEREMY AND SARA ARE WATCHING.
YOU ALWAYS WERE A LOUD BLUSHER.
SCOTT AND BORGMAN 7/12
©2017 ZITS Partnership. Dist. by King Features

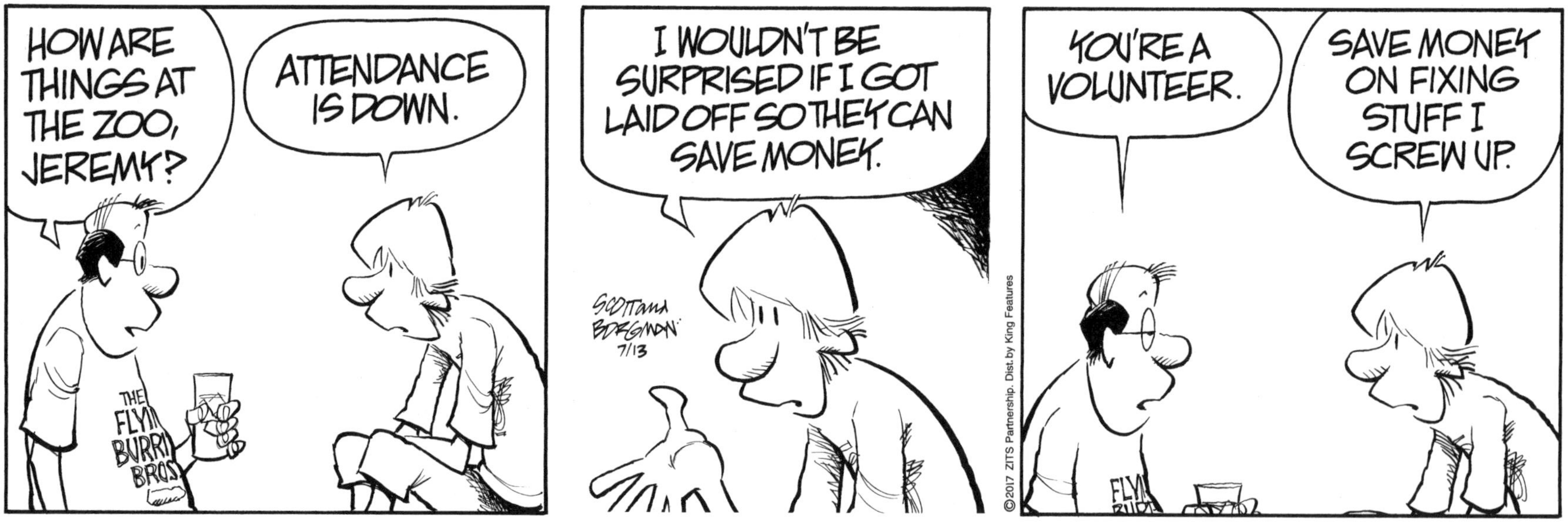
HOW ARE THINGS AT THE ZOO, JEREMY?
ATTENDANCE IS DOWN.
THE FLYIN BURRI BROS
I WOULDN'T BE SURPRISED IF I GOT LAID OFF SO THEY CAN SAVE MONEY.
SCOTT AND BORGMAN 7/13
YOU'RE A VOLUNTEER.
SAVE MONEY ON FIXING STUFF I SCREW UP.
©2017 ZITS Partnership. Dist. by King Features

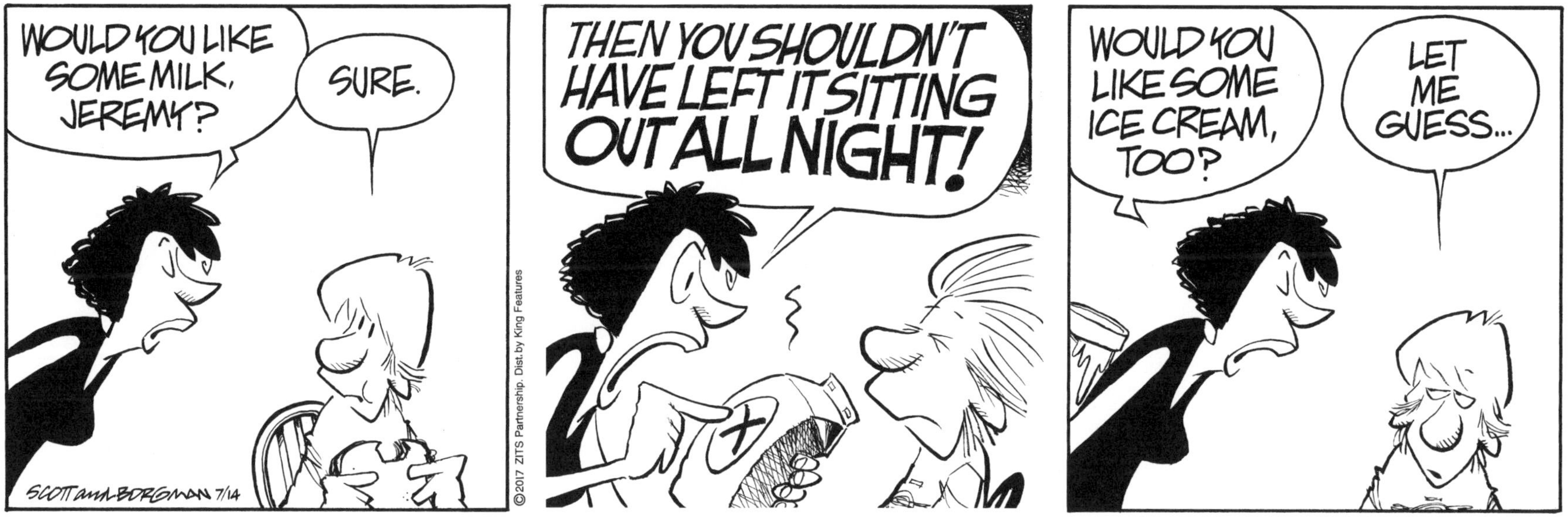
WOULD YOU LIKE SOME MILK, JEREMY?
SURE.
THEN YOU SHOULDN'T HAVE LEFT IT SITTING OUT ALL NIGHT!
WOULD YOU LIKE SOME ICE CREAM, TOO?
LET ME GUESS...
SCOTT and BORGMAN 7/14
©2017 ZITS Partnership. Dist. by King Features

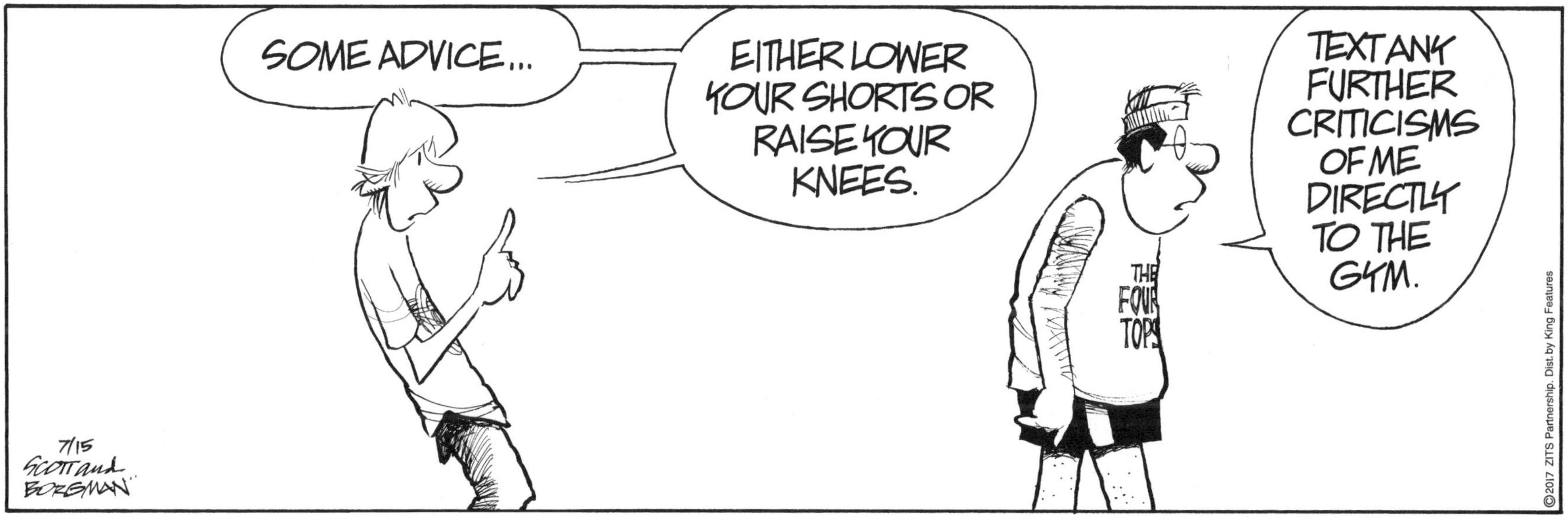
SOME ADVICE...
EITHER LOWER YOUR SHORTS OR RAISE YOUR KNEES.
TEXT ANY FURTHER CRITICISMS OF ME DIRECTLY TO THE GYM.
THE FOUR TOPS
7/15 SCOTT and BORGMAN
©2017 ZITS Partnership. Dist. by King Features

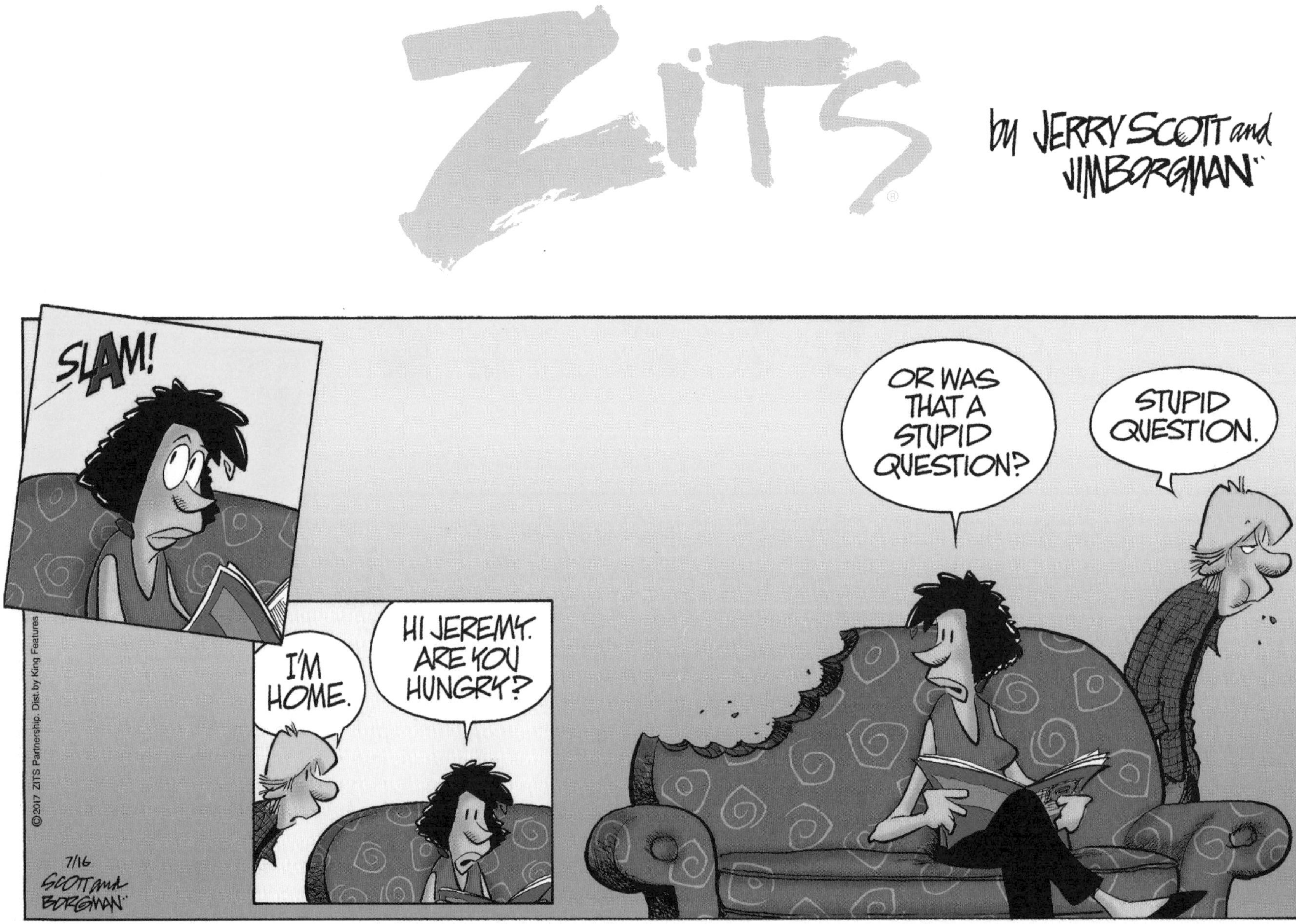
ZITS
by JERRY SCOTT and JIM BORGMAN
SLAM!
I'M HOME.
HI JEREMY. ARE YOU HUNGRY?
OR WAS THAT A STUPID QUESTION?
STUPID QUESTION.
©2017 ZITS Partnership. Dist. by King Features
7/16
SCOTT and BORGMAN

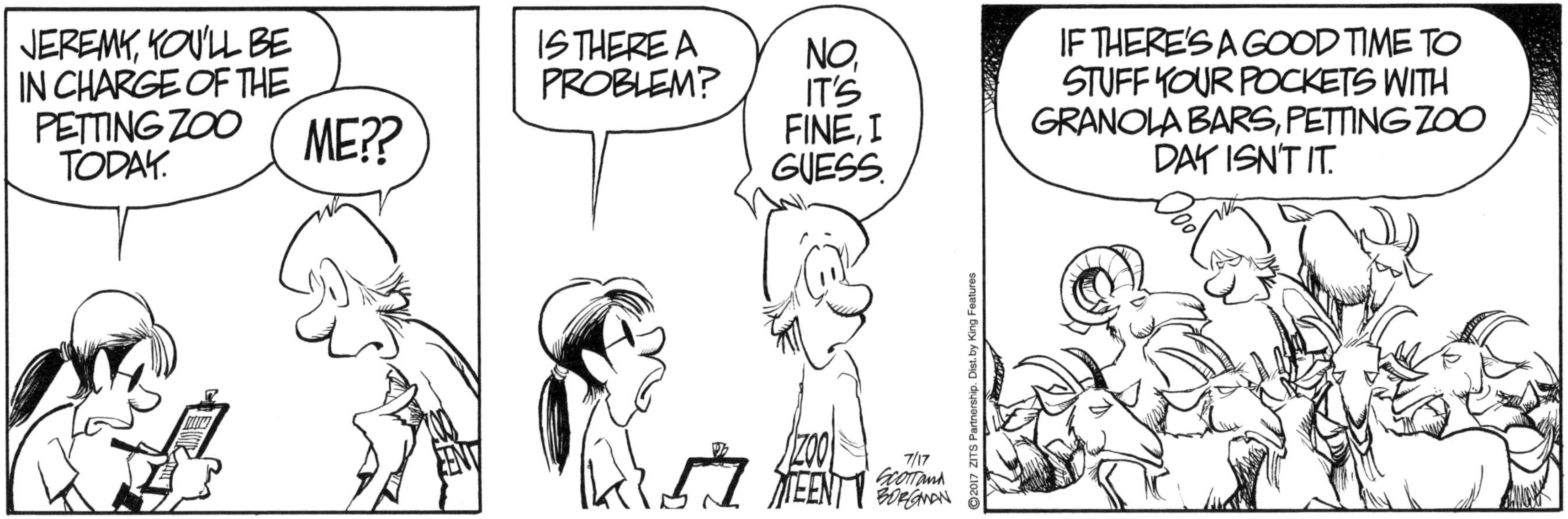
JEREMY, YOU'LL BE IN CHARGE OF THE PETTING ZOO TODAY.
ME??
IS THERE A PROBLEM?
NO, IT'S FINE, I GUESS.
7/17 SCOTT and BORGMAN
IF THERE'S A GOOD TIME TO STUFF YOUR POCKETS WITH GRANOLA BARS, PETTING ZOO DAY ISN'T IT.
©2017 ZITS Partnership. Dist. by King Features

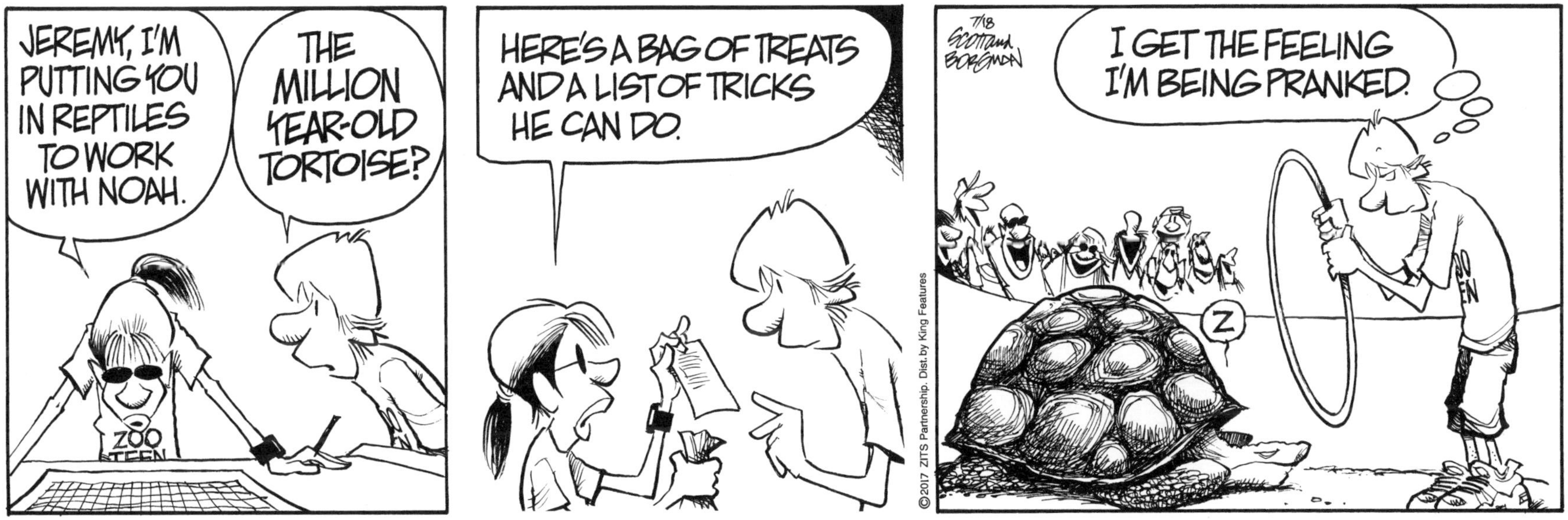
JEREMY, I'M PUTTING YOU IN REPTILES TO WORK WITH NOAH.
THE MILLION YEAR-OLD TORTOISE?
ZOO TEEN
HERE'S A BAG OF TREATS AND A LIST OF TRICKS HE CAN DO.
©2017 ZITS Partnership. Dist. by King Features
7/18 SCOTT and BORGMAN
I GET THE FEELING I'M BEING PRANKED.
Z

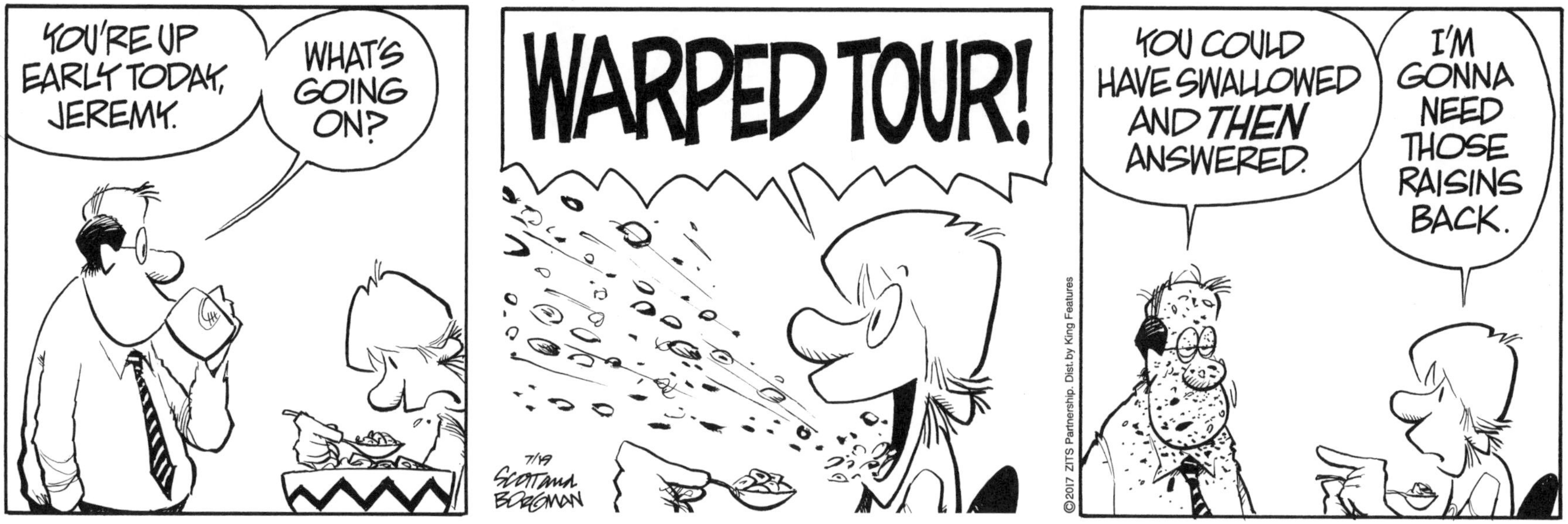
YOU'RE UP EARLY TODAY, JEREMY.
WHAT'S GOING ON?
WARPED TOUR!
YOU COULD HAVE SWALLOWED AND *THEN* ANSWERED.
I'M GONNA NEED THOSE RAISINS BACK.
©2017 ZITS Partnership. Dist. by King Features

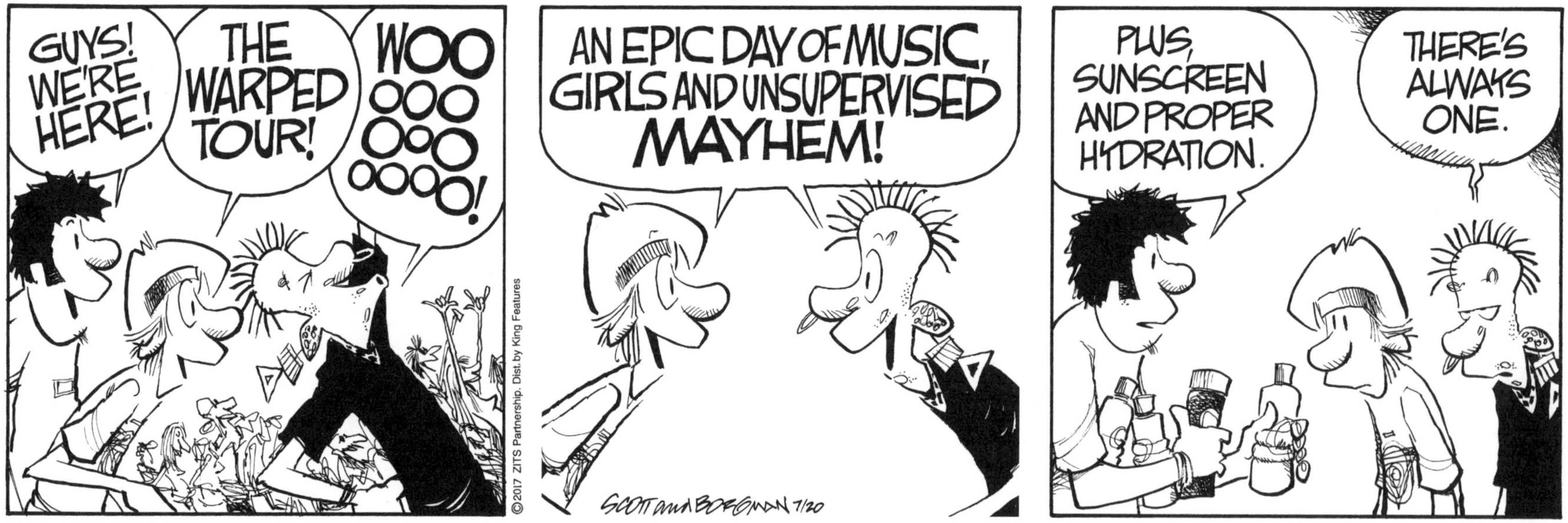
GUYS! WE'RE HERE!
THE WARPED TOUR!
WOO OOO OOO OOOO!
©2017 ZITS Partnership. Dist. by King Features
AN EPIC DAY OF MUSIC, GIRLS AND UNSUPERVISED MAYHEM!
PLUS, SUNSCREEN AND PROPER HYDRATION.
THERE'S ALWAYS ONE.

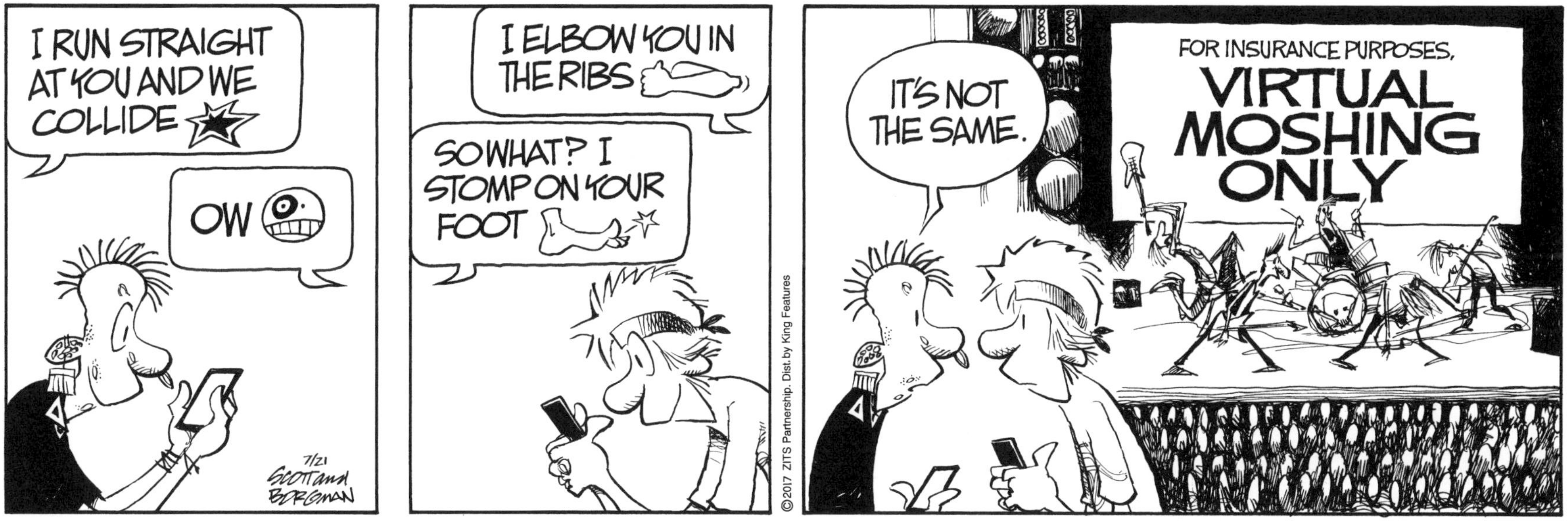
I RUN STRAIGHT AT YOU AND WE COLLIDE
OW
7/21 SCOTT and BORGMAN
I ELBOW YOU IN THE RIBS
SO WHAT? I STOMP ON YOUR FOOT
©2017 ZITS Partnership. Dist. by King Features
IT'S NOT THE SAME.
FOR INSURANCE PURPOSES,
VIRTUAL MOSHING ONLY

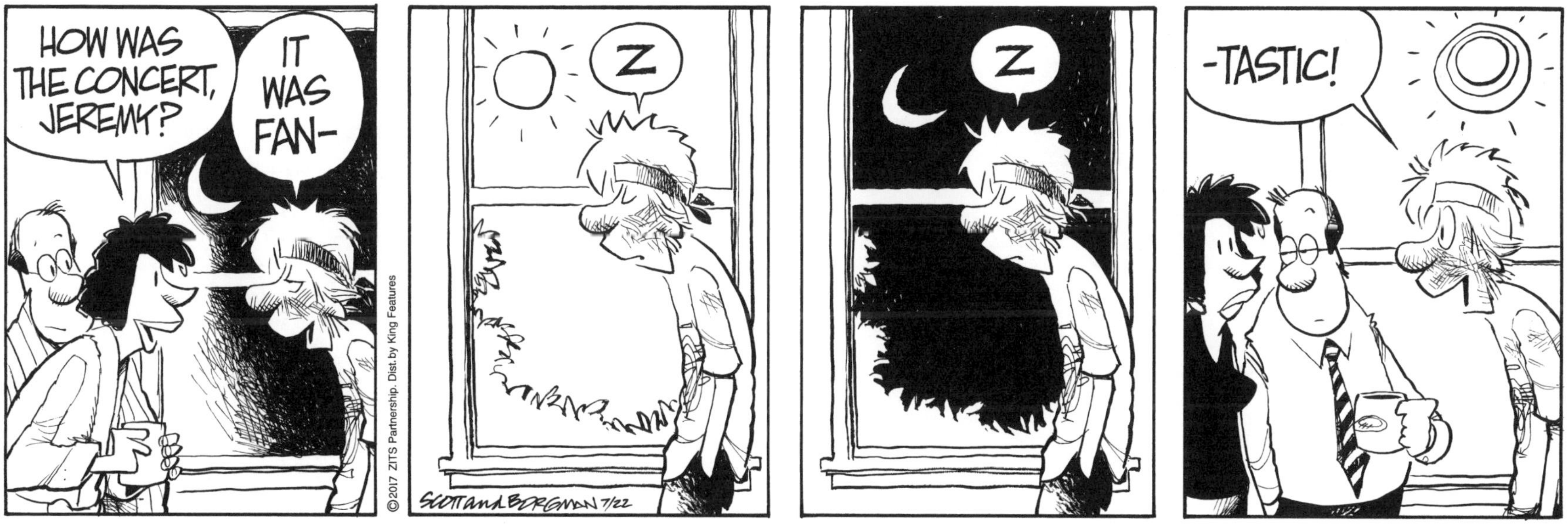
HOW WAS THE CONCERT, JEREMY?
IT WAS FAN-
©2017 ZITS Partnership. Dist. by King Features
Z
SCOTT and BORGMAN 7/22
Z
-TASTIC!

ZITS

by JERRY SCOTT and JIM BORGMAN

DON'T START THE DISHWASHER UNTIL JEREMY CHECKS HIS ROOM FOR DIRTY DISHES.
7/23 SCOTT and BORGMAN
©2017 ZITS Partnership. Dist. by King Features

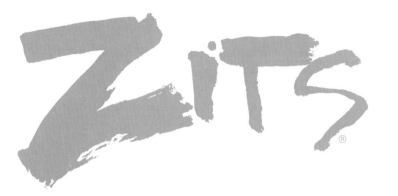

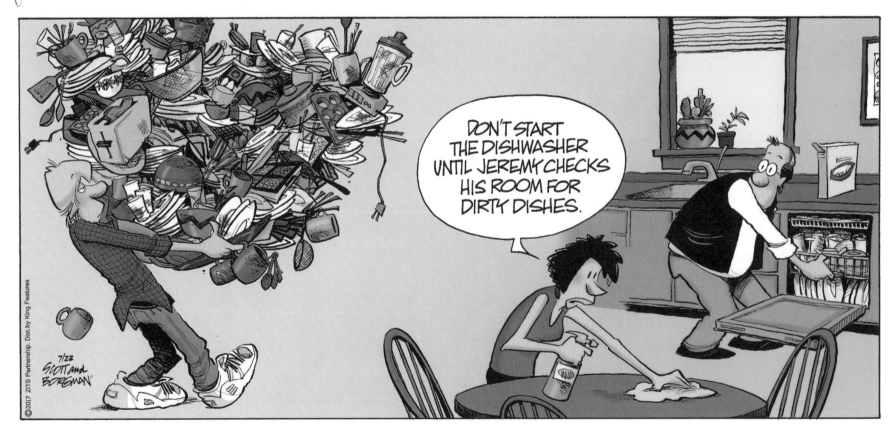

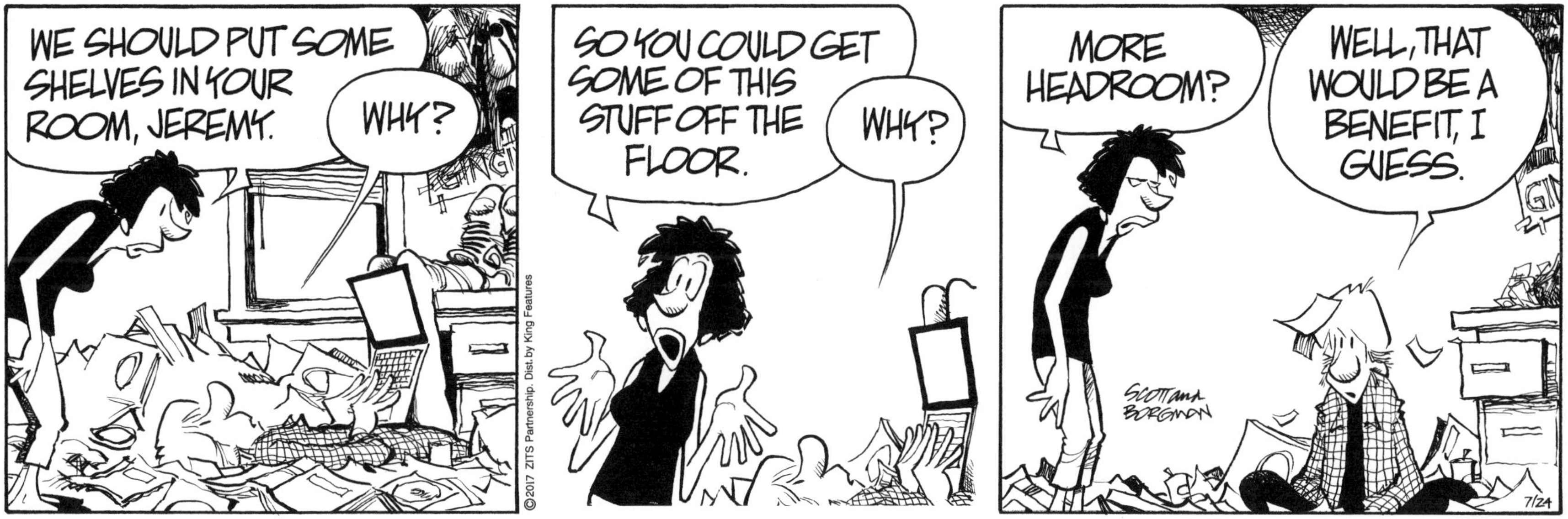
WE SHOULD PUT SOME SHELVES IN YOUR ROOM, JEREMY.
WHY?
SO YOU COULD GET SOME OF THIS STUFF OFF THE FLOOR.
WHY?
MORE HEADROOM?
WELL, THAT WOULD BE A BENEFIT, I GUESS.
© 2017 ZITS Partnership. Dist. by King Features
SCOTT and BORGMAN
7/24

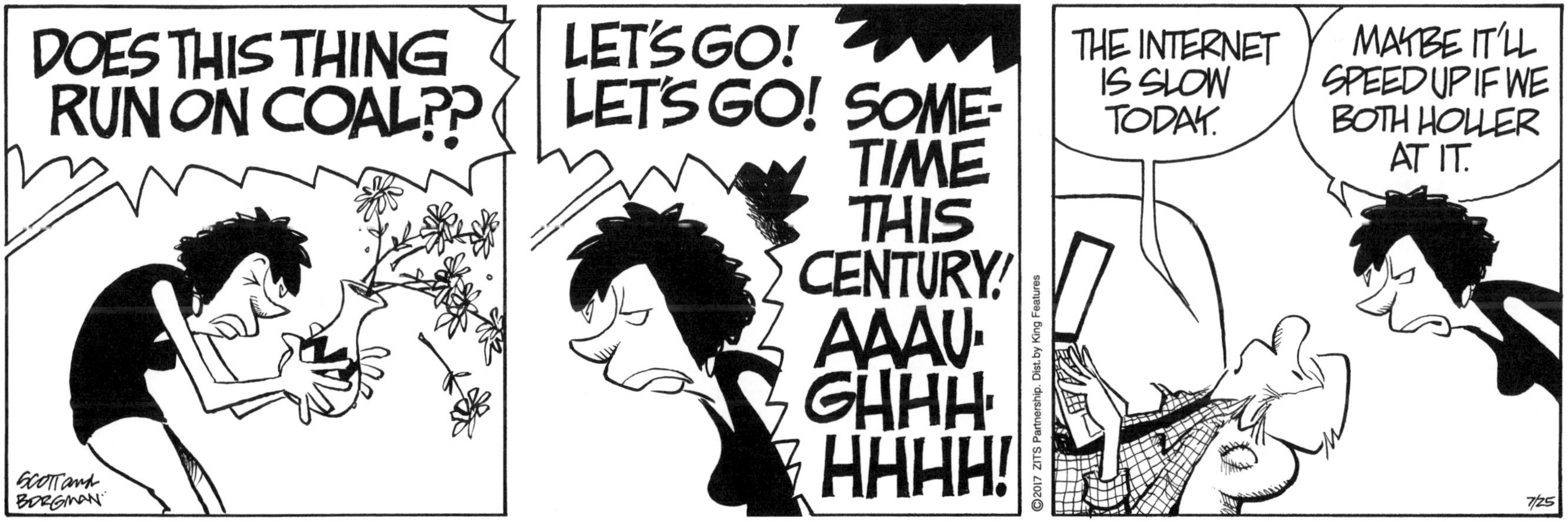
DOES THIS THING RUN ON COAL??
SCOTT and BORGMAN
LET'S GO! LET'S GO!
SOME-TIME THIS CENTURY!
AAAU-GHHH-HHHH!
© 2017 ZITS Partnership. Dist. by King Features
THE INTERNET IS SLOW TODAY.
MAYBE IT'LL SPEED UP IF WE BOTH HOLLER AT IT.
7/25

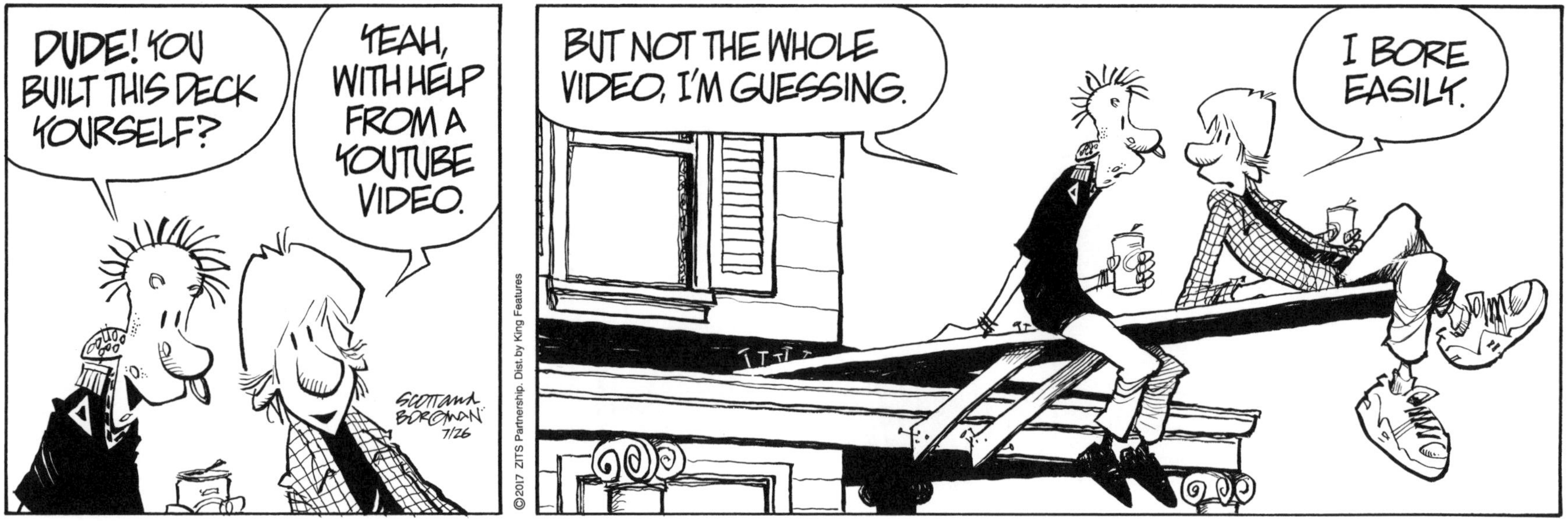

DUDE! YOU BUILT THIS DECK YOURSELF?
YEAH, WITH HELP FROM A YOUTUBE VIDEO.
SCOTT and BORGMAN 7/26
©2017 ZITS Partnership. Dist. by King Features
BUT NOT THE WHOLE VIDEO, I'M GUESSING.
I BORE EASILY.

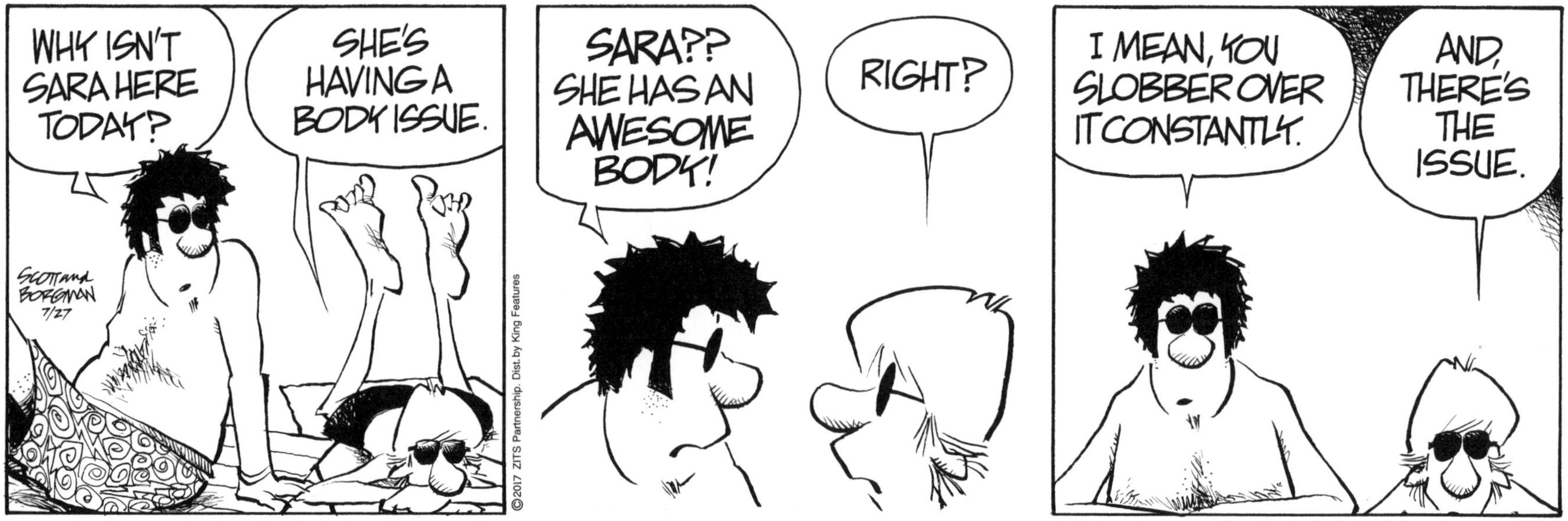

WHY ISN'T SARA HERE TODAY?
SHE'S HAVING A BODY ISSUE.
SCOTT and BORGMAN 7/27
©2017 ZITS Partnership. Dist. by King Features
SARA?? SHE HAS AN AWESOME BODY!
RIGHT?
I MEAN, YOU SLOBBER OVER IT CONSTANTLY.
AND, THERE'S THE ISSUE.

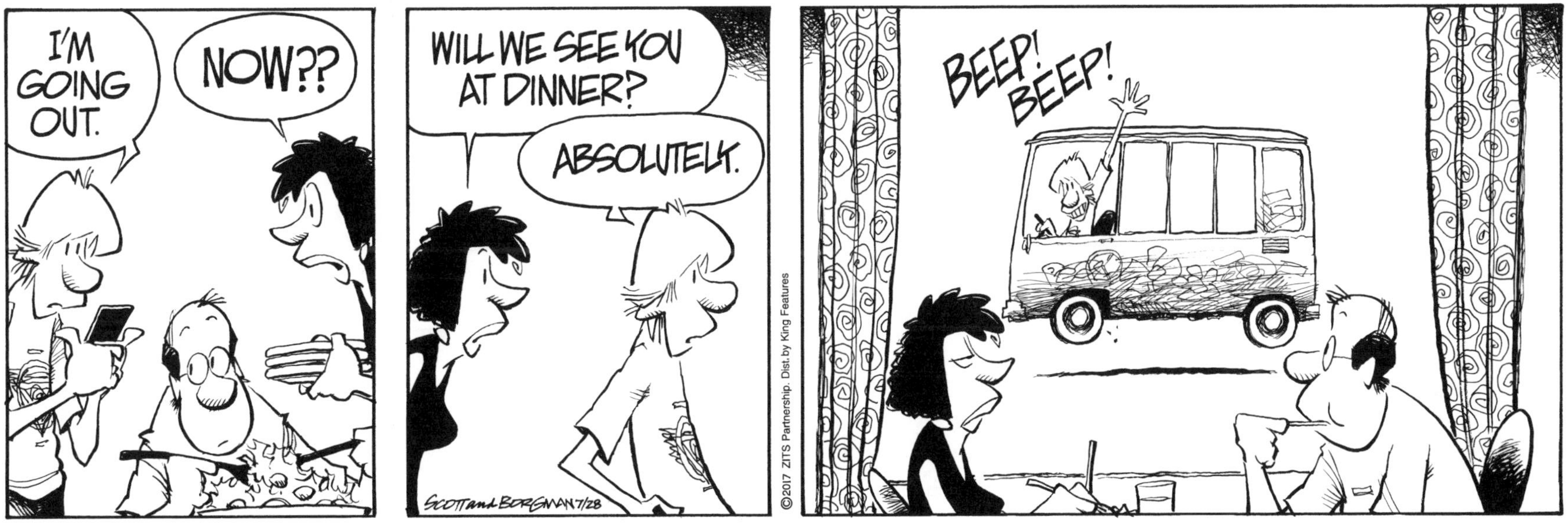
I'M GOING OUT.
NOW??
WILL WE SEE YOU AT DINNER?
ABSOLUTELY.
SCOTT and BORGMAN 7/28
©2017 ZITS Partnership. Dist. by King Features
BEEP! BEEP!

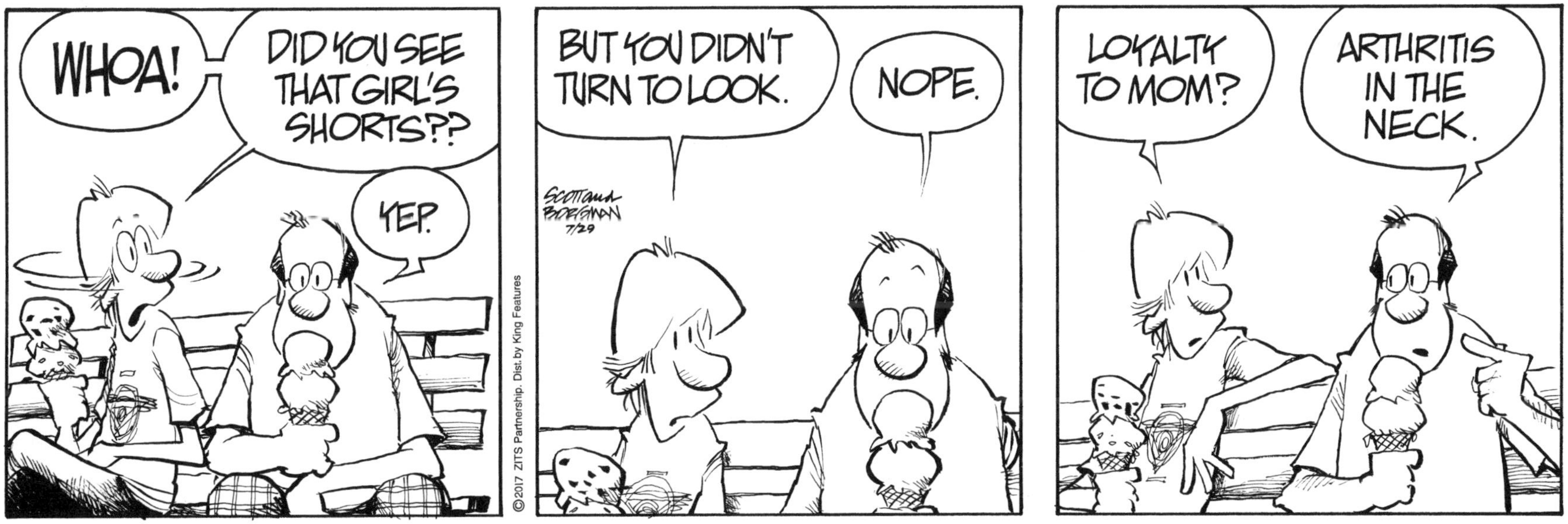
WHOA!
DID YOU SEE THAT GIRL'S SHORTS??
YEP.
©2017 ZITS Partnership. Dist. by King Features
SCOTT and BORGMAN 7/29
BUT YOU DIDN'T TURN TO LOOK.
NOPE.
LOYALTY TO MOM?
ARTHRITIS IN THE NECK.

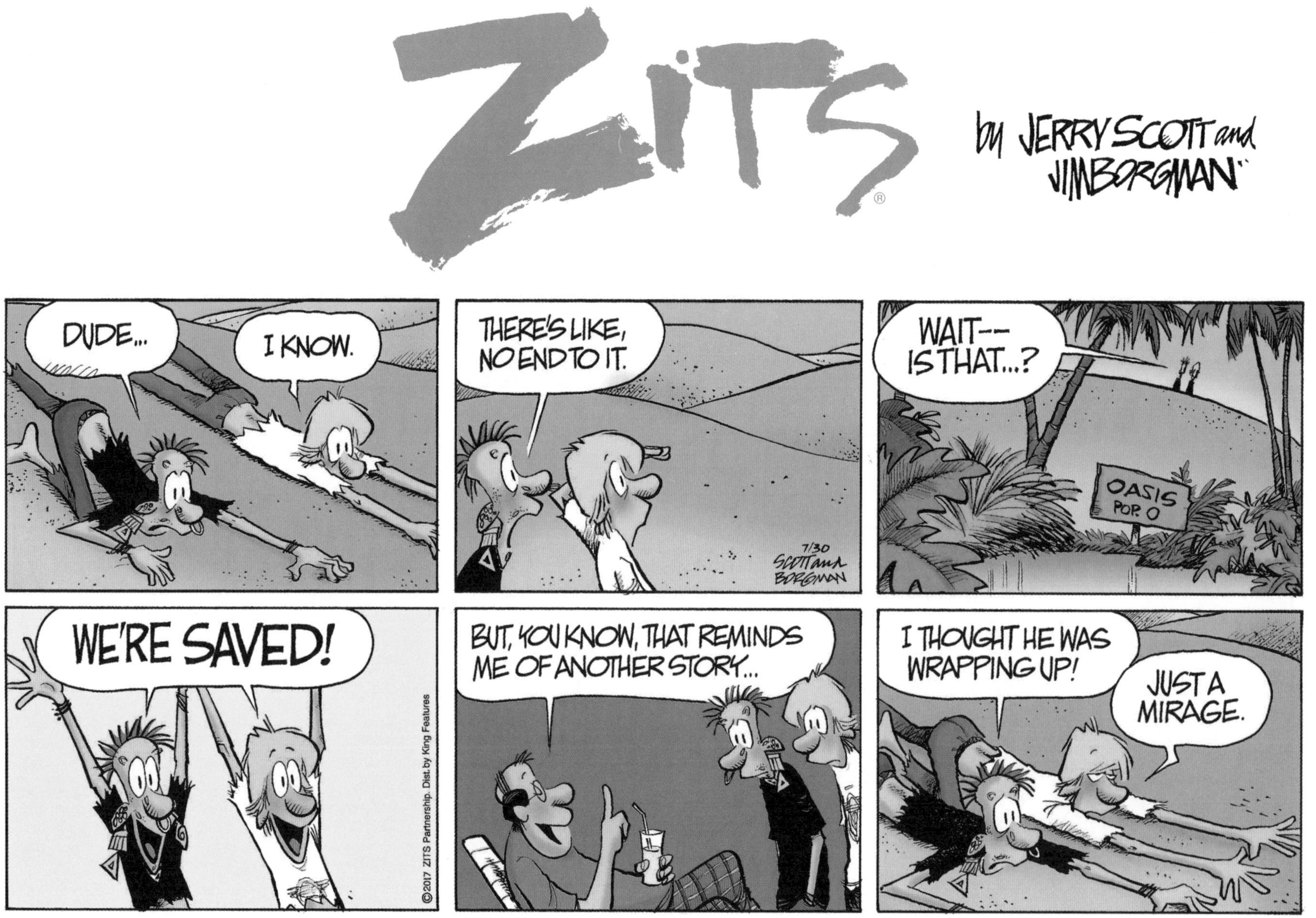
ZITS
by JERRY SCOTT and JIM BORGMAN
DUDE...
I KNOW.
THERE'S LIKE, NO END TO IT.
7/30 SCOTT and BORGMAN
WAIT-- IS THAT...?
OASIS POP. 0
WE'RE SAVED!
©2017 ZITS Partnership. Dist. by King Features
BUT, YOU KNOW, THAT REMINDS ME OF ANOTHER STORY...
I THOUGHT HE WAS WRAPPING UP!
JUST A MIRAGE.

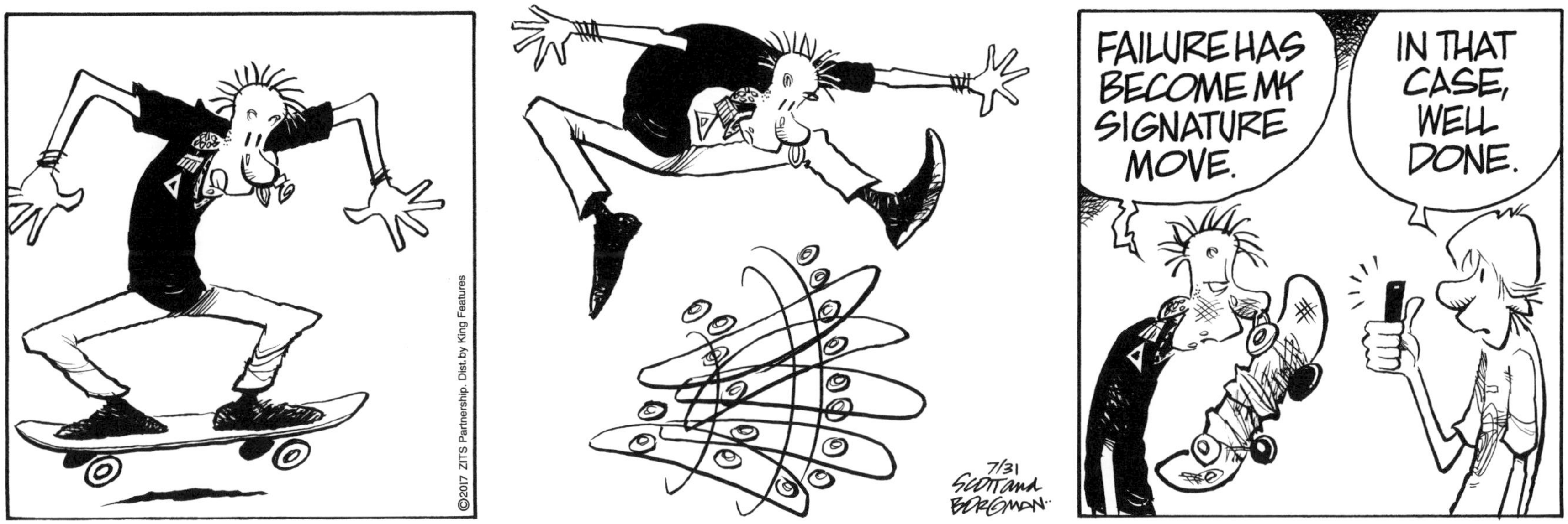
©2017 ZITS Partnership. Dist. by King Features
7/31 SCOTT and BORGMAN
FAILURE HAS BECOME MY SIGNATURE MOVE.
IN THAT CASE, WELL DONE.

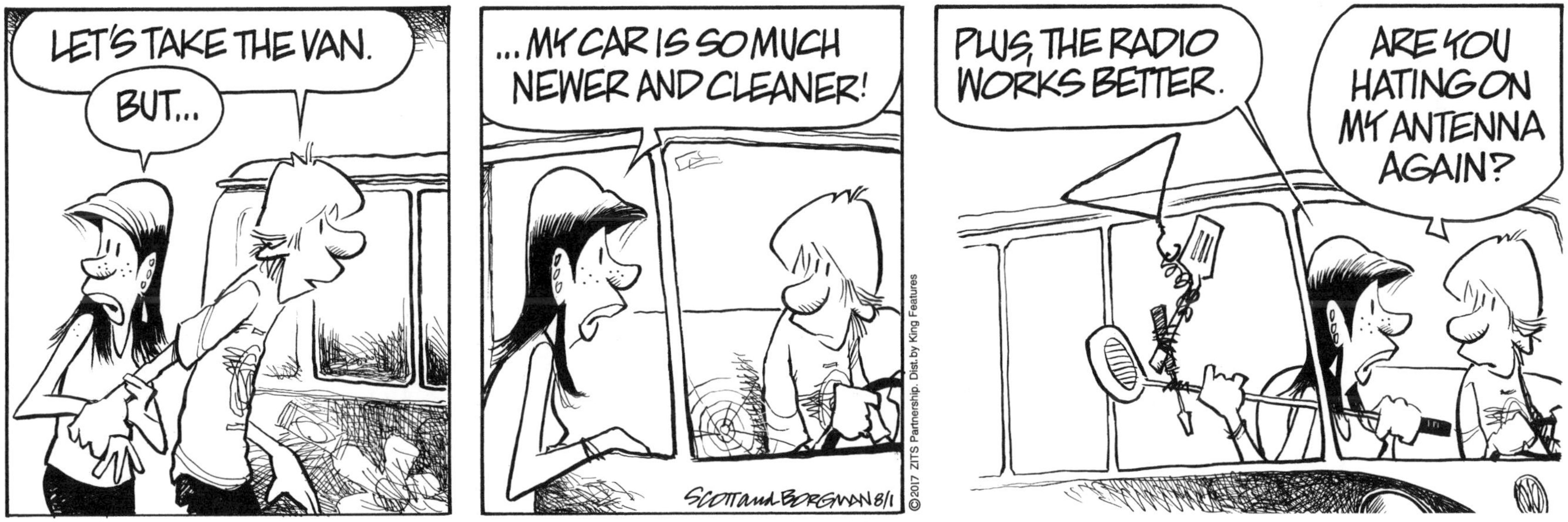
LET'S TAKE THE VAN.
BUT...
...MY CAR IS SO MUCH NEWER AND CLEANER!
SCOTT and BORGMAN 8/1
©2017 ZITS Partnership. Dist. by King Features
PLUS, THE RADIO WORKS BETTER.
ARE YOU HATING ON MY ANTENNA AGAIN?

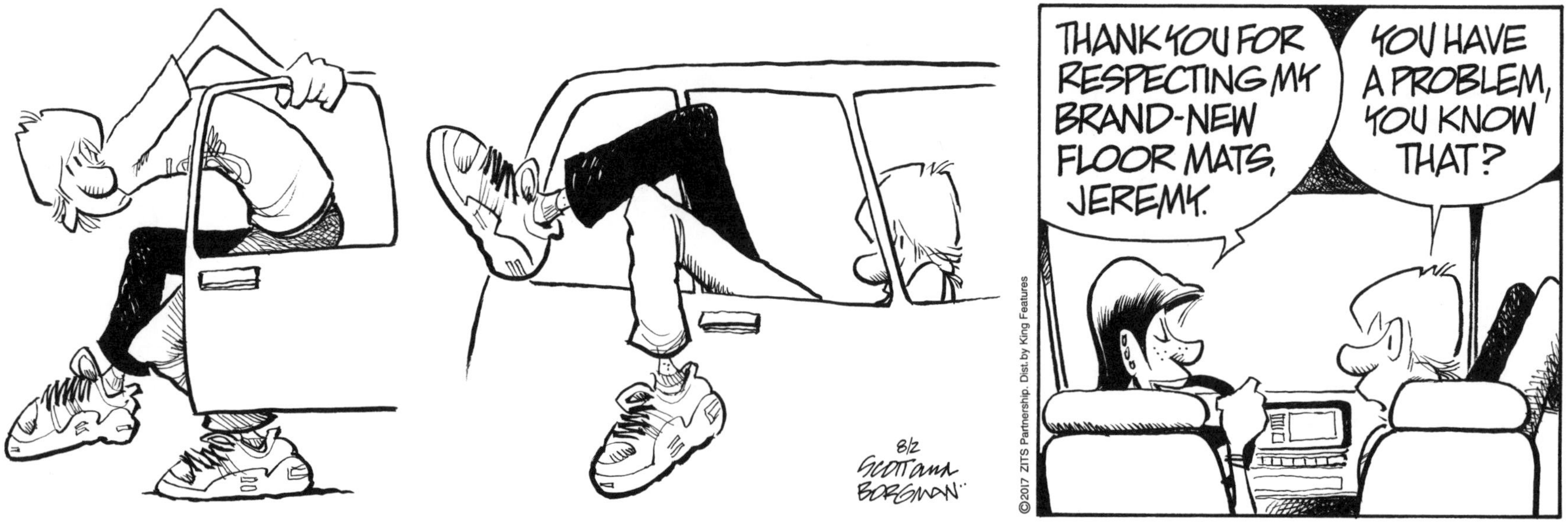
8/2
SCOTT and BORGMAN
THANK YOU FOR RESPECTING MY BRAND-NEW FLOOR MATS, JEREMY.
YOU HAVE A PROBLEM, YOU KNOW THAT?
©2017 ZITS Partnership. Dist. by King Features

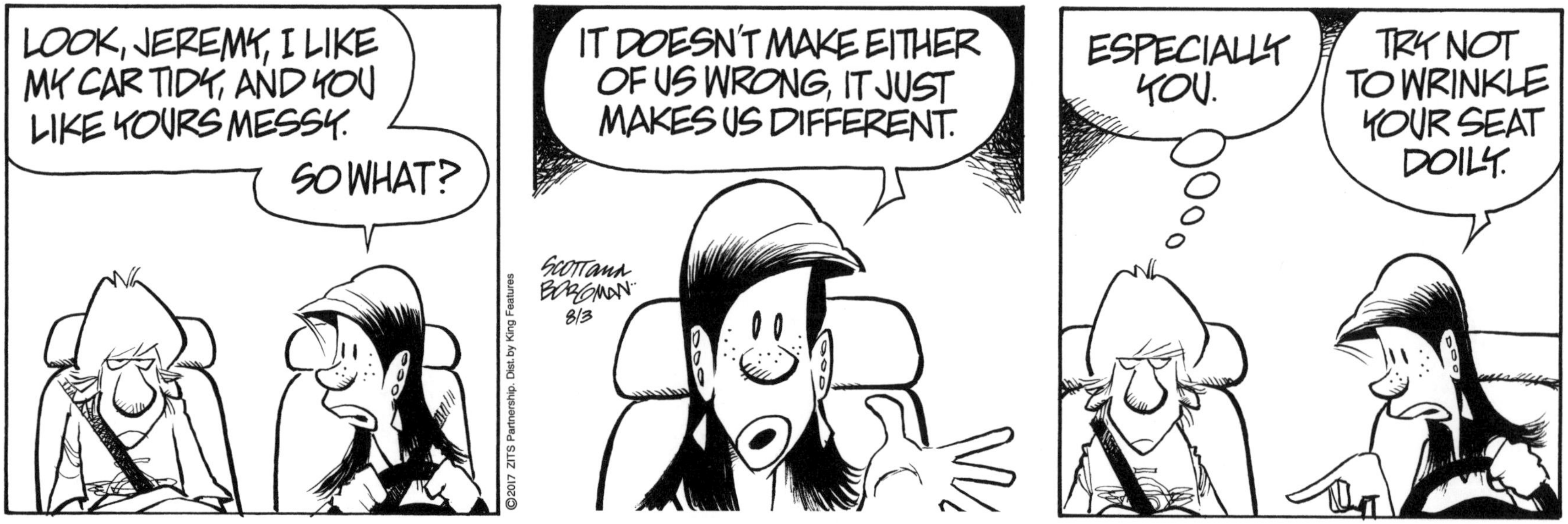
LOOK, JEREMY, I LIKE MY CAR TIDY, AND YOU LIKE YOURS MESSY.
SO WHAT?
©2017 ZITS Partnership. Dist. by King Features
SCOTT and BORGMAN 8/3
IT DOESN'T MAKE EITHER OF US WRONG, IT JUST MAKES US DIFFERENT.
ESPECIALLY YOU.
TRY NOT TO WRINKLE YOUR SEAT DOILY.

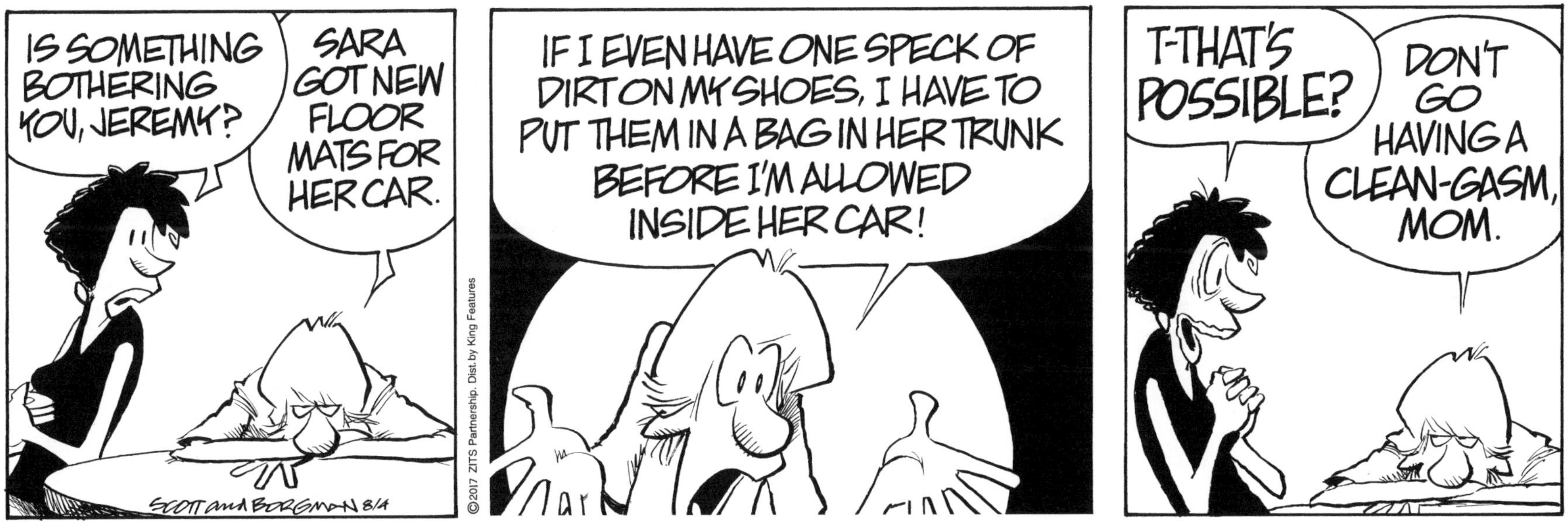
IS SOMETHING BOTHERING YOU, JEREMY?
SARA GOT NEW FLOOR MATS FOR HER CAR.
SCOTT AND BORGMAN 8/4
© 2017 ZITS Partnership. Dist. by King Features
IF I EVEN HAVE ONE SPECK OF DIRT ON MY SHOES, I HAVE TO PUT THEM IN A BAG IN HER TRUNK BEFORE I'M ALLOWED INSIDE HER CAR!
T-THAT'S POSSIBLE?
DON'T GO HAVING A CLEAN-GASM, MOM.

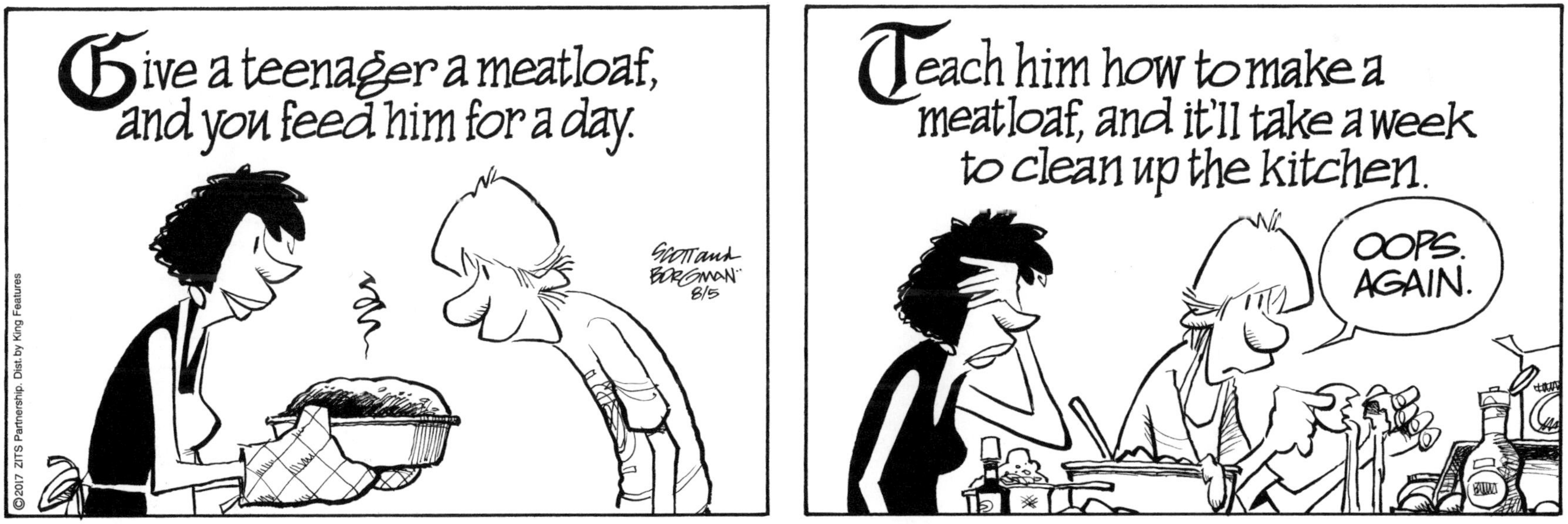
Give a teenager a meatloaf, and you feed him for a day.
SCOTT AND BORGMAN 8/5
© 2017 ZITS Partnership. Dist. by King Features
Teach him how to make a meatloaf, and it'll take a week to clean up the kitchen.
OOPS. AGAIN.

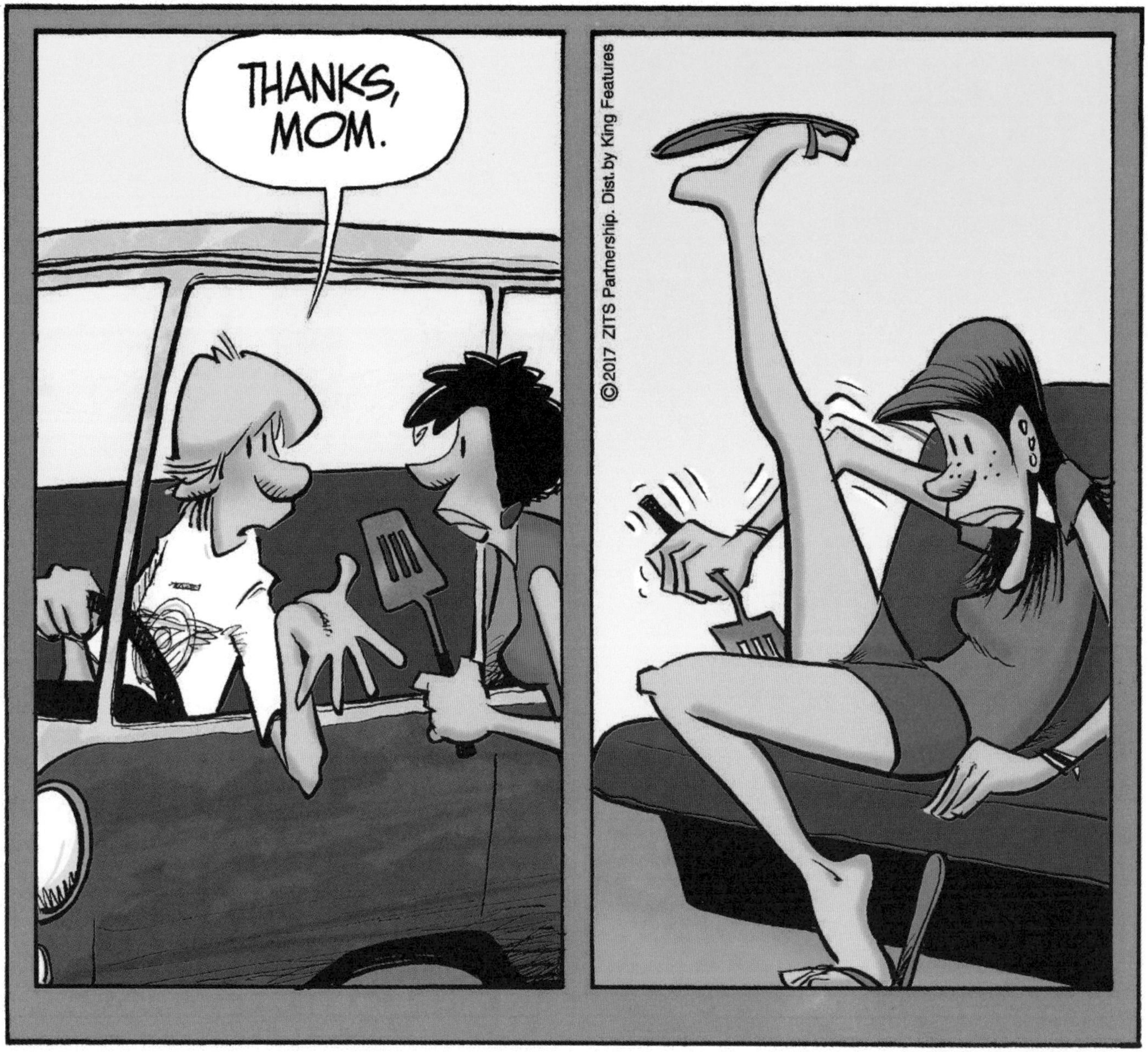
THANKS, MOM.
©2017 ZITS Partnership. Dist.by King Features

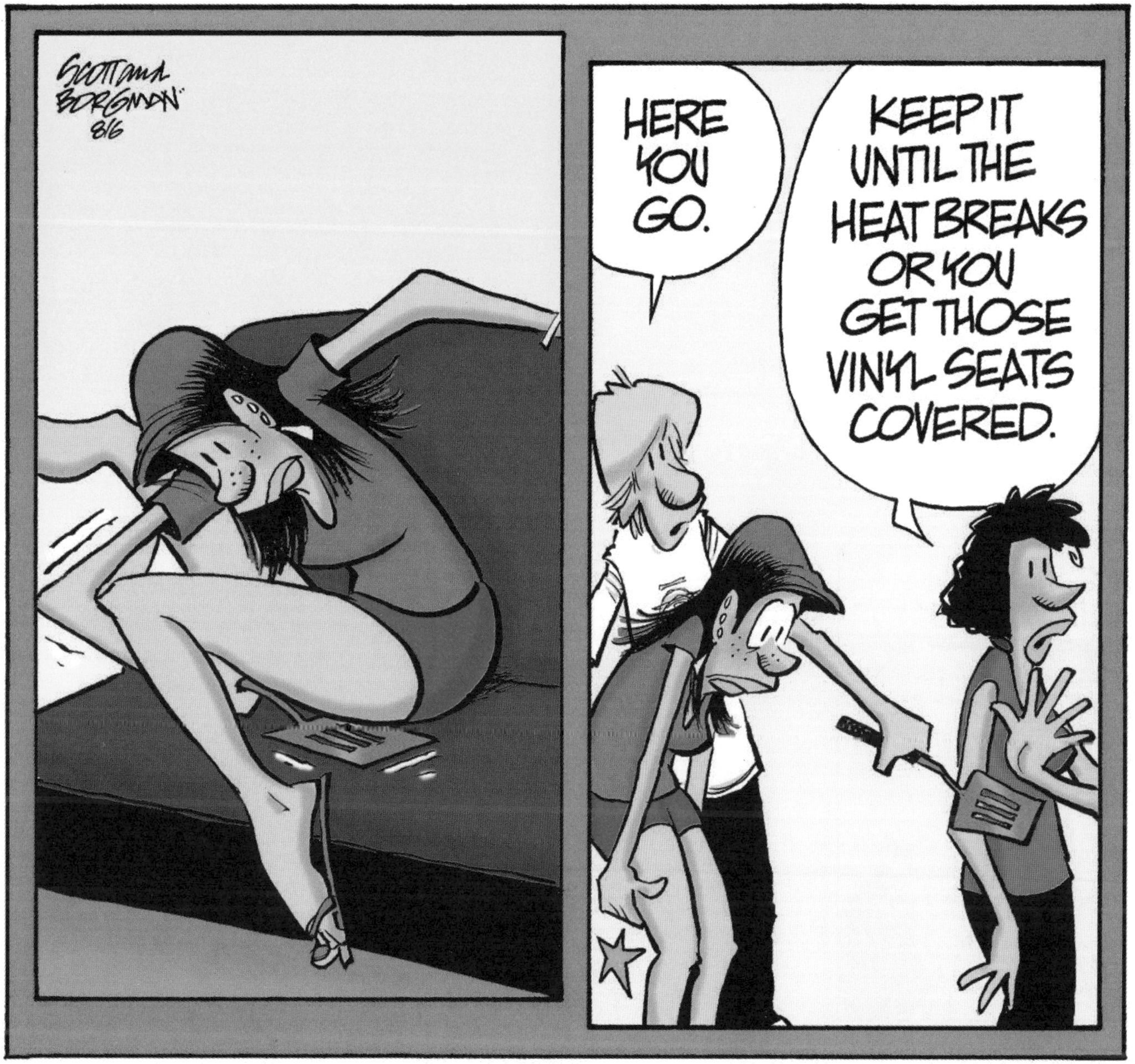
SCOTT and BORGMAN 8/6
HERE YOU GO.
KEEP IT UNTIL THE HEAT BREAKS OR YOU GET THOSE VINYL SEATS COVERED.

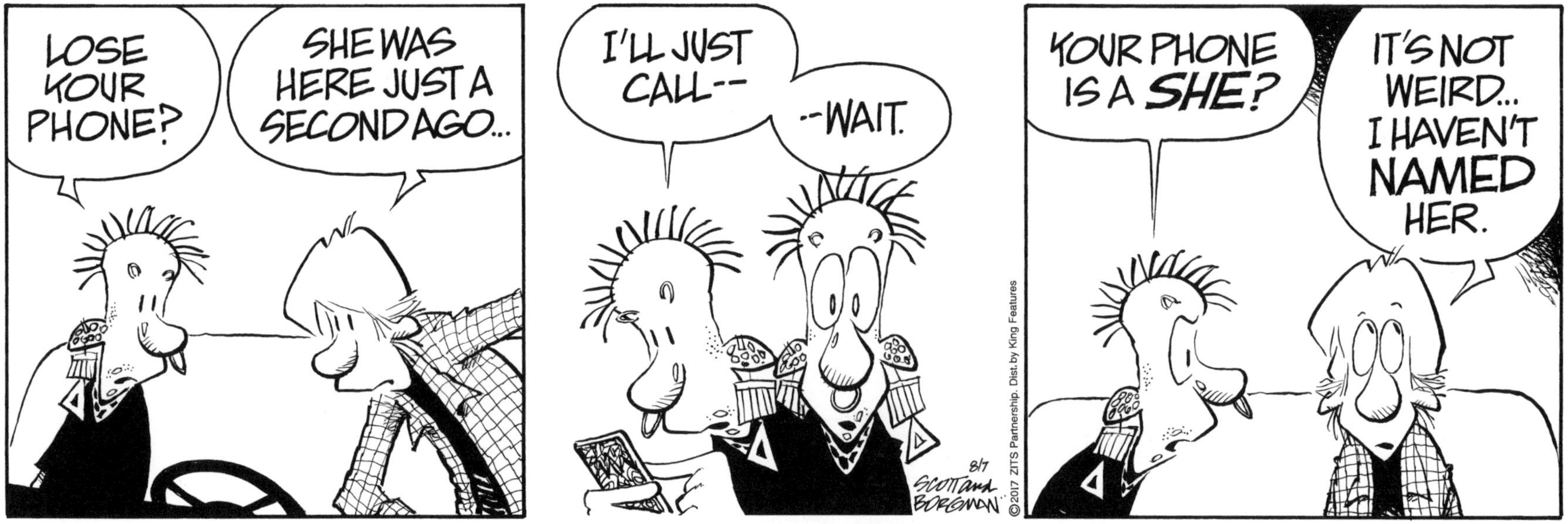
LOSE YOUR PHONE?
SHE WAS HERE JUST A SECOND AGO...
I'LL JUST CALL--
--WAIT.
8/7
SCOTT and BORGMAN
©2017 ZITS Partnership. Dist. by King Features
YOUR PHONE IS A *SHE*?
IT'S NOT WEIRD... I HAVEN'T **NAMED** HER.

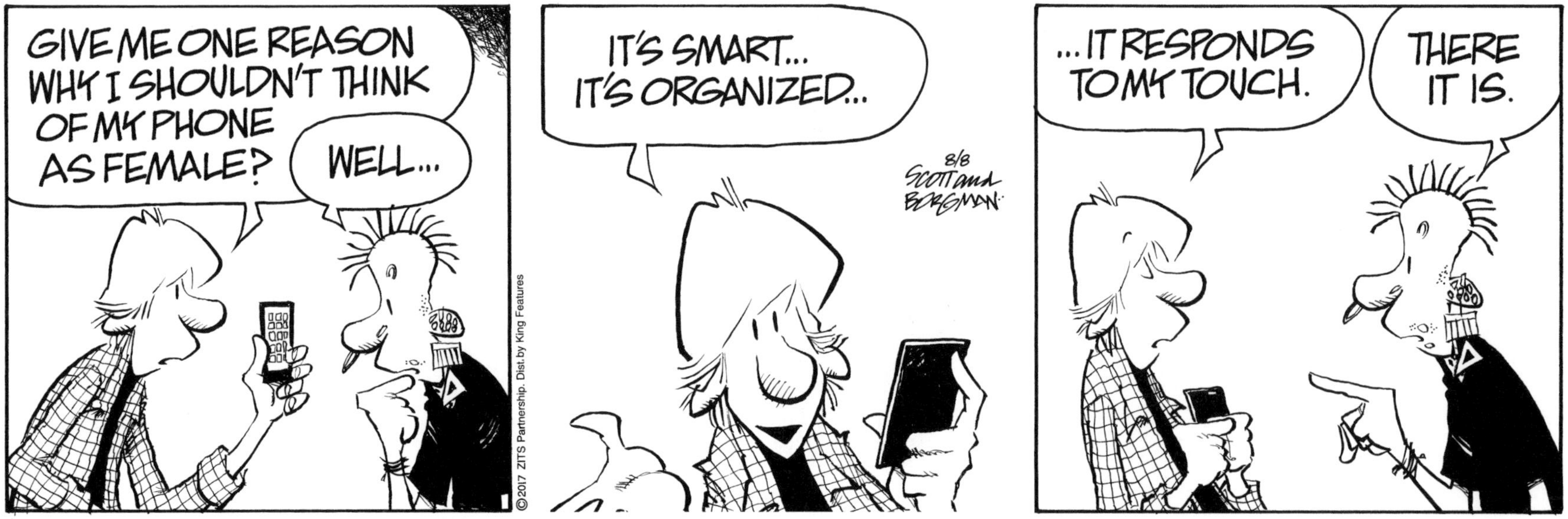
GIVE ME ONE REASON WHY I SHOULDN'T THINK OF MY PHONE AS FEMALE?
WELL...
©2017 ZITS Partnership. Dist. by King Features
IT'S SMART... IT'S ORGANIZED...
8/8
SCOTT and BORGMAN
...IT RESPONDS TO MY TOUCH.
THERE IT IS.

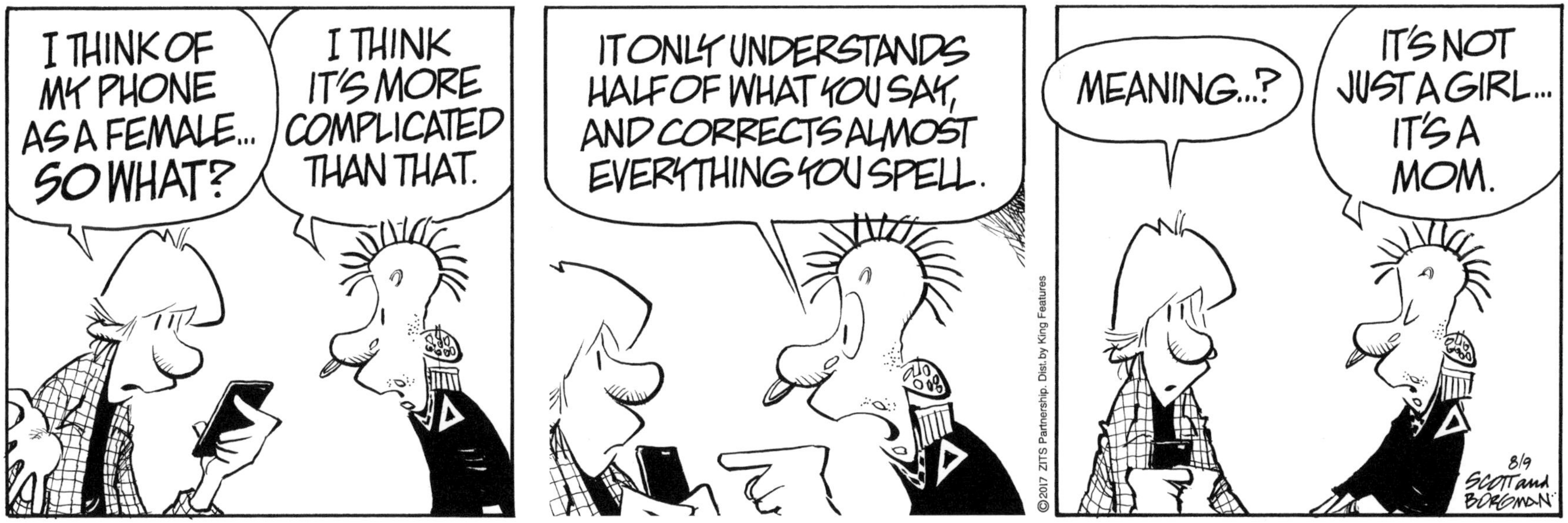
I THINK OF MY PHONE AS A FEMALE... SO WHAT?
I THINK IT'S MORE COMPLICATED THAN THAT.
IT ONLY UNDERSTANDS HALF OF WHAT YOU SAY, AND CORRECTS ALMOST EVERYTHING YOU SPELL.
MEANING...?
IT'S NOT JUST A GIRL... IT'S A MOM.
8/9 SCOTT and BORGMAN
©2017 ZITS Partnership. Dist. by King Features

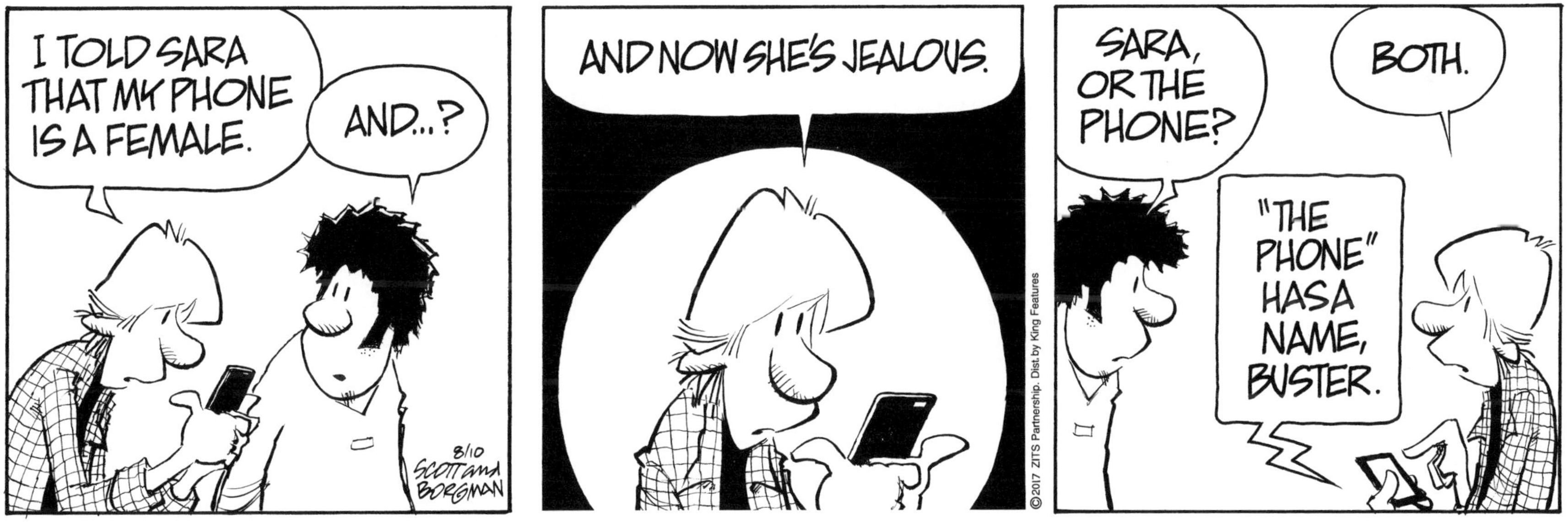
I TOLD SARA THAT MY PHONE IS A FEMALE.
AND...?
8/10 SCOTT and BORGMAN
AND NOW SHE'S JEALOUS.
SARA, OR THE PHONE?
BOTH.
"THE PHONE" HAS A NAME, BUSTER.
©2017 ZITS Partnership. Dist. by King Features

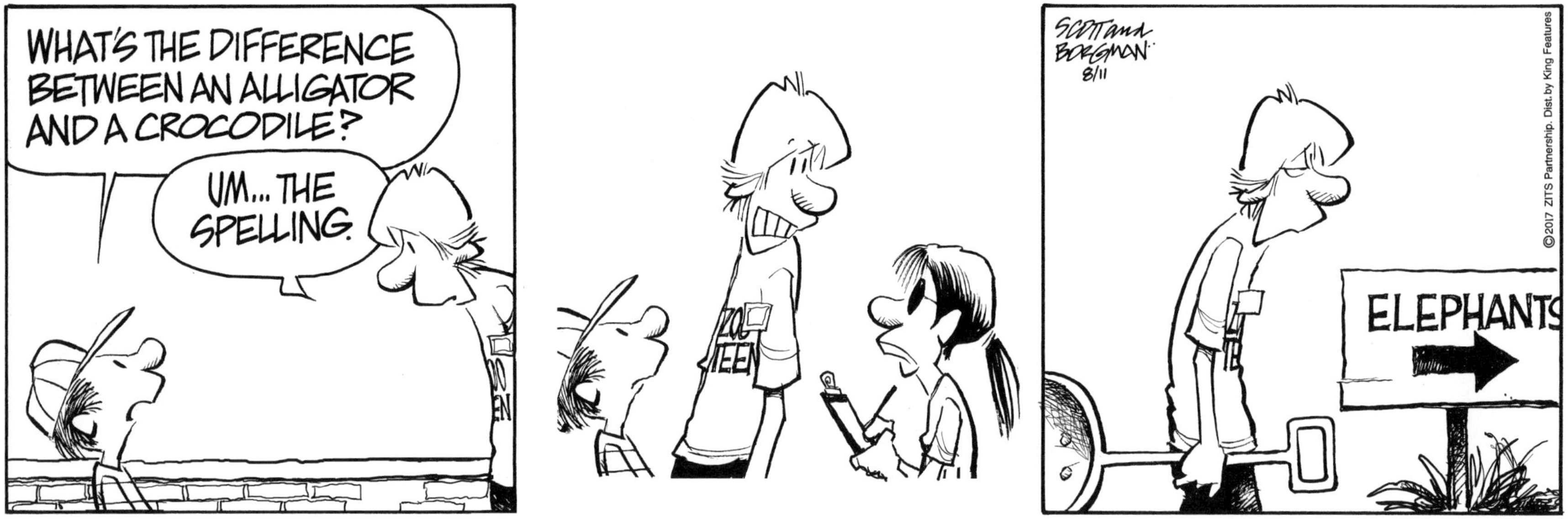
WHAT'S THE DIFFERENCE BETWEEN AN ALLIGATOR AND A CROCODILE?
UM... THE SPELLING.
ZOO TEEN
ELEPHANTS
SCOTT and BORGMAN 8/11
©2017 ZITS Partnership. Dist. by King Features

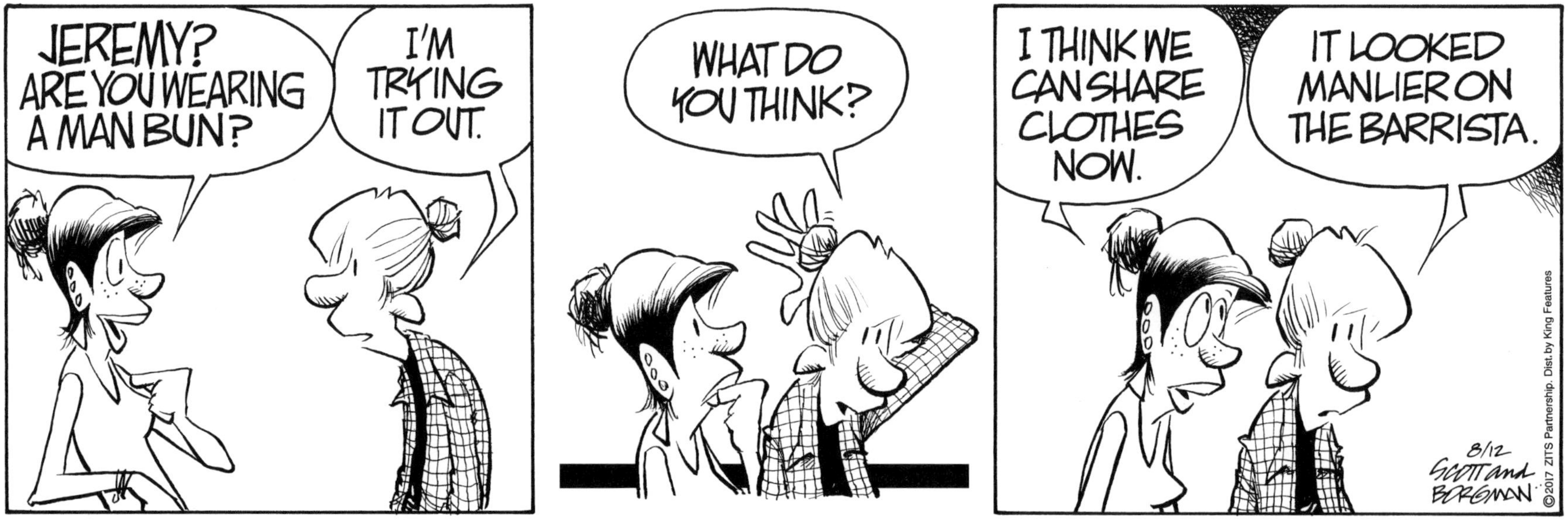
JEREMY? ARE YOU WEARING A MAN BUN?
I'M TRYING IT OUT.
WHAT DO YOU THINK?
I THINK WE CAN SHARE CLOTHES NOW.
IT LOOKED MANLIER ON THE BARRISTA.
8/12 SCOTT and BORGMAN
©2017 ZITS Partnership. Dist. by King Features

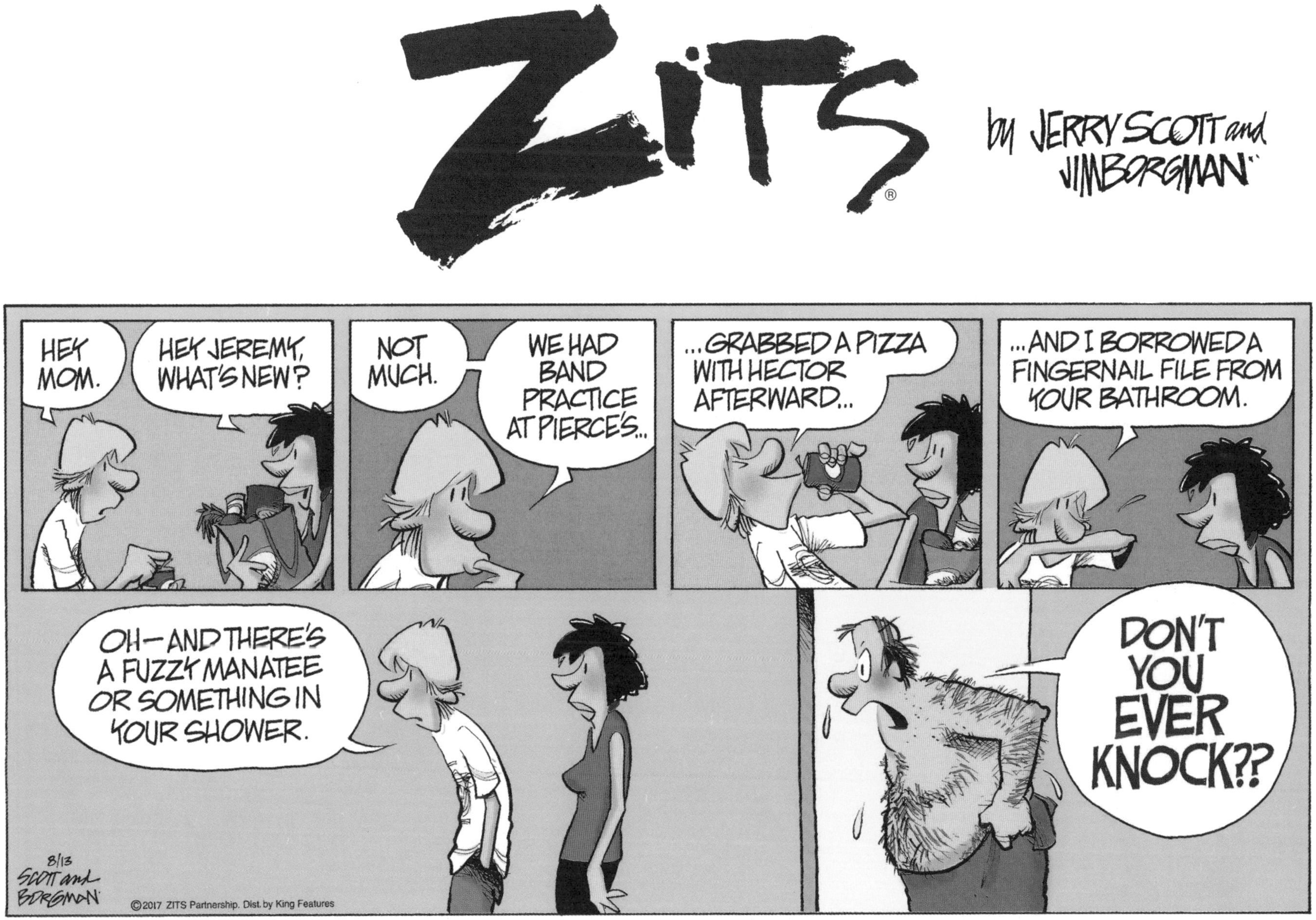
ZITS®
by JERRY SCOTT and JIM BORGMAN
HEY MOM.
HEY JEREMY, WHAT'S NEW?
NOT MUCH.
WE HAD BAND PRACTICE AT PIERCE'S...
...GRABBED A PIZZA WITH HECTOR AFTERWARD...
...AND I BORROWED A FINGERNAIL FILE FROM YOUR BATHROOM.
OH—AND THERE'S A FUZZY MANATEE OR SOMETHING IN YOUR SHOWER.
DON'T YOU EVER KNOCK??
8/13 SCOTT and BORGMAN
©2017 ZITS Partnership. Dist. by King Features

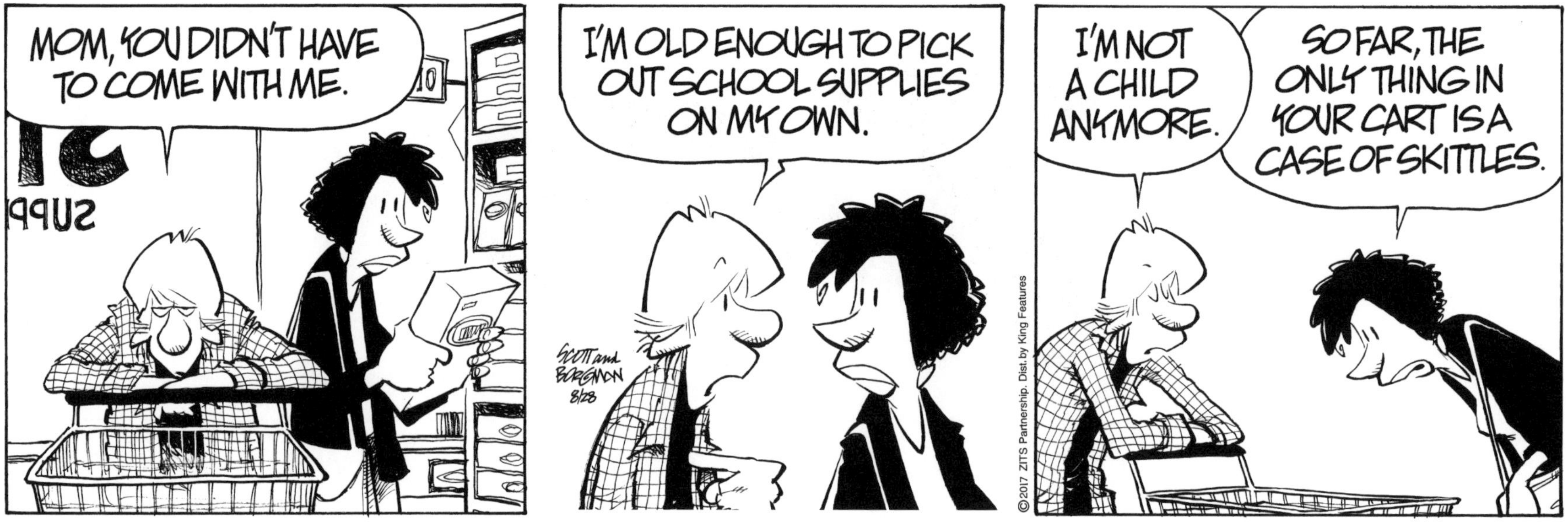
MOM, YOU DIDN'T HAVE TO COME WITH ME.
I'M OLD ENOUGH TO PICK OUT SCHOOL SUPPLIES ON MY OWN.
SCOTT and BORGMAN 8/28
I'M NOT A CHILD ANYMORE.
SO FAR, THE ONLY THING IN YOUR CART IS A CASE OF SKITTLES.
©2017 ZITS Partnership. Dist. by King Features

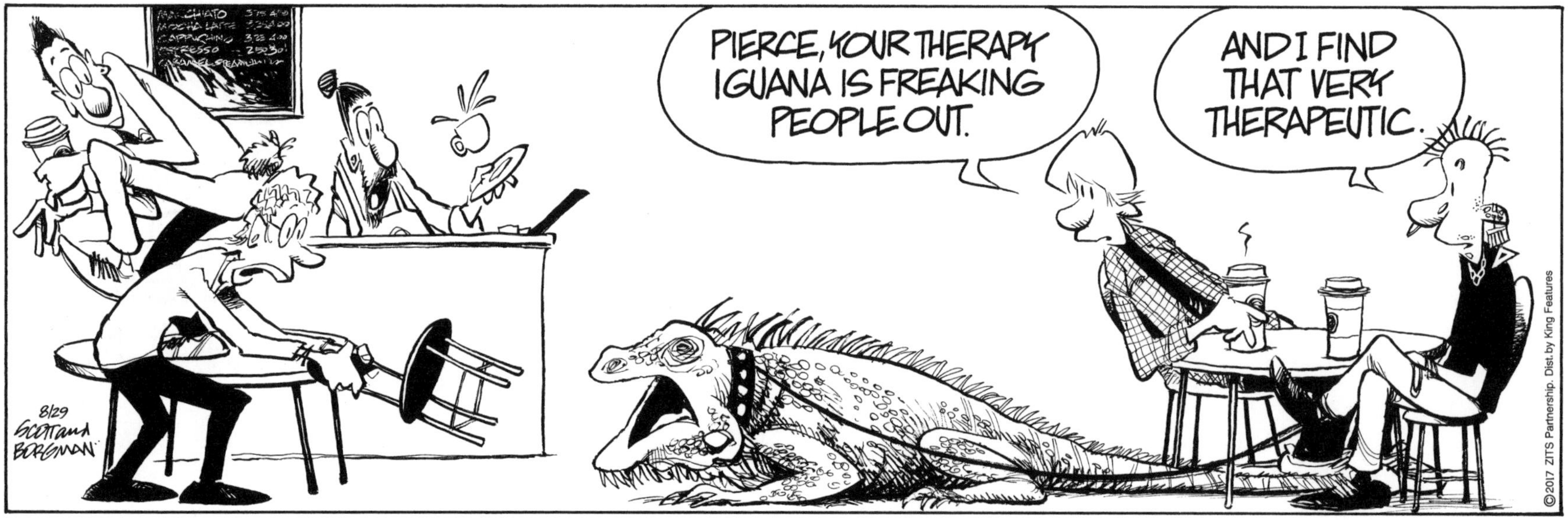
8/29 SCOTT and BORGMAN
PIERCE, YOUR THERAPY IGUANA IS FREAKING PEOPLE OUT.
AND I FIND THAT VERY THERAPEUTIC.
©2017 ZITS Partnership. Dist. by King Features

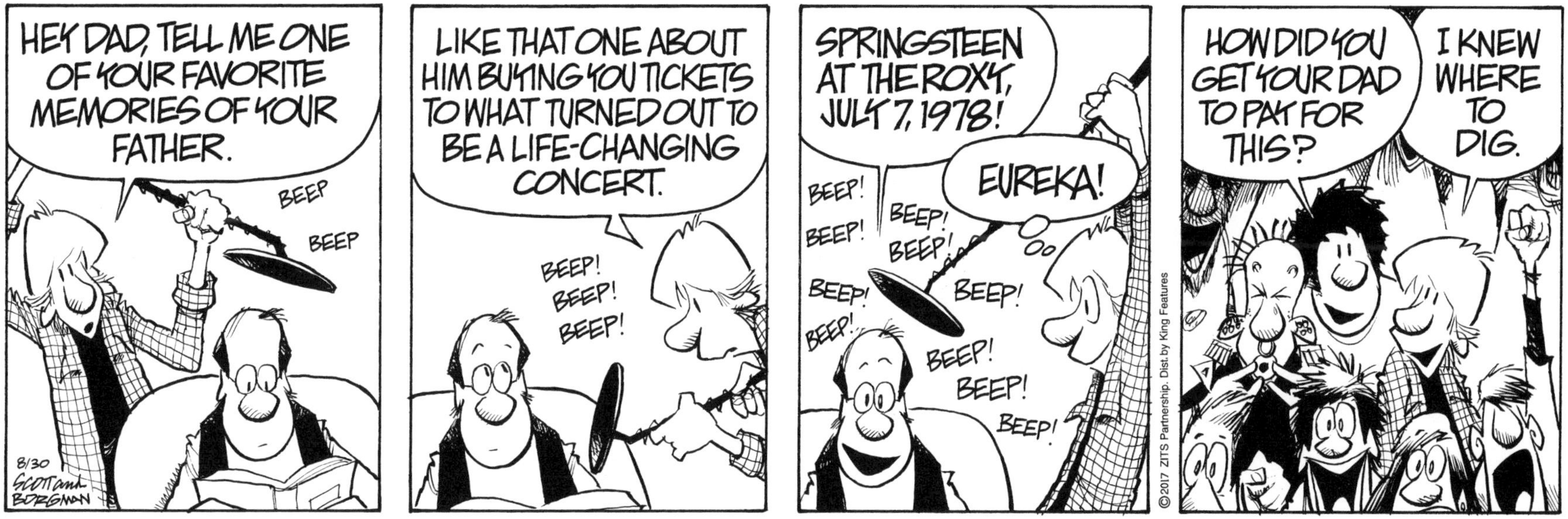
HEY DAD, TELL ME ONE OF YOUR FAVORITE MEMORIES OF YOUR FATHER.
BEEP
BEEP
8/30
SCOTT and BORGMAN
LIKE THAT ONE ABOUT HIM BUYING YOU TICKETS TO WHAT TURNED OUT TO BE A LIFE-CHANGING CONCERT.
BEEP! BEEP! BEEP!
SPRINGSTEEN AT THE ROXY, JULY 7, 1978!
EUREKA!
BEEP! BEEP! BEEP! BEEP! BEEP! BEEP! BEEP! BEEP! BEEP! BEEP! BEEP!
HOW DID YOU GET YOUR DAD TO PAY FOR THIS?
I KNEW WHERE TO DIG.
©2017 ZITS Partnership. Dist. by King Features

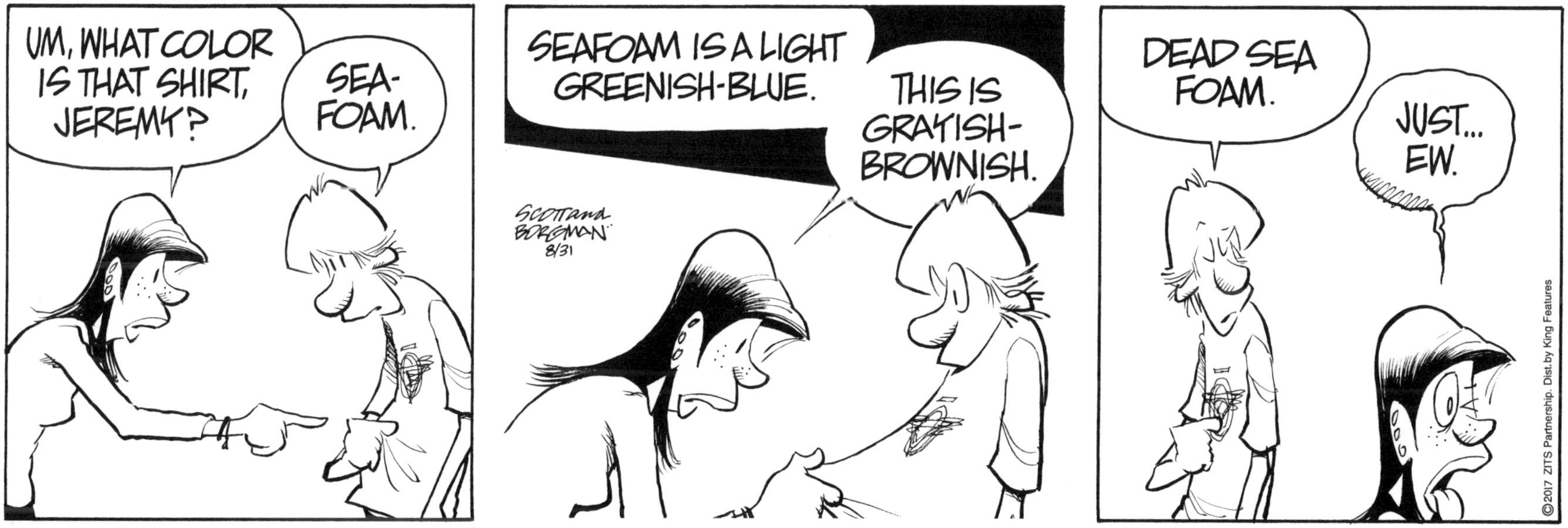
UM, WHAT COLOR IS THAT SHIRT, JEREMY?
SEA-FOAM.
SEAFOAM IS A LIGHT GREENISH-BLUE.
THIS IS GRAYISH-BROWNISH.
SCOTT and BORGMAN 8/31
DEAD SEA FOAM.
JUST... EW.
©2017 ZITS Partnership. Dist. by King Features

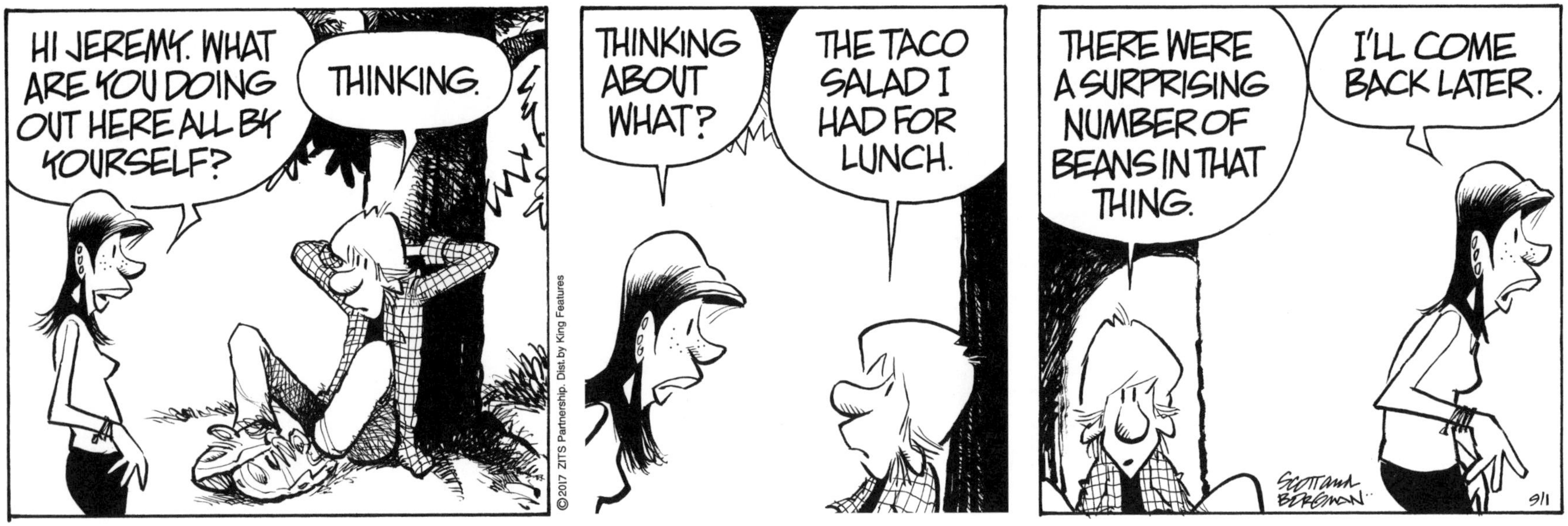
HI JEREMY. WHAT ARE YOU DOING OUT HERE ALL BY YOURSELF?
THINKING.
THINKING ABOUT WHAT?
THE TACO SALAD I HAD FOR LUNCH.
THERE WERE A SURPRISING NUMBER OF BEANS IN THAT THING.
I'LL COME BACK LATER.
SCOTT AND BORGMAN
9/1
©2017 ZITS Partnership. Dist. by King Features

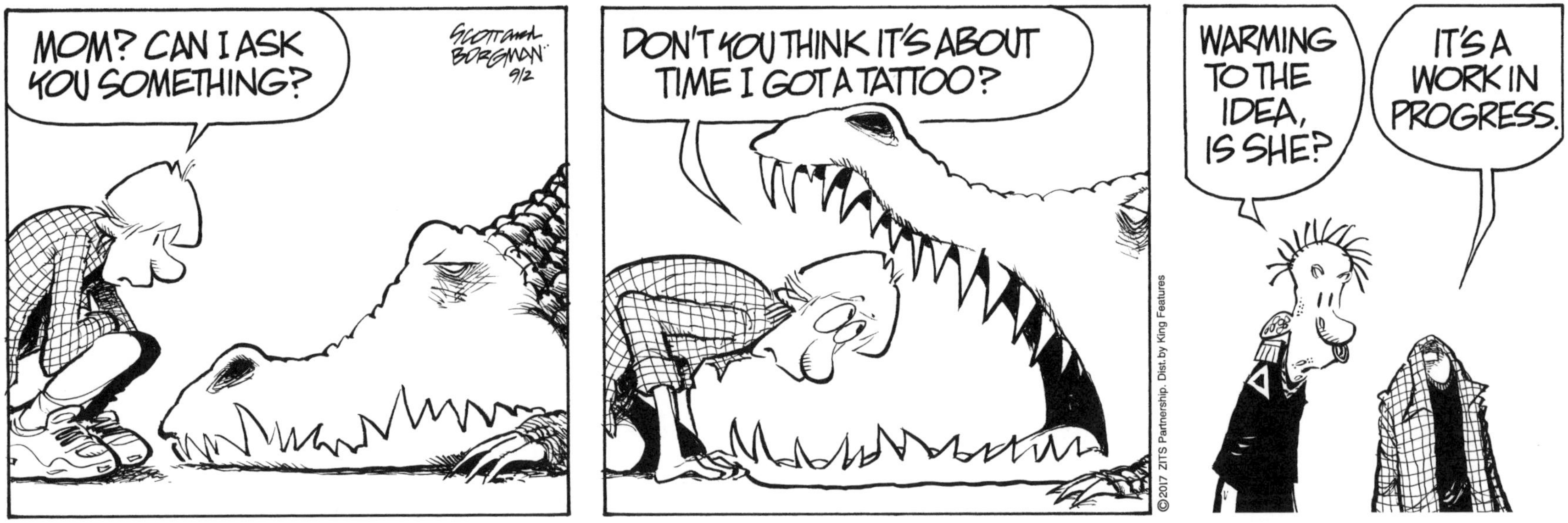
MOM? CAN I ASK YOU SOMETHING?
SCOTT AND BORGMAN
9/2
DON'T YOU THINK IT'S ABOUT TIME I GOT A TATTOO?
WARMING TO THE IDEA, IS SHE?
IT'S A WORK IN PROGRESS.
©2017 ZITS Partnership. Dist. by King Features

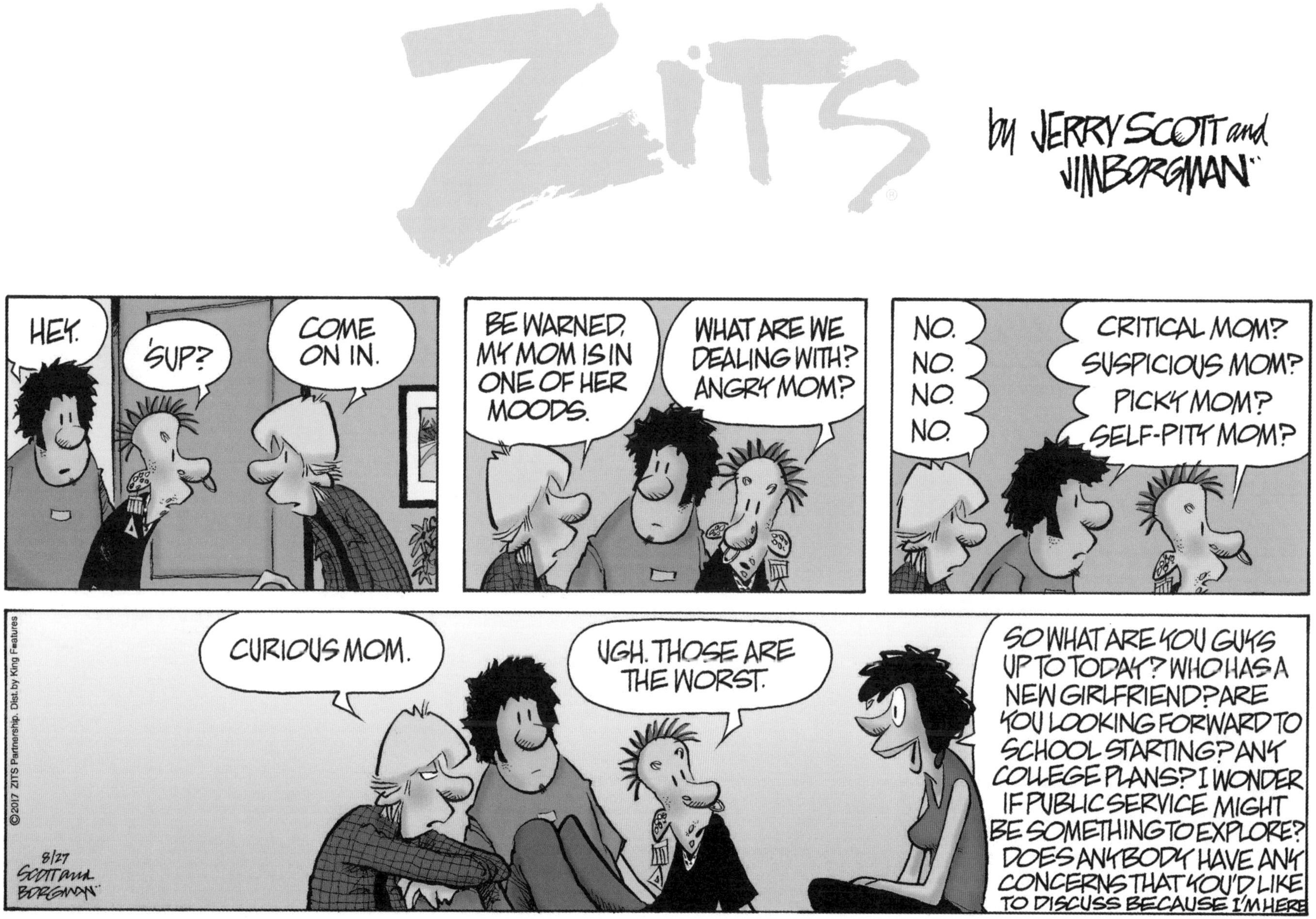

ZITS
by JERRY SCOTT and JIM BORGMAN
HEY.
'SUP?
COME ON IN.
BE WARNED, MY MOM IS IN ONE OF HER MOODS.
WHAT ARE WE DEALING WITH? ANGRY MOM?
NO.
NO.
NO.
NO.
CRITICAL MOM?
SUSPICIOUS MOM?
PICKY MOM?
SELF-PITY MOM?
CURIOUS MOM.
UGH. THOSE ARE THE WORST.
SO WHAT ARE YOU GUYS UP TO TODAY? WHO HAS A NEW GIRLFRIEND? ARE YOU LOOKING FORWARD TO SCHOOL STARTING? ANY COLLEGE PLANS? I WONDER IF PUBLIC SERVICE MIGHT BE SOMETHING TO EXPLORE? DOES ANYBODY HAVE ANY CONCERNS THAT YOU'D LIKE TO DISCUSS BECAUSE I'M HERE
©2017 ZITS Partnership. Dist. by King Features
8/27
SCOTT and BORGMAN

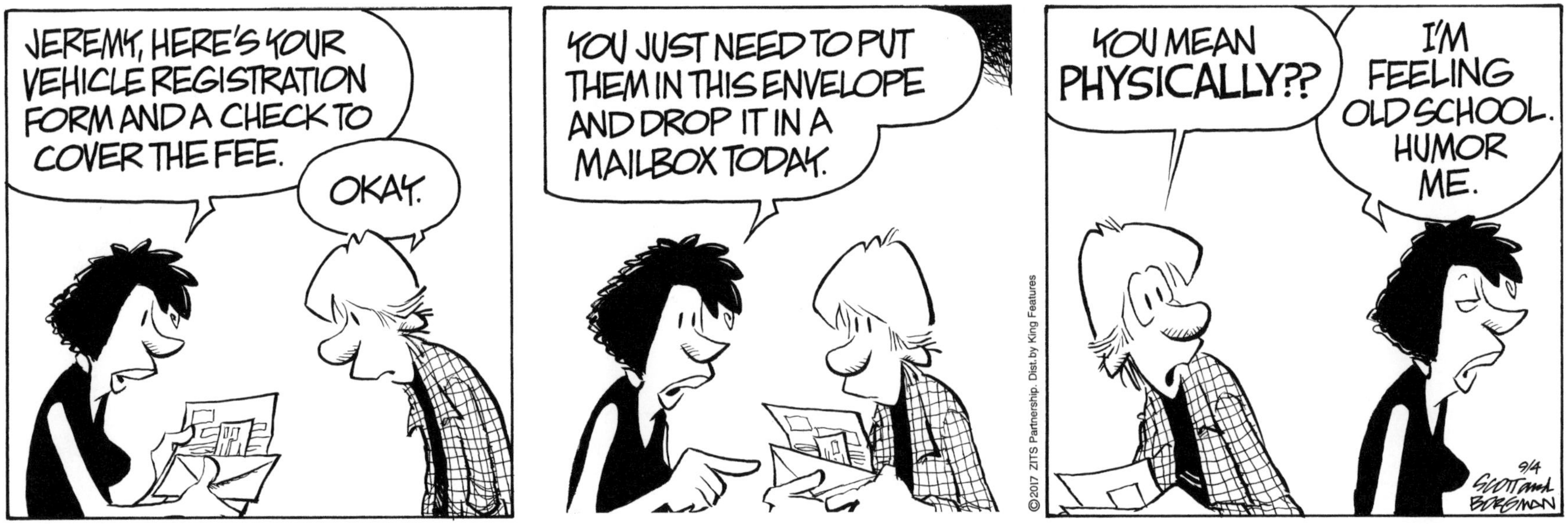
JEREMY, HERE'S YOUR VEHICLE REGISTRATION FORM AND A CHECK TO COVER THE FEE.
OKAY.
YOU JUST NEED TO PUT THEM IN THIS ENVELOPE AND DROP IT IN A MAILBOX TODAY.
YOU MEAN PHYSICALLY??
I'M FEELING OLD SCHOOL. HUMOR ME.
©2017 ZITS Partnership. Dist. by King Features
9/4
SCOTT and BORGMAN

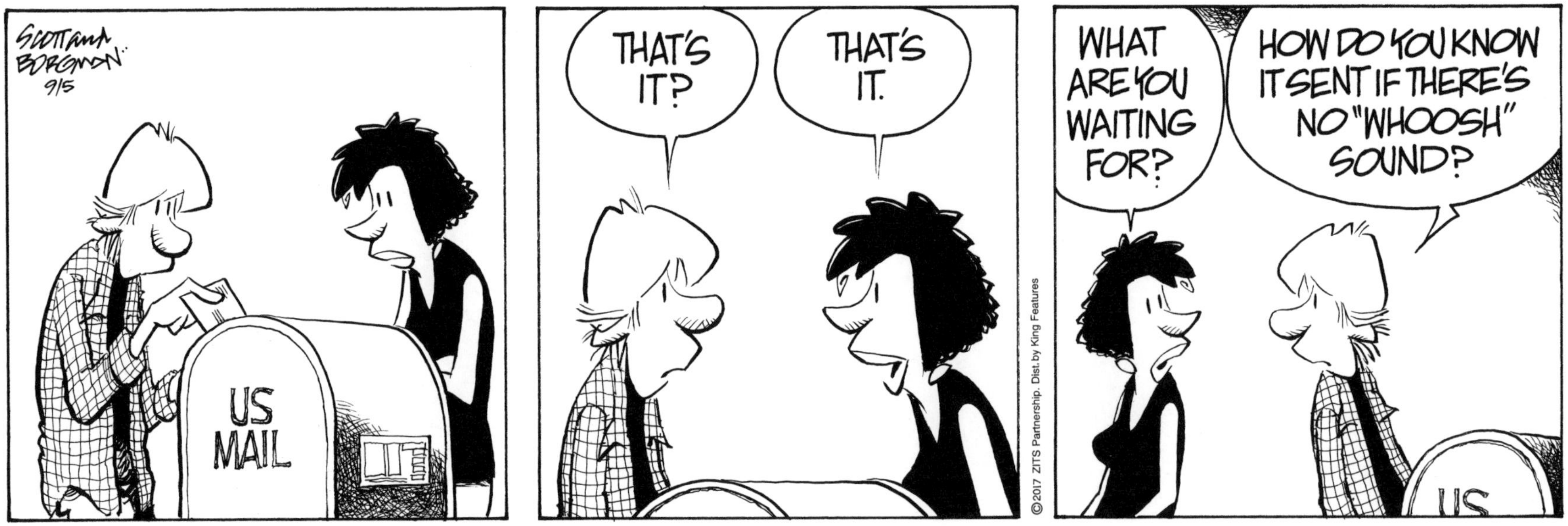
SCOTT and BORGMAN 9/5
US MAIL
THAT'S IT?
THAT'S IT.
©2017 ZITS Partnership. Dist. by King Features
WHAT ARE YOU WAITING FOR?
HOW DO YOU KNOW IT SENT IF THERE'S NO "WHOOSH" SOUND?
US

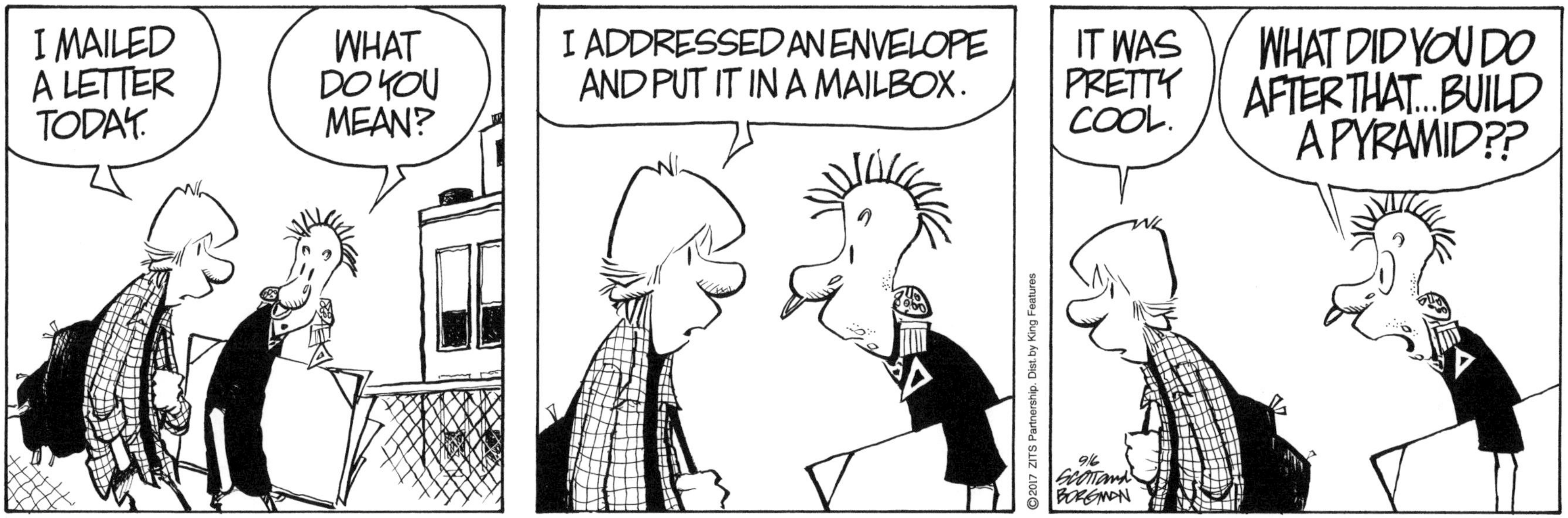
I MAILED A LETTER TODAY.
WHAT DO YOU MEAN?
I ADDRESSED AN ENVELOPE AND PUT IT IN A MAILBOX.
IT WAS PRETTY COOL.
WHAT DID YOU DO AFTER THAT... BUILD A PYRAMID??
9/6 SCOTT and BORGMAN
©2017 ZITS Partnership. Dist. by King Features

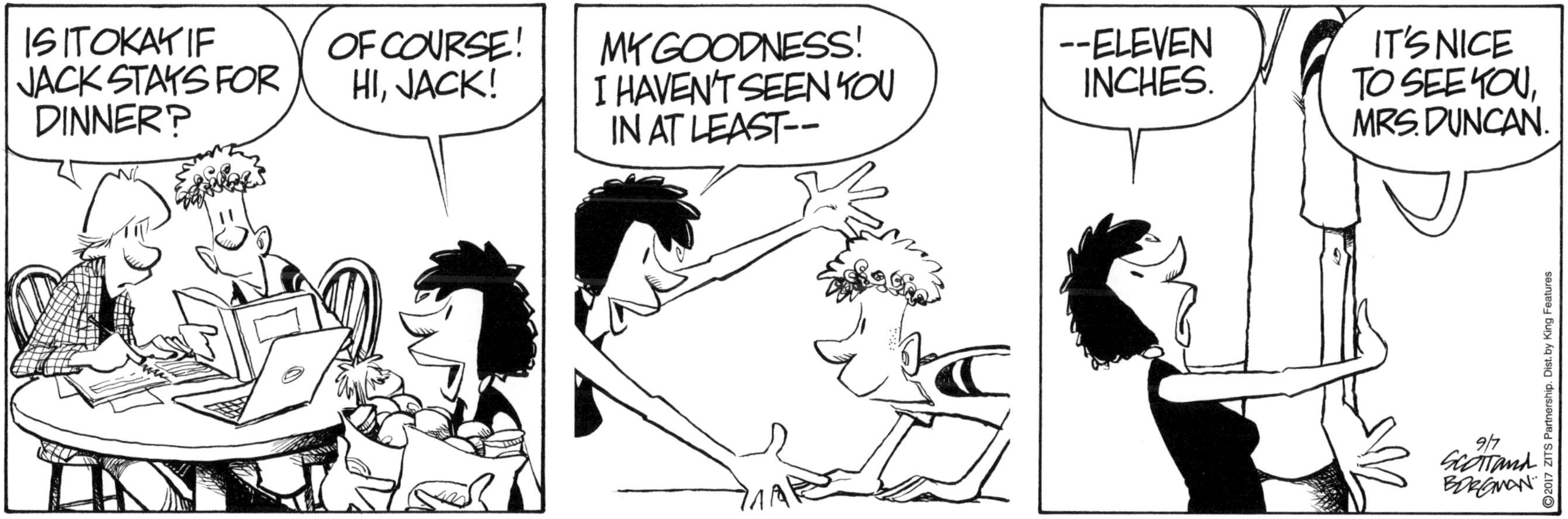
IS IT OKAY IF JACK STAYS FOR DINNER?
OF COURSE! HI, JACK!
MY GOODNESS! I HAVEN'T SEEN YOU IN AT LEAST--
--ELEVEN INCHES.
IT'S NICE TO SEE YOU, MRS. DUNCAN.
9/7 SCOTT and BORGMAN
©2017 ZITS Partnership. Dist. by King Features

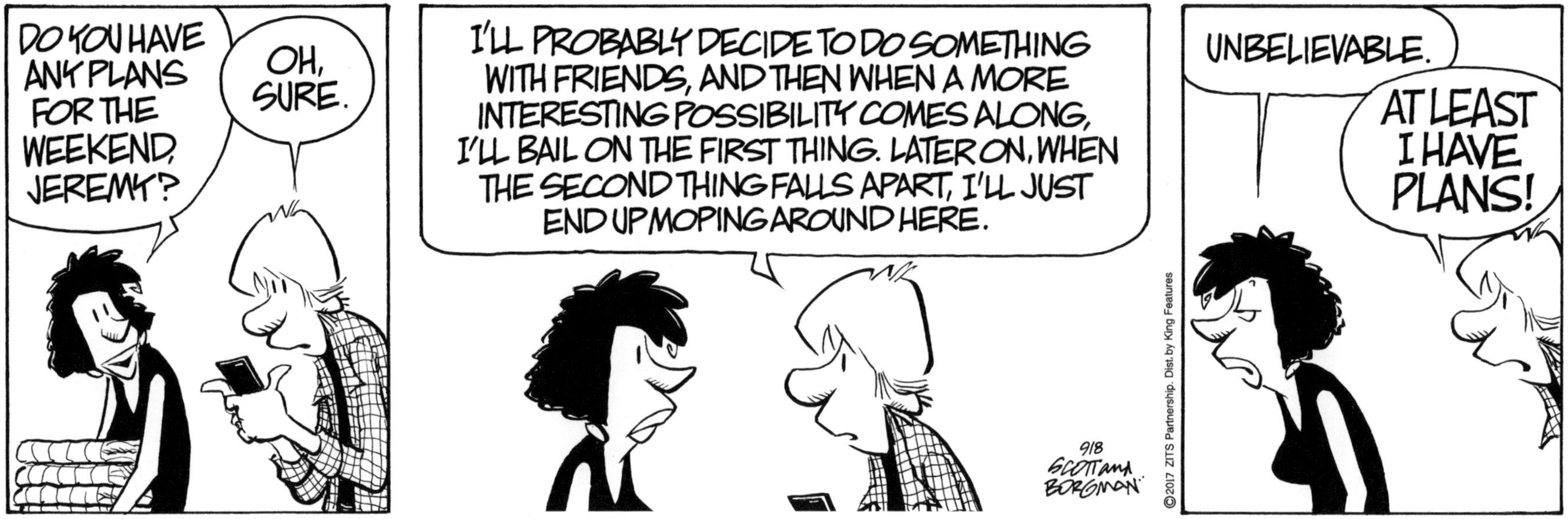
DO YOU HAVE ANY PLANS FOR THE WEEKEND, JEREMY?
OH, SURE.
I'LL PROBABLY DECIDE TO DO SOMETHING WITH FRIENDS, AND THEN WHEN A MORE INTERESTING POSSIBILITY COMES ALONG, I'LL BAIL ON THE FIRST THING. LATER ON, WHEN THE SECOND THING FALLS APART, I'LL JUST END UP MOPING AROUND HERE.
9/18 SCOTT AND BORGMAN
©2017 ZITS Partnership. Dist. by King Features
UNBELIEVABLE.
AT LEAST I HAVE PLANS!

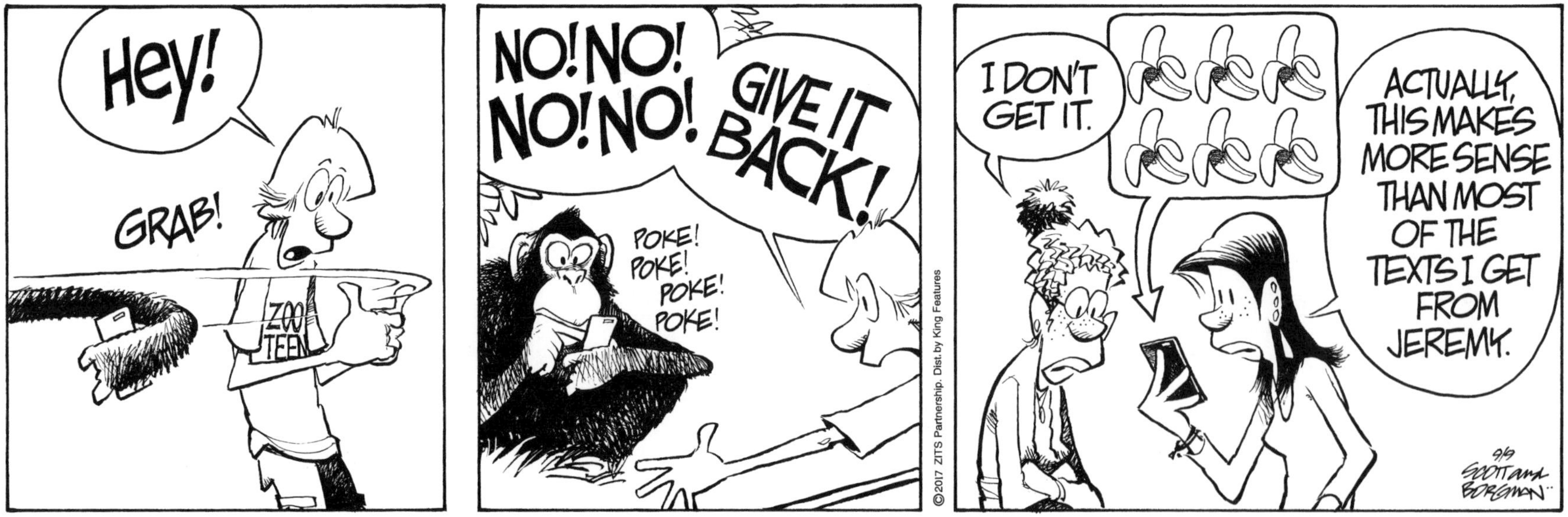
HEY!
GRAB!
ZOO TEEN
NO! NO! NO! NO!
GIVE IT BACK!
POKE! POKE! POKE! POKE!
©2017 ZITS Partnership. Dist. by King Features
I DON'T GET IT.
ACTUALLY, THIS MAKES MORE SENSE THAN MOST OF THE TEXTS I GET FROM JEREMY.
9/19 SCOTT AND BORGMAN

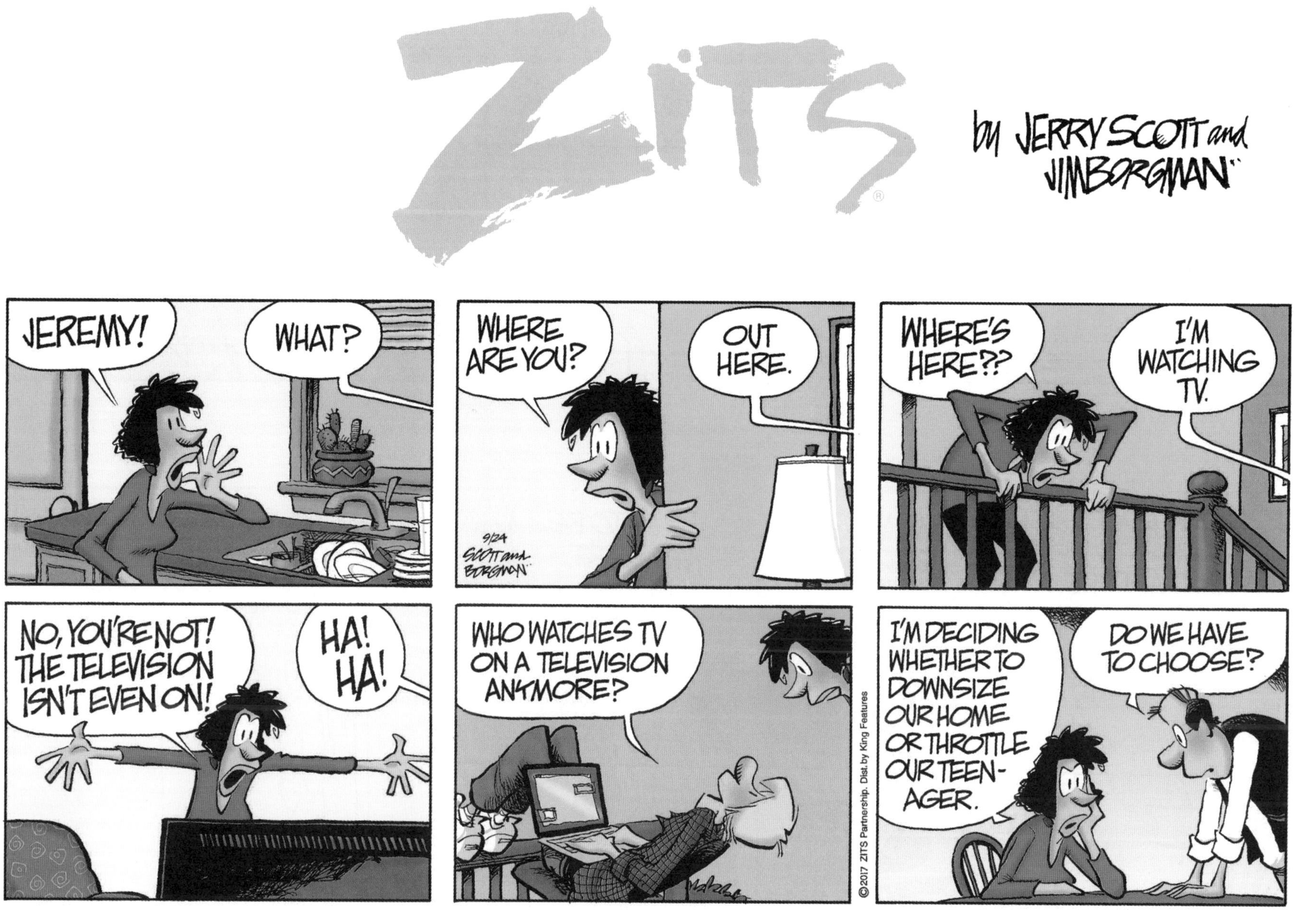
ZITS
by JERRY SCOTT and JIM BORGMAN
JEREMY!
WHAT?
WHERE ARE YOU?
OUT HERE.
9/24 SCOTT and BORGMAN
WHERE'S HERE??
I'M WATCHING TV.
NO, YOU'RE NOT! THE TELEVISION ISN'T EVEN ON!
HA! HA!
WHO WATCHES TV ON A TELEVISION ANYMORE?
© 2017 ZITS Partnership. Dist. by King Features
I'M DECIDING WHETHER TO DOWNSIZE OUR HOME OR THROTTLE OUR TEEN-AGER.
DO WE HAVE TO CHOOSE?

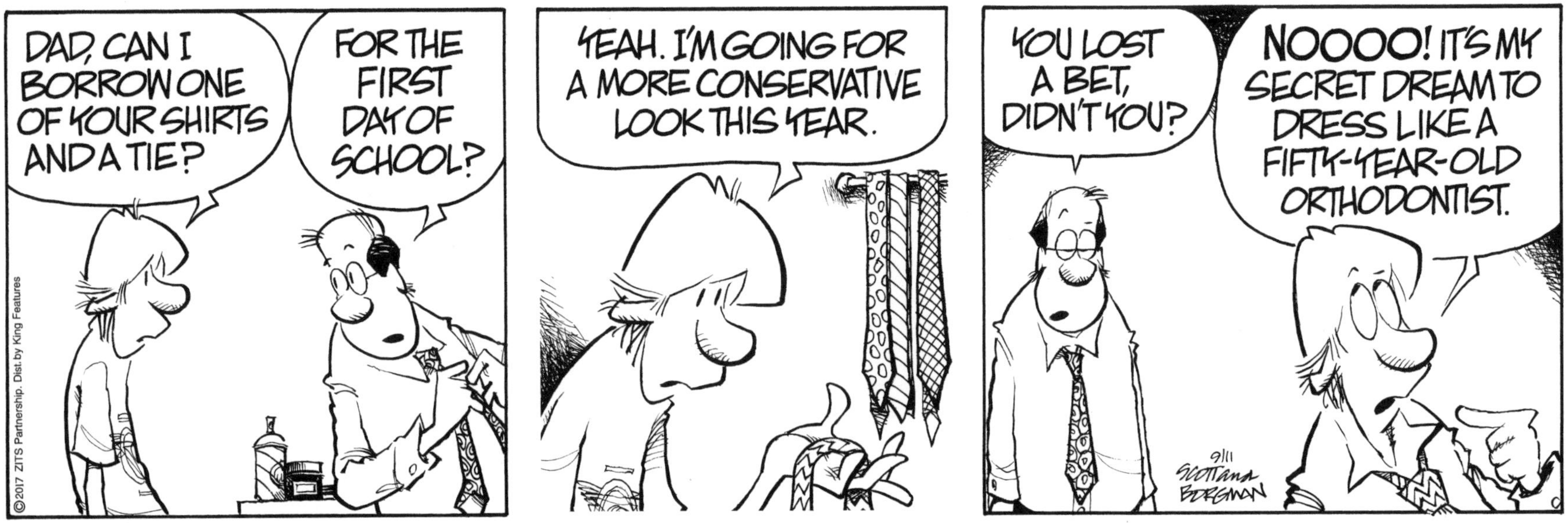
DAD, CAN I BORROW ONE OF YOUR SHIRTS AND A TIE?
FOR THE FIRST DAY OF SCHOOL?
YEAH. I'M GOING FOR A MORE CONSERVATIVE LOOK THIS YEAR.
YOU LOST A BET, DIDN'T YOU?
NOOOO! IT'S MY SECRET DREAM TO DRESS LIKE A FIFTY-YEAR-OLD ORTHODONTIST.
©2017 ZITS Partnership. Dist. by King Features
9/11 SCOTT and BORGMAN

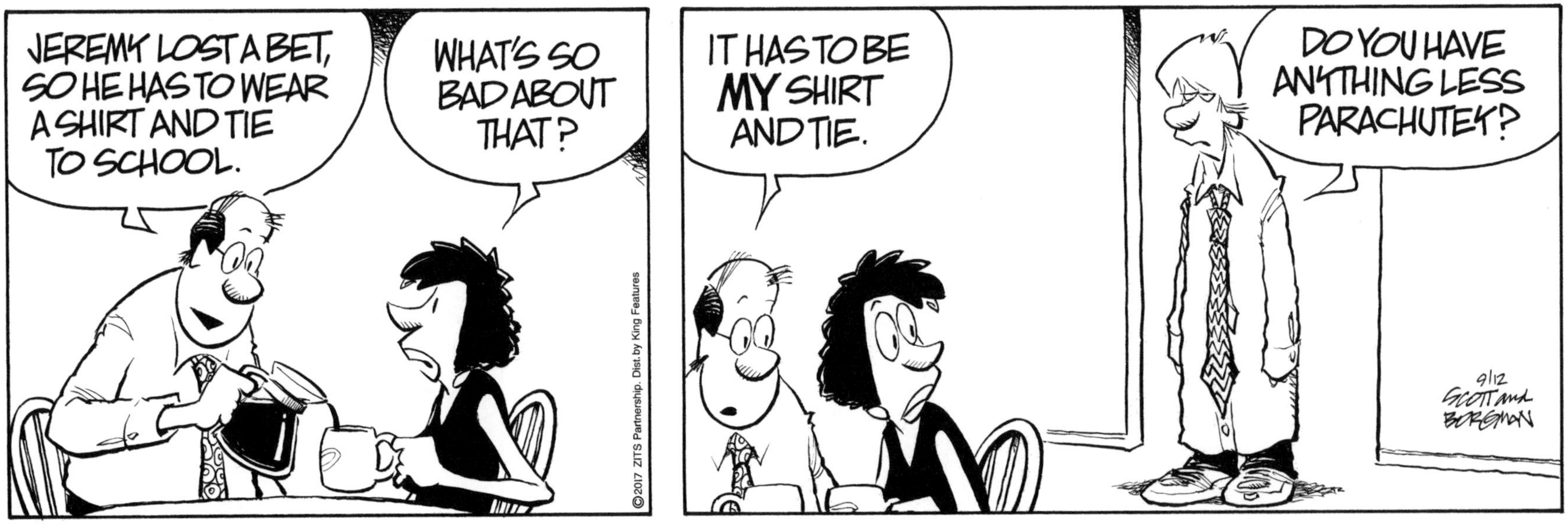
JEREMY LOST A BET, SO HE HAS TO WEAR A SHIRT AND TIE TO SCHOOL.
WHAT'S SO BAD ABOUT THAT?
IT HAS TO BE MY SHIRT AND TIE.
DO YOU HAVE ANYTHING LESS PARACHUTEY?
©2017 ZITS Partnership. Dist. by King Features
9/12 SCOTT and BORGMAN

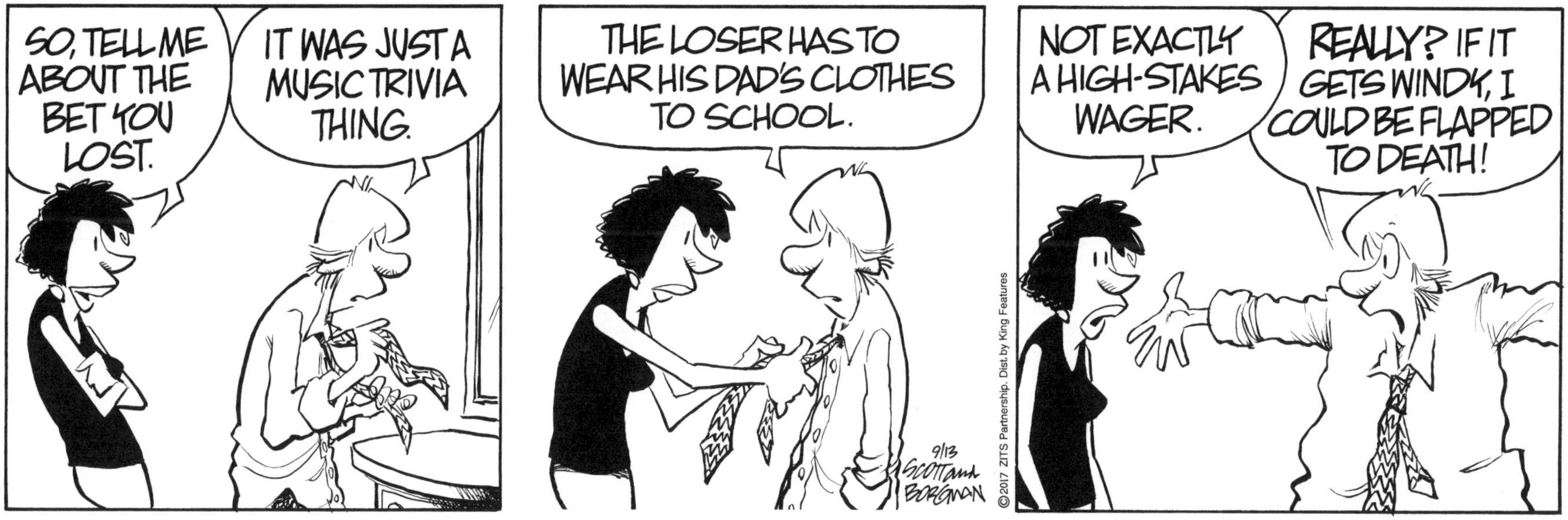

SO, TELL ME ABOUT THE BET YOU LOST.
IT WAS JUST A MUSIC TRIVIA THING.
THE LOSER HAS TO WEAR HIS DAD'S CLOTHES TO SCHOOL.
9/13 SCOTT and BORGMAN
©2017 ZITS Partnership. Dist. by King Features
NOT EXACTLY A HIGH-STAKES WAGER.
REALLY? IF IT GETS WINDY, I COULD BE FLAPPED TO DEATH!

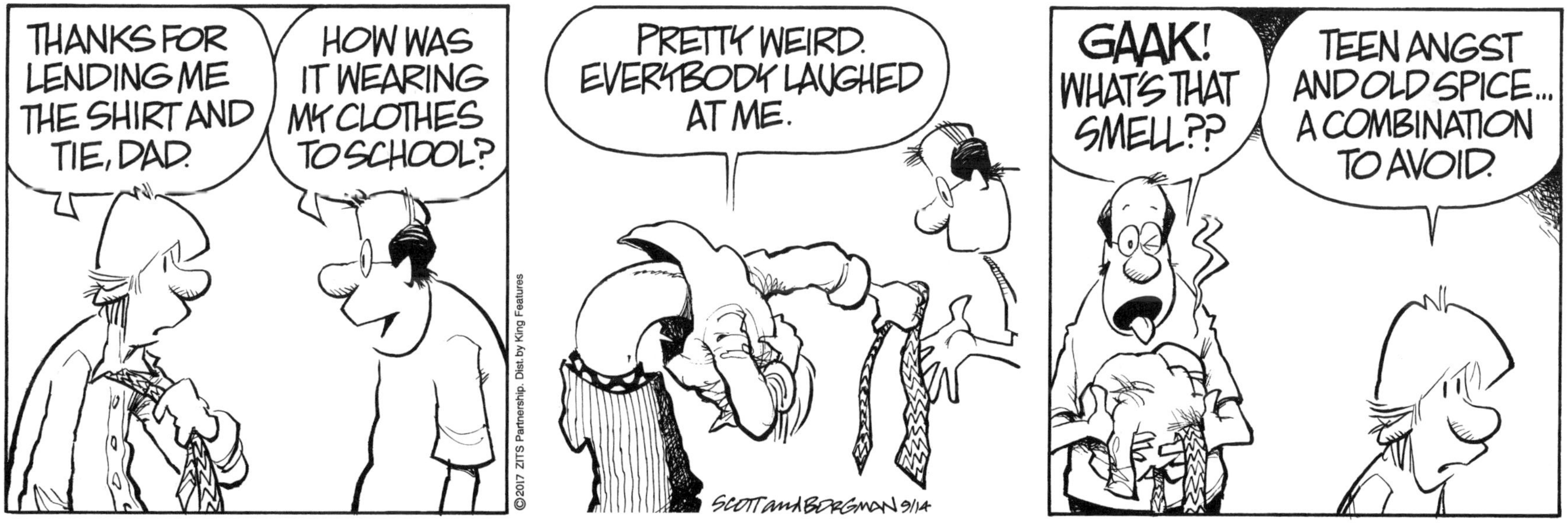

THANKS FOR LENDING ME THE SHIRT AND TIE, DAD.
HOW WAS IT WEARING MY CLOTHES TO SCHOOL?
©2017 ZITS Partnership. Dist. by King Features
PRETTY WEIRD. EVERYBODY LAUGHED AT ME.
SCOTT and BORGMAN 9/14
GAAK! WHAT'S THAT SMELL??
TEEN ANGST AND OLD SPICE... A COMBINATION TO AVOID.

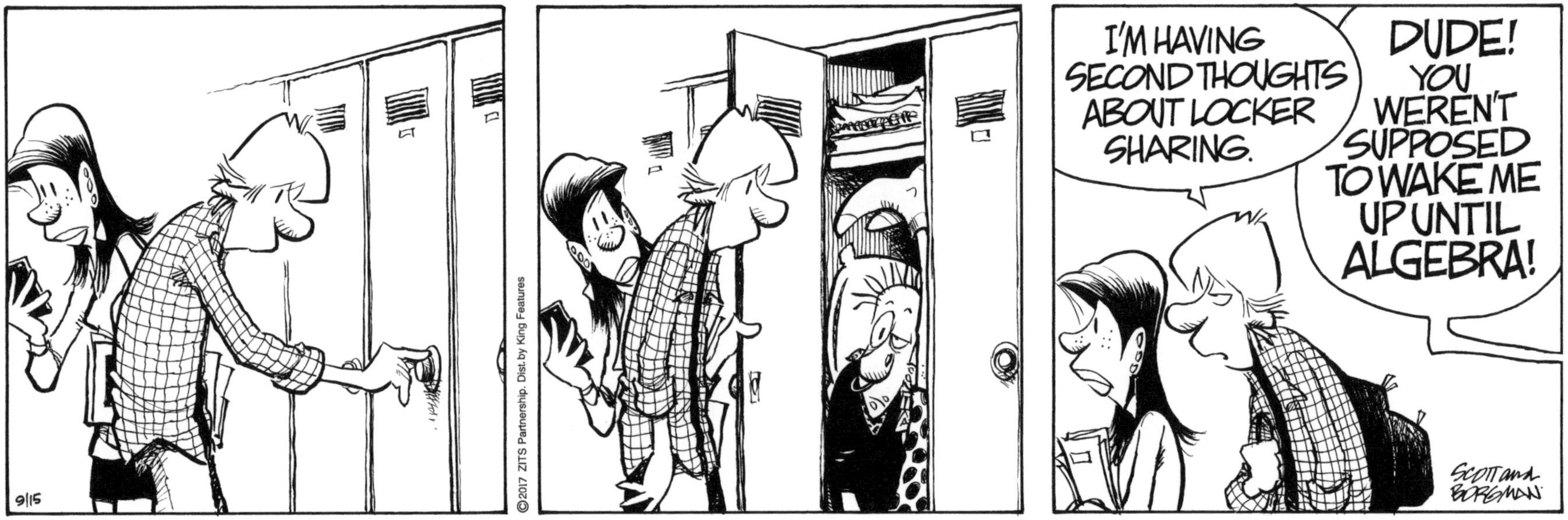
9/15
©2017 ZITS Partnership. Dist. by King Features
I'M HAVING SECOND THOUGHTS ABOUT LOCKER SHARING.
DUDE! YOU WEREN'T SUPPOSED TO WAKE ME UP UNTIL ALGEBRA!
SCOTT and BORGMAN

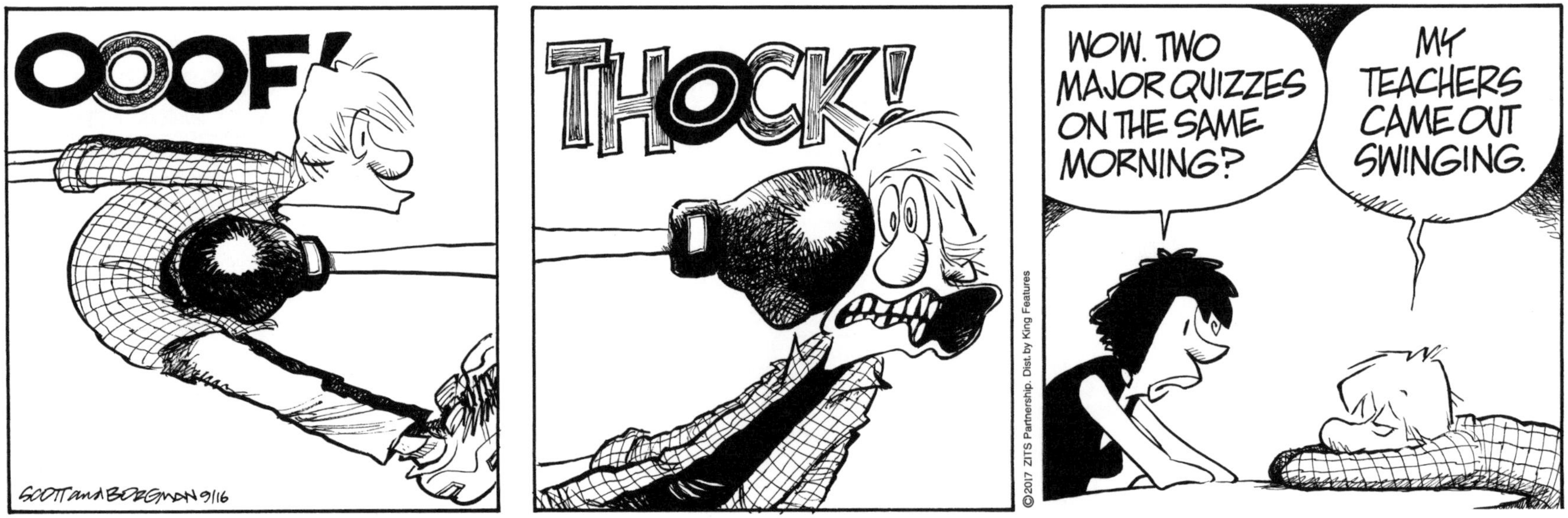
OOOF!
SCOTT and BORGMAN 9/16
THOCK!
©2017 ZITS Partnership. Dist. by King Features
WOW. TWO MAJOR QUIZZES ON THE SAME MORNING?
MY TEACHERS CAME OUT SWINGING.

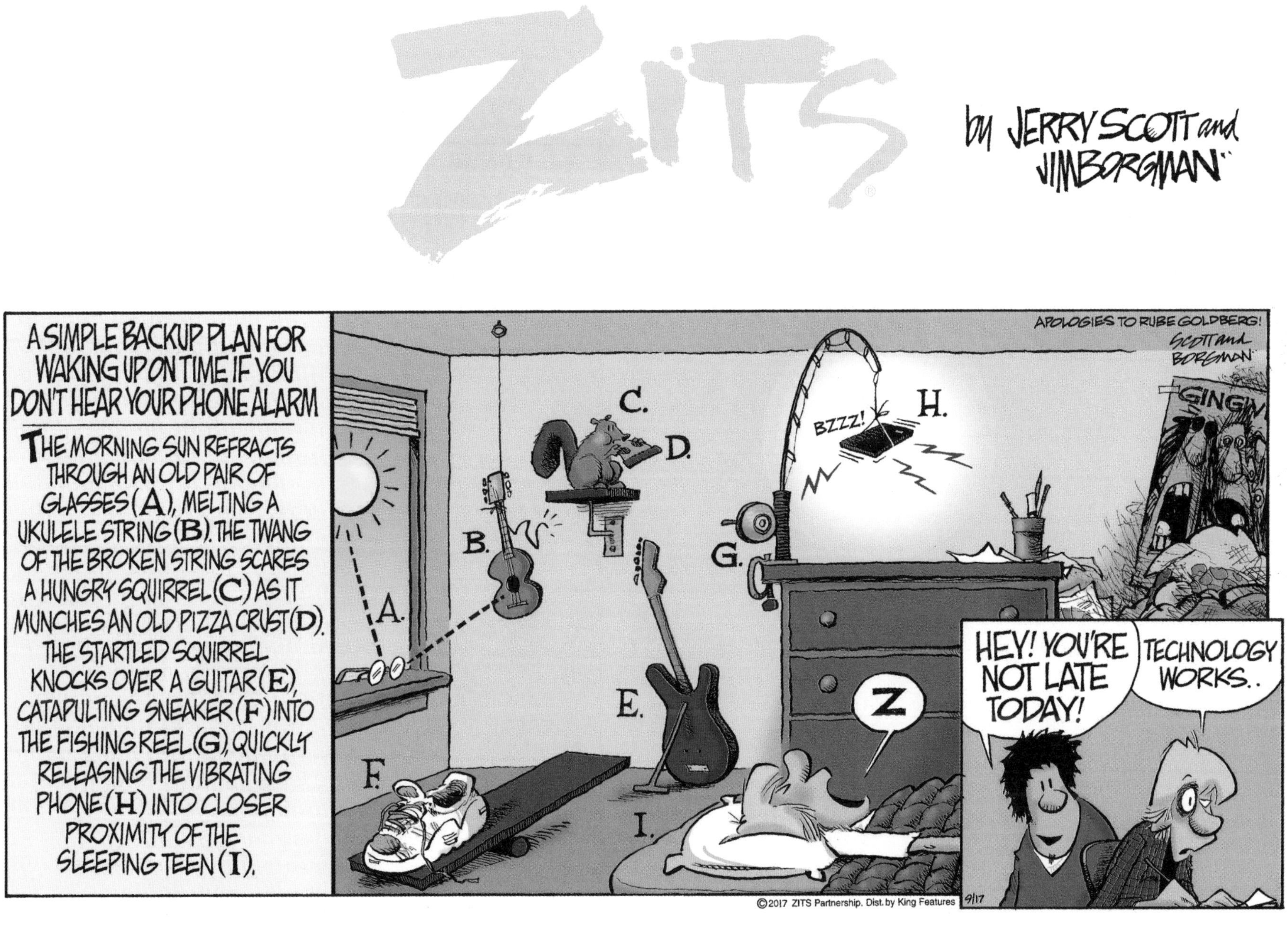
ZITS
by JERRY SCOTT and JIM BORGMAN
A SIMPLE BACKUP PLAN FOR WAKING UP ON TIME IF YOU DON'T HEAR YOUR PHONE ALARM
THE MORNING SUN REFRACTS THROUGH AN OLD PAIR OF GLASSES (A), MELTING A UKULELE STRING (B). THE TWANG OF THE BROKEN STRING SCARES A HUNGRY SQUIRREL (C) AS IT MUNCHES AN OLD PIZZA CRUST (D). THE STARTLED SQUIRREL KNOCKS OVER A GUITAR (E), CATAPULTING SNEAKER (F) INTO THE FISHING REEL (G), QUICKLY RELEASING THE VIBRATING PHONE (H) INTO CLOSER PROXIMITY OF THE SLEEPING TEEN (I).
APOLOGIES TO RUBE GOLDBERG!
SCOTT and BORGMAN
A.
B.
C.
D.
E.
F.
G.
H.
I.
BZZZ!
Z
HEY! YOU'RE NOT LATE TODAY!
TECHNOLOGY WORKS..
9/17
©2017 ZITS Partnership. Dist. by King Features

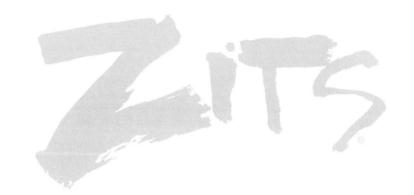

GAAA!
JEREMY!
WHAT?
YOUR SMELLY, DIRTY CLOTHES PILE IS TALLER THAN YOUR AMPLIFIER!
SO?
SCOTT and BORGMAN

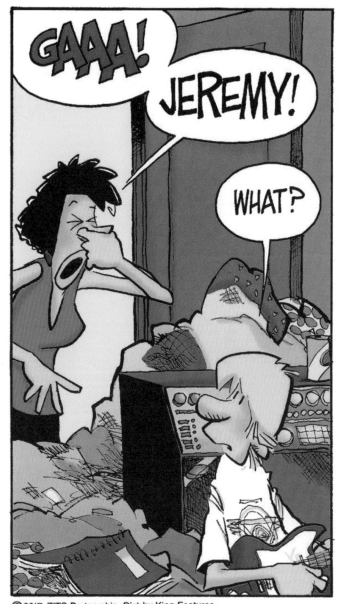

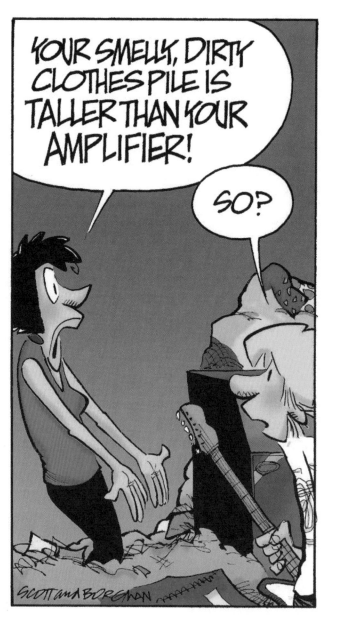

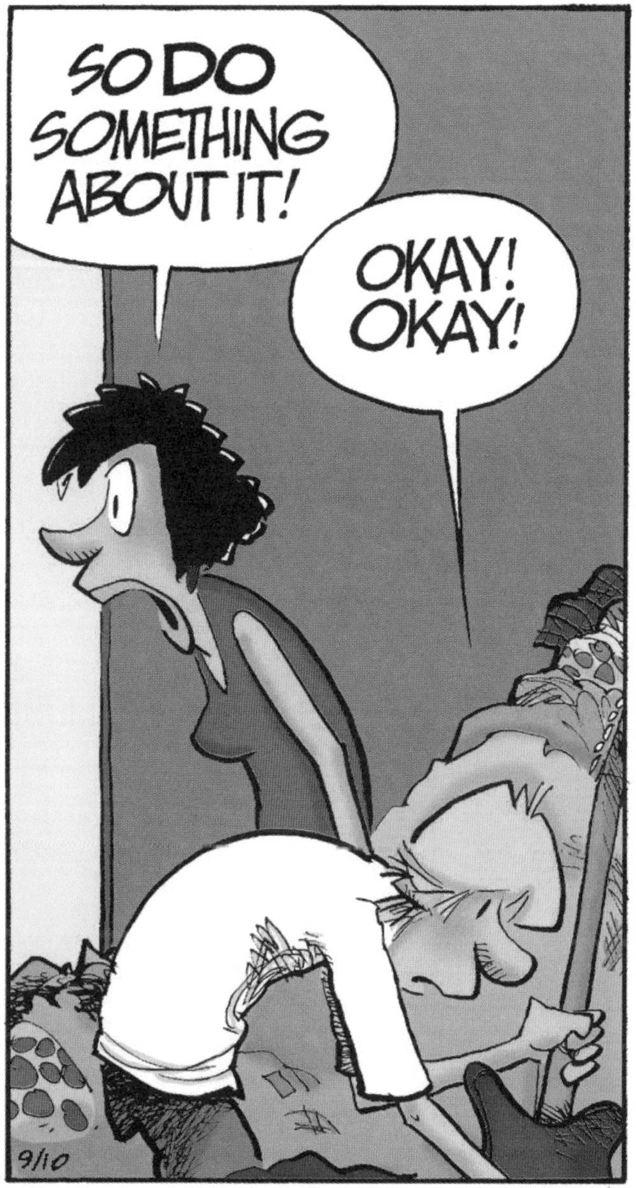
SO DO SOMETHING ABOUT IT!
OKAY! OKAY!
9/10

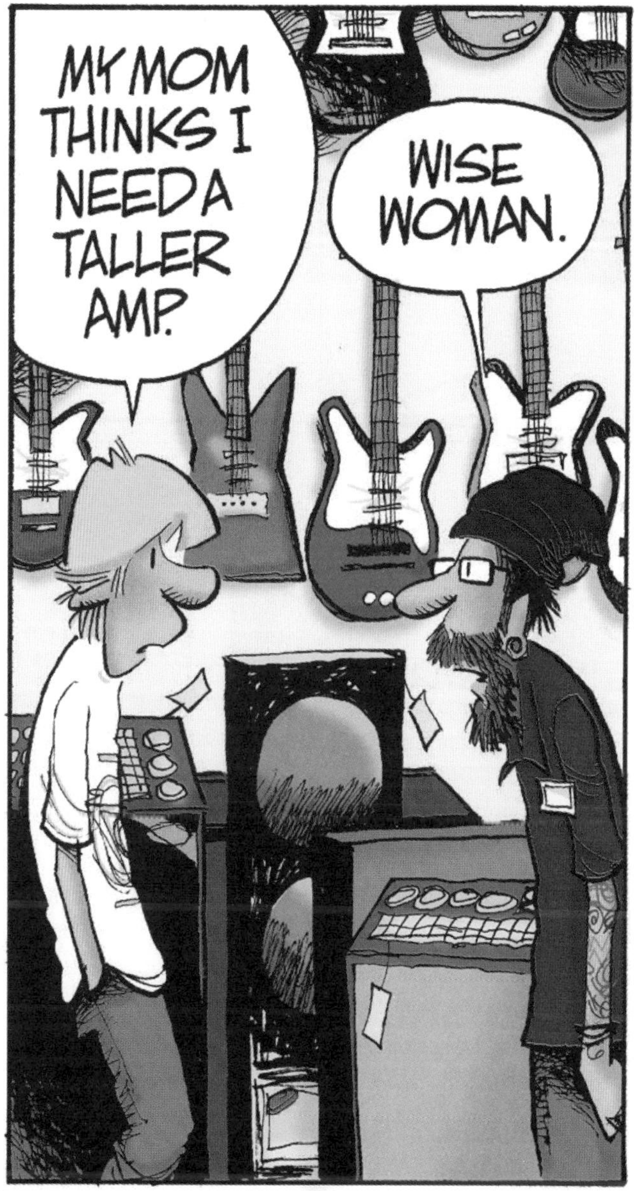
MY MOM THINKS I NEED A TALLER AMP.
WISE WOMAN.

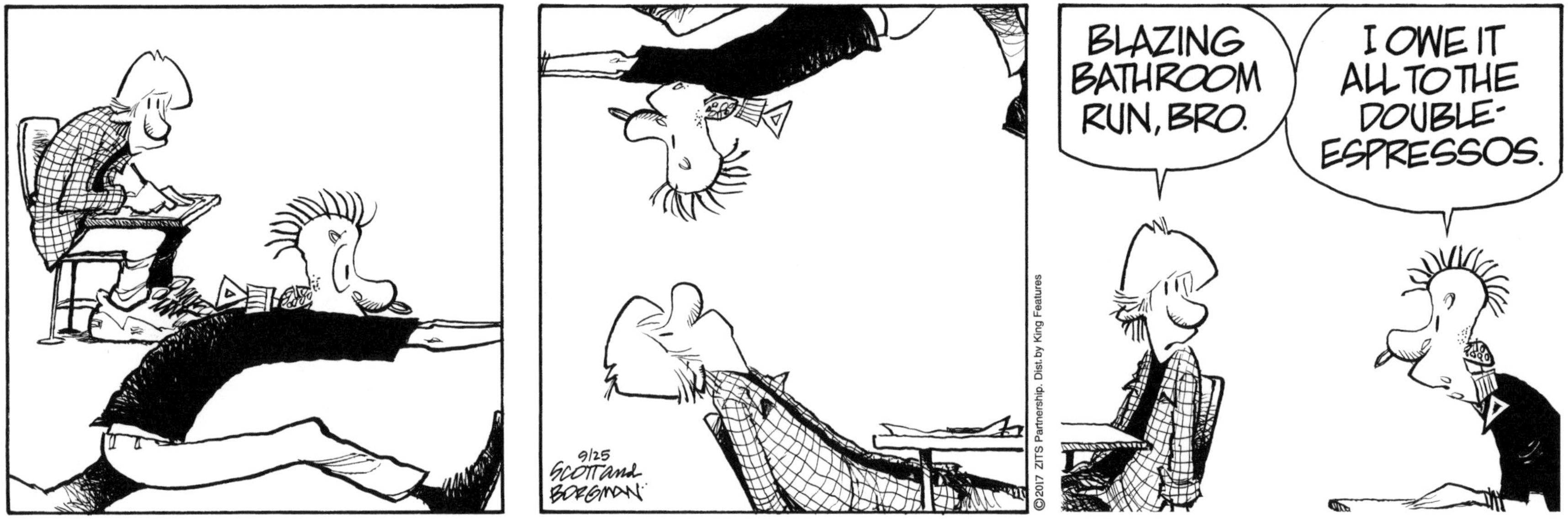
BLAZING BATHROOM RUN, BRO.
I OWE IT ALL TO THE DOUBLE-ESPRESSOS.
9/25 SCOTT and BORGMAN
© 2017 ZITS Partnership. Dist. by King Features

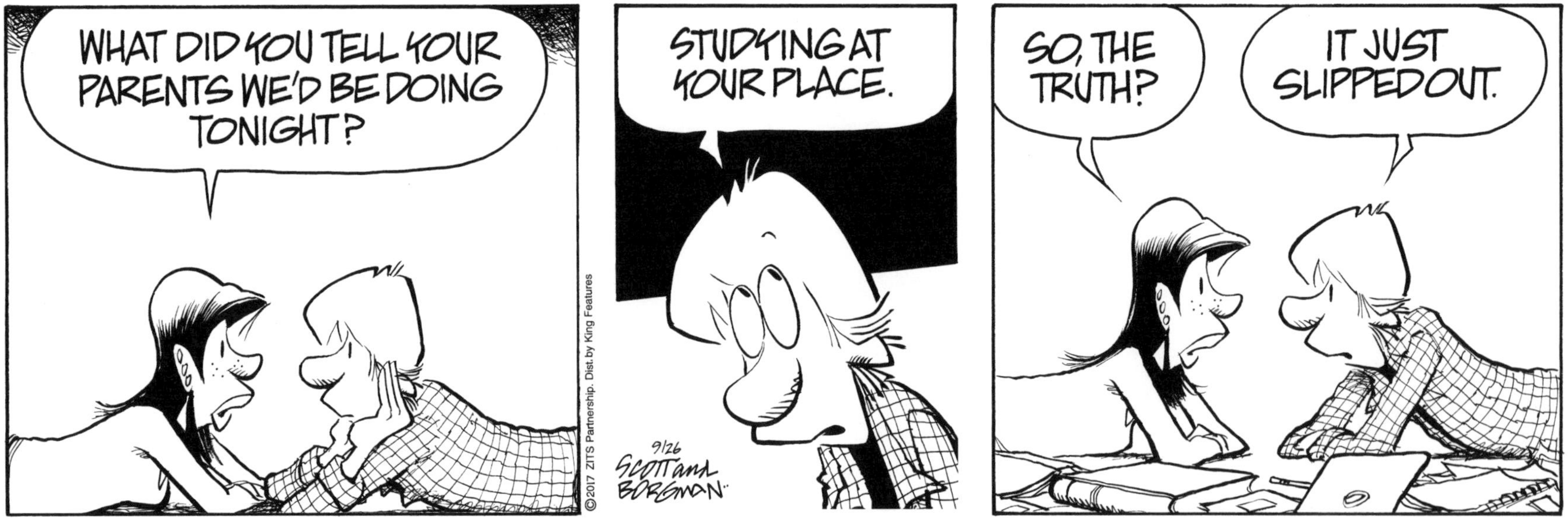
WHAT DID YOU TELL YOUR PARENTS WE'D BE DOING TONIGHT?
STUDYING AT YOUR PLACE.
SO, THE TRUTH?
IT JUST SLIPPED OUT.
9/26 SCOTT and BORGMAN
© 2017 ZITS Partnership. Dist. by King Features

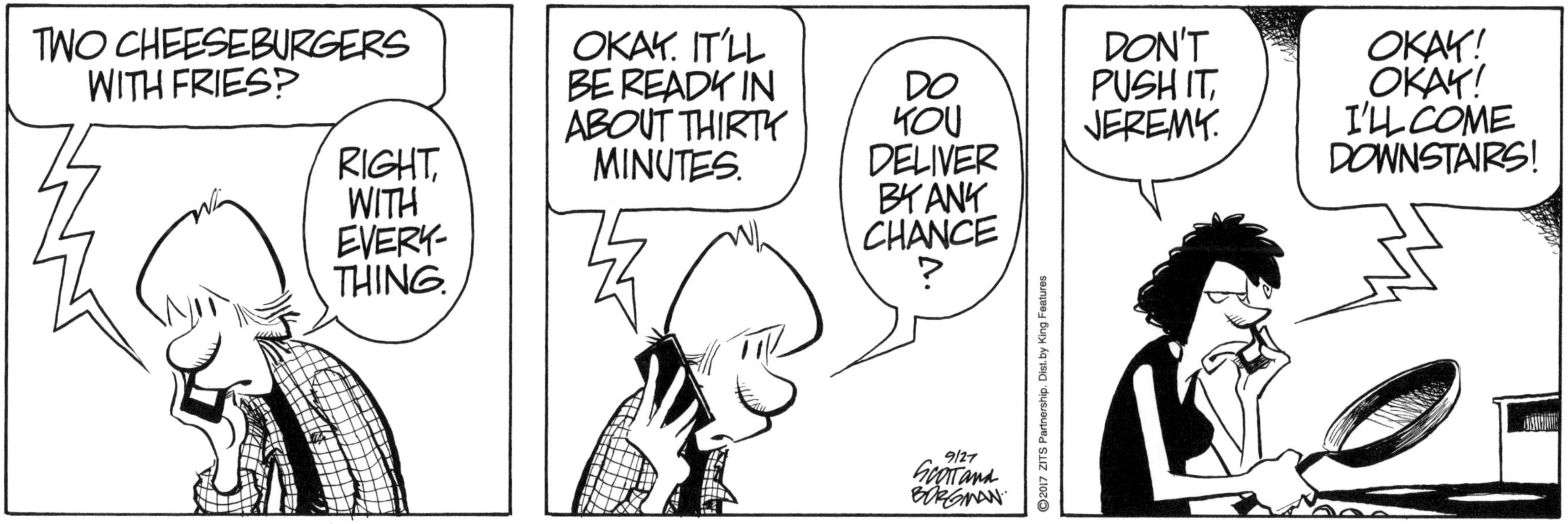
TWO CHEESEBURGERS WITH FRIES?
RIGHT, WITH EVERY-THING.
OKAY. IT'LL BE READY IN ABOUT THIRTY MINUTES.
DO YOU DELIVER BY ANY CHANCE?
DON'T PUSH IT, JEREMY.
OKAY! OKAY! I'LL COME DOWNSTAIRS!
9/27 SCOTT and BORGMAN
©2017 ZITS Partnership. Dist. by King Features

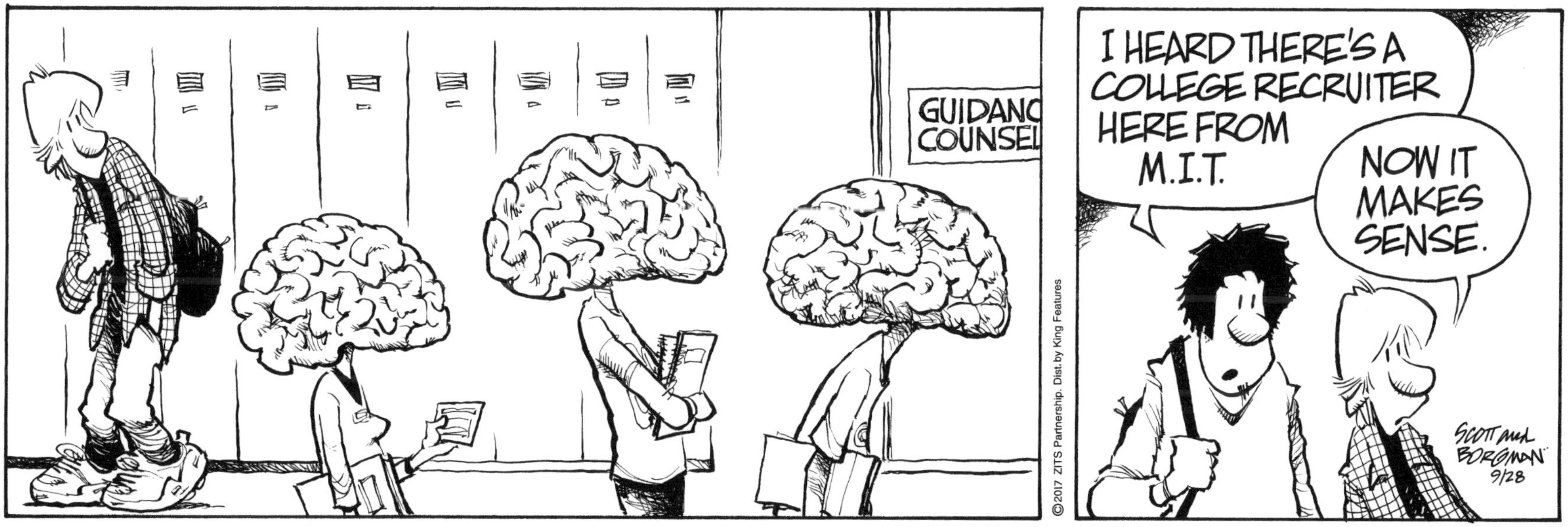
GUIDANC COUNSEL
I HEARD THERE'S A COLLEGE RECRUITER HERE FROM M.I.T.
NOW IT MAKES SENSE.
SCOTT and BORGMAN 9/28
©2017 ZITS Partnership. Dist. by King Features

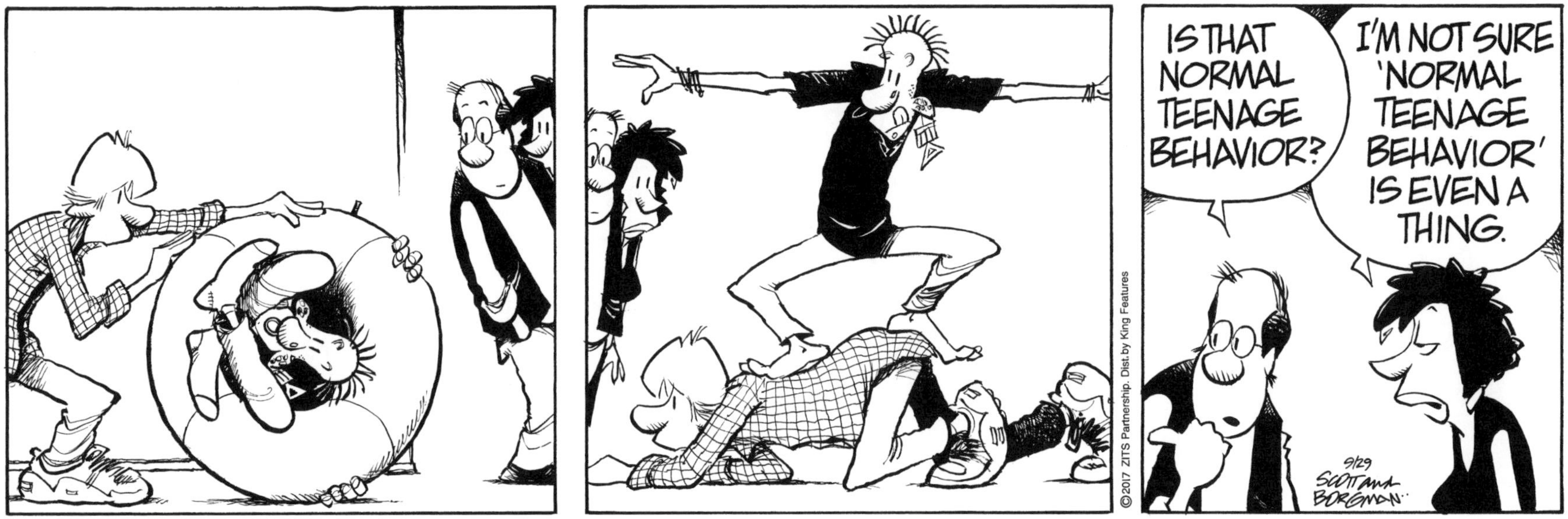
IS THAT NORMAL TEENAGE BEHAVIOR?
I'M NOT SURE 'NORMAL TEENAGE BEHAVIOR' IS EVEN A THING.
9/29
SCOTT and BORGMAN
©2017 ZITS Partnership. Dist. by King Features

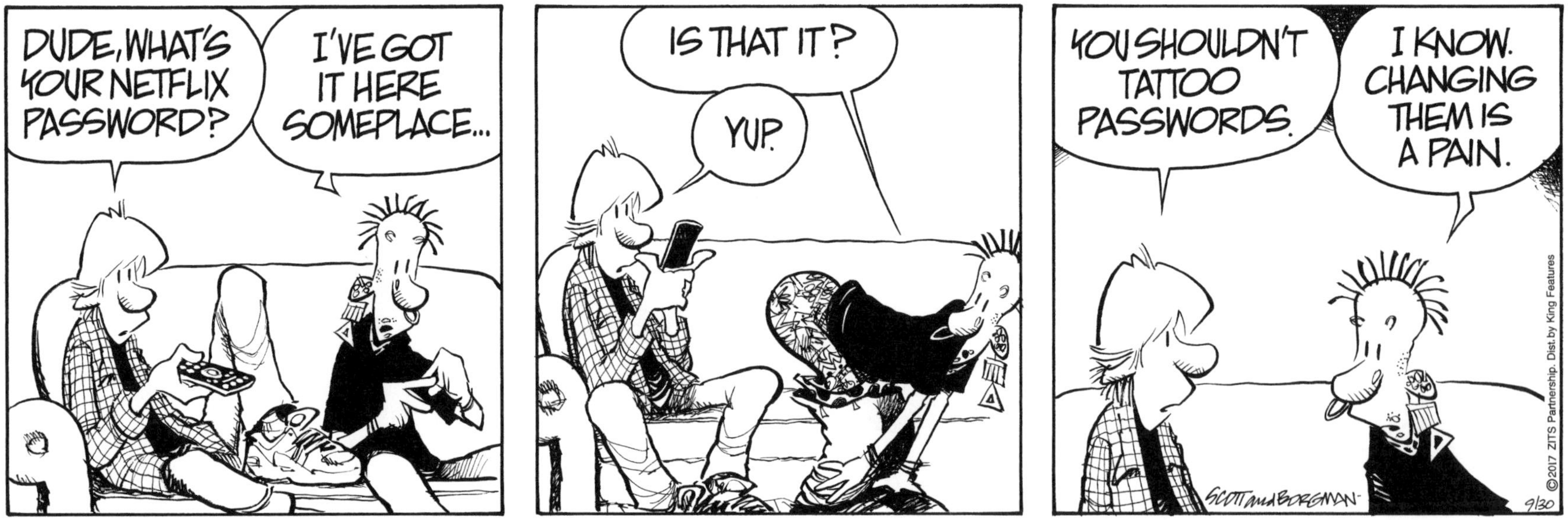
DUDE, WHAT'S YOUR NETFLIX PASSWORD?
I'VE GOT IT HERE SOMEPLACE...
IS THAT IT?
YUP.
YOU SHOULDN'T TATTOO PASSWORDS.
I KNOW. CHANGING THEM IS A PAIN.
SCOTT and BORGMAN
9/30
©2017 ZITS Partnership. Dist. by King Features

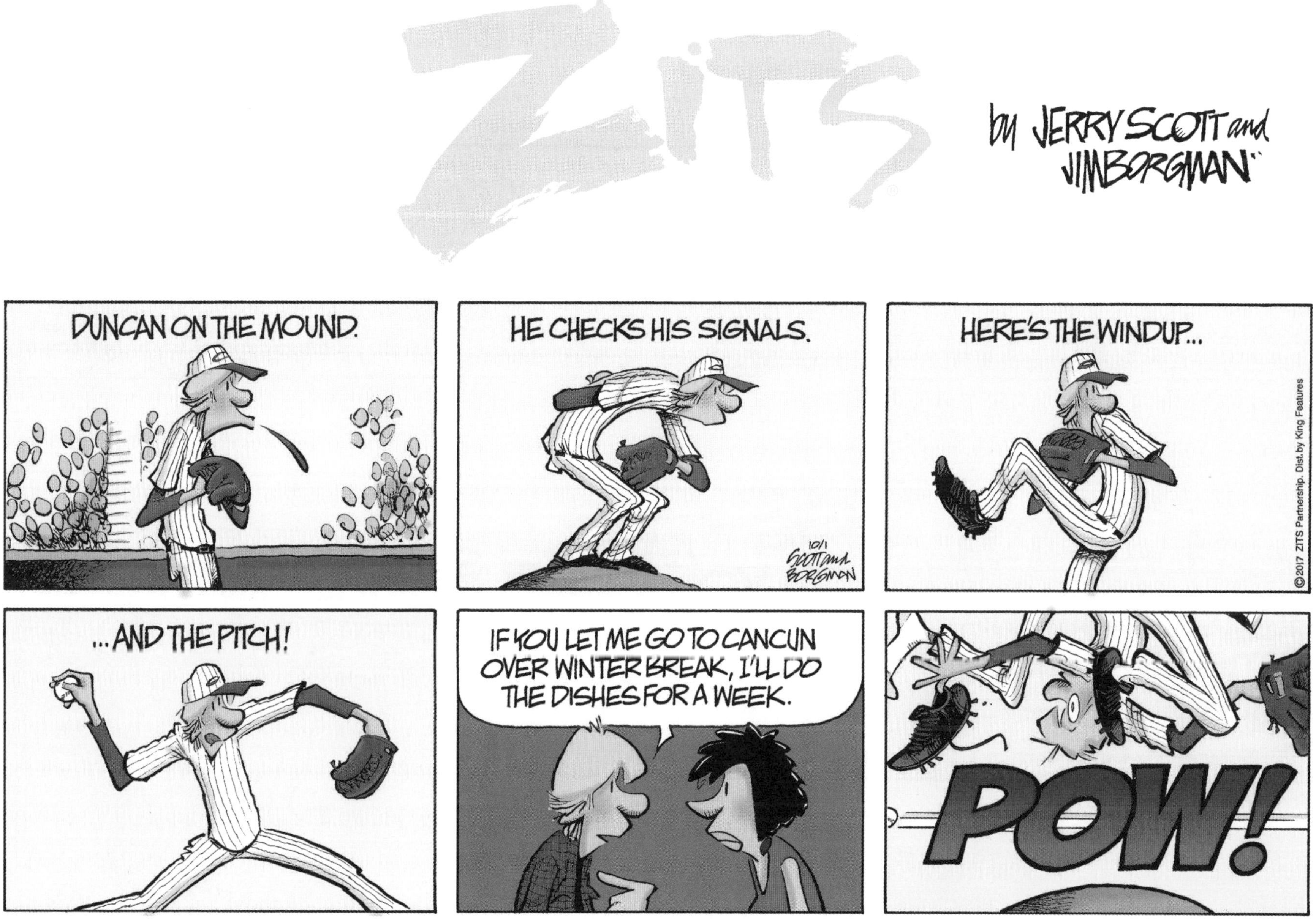
ZITS
by JERRY SCOTT and JIM BORGMAN
DUNCAN ON THE MOUND.
HE CHECKS HIS SIGNALS.
10/1 SCOTT and BORGMAN
HERE'S THE WINDUP...
©2017 ZITS Partnership. Dist. by King Features
...AND THE PITCH!
IF YOU LET ME GO TO CANCUN OVER WINTER BREAK, I'LL DO THE DISHES FOR A WEEK.
POW!

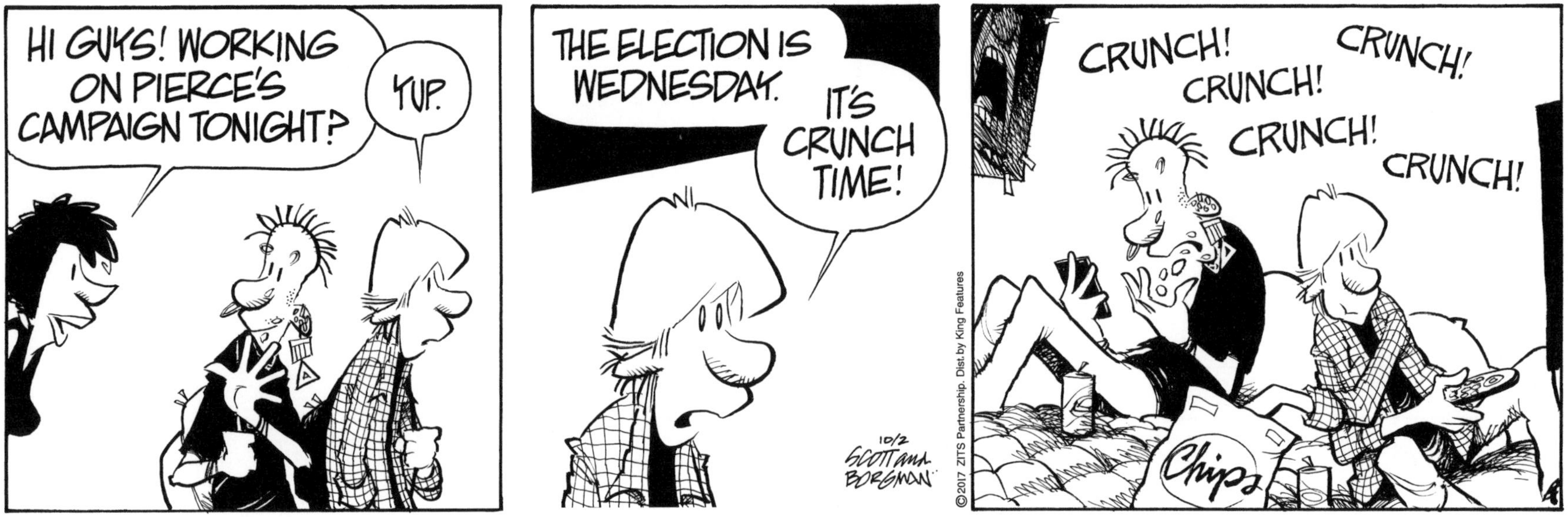
HI GUYS! WORKING ON PIERCE'S CAMPAIGN TONIGHT?
YUP.
THE ELECTION IS WEDNESDAY.
IT'S CRUNCH TIME!
10/2 SCOTT and BORGMAN
©2017 ZITS Partnership. Dist. by King Features
CRUNCH!
CRUNCH!
CRUNCH!
CRUNCH!
CRUNCH!
Chips

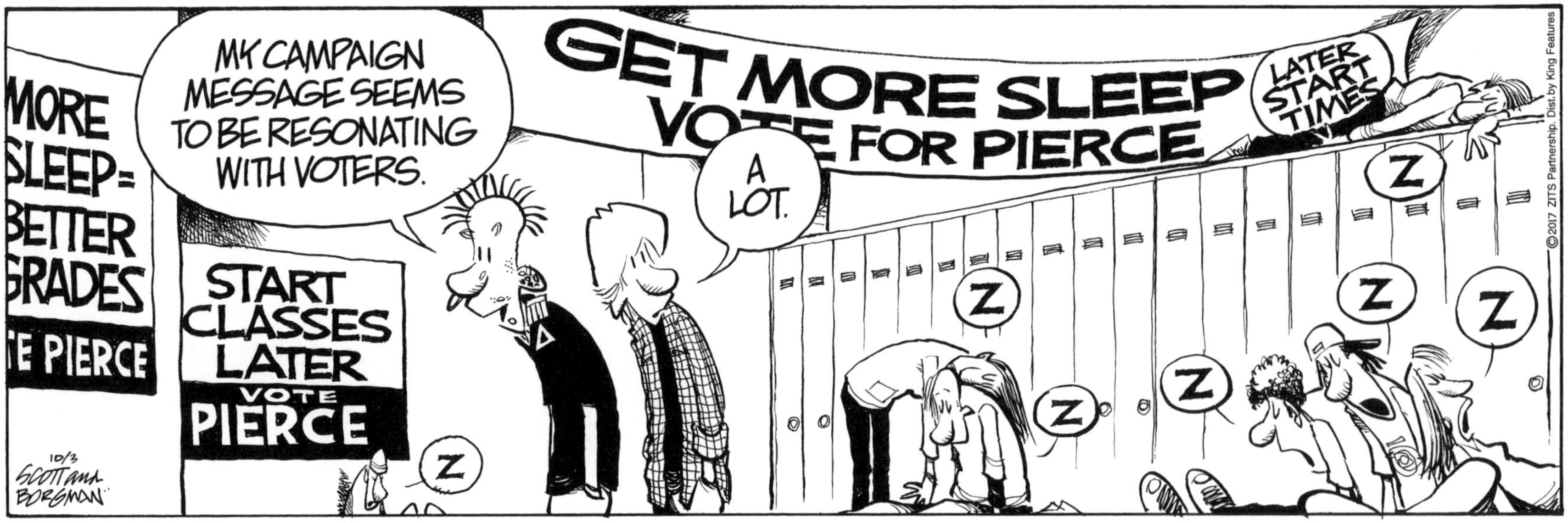
MORE SLEEP= BETTER GRADES
TE PIERCE
MY CAMPAIGN MESSAGE SEEMS TO BE RESONATING WITH VOTERS.
START CLASSES LATER VOTE PIERCE
GET MORE SLEEP VOTE FOR PIERCE
LATER START TIMES
A LOT.
Z
Z
Z
Z
Z
Z
Z
10/3 SCOTT and BORGMAN
©2017 ZITS Partnership. Dist. by King Features

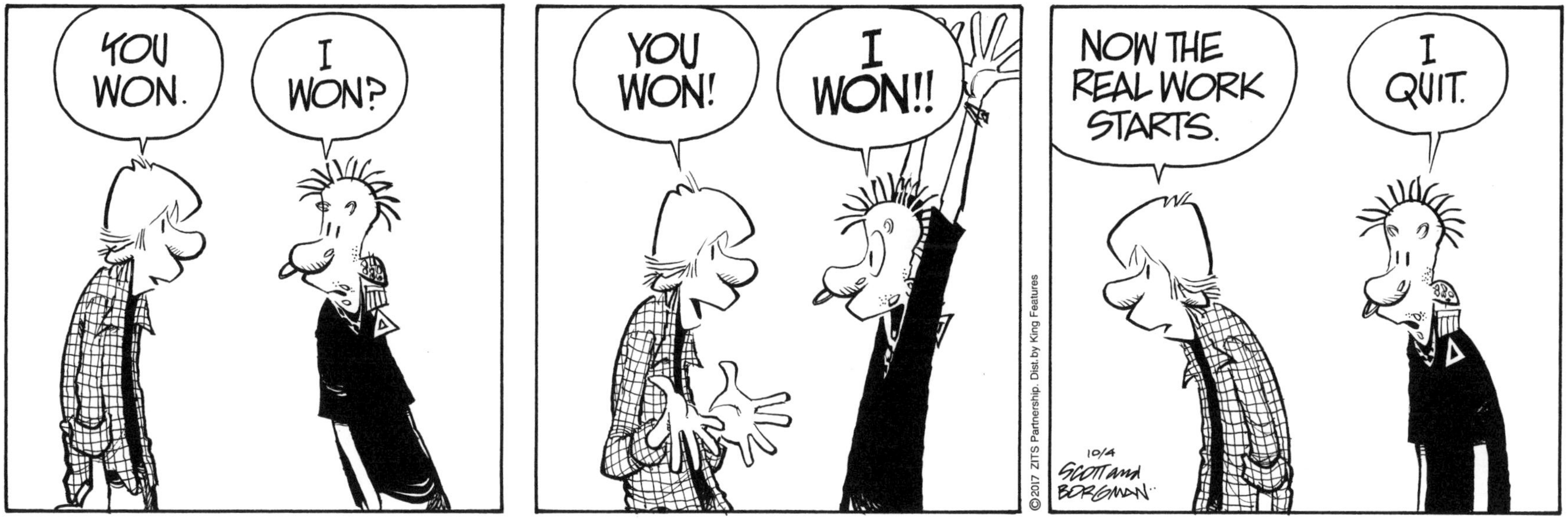
YOU WON.
I WON?
YOU WON!
I WON!!
NOW THE REAL WORK STARTS.
I QUIT.
10/4 SCOTT and BORGMAN
©2017 ZITS Partnership. Dist.by King Features

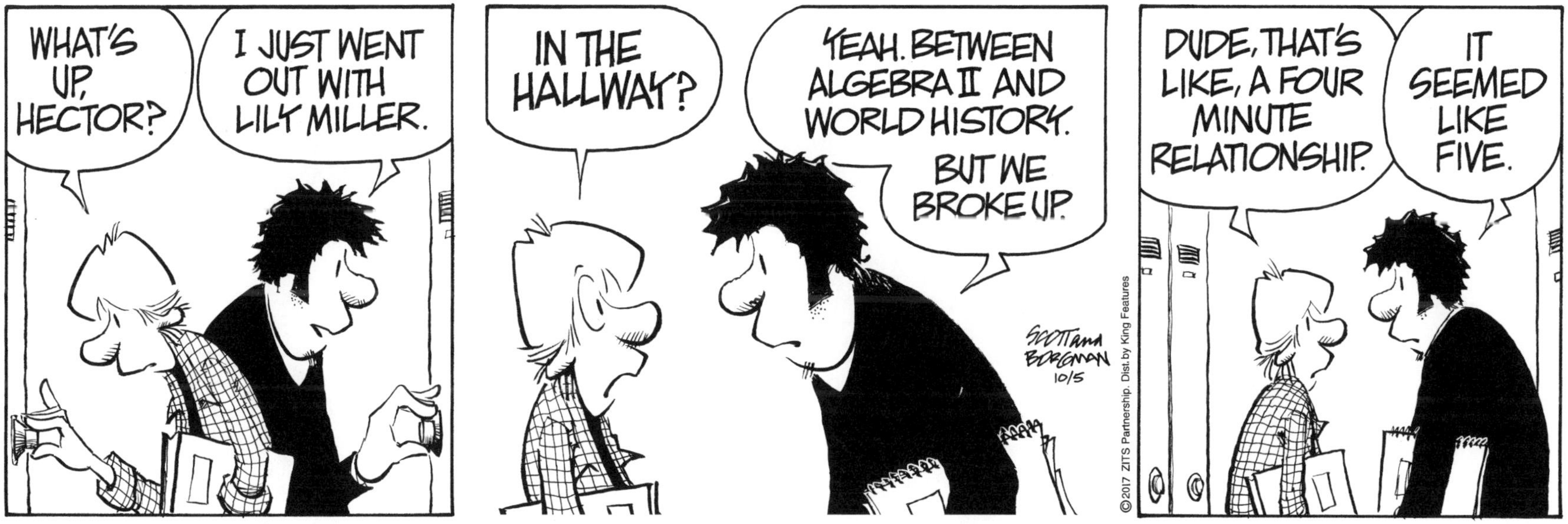
WHAT'S UP, HECTOR?
I JUST WENT OUT WITH LILY MILLER.
IN THE HALLWAY?
YEAH. BETWEEN ALGEBRA II AND WORLD HISTORY.
BUT WE BROKE UP.
DUDE, THAT'S LIKE, A FOUR MINUTE RELATIONSHIP.
IT SEEMED LIKE FIVE.
SCOTT and BORGMAN 10/5
©2017 ZITS Partnership. Dist.by King Features

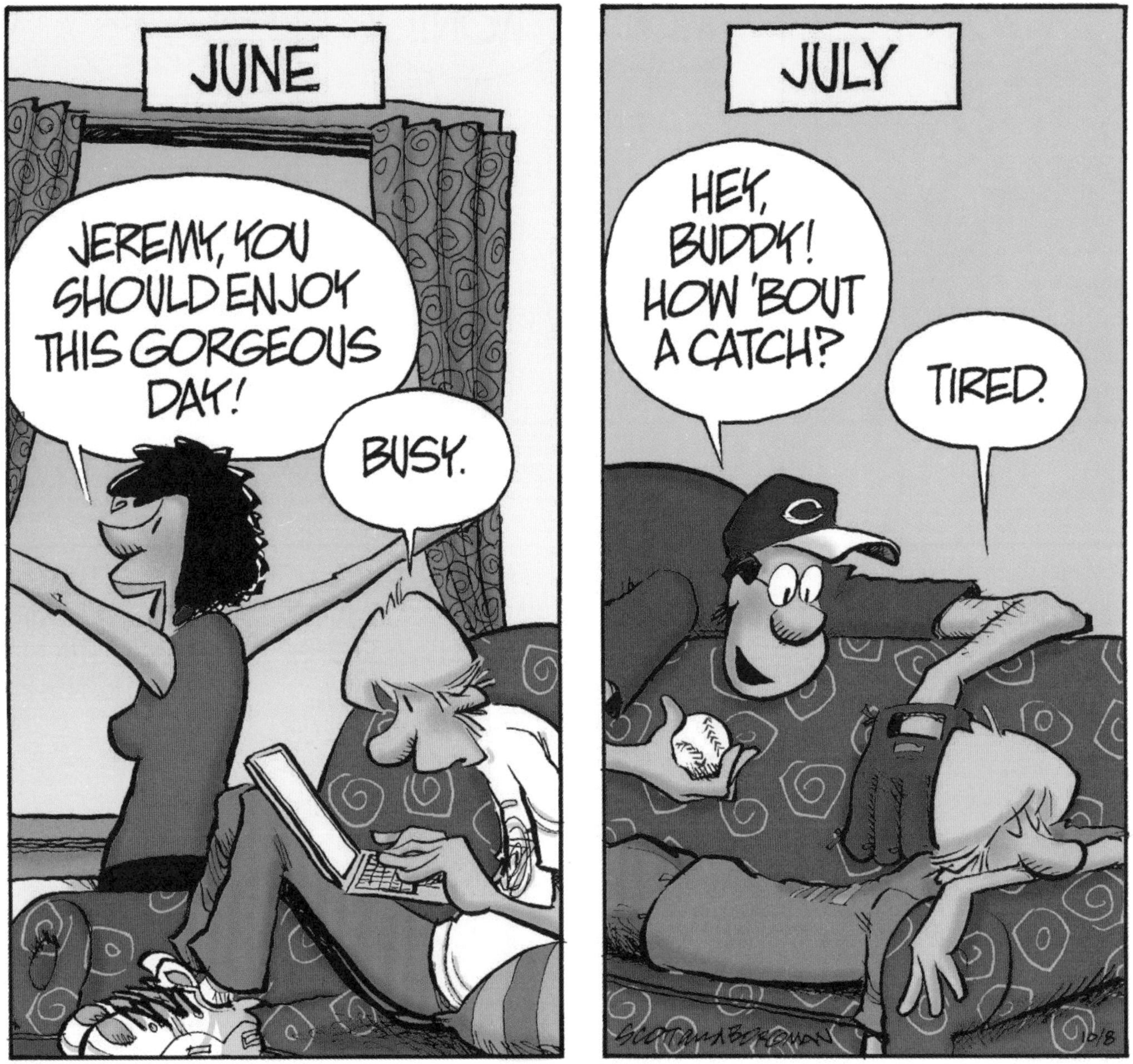
JUNE
JEREMY, YOU SHOULD ENJOY THIS GORGEOUS DAY!
BUSY.
JULY
HEY, BUDDY! HOW 'BOUT A CATCH?
TIRED.
SCOTT JIM BORGMAN

AUGUST
UP FOR A BIKE RIDE?
PASS.
NOW
THE TROUBLE WITH SCHOOL IS THAT WE'RE STUCK INSIDE ALL DAY.
IT'S UNNATURAL.

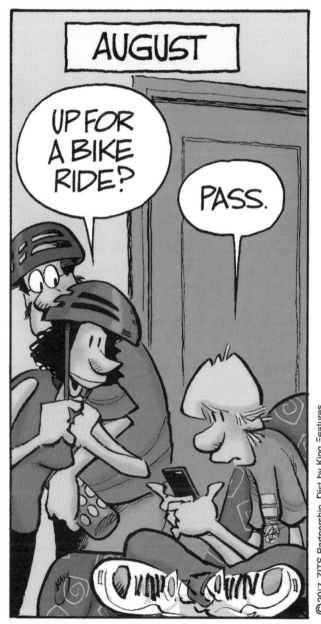

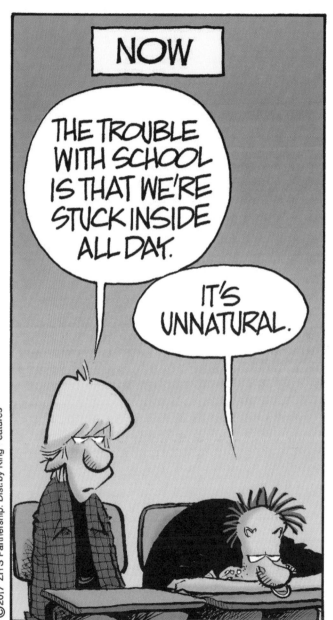

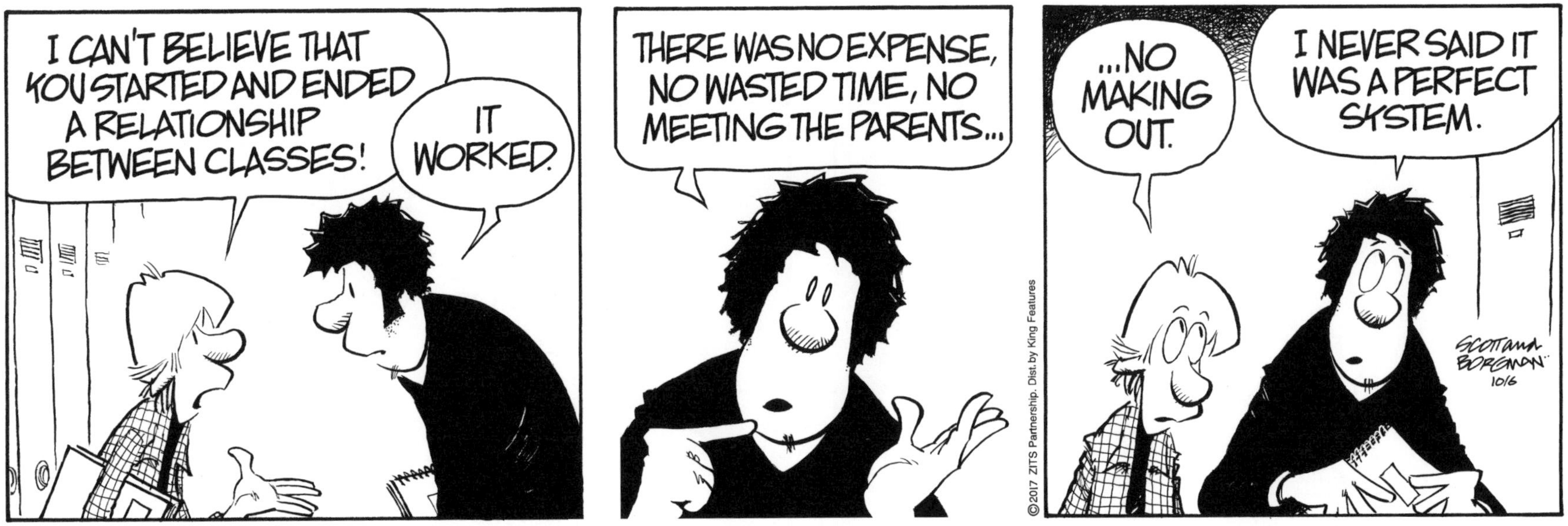
I CAN'T BELIEVE THAT YOU STARTED AND ENDED A RELATIONSHIP BETWEEN CLASSES!
IT WORKED.
THERE WAS NO EXPENSE, NO WASTED TIME, NO MEETING THE PARENTS...
...NO MAKING OUT.
I NEVER SAID IT WAS A PERFECT SYSTEM.
SCOTT AND BORGMAN 10/6
©2017 ZITS Partnership. Dist. by King Features

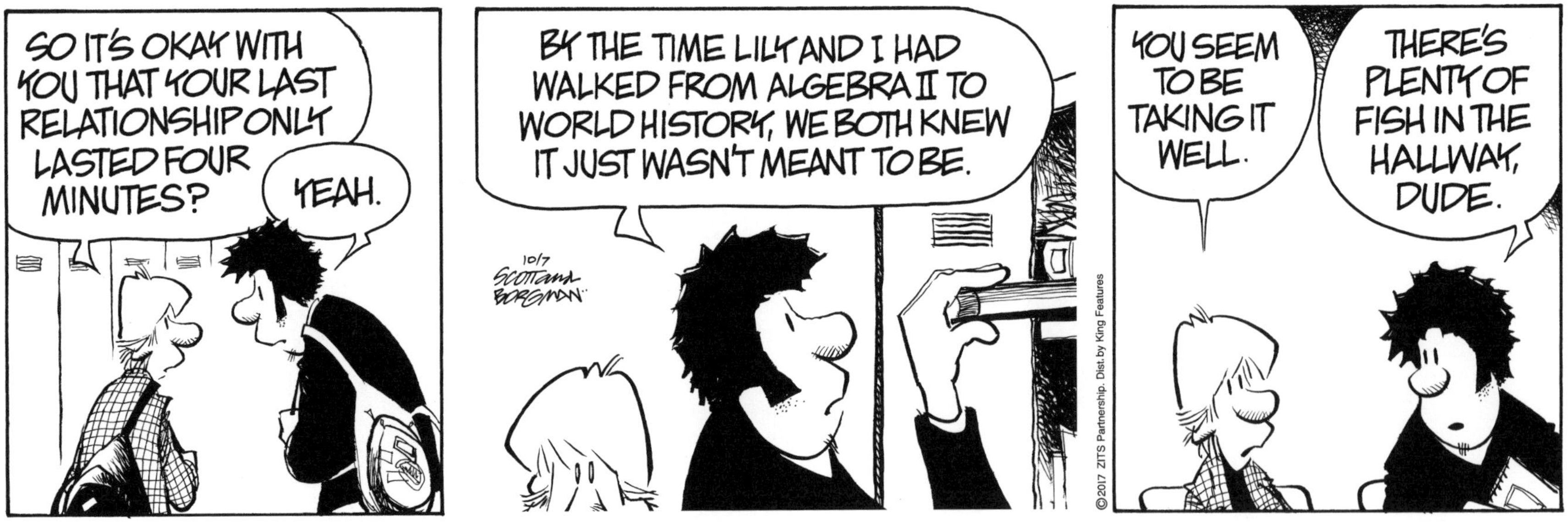
SO IT'S OKAY WITH YOU THAT YOUR LAST RELATIONSHIP ONLY LASTED FOUR MINUTES?
YEAH.
BY THE TIME LILY AND I HAD WALKED FROM ALGEBRA II TO WORLD HISTORY, WE BOTH KNEW IT JUST WASN'T MEANT TO BE.
10/7 SCOTT AND BORGMAN
YOU SEEM TO BE TAKING IT WELL.
THERE'S PLENTY OF FISH IN THE HALLWAY, DUDE.
©2017 ZITS Partnership. Dist. by King Features

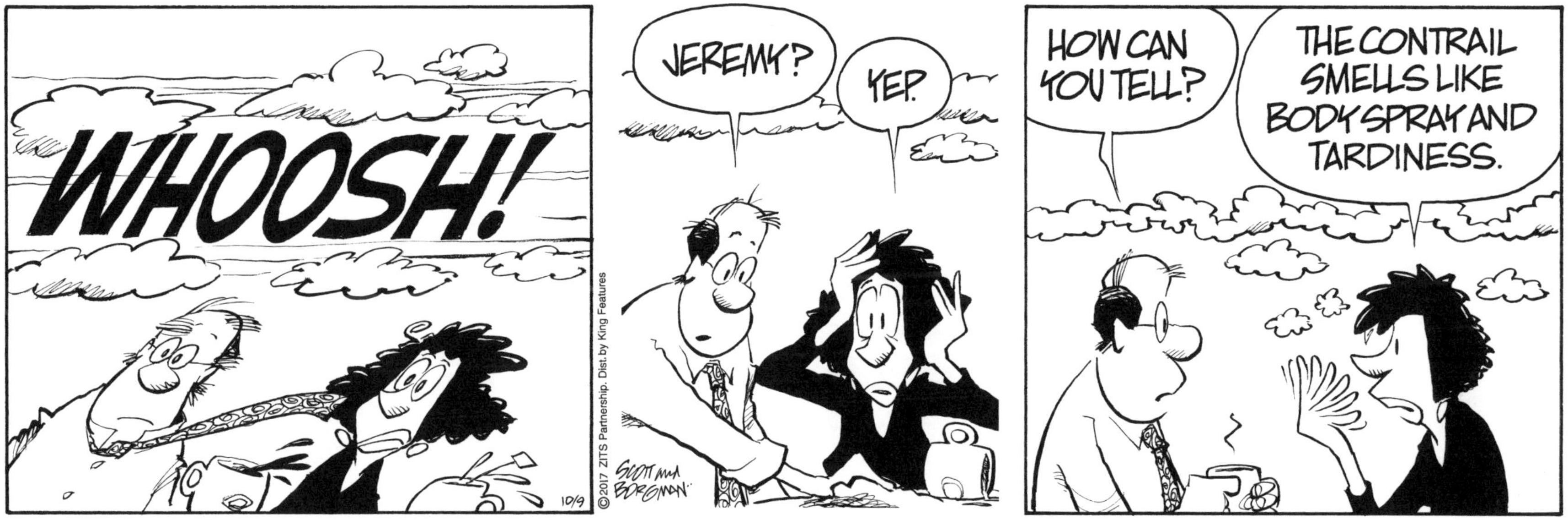
WHOOSH!
10/9
SCOTT AND BORGMAN
©2017 ZITS Partnership. Dist. by King Features
JEREMY?
YEP.
HOW CAN YOU TELL?
THE CONTRAIL SMELLS LIKE BODY SPRAY AND TARDINESS.

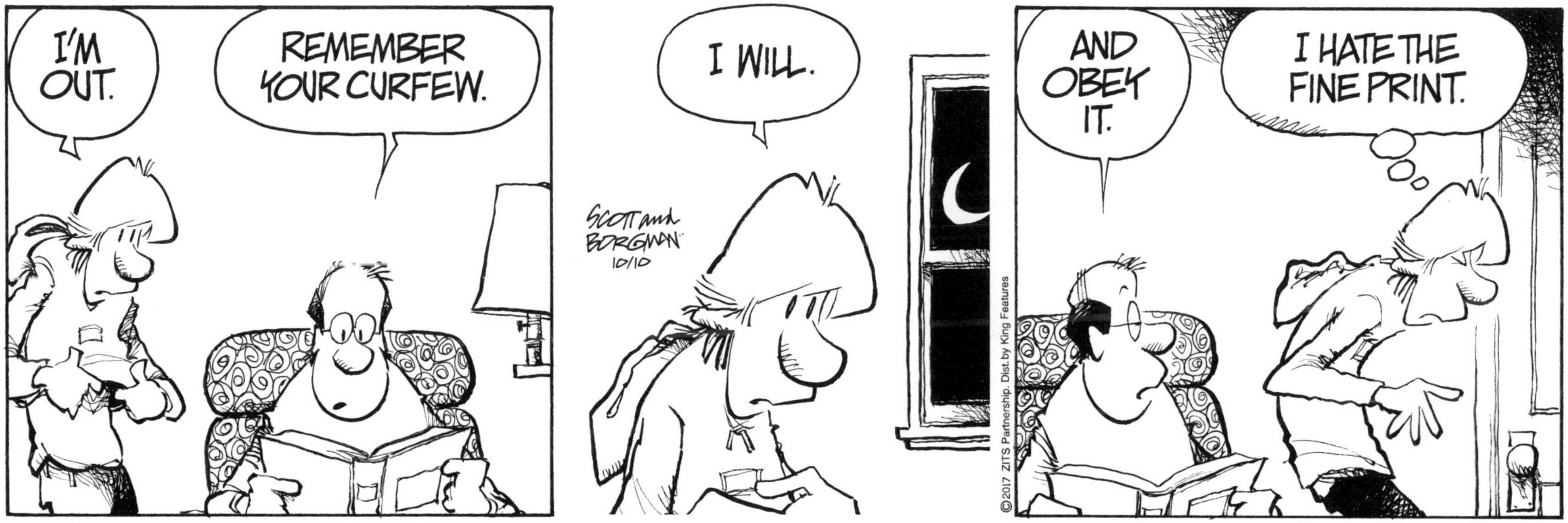
I'M OUT.
REMEMBER YOUR CURFEW.
I WILL.
SCOTT AND BORGMAN
10/10
AND OBEY IT.
I HATE THE FINE PRINT.
©2017 ZITS Partnership. Dist. by King Features

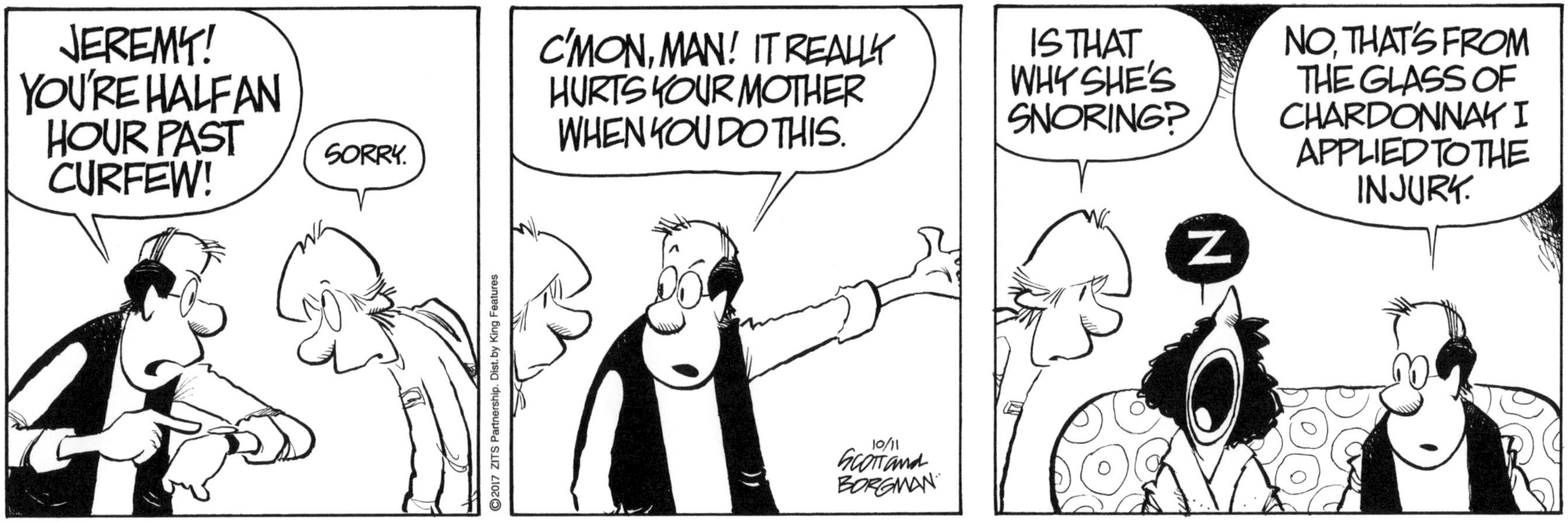
JEREMY! YOU'RE HALF AN HOUR PAST CURFEW!
SORRY.
©2017 ZITS Partnership. Dist. by King Features
C'MON, MAN! IT REALLY HURTS YOUR MOTHER WHEN YOU DO THIS.
10/11 SCOTT and BORGMAN
IS THAT WHY SHE'S SNORING?
Z
NO, THAT'S FROM THE GLASS OF CHARDONNAY I APPLIED TO THE INJURY.

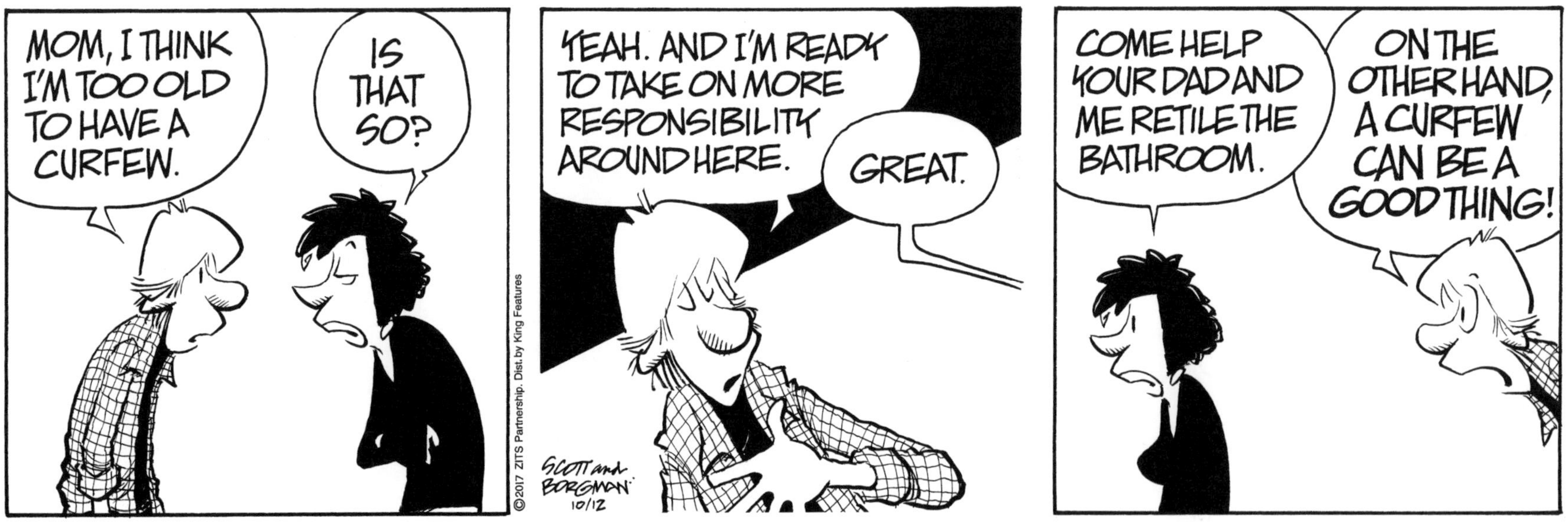
MOM, I THINK I'M TOO OLD TO HAVE A CURFEW.
IS THAT SO?
©2017 ZITS Partnership. Dist. by King Features
YEAH. AND I'M READY TO TAKE ON MORE RESPONSIBILITY AROUND HERE.
GREAT.
SCOTT and BORGMAN 10/12
COME HELP YOUR DAD AND ME RETILE THE BATHROOM.
ON THE OTHER HAND, A CURFEW CAN BE A GOOD THING!

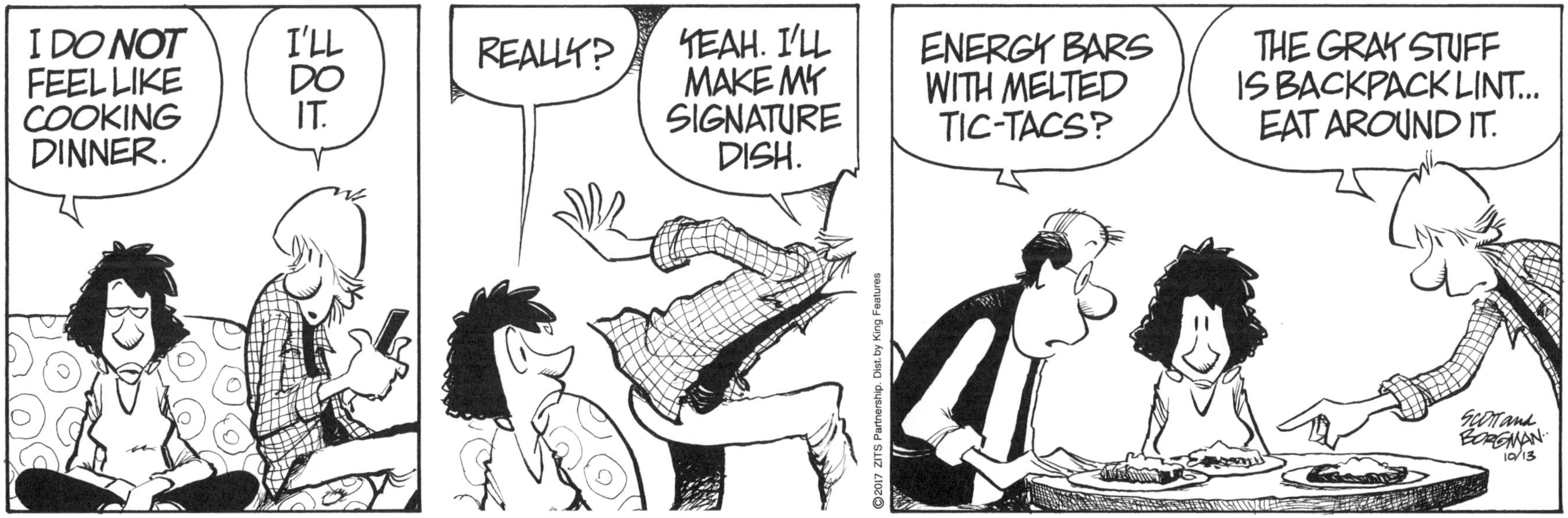
I DO NOT FEEL LIKE COOKING DINNER.
I'LL DO IT.
REALLY?
YEAH. I'LL MAKE MY SIGNATURE DISH.
©2017 ZITS Partnership. Dist. by King Features
ENERGY BARS WITH MELTED TIC-TACS?
THE GRAY STUFF IS BACKPACK LINT... EAT AROUND IT.
SCOTT and BORGMAN 10/13

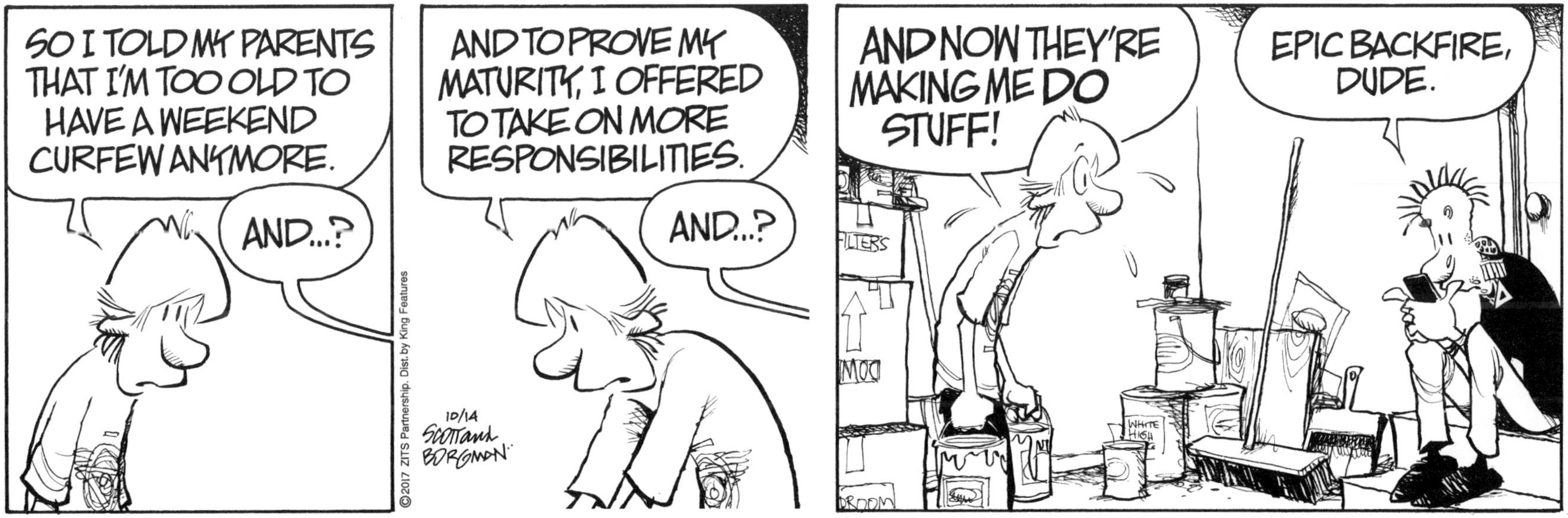
SO I TOLD MY PARENTS THAT I'M TOO OLD TO HAVE A WEEKEND CURFEW ANYMORE.
AND...?
©2017 ZITS Partnership. Dist. by King Features
10/14 SCOTT and BORGMAN
AND TO PROVE MY MATURITY, I OFFERED TO TAKE ON MORE RESPONSIBILITIES.
AND...?
AND NOW THEY'RE MAKING ME DO STUFF!
EPIC BACKFIRE, DUDE.

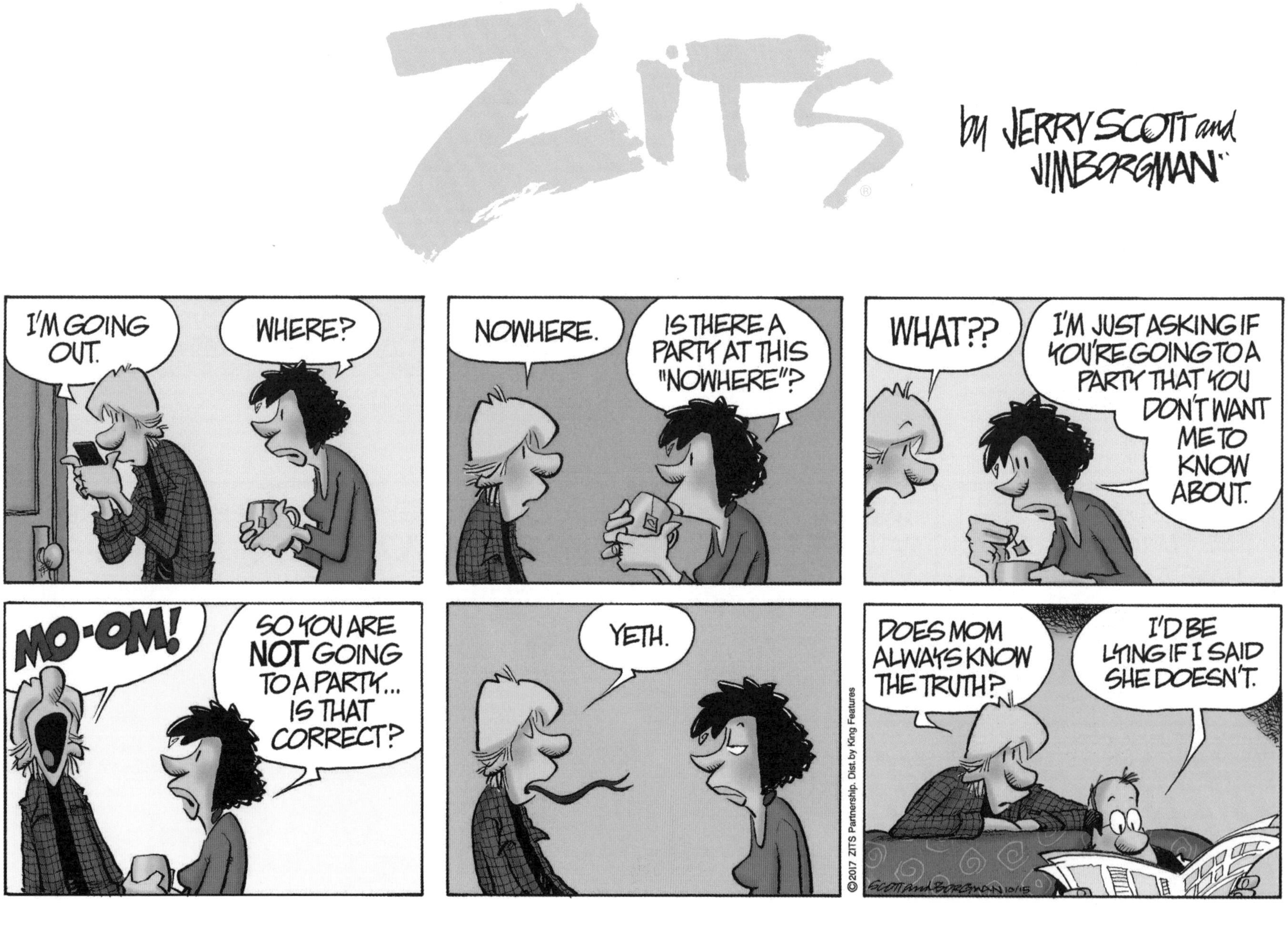
ZITS®
by JERRY SCOTT and JIM BORGMAN
I'M GOING OUT.
WHERE?
NOWHERE.
IS THERE A PARTY AT THIS "NOWHERE"?
WHAT??
I'M JUST ASKING IF YOU'RE GOING TO A PARTY THAT YOU DON'T WANT ME TO KNOW ABOUT.
MO-OM!
SO YOU ARE NOT GOING TO A PARTY... IS THAT CORRECT?
YETH.
DOES MOM ALWAYS KNOW THE TRUTH?
I'D BE LYING IF I SAID SHE DOESN'T.
©2017 ZITS Partnership. Dist. by King Features
SCOTT and BORGMAN 10/15

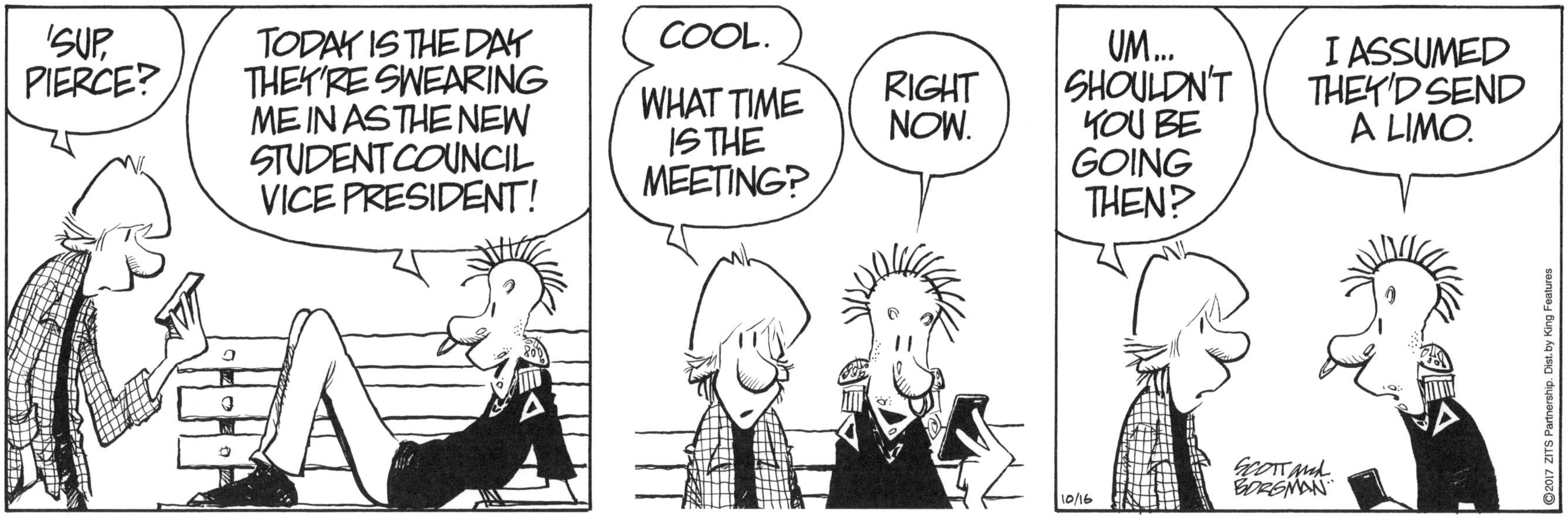
'SUP, PIERCE?
TODAY IS THE DAY THEY'RE SWEARING ME IN AS THE NEW STUDENT COUNCIL VICE PRESIDENT!
COOL.
WHAT TIME IS THE MEETING?
RIGHT NOW.
UM... SHOULDN'T YOU BE GOING THEN?
I ASSUMED THEY'D SEND A LIMO.
SCOTT and BORGMAN 10/16
©2017 ZITS Partnership. Dist. by King Features

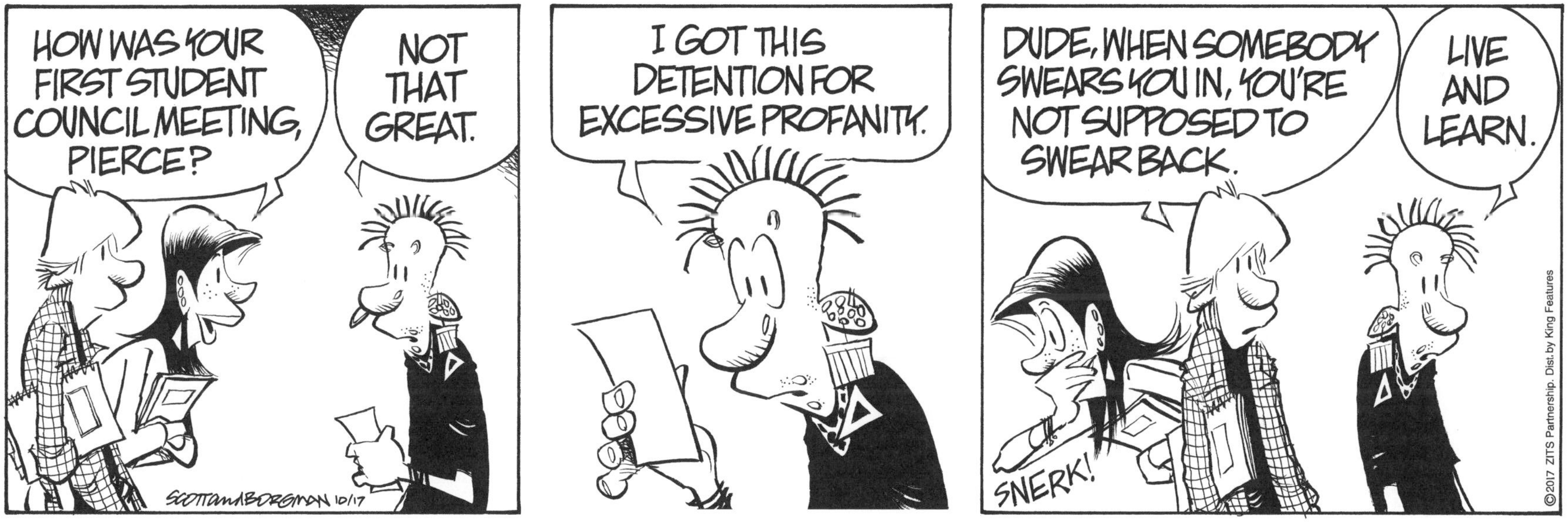
HOW WAS YOUR FIRST STUDENT COUNCIL MEETING, PIERCE?
NOT THAT GREAT.
SCOTT and BORGMAN 10/17
I GOT THIS DETENTION FOR EXCESSIVE PROFANITY.
DUDE, WHEN SOMEBODY SWEARS YOU IN, YOU'RE NOT SUPPOSED TO SWEAR BACK.
LIVE AND LEARN.
SNERK!
©2017 ZITS Partnership. Dist. by King Features

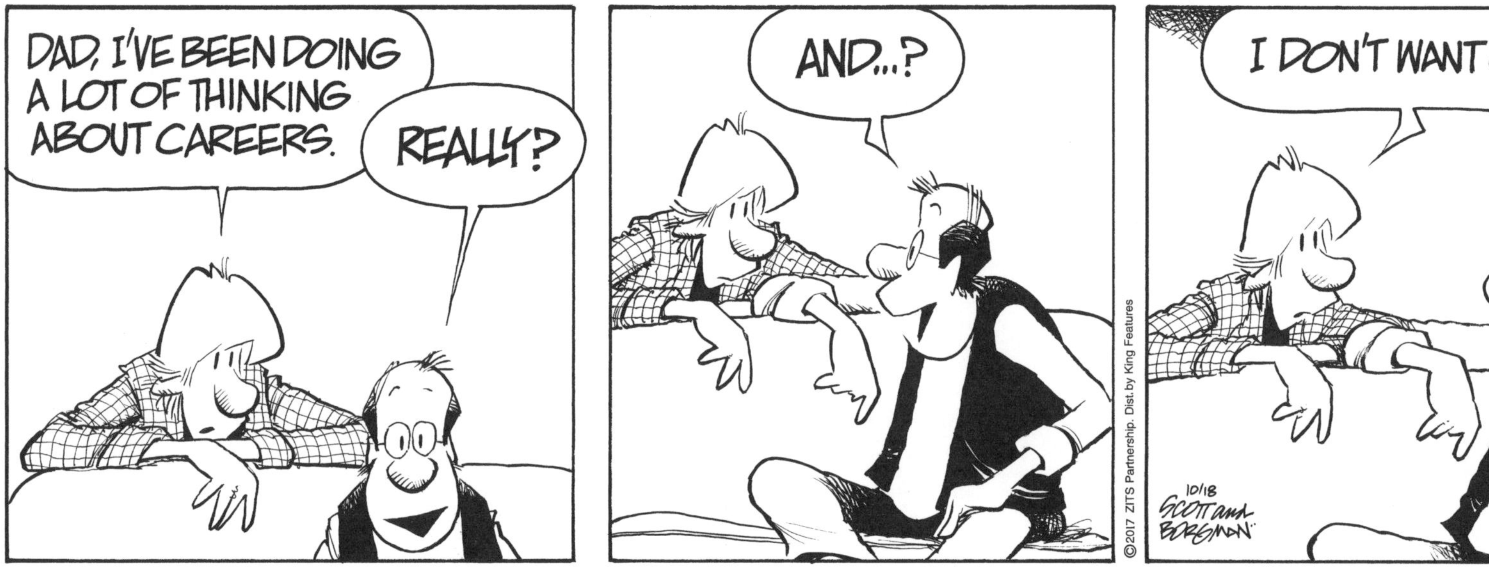
DAD, I'VE BEEN DOING A LOT OF THINKING ABOUT CAREERS.
REALLY?
AND...?
I DON'T WANT ONE.
©2017 ZITS Partnership. Dist.by King Features
10/18 SCOTT and BORGMAN

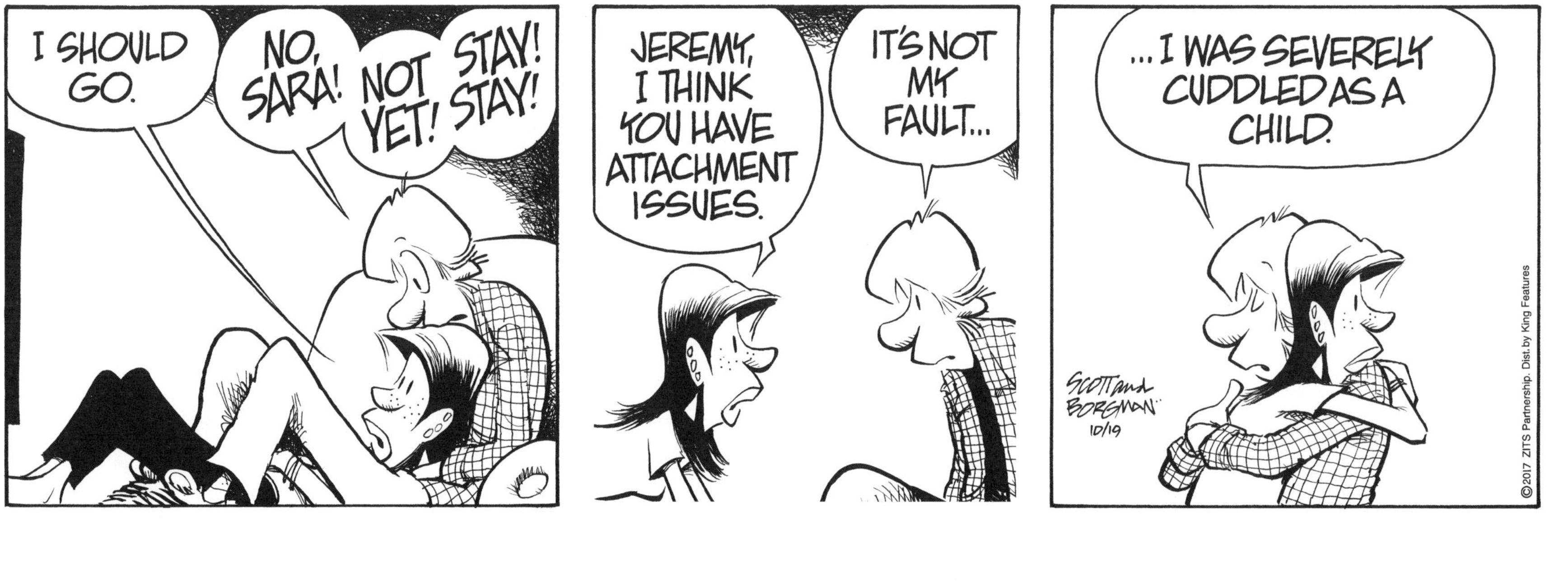
I SHOULD GO.
NO, SARA!
NOT YET!
STAY! STAY!
JEREMY, I THINK YOU HAVE ATTACHMENT ISSUES.
IT'S NOT MY FAULT...
...I WAS SEVERELY CUDDLED AS A CHILD.
SCOTT and BORGMAN 10/19
©2017 ZITS Partnership. Dist.by King Features

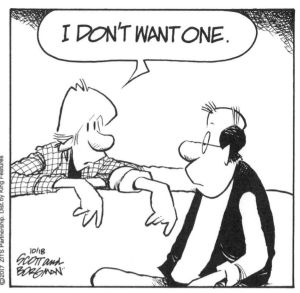

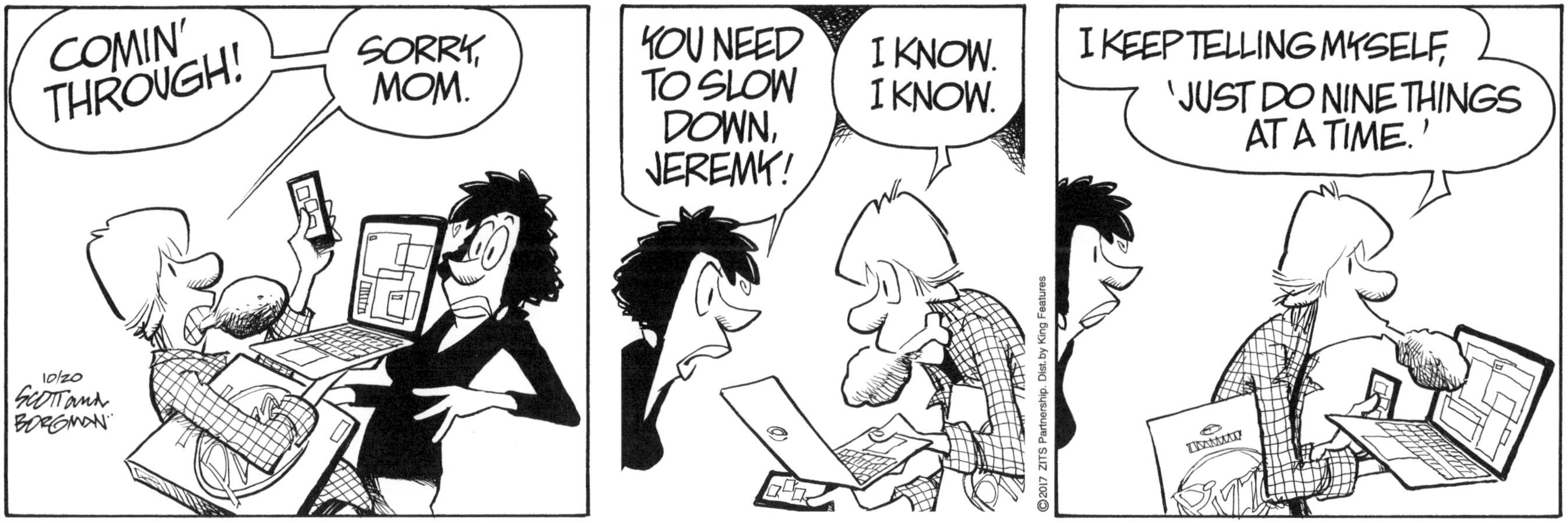
COMIN' THROUGH!
SORRY, MOM.
10/20
SCOTT and BORGMAN
YOU NEED TO SLOW DOWN, JEREMY!
I KNOW. I KNOW.
©2017 ZITS Partnership. Dist. by King Features
I KEEP TELLING MYSELF, 'JUST DO NINE THINGS AT A TIME.'

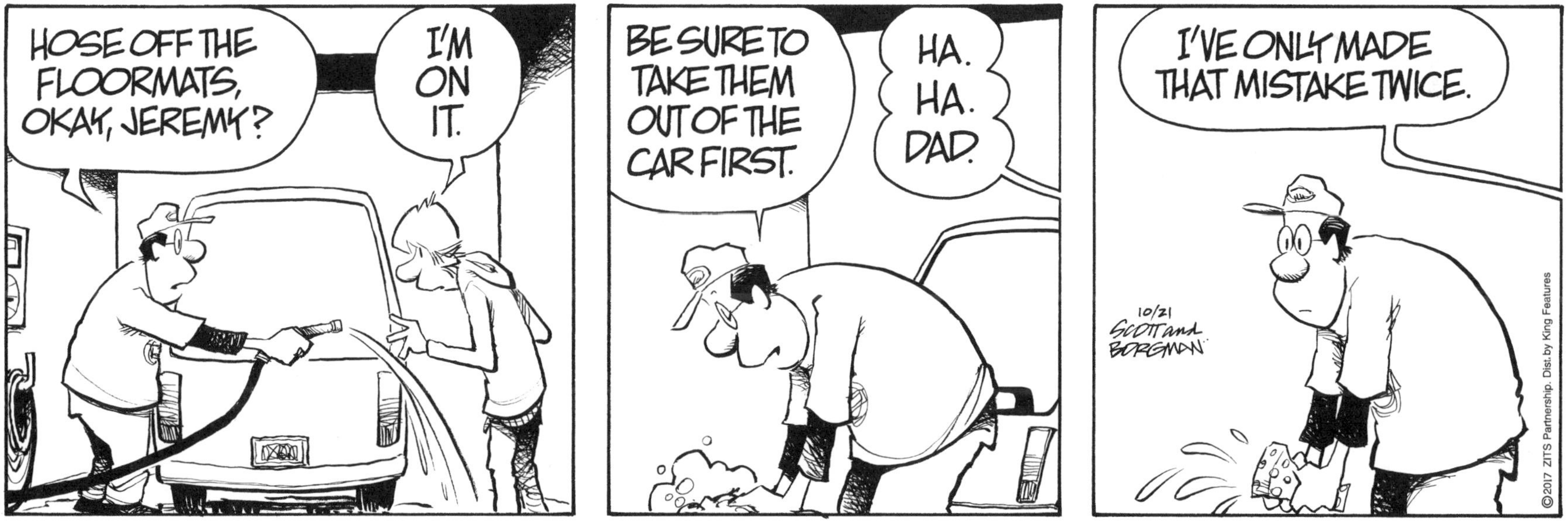
HOSE OFF THE FLOORMATS, OKAY, JEREMY?
I'M ON IT.
BE SURE TO TAKE THEM OUT OF THE CAR FIRST.
HA. HA. DAD.
10/21
SCOTT and BORGMAN
I'VE ONLY MADE THAT MISTAKE TWICE.
©2017 ZITS Partnership. Dist. by King Features

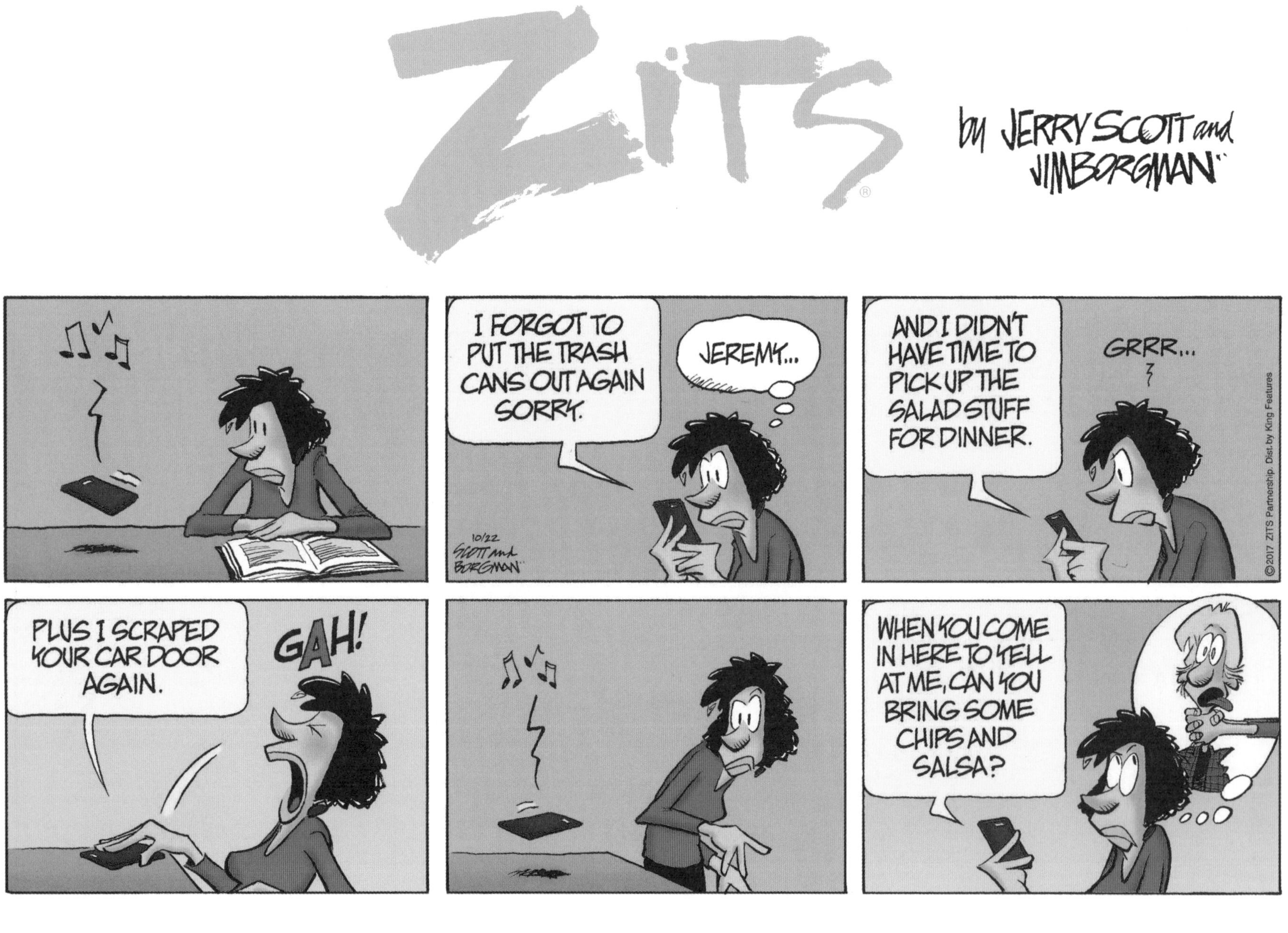
ZITS
by JERRY SCOTT and JIM BORGMAN
I FORGOT TO PUT THE TRASH CANS OUT AGAIN SORRY.
JEREMY...
10/22 SCOTT and BORGMAN
AND I DIDN'T HAVE TIME TO PICK UP THE SALAD STUFF FOR DINNER.
GRRR...
©2017 ZITS Partnership. Dist. by King Features
PLUS I SCRAPED YOUR CAR DOOR AGAIN.
GAH!
WHEN YOU COME IN HERE TO YELL AT ME, CAN YOU BRING SOME CHIPS AND SALSA?

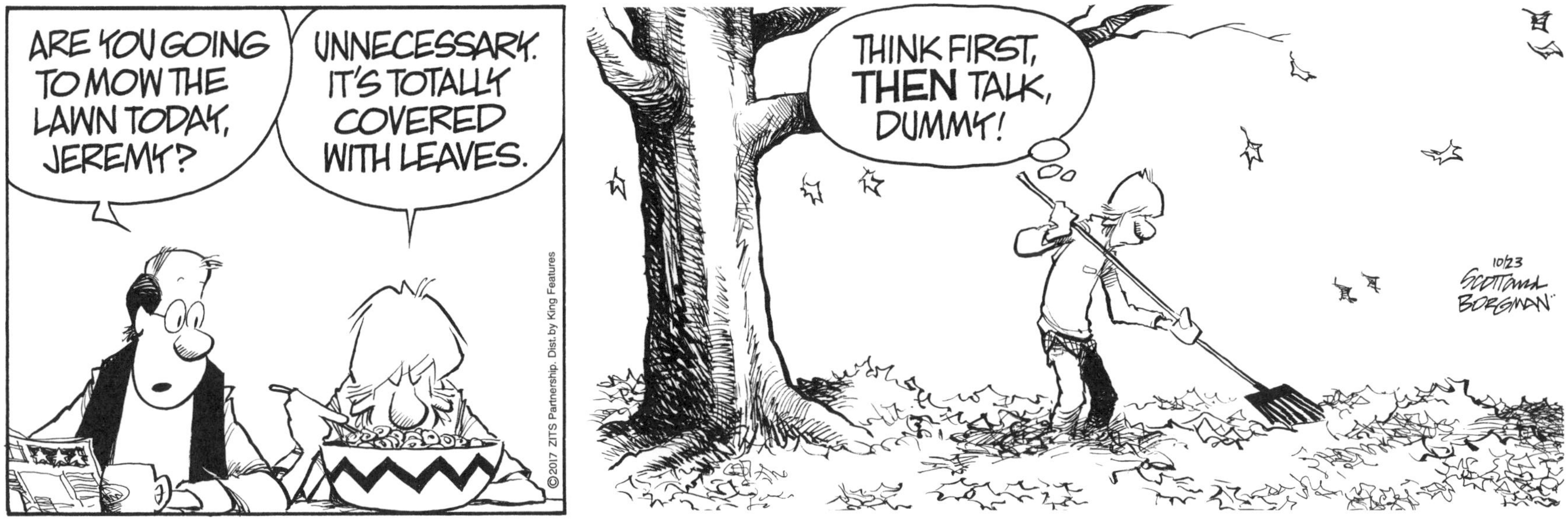
ARE YOU GOING TO MOW THE LAWN TODAY, JEREMY?
UNNECESSARY. IT'S TOTALLY COVERED WITH LEAVES.
©2017 ZITS Partnership. Dist. by King Features
THINK FIRST, THEN TALK, DUMMY!
10/23
SCOTT and BORGMAN

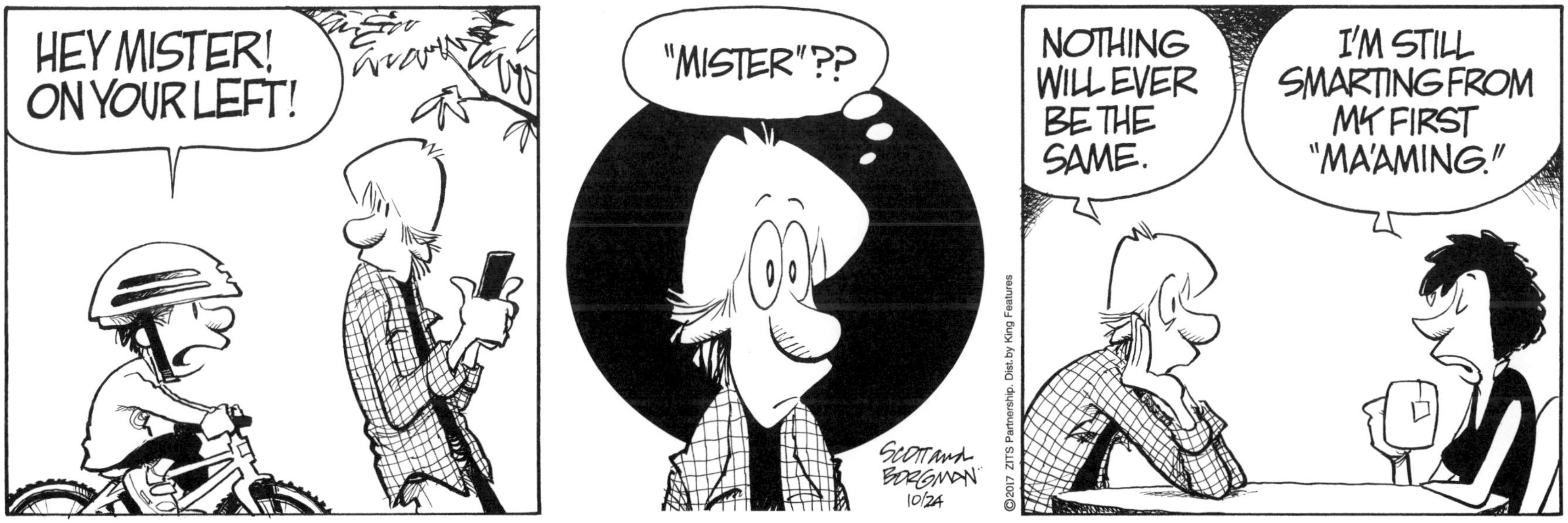
HEY MISTER! ON YOUR LEFT!
"MISTER"??
SCOTT and BORGMAN
10/24
©2017 ZITS Partnership. Dist. by King Features
NOTHING WILL EVER BE THE SAME.
I'M STILL SMARTING FROM MY FIRST "MA'AMING."

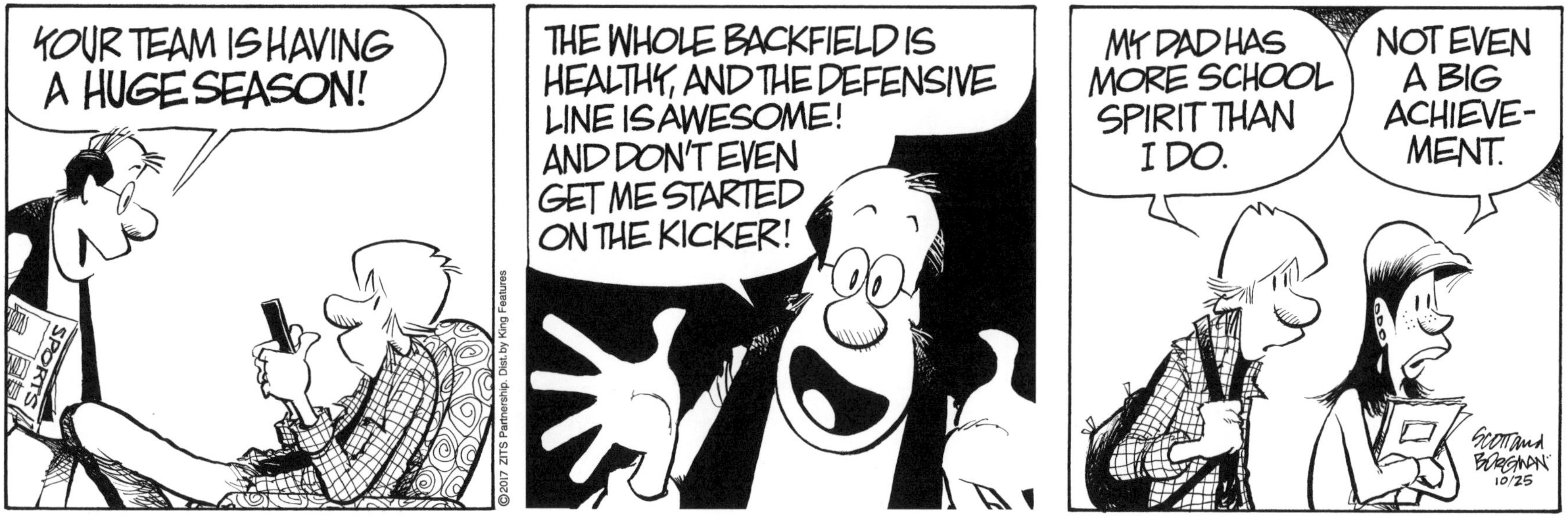
YOUR TEAM IS HAVING A HUGE SEASON!
© 2017 ZITS Partnership. Dist. by King Features
SPORTS
THE WHOLE BACKFIELD IS HEALTHY, AND THE DEFENSIVE LINE IS AWESOME! AND DON'T EVEN GET ME STARTED ON THE KICKER!
MY DAD HAS MORE SCHOOL SPIRIT THAN I DO.
NOT EVEN A BIG ACHIEVEMENT.
SCOTT and BORGMAN 10/25

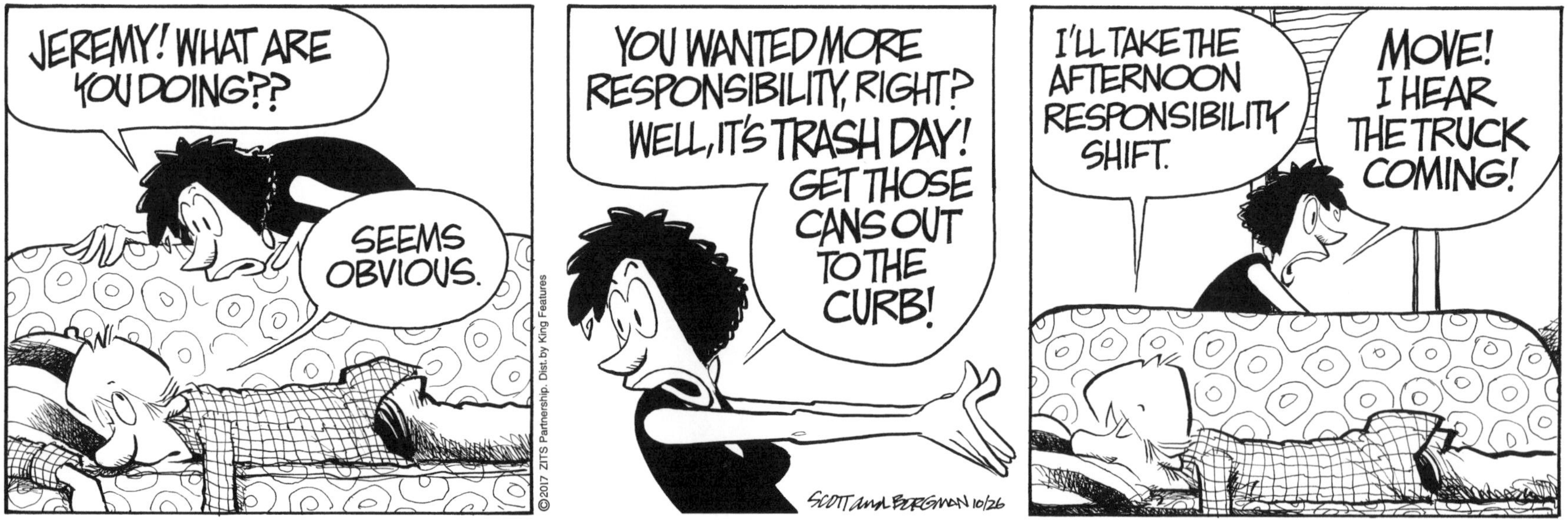
JEREMY! WHAT ARE YOU DOING??
SEEMS OBVIOUS.
©2017 ZITS Partnership. Dist. by King Features
YOU WANTED MORE RESPONSIBILITY, RIGHT? WELL, IT'S TRASH DAY! GET THOSE CANS OUT TO THE CURB!
SCOTT and BORGMAN 10/26
I'LL TAKE THE AFTERNOON RESPONSIBILITY SHIFT.
MOVE! I HEAR THE TRUCK COMING!

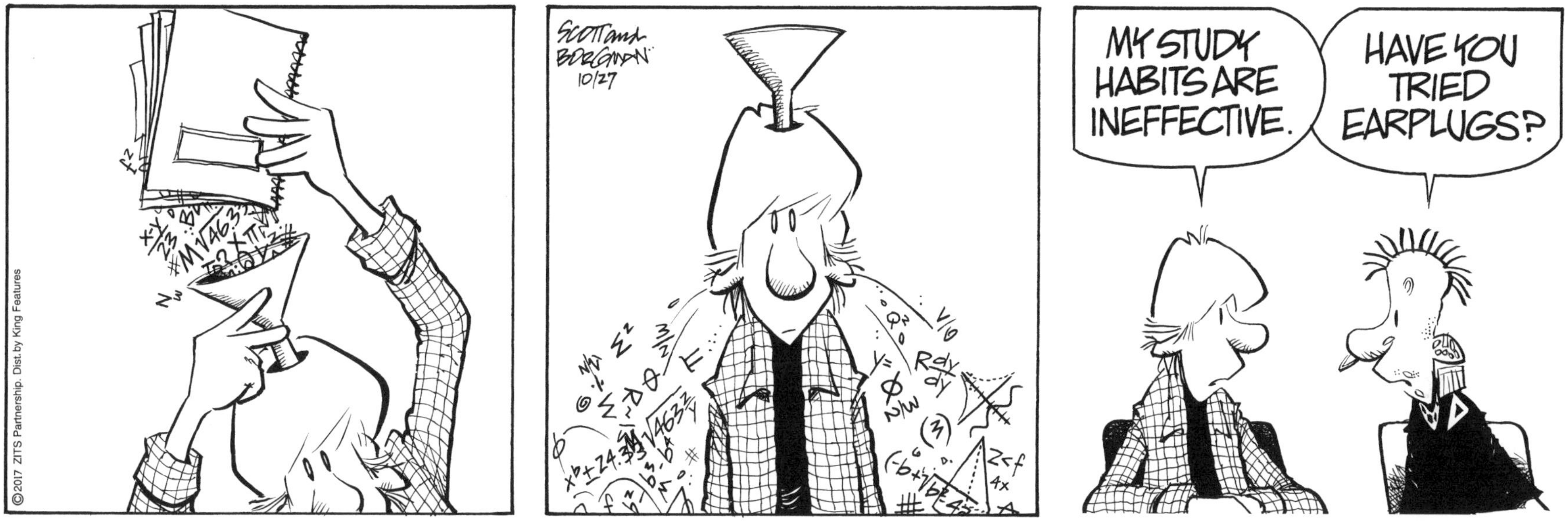
©2017 ZITS Partnership. Dist. by King Features
SCOTT and BORGMAN 10/27
MY STUDY HABITS ARE INEFFECTIVE.
HAVE YOU TRIED EARPLUGS?

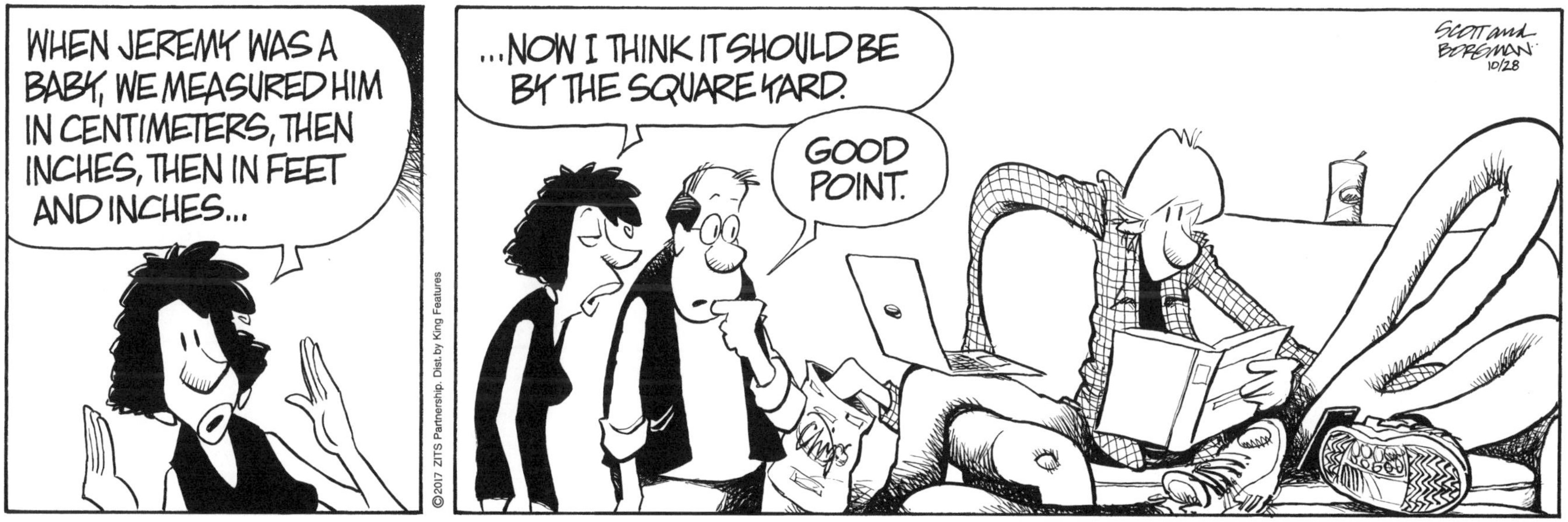
WHEN JEREMY WAS A BABY, WE MEASURED HIM IN CENTIMETERS, THEN INCHES, THEN IN FEET AND INCHES...
©2017 ZITS Partnership. Dist. by King Features
SCOTT and BORGMAN 10/28
...NOW I THINK IT SHOULD BE BY THE SQUARE YARD.
GOOD POINT.

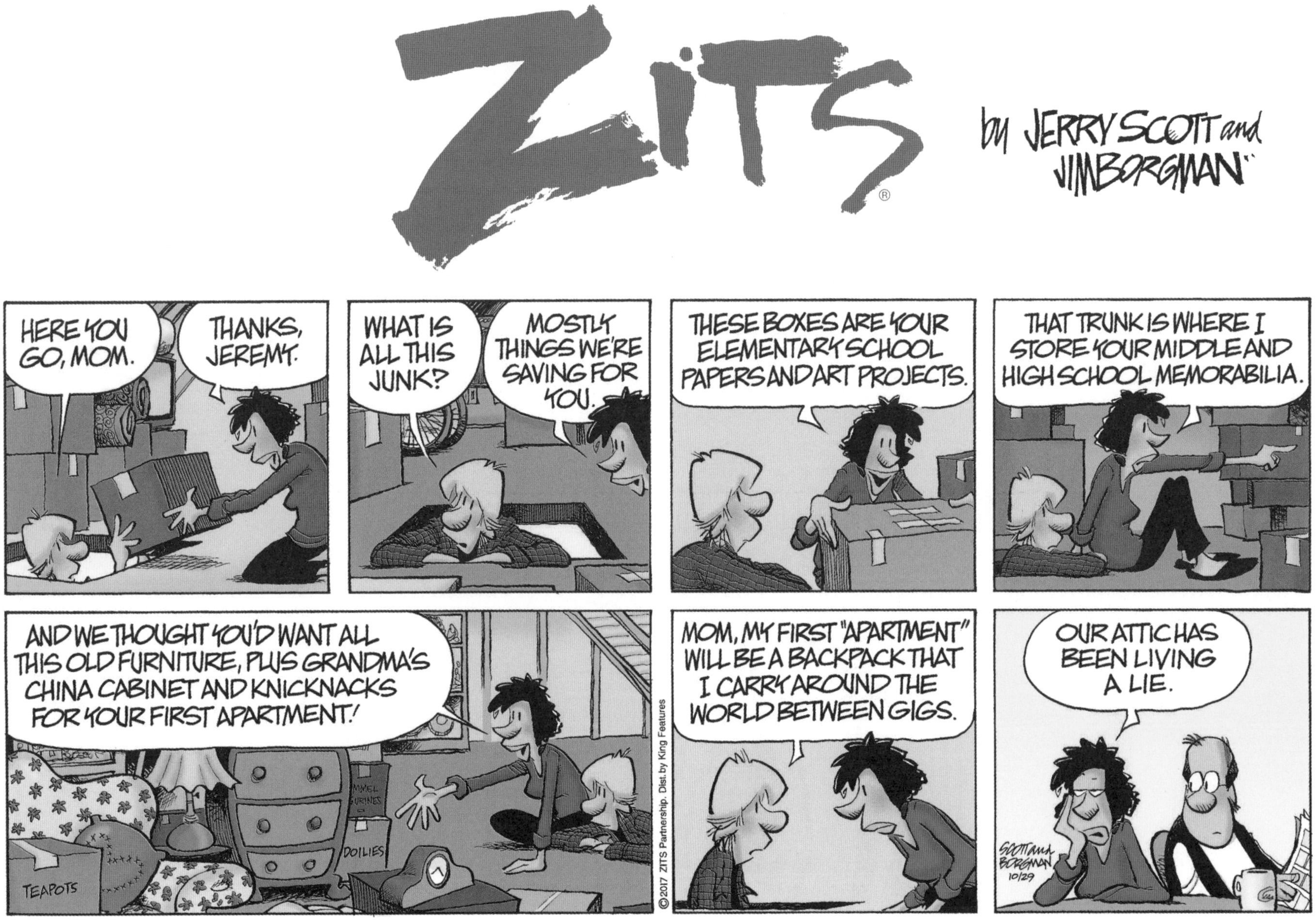
ZITS
by JERRY SCOTT and JIM BORGMAN
HERE YOU GO, MOM.
THANKS, JEREMY.
WHAT IS ALL THIS JUNK?
MOSTLY THINGS WE'RE SAVING FOR YOU.
THESE BOXES ARE YOUR ELEMENTARY SCHOOL PAPERS AND ART PROJECTS.
THAT TRUNK IS WHERE I STORE YOUR MIDDLE AND HIGH SCHOOL MEMORABILIA.
AND WE THOUGHT YOU'D WANT ALL THIS OLD FURNITURE, PLUS GRANDMA'S CHINA CABINET AND KNICKNACKS FOR YOUR FIRST APARTMENT!
DOILIES
TEAPOTS
©2017 ZITS Partnership. Dist. by King Features
MOM, MY FIRST "APARTMENT" WILL BE A BACKPACK THAT I CARRY AROUND THE WORLD BETWEEN GIGS.
OUR ATTIC HAS BEEN LIVING A LIE.
SCOTT and BORGMAN 10/29

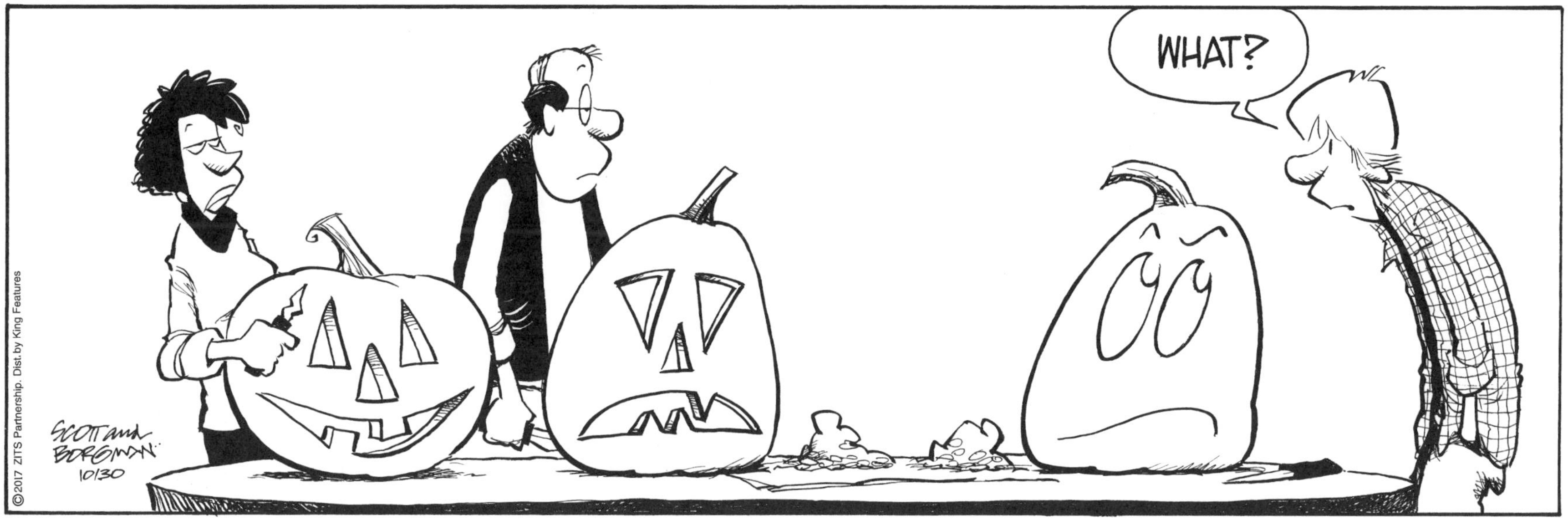
WHAT?
SCOTT and BORGMAN 10/30
©2017 ZITS Partnership. Dist. by King Features

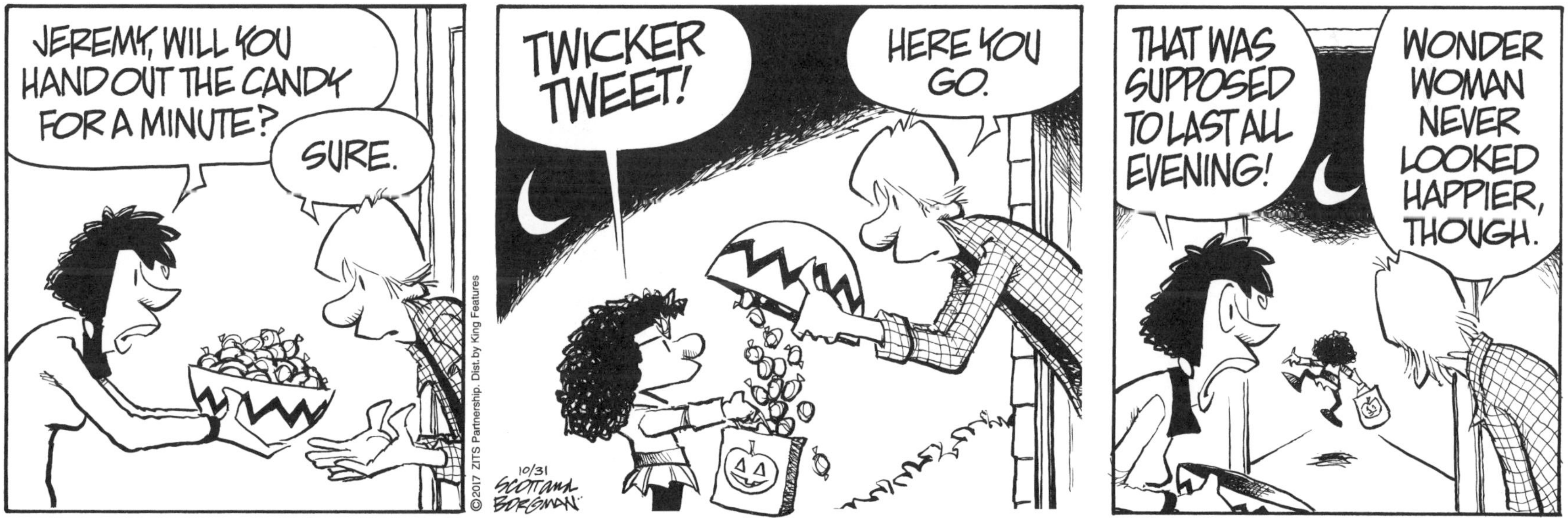
JEREMY, WILL YOU HAND OUT THE CANDY FOR A MINUTE?
SURE.
TWICKER TWEET!
HERE YOU GO.
THAT WAS SUPPOSED TO LAST ALL EVENING!
WONDER WOMAN NEVER LOOKED HAPPIER, THOUGH.
10/31 SCOTT and BORGMAN
©2017 ZITS Partnership. Dist. by King Features

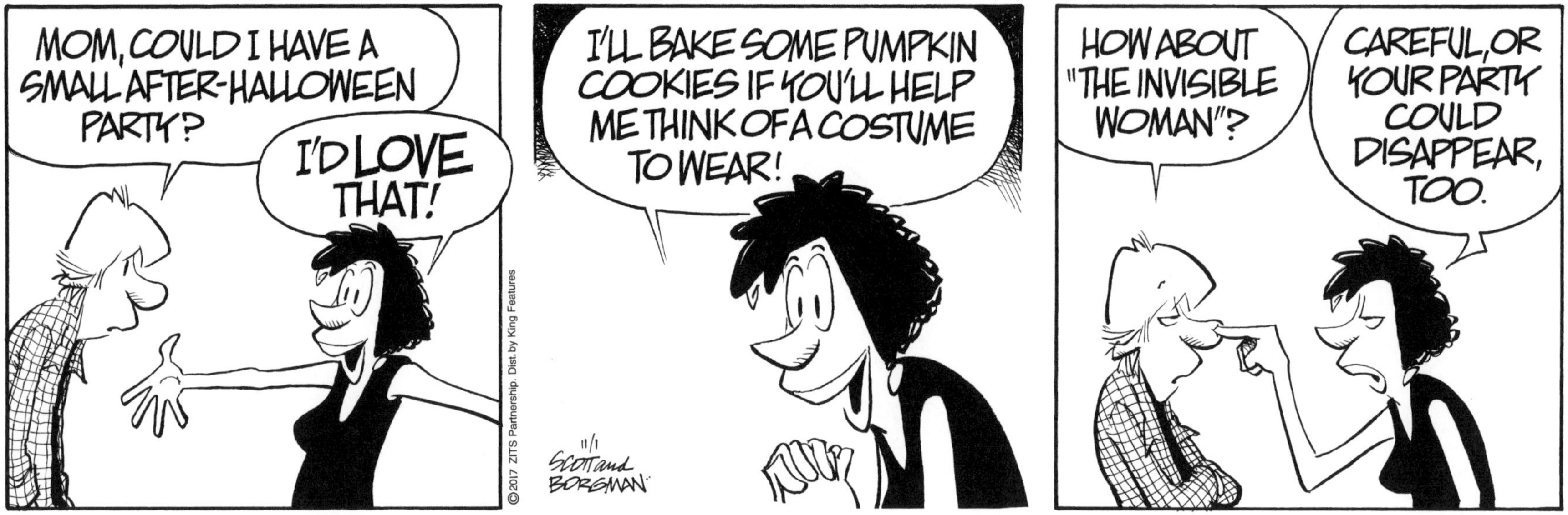
MOM, COULD I HAVE A SMALL AFTER-HALLOWEEN PARTY?
I'D LOVE THAT!
I'LL BAKE SOME PUMPKIN COOKIES IF YOU'LL HELP ME THINK OF A COSTUME TO WEAR!
HOW ABOUT "THE INVISIBLE WOMAN"?
CAREFUL, OR YOUR PARTY COULD DISAPPEAR, TOO.
© 2017 ZITS Partnership. Dist. by King Features
11/1 SCOTT and BORGMAN

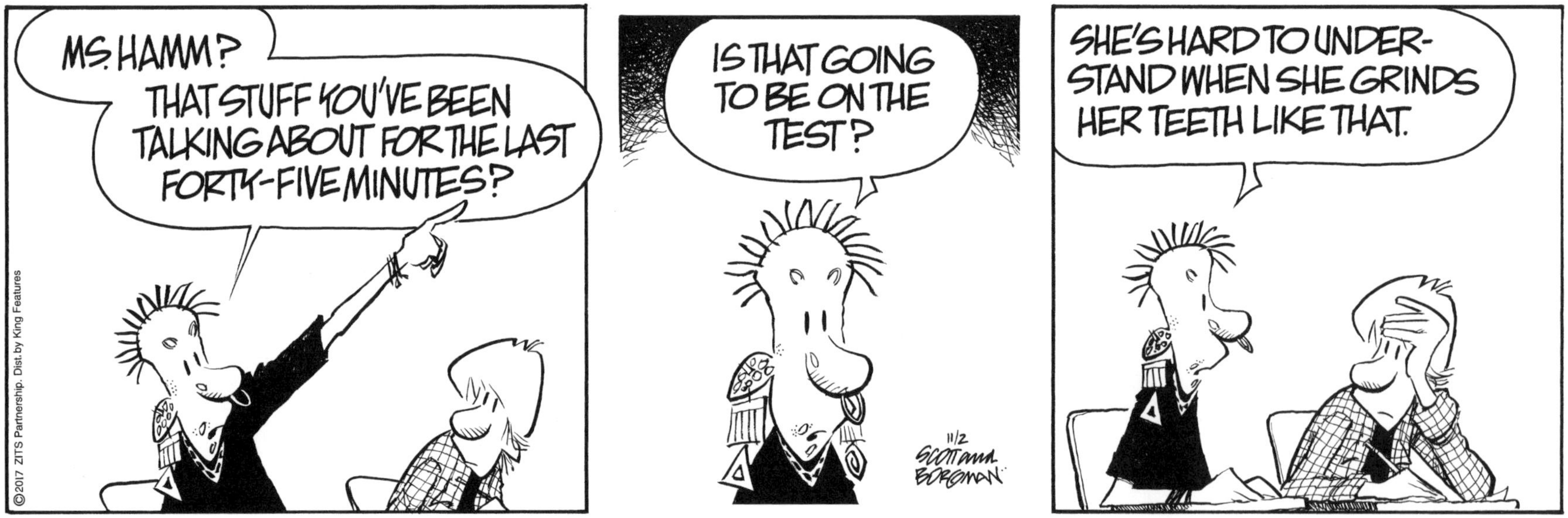
MS. HAMM?
THAT STUFF YOU'VE BEEN TALKING ABOUT FOR THE LAST FORTY-FIVE MINUTES?
IS THAT GOING TO BE ON THE TEST?
SHE'S HARD TO UNDER-STAND WHEN SHE GRINDS HER TEETH LIKE THAT.
© 2017 ZITS Partnership. Dist. by King Features
11/2 SCOTT and BORGMAN

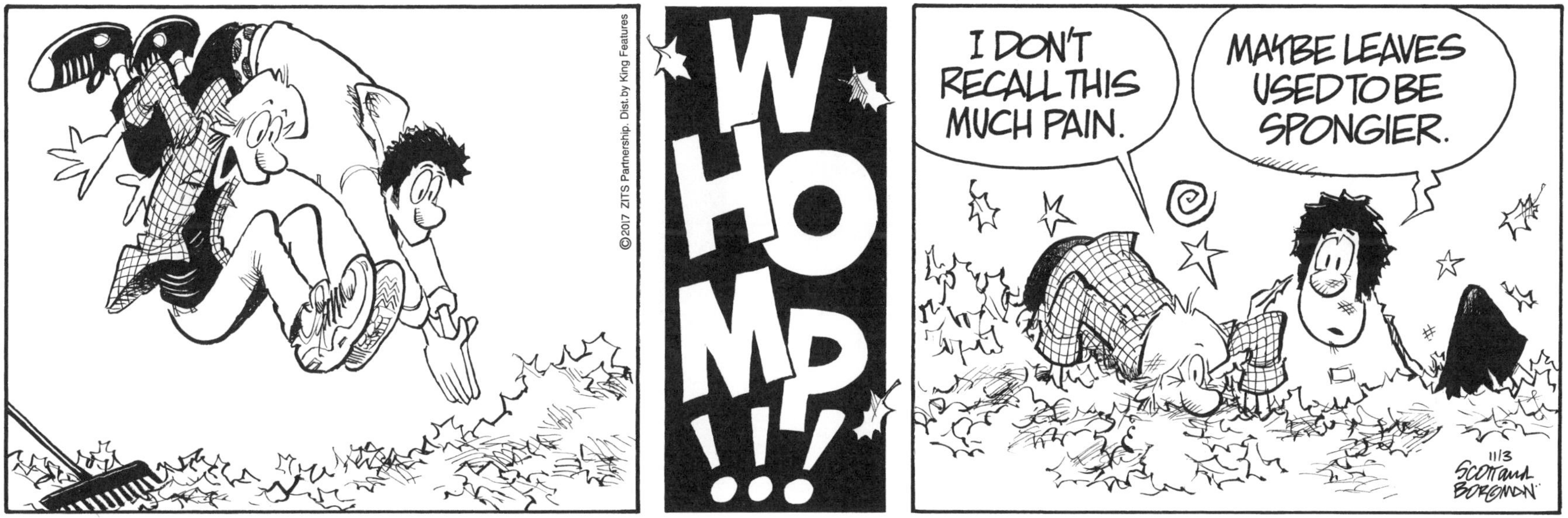
© 2017 ZITS Partnership. Dist. by King Features
WHOMP!!!
I DON'T RECALL THIS MUCH PAIN.
MAYBE LEAVES USED TO BE SPONGIER.
11/3 SCOTT and BORGMAN

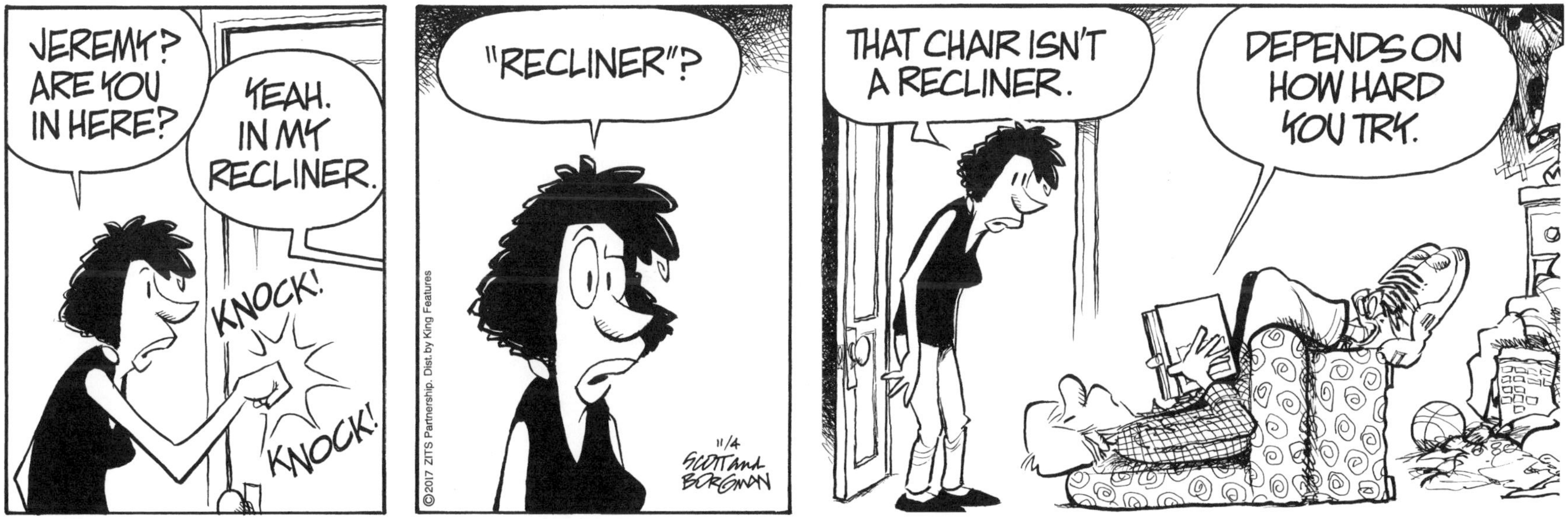
JEREMY? ARE YOU IN HERE?
YEAH. IN MY RECLINER.
KNOCK! KNOCK!
© 2017 ZITS Partnership. Dist. by King Features
"RECLINER"?
11/4 SCOTT and BORGMAN
THAT CHAIR ISN'T A RECLINER.
DEPENDS ON HOW HARD YOU TRY.

MOM, THIS NEW SHIRT IS TOO BIG.
YOU'LL GROW INTO IT.
ZOINK!

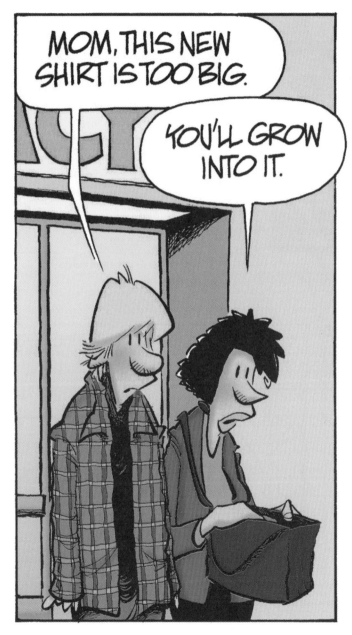

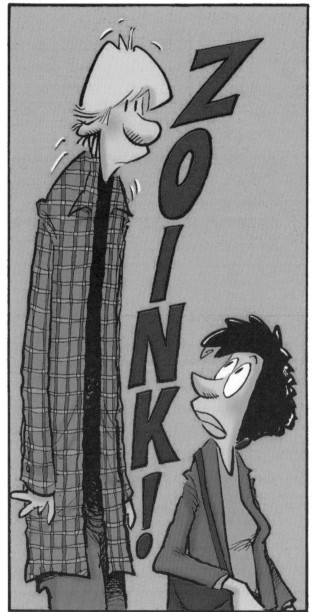

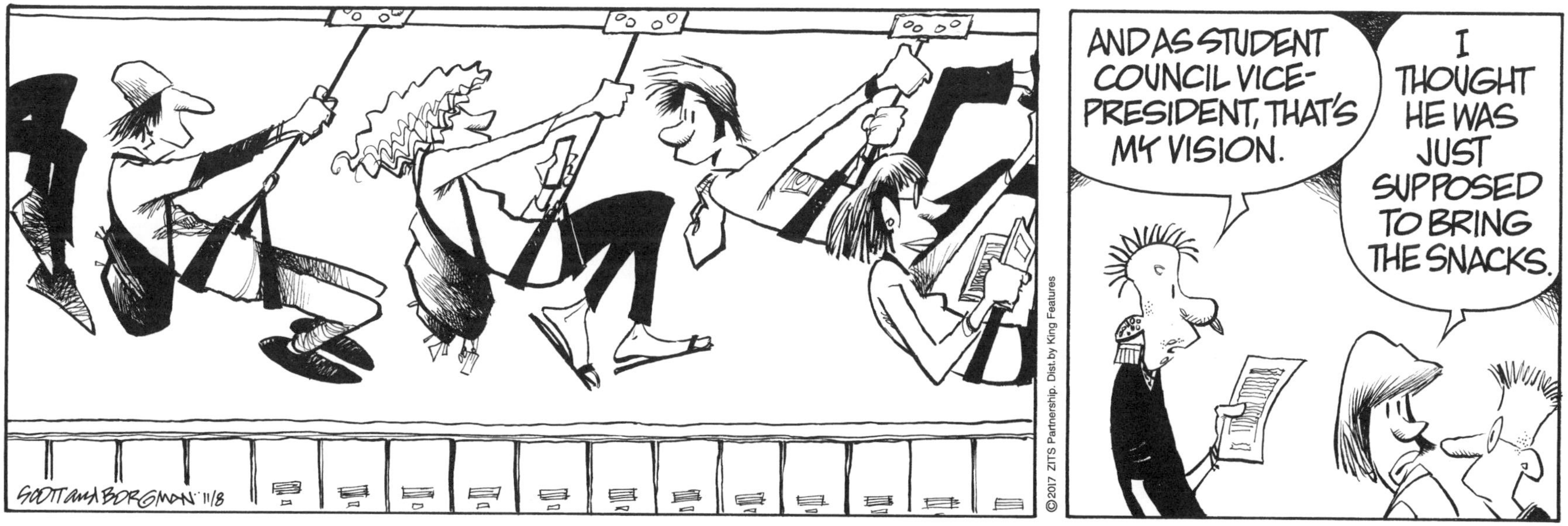
SCOTT and BORGMAN 11/8
© 2017 ZITS Partnership. Dist. by King Features
AND AS STUDENT COUNCIL VICE-PRESIDENT, THAT'S MY VISION.
I THOUGHT HE WAS JUST SUPPOSED TO BRING THE SNACKS.

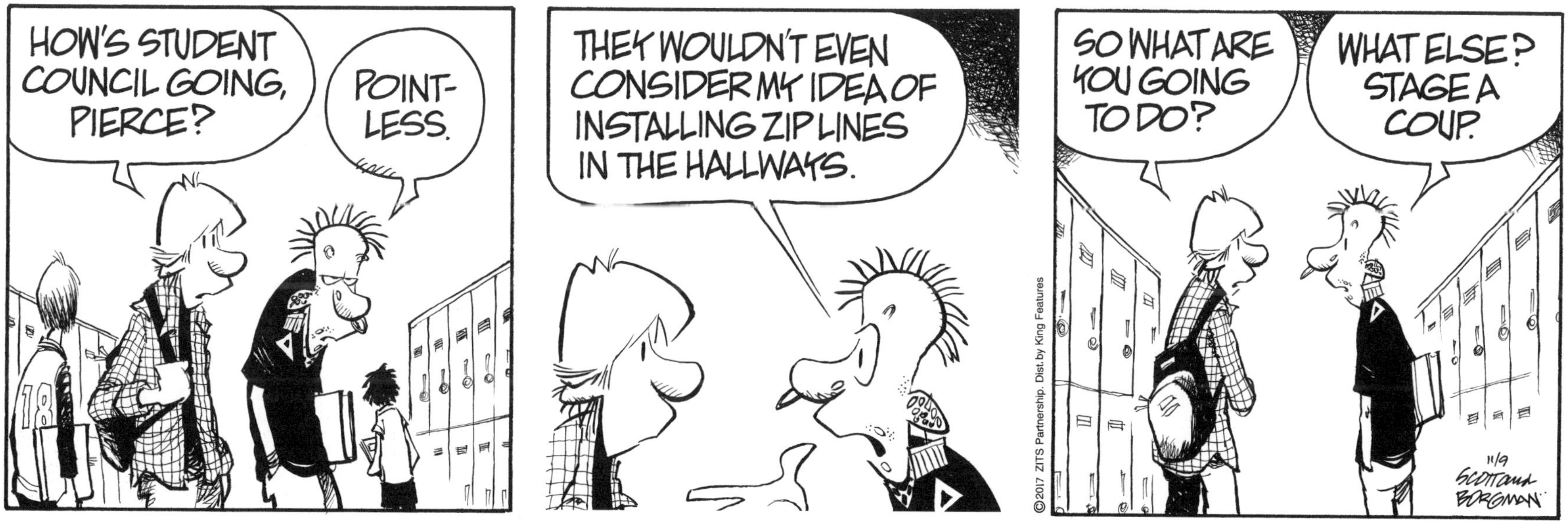
HOW'S STUDENT COUNCIL GOING, PIERCE?
POINT-LESS.
THEY WOULDN'T EVEN CONSIDER MY IDEA OF INSTALLING ZIP LINES IN THE HALLWAYS.
© 2017 ZITS Partnership. Dist. by King Features
SO WHAT ARE YOU GOING TO DO?
WHAT ELSE? STAGE A COUP.
11/9 SCOTT and BORGMAN

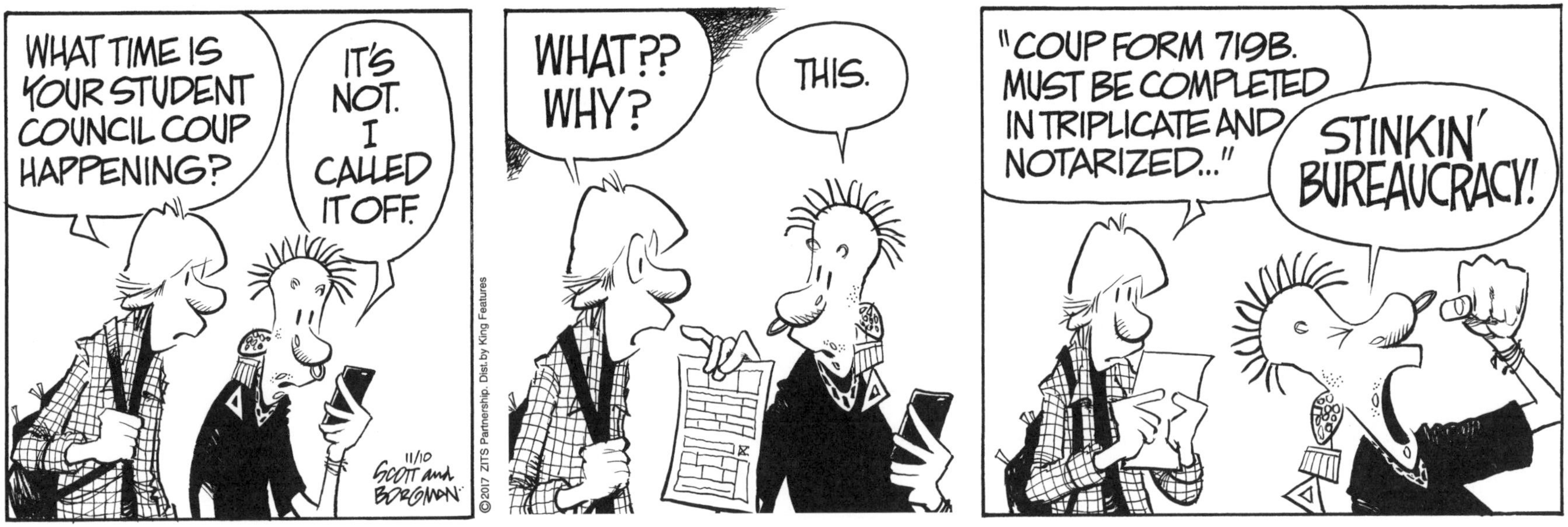
WHAT TIME IS YOUR STUDENT COUNCIL COUP HAPPENING?
IT'S NOT. I CALLED IT OFF.
11/10
SCOTT and BORGMAN
© 2017 ZITS Partnership. Dist. by King Features
WHAT?? WHY?
THIS.
"COUP FORM 719B. MUST BE COMPLETED IN TRIPLICATE AND NOTARIZED..."
STINKIN' BUREAUCRACY!

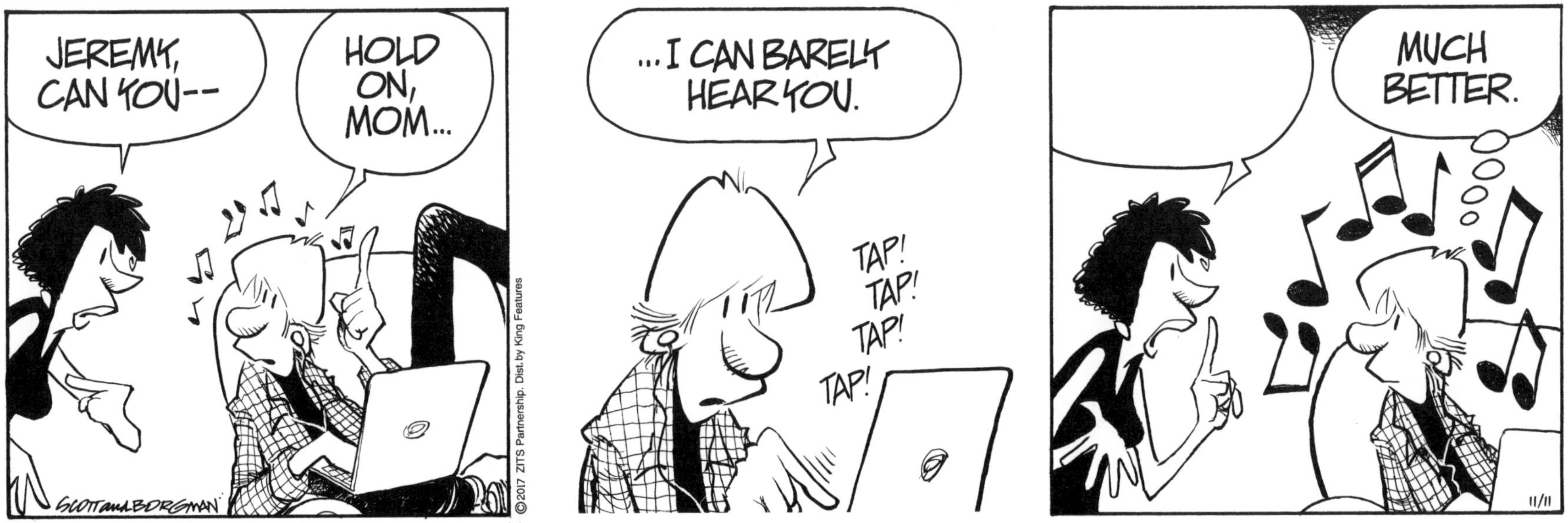
JEREMY, CAN YOU--
HOLD ON, MOM...
SCOTT and BORGMAN
© 2017 ZITS Partnership. Dist. by King Features
...I CAN BARELY HEAR YOU.
TAP! TAP! TAP! TAP!
MUCH BETTER.
11/11

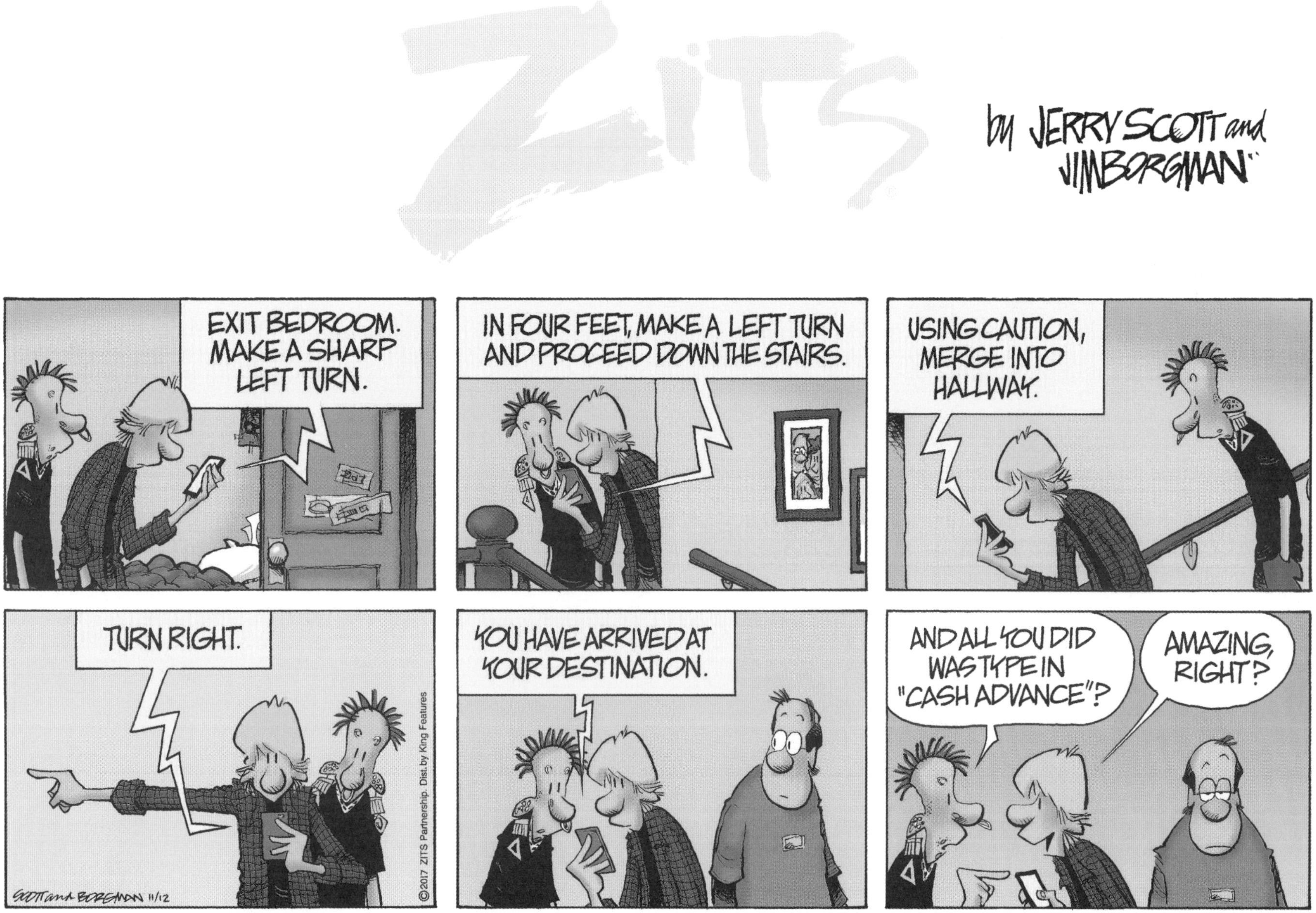

ZITS
by JERRY SCOTT and JIM BORGMAN
EXIT BEDROOM. MAKE A SHARP LEFT TURN.
IN FOUR FEET, MAKE A LEFT TURN AND PROCEED DOWN THE STAIRS.
USING CAUTION, MERGE INTO HALLWAY.
TURN RIGHT.
YOU HAVE ARRIVED AT YOUR DESTINATION.
AND ALL YOU DID WAS TYPE IN "CASH ADVANCE"?
AMAZING, RIGHT?

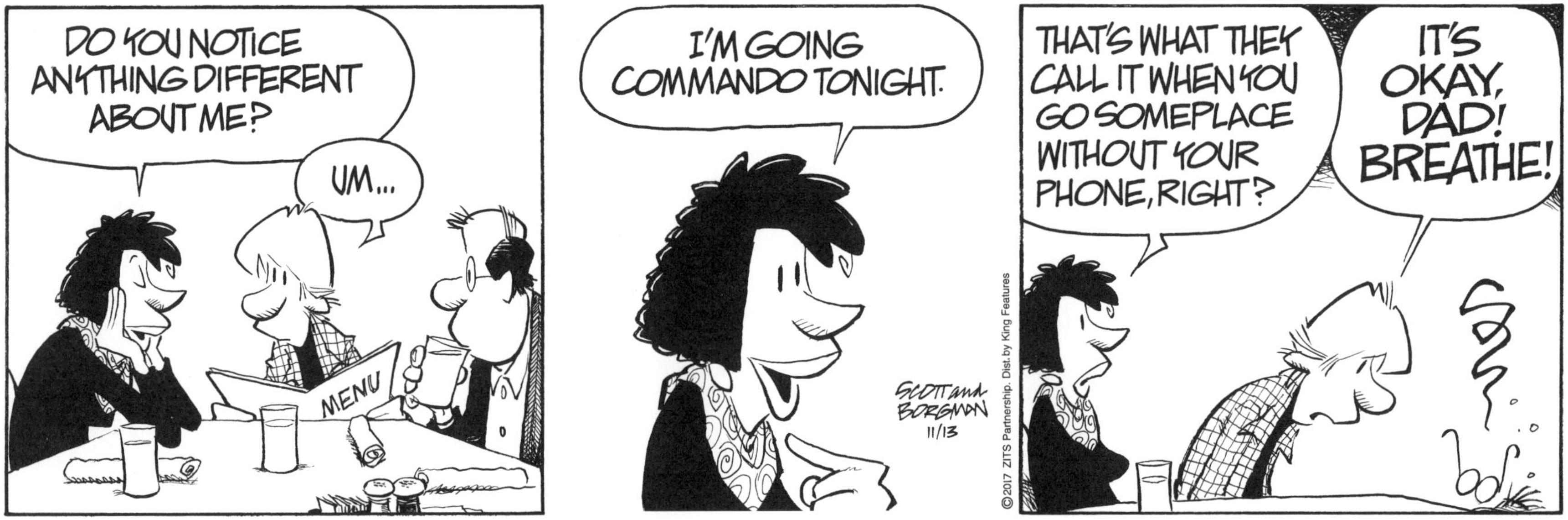
DO YOU NOTICE ANYTHING DIFFERENT ABOUT ME?
UM...
MENU
I'M GOING COMMANDO TONIGHT.
SCOTT and BORGMAN 11/13
THAT'S WHAT THEY CALL IT WHEN YOU GO SOMEPLACE WITHOUT YOUR PHONE, RIGHT?
IT'S OKAY, DAD! BREATHE!
©2017 ZITS Partnership. Dist. by King Features

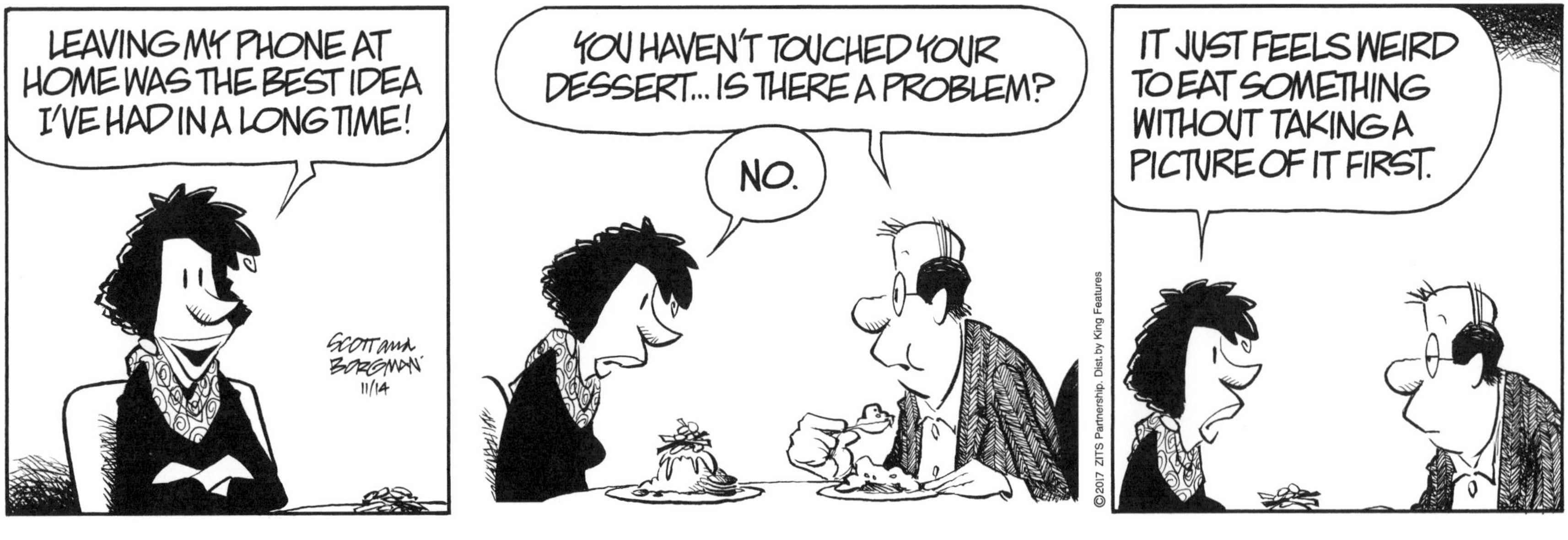
LEAVING MY PHONE AT HOME WAS THE BEST IDEA I'VE HAD IN A LONG TIME!
SCOTT and BORGMAN 11/14
YOU HAVEN'T TOUCHED YOUR DESSERT... IS THERE A PROBLEM?
NO.
IT JUST FEELS WEIRD TO EAT SOMETHING WITHOUT TAKING A PICTURE OF IT FIRST.
©2017 ZITS Partnership. Dist. by King Features

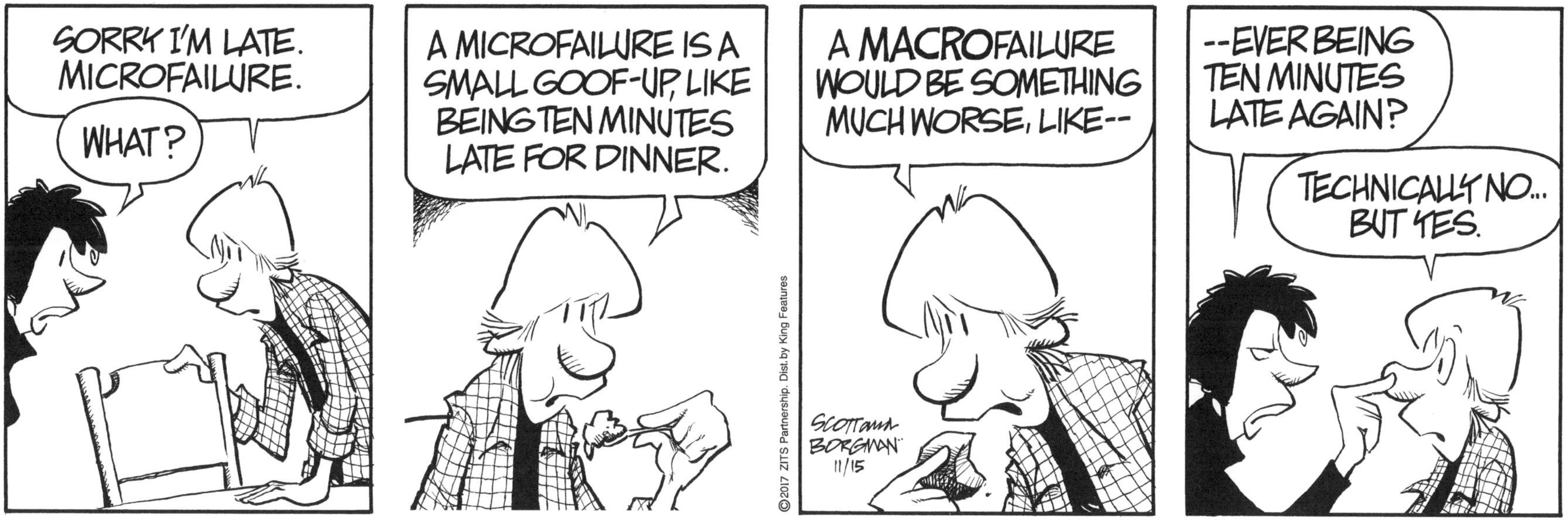
SORRY I'M LATE. MICROFAILURE.
WHAT?
A MICROFAILURE IS A SMALL GOOF-UP, LIKE BEING TEN MINUTES LATE FOR DINNER.
A MACROFAILURE WOULD BE SOMETHING MUCH WORSE, LIKE--
--EVER BEING TEN MINUTES LATE AGAIN?
TECHNICALLY NO... BUT YES.
©2017 ZITS Partnership. Dist. by King Features
SCOTT and BORGMAN 11/15

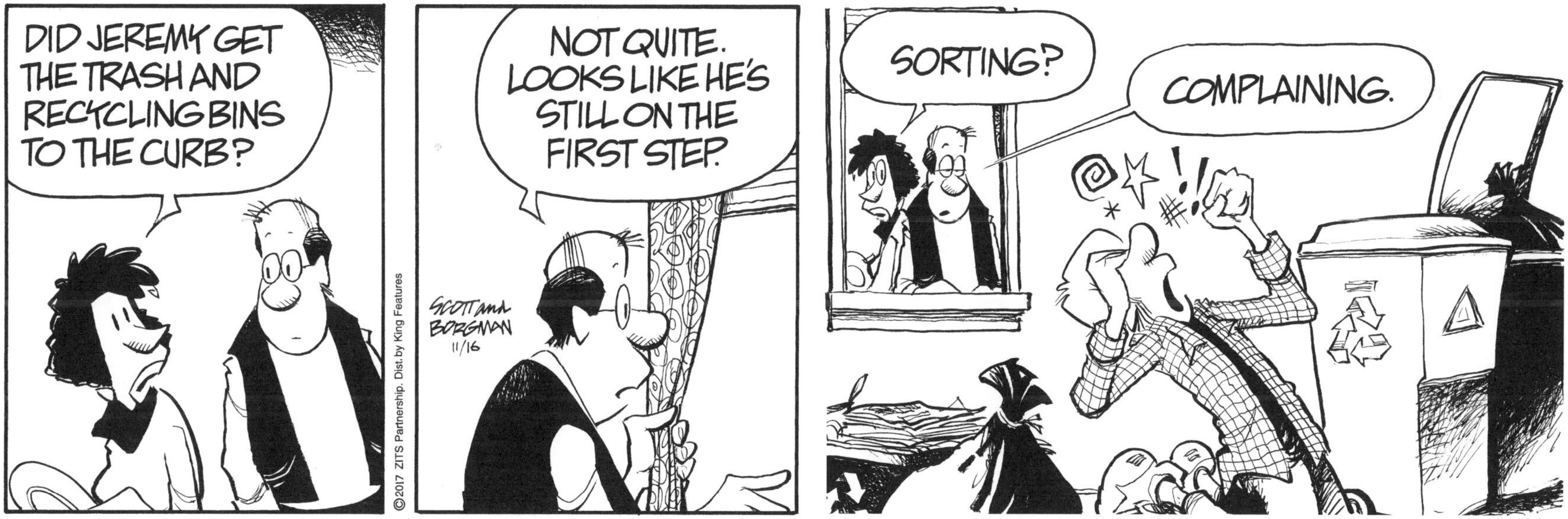
DID JEREMY GET THE TRASH AND RECYCLING BINS TO THE CURB?
NOT QUITE. LOOKS LIKE HE'S STILL ON THE FIRST STEP.
SORTING?
COMPLAINING.
©2017 ZITS Partnership. Dist. by King Features
SCOTT and BORGMAN 11/16

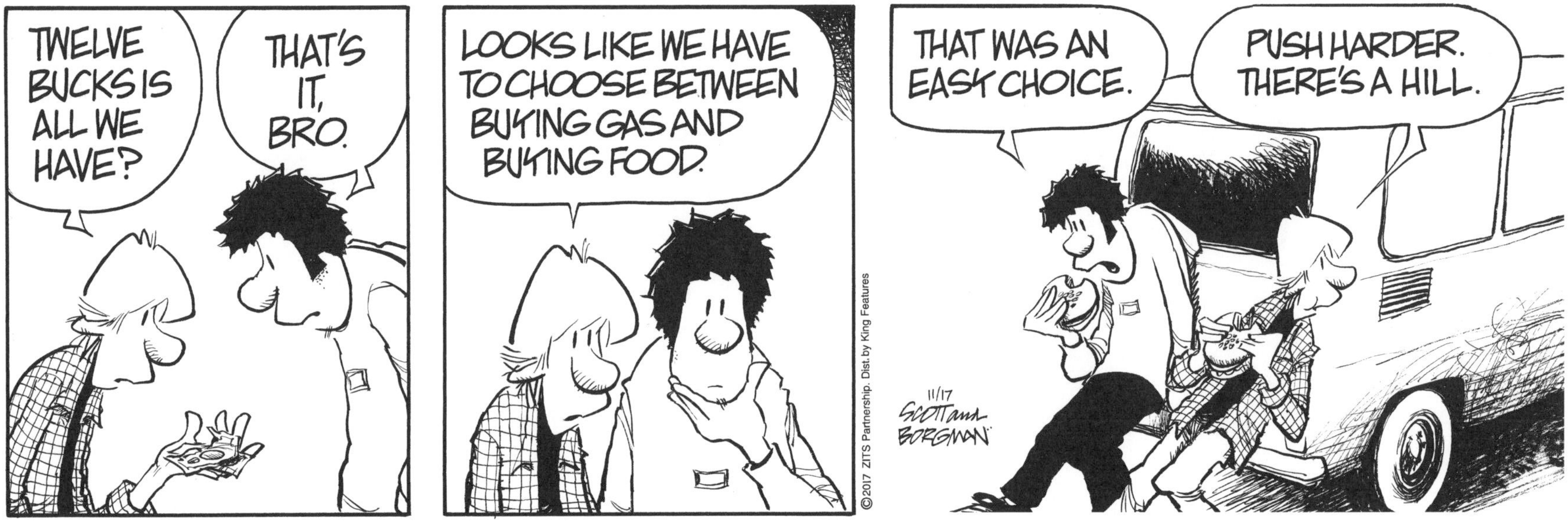
TWELVE BUCKS IS ALL WE HAVE?
THAT'S IT, BRO.
LOOKS LIKE WE HAVE TO CHOOSE BETWEEN BUYING GAS AND BUYING FOOD.
©2017 ZITS Partnership. Dist. by King Features
THAT WAS AN EASY CHOICE.
PUSH HARDER. THERE'S A HILL.
11/17 SCOTT and BORGMAN

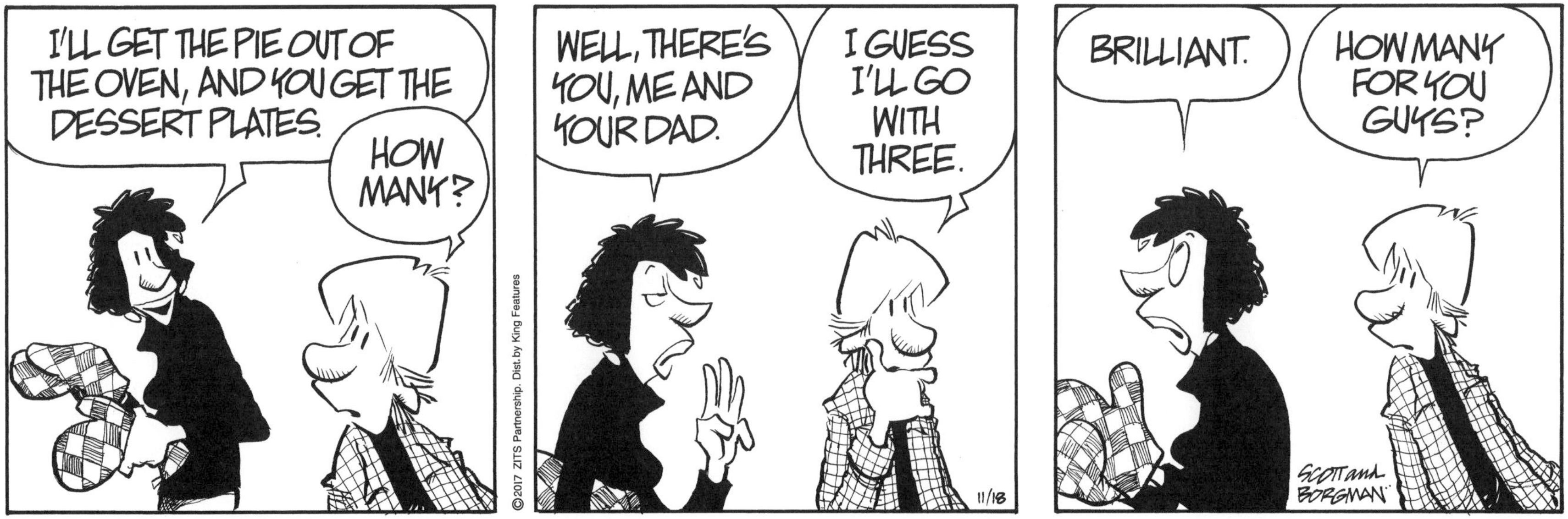
I'LL GET THE PIE OUT OF THE OVEN, AND YOU GET THE DESSERT PLATES.
HOW MANY?
©2017 ZITS Partnership. Dist. by King Features
WELL, THERE'S YOU, ME AND YOUR DAD.
I GUESS I'LL GO WITH THREE.
11/18
BRILLIANT.
HOW MANY FOR YOU GUYS?
SCOTT and BORGMAN

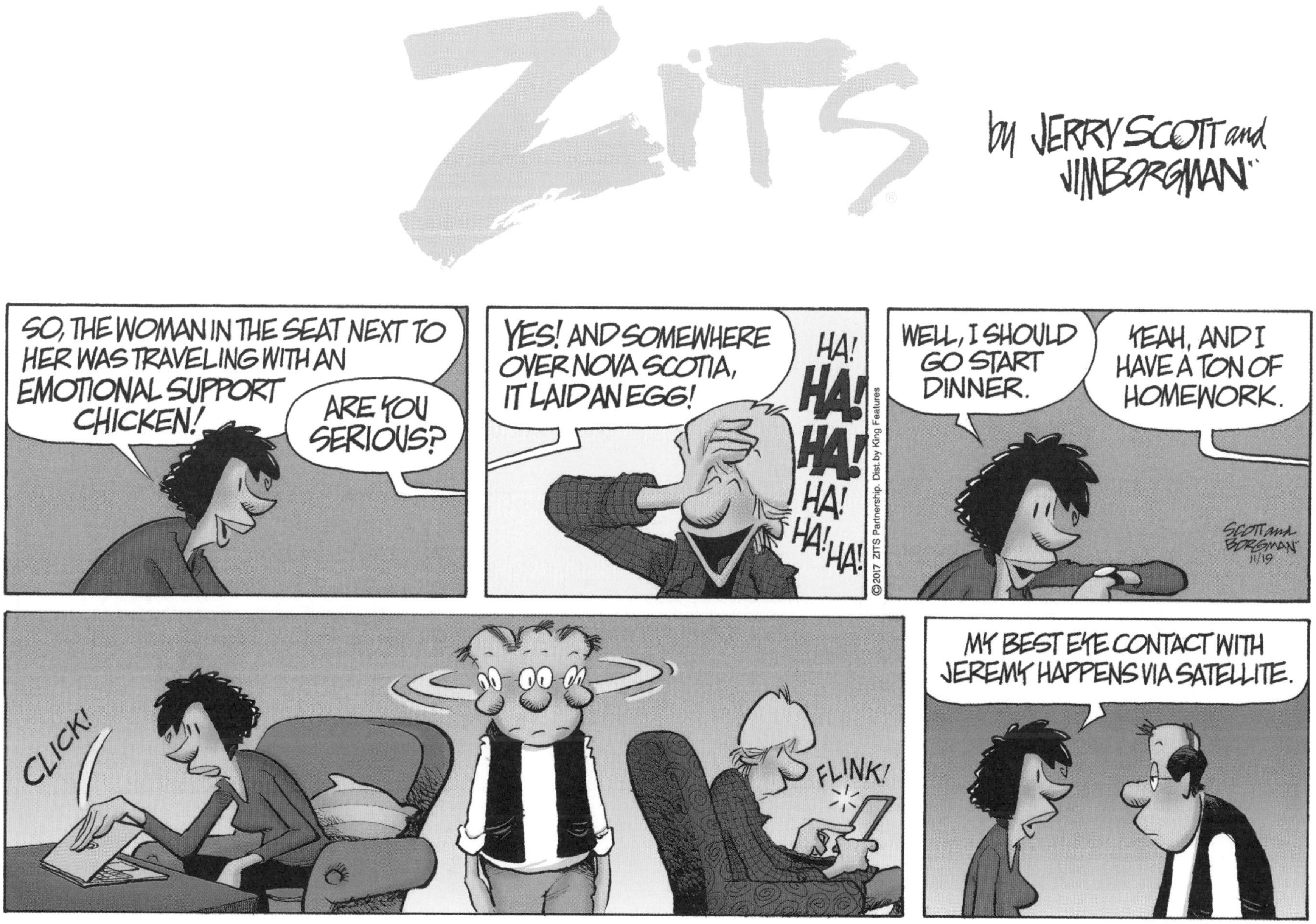
ZITS
by JERRY SCOTT and JIM BORGMAN
SO, THE WOMAN IN THE SEAT NEXT TO HER WAS TRAVELING WITH AN EMOTIONAL SUPPORT CHICKEN!
ARE YOU SERIOUS?
YES! AND SOMEWHERE OVER NOVA SCOTIA, IT LAID AN EGG!
HA! HA! HA! HA! HA! HA!
© 2017 ZITS Partnership. Dist. by King Features
WELL, I SHOULD GO START DINNER.
YEAH, AND I HAVE A TON OF HOMEWORK.
SCOTT and BORGMAN 11/19
CLICK!
FLINK!
MY BEST EYE CONTACT WITH JEREMY HAPPENS VIA SATELLITE.

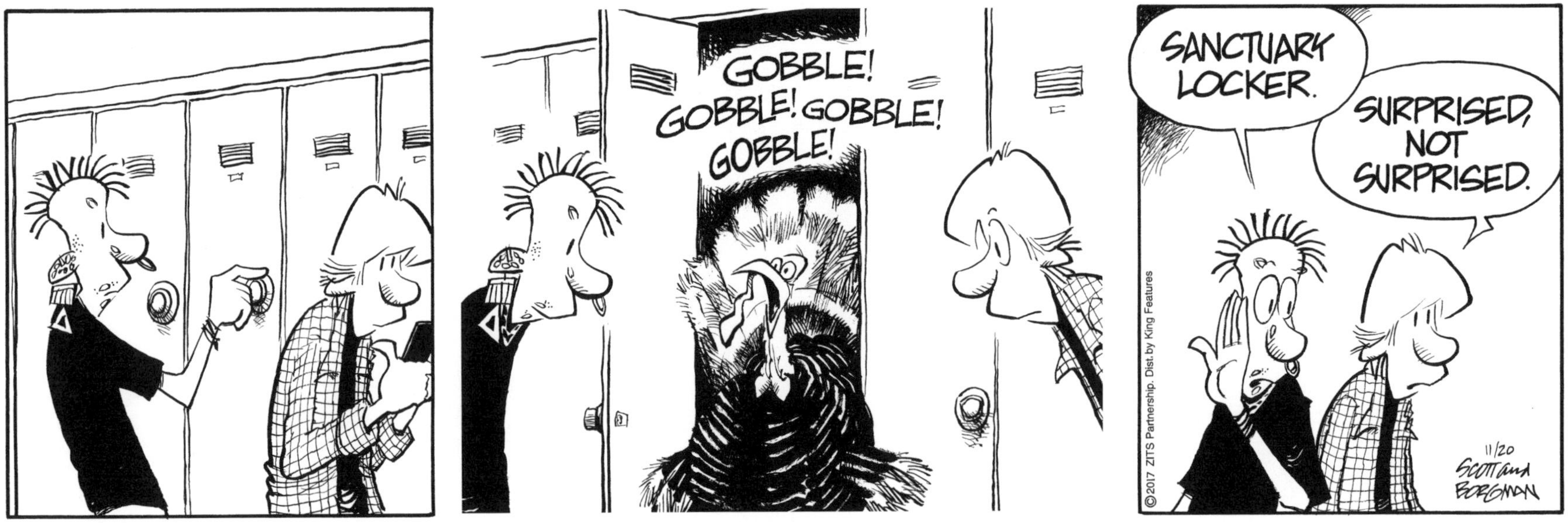
GOBBLE! GOBBLE! GOBBLE! GOBBLE!
SANCTUARY LOCKER.
SURPRISED, NOT SURPRISED.
11/20 SCOTT and BORGMAN
© 2017 ZITS Partnership. Dist. by King Features

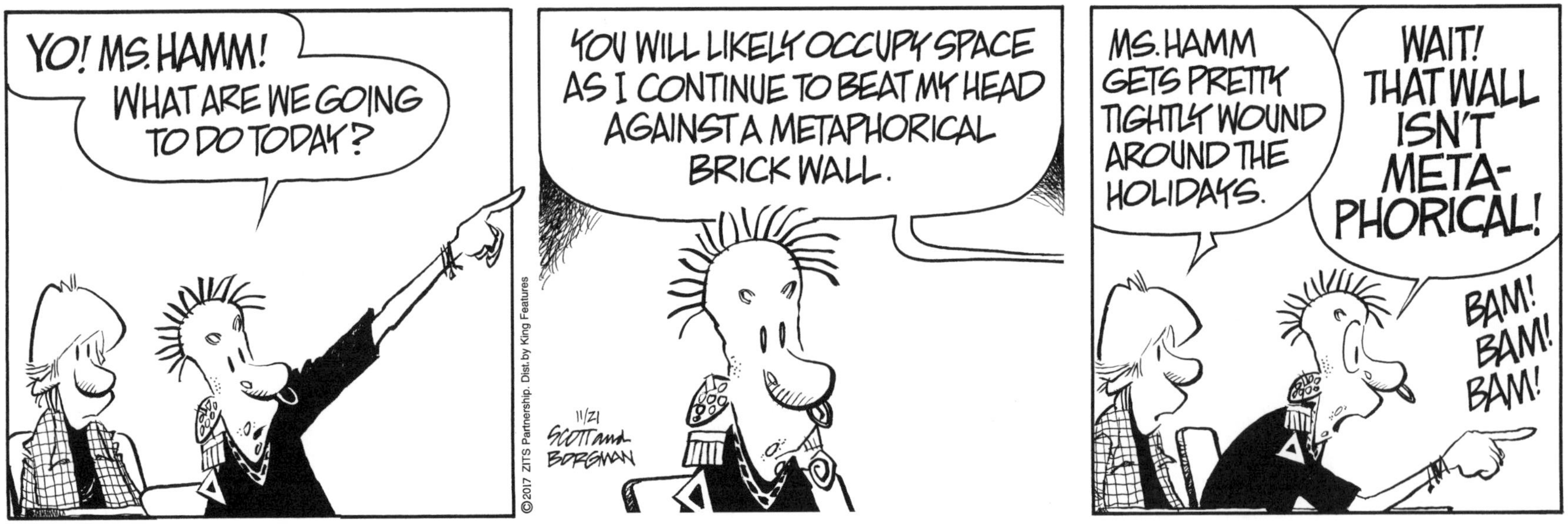
YO! MS. HAMM! WHAT ARE WE GOING TO DO TODAY?
© 2017 ZITS Partnership. Dist. by King Features
11/21 SCOTT and BORGMAN
YOU WILL LIKELY OCCUPY SPACE AS I CONTINUE TO BEAT MY HEAD AGAINST A METAPHORICAL BRICK WALL.
MS. HAMM GETS PRETTY TIGHTLY WOUND AROUND THE HOLIDAYS.
WAIT! THAT WALL ISN'T META-PHORICAL!
BAM! BAM! BAM!

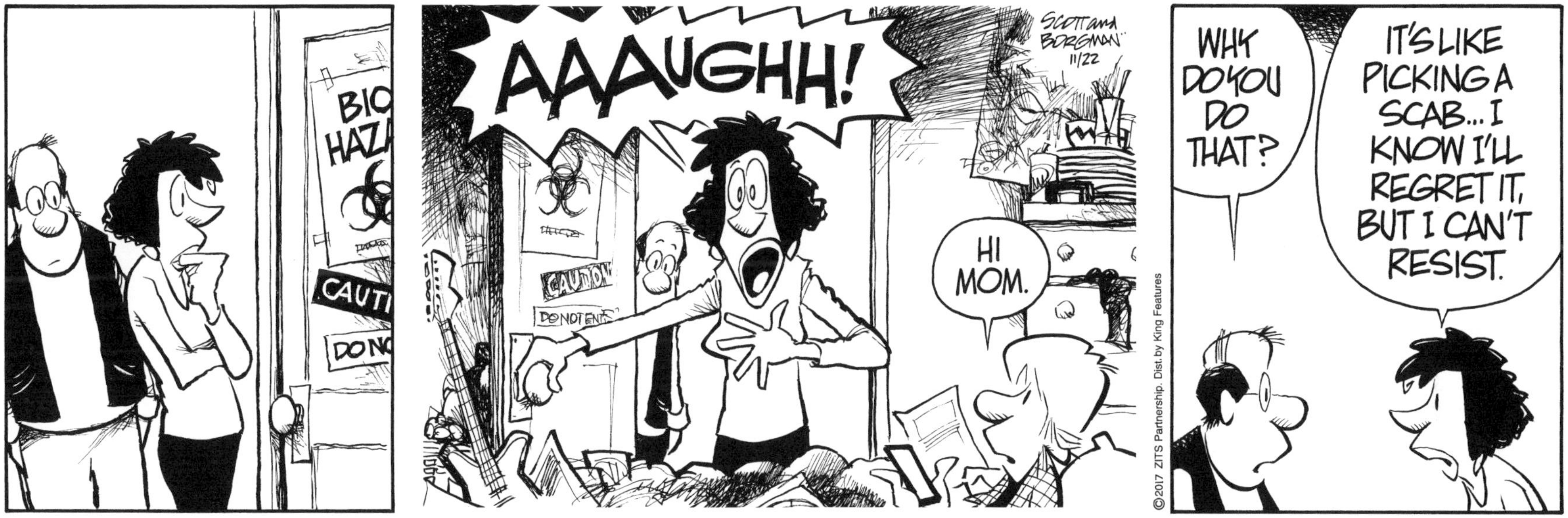
AAAUGHH!
SCOTT and BORGMAN 11/22
HI MOM.
©2017 ZITS Partnership. Dist. by King Features
WHY DO YOU DO THAT?
IT'S LIKE PICKING A SCAB... I KNOW I'LL REGRET IT, BUT I CAN'T RESIST.

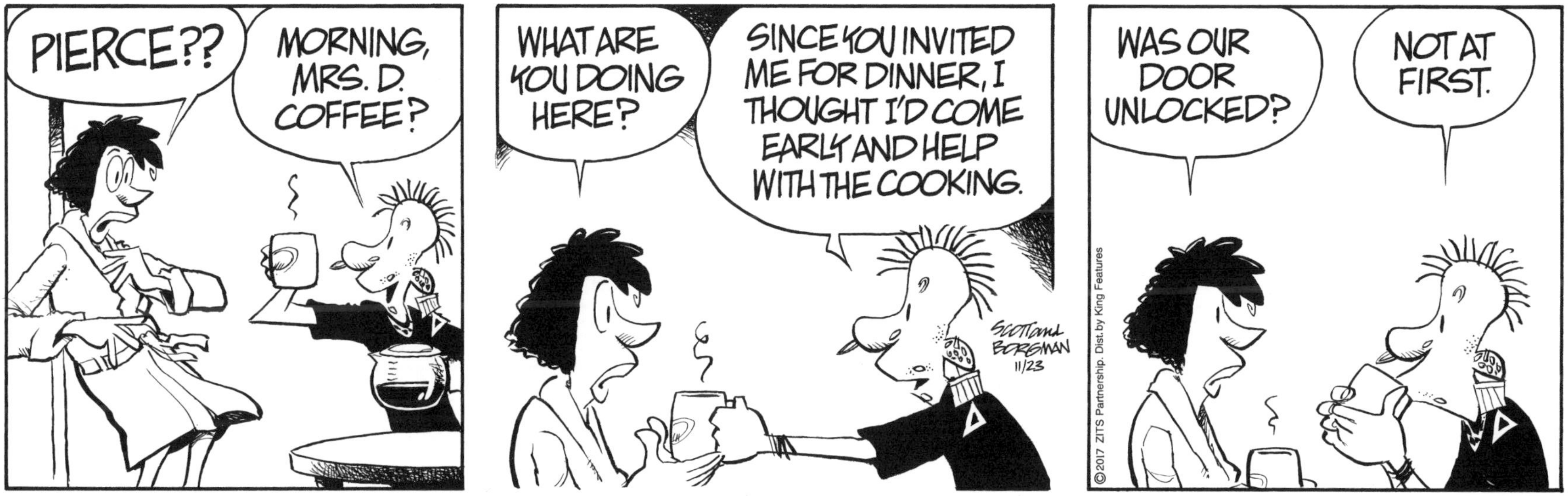
PIERCE??
MORNING, MRS. D. COFFEE?
WHAT ARE YOU DOING HERE?
SINCE YOU INVITED ME FOR DINNER, I THOUGHT I'D COME EARLY AND HELP WITH THE COOKING.
SCOTT and BORGMAN 11/23
©2017 ZITS Partnership. Dist. by King Features
WAS OUR DOOR UNLOCKED?
NOT AT FIRST.

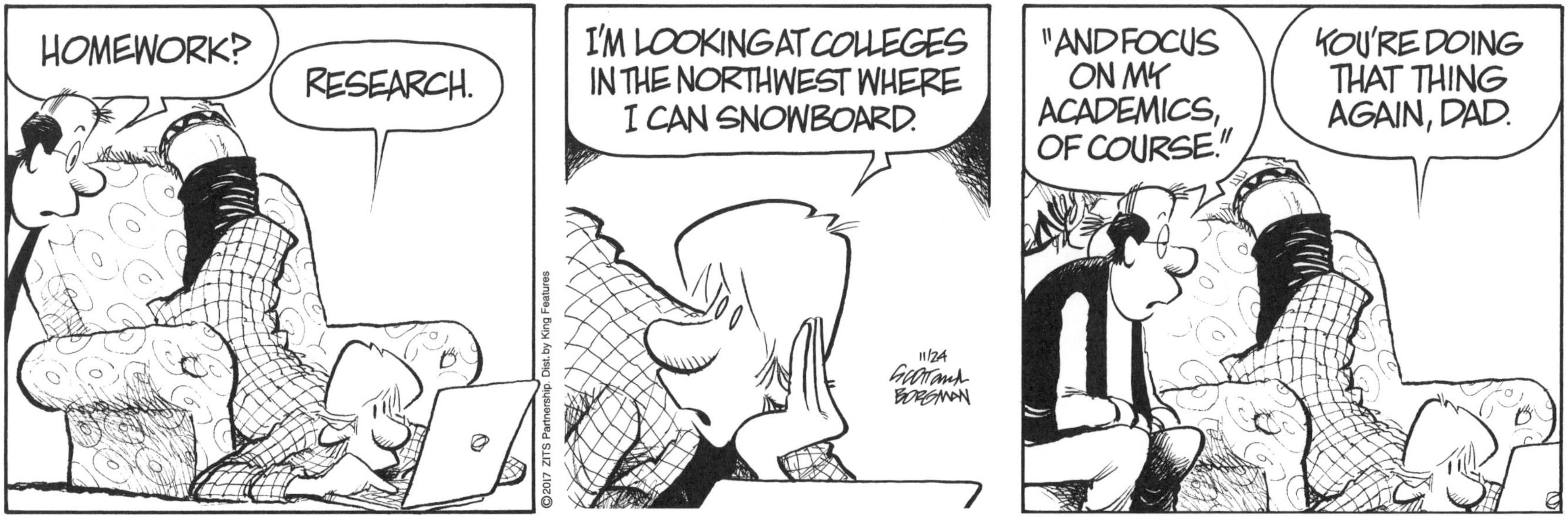
HOMEWORK?
RESEARCH.
©2017 ZITS Partnership. Dist. by King Features
I'M LOOKING AT COLLEGES IN THE NORTHWEST WHERE I CAN SNOWBOARD.
"AND FOCUS ON MY ACADEMICS, OF COURSE."
YOU'RE DOING THAT THING AGAIN, DAD.

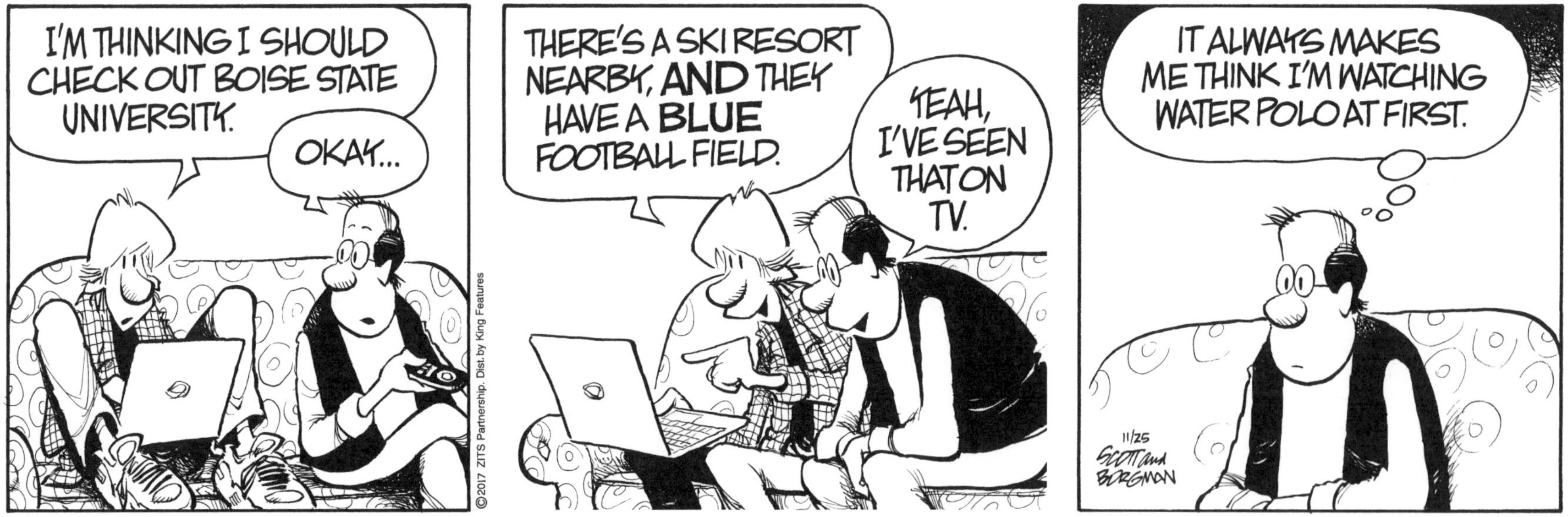
I'M THINKING I SHOULD CHECK OUT BOISE STATE UNIVERSITY.
OKAY...
©2017 ZITS Partnership. Dist. by King Features
THERE'S A SKI RESORT NEARBY, **AND** THEY HAVE A **BLUE** FOOTBALL FIELD.
YEAH, I'VE SEEN THAT ON TV.
IT ALWAYS MAKES ME THINK I'M WATCHING WATER POLO AT FIRST.

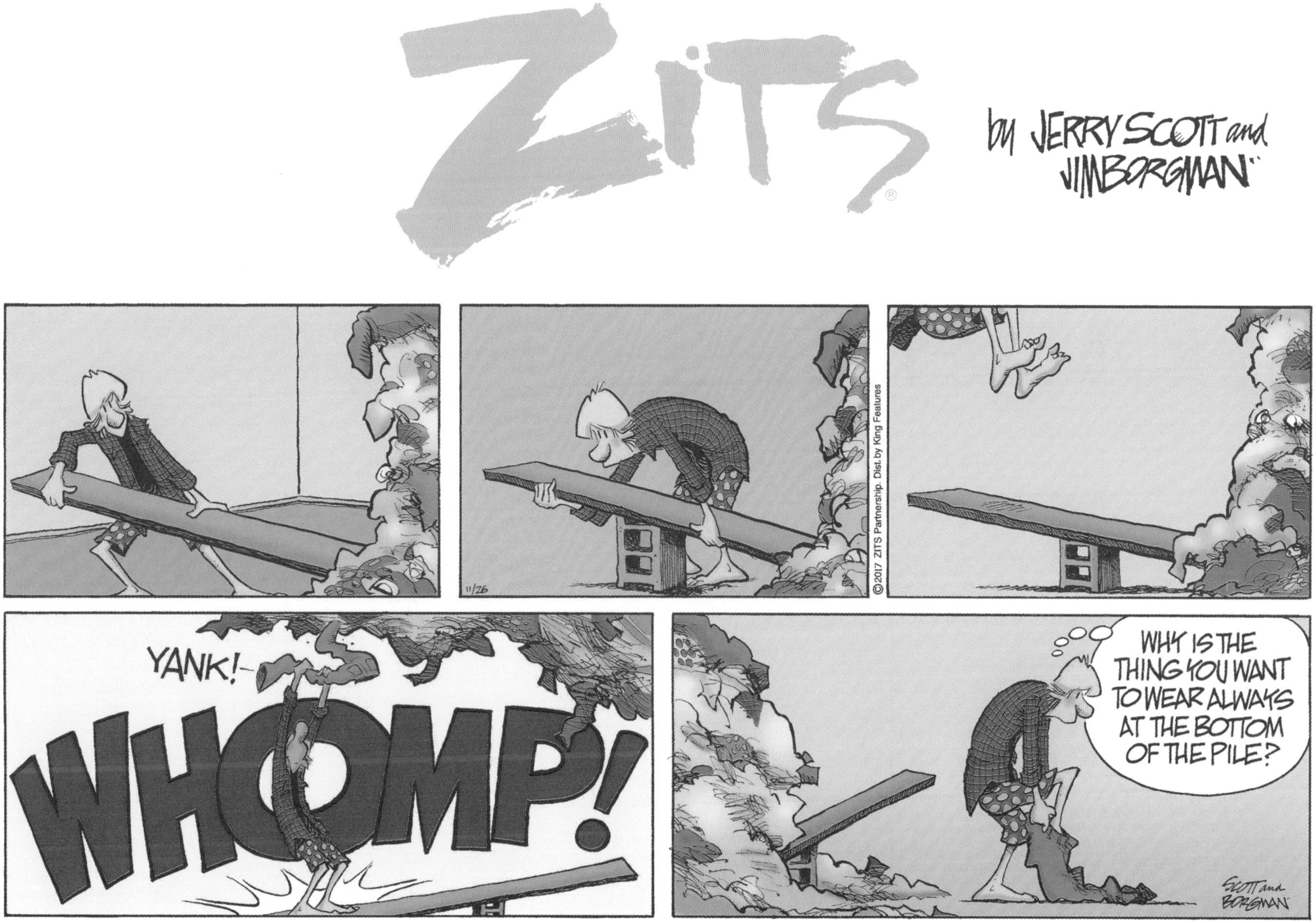
ZITS
by JERRY SCOTT and JIM BORGMAN
11/26
©2017 ZITS Partnership. Dist. by King Features
YANK!
WHOMP!
WHY IS THE THING YOU WANT TO WEAR ALWAYS AT THE BOTTOM OF THE PILE?
SCOTT and BORGMAN

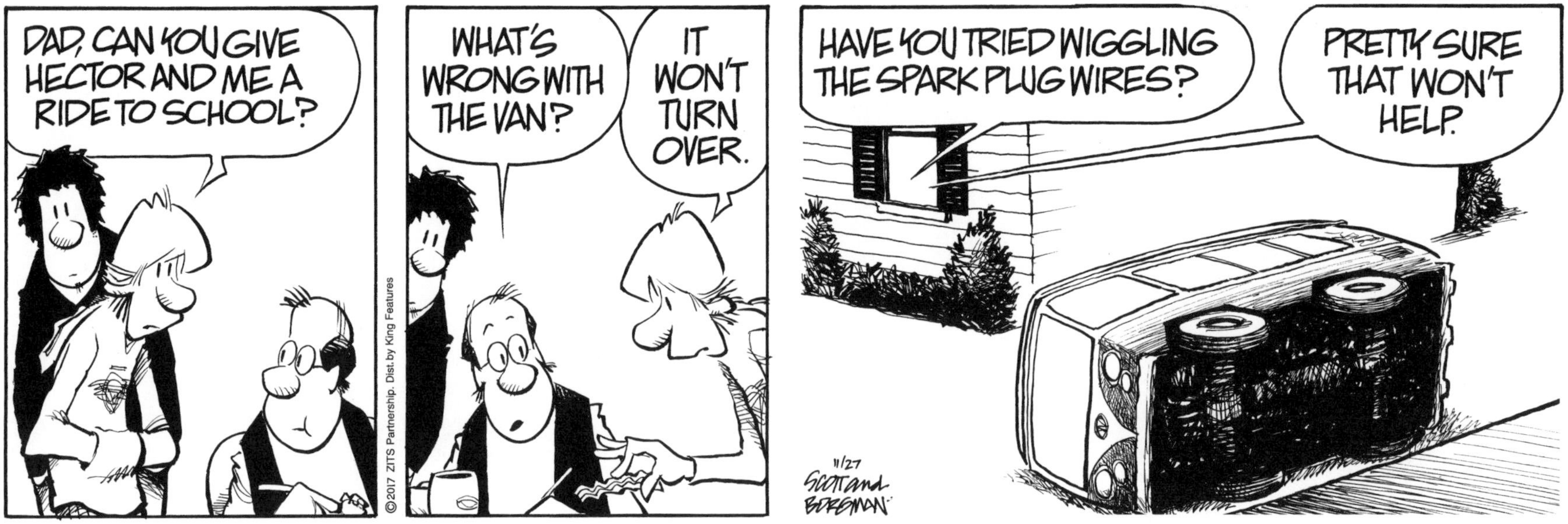
DAD, CAN YOU GIVE HECTOR AND ME A RIDE TO SCHOOL?
WHAT'S WRONG WITH THE VAN?
IT WON'T TURN OVER.
HAVE YOU TRIED WIGGLING THE SPARK PLUG WIRES?
PRETTY SURE THAT WON'T HELP.
©2017 ZITS Partnership. Dist. by King Features
11/27
SCOTT and BORGMAN

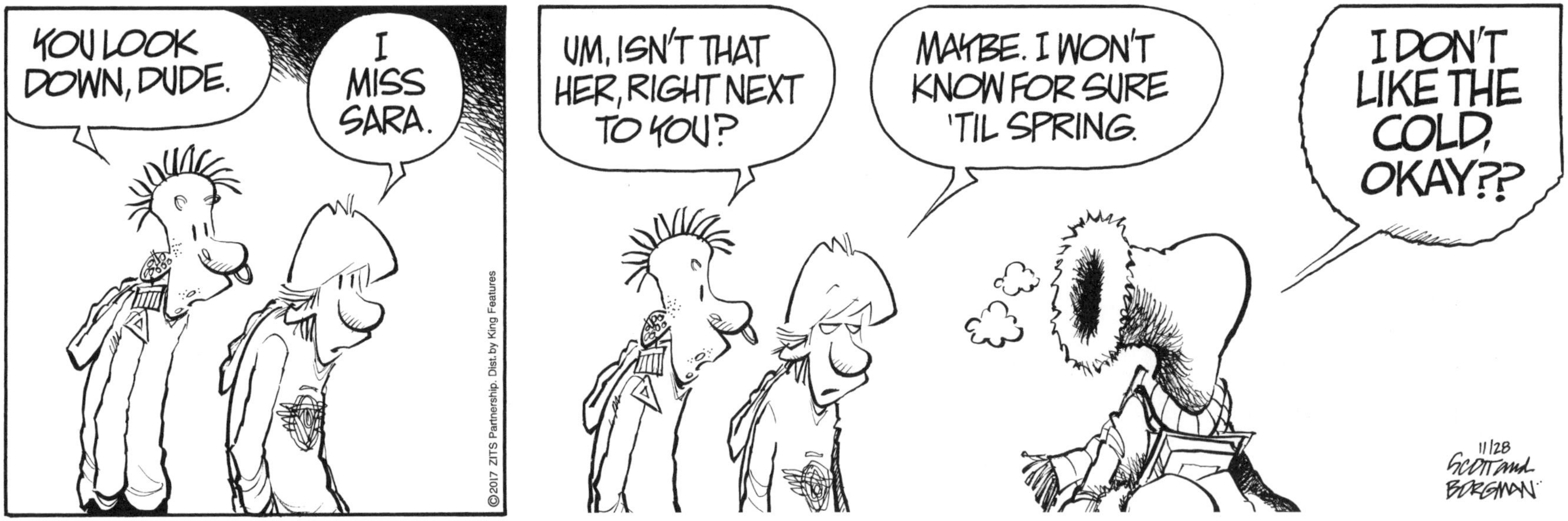
YOU LOOK DOWN, DUDE.
I MISS SARA.
UM, ISN'T THAT HER, RIGHT NEXT TO YOU?
MAYBE. I WON'T KNOW FOR SURE 'TIL SPRING.
I DON'T LIKE THE COLD, OKAY??
©2017 ZITS Partnership. Dist. by King Features
11/28
SCOTT and BORGMAN

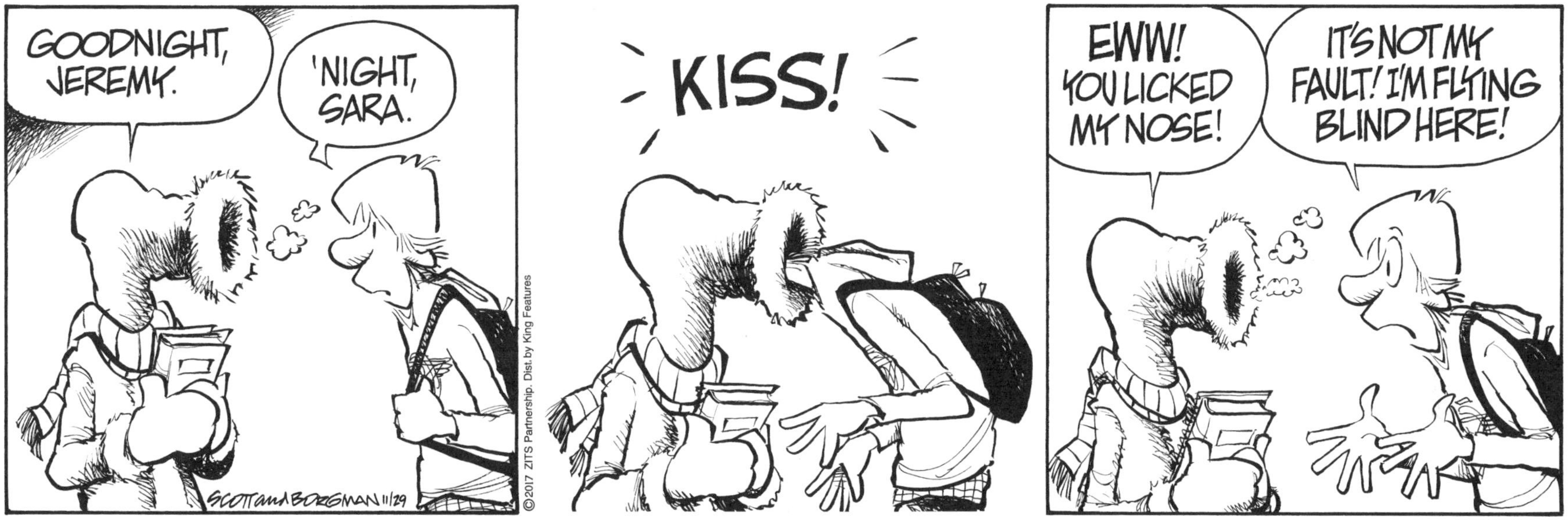

GOODNIGHT, JEREMY.
'NIGHT, SARA.
SCOTT and BORGMAN 11/29
© 2017 ZITS Partnership. Dist. by King Features
KISS!
EWW! YOU LICKED MY NOSE!
IT'S NOT MY FAULT! I'M FLYING BLIND HERE!

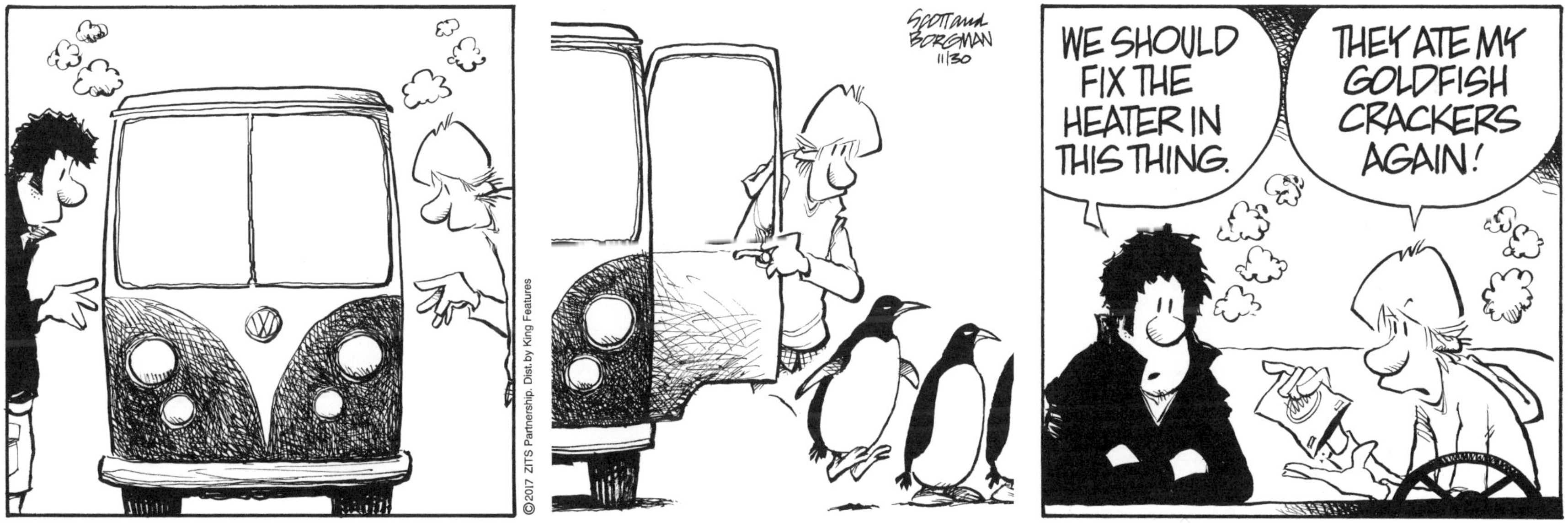

© 2017 ZITS Partnership. Dist. by King Features
SCOTT and BORGMAN 11/30
WE SHOULD FIX THE HEATER IN THIS THING.
THEY ATE MY GOLDFISH CRACKERS AGAIN!

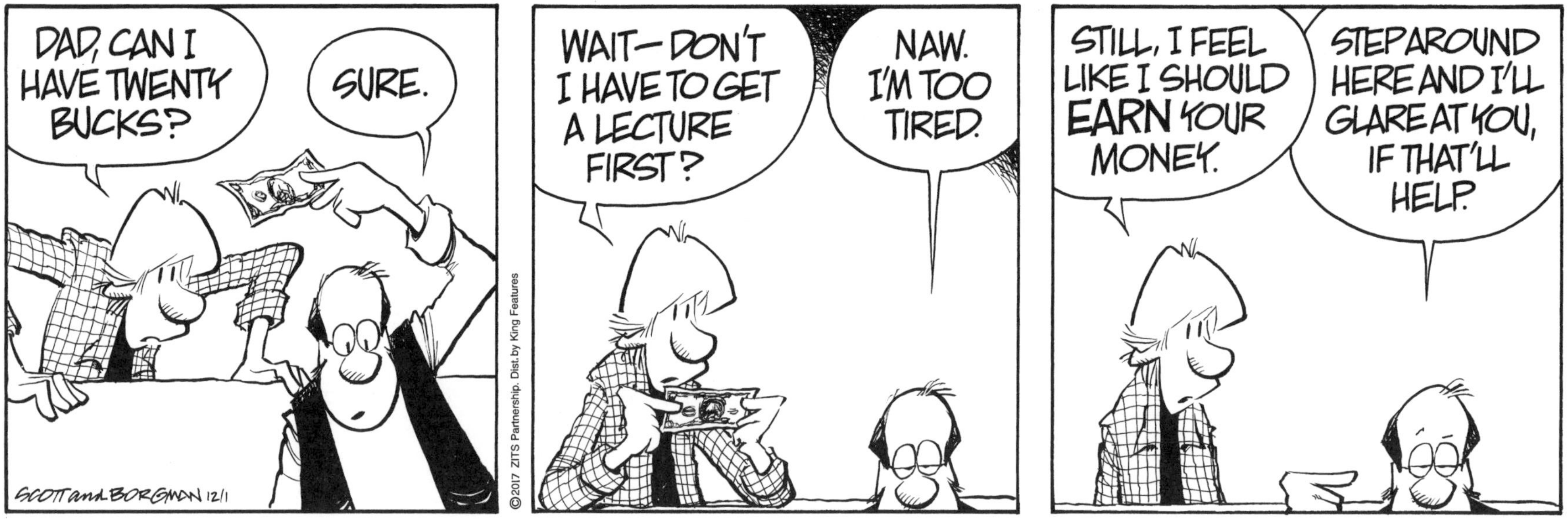
DAD, CAN I HAVE TWENTY BUCKS?
SURE.
SCOTT and BORGMAN 12/1
©2017 ZITS Partnership. Dist. by King Features
WAIT—DON'T I HAVE TO GET A LECTURE FIRST?
NAW. I'M TOO TIRED.
STILL, I FEEL LIKE I SHOULD EARN YOUR MONEY.
STEP AROUND HERE AND I'LL GLARE AT YOU, IF THAT'LL HELP.

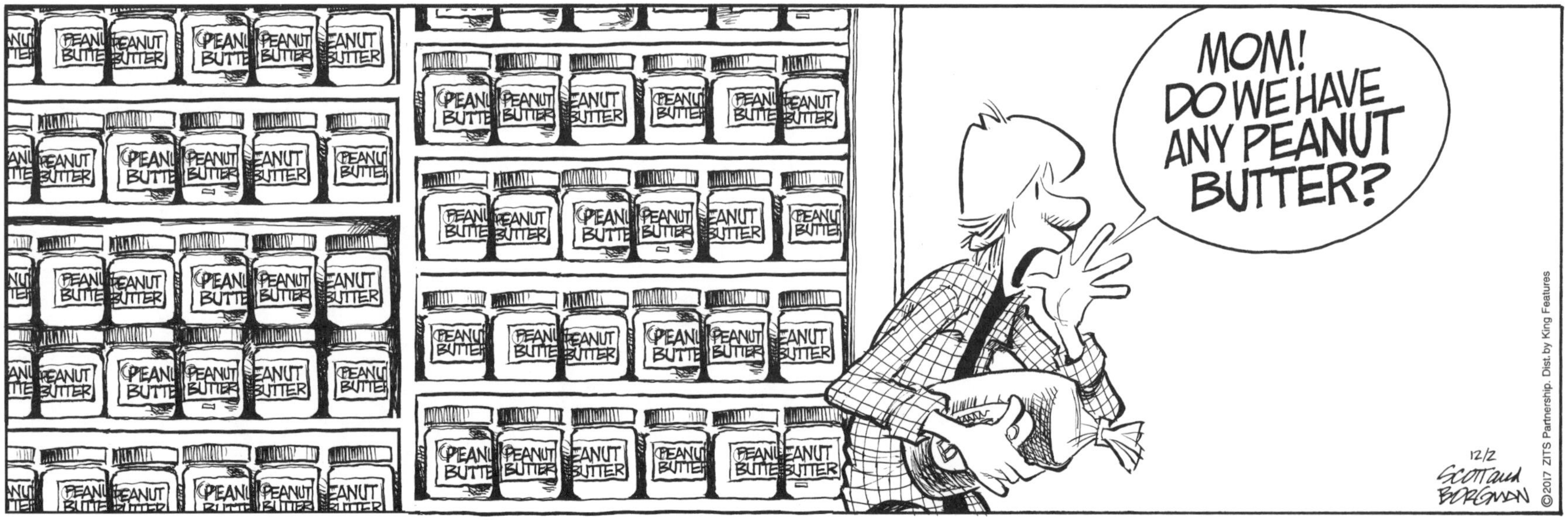
MOM! DO WE HAVE ANY PEANUT BUTTER?
12/2 SCOTT and BORGMAN
©2017 ZITS Partnership. Dist. by King Features

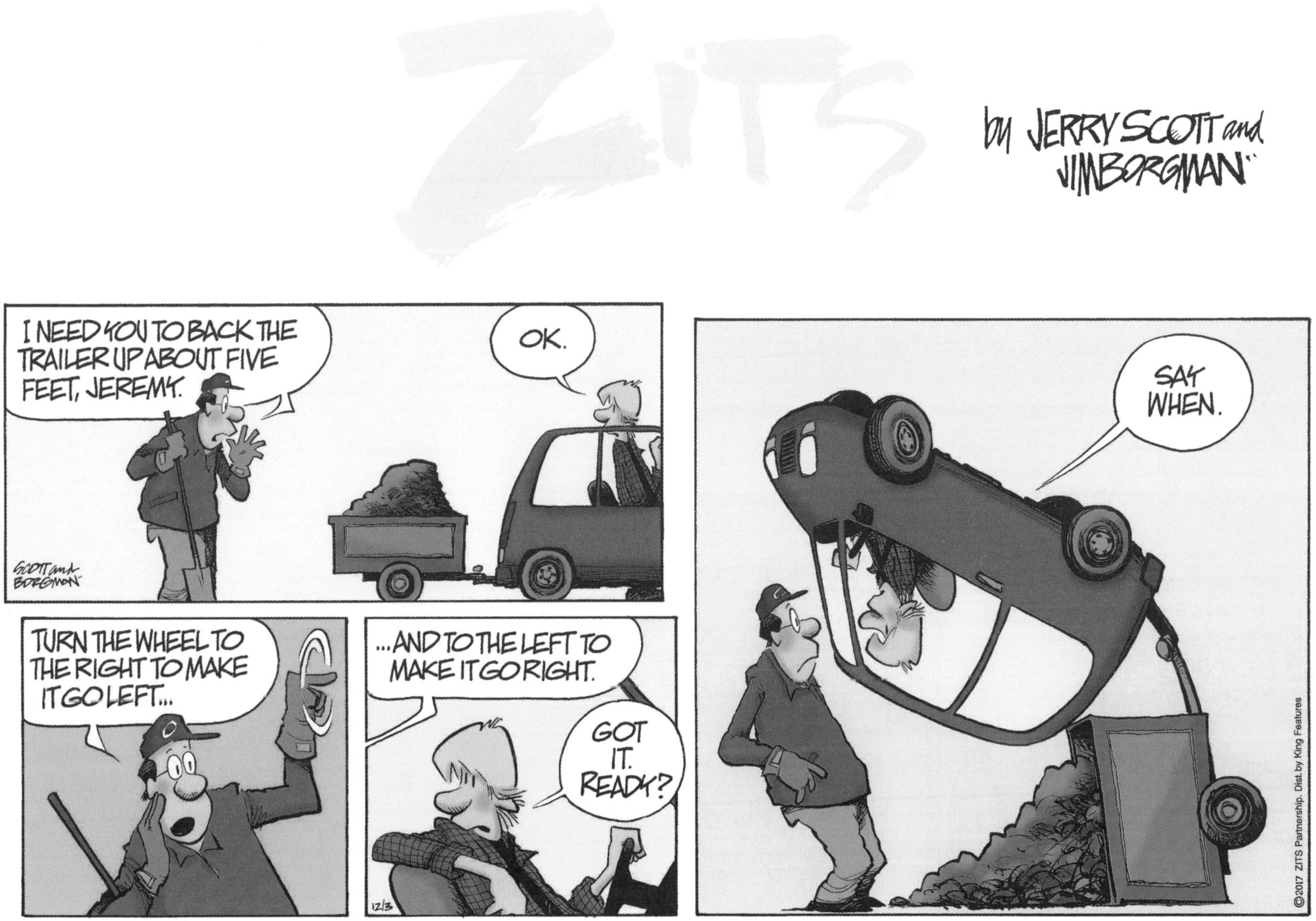
ZITS
by JERRY SCOTT and JIM BORGMAN
I NEED YOU TO BACK THE TRAILER UP ABOUT FIVE FEET, JEREMY.
OK.
SCOTT and BORGMAN
TURN THE WHEEL TO THE RIGHT TO MAKE IT GO LEFT...
...AND TO THE LEFT TO MAKE IT GO RIGHT.
GOT IT. READY?
12/3
SAY WHEN.
©2017 ZITS Partnership. Dist. by King Features

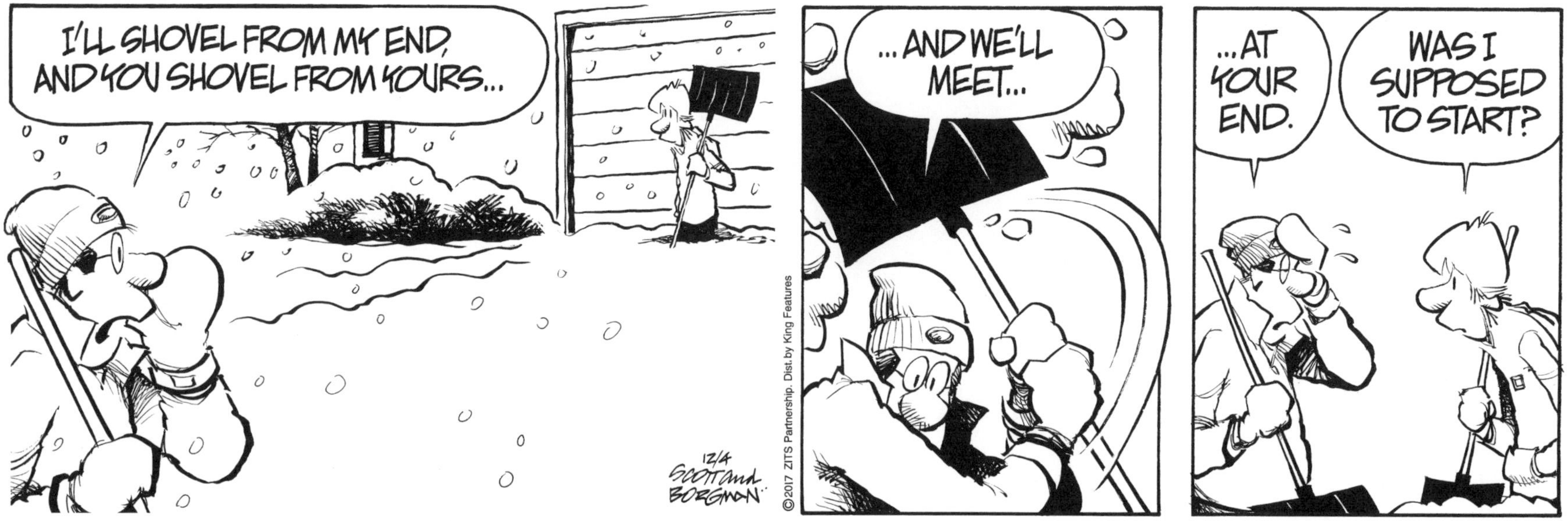
I'LL SHOVEL FROM MY END, AND YOU SHOVEL FROM YOURS...
12/4 SCOTT and BORGMAN
©2017 ZITS Partnership. Dist. by King Features
...AND WE'LL MEET...
...AT YOUR END.
WAS I SUPPOSED TO START?

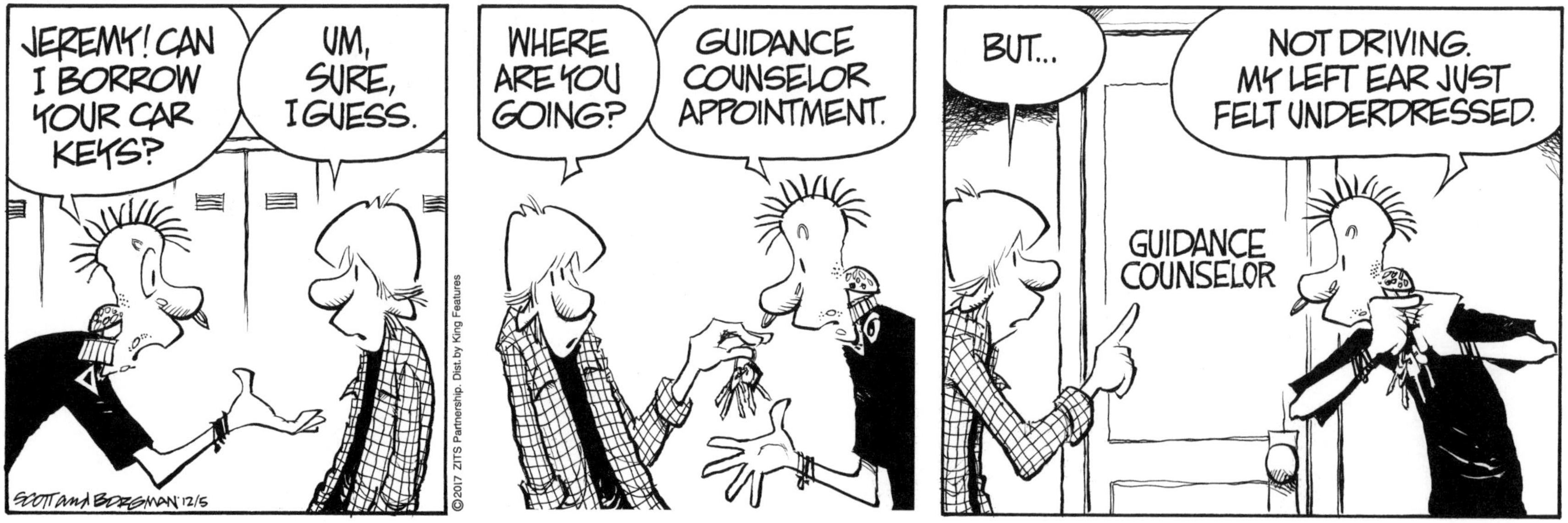
JEREMY! CAN I BORROW YOUR CAR KEYS?
UM, SURE, I GUESS.
SCOTT and BORGMAN 12/5
©2017 ZITS Partnership. Dist. by King Features
WHERE ARE YOU GOING?
GUIDANCE COUNSELOR APPOINTMENT.
BUT...
NOT DRIVING. MY LEFT EAR JUST FELT UNDERDRESSED.
GUIDANCE COUNSELOR

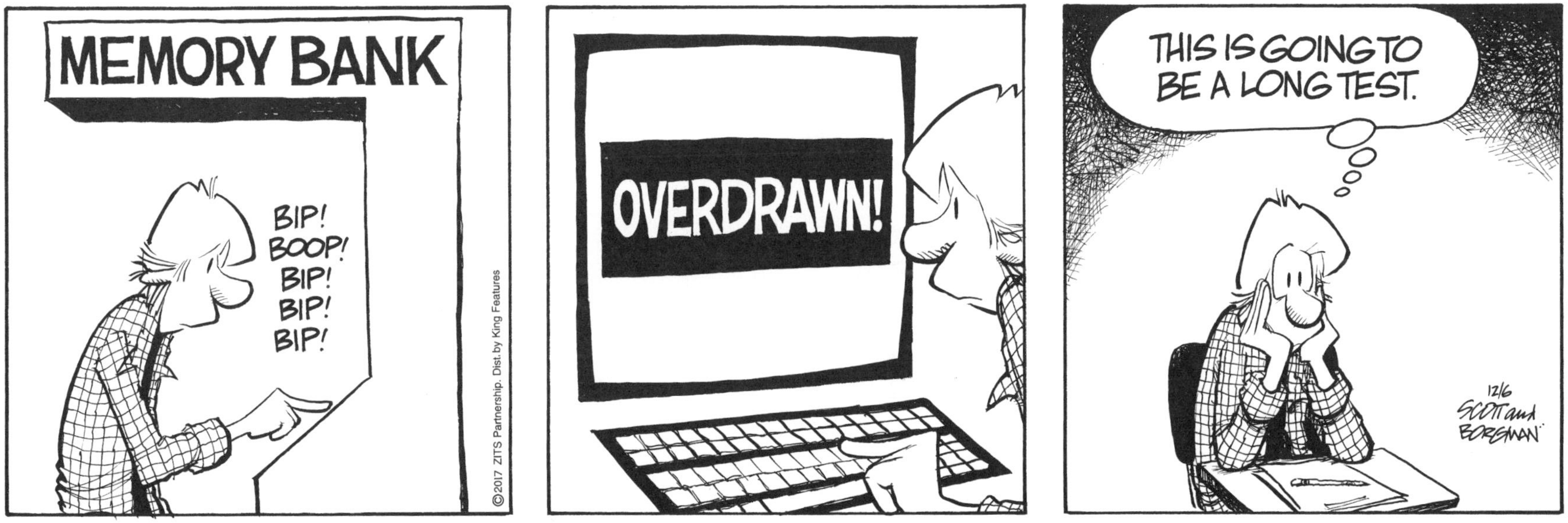
MEMORY BANK
BIP! BOOP! BIP! BIP! BIP!
©2017 ZITS Partnership. Dist. by King Features
OVERDRAWN!
THIS IS GOING TO BE A LONG TEST.
12/6 SCOTT and BORGMAN

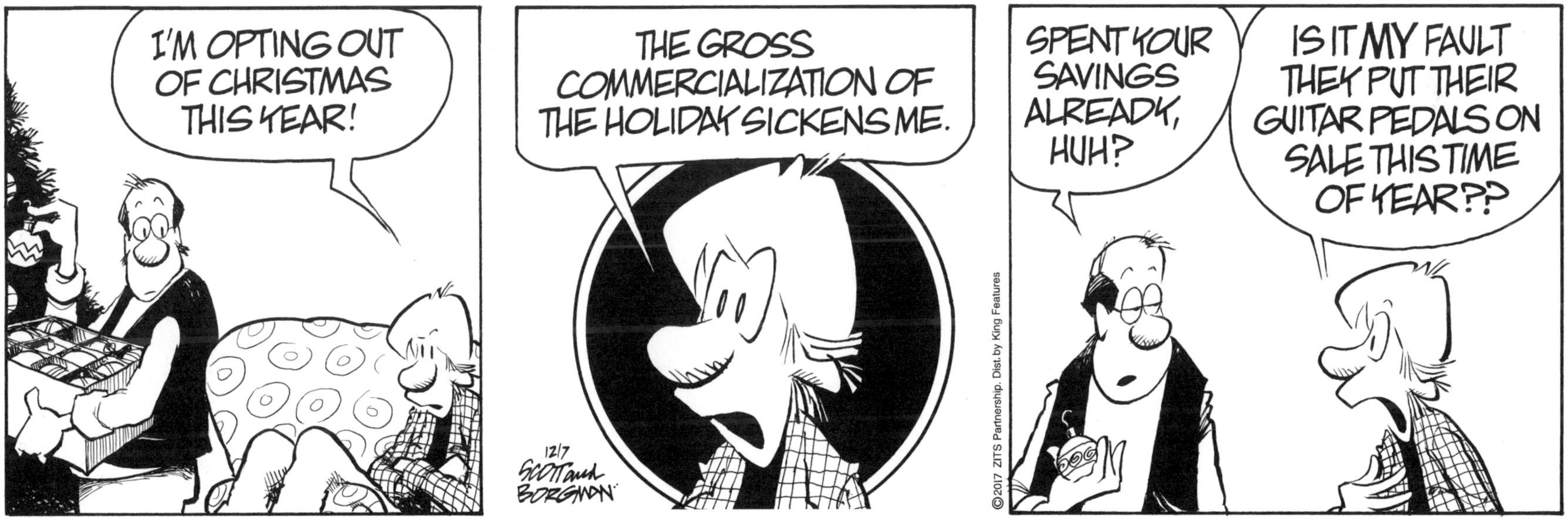
I'M OPTING OUT OF CHRISTMAS THIS YEAR!
12/7 SCOTT and BORGMAN
THE GROSS COMMERCIALIZATION OF THE HOLIDAY SICKENS ME.
©2017 ZITS Partnership. Dist. by King Features
SPENT YOUR SAVINGS ALREADY, HUH?
IS IT MY FAULT THEY PUT THEIR GUITAR PEDALS ON SALE THIS TIME OF YEAR??

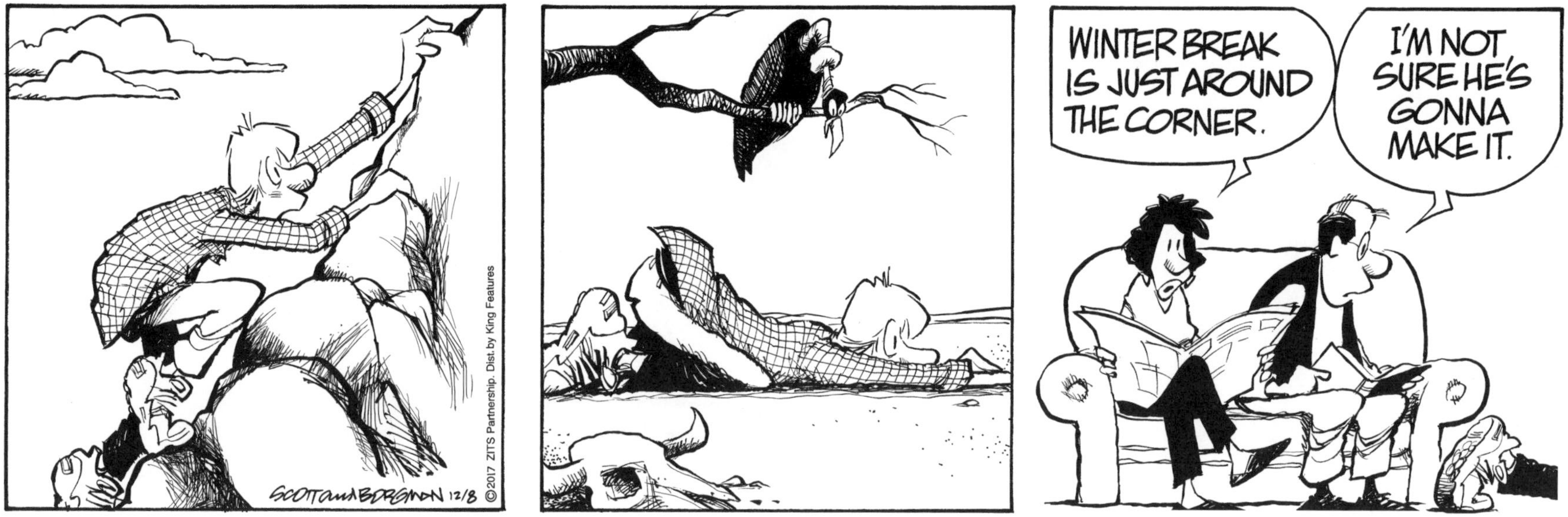
SCOTT and BORGMAN 12/8
©2017 ZITS Partnership. Dist. by King Features
WINTER BREAK IS JUST AROUND THE CORNER.
I'M NOT SURE HE'S GONNA MAKE IT.

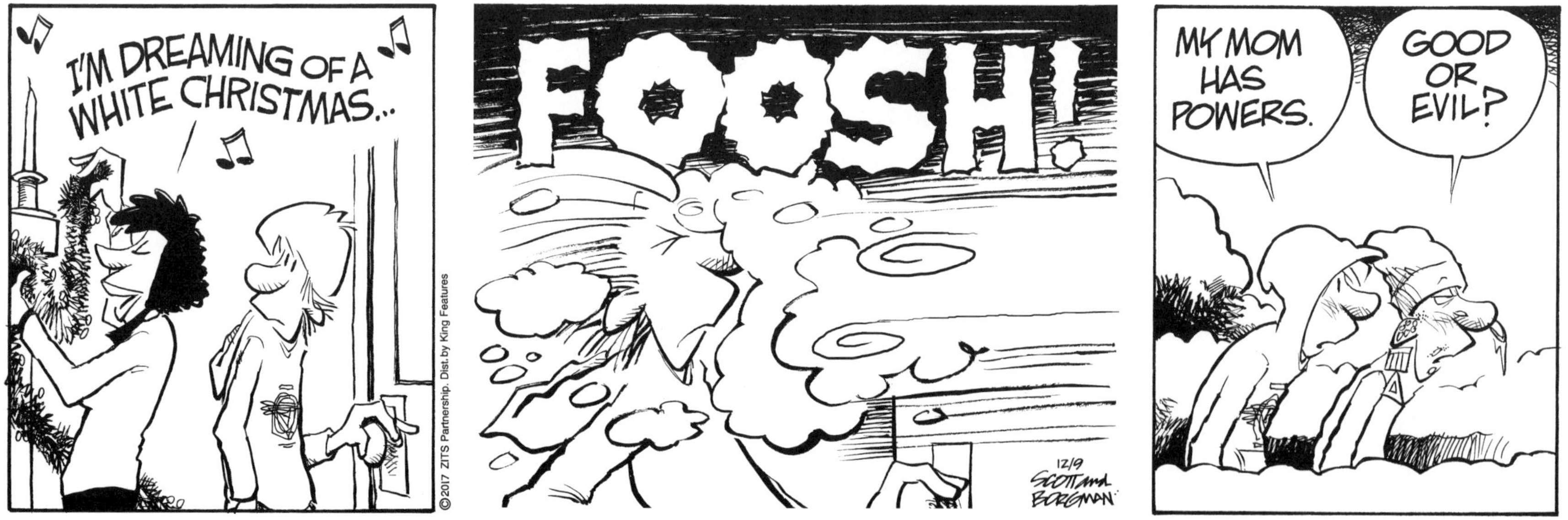
I'M DREAMING OF A WHITE CHRISTMAS...
©2017 ZITS Partnership. Dist. by King Features
FOOSH!
12/9 SCOTT and BORGMAN
MY MOM HAS POWERS.
GOOD OR EVIL?

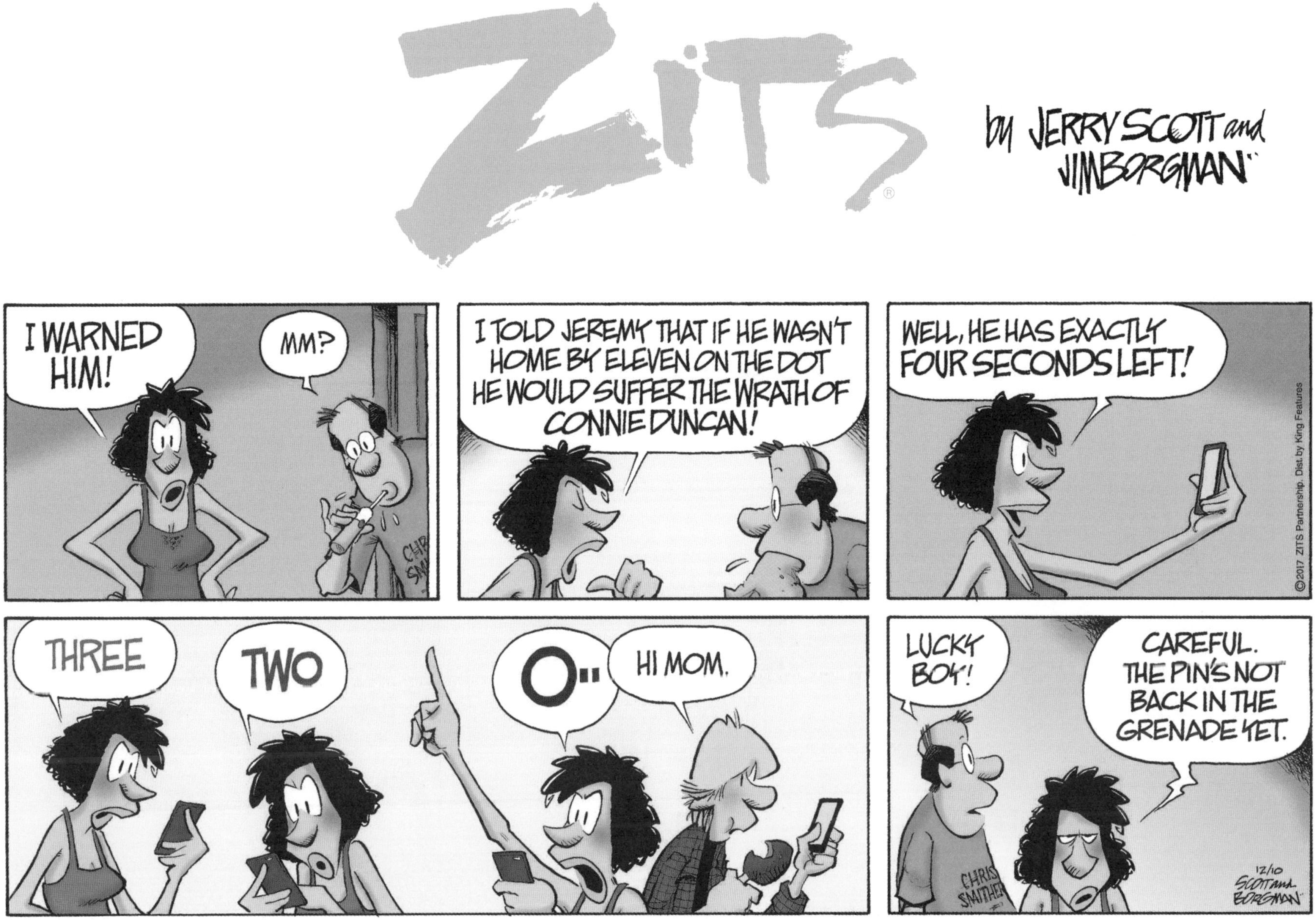
ZITS
by JERRY SCOTT and JIM BORGMAN
I WARNED HIM!
MM?
I TOLD JEREMY THAT IF HE WASN'T HOME BY ELEVEN ON THE DOT HE WOULD SUFFER THE WRATH OF CONNIE DUNCAN!
WELL, HE HAS EXACTLY FOUR SECONDS LEFT!
©2017 ZITS Partnership. Dist. by King Features
THREE
TWO
O..
HI MOM.
LUCKY BOY!
CAREFUL. THE PIN'S NOT BACK IN THE GRENADE YET.
12/10 SCOTT and BORGMAN

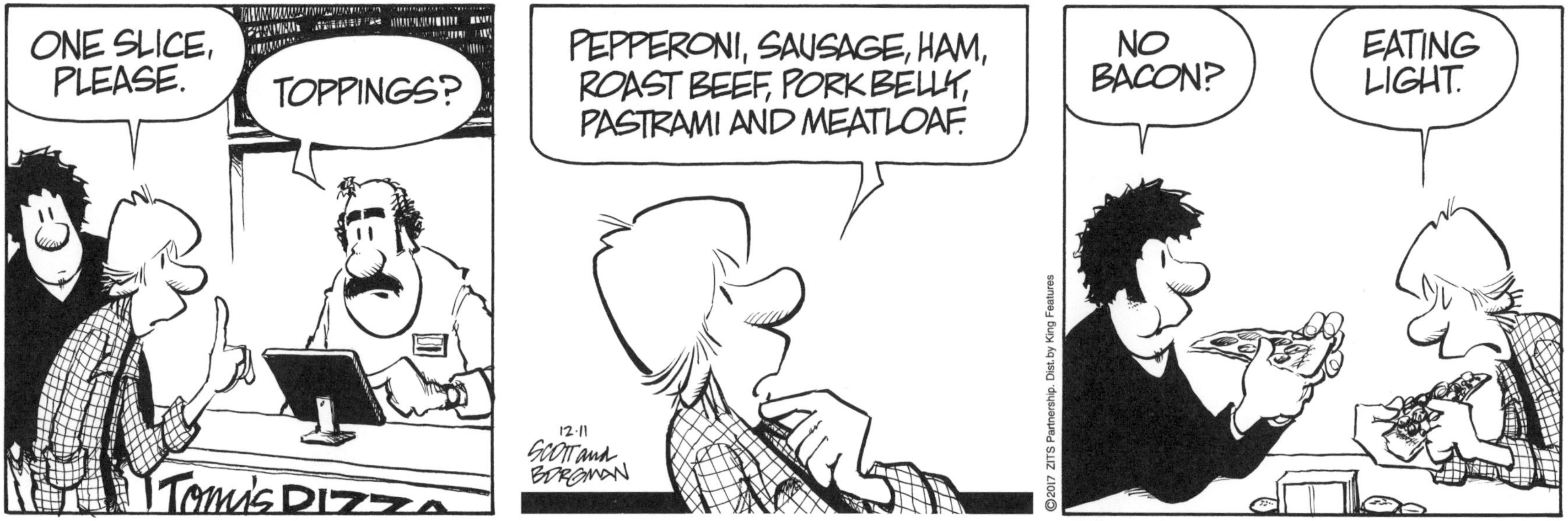
ONE SLICE, PLEASE.
TOPPINGS?
PEPPERONI, SAUSAGE, HAM, ROAST BEEF, PORK BELLY, PASTRAMI AND MEATLOAF.
12·11
SCOTT and BORGMAN
©2017 ZITS Partnership. Dist. by King Features
NO BACON?
EATING LIGHT.

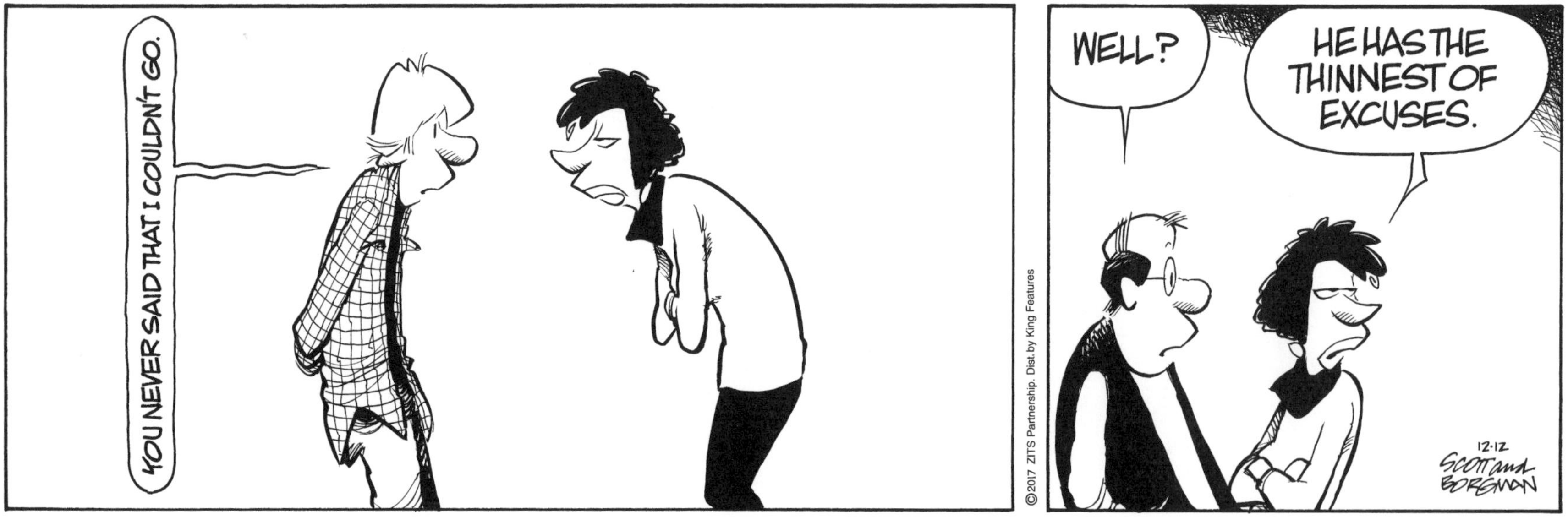
YOU NEVER SAID THAT I COULDN'T GO.
©2017 ZITS Partnership. Dist. by King Features
WELL?
HE HAS THE THINNEST OF EXCUSES.
12·12
SCOTT and BORGMAN

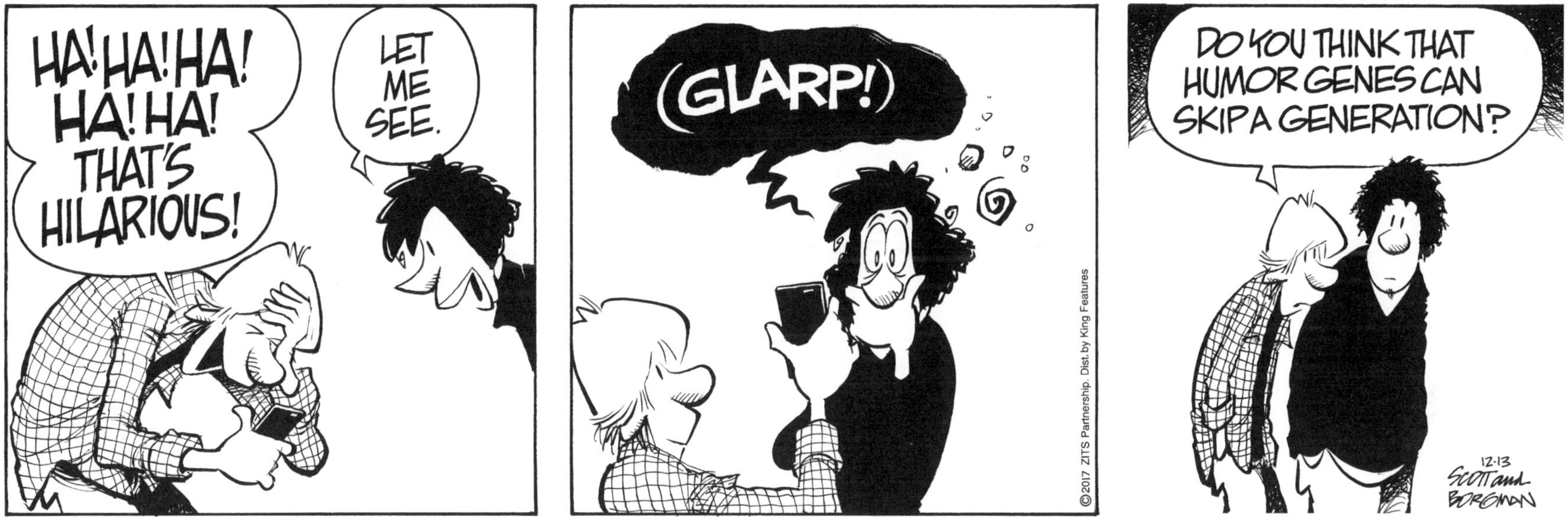
HA! HA! HA! HA! HA! THAT'S HILARIOUS!
LET ME SEE.
(GLARP!)
©2017 ZITS Partnership. Dist. by King Features
DO YOU THINK THAT HUMOR GENES CAN SKIP A GENERATION?
12·13 SCOTT and BORGMAN

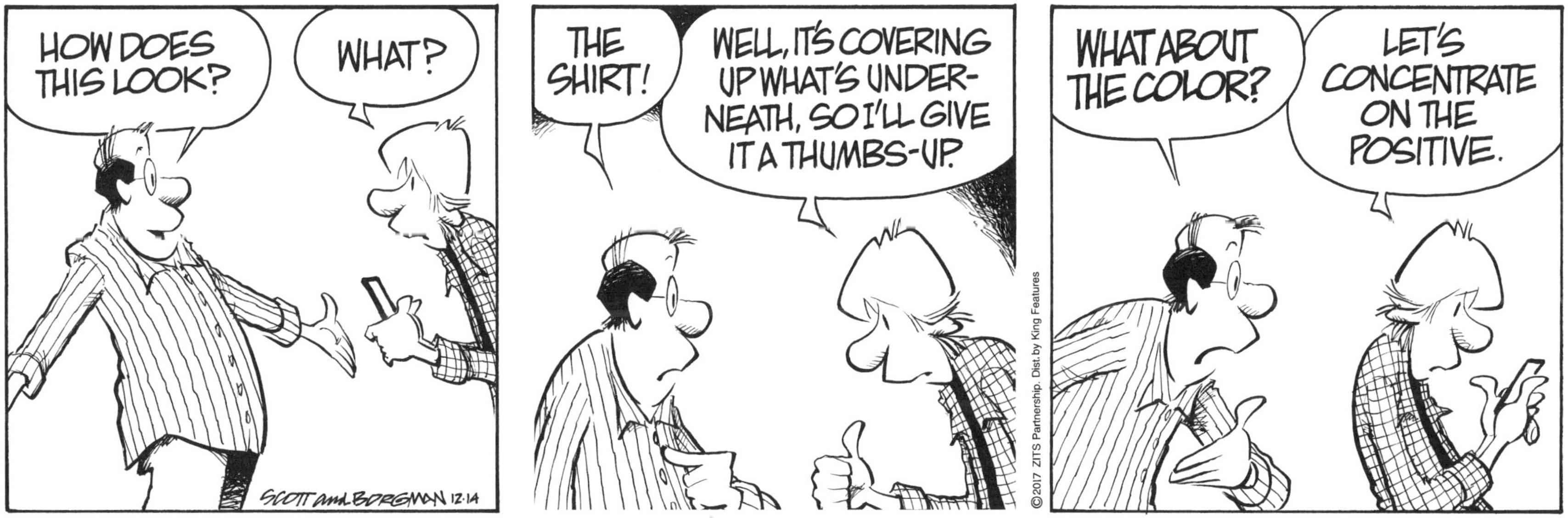
HOW DOES THIS LOOK?
WHAT?
SCOTT and BORGMAN 12·14
THE SHIRT!
WELL, IT'S COVERING UP WHAT'S UNDER-NEATH, SO I'LL GIVE IT A THUMBS-UP.
©2017 ZITS Partnership. Dist. by King Features
WHAT ABOUT THE COLOR?
LET'S CONCENTRATE ON THE POSITIVE.

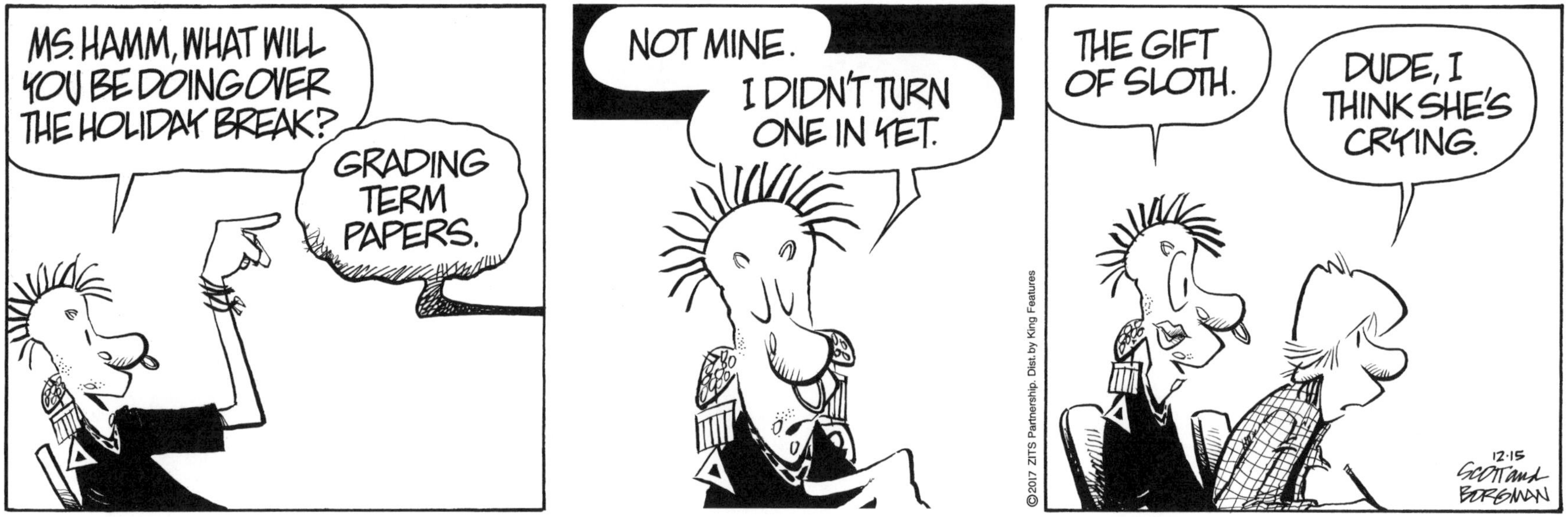
MS. HAMM, WHAT WILL YOU BE DOING OVER THE HOLIDAY BREAK?
GRADING TERM PAPERS.
NOT MINE.
I DIDN'T TURN ONE IN YET.
©2017 ZITS Partnership. Dist. by King Features
THE GIFT OF SLOTH.
DUDE, I THINK SHE'S CRYING.
12·15 SCOTT and BORGMAN

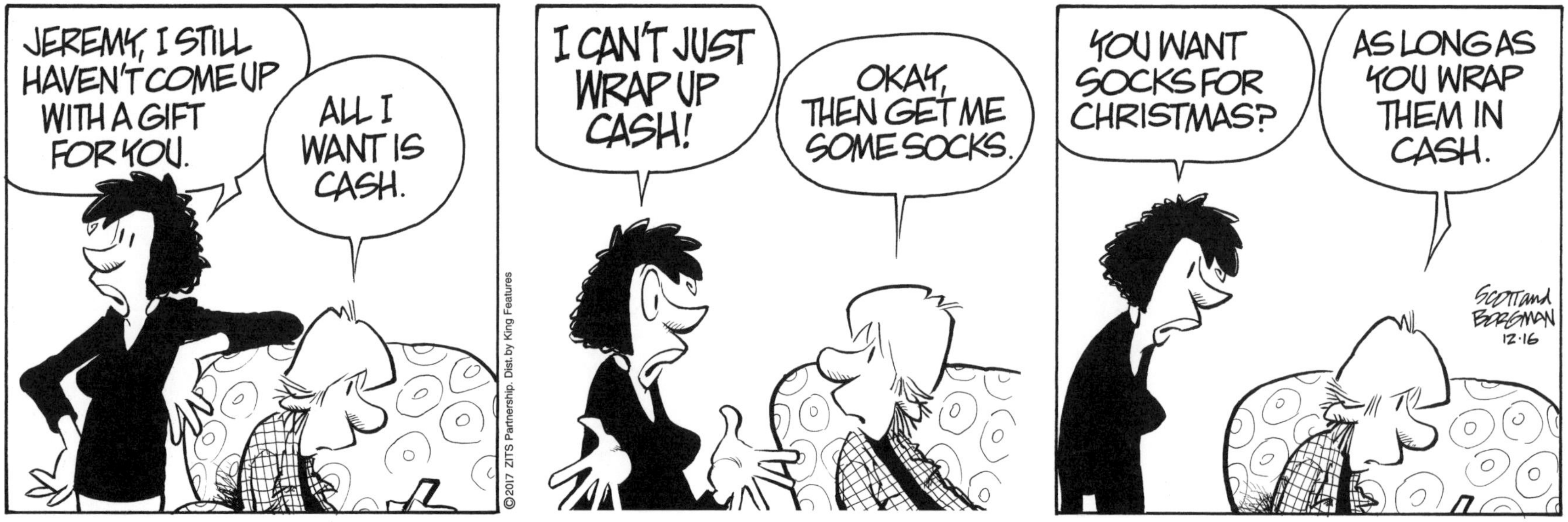
JEREMY, I STILL HAVEN'T COME UP WITH A GIFT FOR YOU.
ALL I WANT IS CASH.
©2017 ZITS Partnership. Dist. by King Features
I CAN'T JUST WRAP UP CASH!
OKAY, THEN GET ME SOME SOCKS.
YOU WANT SOCKS FOR CHRISTMAS?
AS LONG AS YOU WRAP THEM IN CASH.
SCOTT and BORGMAN 12·16

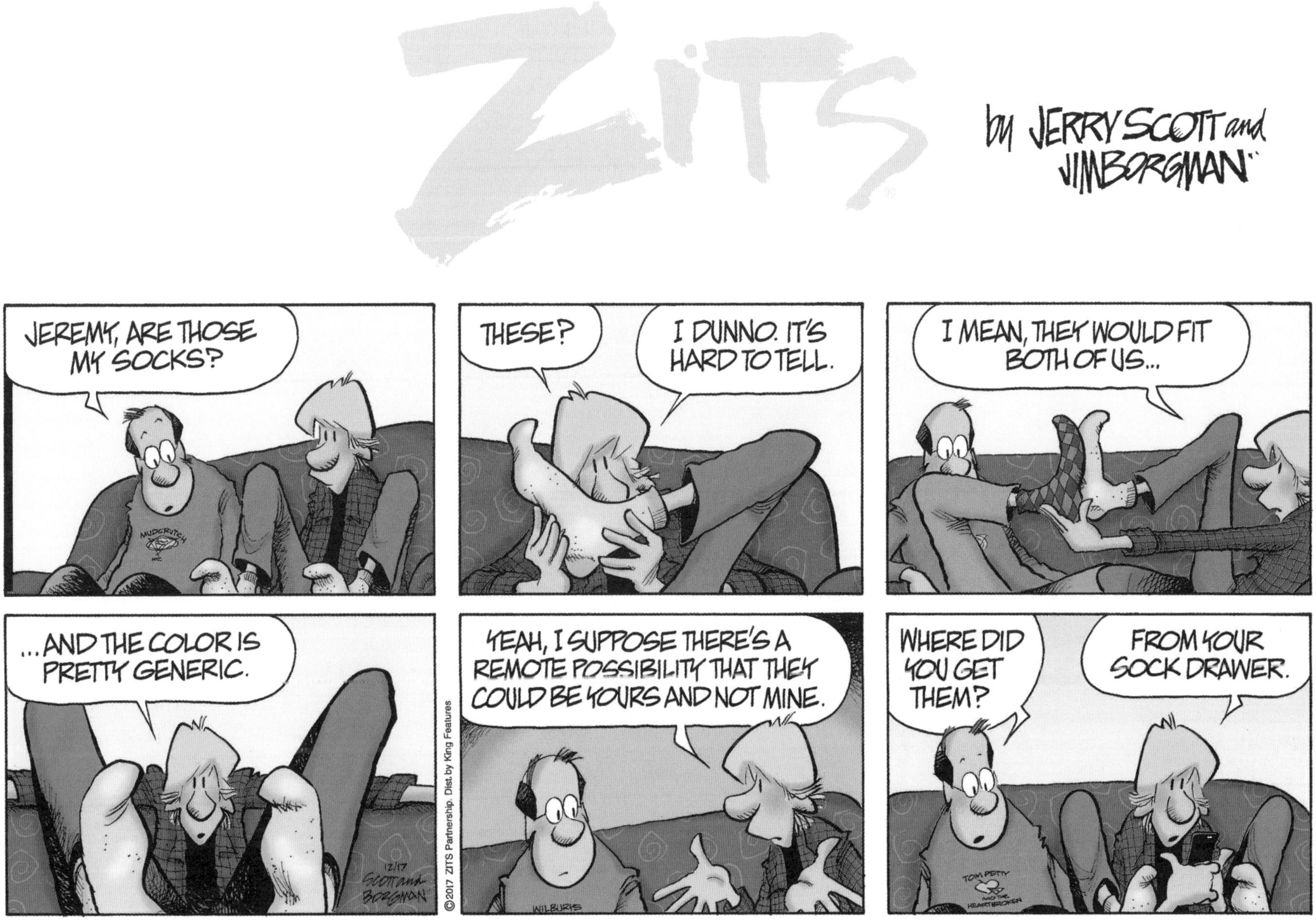
ZITS
by JERRY SCOTT and JIM BORGMAN
JEREMY, ARE THOSE MY SOCKS?
MUDCRUTCH
THESE?
I DUNNO. IT'S HARD TO TELL.
I MEAN, THEY WOULD FIT BOTH OF US...
...AND THE COLOR IS PRETTY GENERIC.
12/17
SCOTT and BORGMAN
©2017 ZITS Partnership. Dist. by King Features
YEAH, I SUPPOSE THERE'S A REMOTE POSSIBILITY THAT THEY COULD BE YOURS AND NOT MINE.
WILBURYS
WHERE DID YOU GET THEM?
FROM YOUR SOCK DRAWER.
TOM PETTY AND THE HEARTBROKEN

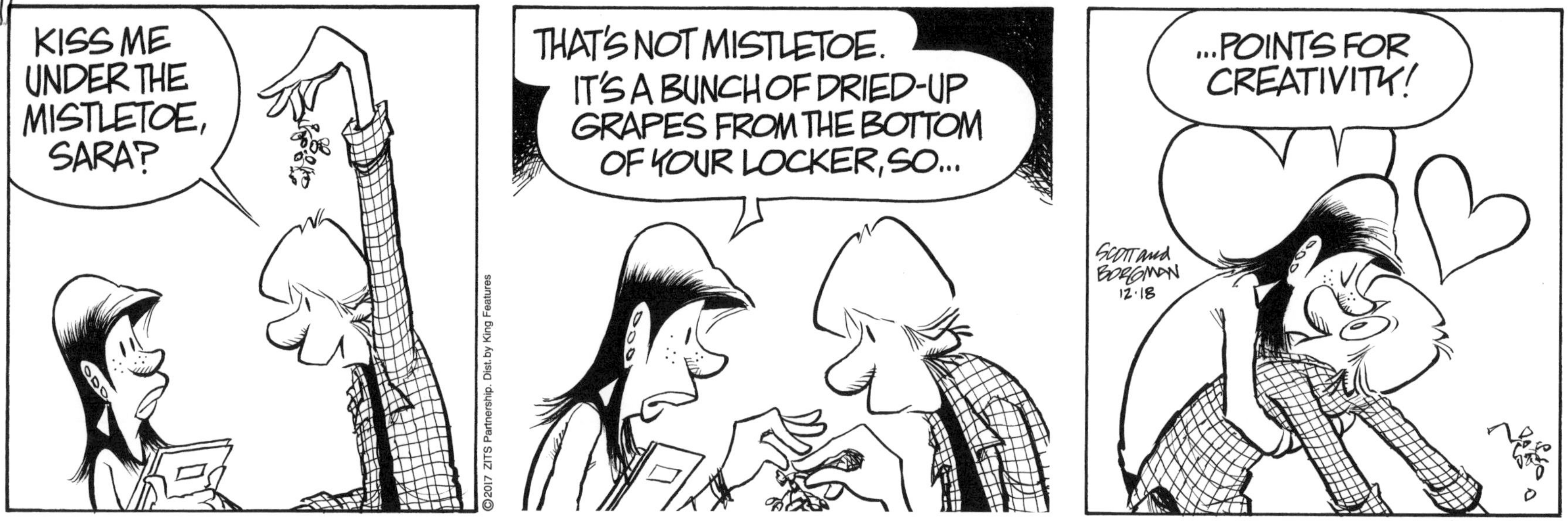
KISS ME UNDER THE MISTLETOE, SARA?
THAT'S NOT MISTLETOE. IT'S A BUNCH OF DRIED-UP GRAPES FROM THE BOTTOM OF YOUR LOCKER, SO...
...POINTS FOR CREATIVITY!
SCOTT and BORGMAN 12·18
©2017 ZITS Partnership. Dist. by King Features

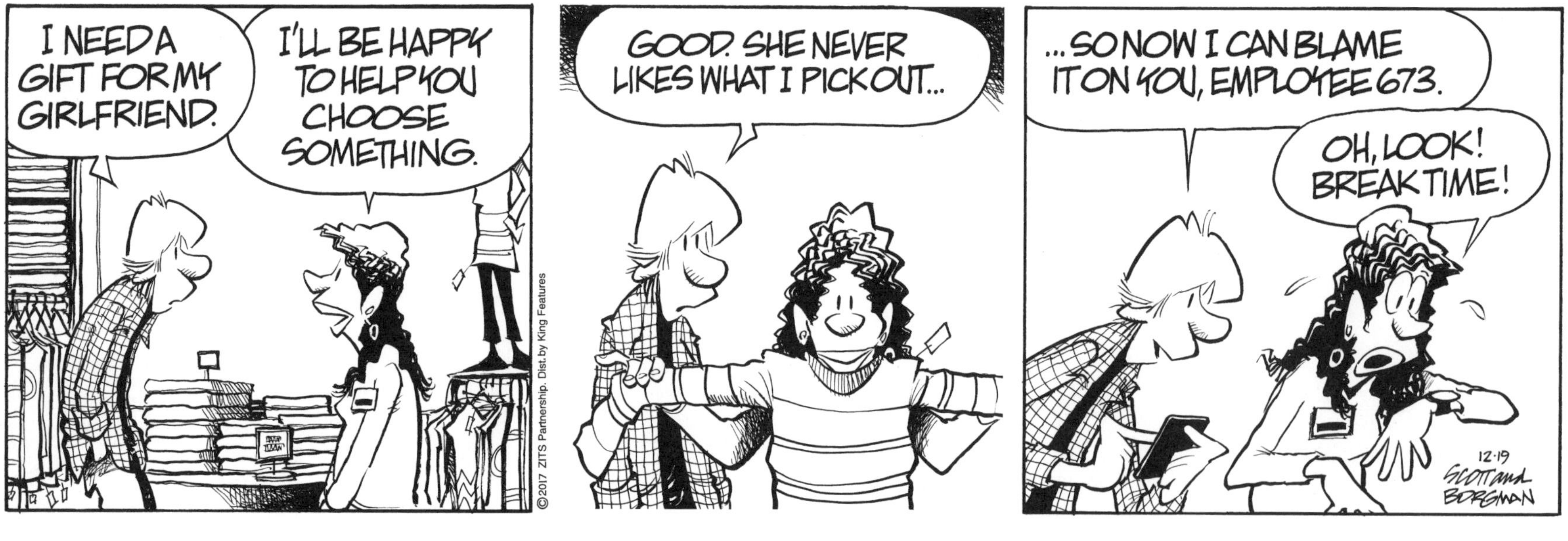
I NEED A GIFT FOR MY GIRLFRIEND.
I'LL BE HAPPY TO HELP YOU CHOOSE SOMETHING.
GOOD. SHE NEVER LIKES WHAT I PICK OUT...
...SO NOW I CAN BLAME IT ON YOU, EMPLOYEE 673.
OH, LOOK! BREAK TIME!
12·19 SCOTT and BORGMAN
©2017 ZITS Partnership. Dist. by King Features

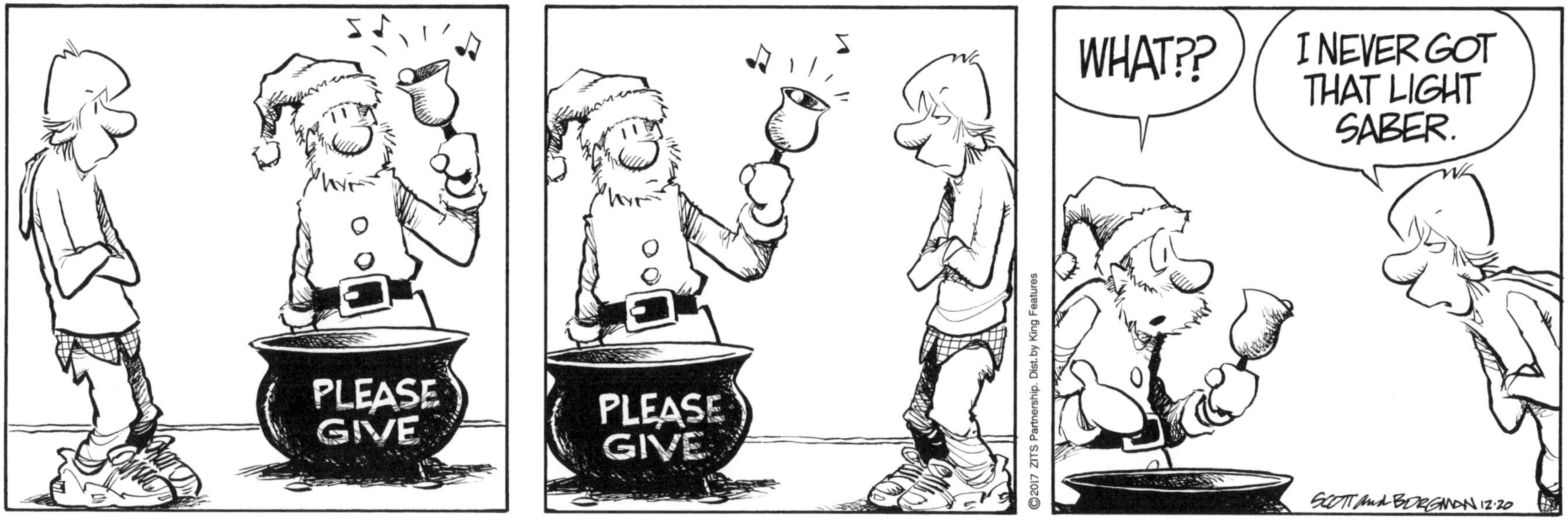
PLEASE GIVE
PLEASE GIVE
WHAT??
I NEVER GOT THAT LIGHT SABER.
©2017 ZITS Partnership. Dist. by King Features
SCOTT and BORGMAN 12·20

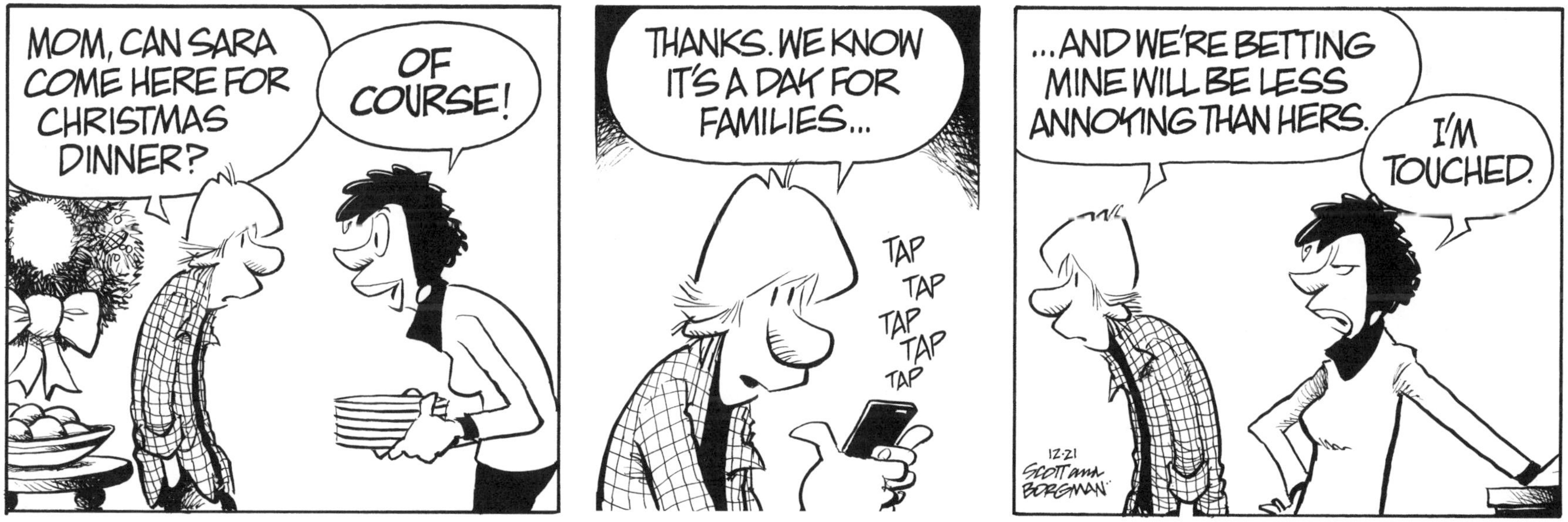
MOM, CAN SARA COME HERE FOR CHRISTMAS DINNER?
OF COURSE!
THANKS. WE KNOW IT'S A DAY FOR FAMILIES...
TAP TAP TAP TAP TAP
...AND WE'RE BETTING MINE WILL BE LESS ANNOYING THAN HERS.
I'M TOUCHED.
12·21 SCOTT and BORGMAN

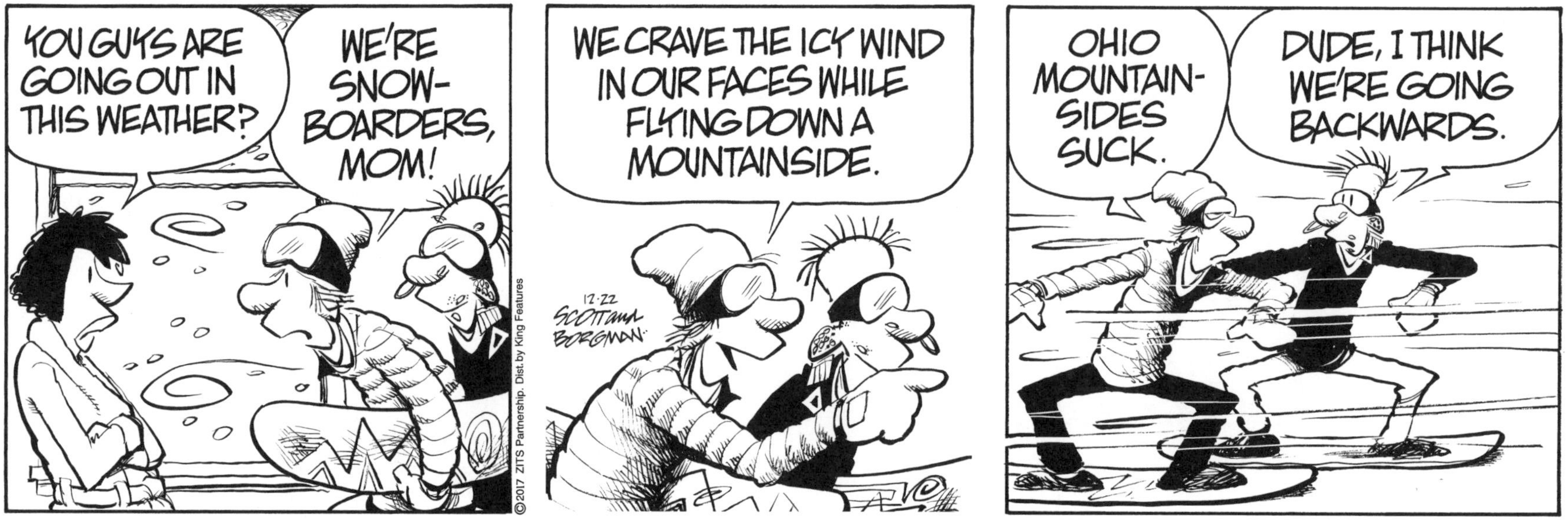
YOU GUYS ARE GOING OUT IN THIS WEATHER?
WE'RE SNOW-BOARDERS, MOM!
WE CRAVE THE ICY WIND IN OUR FACES WHILE FLYING DOWN A MOUNTAINSIDE.
12·22 SCOTT and BORGMAN
©2017 ZITS Partnership. Dist. by King Features
OHIO MOUNTAIN-SIDES SUCK.
DUDE, I THINK WE'RE GOING BACKWARDS.

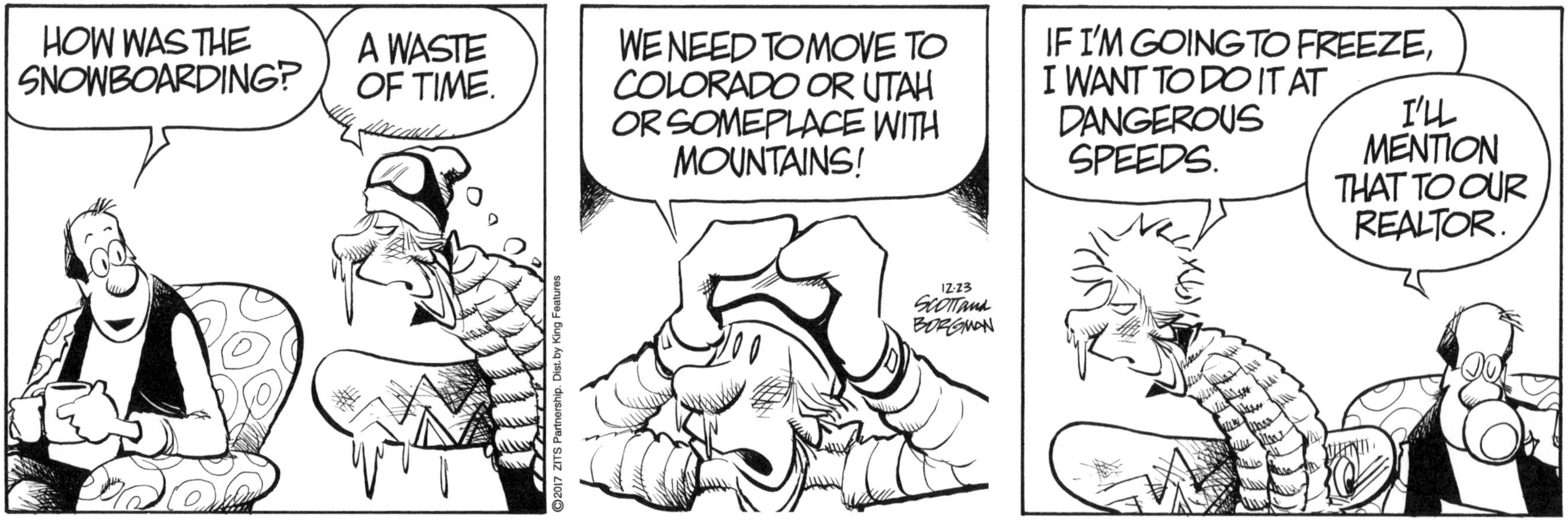
HOW WAS THE SNOWBOARDING?
A WASTE OF TIME.
©2017 ZITS Partnership. Dist. by King Features
WE NEED TO MOVE TO COLORADO OR UTAH OR SOMEPLACE WITH MOUNTAINS!
12·23 SCOTT and BORGMAN
IF I'M GOING TO FREEZE, I WANT TO DO IT AT DANGEROUS SPEEDS.
I'LL MENTION THAT TO OUR REALTOR.

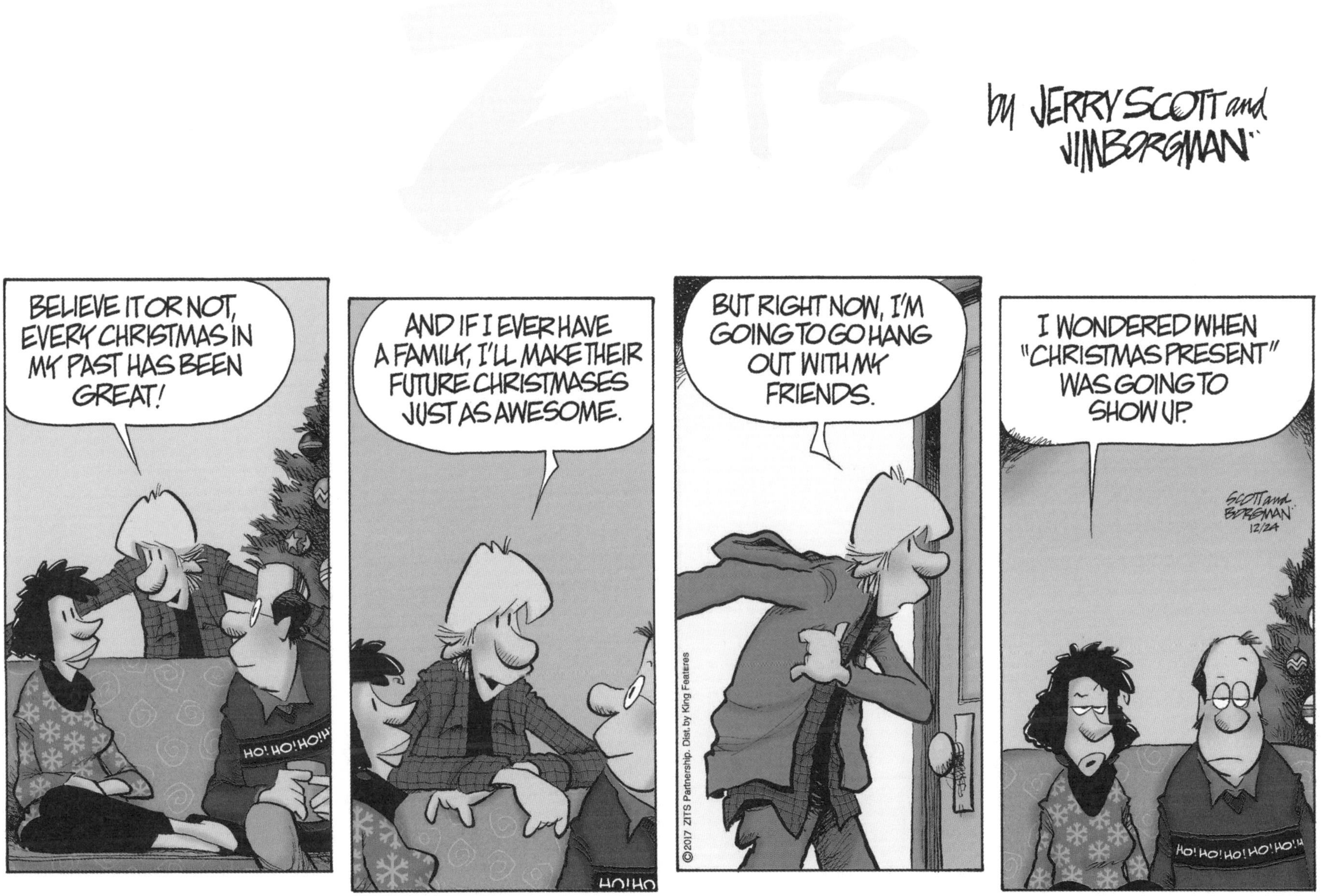
by JERRY SCOTT and JIM BORGMAN
BELIEVE IT OR NOT, EVERY CHRISTMAS IN MY PAST HAS BEEN GREAT!
HO! HO! HO! H
AND IF I EVER HAVE A FAMILY, I'LL MAKE THEIR FUTURE CHRISTMASES JUST AS AWESOME.
HO! HO
©2017 ZITS Partnership. Dist. by King Features
BUT RIGHT NOW, I'M GOING TO GO HANG OUT WITH MY FRIENDS.
I WONDERED WHEN "CHRISTMAS PRESENT" WAS GOING TO SHOW UP.
SCOTT and BORGMAN 12/24
HO! HO! HO! HO! HO! H

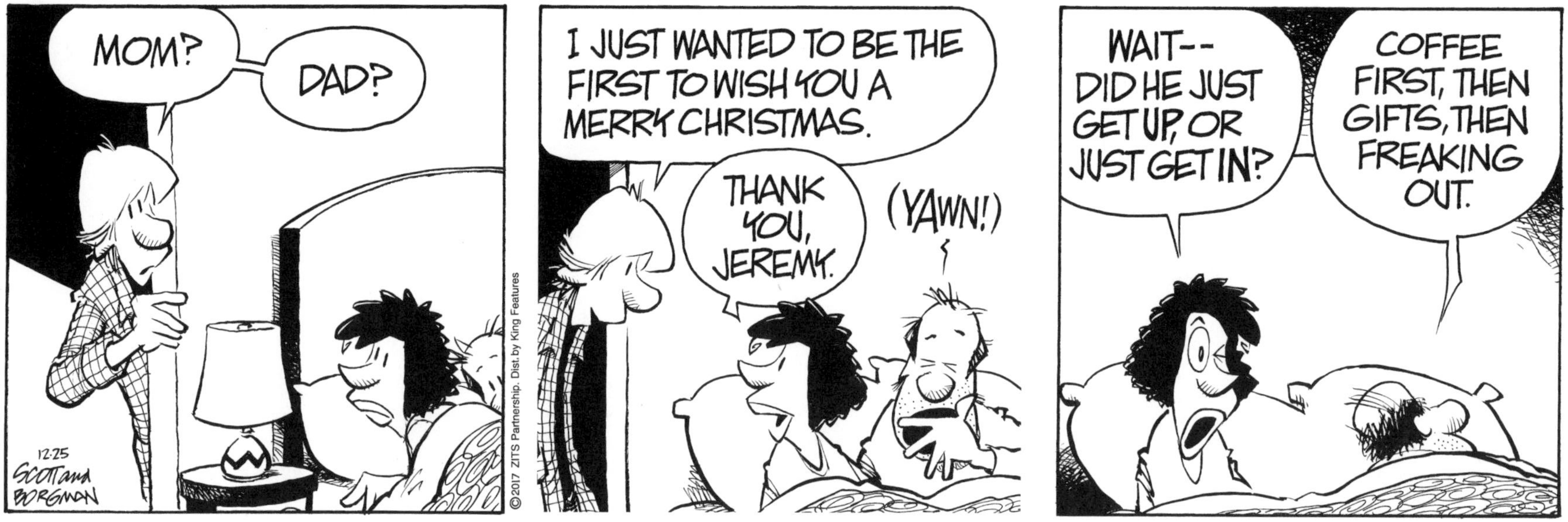
MOM?
DAD?
12·25
SCOTT and BORGMAN
I JUST WANTED TO BE THE FIRST TO WISH YOU A MERRY CHRISTMAS.
THANK YOU, JEREMY.
(YAWN!)
©2017 ZITS Partnership. Dist. by King Features
WAIT-- DID HE JUST GET UP, OR JUST GET IN?
COFFEE FIRST, THEN GIFTS, THEN FREAKING OUT.

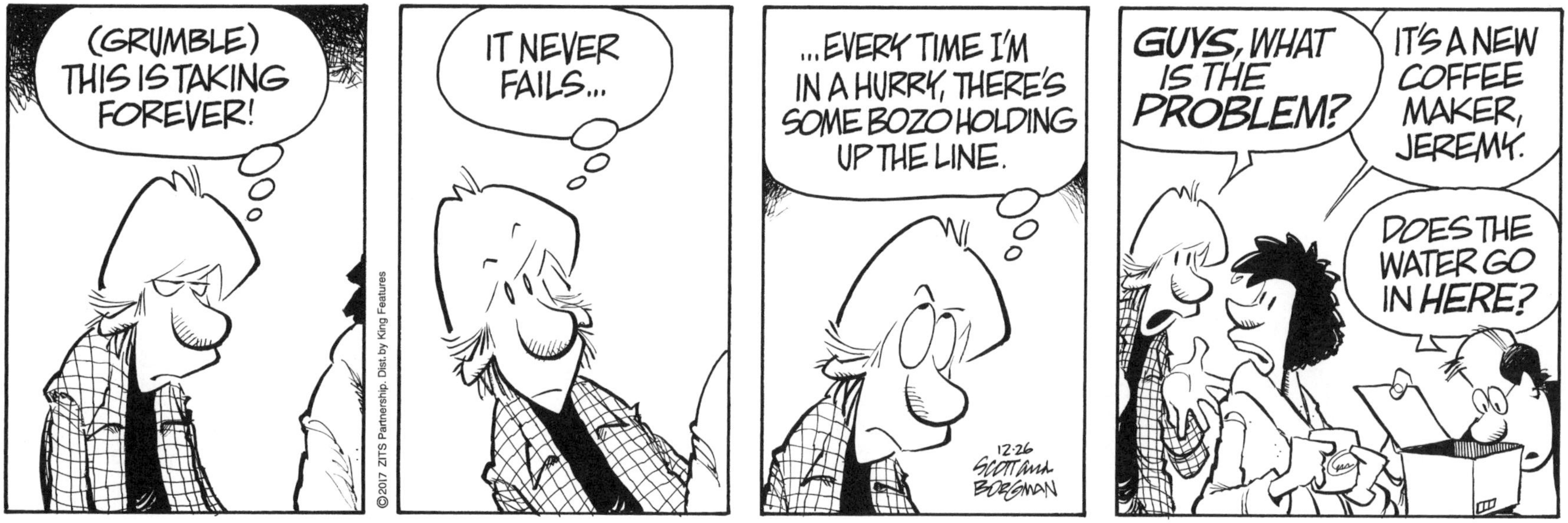
(GRUMBLE) THIS IS TAKING FOREVER!
©2017 ZITS Partnership. Dist. by King Features
IT NEVER FAILS...
...EVERY TIME I'M IN A HURRY, THERE'S SOME BOZO HOLDING UP THE LINE.
12·26
SCOTT and BORGMAN
GUYS, WHAT IS THE PROBLEM?
IT'S A NEW COFFEE MAKER, JEREMY.
DOES THE WATER GO IN HERE?

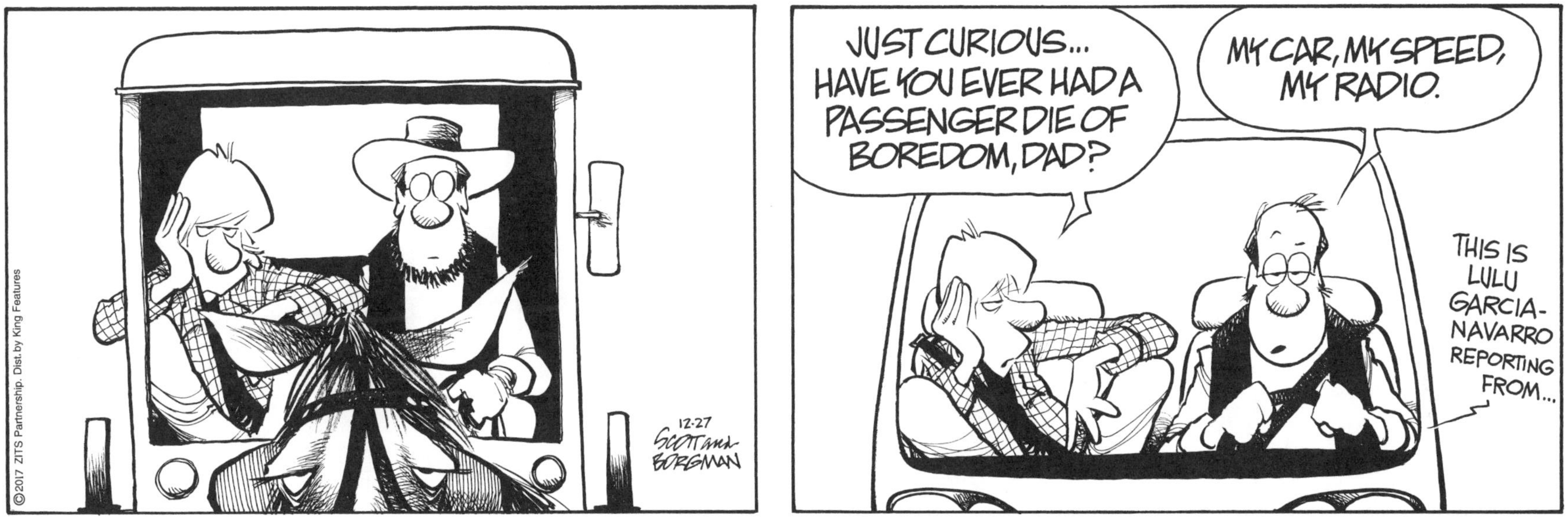
©2017 ZITS Partnership. Dist. by King Features
12·27 SCOTT and BORGMAN
JUST CURIOUS... HAVE YOU EVER HAD A PASSENGER DIE OF BOREDOM, DAD?
MY CAR, MY SPEED, MY RADIO.
THIS IS LULU GARCIA-NAVARRO REPORTING FROM...

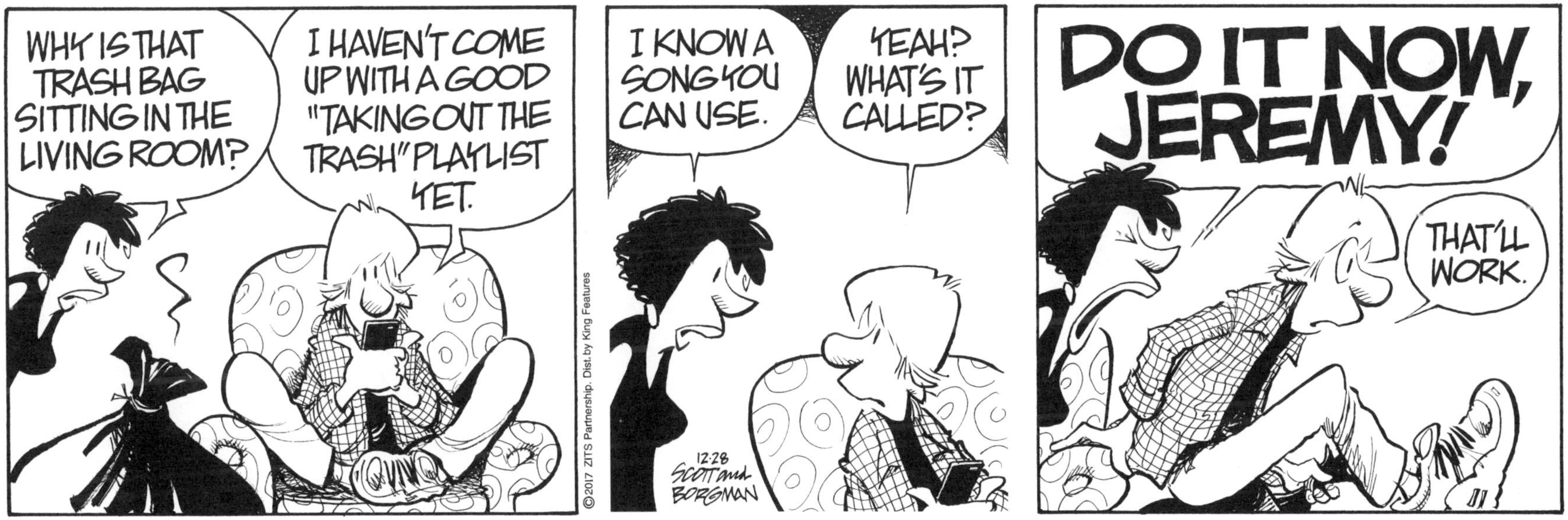
WHY IS THAT TRASH BAG SITTING IN THE LIVING ROOM?
I HAVEN'T COME UP WITH A GOOD "TAKING OUT THE TRASH" PLAYLIST YET.
©2017 ZITS Partnership. Dist. by King Features
I KNOW A SONG YOU CAN USE.
YEAH? WHAT'S IT CALLED?
12·28 SCOTT and BORGMAN
DO IT NOW, JEREMY!
THAT'LL WORK.

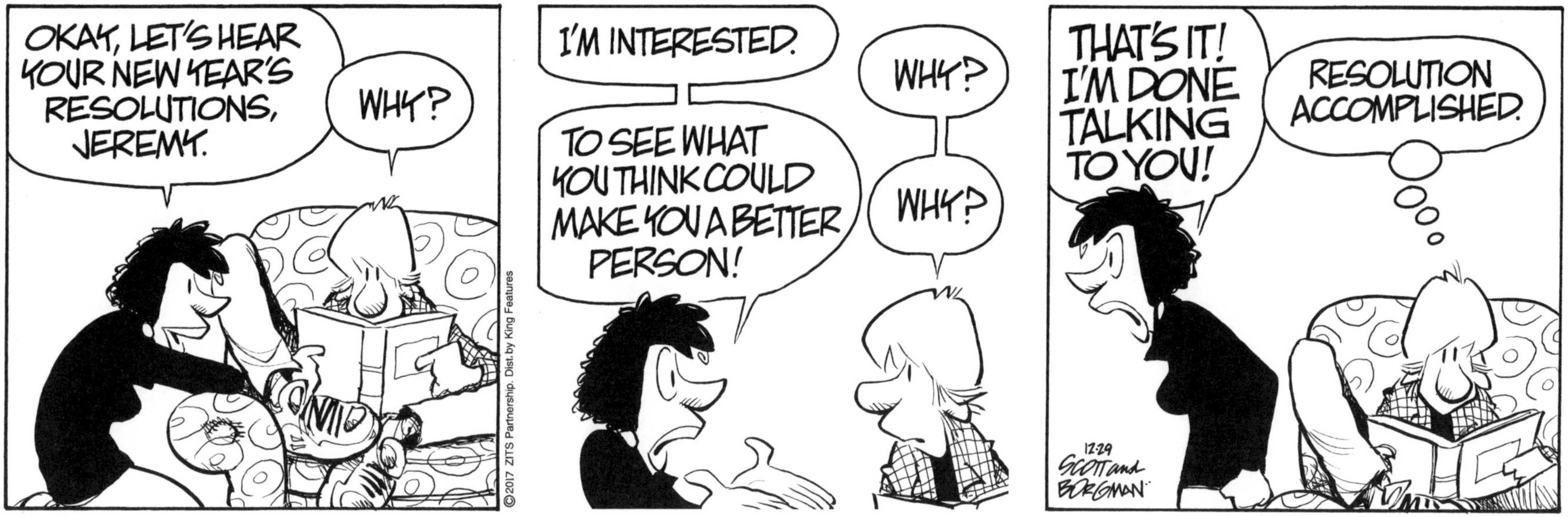
OKAY, LET'S HEAR YOUR NEW YEAR'S RESOLUTIONS, JEREMY.
WHY?
I'M INTERESTED.
TO SEE WHAT YOU THINK COULD MAKE YOU A BETTER PERSON!
WHY?
WHY?
THAT'S IT! I'M DONE TALKING TO YOU!
RESOLUTION ACCOMPLISHED.
12-29 SCOTT and BORGMAN
©2017 ZITS Partnership. Dist.by King Features

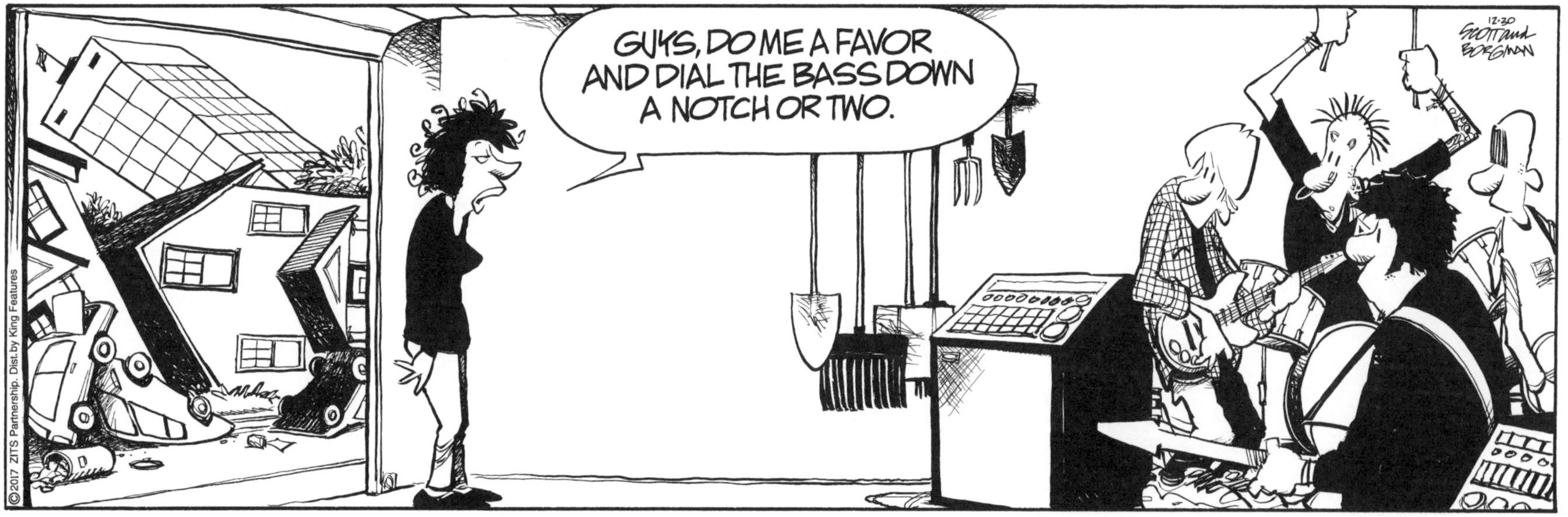
GUYS, DO ME A FAVOR AND DIAL THE BASS DOWN A NOTCH OR TWO.
12-30 SCOTT and BORGMAN
©2017 ZITS Partnership. Dist.by King Features

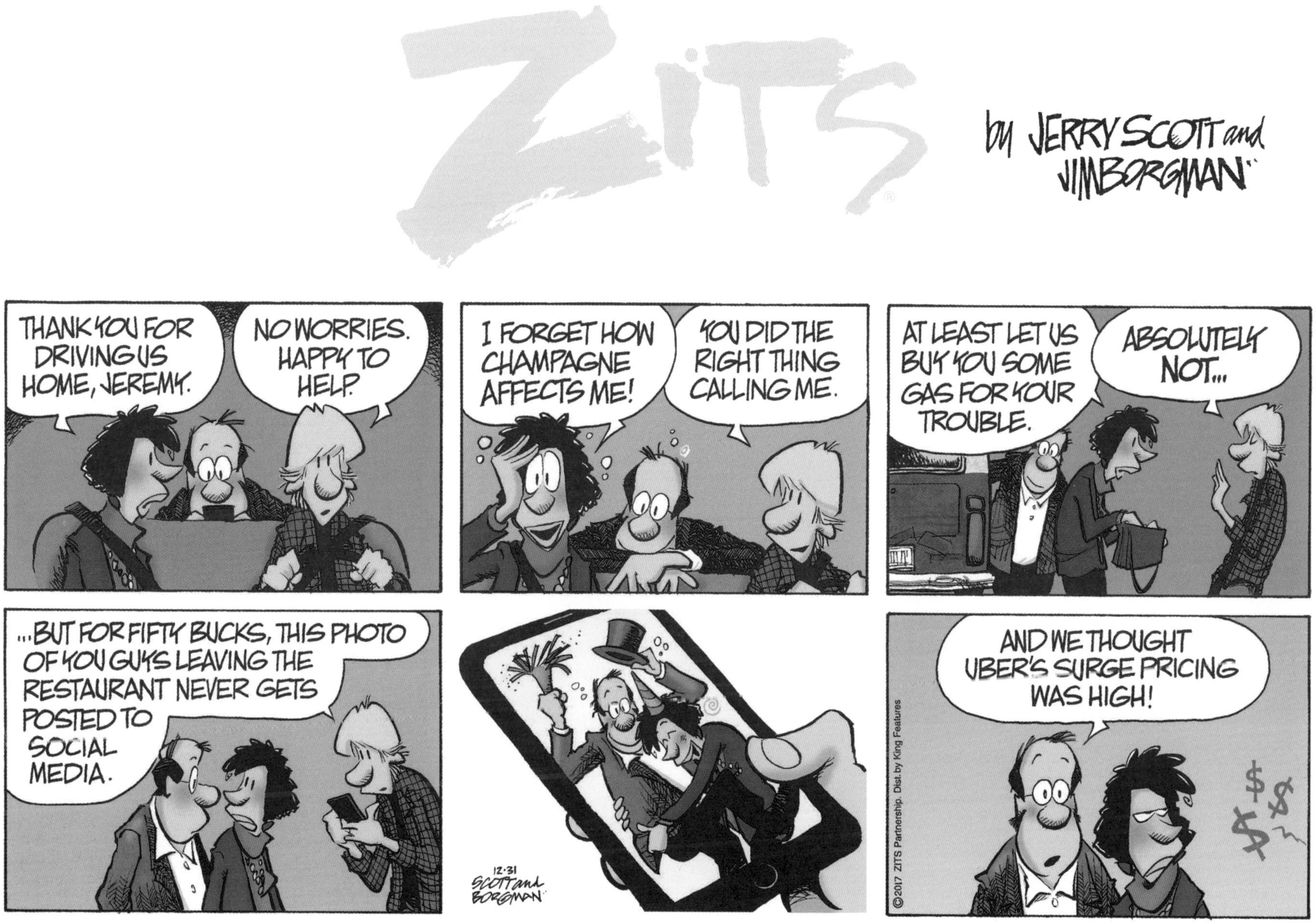

ZITS
by JERRY SCOTT and JIM BORGMAN
THANK YOU FOR DRIVING US HOME, JEREMY.
NO WORRIES. HAPPY TO HELP.
I FORGET HOW CHAMPAGNE AFFECTS ME!
YOU DID THE RIGHT THING CALLING ME.
AT LEAST LET US BUY YOU SOME GAS FOR YOUR TROUBLE.
ABSOLUTELY NOT...
...BUT FOR FIFTY BUCKS, THIS PHOTO OF YOU GUYS LEAVING THE RESTAURANT NEVER GETS POSTED TO SOCIAL MEDIA.
12·31 SCOTT and BORGMAN
AND WE THOUGHT UBER'S SURGE PRICING WAS HIGH!
©2017 ZITS Partnership. Dist. by King Features

Zits® is syndicated internationally by King Features Syndicate, Inc.
For information, write King Features Syndicate, Inc., 300 West Fifty-Seventh Street, New York, New York 10019.

Andrews McMeel Publishing
a division of Andrews McMeel Universal
1130 Walnut Street, Kansas City, Missouri 64106

www.andrewsmcmeel.com

19 20 21 22 23 SDB 10 9 8 7 6 5 4 3 2 1

ISBN: 978-1-5248-5176-7

Library of Congress Control Number: 2019932744

Editor: Lucas Wetzel
Designer/Art Director: Holly Swayne
Production Manager: Chuck Harper
Production Editor: Elizabeth A. Garcia

ATTENTION: SCHOOLS AND BUSINESSES
Andrews McMeel books are available at quantity discounts with bulk purchase for educational, business, or sales promotional use.
For information, please e-mail the Andrews McMeel Publishing Special Sales Department:
specialsales@amuniversal.com

zitscomics.com • facebook.com/zitscomics • instagram.com/zitsguys